Comparative and International Policing, Justice, and Transnational Crime

Comparative and International Policing, Justice, and Transnational Crime

SECOND EDITION

Edited by

Sesha Kethineni

PROFESSOR, DEPARTMENT OF CRIMINAL JUSTICE SCIENCES
ILLINOIS STATE UNIVERSITY

CAROLINA ACADEMIC PRESS
Durham, North Carolina

Library of Congress Cataloging-in-Publication Data

Comparative and international policing, justice, and transnational crime / edited by Sesha Kethineni. -- 2nd ed.
    pages cm
  Includes bibliographical references and index.
  ISBN 978-1-61163-443-3 (alk. paper)
  1. Law enforcement. 2. Criminal justice, Administration of. 3. Transnational crime. 4. International criminal law. I. Kethineni, Sesha, editor of compilation.

  K3465.C66 2014
  364--dc23

                        2014007713

CAROLINA ACADEMIC PRESS
700 Kent Street
Durham, North Carolina 27701
Telephone (919) 489-7486
Fax (919) 493-5668
www.cap-press.com

Printed in the United States of America

Contents

Acknowledgments   xvii
Notes on Contributors   xix
Introduction   xxv

Chapter 1 · Justice Systems in Selected Countries   3
Philip L. Reichel
Introduction   3
Four Legal Traditions   4
   Common Legal Tradition   4
   Civil Legal Tradition   5
   Islamic Legal Tradition   6
   Mixed Legal Tradition   7
   Substantive and Procedural Criminal Law   8
   Substantive Criminal Law   8
   Procedural Criminal Law   9
      The Adversarial Process   9
      The Inquisitorial Process   10
      Mixed Process   11
Justice Systems in Common-Law Countries   11
   England and Wales   11
      Substantive Law: Insanity   12
      Procedural Law: Adjudication   14
   India   14
      Substantive Law: Insanity   15
      Procedural Law: Adjudication   16
Justice Systems in Civil-Law Countries   17
   France   17
      Substantive Law: Insanity   17
      Procedural Law: Adjudication   18
   Germany   19
      Substantive Law: Insanity   19

Procedural Law: Adjudication 20
Justice Systems in an Islamic Law Country 20
  Saudi Arabia 20
    Substantive Law: Insanity 20
    Procedural Law: Adjudication 22
Justice Systems in a Mixed Law Country 22
  People's Republic of China 22
    Substantive Law: Insanity 23
    Procedural Law: Adjudication 24
Conclusion 24
Web Sources 25
Discussion Questions 25
References 26

Chapter 2 · The Roles of International Justice Organizations 31
J.D. Jamieson & Donna Vandiver
Introduction 31
A History of Modern Attempts to Settle International
  Disputes Peacefully 32
The International Court of Justice 34
  Key Features of the International Court of Justice 34
  Jurisdiction of the International Court of Justice 35
  Trial Procedures and Resolution of Contentious Cases 35
  Current Cases between Member States 37
    Belgium v. Senegal 37
    Ecuador v. Colombia 38
    Georgia v. The Russian Federation, 2008 38
    Advisory Proceedings 38
The Permanent International Criminal Court 39
  Key Features of the International Criminal Court 40
  Jurisdiction, Organization, and Administration of the
    International Criminal Court (ICC) 40
    The Office of the President 41
    The Office of the Prosecutor 41
    The Judicial Divisions 42
    The Registry 42
    Administrative Issues: Plenary Sessions 44
  Trial Procedures and Resolution of Cases 45
  Responsibilities of Member States and "States Parties" 46

Current Cases in the International Criminal Court   47
Special Issues of International Courts   48
Conclusion   49
Web Sources   51
Discussion Questions   52
References   52

Chapter 3 · Sovereign Lawlessness: Renditions and Co-Mingling
            of Criminal Justice and Military Justice   55
Sesha Kethineni & Rebecca Lawson
Introduction   55
Historical Overview   55
International Overview   56
Extent of the Problem   61
    Fallout for CIA Agents   63
    The Role of Other Countries   64
    The Opposition   65
Co-Mingling of Criminal Justice and Military Justice   67
    Historical Overview   68
Conclusion   72
Web Sources   74
Discussion Questions   74
References   75

Chapter 4 · International Law Enforcement Organizations   79
Mathieu Deflem & Shannon McDonough
Introduction   79
    The History of International Policing   79
    Contemporary Dimensions of International Policing   83
        Forms   83
        Organizations   84
        Activities   85
    Interpol: The International Criminal Police Organization 89
    Europol: The European Police Office   93
Conclusion   96
Web Sources   97
Discussion Questions   98
References   98

Chapter 5 · Policing in Selected Countries: Organization
        and Structure   103
Harry R. Dammer
Introduction   103
  Policing in a Common Law Country: England   105
    Historical Background   105
    Organization, Structure, and Training   106
    Current Issues of Concern for the Police in England   108
  Policing in a Common Law Country: India   109
    Historical Background   109
    Organization, Structure, and Training   110
    Current Issues of Importance for the Police in India   111
  Policing in a Civil Law Country: France   113
    Historical Background   113
    Structure, Organization, and Training   114
    Current Issues of Concern for French Police   116
  Policing in a Civil Law Country: Germany   117
    Historical Background   117
    Organization, Structure, and Training   118
    Current Issues of Concern for German Police   120
  Policing in a Socialist/Mixed Law Country: China   121
    Historical Background   121
    Structure, Organization, and Training   122
    Issues of Concern for Chinese Police   124
  Policing in an Islamic Law Country: Saudi Arabia   125
    Historical Background   125
    Organization, Structure, and Training   125
    Current Issues of Concern for Saudi Police   127
  Web Sources   128
  Discussion Questions   128
  References   128

Chapter 6 · Policing Subordinate Sovereignties: Policing in
        Democratic Societies   133
L. Edward Wells
Introduction   133
  Policing in Neocolonial Societies   135
    Autocratic Policing of Indigenous Peoples   137
    Neocolonial Policing of American Indians in the United States   139
    The Vassal State Era (late 1770s–1820s)   142

The Removal Era (1830s–1840s) 143
The Enculturation Era (1850s–early 1880s) 144
The Allotment Era (late 1880s–1920s) 146
The Reorganization Era (1930s–1940s) 148
The Termination Era (late 1940s–early 1960s) 149
The Self-Determination Era (late 1960s–present) 150
Contemporary Forms of Tribal Policing 153
Conclusion 156
Web Sources 157
Discussion Questions 158
References 158
Legislation 160

Chapter 7 · Correctional Systems, Philosophies, and Innovations:
A Comparative Perspective 163
Sesha Kethineni & Sarah McCullough
Introduction 163
World Imprisonment Rates 164
Four Goals of Corrections 165
International Standards on Corrections 168
International Covenant on Civil and Political Rights 168
The Second Optional Protocol to the International Covenant
on Civil and Political Rights, Aiming at the Abolition of
Death Penalty 169
UN Standard Minimum Rules for the Treatment of Prisoners 169
Convention against Torture and other Cruel, Inhuman or
Degrading Treatment or Punishment 169
UN Standard Minimum Rules for Noncustodial Measures 170
Optional Protocol to the Convention against Torture
and Other Cruel, Inhuman or Degrading Treatment
or Punishment 170
Sentencing Options 170
Noncustodial Sanctions 171
England 171
China 174
Japan 175
Saudi Arabia 176
Custodial Sanctions 177
England and Wales 178
China 179

Japan 181
Saudi Arabia 182
Conclusion 184
Web Sources 185
Discussion Questions 185
References 185

Chapter 8 · Juvenile Justice: A Comparative Perspective 191
Sesha Kethineni, Sarah McCullough & Richard Charlton
Introduction 191
United Nations' Role and Juvenile Justice 193
The UN Standard Minimum Rules for the Administration
of Juvenile Justice, 1985 193
The UN Convention on the Rights of the Child (CRC),
1989 194
The UN Guidelines for the Prevention of Juvenile
Delinquency, 1990 ("The Riyadh Guidelines") 194
The UN Rules for the Protection of Juveniles Deprived
of Their Liberty, 1990 195
Age of Criminal Responsibility 196
Models of Juvenile Justice 198
Welfare Model 199
India 199
Poland 201
Legalistic Model 202
Indonesia 202
Italy 203
Corporatist Model 205
England and Wales 205
Participatory Model 207
Japan 208
People's Republic of China 209
Conclusion 211
Web Sources 213
Discussion Questions 213
References 213

**Chapter 9 · The Global Normative Order: International Individual
Rights, States and Justice** 219
Gabriel Rubin
Introduction 219

A World of States 220
Rawls's *The Law of Peoples*: A First Encounter 224
Four Problems with Deriving Fundamental Rights at the
    Group Level 225
Should There Be an Individual Right to Democracy? 232
Rawls's *The Law of Peoples*: Decent versus Liberal Peoples 234
Decent Societies and Human Rights 237
Toleration, Liberalism, and Democracy 240
Conclusion 241
Web Sources 243
Discussion Questions 243
References 243

Chapter 10 · International Human Rights Movement 247
Satenik Margaryan
Introduction 247
The History of Human Rights 248
The History of International Human Rights Movement 251
The International Bill of Rights 256
The Universal Declaration of Human Rights 256
International Covenant on Economic, Social, and
    Cultural Rights 262
International Covenant on Civil and Political Rights 264
Other International Human Rights Instruments and Bodies 266
Conclusion 268
Web Sources 269
Discussion Questions 270
References 270

Chapter 11 · War Crimes: International Response to Genocide 275
Ralph Weisheit
Introduction 275
Genocide as an International Crime 276
Genocide: Limits of the Legal Definition 277
Genocide and War Crimes 279
Bosnia-Herzegovina (1992–95) 281
The Aftermath of Genocide in Bosnia 285
Rwanda (1994) 286
The Aftermath of Genocide in Rwanda 289
Sudan (2003–Present) 290
Conclusion 294

Web Sources 296
Discussion Questions 296
References 296

Chapter 12 · Specific Crimes against Humanity: Groups and
Minority Rights 301
Sesha Kethineni & Gail Humiston
Introduction: The Status of Dalits 301
Existing Conditions of Dalits 303
Education 303
Employment Opportunities 303
Migration 304
Specific Instances of Abuse 304
Land Dispute 304
Lack of Civic Facilities 305
The Dalit Rights Movement 305
Economic, Social, and Cultural Rights 307
Empirical Conceptualization of ESC Rights 307
Individual versus Collective Rights 308
India's Efforts to Fulfill Its Commitment to Human Rights 309
Constitutional Provisions 309
Legislative Enactments 309
Implementation and Enforcement of Laws and Policies 310
Land Reforms 310
Employment Reservations Policy 310
Local Government Reservations 311
Prosecution of Offenders 312
Food Programs 313
Health Programs 314
Education Program 314
Work 315
Recommendations 315
Racial Discrimination of Roma/Gypsies of Europe 320
Specific Instances of Violence 323
Social, Economic, and Cultural Discriminations and
Recommendations 325
Web Sources: Dalits 328
Discussion Questions 329
References 329

Chapter 13 · International Terrorism 335
Jeffrey Ian Ross & Michael Stohl
Introduction 335
  Defining Terrorism 336
  Types of Terrorism 337
  Tracing the Historical Trajectory and Contemporary Trends 338
    Introduction 338
    The 1980s: State-Sponsored, Religious Fundamentalist,
      and Single-Issue Terrorism 339
    The 1990s: Narco-Terrorism 340
    The 2000s: Dark Networks 340
  Contemporary Trends in Terrorism 341
    Data Sources 341
    Annual Statistics of International Events 342
    Geographic Spread 343
    Targets 343
    Tactics 344
    Terrorist Groups 345
  Combating Terrorism 345
    Introduction 345
    Contextual Issues 346
    Problems in Combating Terrorism 348
    Typical Measures 348
    Successes and Failures in Fighting Terrorism at Home
      and Abroad 350
  The Future of Terrorism 350
    Future Causes of Terrorism 350
    Future Perpetrators 351
    Future Targets 352
Solutions 352
  What Won't Help? 352
  What May Help? 353
  Tolerating Terrorism 354
Web Sources 355
Discussion Questions 355
References 355

Chapter 14 · Transnational Corruption in the 21st Century:
Context and Countermeasures   361
Michaelene Cox
Introduction   361
   Contextualizing Corruption   362
   Definitions   363
   Causes and Consequences   367
   Measuring the Extent of Corruption   370
   Transnational Corruption   376
   Countermeasures to Transnational Corruption   378
Conclusion   382
Web Sources   384
Discussion Questions   385
References   385

Chapter 15 · International Drug Trafficking   391
Melanie-Angela Neuilly
Introduction   391
International Drug Trafficking and Consumption Patterns
   and Trends   391
   Patterns and Trends   392
      Drug Consumption   392
      Markets   393
   Drug Trafficking as Business   397
      Organized Crime and Drug Trafficking   397
      The Structure of the Drug Trafficking Industry   401
      Money Laundering   401
      Modeling the Drug Trafficking Industry   403
   Responses to the Drug Problem   404
      A Brief History of International Drug Control   404
      Timeline   407
      Institutions of Monitoring, Control, and Enforcement   411
      International Level   411
      Regional Level   412
      National Level: The United States   413
      Range of Responses to the Drug Problem:
        Looking to the Future   414
      The Confusing Case of European Extremes   414
      U.S. Policy   416
Web Sources   416

Discussion Questions 417
References 418

Chapter 16 · International Crimes: *Jus Cogens* and *Obligatio
    Erga Omnes* 423
Jessie L. Krienert, Jeffrey A. Walsh & Kevin Matthews
Introduction 423
Jus Cogens 424
Obligatio Erga Omnes 424
Maritime Piracy 425
    History 426
    Legal Issues: Universal Jurisdiction and *Jus Cogens* 427
    Piracy Today 428
Crimes against Humanity 429
    Apartheid 431
    Enforced Disappearances 432
        An Argentinean Example 433
        Legal Ramifications 434
Gendercide 435
Human Trafficking 437
    Becoming a Victim 438
    Key Players in the Trade 440
Sex Trafficking 441
    Sex Tourism 442
Slavery 443
    Involuntary Servitude 445
The International Organ Trade and Transplant Tourism 446
Legal Response and Universal Jurisdiction 447
Conclusion 448
Web Sources 449
Discussion Questions 449
References 450

Chapter 17 · Other International Crimes: Cyber Crime, Crimes
    against Cultural Heritage, Environmental Crimes,
    and Money Laundering 459
*Murugesan Srinivasan, Solomon Raja Pandian
    & Arockiasamy Enoch*
Introduction 459
Cybercrime 460

Nature and Magnitude of Cyber Crime   463
Global Initiatives to Deal with Cyber Crime   465
Characteristics of Computer Criminals   466
Crimes against Cultural Heritage   467
The Scope of the Problem   467
Challenges in Dealing with Crimes against Cultural Heritage   468
Environmental Crimes   469
Its Gravity   469
Global Response   471
Money Laundering   472
Initiatives of the International Community   474
Conclusion   475
Web Sources   476
Discussion Questions   477
References   477

Overall Conclusion   483

Index   485

Acknowledgments

First, I would like to thank two very important people in my life—my daughter, Gowtami and my parents—who are always supportive of everything I do. I am also grateful to all of the contributors who have made this endeavor possible. In particular, I would like to thank my mentor, Professor Freda Adler, who has been my inspiration since I received my Ph.D. about 22 years ago, and my two best friends, Lois Guyon and Ruth Fennick, for being my confidants and supporters. I would also like to extend my appreciation to David J. Estrin, a freelance editorial consultant, for offering valuable suggestions. Finally, I would like to extend my appreciation to my graduate student, Jeremy Braithwaite, my graduate assistant, Marat Abdukarimov, and my undergraduate assistant Sarah McCullough for their comments and support on this work.

Notes on Contributors

Richard Charlton is a graduate student in the Department of Criminal Justice Sciences at Illinois State University. His research interests include: juvenile justice, gangs, and rhino poaching in South Africa.

Michaelene Cox is an Associate Professor in the Department of Politics and Government at Illinois State University. She received her Ph.D. in political science from the University of Alabama in 2002 with specializations in international relations, public administration, and geography. She was employed more than ten years as a newspaper journalist before beginning a career in academia, and also has degrees in journalism and in visual culture. Her research interests include international law, social capital, quality of governance, and e-government. Her articles have appeared in the *Journal of Peace Research, Journal of Common Market Studies, Transition Studies Review*, and the *International Journal of Social Inquiry*. She has recently edited books about political corruption and violence; social capital and peace-building; and has co-edited a book about sovereignty and human rights.

Arockiasamy Enoch received his Ph.D. in Criminology from the University of Madras in 2009. He is currently a Lecturer at the Madras School of Social Work, Chennai. His research interests include: rehabilitation of drug abusers and reforms in prisons.

Harry R. Dammer is Professor and Chair of the Sociology and Criminal Justice at the University of Scranton. He received his Ph.D. from the Rutgers University School of Criminal Justice. He is the author of a book, *Religion in Corrections* (1999) and co-author of *Comparative Criminal Justice* (2006) and *The Offender in the Community* (2003). He has also published or co-published numerous articles, manuals, and professional reports on a variety of criminal justice topics. In 2009, he was a visiting professor at Ruhr-Bochum University in Germany under the auspices of his second Fulbright Grant. He is the former Chair of the International Section of the Academy of Criminal Justice Sciences (March 2003 to March 2004).

Mathieu Deflem is an Associate Professor at the University of South Carolina. He received his Ph.D. in 1996 from the University of Colorado. His areas of expertise include international policing, terrorism and counter-terrorism, law, and theory. He has published dozens of articles in a wide variety of journals and books, and is the author of *The Policing of Terrorism* (2010), *Sociology of Law* (2008), and *Policing World Society* (2002).

Gail Humiston is a doctoral student in the College of Health and Public Affairs, Criminal Justice track, at the University of Central Florida. Her research interests include corrections, victimology, juvenile justice, human rights, comparative justice, social inequalities and crime, gender and policing, evaluative research methods, and domestic violence.

J.D. Jamieson is a Professor in the Criminal Justice Department at Texas State University, San Marcos. He received his Ph.D. in Criminal Justice from Sam Houston State University in 1981. He has published articles and books on deviant behavior, police and police problem solving, American criminal procedure, and corrections. He is currently involved in cross cultural research with colleagues in Thailand, and is co-authoring books on western criminology theory and family violence as they apply to Asian cultures.

Sesha Kethineni is a Professor in the Department of Criminal Justice Sciences at Illinois State University. She received her Ph.D. in criminal justice from Rutgers, the State University of New Jersey, and her LL.M. degree from the University of Illinois-Urbana/Champaign. Her recent works include female homicide offending in India, status of children in India, domestic violence, and program evaluation. Her co-authored book titled *Comparative Delinquency: India and the United States* received the 1997 Distinguished Book Award by the International Division of American Society of Criminology. She received the college and the university Outstanding Researcher awards.

Jessie L. Krienert is an Associate Professor in the Department of Criminal Justice Sciences at Illinois State University. She received her Ph.D. in criminal justice from the University of Nebraska at Omaha in 2000. Dr. Krienert has published over a dozen articles in top criminal justice journals and has co-authored books on the subculture of prison rape and employment and crime. Her research interests include prison subculture, masculinity, offenders with disabilities, and understudied forms of family violence.

Rebecca Lawson received her M.S. in Criminal Justice from Illinois State University. For more than ten years, she worked as an Intensive Probation Supervision officer, Juvenile Division, McLean County Court Services, Illinois. Currently, she works as an Intelligent Analyst at the Normal Police Department, Illinois. Her research interests include: mental health of inmates, juvenile diversion program, crime analysis, and juvenile diversion program.

Satenik Margaryan is an Assistant Professor at Montclair State University. She received her Ph.D. in criminal justice from Rutgers, the State University of New Jersey. Her research interests include the treatment of prisoners mandated by international human rights instruments; national penal reform processes and penal systems in countries in transition. She has recently published her Ph.D. dissertation as a book which examined the penal reform in the Republic of Armenia since the collapse of the Soviet Union.

Kevin Matthews was a graduate student in the Department of Criminal Justice Sciences at Illinois State University.

Sarah McCullough is an undergraduate student in the Department of Criminal Justice Sciences at Illinois State University. She received her B.S. in Journalism from Illinois State University and is currently pursuing a B.S. in Criminal Justice Sciences. She has published several articles in *The Daily Vidette*, Illinois State University's daily news publication. She was also a co-presenter with Dr. Sesha Kethineni at the Academy of Criminal Justice Sciences Annual Meeting 2014. Her research focuses on international criminology and orders of protection in domestic violence cases.

Shannon McDonough is a Ph.D. candidate in Sociology at the University of South Carolina. Her master's thesis explored the relationship between school surveillance measures and fear. Her research interests include surveillance studies, criminology, and gender inequality.

Melanie-Angela Neuilly is an Assistant Professor at the University of Idaho. She received a Ph.D. in Criminal Justice from Rutgers, the State University of New Jersey, in 2007, and a Ph.D. in Psychology from the University of Rennes II in France in 2008. She has published both in American and French peer-reviewed journals and edited volumes. Her research focuses on international and comparative criminology and criminal justice issues, violent crime and violent deaths, social construction and methodological questions.

Solomon Raja Pandian received his Ph.D. in Criminology from the University of Madras in 2008. He is currently pursuing the specialized course in victimology at the Tokiwa International Victimology Institute, Tokiwa University, Mito, Japan. His research interests include victimological theories and cybercrime victimization.

Philip L. Reichel is a Professor in the Department of Criminal Justice at the University of Northern Colorado. During his 30-plus years in academia, Dr. Reichel has received awards for his teaching, advising, service, and scholarship. He is the author of *Comparative Criminal Justice Systems: A Topical Approach* (2008); co-author with Leanne Alarid of *Corrections: A Contemporary Introduction* (2008); editor of the *Handbook of Transnational Crime and Justice* (2005); and has authored or co-authored more than thirty articles, book chapters, and encyclopedia entries. His areas of expertise include corrections, comparative justice systems, and transnational crime.

Jeffrey Ian Ross received his Ph.D. from University of Colorado-Boulder in 1993. He is an Associate Professor in the Division of Criminology, Criminal Justice and Forensic Studies, and a Fellow of the Center for International and Comparative Law at the University of Baltimore. His areas of expertise include national security, political violence, political crime, violent crime, corrections, and policing for over two decades. Dr. Ross is the author, co-author, editor and co-editor of thirteen books including *Will Terrorism End?* (2006); *Political Terrorism: An Interdisciplinary Approach* (2006); *The Dynamics of Political Crime* (2002); and the forthcoming *Encyclopedia of Religion and Violence*. He has performed consulting services for Westat; CSR; U.S. Department of Defense; Office of Juvenile Justice and Delinquency Prevention; The National Institute of Justice; and U.S. Department of Homeland Security.

Gabriel Rubin is an Assistant Professor in the Justice Studies Department at Montclair State University. He received his Ph.D. in Political Science from the Massachusetts Institute of Technology in 2008. He has attended numerous conferences presenting on issues of terrorism, public opinion, and global justice. His dissertation seeks to explain variation in legislative reactions to terrorist attacks. He resides in Bedminster, New Jersey, with his wife Ariel and son Shai.

Murugesan Srinivasan received his Ph.D. in Criminology from the University of Madras in 1998. He is currently a Reader in the Department of Criminology, University of Madras. He has published more than 30 articles in regional, national, and international journals. He has conducted many research projects sponsored by both national and international funding agencies/institutions. His research and publication focus on the following areas: police administration, victimology, and economic crimes.

Michael Stohl received his Ph.D. in Political Science from Northwestern University in 1974. He is a Professor and Chair of the Department of Communication and Professor of Political Science at the University of California, Santa Barbara (UCSB) and International Partner Investigator for the Centre of Excellence for Policing and Security, a partnership of the Australian National University and Griffith University. Dr. Stohl's research focuses on political communication and international relations with special reference to political violence, terrorism, and human rights. He is the author or co-author of more than one hundred scholarly journal articles and book chapters and the author, editor or co-editor of twelve books. His most recent publications include "Winners and Losers in the War on Terror: The Problem of Metrics," in William Thompson and Rafi Reuveny (eds.), *Coping with Contemporary Terrorism: Origins, Escalation, Counter Strategies and Responses*, published in 2010.

Donna Vandiver is an Associate Professor of Criminal Justice at Texas State University, San Marcos. She received her Ph.D. in Criminal Justice from Sam Houston State University in 2002. She has published over a dozen articles in regional, national, and international journals. She has also co-authored a book, *Juvenile Sex Offenders: What the Public Needs to Know*. Her research interests include human rights issues in developing countries, offenders with special needs, and sexual offenders.

Jeffrey A. Walsh is an Associate Professor at Illinois State University. He received his Ph.D. in Criminal Justice from the City University of New York Graduate School in 2005. Dr. Walsh has published over a dozen articles in some of the leading journals in the field of criminal justice and has co-authored several book chapters on issues ranging from underserved victim populations to teaching pedagogy and practices. His research interests include predatory crime, community social structure and crime, victimization, and understudied forms of family violence.

Ralph Weisheit received his Ph.D. in Sociology from Washington State University. He is currently a Distinguished Professor of Criminal Justice at Illinois State University where he has been teaching and conducting research for over 25 years. He has authored eight books, including *Pursuing Justice, Domestic Marijuana: A Neglected Industry, Crime and Policing in Rural and Small-Town America*, and *Methamphetamine: Its History, Pharmacology, and Treatment*. His current research interests include drugs and crime, rural crime, and international justice.

L. Edward Wells received his Ph.D. in Sociology from the University of Wisconsin, Madison, in 1976. He is currently a Professor in Criminal Justice Sciences at Illinois State University. His publications have covered a variety of topics, but recent research has focused largely on ecological explanations of crime and policing across a broad range of community settings from highly urbanized to remotely rural.

Introduction

The current edition of the book includes five revised and three new chapters (corruption, juvenile justice, and corrections) from a comparative criminal justice perspective. The text is organized into seventeen chapters beginning with "Justice Systems in Selected Countries," which provides the audience a broad understanding of the origin of four legal traditions, their evolution, and their contemporary context. This topic is followed by a chapter addressing the role of international justice organizations (Chapter 2), including the International Court of Justice and the International Criminal Court. Specifically, chapter two outlines the jurisdiction of the courts, their current cases, trial processes, and limitations related to enforceability.

The third chapter offers a discussion of "Sovereign Lawlessness," an interesting and important topic previously underexamined in comparative criminal justice textbooks. The chapter examines the interrelationship between military justice and international criminal justice from historical and comparative perspectives. Using "rendition" as an example, it reviews the involvement of U.S. Intelligence Agencies and other international communities in extrajudicial abductions. Chapter 4 explores international law enforcement organizations (i.e. Interpol and Europol). This chapter also discusses how police autonomy was interrupted by events such as World War I and the Bolshevik Revolution. In addition, highlights include contemporary dimensions of international policing, and how the scope of international policing has been expanded due to a general rise in international crimes.

The next two chapters (Chapters 5 and 6) examine policing topics, including "Policing in Selected Countries," and "Policing Subordinate Sovereignties." The latter topic offers a particularly unique contribution with emphasis on neocolonial societies, specifically American Indians in the United States. The chapter highlights how sovereignty is granted to indigenous tribal groups and how such limited autonomy affected traditional identities and ways of life of native tribal peoples in the United States, Canada, and New Zealand. In addition, fundamental problems of policing subordinate tribal populations are discussed.

The book also includes chapters on correctional systems, philosophies, recent innovations (Chapter 7), and juvenile justice in selected countries (Chapter 8). Chapter 7 provides a thorough description of the goals of corrections, world imprisonment rates, and custodial and non-custodial sanctions in England, China, Japan, and Saudi Arabia. In addition, information is provided on the role of the United Nations in developing guidelines for the treatment of inmates in correctional institutions. Chapter 8 shifts the discussion to juvenile law violators and the role of the United Nations in developing guidelines for their proper treatment. In addition, the four models (i.e., welfare, legalistic, corporatist, and participatory) of juvenile justice and how they are incorporated in the juvenile justice systems of respective countries are addressed.

The next chapter (Chapter 9), "The Global Normative Order," discusses the important, yet neglected topic of international individual rights. The chapter provides challenging, and at times controversial, arguments whether individual rights can be truly maintained in a democracy. The chapter also presents a thought-provoking debate on whether fundamental rights should be derived at the group level or at the individual level.

The discussion continues with preservation of human rights, and atrocities committed in violation of human rights in Chapters 10 through 12. While Chapter 10 focuses on the international human rights movement, Chapter 11 discusses genocide and war crimes in Bosnia, Herzegovina, Rwanda, and Sudan. Group and minority rights, which are rarely included in comparative criminal justice textbooks, are presented in Chapter 12. This Chapter reviews the deprivation of economic, social, and cultural rights of *Dalits* in India, and Roma/Gypsies of Europe.

The last five chapters (Chapter 13 through 17) focus on international crimes including terrorism, corruption, drug trafficking, maritime piracy, cybercrime and several other international crimes. Chapter 13 provides a discussion of laws, treaties, and military-led activities related to international terrorism, focusing primarily on political terrorism. Chapter14 provides an introduction to political, economic and social challenges posed by both public and private corruption. It also discusses specific strategies for controlling increasing transnational corruption. Chapter 15 examines drug trafficking and consumption patterns and trends from a global perspective and its link to organized crime and criminals. It also examines the international responses to the drug problem. Chapters 16 and 17 examine international crimes of piracy, gendercide, maritime piracy, human trafficking, slavery, cybercrime, crimes against cultural heritage, money laundering, and environmental crimes.

Overall, the book includes both essential and traditional topics of international criminal justice as well as several important and emerging novel topic areas that have not been covered in other comparative criminal justice textbooks. This broad and expanded approach gives the audience a deeper understanding of the international criminal justice system, transnational crimes and the role of both international and domestic agencies in past, present, and future crime prevention.

Comparative and International Policing, Justice, and Transnational Crime

Chapter 1

Justice Systems in Selected Countries

Philip L. Reichel

Introduction

The United Nations (UN) counts 193 countries as member states. One thing all those countries have in common is a desire to maintain social order among their citizens. That preservation of order relies on the cooperation of citizens as they go about their daily lives, abiding by rules for how people should behave. Unfortunately, in every society there are some people who do not follow those guidelines and, as a result, the social order is disrupted. The extent of that disruption ranges from minimal (e.g., Molly failed to hold open the door for Sara whose arms were overloaded with books) to extreme (e.g., Harry intentionally kills Sam). When the violation is minor the response by society is likely to be insignificant and informal (e.g., Li frowns at Molly and rushes to help Sara). When the violation is extreme the response is likely to be noteworthy and formal (e.g., Harry is executed or put in prison for life). It is the second type of violation that we are concerned with in this chapter.

Behavior guidelines that society has identified as crucial for maintaining social order will eventually become laws. When a person violates those laws they commit a social wrong or crime. But how does society find out when a crime has been committed and who committed it? If a suspect is identified, how can society be sure he or she is truly the culprit? Once society is convinced they have found the offender, how will the person be punished for his or her wrongdoing? Those questions are ones that all countries must address if social order is to be maintained. Every society must have a means by which their laws can be enforced (i.e., a policing function), a process in which they have confidence that identifies the person who actually broke the law (i.e., an adjudication function), and a way those law violators can be held accountable for their actions (i.e., a corrections function).

The procedures established by a country to accomplish policing, adjudication, and corrections are considered that country's legal system. As you can imagine, with 193 different countries there may well be 193 different legal systems. Some countries might believe policing is best accomplished with a single national police force, whereas another country may prefer multiple national police forces. Others may dislike any sort of national police and prefer a system of decentralization. Similar variations could occur with adjudication (e.g., should we use a professional adjudicator or laypeople?) and with corrections (e.g., is it best to physically separate criminals from the law abiding or to reintegrate them into the community?).

With so many potential variations how can we most succinctly describe how the world's countries have gone about trying to maintain social order? One strategy is to find some broad similarity among the legal systems and to then group systems according to the similarity. We do this by using four broad categories called "legal traditions" into which the various legal systems can be placed. This chapter provides examples of several legal systems (China, England and Wales, France, Germany, India, and Saudi Arabia), placing them in the broader context of their legal traditions (common, civil, Islamic, and mixed).

Four Legal Traditions

Comparative legal scholars do not agree on how many legal traditions exist today nor on what names should be applied to them. Some have suggested as few as three traditions, whereas others have identified as many as sixteen. Regardless of number, two traditions that are invariably included are the civil legal tradition and the common legal tradition. Other popular groupings include religions, socialist, customary, philosphical, and mixed traditions. A four-category strategy is used for this chapter, and they are identified as the common, civil, Islamic, and mixed legal traditions.

Common Legal Tradition

The common law legal tradition is familiar to citizens of the United States because common law was originally developed in England and influenced the law's application in the British colonies. Today, the United States, Canada, Australia, New Zealand, India, and former British colonies in Africa join the United Kingdom in having legal systems counted among those of the common legal tradition.

Although several things distinguish common law from the other legal traditions (Reichel 2013), the key feature is the belief that custom provides the primary source of law. This belief is said to have been established by the Constitutions of Clarendon (1164), which listed customs said to be the practice in England at the beginning of the twelfth century. The idea was that traditional, consistent, and reasonable ways of deciding disputes provided the appropriate source of law. Determining whether something was "customary" fell to members of the community who sat as a jury of peers.

Countries differ in the specific structure and procedures established for their legal system, but if they maintain that law originates in custom they are included among those countries following the Common legal tradition (Dammer, Reichel, & He 2014). Identifying those countries where law is based on custom is often accomplished by reference to the use of precedent or *stare decisis*. Following this principle, decisions in current cases are guided by decisions made on similar points in earlier cases. The rationale for this practice was originally an understanding that earlier court decisions were evidence of custom. Judges were expected to follow legal custom by abiding by prior decisions in similar cases. In this manner, custom could be identified by reliance on the people and through reference to several cases. It is important to note, however, that the case was not referred to as the source of law; it merely provided proof that a legal principle (i.e., a custom) was once applied. Eventually prior cases were used less to prove custom and more to reference authority (typically a higher court).

Civil Legal Tradition

The civil legal tradition is the oldest and most widespread of contemporary legal traditions. Originating in the codes of Roman law (e.g., the *Corpus Juris Civilis*), the civil legal tradition views law as resulting from written codes provided by a political authority. When laws are put in writing, or codified, they are believed to provide a clear statement to citizens regarding their rights and obligations. In addition, written laws allow judges to easily determine if a crime has occurred and to set the appropriate punishment. In this way law is made by legislators (or other political authorities) and the courts simply enforce the law rather than interpret it or make new laws (Reichel 2002a).

Contemporary countries identified as falling in the civil legal family were most likely inspired by the civil codes of France or Germany. The French *Code Napoléon* (1804) was especially influential in continental Europe and Latin America. It was developed to be an easily read and understood handbook that would allow citizens to figure out for themselves (rather than relying on a lawyer) their legal rights and obligations. Like their French contemporaries, nineteenth-century Germans believed codification of law could help pull together a new nation. However, unlike the French, the Germans did not believe it was either desirable or possible to remove lawyers from the legal system. The German Civil Code of 1896 was a historically oriented, scientific, and professional document that assumed lawyers would be needed to interpret and apply the law (Merryman 1985; Reichel 2002a).

Despite some dissimilarity between the French and Germany codes, both incorporated a sharp separation of powers in which the legislator makes law and the judge does not. And that reemphasizes the distinguishing feature of the civil legal tradition—the source of law is codification by a political authority. The role of judges in this tradition is to apply, not make, law.

Islamic Legal Tradition

The Islamic legal tradition is unique among legal families in several respects. First, it views law's source as being sacred rather than secular. The other legal traditions, especially civil and common, have religious links, but they remain distinct and separate from religion. The Islamic legal tradition, on the other hand, is completely reliant on religion.

Islamic law is called the *Shari'a* (the path to follow). Its primary ingredients are the *Qur'an* (Islam's holy book) and the *Sunna* (the statements and deeds of Muhammad). These two elements identify both crimes and punishments but they provide little information regarding the legal process by which offenders are brought to justice. The *Sunna* refers to the way the Prophet Muhammad lived his life. The *Sunna* is reported in *hadiths,* which are statements that provide a narration about the life of the Prophet in terms of what he said, did, or approved. The *hadiths* have been passed on in a continuous and reliable chain of transmission from Muhammad and his companions to later adherents. A *hadith* contains three important parts: the statement itself, an indication of its authority by reference to the chain of reporters (i.e., A heard it from B who heard it from C who heard it from a companion of Muhammad), and a comment regarding the report as being something Muhammad did, said, or approved (Reichel 2013, 94). For example, in reference to kissing during fasting time, Book 18 of Malik's *Muwatta* (Number 18.5.17), reads: "Yahya related to me from Malik from Zayd ibn Aslam that Abu Hurayra and Sad ibn Abi Waqqas used to say that someone who was fasting was allowed to kiss" (Center for Muslim-Jewish Engagement n.d.-b).

In the *Shari'a* Allah (God) identified the crimes and stipulated the penalty, but the law's application fell to humans. Not surprisingly, humans disagreed about how to apply Allah's law. Some Muslims took a strict interpretation and believed that every rule of law must be derived from the *Qur'an* or the *Sunna.* Others believed human reason and personal opinion could be used to elaborate the law. The latter camp suggested that as the centuries progressed from Muhammad's time, there were new behaviors or situations that had not been directly addressed in the early seventh century. Human reason, these Muslims believed, could be used to fill the gaps. The result today is five different schools of law that are linked to either the *Sunni* or *Shi'a* division of Islam. In order to know how Islamic law is applied in a particular jurisdiction, one must know which Islamic school of thought is relevant. For example, in most of the schools the consumption of alcohol is forbidden, but the *Hanafi* school interprets the *hadd* as punishing a Muslim for being drunk—not for drinking. Thus, that school allows the consumption of alcohol until inebriation (Lippman, McConville, and Yerushalmi 1988).

Mixed Legal Tradition

Countries included in the mixed legal tradition are those that incorporate elements from several of the traditions. Also called hybrid systems, the countries in this grouping include those where components of one legal tradition have combined with components from another legal tradition to form a hybrid system (Dammer, et al. 2014).

Palmer (2008) has suggested that countries in this category will have, in a manner obvious to an ordinary observer, the basic elements of two traditions operating so that one predominates in the field of private law (civil law, for example) and the other in criminal law (for example, common law). Mixed legal systems in this sense are rather few in number and exclude countries with mixes of other groups. Castellucci (2008), suggests these other legal traditions might be included if the idea of *mixed* is seen in a more descriptive sense than the classificatory one provided by adherence to three or more categories. Using a family-tree approach, Castellucci describes a forest of legal system family trees wherein the branches and foliage of each tree (each legal system) intertwines with others. Such a forest/family tree model would allow, for example, the existence of a Chinese legal system coming from a mixture of civil law and socialist law. That "tree" intertwines with, for example, Hong Kong's Chinese-common law mix and with a Chinese-customary mix that may describe the North Korea legal system (Dammer, et al. 2014).

China provides a good example of a country representing the mixed legal tradition. There are aspects of socialism wherein law is said to exist to serve the purposes of the socialist revolution, but—especially in the last several years—

China increasingly incorporates features that reflect civil and common legal traditions. Following the lead of Castellucci (2008) and others (Örücü 2008) who consider mixed legal systems as including more than a combination of just a few traditions, China is used here as a country that mixes elements of socialism with those from the civil legal tradition and traditional (or customary) law.

Substantive and Procedural Criminal Law

Even when countries are grouped according to the legal tradition into which they fall, it is convenient to have additional categories by which we may describe the similarities and differences among countries. For example, every country is presented with the dual problem of determining what the laws will be and specifying how they will be enforced. That first problem, determining the law, results in *substantive* criminal law. The second problem, specifying enforcement, refers to *procedural* criminal law. These two essential ingredients of a justice system will be used in this chapter to describe some key features of legal systems representing each of the four legal traditions. For those descriptions to make the most sense, it will be helpful to explain both substantive and procedural criminal law and to identify the particular aspects of each that are used to describe the six countries discussed in this chapter.

Substantive criminal law is the part of law that defines what is criminal and specifies a punishment. The best example of a country's substantive criminal law is its penal or criminal code. Procedural criminal law, on the other hand, is the part of law that specifies how a government will go about enforcing the law. That is, what procedures must be followed by the police, prosecutor, judges, and other criminal justice system actors when someone is believed to have committed a crime? Let us take a more detailed look at each.

Substantive Criminal Law

As noted above, a country's substantive law is best seen by looking at its penal or criminal code. For example, Germany's penal code has this entry for the crime of theft: "Whoever takes moveable property not his own away from another with the intent of unlawfully appropriating the property for himself or a third person, shall be punished with imprisonment for not more than five years or a fine" (Federal Republic of Germany 1998). This is an example of substantive criminal law because Germany has defined what is criminal (taking moveable property from another) and specified the punishment (up to five years in prison or a fine). This seems straightforward, but unfortunately it becomes more complicated as we look closely at what is required for a particular behavior to be considered criminal. Looking again at the German law of theft, we note that beyond simply taking moveable property from another, the law also requires that the person take that property "with the intent of unlawfully appropriating" it. The term "intent" adds a dimension beyond simple taking. Now, the law suggests, the act must occur along with some plan or purpose on the part of the person.

The requirement of intent is part of the fundamental nature of crime. More specifically, crime's core consists of three elements: (1) a criminal act (*actus reus*), (2) a guilty mind (*mens rea*), and (3) a fusion of the two (concurrence). In this manner, the essence of criminal conduct is said to consist of the concurrence of a criminal act with a culpable mental state (Reichel 2013; Schmalleger 2008). Thus, Germany's crime of theft requires both an act ("taking") and a state of mind ("intent of unlawfully appropriating"). The concurrence of these two elements is something the prosecution will try to show in court when attempting to prove guilt.

All three elements play an important role in determining whether someone is guilty of committing a crime, but we will consider only the guilty mind (*mens rea*). More specifically, we will look at those situations where a person committed an act that should be criminal, but the person is considered to be incapable of having criminal intent and so cannot be judged criminal. Several situations of this type are familiar to you (e.g., a person was not old enough to have a guilty mind), but we will consider the insanity defense as our example in each of six countries. Before doing that, however, let us briefly consider the role of procedural criminal law.

Procedural Criminal Law

Just as we must focus on only one aspect of substantive criminal law in the six countries covered in this chapter, so too must we spotlight only one aspect of procedural criminal law. That aspect will be the procedure a country uses to decide whether an accused is guilty of a crime (i.e., a country's adjudication procedure). Broadly speaking, that process is one of two types: (1) an adversarial process, or (2) an inquisitorial process. The former is more typical (but not required) of countries in the common legal tradition. The latter is more often found (but, again, not a requirement) in civil legal tradition countries.

The Adversarial Process

The adversarial system is often considered a substitute for private vengeance. As societies evolve, the power to initiate action first lies with the wronged person (the accuser) then, over time, with the state (e.g., *State of Texas v. Jones*). The setting for the accusation is before an impartial official serving as referee (judge). Because the disputing parties (the state and the accused) behave as if they are engaged in a contest, they are considered adversaries.

Believing that truth in a case will unfold from a free and open competition over which side has the correct facts, the adversarial process positions the prosecution and defense as opponents in a contest. As opponents, the prosecution and defense play an active role by calling witnesses and asking them questions. The two sides rely on cross-examination to challenge or destroy a witness's testimony. Each side has a chance to question the honesty of witnesses, search for biases, and figure out what witnesses actually know instead of what they think they know. The judge serves as a referee in this contest by ensuring that the players abide by the rules. Observing the contest are lay people who were selected as jurors and charged with deciding whether the prosecution has proved its claims against the defendant or if the defense has placed sufficient doubt in the jurors' minds regarding the prosecution's claims (Reichel 2002b).

The Inquisitorial Process

Any discussion of the inquisitorial process, especially for an audience from a common-law country, must begin by distinguishing it from the term "inquisition." The Spanish Inquisition of the late fifteenth century was notorious for its use of torture to compel cooperation in its religious investigations. The only thing it had in common with today's inquisitorial process was the prominent role given to the judges. The judge is at the center of the fact-gathering process in the inquisitorial system, but torture is not.

In contrast to the adversarial process wherein society (represented by the government) takes the victim's place as accuser, the inquisitorial process replaces the idea of accusation with an investigation by the government. This is an important distinction because it means that public officials (whether the defense or the prosecution) are not engaged in a contest. Instead, they are all engaged in an investigation that tries to determine what transpired.

Believing that truth in a case results from everyone working together, the inquisitorial process involves an investigation wherein the police, attorneys, and judges pool their efforts to determine what happened. Trials continue that investigation by providing professional and lay judges with an active courtroom role that includes the calling and questioning of witnesses and the ability to simultaneously consider the defendant's guilt and appropriate punishment.

Mixed Process

Not surprisingly, the great variation among countries in how justice is accomplished makes it impossible to identify each country as being either adversarial or inquisitorial in nature. Instead, many countries have adapted adjudication procedures that reflect aspects of both adversarial and inquisitorial procedures. These mixed systems, almost by definition, cannot be summarized in a paragraph or two, but will be seen in the examples below of India and Saudi Arabia.

With this background we are prepared to review examples of the legal system in countries that fall into one of four legal traditions. Because it is not possible to review all (or even many) aspects of each legal system, we concentrate on one feature of substantive criminal law (*mens rea*) and one feature of procedural criminal law (which adjudication procedure is used). This will allow a comparison of six countries in four different legal traditions. We begin with two countries representing the common legal tradition.

Justice Systems in Common-Law Countries

As noted earlier, a key feature of the common legal tradition is a belief that custom is the source of law and that court rulings should follow legal custom by abiding by prior decisions in similar cases. This issue is relevant to substantive law because it requires the determination of whether the behavior in question constitutes a crime as it is customarily understood. Using the example of *mens rea*, we will see how two common-law countries determine whether an accused is criminally responsible.

In addition to the substantive law question of whether a person's mental state meets the customary definition of crime, there is the related procedural law question of how to best determine whether the accused is actually guilty of committing the crime. On this point, we find that our two common-law countries differ slightly in terms of their preferred adjudication method.

England and Wales

England and Wales have a combined criminal justice system, whereas the two other countries that make up the United Kingdom (Scotland and Northern Ireland) each have their own systems. The criminal justice system of England and Wales is the home of the common legal tradition and, as such, custom has played a primary role in the system's development. During the fifth century, freemen of local communities acted as judges and based their decisions on community perceptions as to how cases should be handled (Carter and Swift 2009; Phillips, Cox, and Pease 1993).

There is no single written constitution for England and Wales, so substantive and procedural law come from statutes, case law, and constitutional conventions. Changes to the criminal justice system occur mostly as constitutional reforms and, since 1997, there have been significant ones. For example, the 800-year-old protection against double jeopardy—one of the oldest legal concepts in Western tradition—was abandoned by the 2003 Criminal Justice Act. Now, a re-trial is allowed for certain serious crimes when new and compelling evidence comes to light (Third time unlucky 2006).

Among other changes, the Ministry of Justice was created on May 9, 2007, as the government department responsible for the justice system. Its head is the Lord Chancellor and Secretary of State for Justice. All criminal cases are heard initially in the magistrates' courts, with the more serious ones transferred to the Crown Court. Appeals from the magistrates' courts go to either to the Crown Court or the High Court, whereas appeals from the Crown Court go to the Court of Appeal, Criminal Division. The final court of appeal for criminal cases in England and Wales is the new Supreme Court for the United Kingdom. Beginning its operation in 2009, the Court's twelve justices serve as the final court of appeal for all U.K. civil cases, and for all criminal cases from England, Wales, and Northern Ireland (Rowe 2010; United Kingdom Supreme Court n.d.).

Substantive Law: Insanity

At the earliest stages of the common legal tradition and well into the thirteenth century, the mentally deranged were treated much like any other criminal. Eventually "insanity" was accepted as a condition that offers an excuse to what would otherwise be criminal responsibility. Yet deciding what constituted insanity remained a problem. The "wild beast test" developed in the thirteenth century was among the first methods used. It said that a madman was one "who does not know what he is doing, who is lacking in mind and reason, and who is not far removed from the brutes" (Hall 1960, 475).

The first long-lasting criteria for determining insanity came in 1843. In that year a court found Daniel M'Naghten not guilty of murdering Edward Drummond because M'Naghten was suffering from delusions. Specifically, M'Naghten felt pursued by several enemies, including Sir Robert Peel, who was England's prime minister at the time. M'Naghten killed Drummond while believing that Drummond was actually Peel. The public outcry in response to the acquittal resulted in a request by the House of Lords for the judges of the Queen's Bench to present their views of the insanity defense. Their response, considered by the judges to be a restatement of existing law rather than an innovation (Hall 1960), was called the *M'Naghten Rules*. They established a "right from wrong" test with the following necessary to show insanity: (1) At the time of the crime the defendant was operating under a defect of reason so as to be unable to know the nature or quality of the act; or (2) if the defendant was aware of the act's nature, he did not know the act was wrong (Moran 1985).

In 1975 a recommendation was presented to the British Parliament that the M'Naghten Rules be replaced by a new defense of "mental disorder." Under this defense a defendant who was suffering from "severe mental illness or subnormality" (both of which had specific definitions) could be found not guilty on evidence of mental disorder (Allnutt, Samuels, and O'Driscoll 2007). However, the recommendation was not acted upon at that time nor was it incorporated into more recent legislation (*Criminal Procedure [Insanity and Unfitness to Plead] Act* 1991). However, the M'Naghten Rules themselves were slightly rewritten, with "defect of reason" being replaced by "mental impairment," which could include intellectual disability and personality disorder. The second arm, relating to knowing the nature and quality of the act or its wrongfulness, was retained and a statement in relation to inability to "control the conduct" was added (Allnutt, Samuels, and O'Driscoll 2007, 293).

England also uses a standard of diminished responsibilities in cases of murder. According to Part 1 of the Homicide Act of 1957,

> Where a person kills or is a party to the killing of another, he shall not be convicted of murder if he was suffering from such abnormality of mind (whether arising from a condition of arrested or retarded development of mind or any inherent causes or induced by disease or injury) as substantially impaired his mental responsibility for his acts and omissions in doing or being a party to the killing (The National Archives n.d.-b).

The Homicide Act was amended by the Coroners and Justice Act 2009, which now requires that a successful defense of diminished responsibility show (The National Archives n.d.-a):

1. An abnormality of mental functioning caused by a recognized medical condition.
2. Which provides an explanation for the defendant's acts or omissions in being party to the killing.
3. Which substantially impaired his/her mental ability to either:
   a. Understand the nature of their conduct or
   b. Form a rational judgment or
   c. Exercise self-control.

A particularly controversial aspect of the diminished responsibilities defense is the role played by the jury. Determination of whether a person is guilty of murder or manslaughter, due to diminished responsibility (thus resulting in such things as hospital admission or a supervision and treatment order) is left to jurors, after hearing the opinion of psychiatric experts. Since expert opinions are often diametrically opposed, jurors are often left in a quandary as to how best to proceed (Summers 2007).

Procedural Law: Adjudication

The legal system in England and Wales is adversarial in all courts, including the juvenile courts (Phillips, Cox, and Pease 1993). Procedurally, England and Wales follow the adversarial process with active lawyers for both prosecution and defense. For serious cases, adjudication is by jury trial with jurors chosen at random from the voter registration list.

Although the British jury would look familiar to Americans, there is a difference in how the jurors came to their seat in each country. The U.S. practice of *voir dire,* wherein both prosecution and defense have limited opportunities to remove potential jurors believed to favor a particular side, is avoided in England. Instead, English jurors arrive at their position without having to suffer questioning by either prosecutor or defense. Actually, there are some limited opportunities to have a potential juror removed, but the typical jury consists simply of the first twelve names called.

India

India, which received independence from the United Kingdom in 1947, retains the common-law tradition established during British colonialism. The Indian Penal Code provides the country's substantive law by defining crime and prescribing appropriate punishments. It was adopted in 1860 and was clearly inspired by English criminal law. Procedural law is found in the Code of Criminal Procedure (enacted in 1861), which established the rules to be followed in all stages of investigation, trial, and sentencing. The Code of Criminal Procedure was replaced with a new code in 1974, but the Penal Code of 1860 remains essentially intact. Along with parts of the Indian Evidence Act of 1872, these three pieces of legislation form the essence of India's criminal law (Raghavan 1993).

The staying power of India's penal code, criminal procedure code, and evidence act is impressive. However, there is increasing pressure for a dramatic revision of the country's criminal justice system. In 2003, a committee formed by the Ministry of Home Affairs (the Malimath Committee) issued a report suggesting that the penal and criminal procedure codes and the evidence act all be examined to determine if they need to be altered to make them more in tune with contemporary issues (Malimath Committee on Reforms of Criminal Justice System 2003). That committee addressed investigation, prosecution, judiciary, and general issues of crime and punishment. A decade later, the majority of the recommendations were still awaiting implementation (Thakur 2013).

As Indians await action by their government on recommendations from either of these committees, their frustration is increasingly apparent—as reflected in one citizen's comment: "The gross reality of the system is that even after 60 years of independence, we are not able to create a people-friendly police system" (Kumar 2008,¶6).

Substantive Law: Insanity

True to its common-law heritage, India recognizes insanity as negating criminal responsibility, and does so with a reliance on the "knowing right from wrong" criterion. Section 84 of the Indian Penal Code stipulates that, "nothing is an offence which is done by a person who, at the time of doing it, by reason of unsoundness of mind, is incapable of knowing the nature of the act, or that he is doing what is either wrong or contrary to law" (*Indian Penal Code* 1860). Reference to unsoundness of mind is considered the same as the M'Naghten Rules, which remain the authoritative statement of law concerning criminal responsibility in India (Chakravarty 2001).

The penal code purposefully refers to "unsoundness of mind" rather than "insane" in this section, although "insane" is used elsewhere in the code (e.g., Sections 89 and 305). In addition, unsoundness of mind is neither defined nor illustrated in the code, except in an example of the crime of abetting (Penal Code Section 108), which makes criminal the acts of a person who encourages another to commit a crime:

> A instigates B to set fire to a dwelling-house. B, in consequence of the unsoundness of his mind, being incapable of knowing the nature of the act, or that he is doing what is wrong or contrary to law, sets fire to the house in consequence of A's instigation. B has committed no offence, but A is guilty of abetting the offence of setting fire to a dwelling-house, and is liable to the punishment provided for that offence.

Greater clarity was provided in 1959 in the case *Lakshmi v. State* wherein an Indian court differentiated between the capacity to know something and what a person knows. What Section 84 protects, the court explained, is a situation wherein:

... a man in whom the guiding light that enables a man to distinguish between right and wrong and between legality and illegality is completely extinguished. Where such light is found to be still flickering, a man cannot be heard to plead that he should be protected because he was misled by his own misguided intuition or by any fancied delusion which had been haunting him and which he mistook to be a reality (Yeo 2008, 248).

This suggests that not every type of unsoundness of mind is encompassed by Section 84. The key feature is that one's cognitive ability must be so destroyed as to render one incapable of knowing the nature of the act or that what one was doing was wrong or contrary to the law. In this manner, irresistible impulse, mental agitation, annoyance, and fury all merely indicate loss of control and are not examples of unsoundness of mind (Chakravarty 2001).

India's continued reliance on its 1860 reference to unsoundness of mind has been criticized by some as being dated and not accommodating recent views about mental illness (Chakravarty 2001). But there seems little chance of any change in the near future because neither of the most recent suggestions for reform of India's criminal justice system have encouraged additional or alternate views on what constitutes unsoundness of mind (Draft National Policy on Criminal Justice 2007; Malimath Committee on Reforms of Criminal Justice System 2003).

Procedural Law: Adjudication

Despite being in the common legal tradition, India relies on a mixed adjudication process. Aspects of the adversarial process are found in the combative role played by prosecution and defense. However, the judge in India has a prominent role as adjudicator and this reflects aspects of the inquisitorial process.

Jury trials were abolished by the Indian government in 1960 following a controversial case (*K. M. Nanavati vs. State of Maharashtra*) in which a defendant charged with shooting his wife's lover was acquitted. The jury's verdict was dismissed by the high court and after a new trial (not before a jury) the defendant was found guilty and sentenced to life imprisonment for premeditated murder (NationMaster n.d.). As a result, formal trials are heard before a professional judge and adjudication is by that judge.

Although no formal juries exist in India today, many minor issues in rural areas are handled by the *panchayats* (village courts). Vincentnathan and Vincentnathan (2007) explain that, although they have existed for millennia, the *panchayats* have been changed by modernization and many have disappeared. The decline in the *panchayats* is occurring at the same time that many in India are increasingly critical of their official criminal justice system—including

India's Supreme Court, which declared the lower courts to be decayed and used only by those people who have no other option (Mahapatra 2009).

Justice Systems in Civil-Law Countries

Codification is the primary source of law in countries of the civil legal tradition, so identification of substantive and procedural law typically requires no more than reviewing the country's criminal code (sometimes called the "penal code") and the code of criminal procedure. We see both types of code used in the following descriptions of the insanity defense in France and Germany.

After reviewing insanity codes in each country, we will look briefly at the adjudication process used in our two sample countries. Because both follow the civil legal tradition it will not be a great surprise to find that they prefer the inquisitorial process.

France

Just as England is home to common law, France can argue for a similar heritage regarding civil law. Like most civil-law countries, France divides its laws into public and private law. The criminal laws are public law, and, as expected in a civil-law system, are the result of specific legislation resulting in a written document. The two primary documents are the Code of Criminal Procedure and the Penal Code. The former specifies how to investigate a case and how to try a person charged with a criminal offense. Substantive law is prescribed in the Penal Code, which identifies the types of offenses and their respective punishments (Reichel 2013).

Substantive Law: Insanity

The French Penal Code (French Republic n.d.-b), which assumes individuals have free will and are rational decision makers, specifies that "No one is criminally liable except for his own conduct" (Penal Code Article 121-1). However, in addition to that conduct (*actus reus*), French law also requires that *mens rea* be present: "There is no felony or misdemeanor [sic] in the absence of an intent to commit it" (Penal Code Article 121-3). Thus, it is possible that a person could commit an act that would otherwise be criminal, but the person would not be considered criminally liable if intent was absent. The Penal Code identifies several circumstances where criminal intent may not have been present (e.g., acts committed by coercion, acts committed in self-defense, acts committed by minors), and one of those is a situation of insanity.

According to Article 122-1 of the French penal code: "A person is not criminally liable who, when the act was committed, was suffering from a psychological or neuropsychological disorder which destroyed his discernment or his ability to control his actions." The French Code of Criminal Procedure (French Republic n.d.-a) explains that if the defense argued that the defendant was not criminally responsible under Penal Code Article 122-1, the court (i.e., judges and lay judges, as explained below) is required to ask two questions (Code of Criminal Procedure Article 349-1): (1) Did the accused commit this act?, and (2) Was the accused's judgment or ability to control his actions destroyed by a psychological or neuropsychological disorder? If the court answers "yes" to the first question and "no" to the second, the accused is declared guilty. If the court answers "no" to the first question and "yes" to the second, it declares the accused to be not guilty (Code of Criminal Procedure Article 361-1).

If a psychological or neuropsychological disorder simply "reduced" rather than "destroyed" a person's judgment or ability to control his actions, he may still be found guilty but the court will take that diminished capacity into consideration when deciding the penalty (Penal Code Article 122-1).

Procedural Law: Adjudication

By the mid-sixteenth century, the inquisitorial method was standardized and required for all French courts. Terrill (2003) identifies the major characteristics of that process as (1) the positioning of the king's prosecutor as a party to the suit in every criminal case and (2) the use of two magistrates during the course of the investigation and the trial. The first point is important because it recognized the state's (i.e., the king's) interest in the case and abolished the accusatory idea of trials as duels between two parties. The second point highlights the primary and active role that judges, rather than attorneys, play in a civil-law system (Reichel 2013).

As with many countries following the inquisitorial process, France relies on a mixed bench of professional and lay judges for adjudication of serious crimes. Specifically, at the Assize Court level the adjudicators consist of three professional judges (one presiding) and nine lay jurors who were chosen randomly from voter rolls. With the presiding judge's approval, the other professional judges and the lay jurors (all sitting together on the bench) may question the accused and the witnesses. Voting by judges and jurors is by secret ballot, with conviction requiring at least eight of the twelve members.

Germany

The German Civil Code, along with the French Napoleonic Code, had a significant influence on the development of the civil legal tradition. Today, the Federal Republic of Germany continues its link to the civil legal tradition and its reliance on codification as the source of law.

The country's original code of substantive law, the Penal Code of 1871, remained relatively intact for over 100 years. There were some important modifications (e.g., the creation of a special juvenile criminal law in 1923), but significant reform did not occur until a series of five Criminal Law Reform Acts beginning in 1969. Those acts emphasized restructuring the sanctions to make them more conducive to the rationale of rehabilitation (Aronwitz, 1993). Today, with its more than 140 years of history, and with nearly 200 major amendments of the law, the contemporary criminal code has a completely different character—but remains the codification of Germany's substantive law (Krehl 2003).

Substantive Law: Insanity

Germany's Penal Code (Federal Republic of Germany 1998) stipulates that "Only intentional conduct is punishable, unless the law expressly provides punishment for negligent conduct" (Section 15). But intent (*mens rea*) is absent in such circumstances as the actor being under age fourteen or if the person was suffering from an emotional disorder. The emotional disorder aspect is Germany's legal criterion for insanity:

> Whoever upon commission of the act is incapable of appreciating the wrongfulness of the act or acting in accordance with such appreciation due to a pathological emotional disorder, profound consciousness disorder, mental defect or any other serious emotional abnormality, acts without guilt (Penal Code Section 20).

The German Penal Code continues, in Section 21, to also excuse persons of "diminished capacity." Here, if the perpetrator's ability either to understand the wrongfulness of his or her conduct or to act in accordance with that understanding is substantially diminished (rather than absent, as in Section 20), he or she is still criminally responsible but subject to a reduced penalty.

According to Section 63 of the German Penal Code, persons who commit an unlawful act but are determined to have lacked *mens rea* (Section 20) or were in a state of diminished capacity (Section 21), may be placed in a psychiatric hospital if a comprehensive evaluation reveals that he or she can be expected to continue committing serious unlawful acts.

Procedural Law: Adjudication

Consistent with its civil legal tradition, Germany relies on an inquisitorial process of adjudication. The German people actually used a jury system in the 1840s, and briefly in Bavaria after World War II. For the most part, however, recent German history has involved the use of citizens as lay judges rather than as jurors. Specifically, the community chooses fellow citizens to serve on the bench with professional judges. These lay judges have full powers of interrogation, deliberation, voting, and sentencing. They serve in courts of limited jurisdiction (one professional judge and two lay judges) and in the higher level courts (three professional judges and two lay judges). Lay judges chosen for a particular trial can be challenged for bias, as can the professional judges, but such challenges are rare (Reichel 2013).

Justice Systems in an Islamic Law Country

The Kingdom of Saudi Arabia is one of only a few countries that fully implement *Shari'a* law (Iran is another). Other countries with a majority Muslim population (e.g., Jordan) use *Shari'a* mostly in private matters such as marriage, divorce, and inheritance. Some criminal laws in those countries reflect traditional Islamic practices (e.g., banning Muslims from drinking alcohol) but other aspects of criminal law are more secular in nature. For this reason, Saudi Arabia is used here as the best single example of a country following the Islamic legal tradition.

Saudi Arabia

Saudi Arabia does not have substantive law in the same sense as other countries. There is no penal code. In fact, as noted in Article 1 of the Basic Law of Government, there is no constitution other than the *Qur'an* and the *Sunna* (Kingdom of Saudi Arabia 1992). Likewise, there is no Saudi Arabia code of criminal procedure. Again, the *Qur'an* and *Sunna* provide basic standards for adjudication, but—as we will see below—there is more possibility for criminal procedure to be influenced by government decisions.

Substantive Law: Insanity

Absent a separate source of substantive law, questions of criminal responsibility in general must be answered by reference to the *Qur'an* and *Sunna*. From those sources, most Muslim scholars find that criminal intent (*mens rea*) has two aspects: (1) general criminal intent and (2) specific criminal intent (Reichel 2013, 116). The former is inferred whenever someone voluntarily participates in criminal conduct, but general intent is not always sufficient to show criminal responsibility. There are times when specific intent must be proven. In this sense, specific intent seems to refer to the need to prove that the person intended to commit the particular act under question and did so without justification or excuse. Because Islamic law will withhold criminal responsibility in such circumstances as coercion and necessity, it is possible for a person to have committed an illegal act with general intent (e.g., he knowingly hit another person) but without specific intent (e.g., he did so only to protect himself from the assailant).

Some of the Islamic reasons for withholding responsibility add an interesting twist on similar ones found in other countries. For example, infancy is a defense to crime under Islamic law, but Muslims believe that criminal capacity increases with age. As a result, criminal capacity is not possible until age seven is reached because younger children are not viewed as able to reason. Children between age seven and the onset of puberty have partial criminal capacity and therefore have some criminal responsibility. After the onset of puberty, a person can be held fully criminally responsible as long as he or she is of sound mind. Because puberty plays such an important role in assigning responsibility, we might expect it to be well defined by Muslim jurists. Sanad (1991), however, reports considerable disagreement. Some scholars say that it is determined by age (either eleven or twelve, depending on the scholar), whereas others say it varies in males and females, and still others argue that some signs of puberty should be used in making the judgment.

The defense of insanity is recognized in Islamic law by reference to such aspects of the *Sunna* as this *hadith* (Center for Muslim-Jewish Engagement n.d.-a): "Commander of the Faithful, do you not know that there are three people whose actions are not recorded: a lunatic till he is restored to reason, a sleeper till he awakes, and a boy till he reaches puberty?" (Sunan Abu-Dawud; Book 38, Number 4385: Narrated Ali ibn AbuTalib). The *Sunna*, therefore, recognizes a need for mental capacity as an aspect of punishment (other translations of this *hadith* use "punishment" rather than "recorded").

According to Sanad (1991) and Souryal (2004), there are two types of insanity in Islamic law: (1) prolonged, which totally destroys or drastically reduces one's awareness, and (2) sporadic, which attacks a person irregularly. Criminal responsibility is said to be absent in the case of prolonged insanity and in cases of sporadic insanity if the act occurred during one of those periods. A person suffering sporadic insanity is held criminally responsible if the act was committed during a period of sanity for that person.

Procedural Law: Adjudication

Because the *Shari'a* does not specify the means used to apprehend the offender and bring him to justice, the adjudicatory process developed at the discretion of the state. The result is a legal tradition that has features of both inquisitorial and adversarial procedure (Reichel 2013). The inquisitorial process is reflected in the tendency for trials to be essentially a continuation of the investigation process. In addition, the defense attorney's role is not as adversarial as it is one of presenting favorable evidence, safeguarding against improper incrimination, and overseeing the criminal judgments. Simultaneously, however, such adversarial provisions as the right to confront accusers, maintain silence, and a modified presumption of innocence reflect adversarial interests.

Adjudication is by a single judge who is directed by the *Qur'an* and *Sunna* in deciding such things as the number of witness to call and the types of testimony needed for conviction. The judge's findings must be based solely on the oral proceedings conducted during the hearing. All motions, pleas, and evidence are presented orally in the presence of the opposing parties and the judge—with opposing parties given the opportunity to challenge. The oral nature of proceedings is said to allow judges opportunities to question the parties and hear details of their pleas. In doing so, the impartiality of the proceedings is more apparent. If judgment is against the defendant, the judge must specify the reasons upon which the decision was based. The judge does not have to follow precedent, not even his own previous rulings, but the decision must have support in the *Qur'an* and *Sunna* (Kingdom of Saudi Arabia n.d.-a; Kingdom of Saudi Arabia n.d.-b).

Justice Systems in a Mixed Law Country

The People's Republic of China is a good example of a country following a mixed legal tradition. Clearly the legal principles of socialism are incorporated into Chinese justice, but so too are aspects from the civil legal tradition (for example, the codification of law) and from Chinese traditional law (for example, a preference for informal justice).

People's Republic of China

With the formation of a communist dictatorship in 1949, the People's Republic of China began a path that would draw heavily from the Soviet Union for ideas. Although a Soviet pattern was followed in the ensuing decades, China was not quick to put its new legal system in writing. Comprehensive codes of substantive and procedural law were generated only in 1979 and revised in 1996. The criminal procedure law was amended in 2012, and some of those amendments show movement by Chinese authorities to incorporate from other legal traditions such features as adversarial proceedings and excluding illegally obtained evidence (Zeldin 2012).

Substantive Law: Insanity

The Criminal Law of the People's Republic of China (Congressional-Executive Commission on China, 2011) recognizes the need for both act and intent. As noted in Article 14:

> An intentional crime refers to an act committed by a person who clearly knows that his act will entail harmful consequences to society but who wishes or allows such consequences to occur, thus constituting a crime. Criminal responsibility shall be borne for intentional crimes.

Criminal responsibility is not attributed to acts by persons under age sixteen (although persons age fourteen or fifteen who commit very serious crimes can be held criminally responsible), persons acting in self-defense, or persons acting under coercion (Criminal Law Article 17).

It should be noted that in addition to identifying persons deemed not criminally responsible Chinese law also lists persons who are still considered to have *mens rea* even if their circumstances might suggest otherwise. For example, intoxicated persons still bear criminal responsibility as does "any deaf-mute or blind person," although this last category could receive a lesser punishment or even be exempted from punishment (Criminal Law Articles 18 and 19).

The insanity defense seems to come into play in China with reference to persons who are "mental patients." Article 18 states: "If a mental patient causes harmful consequences at a time when he is unable to recognize or control his own conduct, upon verification and confirmation through legal procedure, he shall not bear criminal responsibility." The same Article goes on to note that: "If a mental patient who has not completely lost the ability of recognizing or controlling his own conduct commits a crime, he shall bear criminal responsibility; however, he may be given a lighter or mitigated punishment." The specific reference to mental patients could indicate that persons under treatment (a patient in that sense) can use that status to show lack of *mens rea;* but another part of Article 18 explains that "any person whose mental illness is of an intermittent nature shall bear criminal responsibility if he commits a crime when he is in a normal mental state." That suggests that patient status is not a requirement and that the court will consider mental illness itself as a criminal defense.

If a person is determined to have no criminally responsibility because he is unable to recognize or control his own conduct, his family members or guardian will be ordered to keep him under strict watch and control and arrange for his medical treatment. When necessary, the government may compel him to receive medical treatment (Article 18).

Procedural Law: Adjudication

The Chinese system is primarily inquisitorial, but the 2012 amendments to the criminal procedure law have added more adversarial features. The trial is essentially a continuation of the investigation, which is begun by the prosecutor before the trial. When the court has decided to open the court session and adjudicate the case, it must first determine the adjudicators. In each type of court, the adjudicators are a collegial panel of judges and laypersons (called "people's assessors"). In the lower and mid-level courts, that panel consists of three judges or a combination of a total of three judges and people's assessors. If a case in either of those court levels is considered suitable for "simplified procedures" (e.g., cases in which defendant can be sentenced to fewer than three years imprisonment and where the facts of the crime are clear and the evidence sufficient) adjudication can be made by a single judge. For the higher level courts the panel has three to seven judges (but always an odd number) or a combined total of three to seven judges and people's assessors (China Internet Information Center n.d.; People's Republic of China 1997). Examples of adversarial features added in the 2012 amendment include enhancement of the adversarial relationship between defense and the prosecution by, for example, identifying the defense attorney as being responsible for presenting materials and opinions relevant to the defendant's innocence and to safeguard the defendant's procedural rights (Clarke 2012, Article 35).

Conclusion

Categorizing the world's legal systems as falling into one of four legal traditions is one way to make sense of the variation found in criminal justice systems around the world. Being able to compare and contrast legal systems is increasingly important as law enforcement and court personnel find themselves working more and more often with their counterparts in other countries. The growth of transnational crime has required this cooperation as countries work together to combat such activities as human trafficking, terrorism, and piracy. Knowing how the criminal justice systems in other countries operate, especially in comparison to one's own country, can be of immense help when opportunities for cross-national cooperation present themselves.

Web Sources

1. Basic information about a country's legal system is available at:
   http://www.nationmaster.com/graph/gov_leg_sys-government-legal-system
2. A variety of important Muslim texts can be reviewed at:
   http://www.usc.edu/org/cmje/religious-texts/home/
3. China's trial system is described in detail at:
   http://www.china.org.cn/english/Judiciary/31280.htm
4. See what a British courtroom looks like or watch videos of judges explaining their work at:
   http://www.judiciary.gov.uk/interactive-learning

Discussion Questions

1. Distinguish between substantive criminal law and procedural criminal law and provide examples of each.
2. The adversarial process is described as a contest between competing sides, whereas the inquisitorial process is more a continued investigation. Each believes its approach is more likely to find the truth in any given case. Which do you think is more likely to find the truth? Why?
3. Jurors in U.S. jurisdictions are often subjected to questioning (*voir dire*) by both prosecution and defense as each side tries to identify potential jurors who may be biased against their side. British juries are typically the result of the first twelve names called. Which system do you think is more likely to result in a fair jury? Why?
4. Six different ways of describing insanity have been presented in this chapter. Select the country description that you believe is most likely to identify persons who are truly mentally ill and should not be held criminally responsible. Explain your choice.
5. Several different ways of deciding whether a person committed a criminal act have been presented in this chapter. Choosing from the jury system of England and Wales, the mixed bench of China, France, and Germany, and the single judge used by India and Saudi Arabia, which do you think will more accurately identify true culprits and acquit the wrongfully accused? Explain your choice.

References

Allnutt, Stephen, Anthony Samuels, and Colman O'Driscoll. "The Insanity Defence: From Wild Beasts to M'Naghten." *Australasian Psychiatry* 15, no. 4 (2007): 292–298.

Aronwitz, Alexis A. *Germany*. Bureau of Justice Statistics. Accessed April 23, 2013. http://www.bjs.gov/content/pub/html/wfcj.cfm, 1993.

Carter, Sarah, and Hester Swift. "Update: A Guide to the UK Legal System." May 9, 2009. Accessed April 23, 2013. http://www.nyulawglobal.org/globalex/United_Kingdom1.htm.

Castellucci, Ignazio. "How Mixed Must a Mixed System Be?" *Electronic Journal of Comparative Law* 12, no. 1 (May 2008). Accessed April 23, 2013. http://www.ejcl.org/121/art121-4.pdf.

Center for Muslim-Jewish Engagement. "Partial Translation of Sunan Abu-Dawud." Accessed April 23, 2013. http://www.usc.edu/org/cmje/religious-texts/hadith/abudawud/, n.d.-a.

Center for Muslim-Jewish Engagement. "Translation of Malik's Muwatta, book 18." Accessed April 23, 2013. http://www.usc.edu/org/cmje/religious-texts/hadith/muwatta/018-mmt.php, n.d.-b.

Chakravarty, Padmaja. "Review of the Insanity Defense in India: A Case for Reform." *Central India Law Quarterly* XIV(2001). Accessed April 23, 2013. http://services.trueserials.com/CJDB/MERCYHURST/journal/57622.

China Internet Information Center. "China's Judiciary." Accessed April 23, 2013. http://www.china.org.cn/english/Judiciary/25025.htm, n.d.

Clarke, Donald C. "English Translation of Revised Criminal Procedure Law." Accessed April 23, 2013. http://www.typepad.com/services/trackback/6a00d8341bfae553ef0163036246fd970d, 2012.

Congressional-Executive Commission on China. "Criminal Law of the People's Republic of China, 1997." Accessed April 23, 2013. http://www.cecc.gov/pages/newLaws/criminalLawENG.php, 2011.

Criminal Procedure (Insanity and Unfitness to Plead) Act. 1991. Accessed April 23, 2013. http://www.statutelaw.gov.uk/Home.aspx, 1991.

Dammer, Harry R., Philip L. Reichel, and Ni He. "Comparing Crime and Justice." In *Handbook of Transnational Crime and Justice*. 2nd ed., edited by Philip Reichel and Jay Albanese, 23–46. Los Angeles, CA: SAGE Publications, 2014.

Draft National Policy on Criminal Justice. New Delhi, India: Ministry of Home Affairs, Government of India, 2007.

Federal Republic of Germany. "The German Criminal Code." Accessed April 23, 2013. http://www.gesetze-im-internet.de/englisch_stgb/index.html, 1998.

French Republic. Code of Criminal Procedure. "Legifrance Translations." Accessed April 23, 2013. http://www.legifrance.gouv.fr/Traductions/en-English/Legifrance-translations, n.d.-a.

French Republic. Penal code. "Legifrance Translations." Accessed April 23, 2013. http://www.legifrance.gouv.fr/Traductions/en-English/Legifrance-translations, n.d.-b.

Hall, Jerome. *General Principles of Criminal Law*. Indianapolis, IN: Bobbs-Merrill, 1960.

Indian Penal Code 1860. Accessed April 23, 2013. http://www.vakilno1.com/bareacts/indianpenalcode/indianpenalcode.html, 1860.

Kingdom of Saudi Arabia. "Law of the Judiciary 1975. About Saudi Arabia." Accessed April 23, 2013. http://www.saudiembassy.net/about/country-information/laws/, 2009.

Kingdom of Saudi Arabia. "The Basic Law of Governance. About Saudi Arabia." Accessed April 23, 2013. http://www.saudiembassy.net/about/country-information/laws/, 1992.

Kingdom of Saudi Arabia. "The Code of Law Practice. About Saudi Arabia." Accessed April 23, 2013. http://www.saudiembassy.net/about/country-information/laws/, n.d.-a.

Kingdom of Saudi Arabia. "The Law of Procedure before Shari'ah Courts. About Saudi Arabia." Accessed April 23, 2013. http://www.saudiembassy.net/about/country-information/laws/, n.d.-b.

Krehl, Christoph. "Reforms of the German Criminal Code: Stock-taking and Perspectives—also from a Constitutional Point of View." *German Law Journal*, 4, (2003): 421–431. Accessed April 22, 2013. http://www.germanlawjournal.com/article.php?id=267.

Kumar, Ramesh. "Criminal Justice System Crying for Reform." *Merinews*, April 11, 2008. Accessed April 22, 2013. http://www.merinews.com/article/criminal-justice-system-crying-for-reform/132260.shtml.

Lippman, Matthew R., Sean McConville, and Mordechai Yerushalmi. *Islamic Criminal Law and Procedure: An Introduction*. New York: Praeger, 1988.

Mahapatra, Dhananjay. "Criminal Justice System has Collapsed." *Times of India*, February 6, 2009. Accessed April 22, 2013. http://timesofindia.indiatimes.com/articleshow/4083289.cms.

Malimath Committee on Reforms of Criminal Justice System. New Delhi, India: Ministry of Justice, Government of India, 2003.

Merryman, John H. *The Civil Law Tradition*. Stanford, CA: Stanford University Press, 1985.

Moran, Richard. "The Modern Foundation for the Insanity Defense: The Cases of James Hadfield (1800) and Daniel Mcnaughtan (1843)." *Annals of the American Academy of Political and Social Science* 477 (1985): 31–42.

NationMaster. "Encyclopedia: K. M. Nanavati vs. State of Maharashtra." Accessed April 22, 2013. http://www.nationmaster.com/encyclopedia/K.-M.-Nanavati-vs.-State-of-Maharashtra, n.d.

Örücü, Esin. "What is a Mixed Legal System: Exclusion or Expansion?" *Electronic Journal of Comparative Law* 12.1 (May 2008). Accessed April 22, 2013. http://www.ejcl.org/121/art121-15.pdf.

Palmer, Vernon V. "Two Rival Theories of Mixed Legal Systems." *Electronic Journal of Comparative Law* 12.1 (May 2008). Accessed April 22, 2013. http://www.ejcl.org/121/art121-16.pdf.

People's Republic of China. "Criminal Procedure Law." Accessed April 23, 2013. http://en.chinacourt.org/public/detail.php?id=2693, 1997.

Phillips, Coretta, Cox Gemma, and Ken Pease. *England and Wales.* Bureau of Justice Statistics. Accessed April 23, 2013. http://www.bjs.gov/content/pub/html/wfcj.cfm, 1993.

Raghavan, R. K. *India.* Bureau of Justice Statistics. Accessed April 23, 2013. http://www.bjs.gov/content/pub/html/wfcj.cfm, 1993.

Reichel, Philip L. *Comparative Criminal Justice Systems: A Topical Approach* (6th ed.). Boston, MA: Pearson, 2013.

Reichel, Philip L. "Civil Law Legal Traditions." In *Encyclopedia of Crime and Punishment,* edited by David Levinson, 232–237. Thousand Oaks, CA: Sage, 2002a.

Reichel, Philip L. "Common Law Legal Traditions. In *Encyclopedia of Crime and Punishment,* edited by David Levinson, 258–263. Thousand Oaks, CA: Sage, 2002b.

Rowe, Jenny. *The New UK Supreme Court.* Accessed April 23, 2013. http://www.metrocorpcounsel.com/current.php?artType=view&artMonth=January&artYear=2010&EntryNo=10523, 2010.

Sanad, Nagaty. *The Theory of Crime and Criminal Responsibility in Islamic Law: Shari'a.* Chicago: Office of International Criminal Justice, 1991.

Schmalleger, Frank. *Criminal Justice Today: An Introductory Text for the Twenty-First Century.* 10th ed. Upper Saddle River, NJ: Pearson Prentice Hall, 2008.

Souryal, Sam S. *Islam, Islamic Law, and the Turn to Violence.* Huntsville, TX: Office of International Criminal Justice, 2004.

Summers, Chris. 2007. "When Jurors have to Judge Sanity." *BBC News,* December 21, 2007. Accessed April 23, 2013. http://news.bbc.co.uk/2/hi/uk_news/7143252.stm.

Terrill, Richard J. *World Criminal Justice Systems: A Survey.* 5th ed. Cincinnati, OH: Anderson, 2003.

Thakur, Pradeep. "UPA to Tighten Sexual Assault Laws." *The Times of India,* Jan 4, 2013. Accessed April 23, 2013. http://articles.timesofindia.india times.com/2013-01-04/india/36148579_1_law-commission-criminal-justice-system-sexual-assault.

The National Archives. "Coroners and Justice Act 2009." Accessed April 23, 2013. http://www.legislation.gov.uk/ukpga/2009/25/contents, n.d.-a.

The National Archives. "Homicide Act 1957." Accessed April 23, 2013. http://www.legislation.gov.uk/ukpga/Eliz2/5-6/11/contents, n.d.-b.

Third Time Unlucky. *The Economist,* September 16, 2006, 66.

United Kingdom Supreme Court. About the Supreme Court. "The Supreme Court." Accessed April 23, 2013. http://www.supremecourt.gov.uk/about/index.html. n.d.

Vincentnathan, Lynn, and S. George Vincentnathan. "Village Courts and the Police: Cooperation and Conflicts in Modernizing India." *Police Practice and Research* 8, no. 5 (2007): 445–459.

Yeo, Stanley. "The Insanity Defence In The Criminal Laws Of The Commonwealth Of Nations." *Singapore Journal of Legal Studies* (December 2008): 241–263.

Zeldin, Wendy. "China: Amendment of Criminal Procedure Law." *Global Legal Monitor,* April 9, 2012. Accessed April 23, 2013. http://www.loc.gov/lawweb/servlet/lloc_news?disp3_l205403080_text.

Chapter 2

The Roles of International Justice Organizations

J.D. Jamieson & Donna Vandiver

Introduction

Thomas Lubanga lives in a cell in the Haaglanden Prison in The Hague, Netherlands, just a short twenty-minute drive from the offices of the International Criminal Court (ICC) where he was convicted in March of 2012 of recruiting and using child soldiers in the northeastern part of the Democratic Republic of Congo. He is housed by himself in one of the twelve cells reserved in the prison by the ICC for detention purposes. His cell conforms to international standards for incarceration and is billed to the ICC by the Netherlands at a rate of 289 Euros per day. He also has access to an African cook to accommodate his dietary preferences. Mr. Lubanga has been detained at The Hague since March of 2006, after his arrest by United Nations (UN) peacekeeping forces in 2005. He was formally sentenced to a prison term of fourteen years by the ICC, less the six years already spent in detention prior to his sentencing. The ICC has been in operation since July 1, 2002, at a cost of roughly one billion U.S. dollars paid by participating nations. Thomas Lubanga is, so far, the only person tried and convicted by the ICC.

The ICC continues to suffer from the same limitation that has often characterized judicial entities through history: the lack of enforcement power. The ICC must depend on cooperation by participating nations to deliver the indicted accused to trial, or else their mandate cannot be achieved. A glaring case in point is Omar al-Bashir, the current President of Sudan, who has been successfully ignoring an arrest order for genocide and other offenses, issued by the ICC in 2009. The arrest order was significant at the time because it was the first time that the ICC had indicted an active, sitting head of state (Corder 2009). The arrest order raised the possibility that other world leaders could be indicted and brought to trial in order to resolve deadly conflicts as they occur around the world. The prospect of using of the ICC as a proactive mechanism to achieve peace and minimize human suffering was quite exciting, but has proved to be a bit of a false hope, as President al-Bashir's continued defiance illustrates.

It would seem logical that the UN, being a "parent" organization to the ICC, would assume responsibility for enforcing the ICC's orders. Ironically enough, UN personnel in Sudan must continue to cooperate and work with President al-Bashir simply because his government remains in power and is firmly in control of the nation's operating infrastructure. Achieving consensus for forceful action is a complicated, time-consuming process in the UN, and the deployment of UN forces following consensus is usually quite slow. In the meantime, nations with leaders like President al-Bashir continue to operate as they will. Arrest orders issued by the ICC will continue to be difficult to enforce, and the need for global agreement on an effective system of international law and justice will become ever more apparent.

At least seven international courts have been established over time, with different modes of development. For example, after World War II, allied powers developed two tribunals. Also, the UN Security Council for the former Yugoslavia, Rwanda, and Lebanon developed three ad hoc committees. Another was established via an agreement of Sierra Leone's government. Last, the International Criminal Court was developed as a permanent court open to all states (Schabas and McDermott 2012).

A History of Modern Attempts to Settle International Disputes Peacefully

While it might be said that the recognized need for international law and justice dates back to prehistoric times, significant modern attempts to peacefully resolve international disputes involving the USA begin with the Jay Treaty of 1794 between the USA and Great Britain. By this treaty, the two nations established commissions with equal representation, which had the challenge of resolving lingering issues between the nations. While the War of 1812 between the USA and Britain might indicate a failure of the concept, the commissions were used to some advantage through the nineteenth century by nations in the Americas and Europe (Roberson and Das 2008).

During the 1870s, the USA levied complaints about breaches of neutrality against Britain concerning their activities during the American Civil War. International commissions were established to arbitrate the disputes. One of these commissions, composed of five members chosen by the USA, United Kingdom, Italy, Switzerland, and Brazil, applied recognized standards of the duties of neutral governments and concluded that Britain had violated the standards. Britain complied with the orders of the commission and paid compensation (Roberson and Das 2008).

Tsar Nicholas II of Russia was the driving personality behind The Hague Peace Conference of 1899, which was convened with the purpose of exploring possibilities for disarmament and means for peaceful resolution of international problems. The participating nations adopted the "Convention on the Pacific Settlement of International Disputes," as a blueprint for initiating arbitration and mediation between nations. The plan included the establishment of a permanent office at The Hague to enforce the procedural rules of arbitrations and to manage the conduct of nations involved in disputes. The Convention also established a Permanent Court of Arbitration, which had the job of setting up individual arbitration tribunals as they were needed. The Permanent Court of Arbitration commenced operations in 1902 (Roberson and Das 2008).

The mechanisms for international arbitration were revisited in 1907, when the second Hague Peace Convention was convened, this time with participation by more nations from the Americas. The participants were unable to agree on the parameters for establishing an operational permanent court, especially with regard to the proposed court's constitution and procedures for selecting judges. The participants did improve the rules governing the conduct of arbitration hearings under the old system, and the Permanent Court of Arbitration was able to continue organizing tribunals as needed (Roberson and Das 2008).

The work done in these conventions inspired continuing efforts to refine mechanisms for resolving international disputes peacefully. Then, as now, the need for an effective system of international law and justice was quite obvious. World War I demonstrated that need very dramatically.

Following the war, the founders of the League of Nations laid the groundwork for the establishment of a Permanent Court of International Justice (PCIJ), with the understanding that the court would render judgments only in disputes brought to the court by all parties involved. The PCIJ could give opinions in answer to questions submitted by other elements of the League of Nations. Following a laborious process of input and revisions through several advisory committees, the Assembly of the League of Nations adopted the Statute of the PCIJ in December of 1920 (Roberson and Das 2008).

The PCIJ began operations in 1921, following ratification by a majority of the members of the League, and was available to all nations as a forum for settling international disputes. For some types of issues, parties involved had to declare recognition of the PCIJ's jurisdiction before the hearings began, and agree to compulsory compliance with the Court's ruling. The PCIJ was also available for advisory opinions in questions submitted by the League Assembly or the

League Council. The PCIJ had strong procedural rules and an effective permanent mechanism, known as the Registry, for communicating with nations around the world. The PCIJ ultimately heard 29 international cases and delivered 27 opinions to international questions submitted by the League. With the onset of World War II, the offices of the PCIJ were moved to Geneva, Switzerland. During World War II, Allied leaders quickly agreed that an international organization following the war would be necessary, for the purpose of promoting peace and sovereign equality. There was general agreement that an international court would be necessary as well, and some leading jurists recommended that the mandate of the existing PCIJ be continued. Many meetings were held during the war, and allied participants included the USA, Britain, China, the USSR, and jurists from many nations. In 1944, following discussions at the meeting of the Four Powers at Dumbarton Oaks, proposals were published for the postwar establishment of an international court of justice as a component of a proposed new international organization (Roberson and Das 2008).

The International Court of Justice

The UN and the International Court of Justice (ICJ) were both created in 1945 at the San Francisco Conference. In the energetic postwar environment, the PCIJ infrastructure, still safe in Geneva, arranged movement of its archives and records back to the Peace Palace at The Hague where the new ICJ was to reside. The PCIJ judges resigned to pave the way for rapid structuring of the new court. During the first session of the UN General Assembly and the Security Council in February of 1946, the first members of the new ICJ were elected. The ICJ met as an established entity in April of 1946, and received its first international case one year later in May, 1947 (Yacoubian 2003).

Key Features of the International Court of Justice

The International Court of Justice (ICJ) is one of the six principle organs of the UN, although it is not located in New York as are the other principle organs. It is not only a court of justice, but serves as an international communication entity for many States. The ICJ is headquartered in The Hague, in the Netherlands. The official languages of the ICJ are French and English. The ICJ's role is to settle disputes between individual States based on accepted concepts of international law. Sovereign States, therefore, rather than individuals, private entities, or specific government entities, may become litigants in the ICJ as applicants (plaintiffs) and respondents. The Court also has the authority to publish advisory opinions on legal matters referred to the Court by organs of the UN and other specialized agencies. The Court is comprised of fifteen judges who are elected by the UN General Assembly and Security Council for nine-year terms (International Court of Justice 2013).

The administrative organ of the Court is the Registry, and serves to assist the Court with management of international communication and coordination issues. The Registrar and Deputy-Registrar head this organ, and have several specific duties as their mandate. Given that the ICJ is an international court, the Registry assists in administering justice. It also serves as a secretariat of an international commission. Its duties, therefore, may be described as judicial, administrative, and diplomatic at the same time. The Registry is comprised of three Departments which are: legal matters, linguistic matters, and information. The Registry also maintains numerous technical divisions necessary for the routine operation of the Court including: personnel and administration, finance, publications, library, information technology, archives, indexing and distribution, shorthand, typewriting and reproduction, and general assistance. The Registry also houses the official secretaries to the Members of the Courts (International Court of Justice 2013).

Jurisdiction of the International Court of Justice

The ICJ has jurisdiction only over issues relating to sovereign States. Individuals may not petition the Court, and may not be named as respondents in disputes. Only the 192 members of the UN Member States may submit cases to be considered. Thus, the ICJ has no jurisdiction over individuals, non-governmental organizations, corporations, or other private entities. Because the ICJ is an organ of the UN, it accordingly does not have any jurisdiction over States that are not part of the UN (International Court of Justice 2013).

Trial Procedures and Resolution of Contentious Cases

When a case is presented to the ICJ, it must be presented by one of the involved States; thus, the ICJ cannot initiate a case. The phrase "contentious case" refers to cases in which one state has a dispute with another state and desires a legally binding decision. The ICJ also holds advisory proceedings (discussed in the next section), which are designed to address legal questions rather than disputes. The opinions in advisory proceedings are not legally binding.

In contentious cases, both of the States must belong to the UN and must have previously accepted the ICJ's jurisdiction to render a decision. Sovereign States have the freedom to choose how the Court's jurisdiction is specifically applied in the outcome of the case.

Consent for the ICJ is obtained in one of three ways. First, a *special agreement* may be formed between litigating States in which two (or more) States submit a dispute jointly to the ICJ, with the understanding that the ICJ's ruling will be binding. Second, a case may be brought to the ICJ under the authority of a *compromissory clause* in an existing treaty between the States involved in a dispute. This avenue to the Court involves a clause in a pre-existing treaty that requires acceptance of the ICJ's authority to settle disputes that arise between the States. Currently over 300 such treaties exist. Third, a dispute can be brought to the ICJ by a *unilateral declaration*, whereby one State recognizes that they and another State are part of UN and are bound by the authority of the ICJ (International Court of Justice n.d.).

The "applicant" is the State that has initiated the complaint and has submitted the application for action by the Court, and the "respondent" is, of course, the other State named as the source of the problem. If the case was brought to the Court by a *special agreement*, the parties are not referred to as applicant or respondent. Regardless of how a case arrives in the jurisdiction of Court, the parties need agents to represent their respective States before the Court. This State agent may be the nation's ambassador to the Netherlands or may be another appointed senior civil servant (e.g., Legal Adviser to the Ministry of Foreign Affairs). Sometimes a deputy agent is appointed to assist the representative of the State during litigation. The Registrar of the ICC sends all communication regarding the case to the designated representative (International Court of Justice 2013).

During the proceedings, written pleadings are submitted to the Court, followed by oral pleadings made before the Court's judges in a formal hearing forum. Initially, the applicant state files a *Memorial*, which is a written statement of the nature and cause of the accusation. The respondent files a *Counter-Memorial*, which is the respondent's written response to the *Memorial*. The applicant state, if the representative chooses, is allowed to file a *Reply and Rejoinder* in response to the Counter-Memorial. If the case was brought to the Court through a special agreement, each party submits a Memorial and Counter-Memorial and if they choose, both may file a final Reply and Rejoinder. These written documents are not made available to the public prior to the start of the formal hearing. After the appropriate written statements are filed, the oral pleadings begin. These are usually open to the public unless the Court has considered a request to keep the proceedings private and agreed with the reasoning made in the request. The proceedings usually last two to six weeks, depending on the number of witnesses presented by the parties involved. The ICJ's procedures are based on the adversary trial processes found in the justice systems of common-law countries, and include direct examination and cross-examination of witnesses and a re-examining of witnesses when necessary. The Court may also call additional witnesses on its own initiative (International Court of Justice 2013).

The decisions that the ICJ makes are binding to those nations that have demonstrated the appropriate acceptance of the Court's jurisdiction. The decisions are final and cannot be appealed. If any part of the decision is challenged or new information arises that was not known at the time of the hearing, either of the parties can request a revision of judgment. All hearings are open to the public unless special conditions exist and a private hearing has been deemed necessary (International Court of Justice 2013).

Current Cases between Member States

In the past several years the ICJ has heard and rendered opinions in many cases involving disputes between sovereign States. These disputes range from accusations that a State is abusing the environment and harming neighboring states to accusations of harboring alleged criminals who have violated international law, and mass racial discrimination. Below are summaries of some of the cases that were active in 2008 and 2009 in the ICJ.

Belgium v. Senegal

An example of a recent dispute that came before the ICJ is the case of *Belgium v. Senegal*. In this case Belgium, the applicant, requested that the government of Senegal "take[s] steps within its power to keep Mr. Hisséne Habré under the control and surveillance of the Senegalese authorities so that rules of international law with which Belgium requests compliance be correctly applied." Mr. Hisséne Habré is the former President of Chad, and government officials in Belgium want to extradite and prosecute him for criminal acts. He was accused of killing thousands of people through torture. He established a prison in a swimming pool, allowing political prisoners to suffer. The ICJ, in a landmark decision, confirmed Mr. Habré's action violated the Convention against Torture and Other Cruel, Inhuman or Degrading Treatment or Punishment (CAT) and confirmed an obligation to prosecute or extradite Mr. Habré. Subsequently, government representatives from Senegal and the African Union (AU) formally agreed to establish a court in the Senegal justice system with judges appointed by the AU (Human Rights Watch 2013).

Ecuador v. Colombia

A representative of Ecuador petitioned the ICJ about a dispute with Colombia, alleging that persons in Colombia are spraying toxic herbicides "at locations near, at, or across its border with Ecuador." It is stated that the spray has caused damage to crops, animals, people and the natural environment. Officials from Ecuador claim that such damage will continue in the future if the spraying does not cease. They specifically want to recover losses and damages from Colombia for: (1) death and/or injury to health of persons affected, (2) damaged/lost property, (3) environmental damage/depletion of natural resources, (4) costs to identify and assess future harm/damage caused, and (5) any other loss/damage caused by the spraying of toxic herbicides. The decision on this case is also pending (International Court of Justice 2011).

Georgia v. The Russian Federation, 2008

On August 14, 2008, the Republic of Georgia requested the ICJ hear a case against the Russian Federation. It is alleged the Russian Federation has engaged in mass racial discrimination. It is noted that beginning in the 1990s, the Russian Federation has engaged in a systematic policy of racial discrimination with their action directed at the ethnic Georgian population and other groups in South Ossetia and Abkhazia. The Republic of Georgia alleges that the Russian military invaded Georgia in violation of the International Convention on Elimination of All Forms of Racial Discrimination (CERD). The military invasion led to extensive damage and destruction to property, loss of hundreds of civilians' lives, and displacement of the ethnic Georgian population in South Ossetia. Although Georgia withdrew its forces and declared a ceasefire, the Russian military continued its military action. In October of 2008, ICJ (in an eight to seven vote) delivered its provisional measures, ordering that "both parties shall refrain from any act of discrimination and from sponsoring, defending, or supporting such acts; that they shall facilitate humanitarian assistance; and that they shall refrain from any action which might prejudice the respective rights of the Parties or might aggravate or extend the dispute" (International Court of Justice 2008).

Advisory Proceedings

Only about one-fifth of the cases heard by the ICJ are advisory in nature. The ICJ noted in a recent report that "The advisory procedure is available to certain public (offices) in international organizations (namely organs and specialized agencies of the UN) and enables them to request an advisory opinion from the Court on a legal question" (International Court of Justice 2000, 42).

Slightly more than half of the advisory opinions are the result of a request from the UN General Assembly. Although non-governmental agencies can request an advisory hearing, the Court can decline to give an advisory opinion. Advisory proceedings are similar in some ways to the contentious proceedings. For example, in both proceedings a list of those States that could provide relevant information are created and the hearings are public; however the decision of ICJ in advisory proceedings are not binding to the States involves. Advisory proceedings occur in a more expedited manner, being less adversarial, and the end result of a hearing is the delivery of an advisory opinion. The opinion is formed behind closed doors and is written in a summary format that includes the Court's reasoning. The opinion summary is usually about 30 pages in length, and is read without delay to the public hearing (International Court of Justice 2000).

The Permanent International Criminal Court

In 1998, the UN convened a meeting entitled "the United Nations Diplomatic Conference of Plenipotentiaries on the Establishment of an International Criminal Court." Because the conference was held in Rome, the statute creating the International Criminal Court (ICC) is often referred to as the Rome Statute. Initially, member nations in the UN were enthusiastic about the development of the ICC, and the USA, under President William (Bill) J. Clinton's administration, played a leading role in establishing the court. By 2002, however, many nations including the USA, China, Russia, and most nations in Asia and the Middle East, had declined to continue on as participating members of the ICC. The main concern at this time for the USA was resistance by member nations to the concept of exempting U.S. citizens and soldiers from prosecution by the ICC. During George W. Bush's administration, with continuing warfare involvement in Iraq and Afghanistan, the President and the U.S. Congress worried that the ICC would be used as a forum to criminalize the participation by U.S. military personnel and contractors in the conflicts (Yacoubian 2003). The U.S. Congress passed legislation intended to interfere with the ICC's jurisdiction, and President Bush signed documents declaring that the USA would no longer be bound by the agreement to participate made by the previous administration. Despite this rocky start, the ICC continues to receive cases and prosecute according to its mandate (Roberson and Das 2008).

Key Features of the International Criminal Court

The International Criminal Court serves as a permanent court. It commenced operations with 60 participating nations and was later joined by another 48. Currently, representatives of 122 countries have active signatures on the treaty and participate as member nations of the court. The ICC has the authority to bring individuals to trial for only the gravest categories of crimes, including genocide, crimes against humanity, and war crimes. If a particular criminal accusation is already being investigated by a country's judicial system, or if proceedings against an accused are in progress in another venue, the ICC will not act. The only exception to this is if the judicial action taken is determined to be merely superficial. The ICC is based in The Hague, Netherlands, and is governed by provisions in the Rome Statute. Some of the hallmarks of the ICC's mandate are "due process, procedural safeguards to protect an accused from abuse, and to further victims' rights and gender justice under international law" (International Criminal Court 2013).

The ICC is different from the International Court of Justice (ICJ) in that the ICJ lacks jurisdiction to prosecute *individuals*, that is, the ICJ only adjudicates disputes between member states. Also, the ICC is an independent court, whereas the ICJ is an entity of the UN.

Jurisdiction, Organization, and Administration of the International Criminal Court (ICC)

The overall objective of the ICC is "to end impunity for the perpetrators of the most serious crimes of concern to the international community as a whole, and thus to contribute to the prevention of such crimes" (International Criminal Court 2013, 1). The ICC has jurisdiction to prosecute crimes of genocide, crimes against humanity, and war crimes. Thus, it has jurisdiction over those who are directly involved in these crimes as well as those who assist in committing these crimes (e.g., aiding, abetting, or assisting in other ways) (Roberson and Das 2008). Additionally, several criteria must be met for the ICC to have jurisdiction to proceed with an accusation. First, the individual must have citizenship in a state party that has accepted the jurisdiction of the court. Thus, the individual must be a national of one of the 122 countries that has signed the treaty. The crime must have taken place within one of those 122 countries after July, 2002. Also, the UN Security Council must have referred the incident to the Prosecutor of the ICC.

There are four entities (often referred as "organs") of the ICC: 1) Office of the Presidency, 2) Office of the Prosecutor, 3) Judicial Division, and the 4) Registry (see Figure 1).

The Office of the President

All judicial operations of the ICC, with the exception of the Office of the Prosecutor, are administered by the Office of the President. Three judges are elected for three-year terms by their fellow judges, and together the three comprise the Presidency. The judges are designated as the President, first Vice-President, and Second Vice-President of the Court. The current judges in the Presidency are from the Republic of Korea (Judge Sang-Hyun Song, who serves as the President), Botswana (Judge Sanji Mmasenono Monageng, who serves as First Vice-President), and Italy (Judge Cuno Tarfusser, who serves as the Second Vice-President) (International Criminal Court 2013).

The Office of the Prosecutor

The Office of the Prosecutor is one of four entities of the ICC, and has authority for investigations and prosecutions and also for managing cooperation, coordination, and jurisdictional issues between nations. The Prosecutor oversees the office and is elected by the State Parties for a nine-year term. The Prosecutor has full authority for the management of the office. The current Prosecutor is Ms. Fatou Bensouda, from the West African nation of The Gambia, who is serving a nine-year term in office. There is also a Deputy Prosecutor, Mr. James Kirkpatrick Stewart of Canada, who is in charge of the Prosecutor Division of the Office of the Prosecutor (International Criminal Court 2013).

There are three divisions within the Office of the Prosecutor. The first division, the Investigative Division, collects evidence, questions involved persons for both incriminating and exonerating facts. Essentially, this division is responsible for collecting facts, conducting the investigation, and assessing the veracity of evidence in preparation for trial. The second division, the Prosecution Division, has some involvement in the investigative process, but has the primary duty for litigating the case before the court. The third division, the Jurisdiction, Complementarity and Cooperation Division, works with the Investigation Division and assists in facilitating communication, obtaining needed cooperation between nations, and establishing jurisdiction for the ICC to ultimately try cases (International Criminal Court 2009).

The Judicial Divisions

Eighteen elected judges are divided between the Pre-Trial Division of the Court, the Trial Division, and the Appeals Division. Each division includes a "chamber," or panel of assigned judges that conducts specific hearings. Judges are assigned to divisions based on qualifications and expertise; the goal is to ensure that each division has an appropriate combination of judges with experience in criminal law and procedure, along with international law.

In 2003, the Assembly of State Parties elected the current judges for terms of three, six, or nine years. Two lists of qualified candidates were created and the judges were elected from both lists. List A candidates include those with "established competence in criminal law and procedures, and the necessary relevant experience, whether as judge, prosecutor, advocate, or in other similar capacity in criminal proceedings" (International Criminal Court 2009, n.p.). List B candidates include those with "established competence in relevant areas of international law, such as international humanitarian law and the law of human rights, and extensive experience in a professional legal capacity which is of relevance to the judicial work of the Court" (International Criminal Court 2009, n.p.).

The current judges were elected from the Western European and Other Group of States, the Asian Group of States, the Group of Eastern States, and the African Group of States (see Table 1 below). The seventeen Judges, therefore, are from a wide range of countries (International Criminal Court 2013).

Ten of the judges are female and seven are male. Scholars have noted that the number of women who serve as justices is unprecedented and can assist in making the ICC a women-friendly institution, especially given that many cases of war crimes heard in this court involve female sexual victims (Booth and du Plessis 2005).

The Registry

The Registry oversees all non-judicial matters in the administration of the ICC. The Registrars serve as the principal administrative officers of the court and their duties fall under the supervisory authority of the President of the Court. They are appointed for five-year terms. (International Criminal Court 2013).

Several semi-autonomous offices also exist. These include the Office of Public Counsel for Victims and the Office of Public Counsel for Defense. Although their responsibilities fall under the Registry for administrative purposes, they function as an independent office. The Trust Fund office also services the needs of victims and families of victims (International Criminal Court 2013).

Table 1 International Criminal Court Elected Judges

Judge Sang-Hyun SONG President	Republic of Korea
Judge Sanji Mmasenono MONAGENG First Vice-President	Botswana
Judge Cuno TARFUSSER Second Vice-President	Italy
Judge Hans-Peter KAUL	Germany
Judge Akua KUENYEHIA	Ghana
Judge Erkki KOURULA	Finland
Judge Anita UŠACKA	Latvia
Judge Ekaterina TRENDAFILOVA	Bulgaria
Judge Joyce ALUOCH	Kenya
Judge Christine VAN DEN WYNGAERT	Belgium
Judge Silvia Alejandra FERNÁNDEZ DE GURMENDI	Argentina
Judge Kuniko OZAKI	Japan
Judge Miriam DEFENSOR-SANTIAGO	Philippines
Judge Howard MORRISON	United Kingdom
Judge Olga HERRERA CARBUCCIA	Dominican Republic
Judge Robert FREMR	Czech Republic
Judge Chile EBOE-OSUJI	Nigeria

The Judges from the Pre-Trial Division and Trial Division normally are chosen for their demonstrated criminal trial expertise. They typically serve for three years, but will serve longer if they are involved in cases that are not completed at the time that their terms officially end. Hearings in the Pre-Trial Chamber may be conducted by a single judge, or a bench of three judges in more complex matters. Hearings in the Trial Chamber are conducted by panels of three judges (see Figure 1 below). They have the responsibility of adopting the procedures established by the Pre-Trial Chamber and ensuring the procedures are fair, expeditious, and fully acknowledge the rights of the accused and victim(s).

The President can serve in the Trial Division for purposes of effective workload management; however, no judge who is serving in the Pre-Trial Division can serve simultaneously in the Trial Division. The Trial Chamber hears the case

**Figure 1 Organization and Administration of the
International Crime Court**

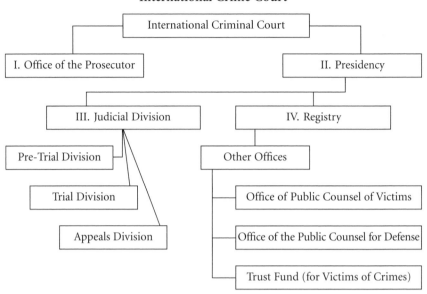

and determines the adjudication (innocent or guilty) of the accused. The Trial Chamber cannot impose a sentence of imprisonment that exceeds 30 years, or a "life sentence." They are authorized to impose financial penalties, including compensation to the victims. The trial must be open to the public, unless a special circumstance exists (International Criminal Court 2013).

The majority of the Judges in the Appeals Chamber have experience predominantly in international law (rather than criminal trial expertise). All of the five judges who are assigned to the Appeals Division make up the Appeals Chamber (International Criminal Court 2013).

Administrative Issues: Plenary Sessions

The Rome Statute, along with the Rules of Procedure, requires that all of the judges meet together at least once a year. In this meeting of the judges, matters that require the consideration of the entire Court are discussed. A majority of the judges must be present to convene the meeting, and a quorum for each session of two-thirds of the judges is required for votes. If there is a tie vote, the President (or the judge acting in the place of the President) can cast the deciding vote.

Since 2003, there have been two plenary sessions of the Court; first to elect the President and two Vice-Presidents, and second to assign judges to the three divisions: Pre-Trial Division, Trial Division, and Appeals Division (International Criminal Court 2013).

Trial Procedures and Resolution of Cases

The duties of the Office of the Prosecutor include conducting investigations and prosecutions against crimes that fall within its jurisdiction (genocide, crimes against humanity, and war crimes). After the office receives a referral, the Prosecutor verifies existing evidence in the case. Cases are brought to the court in one of two ways. First, a special agreement must exist between the State parties involved. This agreement includes language that allows the ICJ to have jurisdiction to proceed and render a judgment in the case. Second, an application is made (unilateral action) by one State against the accused.

After a case is presented and the Prosecutor confirms there is sufficient evidence to warrant inquiry, the Prosecutor presents the information and evidence to the Pre-Trial Division. Judges in the Pre-Trial Chamber serve two primary functions at this point: (1) to confirm or reject the authority to begin an investigation and (2) to decide whether the matter falls under the jurisdiction of the ICC. After a decision is rendered, the Prosecutor can decide whether to proceed with the investigation, or in case of a rejection, to present additional information to the Pre-Trial Chamber (International Criminal Court 2013).

Those in the Pre-Trial Chamber also have the authority to review the decision of the Prosecutor not to commence an investigation. They also have the authority to issue warrants of arrest, summons to appear before the Court, and orders to grant rights of the parties of the proceedings. The Chamber also defines the procedures to be followed during the proceedings. The accused will have a hearing with the Prosecutor present and the accused (with the assistance of counsel) can reject or confirm the charges. The Prosecutor's role at this hearing is to provide sufficient documentation or summary evidence to establish that the person committed the crime. The accused can object to the charges and/or challenge the evidence presented (International Criminal Court 2013).

Unlike the USA court system, both the prosecutor and the defendant may appeal a decision. The Appeals Division then handles the case. Cases are appealed for many reasons, including, but not limited to, procedural error, error of fact, and/or error of law. The Appeals Chamber can decide to reverse or amend the decision, sentence and/or order a new trial. If a new trial is ordered, it will be held before a different Trial Chamber. A sentence is typically requested when new evidence is presented that was not available at the time of the original trial (International Criminal Court 2013).

Responsibilities of Member States and "States Parties"

State Parties are those 122 countries (as of May 1, 2013) that have signed the treaty and have accepted the authority of the ICC. Only those States that consent to the provisions are bound by the terms of the ICC. The State Parties are expected to assist in any active cases; that is, the State Parties assist in "arresting persons wanted by the court, providing evidence for use in proceedings, relocating witnesses, and enforcing the sentences of convicted persons" (Roberson and Das 2008, 230).

In addition to the 122 State Parties, the UN also plays an important role in the ICC. For example, in 2004 the ICC and UN formed the Negotiated Relationship Agreement (Roberson and Das 2008). The Agreement further defined the independence of the ICC while establishing reassurance of UN support. The Agreement includes four sections: the first section (Article 1 through 3) outlines the basic purpose of the Agreement. More specifically, the Agreement assures that the two entities "shall cooperate closely, whenever appropriate with each other and consult with each other on matters of mutual interest ..." (International Criminal Court and the United Nations 2004).

The second section (Articles 4 through 14) establishes institutional relationships. This includes requiring that the ICC will submit reports to the UN, and propose items to the UN, where appropriate. Also, the UN will consult with the ICC regarding personnel matters (i.e., consult with the ICC regarding personnel matters where there is a mutual interest). The ICC and UN will efficiently use facilities and services by consulting with each other to avoid duplicating efforts and spending resources inefficiently. The UN will provide members of the ICC access to the UN headquarters when necessary. The Agreement also allows certain members of the ICC to have access to a Laissez-passer, a passport that ensures the recipient's authority to re-enter the country of origin. The Agreement also requires that any financial support provided by the UN to the ICC must first be approved by the General Assembly of the UN. Any agreements made by the ICC with other international organizations must be filed with the UN (International Criminal Court and the United Nations 2004).

The third section of the Agreement (Articles 15 through 20) further defines cooperation and judicial assistance, including establishing cooperation between the UN and the Prosecutor of the ICC, allowing immunity of UN members to be waived, and allowing the disclosure of confidential information if deemed necessary. The last section of the Agreement (Articles 21 through 23) allows Amendments to be made to the Agreement and outlines the procedures for doing so (International Criminal Court and the United Nations 2004).

Current Cases in the International Criminal Court (*www.icc-cpi.int/EN*)

The Prosecutor may open an investigation under three circumstances:

- when a situation is referred by a state party (member nation);
- when a situation is referred by the UN Security Council, acting to address a threat to international peace and security;
- when the Pre-Trial Chamber authorizes her to open an investigation on the basis of information received from other sources, such as individuals or non-governmental organizations.

Victims thus have the possibility under the Statute to present their views and observations before the Court. Also, the ICC heavily depends on Non-Government Organizations (NGOs) for its operations. NGOs and nations may seek to initiate ICC investigations by providing information on crimes to the Prosecutor, and by helping to locate victims and witnesses. The ICC depends on NGOs to interact with local populations. The NGO Coalition for the ICC has served as a sort of umbrella for NGOs to coordinate delivery of information to the ICC.

The Court has received complaints about alleged crimes in at least 139 countries. Currently, the Prosecutor of the Court has opened official investigations into eight situations in Africa: Democratic Republic of the Congo; Uganda; the Central African Republic; Mali; Darfur, Sudan; the Republic of Kenya; the Libyan Arab Jamahiriya, and the Republic of Côte d'Ivoire. Of these eight, four were referred to the Court by the states parties (Uganda, Democratic Republic of the Congo, the Central African Republic, and Mali), two were referred by the UN Security Council (Darfur and Libya) and two were begun by the Prosecutor (Kenya and Côte d'Ivoire).

The Prosecutor currently is conducting preliminary investigations in Afghanistan, Colombia, Georgia (former Soviet republic), Guinea, Honduras, Nigeria, and South Korea. Preliminary investigations have been conducted and closed in Venezuela, Iraq, and Palestine.

The ICC has the following cases currently active and in some stage of development:

The Prosecutor v. Germain Katanga,
The Prosecutor v. Callixte Mbarushimana,
The Prosecutor v. Mathieu Ngudjolo Chui,
The Prosecutor v. Sylvestre Mudacumura, (Democratic Republic of the Congo),

The Prosecutor v. Jean-Pierre Bemba Gombo, (Central African Republic),
The Prosecutor v. Joseph Kony, Vincent Otti, Okot Odhiambo, and Dominic Ongwen, (Uganda),
The Prosecutor v. Ahmad Muhammad Harun ("Ahmad Harun") *and Ali Muhammad Ali Abd-Al-Rahman* ("Ali Kushayb"),
The Prosecutor v. Omar Hassan Ahmad Al Bashir,
The Prosecutor v. Bahar Idriss Abu Garda,
The Prosecutor v. Abdallah Banda Abakaer Nourain and Saleh Mohammed Jerbo Jamus,
The Prosecutor v. Abdel Raheem Muhammad Hussein, (Darfur, Sudan),
The Prosecutor v. William Samoei Ruto and Joshua Arap Sang, The Prosecutor v. Uhuru Muigai Kenyatta, (Republic of Kenya),
The Prosecutor v. Saif Al-Islam Gaddafi and Abdullah Al-Senussi, (Libya),
The Prosecutor v. Laurent Gbagbo,
The Prosecutor v. Simone Gbagbo, (Republic of Côte d'Ivoire).

Also, it was not until six years after the International Criminal Court was established that it heard its first case. Thus, the Court is rather new and the ability of the Court to achieve its mandate cannot yet be determined. The first case was against Thomas Lubanga, who was a Congolese Warlord. He was accused of war crimes, which included supervising child soldiers, some of whom were as young as nine years old. The proceedings in this initial case were not without problems. Before the case was tried, the judges of the Court found that the Prosecutor made several procedural errors. Evidence in the case was also seriously mishandled. The judges went as far as saying that it was not possible to have a fair trial because of the mistakes that had been made. Despite this, the trial did begin (Simons 2009), and Lubanga was subsequently found guilty.

Special Issues of International Courts

Although the formation of the International Courts is seen as a way to address human rights issues on an international stage, the process established has several problems. These include, but are not limited to, handling instances in which illegal means were used to deliver persons physically to the Court, and meeting other standards set by international courts.

First, scholars have examined the issue of handling witnesses who arrived at the Court through a questionable or outright illegal extradition. This involves abducting someone in defiance of procedures defined in a nation's laws (see generally: Currie 2007). In general, an extradition must be carried out in accordance with international law, and violation of this constitutes a human rights violation; the very type of incident that international courts are intended to prevent and address. Illegal renditions have occurred, for example, in *Lopez Burgos,* where Uruguayan officials abducted (without a legal right) a Uruguayan refugee. Later, the UN Human Rights Commission found this to be a human rights violation. It appears, however, that the UN and the European Court of Human Rights (ECHR) and the UN Human Rights Committee (HRC) view the issue differently. The HRC finds the illegal abduction irrelevant. The ECHR views this as a human rights violation, but only when the State (where the individual is retrieved) does not consent to the extradition, and when any applicable law (i.e., treaty or international law) has been violated.

Second, experts have noted that it is rather difficult to get a case investigated by the ICC because the threshold for jurisdiction is so high. A case cannot be heard by the ICC unless a national court is not able or not willing to handle the case. Also, the definition for what constitutes prosecutable criminal behavior is very specific; the accused must be part of a government policy or plan. Thus, any local commander or individual who takes criminal action on his own volition (murder, rape, torture, etc.) would not be included in the ICC's jurisdiction. Additionally, the damage caused by the crime must be "clearly excessive." If the ICC Prosecutor makes the decision to conduct an investigation, the ICC will notify the suspect's government, and that government has six months to conduct its own investigation, which becomes a very time consuming process (*Times Topics: International Criminal Court* n.d.).

Conclusion

Even though the ICC appears to be the "go to" forum for seeking accountability internationally for significant criminal activity and abuse of human rights, the idea that the Court might be able to actually provide such accountability may not be possible at this current time. And so, the search continues for an effective model of international law and justice. In recent history, each new model of international justice has enjoyed initial short periods of enthusiasm and perhaps some success in resolving problems, followed by waning interest as influential and powerful nations exercise preference for self-interest and primary sovereignty in decisions to subject their own citizens to justice. This cycle of creation and decline is likely to characterize attempts to develop effective international justice mechanisms in the foreseeable future, for two basic reasons:

1. Judicial entities at all levels lack the means and authority to enforce their decisions;
2. Nations, and more specifically, the leaders of nations, large and small, have no compelling reason to submit to a system of justice that is antagonistic to personal interests or the best interests of their countries.

It is easy to ignore a judicial decision, provided the decision is unpopular and contrary to the interests of the Executive Branch of government. The U.S. President James Madison is credited with saying, "It is their decision, let them enforce it" in response to an action by the U.S. Supreme Court early in U.S. history. He didn't like the decision, so he allowed it to remain unenforced. In such an environment, any court may quickly become a joke; a tiny barking dog that is easily ignored. Today, the U.S. Supreme Court may be confident in its authority because of our post-Madison tradition of support for court rulings by the other branches of government. Their rulings WILL BE ENFORCED, by whatever means necessary, and so the United States Supreme Court enjoys respect, dignity, and power. It is a bit sobering to realize, however, that the robes and dignity might remain, but the power could vanish quickly in a changing political environment.

And so, the ICC took a risk when it issued the arrest warrant for President al-Bashir of Sudan. The court's order has been openly defied for years, the UN has continued to cooperate with Mr. al-Bashir, and the ICC continues aggressive pursuit of justice in regions where the Prosecutor has an interest and individual nations are actually willing to deliver accused persons to the Court's jurisdiction. What is the future for such a court in such an environment? Timely response and cooperation by the UN is unlikely. During the Rwandan genocide of the early 1990s, the UN took months to formulate a response and deploy forces effectively, to the certain dismay of hundreds of thousands who were hacked to death in the meantime. The ICC does the best it can with the limited resources and meaningful support that it has. The good news for the ICC is that it is all that the international community has as a recognized instrument of criminal justice.

To be an effective instrument of justice, a court must have dependable and timely enforcement. The ICC obviously does not yet have it, and consequently will not be effective, or dignified, or respected, or powerful until it does. Perhaps in the future this international court will receive more support and be more effective, as it is a relatively new arena for international court systems.

National leaders have been motivated in their behaviors by various incentives. The list is, perhaps, endless but has certainly included unfortunate characteristics like greed, vanity, ego, madness, paranoia, lust for power, fear of losing power, hatred, bias, etc. Surely a few good characteristics may be added to the mix, such as altruism, love of country, honesty, determination to protect the nation, loyalty to the men and women in the armed forces, and confidence in decisions made in the nation's best interests. Of course, such motivations appear to be acceptable from some points of view, and criminal from others. Leaders will rarely sacrifice personal interests, the interests of their citizens and soldiers, or national interests to serve a nebulous benefit to mankind globally, especially if they can get away with it easily. Mr. al-Bashir, Mr. Bush, and the leaders who have declined to participate in the ICC have nothing to lose by choosing to remain outside the court's jurisdiction. There is no "big stick," no compelling reason for them to subject themselves, their people, or their nations' interests to international law and justice. Sadly, short-term status quo is the smart move.

A global system of international law, justice, and dispute resolution is obviously needed and ultimately, necessary for peace in the long term (Shany 2010). Most nations agree on this necessity, but many, including the USA, are unwilling to jeopardize national interests in the greater interest of global justice and peaceful resolution of conflict between nations.

Perhaps our planet needs a benevolent bully, jedi knights or whatever, with the authority and ability to compel compliance with international law by any necessary means. The UN is not up to the job, as we have witnessed in the last 60 years. The hope that nations will realize the importance of voluntary compliance and make the appropriate sacrifices is unrealistic. Without the "big stick," we will continue to experience the cycles of development and decline of mechanisms that we have seen in the past.

Web Sources

1. Information on the International Criminal Court available at: http://www.icc-cpi.int/en_menus/icc/Pages/default.aspx
2. Information on the International Court of Justice available at: http://www.icj-cij.org/homepage/index.php?lang=en
3. A list of International Court of Justice cases is available at: http://www.icj-cij.org/docket/index.php?p1=3&p2=2
4. Information about the structure of the International Criminal Court is available at: http://www.icc-cpi.int/en_menus/icc/structure%20of%20the%20court/Pages/structure%20of%20the%20court.aspx
5. Information on the Jay Treaty can be found at: http://www.loc.gov/rr/program/bib/ourdocs/jay.html

Discussion Questions

1. What is the historical significance of the Jay Treaty?
2. What is the function of the International Court of Justice (ICJ)?
3. What is the function of the International Criminal Court (ICC)?
4. Distinguish between the ICJ and the ICC. In what ways are they similar? In what ways do they differ?
5. Discuss the process of how cases are processed in the International Criminal Court versus the International Court of Justice.

References

Booth, Cherie, and Max du Plessis. "The International Criminal Court and Victims of Sexual Violence." *South African Journal of Criminal Justice* 18, no. 3 (2005): 241–258.

Corder, Mike. "Court Orders Sudan Leader's Arrest." *Austin American Statesman,* March 5, 2009, A3.

Currie, R. J. "Abducted Fugitives before the International Criminal Court Courts: Problems and Prospects." *Criminal Law Forum* 18, no. 3–4 (2007): 349–393.

Human Rights Watch. "The Case Against Hisséne Habré, an 'African Pinochet'." Accessed March 1, 2013. http://www.hrw.org/habre-case, 2013.

International Court of Justice. "International Court of Justice." Accessed May 1, 2013. http://www.icj-cij.org/. 2013.

_____. "Understanding the International Criminal Court." Accessed May 1 2013. http://www.icccpi.int/iccdocs/PIDS/publications/UICCEng.pdf, 2013.

_____. "Press Release: Extension of the Time-Limit for the Filing of Colombia's Rejoinder." International Court of Justice. Accessed January 1, 2013. http://www.icj-cij.org/docket/files/138/16727.pdf.

_____. "Press Release: Questions Relating to the Obligation to Prosecute or Extradite (Belgium V. Senegal), Request for the Indication of Provisional Measures, Court to Deliver Its Order on Thursday 28, May 2009 At 10 A.M". International Court of Justice. Accessed April 1, 2009. http://www.icj-cij.org/docket/files/144/15139.pdf, 2009.

_____. *International Court of Justice: Questions and Answers about Principal Judicial Organ of the United Nations.* The Hague, The Netherlands: The International Court of Justice, 2000.

_____. "Press Release: Application of the International Convention on the Elimination of All Forms of Racial Discrimination (Georgia V. Russian

Federation). International Court of Justice October 15, 2008." Accessed May 1, 2009. http://www.icj-cij.org/docket/files/140/14803.pdf, 2008.

_____. "Press Release: Ecuador Institutes Proceedings Against Colombia with Regard to a Dispute Concerning the Alleged Aerial Spraying by Columbia of Toxic Herbicides Over Ecuadorian Territory. International Court of Justice, April 1, 2008." Accessed May 1, 2009. http://www.icj-cij.org/docket/files/138/14470.pdf, 2009.

_____. "International Criminal Court: Situations and Cases." International Criminal Court, 2009. Accessed May 1, 2009. http://www.icc-pi.int/Menus/ICC/Situations+and+Cases/, 2009.

International Criminal Court and the United Nations. "Negotiated Relationship Agreement Between the International Criminal Court and the United Nations 2004." Accessed March 1, 2009. http://www.icc-cpi.int/NR/rdonlyres/916FC6A2-7846-4177-A5EA-5AA9B6D1E96C/0/ICCASP3Res1_English.pdf, 2009.

Roberson, Cliff, and Dilip K. Das. *An Introduction to Comparative Legal Models*. Boca Raton, FL: CRC Press, 2008.

Schabas, William, and Yvonne McDermott. "International Criminal Courts." In *Wiley-Blackwell Encyclopedia of Globalization*, edited by George Ritzer, 1114–1118. Chester, UK: Wiley-Blackwell, 2012.

Shany, Yuval. "Compliance with Decisions of International Courts as Indicative of Their Effectiveness: A Goal-Based Analysis." Hebrew University of Jerusalem Faculty of Law Research Paper No. 04-10. Accessed May 1, 2011. http://www.effective-intl-adjudication.org/admin/Reports/b9e3ecd149906 8e738666d041bd05459Shany_ESIL2010_Draft_Paper.pdf, 2010.

Simons, Marlise. "International Court Begins First Trial." *New York Times*, January 26, 2009, A10.

"Times Topics: International Criminal Court." *New York Times*. Accessed May 26, 2009. http://topics.nytimes.com/top/reference/timestopics/organizations/i/international_criminal_court/index.html?offset=54&s=newest.

Yacoubian, George S. Jr. 2003. "Should the Subject Matter Jurisdiction of the International Criminal Court Include Drug Trafficking?" *International Journal of Comparative Criminology* 3, no. 2 (2003): 175–190.

Chapter 3

Sovereign Lawlessness: Renditions and Co-Mingling of Criminal Justice and Military Justice

Sesha Kethineni & Rebecca Lawson

Introduction

"Irregular rendition," a contemporary extralegal international intelligence gathering and enforcement practice used with increasing regularity by agents of the United States in its global fight against narco- and political terrorism, has a long and sordid history in U.S. law. Irregular rendition involves the forcible abduction (i.e., kidnapping) and/or transfer of subjects from a sovereign foreign jurisdiction (i.e., the asylum state) by agents of an external sovereignty (i.e., the demanding state), for the purpose of transporting a subject or subjects to the demanding state where the subject(s) will be tried for alleged crimes. In some instances the subject(s) will be transported to a third sovereign jurisdiction, where the use of torture is permissible during interrogations, in an attempt to extract intelligence (Amnesty International 2006). The practice is variously known as extraordinary rendition, extraterritorial rendition, extraterritorial abduction, judicially sanctioned kidnapping, rendition to torture, and torture by proxy.

Historical Overview

In the United States, extraordinary renditions have been a historic practice. During the antebellum period (the years immediately preceding the U.S. Civil War), runaway slaves from the Southern states, who were found living in northern anti-slavery states, were forcibly abducted by Southern agents and transported back to their owners in the South. The lawful process to return a wanted fugitive back to another state is known as "rendition," although commonly, albeit improperly, referred to as "extradition" (Falcone 2005).

On February 12, 1793, the federal government passed a bill titled, "An Act Respecting Fugitives from Justice, and Persons Escaping from the Service of their Masters." The Act was the result of the murders of four Delaware Indians near the Big Beaver Creek by a band of Virginians on March 9, 1791. These murders were the result of earlier murders and kidnappings that they had allegedly committed. The Virginians who killed the Indians believed to have mistakenly identified these particular four as Delawares when they came upon some Indians in Beaver County, Pennsylvania, and not in Ohio County, Virginia, where the original murders took place. At that time neither the federal government nor state governments had a law that allowed the transfer of fugitives from one state to another. Then attorney general of Virginia, James Innes, argued that "there had to be a positive law for acquiring control over a person, delivering him up, and removing him from a state" (Leslie 1951, 72). Referring to the case, Innes stated that every free man in Virginia is entitled to enjoy his liberty, unless it is taken away by the laws of the United States or the U.S. Constitution or by the constitution or laws of Virginia (Leslie 1951).

This curious and extralegal process went unabated until 1850, when the Fugitive Slave Act curtailed the practice by requiring that asylum states honor the requests of the demanding states for the return of their slaves. As a result, extralegal renditions between states within the Union fell largely into dormancy. Despite the fact that forcible renditions (state-sponsored kidnappings) were in conflict with long-standing legal principles in U.S. and Anglo-Saxon jurisprudence, the practice was tolerated by the U.S. appellate courts.

International Overview

Despite its domestic roots, the issue of rendition was not limited to fugitives within the country. The United States also sought wanted felons hiding in other countries. For example, immediately following the assassination of President Abraham Lincoln, at the close of the Civil War, one of the co-conspirators, John Surratt, fled the country and was assisted by Southern sympathizers in numerous nations across the Western world in his escape and concealment. Eventually finding himself a member of the Papal Zouaves (army) in 1866, Surratt journeyed to Alexandra, Egypt, where U.S. agents had been informed of his whereabouts. He was forcibly abducted and rendered back to the United States, where he stood trial in 1867 as a principal in the murder of the late president, his unlawful abduction and legal protestations notwithstanding (Jordan and Litwack 1987). Although the historical record is not entirely clear concerning the details of Surratt's defense, it seems reasonable to assume that the trial court did not allow his defense of unlawful abduction, as Egypt had not protested Surratt's improper seizure and its attendant sovereignty violation through diplomatic channels. All of Surratt's co-conspirators, including his mother Mary Surratt, had been tried and convicted by a military commission in 1865, with limited constitutional protections. Four co-conspirators (Mary Surratt, Lewis Powell, George Atzerodt, and David Herold) received death penalty; three (Samuel Arnold, Dr. Samuel Mudd, and Michael O'Laughlen) were sentenced to life imprisonment; and one (Edman Spangler) was given a six-year sentence (Linder 2009).

Unlike the co-defendants, Surratt enjoyed the benefits of a civilian court trial and full constitutional protections because of the Supreme Court's decision in 1866 in *Ex Parte Milligan*. The Court ruled that when the civilian courts are operational a military tribunal may not be used to adjudicate nonmilitary U.S. citizens. Finally, the trial of Surratt ended with a hung jury; the government never sought a retrial. The issue of irregular renditions had had a brush with the courts, but only indirectly, and the issue was not directly addressed until an Illinois man (Ker) appealed his conviction, based on his unlawful rendition from South America.

The issue of unlawful abduction and seizure from foreign soil for the purpose of domestic criminal prosecutions resurfaced only two decades after *Ex Parte Milligan* in *Ker v. Illinois* (1886). Frederick Ker had fled Illinois after his indictment on felony charges of embezzlement, larceny, and receiving stolen property, to the nation of Peru. With legal writs in hand, Henry G. Julian of the Pinkerton Detective Agency was dispatched by the U.S. State Department, in compliance with a valid extradition treaty, and with the full knowledge and cooperation of the Peruvian authorities, to apprehend Mr. Ker. At the time of the agent's arrival, however, Peru and Bolivia were fighting Chile in the War of the Pacific (1879–84). Julian could not locate a civil authority that could provide assistance in the Peruvian capital of Lima (DiMento and Geis 2006). Given the exigency of the circumstances, the agent forcibly abducted Ker, who was transported back to Illinois where he stood trial and was convicted only of embezzlement (*Ker v. Illinois* 1886).

On appeal, Ker argued before the U.S. Supreme Court that he had been kidnapped by Julian in violation of the extant extradition treaty between the United States and Peru. He further argued that he was denied the protections of due process of law and that his unlawful apprehension and forcible abduction nullified the trial court's jurisdiction. The Supreme Court failed to sustain his claim of unlawful seizure, claiming that jurisdiction existed for the trial court to hear the case of a defendant standing before it, thereby reinforcing the maxim *mala captus bene detentus* (improper capture but lawful detention) (Falcone 2005). The Court, however, stated that Ker could extradite Julian to Peru to be tried there for kidnapping and other charges.

The *Ker* decision set the stage for future rendition decisions, as observed in *Frisbie v. Collins* (1952). In 1951, Shirley Collins, wanted on felony violations, was forcibly abducted in Chicago, Illinois, by the local police and returned to Michigan to stand trial. He was convicted of murder and received a life sentence. Collins claimed his due process rights were violated when he was illegally taken from Chicago to Michigan without legal process, and thus his conviction should be overturned. The defense attorney, citing the 1937 Federal Kidnapping Act, argued that the police tactic is rendered unacceptable under the Act (DiMento and Geis 2006). The Supreme Court upheld the view of the district court by adhering to the rule that jurisdiction to try a person for a crime is not impaired by the fact that he is brought to the court as a result of forcible abduction. This rule was held not to have been changed by the Federal Kidnapping Act.

The *Ker* decision (1886) and its later companion, *Frisbie v. Collins* (1952), together created the *Ker-Frisbie* doctrine, which gives tacit judicial imprimatur for irregular renditions. In other words, the Supreme Court made clear that its interest was focused on the authority of the trial court to hear the case when the defendant stands before it, the illegality of his or her seizure/apprehension notwithstanding. In other words, how a person was brought before the court, legally or illegally, did not affect the court's authority to try the defendants in a given case. The ruling in this case could have been influenced by the seriousness of the charge, judicial restraint, and a "bow to legislative power" (DiMento and Geis 2006, 53).

Following the precedent set in *Ker-Frisbie*, some U.S. courts were hesitant to approve renditions when torture was used (DiMento and Geis 2006). For example, in the *United States v. Toscanino* (1974), the U.S. Court of Appeals for the Second Circuit refused to accept jurisdiction of Francisco Toscanino and remanded the case to the District Court of Eastern New York to hold an evidentiary hearing with respect to Toscanino's allegation of forcible abduction by U.S. agents. The Appellate Court further stated that when "[F]aced with a conflict between the two concepts of due process, the one being the restricted version found in *Ker-Frisbie* and the other the expanded and enlightened interpretation expressed in more recent decisions of the Supreme Court, we are persuaded that to the extent that the two are in conflict, the *Ker-Frisbie* version must yield" (*U.S. v. Toscanino* 1974).

In this case, Francisco Toscanino, an Italian citizen charged with conspiracy to import heroin, appealed the lower court's decision, claiming "that the entire proceedings in the district court against him were void because his presence within the territorial jurisdiction of the court had been illegally obtained" (*U.S. v. Toscanino* 1974). Toscanino was kidnapped from Montevideo, Uruguay, where he was tortured by local police who were paid by U.S. agents, then taken to Brazil where he was further tortured for seventeen days at the insistence of the agents. During the entire process, no effort was made to legally extradite him. He alleged that the U.S. narcotic agents used wiretapping, torture, and illegal abduction. The trial court convicted and sentenced him to twenty years in prison and claimed "that the court's jurisdiction was not adversely affected by the manner in which the defendant was brought before the court" (Evans 1975, 406).

Almost twenty years later, the U.S. Supreme Court, following the *Ker-Frisbie* doctrine, ruled in *U.S. v. Alvarez-Machain* (1992) that U.S. courts have jurisdiction over defendants abducted abroad (Bush 1993). Alvarez, a Mexican doctor, was illegally and forcibly abducted in Mexico by four Mexican nationals, bounty hunters who had been working for the Drug Enforcement Agency (DEA). They then brought him to El Paso, Texas, where DEA agents arrested him. Alvarez was to stand trial for his role in the torture and murder of a DEA special agent (Enrique Camarena-Salazar) in Mexico in 1985. According to the complaint, the doctor kept the agent alive in order to extract more information.

Alvarez was in federal custody for two years. During this time, Alvarez attempted to gain his release on the ground that the U.S. government violated the extradition treaty between the two countries. The federal district court in central California ruled that the United States had violated the 1978 Extradition treaty between the United States and Mexico and that the court had no jurisdiction over the case and ordered his release. The Court of Appeals for the Ninth Circuit agreed with the lower court's decision, but the U.S. Supreme Court, citing *Ker,* noted its authority to try Alvarez irrespective of how he was brought into the United States for trial. Finally, he was acquitted due to lack of evidence. Alvarez attempted to gain redress for the illegal manner in which he was brought to the United States under the Federal Tort Claims Act (FTCA) (1946) and Alien Tort Statute (ATS) (1789). Under FTCA private parties are allowed to sue the federal government in federal courts for torts arising out of negligence acts committed by the agents of the United States, whereas ATS (adopted in 1789 as part of the original Judicial Act) allows law suits by aliens for torts in federal district courts, committed in violation of the U.S. laws or a treat of the United States. The U.S. Supreme Court reversed the decision of the lower court and ruled that Alvarez had no recourse under FTCA because the Act precludes claims arising out of actions committed in a foreign country (*U.S. v. Alvarez-Machain* 2004).

No matter what the Court's rationale, this process has been heavily criticized by respected jurists and courts across the globe stating that it is in direct contravention of international conventions on human rights and torture. Most importantly, under Article VI of the U.S. Constitution, international law (i.e., treaties) to which the United States is a signatory become "the law of the land" and are as binding as the Constitution and federal statutory law itself (*Valentine v. U.S.* 1936). Despite the controversy, the U.S. government was involved in illegally extraditing wanted individuals to other nations for the purpose of interrogation and torture. Stating the prohibition against ill-treatment of persons in custody, the Human Rights Watch (2004) reported,

> International and U.S. law prohibits torture and other ill-treatment of any person in custody in all circumstances. The prohibition applies to the United States during times of peace, armed conflict, or a state of emergency.... It is irrelevant whether the detainee is determined to be a prisoner-of-war, a protected person, or a so-called "security detainee" or "unlawful combatant." And the prohibition is in effect within the territory of the United States or any place anywhere U.S. authorities have control over a person. In short, the prohibition against torture and ill-treatment is absolute (1).

When subjects are transported to a third nation for the purpose of interrogation, they are frequently held in "black sites," where detainees are tortured by agents of the receiving sovereignty at the behest of U.S. intelligence and/or law enforcement agents (Preist 2005). The use of black sites, where torture is employed, is a technique intended to avoid criminal culpability, as both U.S. law and international conventions forbid the use of torture (see Federal Anti-Torture Statute 1994; War Crimes Act 1996; Universal Declaration of Human Rights 1948; United Nations [UN] Convention Against Torture 1984; and the UN Code of Conduct for Law Enforcement Officials 1979). Some of the domestic laws violated under the rendition process employed by the United States today include the Constitution's Eighth Amendment's prohibition against cruel and unusual punishment, the Federal Anti-Torture Statute (1994), and the War Crimes Act (1996).

Extent of the Problem

Although the exact number of extraterritorial abductions remains a "dark figure," watchdog agencies have argued that many of those who have been forcibly abducted, approximately 100–150 between September 11, 2001 and 2006, and have been held in black sites, which operate in at least eight countries (Zagaris 2005; Amnesty International 2005; Whitlock and Linzer 2005). These black sites were in existence prior to September 11, 2001, although the frequency of extrajudicial renditions has considerably increased since 2001. In 1995, for example, U.S. agents kidnapped Talaat Fouad Qassem, one of Egypt's most wanted terrorists. He was arrested in Croatia by the Croatian police, who handed him over to U.S. intelligence agents. The agents interrogated Qassem aboard a ship that was traveling in the Adriatic Sea for information that the Islamic Group was planning to assassinate President Clinton. Qassem was handed over to Egyptian officials and now it seems he has disappeared.

The tactics used by the United States under the disguise of the "war against terrorism" have stimulated a renewed interest in renditions (Fitzpatrick 2003). Since 9/11, thousands have been illegally rendered from outside the United States and transferred to detention facilities, including the military base in Guantanamo Bay, Cuba. The detainees have not been afforded legal rights in violation of the Geneva Convention, yet many have been held for years.

As an example, Abu Zubaydah and Ramzi Bin al Shibh, alleged Al-Qaeda operatives, were captured in Pakistan in March 2002 with the cooperation from Pakistan government. The two suspects were transported across international borders and detained at an unknown location. In other instances, U.S. agents have crossed into Pakistan without the cooperation of the Pakistani government, captured suspected Al-Qaeda supporters and transferred to detention facilities. Many other examples exist, such as the case of Abdul Rahim al-Nashiri, who was allegedly involved in the bombing of the USS Cole in 2000 in Yemen. Al-Nashiri was brought into custody in the United Arab Emirates and then taken to Jordan where he was detained and interrogated (Fitzpatrick 2003).

On December 18, 2001, two Egyptian asylum seekers, Muhammad Zery and Ahmed Agiza, were apprehended at Stockholm's Bromma Airport by several hooded men. Zery and Agiza were then stripped down, given a sedative through a suppository, placed in diapers and redressed in orange jumpsuits. The two were restrained by handcuffs and shackles, blindfolded and then flown, via a U.S. registered airplane, to Cairo. The suspects were reportedly tortured with electrical shocks to their genitals. Zery was released after two years, but

Agiza was eventually convicted of terrorist acts and sentenced to twenty-five years in prison (Mayer 2005).

The preceding cases involve moving suspects between countries other than the U.S. However, the U.S. has also taken suspected terrorists from the United States and detained them in other countries. Maher Arar, a Canadian-Syrian national, was apprehended at a U.S. airport while traveling home to Canada because his name was on a terrorist suspect list. After being held in the United States for thirteen days, Arar was taken to Syria where he was interrogated, tortured and detained. After ten months, Arar was released without charges. After his release, he comments, "Sometimes I have the feeling that I want to go and live on another planet.... A completely different planet than planet Earth. You know?" (Herbert 2006, A27). Arar was referring to the fact that his life has been forever transformed and destroyed, and he no longer feels he has a place in the world. Herbert concludes by stating, "The rendition program is one more example of the way the United States, using the threat of terror as an excuse, has locked its ideals away in a drawer somewhere" (A27).

Often times, the business of extraordinary renditions involve private company. For example, "a private jet allegedly leased by the U.S. government to skirt extradition protocol by secretly ferrying suspected terrorists around the globe is registered to a Massachusetts company" (Boston Herald 2004, ¶1). The company, Premier Executive Transport Services, has been used since at least 2001 to secretly transport two Al-Qaeda suspects from Sweden to Egypt. According to the suspects' lawyer, the suspects were tortured once they arrived in Egypt. The Associated Press reported that a classified report showed 300 flights from the United States that landed in forty-nine countries, including three that are reported to allow torture.

Despite documented rendition cases, President Bush maintained that the United States follows the Geneva Convention policy of "nonrefoulement," which means that detainees will not be taken to countries where it is known that they violate human rights through torture. Those held at "black sites" become politically problematic for the United States, as they are of little value after intelligence has been extracted. Returning them to their countries of origin or another nation, where violence or torture are likely, is forbidden under international treaty as an act of "refoulement" and a direct violation of the principle of *jus cogens*. *Jus cogens* offenses include those acts that are forbidden by the majority of the international community and that become "international common law" binding on all nations, including the United States, whether or not there is a written international law prohibiting it. Coupled with the U.S. Constitution's Article VI provision, *jus cogens* prohibitions are binding on U.S. courts under some circumstances. Then U.S. Attorney General Alberto Gon-

zales argued that the United Nations' (UN) ban on cruel treatment of terrorist suspects does not apply to U.S. interrogations of foreigners conducted abroad
(Mayer 2005).

The Central Intelligence Agency's (CIA) officials justify the use of extraordinary rendition policies by saying it is a way of protecting their intelligence
sources and the methods by which they gather their information. Further, the
CIA fears that foreign governments will not cooperate if they are required to
come to the United States and testify regarding their role in locating suspects;
these governments fear reprisals from their own citizens if their cooperation
were to be made public.

Currently, many persons who are captured through extraordinary renditions
are warehoused at the U.S.-run prison camp in Guantanamo Bay, Cuba. In 2005,
there were approximately 550 detainees at Guantanamo Bay, most of whom had
been either captured, kidnapped, or arrested during U.S. military operations in
Afghanistan after September 11, 2001 (Ratner 2005, 31). Most of the detainees
have been held for more than two years, have not been afforded access to an attorney or their families, and have not been formally charged with a crime. This
treatment of detainees has become a historic practice dating back to the presidency of Ronald Reagan and continuing through the first Bush administration,
Clinton administration, and the second Bush administration. During the Reagan administration extraordinary rendition was approved to make a point that
terrorists who attack U.S. interests/citizens could not escape their "day in U.S.
court" (Naftali 2005). It was "extraordinary" because no foreign country assisted
the United States in the kidnappings and it was used infrequently (DiMento and
Geis 2006). In the first Bush administration, Guantanamo Bay was used to house
Haitian refugees; during that time, the first HIV-positive refugee camp was created. The creation of these refugee camps was to prevent the Haitians from coming into the United States. Ratner (2005, 33) stated that,

> [T]he Bush II administration have all operated as if no court in the world
> could hear a case brought on behalf of a Guantanamo refugee or de-
> tainee. In effect this meant that the U.S. government could treat
> refugees and detainees however it wished; it could beat them, punish
> them, detain them forever or send them back to their oppressors in Haiti,
> and there was nothing anyone could do about it.

Fallout for CIA Agents

Generally speaking, CIA agents are the ones who executed President Bush's
order to capture and detain certain individuals whom he believed to be ter-

rorist suspects. The consequences of this are quite severe for many CIA agents, who now face arrest should they ever leave the United States. In January 2007, courts in Germany issued arrest warrants for thirteen CIA agents whom they believed to be involved in the secret transfer of a German citizen believed to be a terrorist suspect. Khaled el-Masri was apprehended in Macedonia in 2003. He was taken to Afghanistan and detained for five months where he says he was tortured. Despite his alleged ties to Al-Qaeda, El-Masri was eventually released without charges. Further, Italian prosecutors are seeking indictments against twenty-five CIA operatives and a former Italian intelligence chief for the kidnapping of an Egyptian militant cleric, Osama Nasr Mostafa Hassan, also known as Abu Omar, in 2003 (Landler 2007). All of the arrest warrants are valid throughout Europe. Thus, any CIA agent named on a warrant would not be able to travel to any European Union (EU) member nation without facing the possibility of arrest.

In addition to being named on arrest warrants, many CIA agents now face legal action through the filing of civil law suits. Khaled el-Masri and Maher Arar (a Canadian-Syrian national) both filed suits against CIA agents and/or the United States. Neither has been compensated by the United States for having been illegally rendered to another country, tortured, and released without charges. Canada awarded Maher Arar $10 million dollars for its role in his kidnapping by the United States. The United States, however, cites national security as its reason for not hearing the cases. The American Civil Liberties Union (ACLU) reported that in declining to hear El-Masri's case, the government was invoking the "state secretes" privilege. Despite the government's claim of national security protection, the ACLU (2007a), arguing on behalf of el-Masri, said, "the government is invoking the state secrets privilege to avoid accountability for the abuses it perpetrated against El-Masri rather than to protect sensitive national security interests" (9).

The Role of Other Countries

The European parliament denounced the use of extraordinary renditions. Nonetheless, there is evidence that many member nations have either participated in and/or had knowledge of renditions and torture of suspects (European Parliament 2009). European countries reported to have known about the black sites where kidnapped persons were being detained. Further, these countries were impeding an investigation into the link between these secret detention camps and the CIA. A European Parliament report, issued in November 2006, indicated that despite Italy claiming it had no involvement in the kidnapping of Abu Omar, this was untrue. In fact, the Parliament report stated that the truth was concealed, and that in fact Nicolo Pollari, former head of Italy's intelligence service, was involved, leading them to believe that the Italian government must have also known about the kidnapping. U.S. Secretary of State Condoleezza Rice acknowledged that European member nations had knowledge of the U.S. extraordinary rendition program as well as the use of secret prisons (European Parliament 2006).

Egypt, Syria, Morocco, Yemen, Pakistan, and Jordan, among others, have assisted the United States with the rendition program by allowing the detention of captured persons in their respective countries. Each of these countries has a known history of torture and has been cited for human-rights violations in the past. Although Britain minimizes its knowledge and involvement in the U.S. rendition program, it has granted permission to CIA to utilize its air space to transport suspects seized overseas (Charter, 2006).

The Opposition

In January 2007, U.S. Congressmen Edward J. Markey (D-Mass.), a member of the Homeland Security Committee, issued a statement on his Web site in which he discussed the U.S. practice of "outsourcing torture." Markey (2007) is asking the United States to stop its practice of extraordinary rendition. He is quoted as saying,

> Today's case sheds more light on the ugly U.S. practice of extraordinary rendition. Germany now joins Italy, and Sweden in investigating extra-legal actions by the United States on the streets of sovereign allies. In Italy indictments have been issued against 25 CIA agents for the kidnapping and transfer of a man to Egypt. President Bush needs to put an end to the practice of outsourcing of torture, his defense of this illegal practice jeopardizes U.S. officials who are now caught in the middle of an international kidnapping scandal. Rep. Markey noted, The War on Terror must be won, but it will not be won by scooping up innocent foreign citizens and sending them to secret prisons around the world. This is an outrageous practice (2).

Congressman Markey, author of the Torture Outsourcing Prevention Act, attempted to make an amendment to Bush's policy on renditions, which would ban funding in the Intelligence Authorization Acts' extraordinary renditions program that allowed for outsourcing of torture. However, in April 2006, the House Republicans blocked a vote on the amendment.

In the fall of 2005, Senator John McCain introduced an Amendment to the Defense Departments Appropriations bill to Congress that would require Americans abroad to treat detainees the same as they would at home as per the U.S. Constitution. The bill was favorably voted for 90–9, despite President Bush's opposition to it. Congressman Earl Blumenauer has also sponsored an amendment to legislation, which was adopted by the House of Representatives, will prohibit the funds for being used in a way that contravene the UN Convention Against Torture (Robinson 2005).

As it can be imagined, organizations like Amnesty International and the ACLU strongly oppose extraordinary renditions. On January 11, 2007, Amnesty International asked the European Union to use the fifth anniversary of Guantanamo Bay as a way to revisit the issue of extraordinary renditions. Pleading to the German presidency of the European Union, Amnesty International indicated that it was a prime opportunity for Germany to address this issue, in light of German citizens who have been abducted through extraordinary renditions. Amnesty International also reports disgust with member countries of the European Union as it has been revealed that many are participating, at least to some degree, in extraordinary renditions.

Amnesty International (1999) has also called for nations to enact universal jurisdiction laws or amend current ones to make them more effective. Universal jurisdiction laws give countries the right to prosecute offenses that did not occur within their sovereign territories. Prosecutable offenses under universal jurisdiction would include violations of the Geneva Convention, including incidents of torture that other nations refuse to prosecute.

In a call to stop extraordinary renditions, the ACLU (2007a) appealed to the federal government in February 2007, criticizing the Bush administration for its refusal to sign an international accord prohibiting secret detentions and forced disappearances. The ACLU goes on to say, "No president should ever be given the power to call someone an enemy, wave his hand, and lock them away indefinitely" (Kairi 2007, 5). Since 9/11, President Bush has created the Military Commissions Act, which has changed the legalities of *habeas corpus*. The Military Commissions Act now allows the U.S. government to imprison people without charge or legal ramification, including denying detainees any court review of their imprisonment. Furthermore, the Act allows the government to redefine torture and abuse, ignoring the Geneva conventions or any other human rights acts (ACLU 2007b). In addition to the Military Commissions Act, the U.S. Patriot Act (2001) was revised to increase the surveillance and investigative powers of law enforcement agencies in the United States.

The Patriot Act now intrudes on several constitutional rights including the First Amendment freedom of speech, religion, etc.; the Fourth Amendment right to protection from unreasonable searches and seizures; the Fifth Amendment, no person shall be deprived of life, liberty or property without due process; the Sixth Amendment right to a speedy trial; the Eighth Amendment right to protection from cruel and unusual punishment; and the Fourteenth Amendment, due process to all citizens and noncitizens. Due to provisions of the Patriot Act, all these rights can be removed should the government find it necessary for intelligence gathering purposes.

The Patriot Act has affected both the U.S. federal and domestic law enforcement, as it calls for a collaboration between federal and local officers. The federal government is now relying, in part, on domestic officers to relay information they gather in the course of their routine investigations, to federal officers, which will assist with foreign intelligence gathering.

The increased responsibility of assisting the federal government in tracking down suspected terrorist is inevitably going to change the face of the domestic officers' law enforcement responsibilities. Many domestic law enforcement agencies have implemented, in part, militaristic type tactics, such as SWAT teams. Implementation of such tactics has increased since 9/11 and is reinforced by the governments call for local agencies to assist the federal government in its "War on Terrorism."

Thus, it would not be a far stretch to state that when a local law enforcement officer sees the federal government trample on citizen's civil liberties, they in turn feel that practice will be tolerated. When the agents of the federal government kidnap, torture, and illegally detain suspects, local officers are sure to see that this is an effective way to police the community. From the community perspective, if the citizens feel they cannot trust the federal government, how can they be expected to trust and respect their local officers?

Co-Mingling of Criminal Justice and Military Justice

As countries attempt to import core international crimes into national criminal law, the United States is confronted with the jurisdictional issue of military courts in trying suspected foreign terrorists or so called "enemy combatants." The unlawful interrogation techniques, indefinite detention without formal charges, and trial by military commissions of Guantanamo Bay detainees came under criticism internationally as well as by President Obama's administration. Trials by military commissions limit due process rights of accused and death penalty can be liberally applied.

Historical Overview

The subject of jurisdiction of military commissions to try civilians was not fully tested in the United States until the Civil War (Young 2002). In 1863, the issue was challenged in *Ex Parte Vallandigham*. Mr. Vallandigham, a resident of Ohio, was arrested and later arraigned before a military commission on charges of showing sympathies for those in arms against the U.S. government by uttering disloyal statements and opinions at a public meeting. The commission, consisting of seven members, tried Mr. Vallandigham and found him guilty and sentenced him to imprisonment. Justice Wayne, who delivered the opinion for the court, made a distinction as to the type of cases that are tried under court-martial and those that can be tried by military commission. Military offenses that fall under the statute are to be tried in a manner as stated in the statute by "court-martial," whereas those that do not fall under the statute must be tried in accordance with the common law of war, meaning the military commissions.

The Supreme Court revisited the subject of the jurisdictional issue in a number of cases. For example, the U.S. government applied military justice in the trial of Mrs. Mary E. Surratt, mother of John Surratt, and other conspirators in the assassination of President Abraham Lincoln. At the conclusion of the trial and before Mrs. Surratt's execution, the counsel attempted to secure the writ of *habeas corpus* (Turner 1991) on several grounds. First, the counsel claimed that Mrs. Surratt was charged, against her protest, by the military commission without warrant. Second, at the time of the commission of the said offense, Mr. Surratt was a private citizen of the United States and in no way connected to the military authority. Third, the said offense was committed in the District of Columbia and not in an enemy's territory. Fourth, the said offense was an offense against the peace of the United States and not an act of war. Fifth, that all crimes claimed to have been committed were under the constitution and laws of the United States where she was entitled to an investigation by a grand jury and a trial by jury before a criminal tribunal (Pitman 1865). Judge Andrew B. Wylie issued the writ but President Andrew Johnson ordered a proclamation suspending the writ. Unlike his mother, who was tried before the military commission, John Surratt was tried in a civilian court because of the Supreme Court's decision in *Ex Parte Milligan* (1866) in which the Court ruled that a civilian court, and not military court, has jurisdiction in civilian cases if civilian courts are open and operational.

The landmark decision by the Supreme Court in *Ex Parte Milligan* temporarily settled the jurisdiction of military courts. In this case, Lambdin P. Milligan, a citizen of the United States and a resident of Indiana, was arrested and charged with conspiracy against the government, affording aid to rebels, and inciting insurrection, and violations of the laws of the war, among other charges (*Ex Parte Milligan* 1866). He was tried by a military commission and sentenced to death by hanging. Milligan filed his petition of *habeas corpus* for his release in the Circuit Court of the United States for the District of Indiana. The court split on the question of jurisdictional authority of the civilian courts to hear appeals from military tribunals. The Supreme Court cleared the path by affirming the right of the civilian courts over military courts if civilian courts are open and operational.

Subsequent decisions by the Supreme Court primarily dealt with foreign nationals who were detained during war times, military personnel charged with crimes while stationed at U.S. military bases, and civilians tried by military tribunals when the martial law was in place. In *Ex Parte Quirin* (1942), the Supreme Court denied the leave to file petitions for *habeas corpus* by eight Germans accused of violating the laws of war, sabotage, and spying. All of the petitioners were born in Germany, lived in the United States, and returned to Germany from 1933–41, during which the United States was at war with Germany. All except petitioner Haupt were citizens of Germany. Haupt came to the United States when he was young and gained citizenship by virtue of his parents' naturalization and never relinquished his citizenship. The government, however, took the position that he maintained German allegiance and carried out acts against the United States and by his very conduct he renounced the U.S. citizenship. The Court based its decision on three key factors: 1) the charges against petitioners on which they are being tried by military commission were authorized by the order of the president; 2) the military commission was lawfully constituted; and 3) the detention of the petitioners was lawful.

In *Duncan v. Kahanamoku* (1946), the issue was whether military tribunal created during wartime in Hawaii had the authority to sentence civilians during the peace time. Petitioner White was a stockbroker in Honolulu charged with embezzling funds from another civilian. He was arrested by military police more than eight months after the Pearl Harbor attack. He was tried before a military tribunal known as the Provost Court, which sentenced him to five years in prison, although this was later reduced to four years. The second petitioner, Duncan, was a civilian shipfitter employed at the Navy yard at Honolulu. He was charged with brawling with two armed Marine sentries at his place of employment. He was tried by the military tribunal and received a six-month sentence. This incident occurred on February 24, 1944, more than two years after the attack on Pearl Harbor.

Both petitioners filed *habeas corpus* petition before the U.S. District Court for Hawaii. The court held that the military tribunal had no such power and ordered their release. The Circuit Court of Appeals reversed the ruling of the District Court against the argument of the petitioner that "martial law" that was imposed during wartime (attack on Pearl Harbor) did not authorize the military tribunals to try and punish civilians. The Supreme Court recognized the importance of civil courts in protecting constitutional rights and ruled "that martial law alone was no excuse for replacing civilian courts with military commissions" (Young 2002, ¶ 10). The Supreme Court took a similar stand in *U.S. Ex Rel. Toth v. Quarles* (1955).

The question of the jurisdiction of military tribunals resurfaced during President George W. Bush's tenure. After the terrorists' attacks of September 11, 2001, President Bush issued a military order, "Detention, Treatment and Trial of Certain Non-Citizens in the War Against Terrorism," authorizing the detention and trial of suspected terrorists who are noncitizens by a military commission. According to the Order, reviews of convictions would be done either by the Secretary of Defense or by the President of the United States and not by the judiciary. Tim Golden of *The New York Times* commented that "[T]he Administration claims of authority to set up military commissions ... was guided by a desire to strengthen executive power" (Golden 2004, ¶ 14).

Using the "sense of urgency" as a rationale, the CIA captured many suspected Al-Qaeda fighters, who were not members of Taliban armed forces, and denied them status as prisoners of war. Some of these captives were detained at U.S. military bases in Afghanistan and others were transported to Guantanamo Bay, Cuba. Except for few, an estimated 3,000 detainees at Guantanamo Bay were not charged with a "recognizable criminal offense" (Fitzpatrick 2003, 460). Many of them were labeled as "enemy combatants" so that the protections under the Geneva Convention could be avoided. Some of the states involved in transporting the captives to U.S. custody were not parties to the human rights treaties, and therefore could not be held responsible for denying human rights, such as refoulement.

According to Fitzpatrick (2003), the prisoner of war, such as regular Taliban soldiers, should be accorded full rights under the Third Geneva Convention, including repatriation. Under privileged combatants, such as Al-Qaeda fighters who are not members of the Taliban Armed Forces, should be given protection under the customary international law by repatriating them to Afghanistan when the Afghan conflict ceases. If further detention is necessary, they should be charged with criminal offenses and be given a fair trial (Fitzpatrick 2003, 491–492).

Although the Bush administration insisted that the detainees at Guantanamo Bay are not entitled to any of the protections of the Geneva Convention, the U.S. Supreme Court in *Hamdan v. Rumsfeld* (2006) ruled that they were entitled to minimal protections listed under Article 3 of the Geneva Convention (see Oyez Project 2006). Salem Ahmed Hamdan, a former chauffeur of Osama bin Laden, was captured in Afghanistan and detained in Guantanamo Bay. He filed a *habeas corpus* petition challenging his detention in a federal district court. Although his petition was pending before the district court, the military commission that heard his case designated him an enemy combatant. The District Court allowed his petition and ruled that a hearing must first be held to determine whether he was a prisoner of war and therefore entitled to protection under the Geneva Convention before he can be tried by a military commission. The Circuit Court of Appeals reversed the decision stating that the military tribunals were authorized by Congress and therefore not unconstitutional. The Supreme Court reversed the Circuit Court's decision and held that,

> [N]either an act of Congress nor the inherent powers of the Executive laid out in the Constitution expressly authorized the sort of military commission at issue in this case. Absent that express authorization, the commission had to comply with the ordinary laws of the United States and the laws of war. The Geneva Convention, as a part of the ordinary laws of war, could therefore be enforced by the Supreme Court, along with the statutory Uniform Code of Military Justice (Oyez Project, *Hamdan v. Rumsfeld* 2006, 4).

The jurisdictional debate continued to haunt the current administration. President Barack Obama signed an order on January 22, 2009, suspending the proceedings of the military commission at Guantanamo Bay for 120 days, including the closure of the facility and review of cases. On May 2009, the president reversed his earlier decision, stating that the military trials will resume, however, they will be based on five rule changes that will make the commission a legitimate one (Mazzetti and Glaberson, 2009).

President Obama authorized an interagency Guantanamo Bay Task Force to review the cases. The first case eligible to be tried in civilian court under the new policy was that of Ahmed Ghailani, a Tanzanian accused in two U.S. Embassy bombings in Tanzania and Kenya in 1998 that killed 224 people, including twelve Americans. He was handed over to U.S. Marshals by the Department of Defense and was brought to the Southern District of New York on June 9, 2009. The future will tell how these cases will be handled (USA Today, 2009).

Conclusion

The use of irregular renditions has a long history in the United States, and its approval by the judiciary has led to the current international crisis regarding this issue. It seems certain that the nation's present course concerning this issue will not be altered by those in either the executive or judicial branches. Therefore, if the United States is to claim the moral "high ground" in its global battle against terrorism, it must conduct this battle within the parameters of the law at both the national and international levels. That means: (1) enforcing domestic legislation that proscribes this activity, and (2) complying with applicable international treaties that proscribe irregular renditions, the use of secret detention sites, and torture.

Just as with other "legal" processes that were found to be offensive to a democratic state (e.g., asset forfeiture) the task of righting wrongs ultimately lies with the legislature, given the conservative orientation of the present-day executive and judicial branches. Although this approach to correcting the national trajectory is difficult, no other means appears viable in the current environment. We posit that the polity must "think globally and act locally" to begin the process of convincing the legislatures in this republic to act in this important matter.

In the U.S. scheme of government, if the people collectively disagree with either the practices of the executive branch or the rulings of the judicial branch, they may seek redress through the legislative branch, to which both the executive and judicial branches must be compliant. In such situations, the legislature (in this instance Congress) may create new laws that overrule executive practices and executive orders that have been ruled legal/constitutional by the Supreme Court through its inherent powers of judicial review (see *Marbury v. Madison* 1803). That is, the Court may interpret existing laws and/or the constitutionality of executive powers and practices. In *Marbury v. Madison*, the U.S. Supreme Court, under Chief Justice John Marshal, held that the judiciary had the right to review and determine whether the legislative or executive branches have legislated or acted within the parameters of the U.S. Constitution. The case stands as the cornerstone underpinning the judicial branch as a full partner in the federal scheme of government.

Should the people strongly disagree with those existing practices, which have been condoned by the appellate courts, they may petition the legislature to create new laws that will supersede and annul existing statutes or judicially generated case law that allow(s) the practice(s), upon which that practice or practices is/are made legally justifiable and permissible.

Given the right-leaning posture of the U.S. Supreme Court, especially after the appointment of Chief Justice John Roberts, Jr., in 2005 and Associate Justice Samuel Alito, in 2006, both of whom are conservatives, neither the executive branch nor the judiciary are likely to discontinue the practice of irregular renditions, foreign abduction/seizures, interrogations at black sites, or torture by proxy.

The only viable escape from the corner into which this nation has painted itself is through the citizenry demanding that the Congress pass federal legislation forbidding irregular renditions and their attendant and related nefarious activities. Further, any such legislative bills must include a stipulation disallowing any form of presidential exception (a signing statement) allowing the executive branch to be immune to the requirements of the new statute, as this has been a favorite loophole for the current administration in its attempts to avoid congressional accountability in what appears to be a growing trend toward an imperial presidency. This translates into: The president is not subject to the statute he has signed into law. In fact, President George W. Bush's administration used this technique (a technique upon which the Constitution is silent) to avoid legal liability imposed by the statute more than any president in the nation's history. That is, he has used "signing statements" 108 times in the five years of his presidency; his Republican predecessor, Ronald W. Reagan, used signing statements only 75 times in his entire eight-year tenure (Dahlia 2006).

Although all legal scholars agree that signing statements are not explicitly permitted under the Constitution, they are somewhat divided as to the legality of the process as an implied "war power" of the president. The question of the processes' legality (constitutionality) is one upon which the Supreme Court must eventually make a ruling, if the practice is litigated against. Once again, the conservative posture of the Court would suggest a positive ruling for the chief executive at this time. Thus, if legislative supremacy is to have any meaningful impact on current U.S. policy and the controlling case law supporting irregular renditions, any proposed legislation must explicitly disallow use of any signing statement authority.

As is so often the case in the United States, it is at the state and local level where legislative experimentation must begin. Although this would have no direct bearing on federal law or foreign policy, it would disallow the use of irregular renditions in state courts and build political momentum against its use in federal courts and foreign policy concerning irregular renditions. Moreover, this course of action, at the state level, would demand the attention of the U.S. Department of Justice and the executive branch, as inattention to this matter holds the potential for a "nullification crisis," something the federal government truly wants to avoid. This would be just one more area in which state law (both constitutional and statutory) provides criminal defendants with more protections than that found at the federal level—a situation that has existed for over two decades. After sufficient political support has developed at the state and local levels, the effort to press for federal legislation would have a viable chance.

Web Sources

1. Uniform Code of Military Justice is available at:
    http://www.au.af.mil/au/awc/awcgate/ucmj.htm
2. Military Justice Fact Sheets are available at:
    http://sja.hqmc.usmc.mil/JAM/MJFACTSHTS.htm
3. National Institute of Military Justice is available at:
    http://www.nimj.org/home.aspx
4. ACLU fact sheets on extraordinary rendition is available at:
    http://www.aclu.org/safefree/extraordinaryrendition/22203res20051206.html
5. Videos of extraordinary renditions are available at:
    http://video.google.com/videosearch?hl=en&rls=com.microsoft:en-us:IE-SearchBox&rlz=1I7GGLL_en&q=Extraordinary+renditions&um=1&ie=UTF-8&ei=mZyVSvDaI4aYMce26PkH&sa=X&oi=video_result_group&ct=title&resnum=4#

Discussion Questions

1. Discuss the origin of rendition in the United States.
2. What are the legal and policy justifications of extraordinary renditions?
3. What is the U.S. Supreme Court's position on extraordinary renditions?
4. What international laws are presumed to be violated by the detention of "enemy combatants" at Guantanamo Bay?
5. Discuss the jurisdictional issues pertaining military trials in civilian cases.

References

American Civil Liberties Union (ACLU). "Federal Appeals Court Denies Day in Court for Victim of C.I.A. Kidnapping, Citing State Secrets." Accessed April 17, 2007. http://aclu.org/safefree/extraordinaryrendition, 2007a.

American Civil Liberties Union (ACLU). "Military Commission Act." Accessed February 10, 2009. http://aclu.org/safefree/detention, 2007b.

Amnesty International. "Universal Jurisdiction: Four Principals on the Effective Exercise of Universal Jurisdiction." Accessed April 17, 2007, http//web.amnesty.org/library, 1999.

Amnesty International. "A Deadly Interrogation: Can the C.I.A. Legally Kill a Prisoner?" Accessed February 18, 2007. http://newyorker.com, 2005.

Amnesty International. "'Rendition' and Secret Detention: A Global System of Human Rights Violation." Accessed April 17, 2007. http://web.amnesty.org/library, 2006.

Boston Herald. "Plane Allegedly Used By Government Owned By Mass. Company." *Boston Herald,* November 29, 2004. Accessed February 18, 2007. http://www.freedomunderground.net/view.php?v=3&t=3&aid=12134.

Bush, Jonathan A. "How Did We Get There? Foreign Abduction after Alvarez-Machain." *Stanford Law Review* 45 (1993): 939–978.

Charter, David. "Britain Accused on Secret CIA Flights." *Timesonline*, November 29, 2006. Accessed August 20, 2009. http://www.timesonline.co.uk/tol/news/world/us_and_americas/article653418.ece.

Dahlia, Lithwick. "Sign Here: Presidential Signing Statements Are More Than Just Executive Branch Lunacy." Accessed June 16, 2009. http://www.slate.com/id/2134919/, 2006.

DiMento, Joseph F. C., and Gilbert Geis. "The Extraordinary Condition of Extraordinary Rendition: The C.I.A., the D.E.A., Kidnapping, Torture, and the Law." *War Crimes, Genocide, and Crimes against Humanity* 2 (2006): 35–64.

Duncan v. Kahanamoku, 327 U.S. 304 (1946).

European Parliament. "Extraordinary Renditions: EU Member States Are Also Responsible, MEPs Say." Accessed August 10, 2009. http://www.europarl.europa.eu/news/expert/infopress_page/019-49769-047-02-08-902-2009 0218IPR49768-16-02-2009-2009-false/default_en.htm, 2009.

Evans, Alona E. Judicial decisions: *United States v. Toscanino.* 500 F.2d 267. *American Journal of International Law* 69, no. 2 (1975): 406–415.

Ex parte Milligan, 71 U.S. 1 (1866).

Ex Parte Quirin, 317 U.S. 1 (1942).

Ex Parte Vallandigham, 68 U.S. 243 (1863).

Falcone, David N. *Dictionary of American Criminal Justice, Criminology, and Criminal Law*. Upper Saddle River, N.J.: Pearson/Prentice Hall, 2005.

Federal Anti-Torture Statute. 18 U.S.C., Chapter 113C §2340A, 1999.

Fitzpatrick, Joan. "Rendition and Transfer in the War Against Terrorism: Guantanamo and Beyond." *Loyola of Los Angeles International and Comparative Law Journal* 25 (2003): 457–492.

Frisbie v. Collins, 342 US 865 (1951).

Golden, Tim. "Threats and Responses: Tough Justice; after Terror, a Secret Rewriting of Martial Law." *The New York Times*, October 24, 2004. Accessed August 10, 2009. http://query.nytimes.com/gst/fullpage.html?res= 9A07EFDD163DF937A15753C1A9629C8B63.

Herbert, Bob. "No Justice, No Peace." *New York Times,* February 23, A27, 2006.

Human Rights Watch. "Summary of International and U.S. Law Prohibiting Torture and Other Ill-Treatment of Persons in Custody." Accessed February 20, 2008. http://www.hrw.org, 2004.

Jordan, Winthrop D., and Litwack, Leon F. *The United State* (Combined ed.), Englewood Cliffs, N.J.: Prentice Hall, 1987.

Kairi, A. "Amnesty International and ACLU Announce Plans for a Rally in Washington D.C." Accessed June 9, 2009. http://www.associatedcontent.com/ article/281209/amnesty_international_and_aclu_annoanno.html, 2007.

Ker v. Illinois. 119 U.S. 436 (1886). Accessed March 24, 2009. http://scholar. google.com/scholar_case?case=4222245513236373620&hl=en&as_sdt= 6&as_vis=1&oi=scholarr, 1886.

Landler, Mark. "German Court Seeks Arrest of 13 C.I.A. Agents." Accessed January 31, 2008. http://www.nytimes.com/2007/01 /31/world/europe/31 cnd-germany.html, 2007.

Leslie, William R. "A Study in the Origins of Interstate Rendition: The Big Beaver Creek Murders." *American Historical Review* 57 (1951): 63–76.

Linder, Doug. "The Trail of the Lincoln Assassination Conspirators." Accessed July 10, 2009. http://www.law.umkc.edu/faculty/projects/ftrials/lincolnconspiracy/lincolnaccount.html, 2009.

Marbury v. Madison. 5 U.S. 137 (1803).

Markey, Ed. "Markey: Germany's Arrest Warrants for CIA Officials Sheds More Light on U.S. Practice of Outsourcing Torture." Accessed June 10, 2009. http:// markey.house.gov, 2007.

Mayer, Jane. "Outsourcing Torture: The Secret History of America's "Extraordinary Rendition" Program." Accessed February 10, 2008. http://web.lexisnexis.com, 2005.

Mazzett, Mark, and Glaberson William. "Obama Issues Directive to Shut Down Guantánamo." *The New York Times*, January 21, 2009. Accessed August 20, 2009. http://www.nytimes.com/2009/01/22/us/politics/22gitmo.html.

Naftali, Tim. "Milan Snatch: Extraordinary Rendition Comes Back to Bite the Bush Administration." Accessed June 30, 2009, http://www.slate.com/id/2121801/, 2005.

Oyez Project. *Hamdan v. Rumsfeld*, 548 U.S. 557 (2006), Accessed August 2009. http://www.oyez.org/cases/2000-2009/2005/2005_05_184.

Pitman, Benn. *The Assassination of President Lincoln and the Trial of Conspirators*. New York: Moore, Wilstach & Baldwin. Accessed August 20, 2009. http://books.google.com/books?id=LHwsYcwmH-8C&printsec=frontcover&source=gbs_book_other_versions_r&cad=6, 1865.

Preist, Dana. "CIA Holds Terror Suspects in Secret Prisons." *Washington Post*, November 2, A01, 2005. Accessed April 10, 2009. http://www.washingtonpost.com.

Ratner, Michael. "Guantanamo Prisoners." In *America's Disappeared: Secret Imprisonment, Detainees, and the "War on Terror,"* edited by Rachel Meeropol, 31–59. New York: Seven Stories Press, 2005.

Robinson, Dan. "Lawmakers Oppose Practice of Extraordinary Rendition." Accessed July 10, 2009. http://cageprisoners.com/articles.php?id=5942, 2005.

Turner, Thomas R. *Before the People Weeping: Public Opinion and the Assassination of Abraham Lincoln*. Baton Rouge: Louisiana State University Press, 1991.

USA Patriot Act. H.R. 3162, Public Law (2001): 107–156.

USA Today. "1st Gitmo Detainee in U.S. Court Pleads Not Guilty." *USA Today*, June 9, 2009. Accessed June 10, 2009. http://www.usatoday.com/news/washington/2009-06-09-gitmo-detainee_N.htm.

United Nations Code of Conduct for Law Enforcement Officials, G.A. Res. 34/169 at 186 U.N. Doc. A/34/461 (1979).

United Nations Convention Against Torture, G.A. 51 at 197, U.N. Doc. A/39/51 (1984).

United States Ex Rel. Toth v. Quarles. 350 US 11 (1955).

United States v. Alvarez-Machain. 504 US 655 (1992).

United States v. Toscanino. 500 F.2d 267 (1974).

Universal Declaration of Human Rights, G.A. Res. 217A (III), U.N. Doc. A/810 at 71 (1948).

Valentine v. United States. 299 U.S. 5 (1936).

War Crimes Act. Title 18 USC § 2441 (1996).

Whitlock, Craig, and Dafna Linzer. "Italy Seeks Arrests of 13 in Alleged Rendition." *Washington Post,* June 25, A01, 2005. Accessed January 10, 2006. http://www.washingtonpost.com/wp-dyn/content/article/2005/06/24/AR2005062400484_pf.html.

Young, Stephen. "Features—United States Military Commissions: A Quick Guide to Available Resources." Accessed June 9, 2009. http://www.llrx.com/features/military.htm, 2002.

Zagaris, Bruce. "U.S. Extraordinary Renditions Subject to Foreign and U.S. Investigations and Oversight." *International Enforcement Law Reporter,* 21 (2005): 188. Accessed February 19, 2007. http://web.lexis-nexis.com.

Chapter 4

International Law Enforcement Organizations

Mathieu Deflem & Shannon McDonough

Introduction

The police function, primarily organized in law enforcement agencies at the local and national level, reveals a variety of characteristics in different jurisdictions. As discussed in the previous chapter, there are important variations in policing practices and organizational styles in different nations. However, the practice and function of policing has become internationalized, which has brought about important mechanisms and structures, in general, and international police cooperation in particular. Although the internationalization of police work has accelerated tremendously since the 1980s, this chapter will show that the recent growth of international police activities has important historical antecedents. Moreover, contemporary dimensions of international policing vary in terms of functions and modalities. In particular, among the efforts to organize international police work are the international law enforcement organizations that exist to structure police cooperation on a broad, multilateral scale. This chapter will discuss two important examples of such organizations: Interpol and Europol.

The History of International Policing

A review of some of the key historical developments in international law enforcement and cooperation among industrialized nations reveals two important trends (Deflem 2002, 2007a, 2007b). First, early manifestations of international policing had a strong focus on the political objectives of particular governments, but international policing gradually evolved toward a concentration on criminal objectives as police institutions achieved a certain level of autonomy. Second, the structure of international policing progressed from exclusively unilaterally enacted transnational activities and temporary and limited forms of cooperation to the development of more permanent and structured organizations with wide multilateral participation.

The origins of international policing date back to at least the nineteenth century amidst the expanding formation of large national states, especially in Europe. In the United States, international police activities were historically restricted to regional issues, such as immigration and the changing borders of the United States. By contrast, Europe experienced greater development of international police practices because of the multitude of countries existing in close proximity to one another as well as the general political conditions of the time. International policing activities in Europe during the nineteenth century initially emerged to suppress political threats to established autocratic regimes. These activities were mostly conducted unilaterally through the employment of agents abroad, either secretively or as representatives in foreign embassies. Bilateral and multilateral cooperation occurred only on a limited and temporary basis in specific investigations.

The first effort to organize international police cooperation on a more permanent basis took place in 1851 with the formation of the Police Union of German States. Consisting of police from seven German-speaking nations that shared similar political objectives, the Police Union engaged in the gathering of political intelligence and created systems of information exchange on suspect political groups (e.g., democrats, anarchists, and socialists) to thwart the threat they were thought to pose to the participating members' governments. Because the Union was organized around political rather than criminal enforcement objectives, the organization gradually declined as the governments of its member agencies began to diverge politically. The Union was dissolved in 1866 when war broke out between its two primary members, Prussia and Austria. This failure to create a more enduring international police organization illustrates the inherent limitations of policing for political objectives and shows the importance of securing the autonomy of police agencies with exclusively criminal objectives.

In the second half of the nineteenth century, police institutions became subject to bureaucratization through the gradual development of professional systems of knowledge about crime, including its increasing international dimensions, and the attainment of expertise about the proper means of policing. This process of bureaucratization was manifested by a growing emphasis on criminal enforcement tasks rather than the political objectives of national governments. In response to the political disorder produced by anarchism, however, national governments' political demands remained in force until nearly the end of the nineteenth century, which impeded attempts to establish more permanent forms of international police cooperation. For example, amidst increasing violence directed against autocratic regimes in Europe in the final decade of the nineteenth century, the Italian government arranged for an international conference in Rome to organize the fight against anarchism. From November 24 to December 21, 1898, fifty-four delegates from twenty-one European nations attended "The International Conference of Rome for the Social Defense Against Anarchists," which was focused on suppressing the anarchist movement. The conference encouraged police to keep watch over anarchists through establishing specialized surveillance agencies in each country along with systems of information exchange. Yet, although the conference was organized around explicitly political objectives, police officials established only practical standards of cooperation and law enforcement, e.g., adopting a shared method of criminal identification and a procedure for extraditing persons involved in assassination attempts of a sovereign or head of state. In March 1904, the Russian government revived the anti-anarchist program at a follow-up meeting in St. Petersburg where a "Secret Protocol for the International War on Anarchism" was drafted. The Rome and St. Petersburg conferences, however, failed to produce any long-term forms of international police cooperation because of their political foundations and the ideological divisions of the participating countries. In particular, these conferences failed to create a central anti-anarchist intelligence bureau that would allow for more efficient information exchange between nations.

During the twentieth century, international policing continued to move away from political objectives toward a focus on the policing of crimes with international dimensions. The progress towards criminal enforcement activities was fostered by structural conditions that allowed police agencies to gain institutional autonomy from their respective governments, which enabled them to function as independent, professional institutions. Following the work of sociologist Max Weber (1922), it can be argued that this position of autonomy was achieved as a result of a bureaucratization process by which police institutions began to rely on a purposive-rational logic to find and use the most efficient means to achieve given objectives of criminal law enforcement (Deflem 2002). The trend towards autonomy was periodically interrupted by re-politicization attempts instigated by incidents of political disruption, e.g., World War I (1914–1918) and the Bolshevik Revolution (1917). However, police institutions became more resistant to such influences as they gained higher degrees of autonomy, which fostered the establishment of more permanent forms of international policing with multilateral participation. Furthermore, a variety of globalization trends accelerated attempts to organize police internationally because of the growing interdependence of societies and the increase in opportunities for crimes with global implications.

Among the earliest historical manifestations of the change toward criminal concerns in international police work was the focus on the suppression of the international trafficking of prostitutes, the so-called "White Slave" trade. The first attempt to organize international police activities against the White Slave trade was organized by France at a conference in Paris in 1902. This meeting eventually led to the "International Agreement for the Suppression of White Slave Traffic" in 1904, which was signed by twelve European nations and several other nations, including the United States. In addition, in 1910, the "International Convention for the Suppression of the White Slave Traffic" was signed by thirteen nations. These conventions, however, failed to take into account the bureaucratization of police institutions, nor did the participants consult with police officials; therefore, neither the conference nor the agreements had any significant impact on actual international police activities.

Other attempts to establish an international police organization likewise failed due to their exclusion of representatives from police agencies. For example, in Monaco in 1914, politicians and legal officials failed to establish an international police organization during the "First Congress of International Criminal Police," because they excluded police officials and only focused on criminal police duties as a function of legal principles already abandoned by police institutions. World War I began soon after the meeting and the program did not recommence after the war had ended. Other efforts to set up an international police organization that did include police officials were relatively insignificant because they emphasized professional standards of police reform rather than international criminal policing objectives. Such attempts included the International Association of Chiefs of Police, formed in Washington, D.C., in 1901; police conferences in Buenos Aires in 1905 and 1920, and Sao Paolo in 1912; and the International Police Conference in New York in 1922.

The most successful effort to organize an international police organization was the International Criminal Police Commission (ICPC), which was established in 1923 in Vienna, and which is today widely known as Interpol (Deflem 2002). The ICPC was independently organized by police officials to facilitate cooperation in the policing of international crime, explicitly excluding political violations. To that end, the organization established a headquarters and various systems of information exchange. The ICPC became the most developed international law enforcement organization with multilateral membership, although the organization was initially a predominantly European organization. In the years leading up to World War II, the ICPC was taken over by the Nazi regime after the annexation of Austria in 1938. The Nazi-appointed president of the Viennese police was assigned to the ICPC presidency and, a few years later, the headquarters was relocated to Berlin. In 1946, the ICPC was revived at a police meeting in Brussels, Belgium, and renamed the International Criminal Police Organization, and the headquarters were relocated to France. As will be discussed in more detail below, today Interpol is the largest international law enforcement organization with member agencies representing 187 nations.

Contemporary Dimensions of International Policing

The attainment of bureaucratic autonomy by police institutions has facilitated the development of more permanent forms of international cooperation based on systems of information exchange and a shared understanding of criminal enforcement goals. The apolitical nature of international police organizations allows for the cooperation of police from nations with different political and legal systems. At the same time, however, nationality remains a persistent element in international policing in terms of forms and objectives.

Forms

International law enforcement emerges within the context of important societal developments such as political and economic transformations (notably, the spread of capitalism and democratization), which affect the organization and practices of police institutions across nations (Deflem 2007b). These societal developments allow police institutions to engage in transnational operations involving foreign citizens within their own jurisdictions or through police work concerned with nationals or foreigners abroad. International policing can also involve various types of collaboration among police institutions of different nations, including temporary or permanent bilateral and multilateral arrangements, in the form of investigative enforcement tasks, the sharing of operational and organizational methods and techniques, or more permanent multilateral international police organizations.

Whatever the form, the nationality of police organizations is persistent, and is manifested in three ways (Deflem 2007a). First, police organizations prefer to conduct international policing unilaterally rather than through cooperation with foreign police. This is especially the case with police institutions (e.g., those in the United States) that have sufficient resources to operate alone. Second, arrangements of cooperation are most often made on a temporary basis, rather than through multilateral organizations, and occur in the context of specific investigations in which cooperation is necessary to accomplish criminal objectives. Third, police cooperation in the context of a permanent multilateral organization does not involve the formation of a supranational police force. Rather, police institutions of different nations engage in collaborative efforts with one another to attain their respective nationally or locally defined goals.

The persistence of nationality in international policing activities is most evident in the case of U.S. agencies because they are heavily involved in unilateral transnational police work (Cottam and Marenin 1999; Deflem 2001, 2004a, 2005). In the context of international cooperation involving U.S. law enforcement organizations, there is a relative lack of cooperation due to the U.S. police's lack of trust in foreign law enforcement agencies and suspicions of corruption and unprofessionalism. Police organizations in the United States, especially those at the federal level, are generally more heavily involved in international policing activities than police from any other nation, due mainly to concerns over the international drug trade, illegal immigration and border control, and international terrorism. The dominant role of the United States today—in stark contrast to the conditions of the nineteenth and early twentieth centuries—signifies an "Americanization" of international police activities (Nadelmann 1993). This Americanization can be observed in various aspects of foreign police organizations and activities, such as the adoption of policing methods and principles originally developed in the United States, the reliance on U.S. assistance in the formation of specialized drug units and the organization of police training and investigative work, and the influence of U.S. agencies on the legalization of certain police techniques in foreign countries. Reviewing the most prominent organizations involved in international policing, the dominance of the United States becomes evident in terms of the level of participation and assistance that U.S. police institutions bring to international policing. At the same time, however, there is still some development of autonomous international police organizations (e.g., Europol) that are directed toward specific local and regional concerns outside of U.S. interests.

Organizations

Many law enforcement organizations are involved in international operations. At the international level, Interpol and Europol (the European Police Office) are among the most prominent international police organizations with permanent multilateral structures (see below). Among the many U.S. federal agencies involved in international policing activities, the Federal Bureau of Investigation (FBI) and the Drug Enforcement Administration (DEA) have the greatest international impact and presence (Deflem 2001, 2004a, 2005, 2007b). The FBI serves the investigative function of the Department of Justice and is responsible for the policing of federal crimes, e.g., terrorism and drug trafficking. The Bureau manages a system of legal attachés (or legats), employed in at least fifty-two countries, who participate in investigations and help foreign police forces make arrests. The FBI also oversees international training programs for foreign police at the FBI National Academy in Quantico, Virginia, and, in cooperation with the Diplomatic Security Service, at the International Law Enforcement Academy in Budapest, Hungary.

The DEA is the U.S. agency primarily responsible for policing the drug trade. Through the enforcement of U.S. drug laws, the DEA engages in many international activities at the borders and abroad, including regular communication with international organizations concerned with drug control. The DEA Operations Division includes an Office of International Operations, which organizes international missions, and a foreign liaison system, which is even more extensive than the FBI's, with at least seventy-eight offices in fifty-eight countries. The U.S. law enforcement organization with the largest overseas presence is the Bureau of Diplomatic Security, which, amongst other things, is in charge of security at U.S. embassies around the world.

Although U.S. agencies prefer to work unilaterally or bilaterally in international police activities, the United States is represented in the multilateral organization Interpol through the National Central Bureau (NCB) in Washington, D.C. (Deflem 2001, 2005). Also known as Interpol Washington, the NCB is organized into five divisions: the Alien/Fugitive Enforcement Division, which deals with international fugitives; the Financial Fraud/Economic Crimes Division, which involves the policing of economic crimes; the Criminal Investigations Division, which oversees activities involving a variety of international crimes; the Drug Investigations Division, which deals with drug crimes; and the State Liaison Division, which maintains relations with various state and federal police agencies in the United States.

Many U.S. federal agencies are involved in international policing activities (Deflem 2001). Besides the FBI and the DEA, they include U.S. Citizenship and Immigration Services (USCIS), the Bureau of Alcohol, Tobacco, Firearms, and Explosives (ATF), the Secret Service, the Internal Revenue Service (IRS), the Postal Inspection Service, the Criminal Division's Office of International Affairs in the Justice Department, and the Bureau of Diplomatic Security. Besides these federal agencies, various local and state police forces, especially those located close to the borders, also have international policing duties.

Activities

The current era of globalization has produced an increase in international criminal activities, which have greatly expanded the scope of international policing. Moreover, advances in technology have shaped the nature and forms of international crime and its control. Thus, the internationalization of crime, along with the important organizational and technical developments of police agencies (i.e., bureaucratization and institutional autonomy), have facilitated international police activities and cooperation in the fight against international crime. In particular, growing concerns over border control, illegal immigration, drug trafficking, international money laundering, cybercrimes, and international terrorism have steadily affected the development of international police cooperation (Deflem 2001, 2007b; James 2005; McGillis 1997; Nadelmann 1993).

Border control has become a special focus of international policing activities with the rise of international crimes such as smuggling and illegal immigration. In the United States, the Citizenship and Immigration Services (formerly called the Immigration and Naturalization Service) and the Border Patrol within Customs and Border Protection enforce immigration laws through various prevention strategies and the apprehension of smugglers and illegal aliens. As border policing becomes increasingly redefined as a "militarized" national security issue (Dunn 1996), there has been an increase in the deployment of military forces at the U.S. border as well as an upgrade in the weaponry used by border patrol agents (e.g., semiautomatic guns). Likewise, ATF manages a division of agents that specialize in border control issues such as gun and liquor smuggling. The United States also cooperates bilaterally with Mexican and Canadian police agencies in the patrol of their respective borders and related law enforcement activities.

To prevent illegal immigration and smuggling, the main strategy of Border Patrol since the 1990s has been to increase the number and visibility of local and federal police agents stationed at the borders in an effort to deter aliens from attempting to enter the country illegally. Other activities include the search and identification of criminal and illegal aliens, the inspection of passengers aboard ships and airplanes entering the country, and the investigation of drug, liquor, and gun smuggling. To enhance the effectiveness and efficiency of these activities, border police rely on advanced technologies such as computerized fingerprint tracking systems.

Intimately related to border control and placed in the context of the United States' "war on drugs," international drug trafficking is another major focus of international policing. The drug trade was, in fact, the original driving force behind the increased participation of U.S. police agencies in international policing activities, the Americanization of policing abroad, and the continued dominance of U.S. police in international efforts (Deflem 2001, 2004a, 2007a). International police work targeting the drug trade involves a large number of U.S. agencies. The primary U.S. drug enforcement agency is the DEA, which handles violations of drug laws within the United States as well as at the nation's borders and abroad in collaboration with other U.S. agencies and foreign police. Related to the enforcement of drug laws, the DEA participates in various forms of international cooperation, including functioning as a liaison in a number of international organizations involved in drug control and an international network of more than 500 DEA agents stationed abroad, mostly in notorious drug-producing nations, who collaborate with foreign police in drug investigations and training programs.

In addition to the DEA, the escalating emphasis on controlling the drug trade in the United States' "war on drugs" has led to an increase in the international orientations of other U.S. agencies. For instance, the FBI includes drug trafficking among its federal crime enforcement responsibilities. Other U.S. agencies involved in international activities related to policing the drug trade include the Marshals Service, the Coast Guard, and the Border Patrol. Furthermore, all branches of the U.S. military have anti-drug units and there are joint military task forces aimed at fighting drug operations at the U.S.-Mexico border (Defenselink 1996). Multilateral cooperation occurs through the Drug Investigations Division of Interpol Washington, which coordinates investigations of drug-related international crimes.

International money laundering is related to drug trafficking and terrorism, which has increased along with a general rise in organized crime (Deflem and Irwin 2008). Money laundering is often used to conceal illegal income, including its sources and applications. The policing of international money laundering occurs in conjunction with international regimes aimed at suppressing money laundering through the implementation of policies and regulations at bilateral and multilateral levels between countries. These global regimes formally prohibit and criminalize money laundering, whereas police agencies enforce the respective laws and regulations. The hidden and technologically advanced nature of money laundering activities presents additional obstacles and therefore requires specialized means and police agencies to control them.

In the United States, the FBI and the DEA include specialized operations divisions against money laundering among their overall international policing activities. The Financial Crime Section of the FBI includes a Money Laundering Unit, which oversees activities aimed at disrupting and dismantling money laundering operations identified in relation to the FBI's enforcement of white-collar crimes, organized crime, and drug and violent crimes. The FBI also maintains relationships with other police agencies at the local, state, and federal level and organizes special task forces aimed at domestic and international money laundering concerns. The DEA engages in similar activities focused on the money laundering activities and capabilities of major drug-trafficking organizations.

It is important to note that U.S. authorities perceive of money laundering as an international security threat and view some vulnerable foreign governments as incapable of avoiding the risk or temptation of allowing illegal monetary transactions in their countries. Therefore, U.S. law enforcement agencies also set up sting operations within these countries unilaterally, without the knowledge of the host country, or bilaterally, to thwart money-laundering activities. International cooperation also occurs at the multilateral level. For example, Interpol has facilitated the cooperation among member nations in identifying, tracing, and seizing the assets of money launderers through the exchange of information. Private organizations, such as financial institutions, also cooperate with law enforcement in the identification of money-laundering crimes.

Since the late twentieth century, international policing has shifted its focus towards more technologically advanced crimes (Deflem 2007a). Advancements in computer technology have brought about new opportunities for crimes involving the Internet and information technology, transcending national borders and affecting multiple national jurisdictions. The transnational nature of cybercrime requires international policing activities ranging from unilateral activities to the establishment of bilateral agreements and multilateral law enforcement regimes. Unilateral transnational police activities are sometimes necessary because the legal systems of nations do not always harmonize. Law enforcement agencies from different countries do cooperate to police cybercrimes, but collaborative efforts may be hindered when laws related to cybercrimes differ among the nations involved. Thus, international legal frameworks have been developed to facilitate cooperation among nations. For example, the Council of Europe's Convention on Cybercrime serves to organize procedures of cooperation to aid in the policing of cybercrimes (Council of Europe 2001). Multilateral organizations (e.g., Interpol and Europol) also support collaborative efforts in the policing of cybercrimes. For instance, Interpol has instigated a number of activities related to cybercrime, including a system of working parties around the world that specialize in information technology crimes, to facilitate the sharing of information on computer security-related matters between member nations.

The most important development in international policing in the current era is the proliferation of terrorism. From the 1980s onwards and, especially in the aftermath of the events of September 11, 2001, international terrorism has been the central catalyst of increased international police cooperation and an expansion of policing powers across the world (Deflem 2004b, 2005, 2007a, 2007b). Various newly developed anti-terrorism agreements and laws have facilitated these developments. In the United States, for example, the USA PA-

TRIOT Act ("Uniting and Strengthening America by Providing Appropriate Tools Required to Intercept and Obstruct Terrorism") of 2001 extended the authority of police. Across the globe, similar anti-terrorism agreements and laws have been passed. The strengthening of the police function has also affected various jurisdictions of authority and, as a result, has intensified cooperation among police at local, state, federal, and international levels. Police cooperation has also been enhanced by a focus on the most efficient means to accomplish counterterrorism objectives. Furthermore, the increase in international police cooperation motivated by counterterrorism objectives has reinforced the centrality of U.S. police institutions in international police activities.

In the wake of increasing concerns over terrorism, police agencies have been afforded greater powers in terms of the means of policing, equipment, personnel, and budget, and have brought about a realignment of police agencies with military forces (Deflem 2004b). Terrorism has also been conceptualized in terms related to war and national security, leading to a militarization of the police function (Kraska 2001; Sievert 2003). For example, on November 13, 2001, U.S. President George W. Bush approved an order to allow military trials for foreign suspects of terrorism. Moreover, the reorganizations and realignments of police institutions that are presently justified in terms of the terrorism threat may lead to lasting structural readjustments long after the immediate repercussions of events such as 9/11 have faded.

The reorganization of policing across the world since 9/11 is reminiscent of past politicization attempts of police activities during periods of societal turmoil. However, in the present era, modern police institutions have attained an unprecedented level of bureaucratic autonomy, allowing police to remain resistant to politicization attempts and continuing to rely on professional standards of police technique and expertise. Modern-day police institutions may therefore continue to exhibit a high degree of autonomy in determining the means and objectives of counterterrorist police work even when facing political pressure to conform to the goals of their respective governments.

Interpol: The International Criminal Police Organization

Since its establishment as the International Criminal Police Commission in 1923, Interpol has steadily expanded its membership to become the most prominent international police organization (Deflem 2002, 2006a). Relying on a collaborative model of policing, the formal objectives of the organization are to facilitate and ensure cooperation between the police of different nations within the limits of their respective national laws while adhering to the Universal Declaration of Human Rights. Since the organization's reformation after World War II, Interpol's focus on criminal violations has explicitly excluded political, racial, and religious matters. Historically, however, Interpol has not always been invulnerable to political conditions. During the Cold War era, the Soviet control over Eastern European nations that were members of the organization led the FBI, which had joined the organization in 1938, to terminate its participation in 1950. U.S. participation in Interpol was thereafter secured on an informal basis by the Treasury Department. The United States has reestablished formal ties with Interpol, represented jointly by the Departments of Justice and the Treasury.

Originally founded in response to increasing concerns over the internationalization of crime due to rapid social change and technological progress, Interpol was created to serve as a communication network to facilitate law enforcement cooperation via a headquarters through which information could be exchanged among police agencies from different countries. Information exchange was further accomplished through printed publications, a radio and telegraphs system, and regularly held meetings of police representatives. The headquarters in Vienna contained divisions specializing in the falsification of passports, checks and currencies, fingerprints and photographs, and other pertinent systems of knowledge. The emphasis on swift methods of information exchange has basically remained unaltered since the headquarters were moved to France (first to Paris and, in 1989, to Lyon), although the technical sophistication of these methods has advanced greatly. Since the 1970s and, especially, the 1980s, Interpol accelerated its activities. International terrorism has been a central driving force in this expansion. As early as 1984, Interpol decided on a resolution that encouraged its members to cooperate on terrorism matters, and by the late 1990s, Interpol viewed international terrorism as one of its primary concerns.

The structure of Interpol consists of a General Assembly, an Executive Committee, a General Secretariat, and National Central Bureaus. The General Assembly functions as the main governing component, which includes delegates, appointed by member agencies, who meet annually. The Assembly votes on all major decisions related to Interpol's policies, resources, methods, finances, and activities. The Executive Committee, elected by the General Assembly, consists of a president, three vice presidents, and nine delegates representing Africa, the Americas, Asia, Europe, the Middle East, and North Africa.

The General Secretariat is located at the Interpol headquarters in Lyons, France. Regional offices are located in Argentina, El Salvador, the Ivory Coast, Kenya, Thailand, and Zimbabwe, and there is a liaison office at the UN in New York. Since 1996, Interpol has formal agreements with the UN, and entertains similar agreements with Europol, the International Criminal Court, and other police and legal organizations, which provide it observer status in sessions of the UN General Assembly. Interpol's secretary general oversees the General Secretariat and assigns membership in the organization to police agencies chosen by the governments of their respective nations to be participants in the organization.

The National Central Bureaus are maintained by each of Interpol's member agencies in their respective countries. They serve as contact points for communication between the regional offices of the General Secretariat and other member agencies concerning all official Interpol police communications about international crime investigations and the location and capture of fugitives. Communication occurs on the basis of a color-coded notification system with each of six colors representing a specific type of request. For example, a red notice is a request to arrest a fugitive under the process of extradition, whereas a blue notice is a request to gather information about an individual related to a crime. A green Interpol-UN Special Notice has most recently been added, and it concerns group or individual actions formally sanctioned by the UN against Al Qaeda and the Taliban.

Interpol's functions fall into three main categories. First, Interpol organizes a system of information exchange regarding international policing among its members. Communications were originally handled by mail, but since 2003 use an encrypted Internet-based system (I-24/7) that connects the General Secretariat with the National Central Bureaus. Second, Interpol functions as a source of operational data and databases, including names, fingerprints, and DNA profiles on international fugitives and information concerning stolen property, such as passports and works of art. Third, Interpol provides its member agencies with operational assistance with investigations in priority areas. For example, Interpol coordinates a Command and Coordination Center, which acts as the primary point of contact for member agencies seeking immediate assistance. Also, the Crisis Support Group, the Criminal Analysis Unit, and the Incident Response Teams, and Disaster Victim Identification Teams offer operational support at the request of a member agency.

Interpol emphasizes certain categories of international crime, rather than taking on tasks it is not equipped to handle. The organization prioritizes crimes involving terrorism and public security, drugs and organized crime, financial and high-tech crimes (e.g., money laundering and cybercrimes), fugitives, and the trafficking of human beings (Anderson 1997; Deflem 2006a; Interpol 2009). Since the 1970s, a primary concern of Interpol has been international terrorism, and various resolutions have been passed to combat terrorism and terrorist activities. Initially, Interpol passed a number of resolutions related to crimes involving terrorist activities, e.g., plane hijackings and holding hostages. In 1984, Interpol expanded its counterterrorism focus in a resolution concerning "Violent Crime Commonly Referred to as Terrorism," which encouraged member agencies to cooperate in the fight against terrorism within the context of their respective nations' laws. The political motivations of terrorist incidents are to be delineated from the criminal elements, which, once identified, can be subjected to police investigations. In 1985, a Public Safety and Terrorism Sub directorate was established to further facilitate cooperation in matters of international terrorism.

During the 1990s, Interpol accelerated its counterterrorism initiatives following an increase in terrorist attacks around the world. In 1998, at a General Assembly meeting in Cairo, Interpol announced its commitment to combat international terrorism through a "Declaration against Terrorism," which emphasized the threat of terrorism to public security, democracy, and human rights. Interpol's primary concern with international terrorism was reaffirmed in 1999 at a General Assembly meeting in Seoul, when a resolution was passed condemning the financing and support of terrorism. The terrorist attacks of September 11, 2001, strengthened the focus on terrorism as well as Interpol's infrastructure. Immediately following the attacks, on September 14, 2001, Secretary General Ronald Noble announced the formation of an 11 September Task Force in order to coordinate international criminal police intelligence regarding the attacks. Interpol also circulated fifty-five red notices for terrorists connected to the attacks and increased the circulation of blue notices to obtain information about the location of suspects, nineteen of which concerned the hijackers who committed the attacks.

A few weeks after September 11, at a General Assembly meeting in Budapest, Interpol passed a resolution regarding the attacks, which condemned the "murderous attacks perpetrated against the world's citizens in the United States of America on 11 September 2001" as a "cold-blooded mass murder [and] a crime against humanity" (Interpol 2001). Interpol also prioritized the red notices for terrorists connected to the attacks to combat terrorism and organized crime more effectively.

A number of important aspects of Interpol's organization changed following the September 11 attacks. Interpol strengthened its infrastructure through the establishment of the aforementioned I-24/7 communications system and a permanent General Secretariat Command and Coordination Center. Also set up was a Financial and High Tech Crimes Sub-Directorate, which specializes in money laundering. In April 2002, Interpol announced the formation of an Interpol Terrorism Watch List, which equips the police member agencies with direct access to information on fugitives and suspected terrorists.

As an international police organization, Interpol serves a unique yet limited function by maintaining an international network relying solely on the participation of member agencies rather than a supranational police force. Obstacles to cooperation can occur because of the sensitive nature of some relevant information and the fact that not all police agencies are equipped with the necessary infrastructure, personnel, and/or finances needed for international communications. Furthermore, the ideological diversity of Interpol's member agencies may engender feelings of distrust and suspicion. The primary goal of efficiency and the focus on international crime in the absence of a formal legal system may also lead to problems of democratic accountability. However, the main advantage of Interpol is its broad multilateral reach, which maintains communications between countries that otherwise would be unavailable. The emphasis on methods of information exchange reflects a shared concern among Interpol's member agencies regarding efficiency in international police work unhindered by international politics. Thus, Interpol can ensure cooperation in international criminal matters between the police of countries with differing political ideologies and legal standards.

Europol: The European Police Office

The formation of the European Police Office (Europol) was brought about to promote cooperation among police agencies in the European Union (EU) when policing serious international crimes (Deflem 2006b). Europol facilitates cooperation between EU member nations through a headquarters that employs some 600 personnel, more than 100 of which are Europol Liaison Officers from various police and security agencies, including the national police, customs, and immigration services from EU member states. Europol was formally established in 1992, but, as discussed above, the organization has roots dating back to the earlier efforts to organize international policing in the nineteenth century onwards. Since the 1970s, efforts to control terrorism accelerated international policing activities within Europe and led to the formation of the "Terrorism, Radicalism, Extremism, and International Violence" group (TREVI) by European police officials in order to facilitate the exchange of information and cooperation on international crimes related to terrorism. On February 7, 1992, in Maastricht, The Netherlands, the formation of Europol was officially outlined in the Treaty on the European Union (also known as the "Maastricht Treaty") (Europol Convention 1995; Laveran's 2003; Occhipinti 2003; Winer 2004). The Treaty specified the establishment of a European Police Office, which framed Europol's governance structure and defined its function as supporting cooperation among police agencies in the EU. Initially, operations began on a limited basis in The Hague through the Europol Drugs Unit, which focused on international drug crimes. Other forms of international crime were gradually addressed as well. A Europol Convention was formally organized in Brussels on July 18, 1995, which activated Europol on October 1, 1998. The organization was ratified by all the EU member states, and became fully operational on July 1, 1999.

The Europol Convention of 1995 specified that Europol's function was to enhance the effectiveness and efficiency of cooperation among police agencies from EU countries in the prevention and control of international organized crime without the formation of a supranational police force (Europol Convention 1995). Europol's mission is restricted to criminal activities involving two or more member nations of the EU, especially those committed by criminal organizations. More specifically, Europol's activities concern the investigation of international crimes, e.g., the illegal trafficking of drugs, human beings, and vehicles; child pornography; the forgery of money; money laundering; cybercrimes; organized robbery; swindling and fraud, corruption; environmental crime; and terrorism.

Europol provides its member agencies with various systems of international policing. First, Europol facilitates communications between the Europol Liaison Officers, who represent the national police of the member states at the Europol headquarters in The Hague. Each EU nation designates a particular police agency to function as the Europol National Unit, which acts as the contact point for Europol communications. Second, Europol provides operational analyses to assist international police activities, and draws up strategic reports (e.g., threat assessments), and crime analyses utilizing information collected by the police of member states or generated by Europol headquarters. Third, Europol offers technical support for police investigations initiated by the police of EU member states. Finally, Europol manages the Europol Computer System, which is used for analyzing data on people's behavior and movements. The Europol Computer system is supplemented by the EU Customs Information System, which affords customs agencies the ability to exchange information on smuggling, and the Identification File of Customs Investigations, which contains information on individuals involved in criminal investigations.

The structure of Europol includes a governing body, called the Directorate, consisting of a director and three deputy directors, who are all appointed by the EU Council of Ministers for Justice and Home Affairs. The director serves a five-year term, which is renewable once for four years, whereas the deputy directors serve a four-year term, which is also renewable once. The EU Council approves Europol's budget and acts as a regulatory body, and forwards an annual report about Europol's activities to the European Parliament. The Europol Management Board, made up of one representative from each member state, supervises day-to-day operations and meets at least twice a year to discuss the activities and future direction of the organization. Europol's operations are also overseen by a Joint Supervisory Body, which consists of appointed representatives of the national supervisory bodies in the EU member states, to ensure that the rights of individuals are not violated by Europol's handling of data and information exchange.

Europol primarily differs from Interpol in terms of its political and legal framework because it is formally sanctioned and organized within EU governmental structures. Yet, although Europol is formally mandated by the EU and overseen by its regulatory bodies, Europol maintains a level of bureaucratic autonomy similar to other international police organizations through the coordination of activities of the National Units. Europol's operations are primarily guided by a concern for efficiency in the control of crime and police cooperation, which is implemented through a number of measures. Europol depends on the expertise and participation of existing police institutions from EU member states to staff Europol headquarters and the Europol National Units with qualified personnel. This ensures that Europol personnel are police officials who are familiar with a highly professionalized and independent European police culture. Efficiency of operations is also achieved by emphasizing the importance of effective and speedy communication among participating police agencies. Europol also promotes efficiency through managing agreements with non-EU nations, such as the United States, to facilitate cooperation with a broader range of police organizations. For instance, Europol has a liaison office in the United States to maintain relations with U.S. law enforcement agencies.

Similar to Interpol, international terrorism is currently one of Europol's main concerns. The Europol Convention of 1995 already listed terrorism as one of the central justifications for establishing a European police organization. The terrorist attacks of September 11, 2001, further accelerated international police cooperation aimed at terrorism and led to a prioritization of counterterrorism among Europol's activities (Deflem 2006b; Den Boer and Monar 2002; Fijnaut 2004; Lavranos 2003). Immediately following the attacks, Europol set up a Europol Operational Centre to enable a twenty-four-hour-a-day information exchange. In November 2001, a new Counterterrorism Task Force became fully operational at the Europol headquarters. The Task Force functions as a specialized counterterrorism unit, consisting of terrorism experts and liaison officers from various police and intelligence agencies of EU member states. In 2002, the Task Force was incorporated into Europol's Serious

Crime Department, but it became a separate entity again after the terrorist bombings in Madrid on March 11, 2004. The Task Force accumulates and analyzes information and intelligence related to terrorism, performs operational and strategic analyses, and produces a terrorism threat assessment, including targets, modus operandi, and security consequences (Europol 2006). Since its formation, the Task Force has produced several threat assessments pertaining to existing counterterrorism security measures in the EU and the presence of terrorist groups in Europe, including information on the financing of terrorism and the formation of an Arabic-to-English translation system.

In addition to the Counter-Terrorism Task Force, Europol has established other programs to combat terrorism. A Counter-Terrorism Program functions to coordinate all Europol counterterrorism activities, such as information gathering and threat assessments. The Counter-Proliferation Program handles all forms of illicit trafficking, including nuclear materials, arms, and explosives. The Networking Program coordinates communication among the experts of these programs and other international organizations and police in non-EU member states. The Preparedness Program organizes multilateral counterterrorism investigative teams for terrorist incidents in the EU. Finally, the Training and Education Program supports the terrorist intelligence and investigative programs by providing training to relevant personnel in the EU.

Europol's counterterrorist efforts focus on terrorist groups insofar as they are active in or otherwise relevant to Europe. Thus, Europol maintains a regional focus in international policing, concentrating on concerns specific to the EU. The political decision-making process within the EU framework does not always ensure smooth police cooperation through Europol. Instead, political-ideological conflicts among EU member nations still occasionally hamper cooperation and restrict the organization's structure and capabilities, for instance in passing and implementing legislation (Deflem 2006b).

Conclusion

The world of international policing varies in terms of practices and structures. International police work has been transformed from a preoccupation with political violations to a focus on international crimes. Moreover, unilaterally enacted transnational activities and bilateral cooperative networks have been gradually supplemented with multilateral international law-enforcement organizations. The recent past has witnessed a general expansion of international policing in the wake of global concerns surrounding border controls, illegal immigration, the drug trade, money laundering, crimes relying on advanced border-transcending technologies, and terrorism. Despite the growth of international police initiatives, the persistence of nationality is revealed in that police agencies prefer to work unilaterally, engage in relatively small and temporary bilateral cooperation, or participate in large multilateral organizations only on the basis of a collaborative model from which they seek to benefit in terms of nationally delineated enforcement concerns. The persistence of nationality of police participating in international activities is most advantageous to agencies from powerful nations. Thus, it is no surprise that the strong global presence of U.S. law enforcement has brought about an Americanization of international police work.

Interpol and Europol are two of the most prominent international law-enforcement organizations. Interpol has steadily developed since its formation in 1923 to become the largest international police organization, with a membership drawn from 187 nations. The organization relies on a collaborative model of cooperation to facilitate technologically advanced systems of information exchange and communication among its member agencies. Since the events of September 11, 2001, international terrorism has become a key concern for Interpol. In the EU, Europol has also expanded its activities in the wake of concerns over global security and the proliferation of serious crimes affecting EU member nations. Although Europol's function and organization are subject to political control from the EU leadership, the organization relies, like Interpol and other international police organizations, on police professionals drawn from highly bureaucratized agencies that claim expertise and institutional independence.

The current era of globalization, which affects all aspects of life, can be expected to continue to necessitate international police activities. Despite the proliferation of international police work, however, it should be noted that the police function within larger jurisdictions also is organized at smaller, regional levels, such as in the subordinate sovereignties that will be discussed in the next chapter.

Web Sources

1. Bureau of Alcohol, Tobacco, Firearms and Explosives (ATF):
   http://www.atf.gov/
2. Bureau of Diplomatic Security:
   http://www.state.gov/m/ds/
3. Drug Enforcement Administration (DEA):
   http://www.usdoj.gov/dea/

4. European Police Office (Europol):
   http://www.europol.eu.int/
5. Federal Bureau of Investigation (FBI):
   http://www.fbi.gov/
6. International Criminal Police Organization (Interpol):
   http://www.interpol.int/
7. International Law Enforcement Academy, Budapest:
   https://www.ilea.hu/
8. U.S. Citizenship and Immigration Services (USCIS):
   http://www.uscis.gov/
9. U.S. Coast Guard:
   http://www.uscg.mil/
10. U.S. Customs and Border Protection:
    http://www.cbp.gov/
11. U.S. Marshals Service:
    http://www.usmarshals.gov/
12. U.S. Postal Inspection Service:
    http://postalinspectors.uspis.gov/
13. U.S. Secret Service:
    http://www.secretservice.gov/

Discussion Questions

1. What are the most important conditions that have historically influenced the internationalization of law enforcement?
2. How do contemporary developments in international police work affect law enforcement efforts at the local and national level among different nations?
3. What needs to happen if Interpol is to be more effective in fulfilling its mission?
4. How would you defend the view that Europol is like a European FBI?
5. Given contemporary concerns over a variety of international crime issues, how should international law enforcement organizations be developed in the coming decades?

References

Anderson, Malcolm. "Interpol and the Developing System of International Police Cooperation." In *Crime and Law Enforcement in the Global Vil-*

lage, edited by William F. McDonald, 89–102. Cincinnati, OH: Anderson, 1997.

Baker, Nancy V. "The Law: The Impact of Antiterrorism Policies on Separation of Powers." *Presidential Studies Quarterly* 32, no. 4 (2002): 765–778.

Cottam, Martha L., and Otwin Marenin. "International Cooperation in the War on Drugs: Mexico and the United States." *Policing and Society* 9 (1999): 209–240.

Council of Europe. "Convention on Cybercrime." Budapest, November 23, 2001. Accessed August 28, 2009. http://conventions.coe.int/Treaty/EN/Treaties/Html/185.

Defenselink. *Joint Task Force Supports Nation's War on Drugs.* American Forces Press Service, U.S. Department of Defense. Accessed August 28, 2009. http://www.defenselink.mil/news/newsarticle.aspx?id=40734, 1996.

Deflem, Mathieu. "International Police Cooperation in Northern America: A Review of Practices, Strategies, and Goals in the United States, Mexico, and Canada." In *International Police Cooperation: A World Perspective,* edited by Daniel J. Koenig and Dilip K. Das, 71–98. Lanham, MD: Lexington Books, 2001.

_____. *Policing World Society: Historical Foundations of International Police Cooperation.* Oxford: Oxford University Press, 2002.

_____. "The Boundaries of International Cooperation: Problems and Prospects of U.S.-Mexican Policing." In *Police Corruption: Challenges for Developed Countries — Comparative Issues and Commissions of Inquiry,* edited by Menachem Amir and Stanley Einstein, 93–122, Huntsville, TX: Office on International Criminal Justice, 2004a.

_____. "Social Control and the Policing of Terrorism: Foundations for a Sociology of Counter-Terrorism." *American Sociologist* 35, no.2 (2004b): 75–92.

_____. "International Policing: The Role of the United States." In *The Encyclopedia of Criminology,* edited by Richard A. Wright and J. Mitchell Miller, 808–812. New York: Routledge, 2005.

_____. "Global Rule of Law or Global Rule of Law Enforcement? International Police Cooperation and Counter-Terrorism." *Annals of the American Academy of Political and Social Science* 603 (2006a): 240–252.

_____. "Europol and the policing of international terrorism: Counter-terrorism in a global perspective." *Justice Quarterly* 23, no. 3 (2006b): 336–359.

_____. "Policing." In *Encyclopedia of Globalization,* edited by R. Robertson and J. A. Scholte, 970–973. New York: Routledge, 2007a.

_____. "International Policing." In *The Encyclopedia of Police Science* (3rd Ed.), edited by Jack R. Green, 701–705. New York: Routledge, 2007b.

Deflem, Mathieu, and Kyle Irwin. "International Money Laundering Control: Law Enforcement Issues." In *Organized Crime: From Trafficking to Terrorism,* edited by Frank G. Shanty, 243–246. Santa Barbara, CA: ABC-CLIO, 2008.

Den Boer, Monica., and Jörg Monar. "11 September and the Challenge of Global Terrorism to the EU as a Security Actor." *Journal of Common Market Studies* 40 (2002): 11–28.

Dunn, Timothy J. *The Militarization of the U.S.-Mexico Border, 1978–1992.* Austin, TX: CMAS Books, 1996.

Europol. "An Overview of the Counter Terrorism Unit Activities, January 2006." Accessed August 28, 2009. http://www.europol.europa.eu/publications/ Serious_Crime_Overviews/overview_SC5.pdf, 2006.

Europol Convention. "Convention on the Establishment of a European Police Office." Brussels, July 26, 1995. Accessed August 28, 2009. http://www.europol.europa.eu/legal/Europol_Convention_Consolidated_version.pdf.

Fijnaut, Cyrille. "The Attacks of 11 September 2001, and the Immediate Response of the European Union and the United States." In *Legal Instruments in the Fight against International Terrorism,* edited by Cyrille Fijnaut, Jan Wouters, and Frederik, 15–36. Leiden, The Netherlands: Martinus Nijhoff, 2004.

Interpol. "Resolution no. AG-2001-RES-05: Terrorist Attack of 11 September 2001." Accessed August 28, 2009. http://www.interpol.int/Public/ICPO/ GeneralAssembly/AGN70/Resolutions/AGN70RES5.asp, 2004.

Interpol. "Interpol's Four Core Functions." Accessed August 8, 2009. http:// www.interpol.int/Public/icpo/about.asp, 2009.

James, Adrian. "Criminal Networks, Illegal Immigration and the Threat to Border Security." *International Journal of Police Science & Management* 7, no. 4 (2005): 219–229.

Kraska, Peter, B. (Ed.). *Militarizing the American Criminal Justice System: The Changing Roles of the Armed Forces and the Police.* Boston: Northeastern University Press, 2001.

Lavranos, Nikolaos. "Europol and the Fight against Terrorism." *European Foreign Affairs Review* 8, no. 2 (2003): 259–275.

McGillis, Daniel. "U.S. Government International Justice Assistance: Overview of Major Activities." In *Policing in Emerging Democracies: Workshop Papers and Highlights,* 75–88. Washington, D.C.: U.S. Department of Justice, Office of Justice Programs, 1997.

Nadelmann, Ethan A. *Cops across Borders: The Internationalization of U.S. Criminal Law Enforcement.* University Park: Pennsylvania State University Press, 1993.

Occhipinti, John D. *The Politics of EU Police Cooperation: Toward a European FBI?* Boulder, CO: Lynne Rienner, 2003.

Sievert, Ronald J. War on Terrorism or Global Law Enforcement Operation? *Notre Dame Law Review* 78, no. 2 (2003): 307–353.

Weber, Max. *Economy and Society: An Outline of Interpretive Sociology.* Berkeley and Los Angeles: University of California Press, 1922. (Reprint published in 1978.)

Winer, Jonathan M. "Cops across Borders: The Evolution of Transatlantic Law Enforcement and Judicial Cooperation." Paper presented at the Council on Foreign Relations, September 1, 2004. Accessed August 28, 2009. http://www.cfr.org/pub7389/presentation/cops_across_borders_the_evolution_of_transatlantic_law_enforcement_and_judicial_cooperation.php.

Chapter 5

Policing in Selected Countries: Organization and Structure

Harry R. Dammer

Introduction

Traditionally, police have been asked to perform a variety of functions: crime prevention, apprehension of lawbreakers, riot control, community service, and protection against internal security threats. More recently, however, other issues have become equally important for police, such as terrorism, corruption, and organized crime. To complicate matters further, these crimes are often international in scope so police agencies must improve communications and keep abreast of the various technological advances. And while performing these tasks, they must always keep in mind the complexities of global human rights. As a result of these developments, modern policing has also become extremely expensive.

The style and quality of policing varies greatly across the globe. What we do know about modern policing may be expressed in at least three generalizations. First, that the police perform two major functions in modern societies: deviance control and civil order control. Both of these functions are necessary to ensure that people feel secure and able to carry out their everyday business without fear and major disruption. *Deviance control* refers to the police mission to reinforce community values and laws and typically involves several tasks. Police personnel must protect citizens against lawbreakers. In addition, the police seek to discourage alarming or threatening behavior that tends to make people uneasy or insecure. For example, police are carrying out this mission when they arrest known criminals, work with troubled juveniles, or remove drunks from the streets.

The *civil order control* function of policing refers to the duty of police to respond to, supervise, or control two or more citizens in any situation that may disrupt the peace and tranquility of a society (Dammer, Fairchild, and Albanese 2006). Modern police forces generally organize to accomplish the functions of civil order control and deviance control in one of two ways. By far the most common arrangement is to have these functions performed by different divisions within the larger organization. Among our selected countries, this is the arrangement favored by Germany, France, China, India, and Saudi Arabia. By contrast, in England (and in the United States) civil order control is not organizationally separated from deviance control but is performed by regular street police. Military units may also be used in extreme cases on an ad hoc basis. Although no democratic country wants to use its military to maintain order internally, the military remains the last resort in a civil order crisis in any country.

The second thing we know about policing around the world is that the formation of policing in any country, as well as its daily operations, is directly associated with a variety of cultural, historical, and economic factors. Because of these factors police are a "mirror image of their parent society and often vice versa—that is a change in one often gets reflected in the other" (Dhillon 2005, 25). For example, with the growth of the democratic ideas brought forth by the Age of Reason and the Enlightenment, policing in England evolved during the nineteenth century following a model that emphasized the provision of services and operating in consent of the citizenry within the context of a solid democracy.

Third and finally, we know that police around the world are generally classified into three types or systems or structures: centralized, semi-centralized, or decentralized (United Nations Asia and Far East Institute 2003, 182–183). *Centralized police systems* are agencies where there is a national police force that is centrally commanded and controlled and has unlimited jurisdiction in the country. *Semi-centralized police systems* place the tasks of policing jointly in the hands of states or provinces along some oversight by the central (federal) government. The third type, *decentralized policing,* places the responsibility of policing solely in the hands of state or provinces. Each country in the world has developed one or a variation of these three types of systems based on their own particular historical, political, and, in some cases, economic situation.

In this chapter, we briefly trace the historical development of the police as well as how each of our six selected countries are organized and structured, including how the police handle civil order and deviance order control functions. We will conclude with some comments on the most pressing issues of concern for the police as we proceed into the twenty-first century. The chapter will begin with the Common Law countries of England and India, proceed to the Civil Law countries of Germany and France, then to the Socialist Law example of China, and finally the Islamic Law example of Saudi Arabia.

Policing in a Common Law Country: England

Historical Background

The modern English police force dates back to 1829, when Prime Minister Sir Robert Peel urged Parliament to establish the London Metropolitan Police. Previously, because of the general British repugnance toward the idea of a police agency (such as existed in France) that might be used by the government to stifle dissent, Parliament had refused to set up a formal police agency.

The unrest, crime, and disorderliness that accompanied urbanization and industrialization in nineteenth-century London led to the establishment of the Metropolitan Police. Because the genesis of the police in England came from democratic ideals, and opposition to the form of policing used by the French, the English police have tried to develop the image of being "civilians in uniform": friendly, helpful, and capable. Another way to explain the police reforms put forth by the English was to gain support of the public by consent rather than by force.

The model of "policing by consent" remained a staple of British policing through the twentieth century. Whether the model was totally effective has been debated but we do know that in general the confrontations between the police and the public, as well as the abuse of power by the police, abated during the twentieth century, especially after World War II. We also know that the recorded crime rates following World War II were, by any standard, very low. Finally, we are aware that many other democratic nations, including the United States, have adopted, at least in part, a number of the democratically oriented police methods first adopted by the British—most notably community policing.

Since the early 1800s, community policing has remained a staple of policing in England. However, community policing has undergone many changes in England, especially during the last twenty-five years. For example, during the 1980s the police introduced problem-oriented policing (POP) as a strategy. In the late 1990s sector policing was initiated. Much like the *Compstat* police program in New York City, sector policing held individual police commanders responsible for the control of crime in their geographic areas. *Neighborhood policing,* or the emphasis on the delivery of policing to specific (i.e., local) communities based on their own particular needs, came about in 2003 when the Home Office of England called for a move away from policing with consent and toward policing that attempts to gain "active cooperation" of the public (Home Office 2003). This new emphasis soon led to the formation of *reassurance policing.* Reassurance policing calls for the focus of policing to be on the addressing "signal crimes and disorders" that would increase fear of crime and eventually have an "adverse effect on people's sense of security and cause them to alter their beliefs or behavior" (Joyce 2006, 136). It is likely that the further modifications of community policing in England will be implemented as we proceed into the twenty-first century.

Organization, Structure, and Training

For almost 180 years the English police have traditionally been decentralized, with each city or town making rules and providing funds for its own police operations and controlling the hiring, firing, and compensation of police personnel. At present, there are forty-one large provincial police forces in England and Wales. The provincial police, also called "territorial police forces," are funded by local districts and regions (50 percent) and by the central government (50 percent). In the local districts policing is delivered through the formation of basic command units (BCUs). The BCUs are able to more easily deliver the various forms of community policing that are so vital to service role of the British police and the need to solicit citizen cooperation for crime prevention.

In addition to the provincial police there are two police forces in greater London: the Metropolitan Police Force (with 31,500 officers) and the London City Police (900 officers). To assist the regular police in the area of London are two other kinds of law enforcement. First, the Metropolitan Special Constabulary (MSC) was created over 175 years ago. The 2,500 members of the MSC operate in Greater London and although they are not paid they have the full powers of an officer (constable). Also, beginning in 2002 the British deployed around 4,000 Police Community Support Officers (PCSO). The PCSOs are uniformed officers who work along with regular officers in neighborhood policing areas; however, they are less trained, receive lower pay, have less equipment, and have less legal power than officers. PCSOs generally "perform routine duties, assisting and supporting Police Officers, gathering intelligence, carrying out security patrols and, through their presence alone, reassuring the public. Where possible, they also attend to matters not requiring police powers" (Metropolitan Police 2009). The PCSOs cost 25 percent less than regular officers and they operate throughout London and adjoining suburbs (Muir 2003). Finally, the British also deploy "special" police, like the British Transport Police, the Ministry of Defence Police, and the Port of London Authority Police, that have specific jurisdictional responsibilities.

In England there are forty-three Police Authority Boards, a uniquely English committee made up of local elected officials and judicial officials appointed by the Home Secretary. The Police Authority hears citizen complaints about alleged police abuses and consults about police practices. It is also involved in hiring the local chief constable and setting his or her compensation (Gregory 1985). The chief constable is the main administrator for each of the forty-one provincial forces. For the Metropolitan Police, the overseeing body is the Metropolitan Police Authority, established in 2001. Many have heard of the famous English police term "Scotland Yard." Scotland Yard is actually the location for the Metropolitan Police Force of London; it serves as a national repository for crime statistics, information on criminal activity, missing persons reports, fingerprints, and juvenile delinquent data.

The English police have a much different way than most countries, including their Common Law partner India, for carrying out the two main functions of police. The regular police, i.e., the provincial police outside London and the Metropolitan or London police within, each carry out the deviance control function of police. It is interesting to note, however, there is no separate agency or even well-defined way to deal with civil order control problems in England. This does not mean that England has no such problems. In the twentieth century, there have been many occasions of major social upheavals, including labor troubles, student protests, and riots of various kinds. Always the first line of defense has been the local police agency, acting in a civil order control rather than a deviance control capacity. Traditionally, the police in England did not receive extensive training related to crowd control. However, additional training and strategic planning to riot control and weapons use has been implemented, partly in response to the British Crime Survey of 1988, which revealed a declining support for British police (Mayhew, Elliot, and Dowds 1989). In effect, there is a strong tradition against the use of the military in less-than-regime-threatening situations.

Police leaders are given fairly extensive training in dealing with civil disorder situations. For example, in the three-month Intermediate Command Course at Bramshill, police administrative trainees receive instruction in civil order maintenance. Likewise, the three-month Senior Command Course, which trains the highest-ranking police officials, emphasizes "policing in a changing society, with particular reference to the delicate task of maintaining the peace in an inner-city environment" (Watt 1988, 11).

Recent events, like the May Day riots of 2001 and the tragic events of April 1, 2009, are sure to increase discussions about how the British should attend to riot control. On the latter date there were extensive protests outside the Bank of England during the G-20 London Summit. During the demonstration a British citizen, Ian Tomlinson, died shortly after being struck by a police baton and pushed to the ground by an officer. Although the matter is still under investigation, it will likely cause a review of what is allowable behavior for British police in civil order control situations.

Training for constables entails a fourteen-week course during which recruits learn theoretical and practical information on a variety of topics, followed by ten weeks of field experience under the supervision of an experienced constable. After the twenty-four-week period, the new constable remains on probation for the first two years of service while gaining additional classroom training and supervision. Those who aspire to become police administrators attend the police staff college at Bramshill, the central police leadership training college in Britain.

Current Issues of Concern for the Police in England

Recent social, economic, and technological changes in England have created new crime problems and have called for new and improved methods of policing. In the past the social cohesion created by the factory, the church, and the local pub have diminished and neighborhoods can no longer rely on informal social control mechanisms and the local constable to keep crime under control. The police have recently been called up to do more to keep the social fabric of communities under control and to provide safety for its citizens. As discussed above, the police in England have tried to adapt to social changes through the adoption of a plethora of community policing strategies. In addition, the rise of criminal gangs and organized crime, nationally and internationally, are further examples of the increasing complexity of crime in England. More specifically, crimes such as illegal immigration, human trafficking, drug trafficking, and computer fraud have inspired a call for a police force that is more flexible, technologically savvy, and able to cross jurisdictional borders. Some of the common tools used for law enforcement that have evolved since the 1990s include more sophisticated computer technology to identify and catch criminals, better use of DNA testing, and the extensive use of closed circuit television. The British have also moved to address national and international crime issues through the formation of new national police organizations, e.g., the National Crime Squad (NCS), the National Criminal Investigation Service (NCIS), the National Security Service (MI5), and the Serious Organized Crime Agency (SOCA). These agencies have played an important role in enhancing the communication between law enforcement agencies in England and other law enforcement agencies of the European Community, e.g., Europol and the Trevi Group. Such cooperation is especially important since the end of the Cold War and opening of the borders of Eastern and Central Europe.

Another major issue for the police in England is the recent explosion in the use of private policing. Private security companies are used extensively in England and it is estimated that there are now more private security officers than sworn police officers: around 300,000 (Southgate 1995; Jones and Newburn 2002). There are a number of problems that have surfaced with the proliferation of private police in England. Among the most important of these are the lack of standards for the hiring and training of private police as well as the need for better coordination with the local public police. Fortunately, the British government has passed legislation to improve the quality and accountability of private security forces (Joyce 2006).

Policing in a Common Law Country: India

Historical Background

The history of policing in India is an interesting and curious one. It may be easiest to view the long history of Indian policing in three time periods. We will refer to them as early, colonial, and modern periods of policing. In the early period we know of the ancient Hindu rulers who passed legal matters to the *Mauryas,* who began their rule during the fourth century CE. In the eighth century India was subjected to a series of invasions by the Muslims, which eventually led to the power being passed to the Moghuls, who in 1526 organized a new empire that demanded following Islamic law. During this early period and up until the seventeenth century the police in India served the king, who assumed the responsibility of preserving peace and order and dealing with wrongdoers. The reigning powers often used the police to serve imperial goals and the result was a separation from the public and a lack of accountability to the citizenry. These conditions eventually led to excesses in use of power and various forms of corruption. This corruption were exacerbated by the formation of small police districts and stations formed by local officials, then called *darogas, thanedars,* and *kotwals,* who held the rural and urban areas under their strict control and who were prone to corruption and brutality (Dhillon 2005).

Policing in this manner lasted until the early 1600s when the British arrived to form the East India Trade Company. The British company slowly acquired territories, first purely for financial gain but this eventually led to governance. During this time the British slowly tried to reform the Indian system, moving it away from the local tribal and draconian Islamic laws that had existed for centuries. In effect, beginning when the East India Company gained political power in Eastern India in 1765, the British controlled the country. This began the colonial era of Indian policing.

One of the reform efforts during this colonial time period was by Sir Charles Napier, who in 1845 tried to establish a police force modeled after the Royal Irish Constabulary that had been implemented in Ireland—another British occupied territory. But even with such efforts policing in India remained primitive and disorganized and served only to keep minimal peace, control the colonized populace, and support the economic needs of the East India Trade

Company. In fact, even after the full transfer of power to the British in 1857, the remnants of the former corrupt system of the Moghuls, including the use of the *kotwals, thanedars,* and *darogas,* was retained in many parts of the country. At first the British seemed to benefit from this continuing system but eventually the problems of corruption and abuse, as well as other weaknesses of the system, led to citizen unrest and, eventually, the 1857 war for independence. These developments were embarrassing to the British who viewed themselves not as tyrannical dictators but as benevolent rulers concerned about the good of the masses. The revolt made it clear to the British that reform was necessary. What resulted was the single most important event to date in the history of Indian policing—the Police Act (V) of 1861. This Act signaled what we now call the modern era of Indian policing.

The Indian Police Act of 1861 was the effort to professionalize, formalize, and streamline the administration of the Indian police. Specifically, it prescribed duties for police officers as well as the process the police were expected to follow when carrying out the orders of the lawful (read: British) authority. The Act also set out to organize the police by state and districts and determined who would carry out the administration of those districts.

Much of the district structure of the police, set up by the Police Act of 1861, remains to this day under the umbrella agency called the Indian Police Service (IPS). What also remains is the reliance within the districts on the local police station (PS) to handle the daily deviance order functions of the police. This is where the majority of police work is still carried out. The PS is headed by an inspector or sub-inspector and staffed by a number of line officers called constables. The number of police stations per district, as well as the number of constables, is determined by the size of the district. Some police stations have small mini-stations called outposts that serve remote or high-crime areas.

Organization, Structure, and Training

The centralized IPS is now under the administration of Federal (Central) Ministry of Home Affairs, which is responsible for all matters concerning the maintenance of peace and public order as well as the staffing and administration of public services, supervision of boundaries, and administration of union territories (Hakeem 2008, 176). The IPS is divided into state and federal police organizations. The state police organizations fall into one of two groups: the aforementioned state district system, or the Commissionerate system. The *Commissionerate system* was formed by the British to handle deviance order control in large metropolitan areas, e.g., Calcutta, Bombay, Madras, and Hyderabad. It was thought that these regions should be placed under the control of their respective police commissioners because the British believed that the district system would not work well in areas that have serious crime and disorder problems. Since full independence in 1947 the Commissionerate system has been extended to other large areas throughout India.

The second large group of bureaucratic police entities under the IPS are the special police agencies under the central (Federal) government. There are two groups of these: the Central Paramilitary Forces (CPF) and the various agencies under the category of unarmed forces. Each of these will be discussed in more detail below.

As of January 2001 there were 1,449,761 police in India: 141.2 police per 100,000 persons. Those performing deviance control or the regular police functions made up 1,077,415 of these. The remainder are in the armed police, either on state or federal levels, and their primary function is civil order control. There are twenty-eight states and seven union territories in India, with a population of over one billion people. Within those states are 635 districts and 12,248 police stations. The Commissionerate system is present in over thirty large cities or jurisdictions (Commonwealth Human Rights Initiative 2003).

The recruitment and training of police in India varies considerably depending on the entry level and the type of agency. The three levels of entry are constable, sub-inspector, and superintendent. For constables, a high school diploma is generally required and one must be at least seventeen years of age. The training varies from state to state, but all recruits have some physical training and classroom training. Sub-inspectors must have a university degree, some physical training, and attend the state police college for one year. Superintendent level appointments are given through an extensive process of exams, one year training at the National Police Academy, and an in-service probation training period. (For a detailed description of such training, see Diaz 1994.)

Current Issues of Importance for the Police in India

Unfortunately, the Police Act of 1861, subsequent reforms, and even gaining independence from the British in 1947 failed to fully democratize the police or improve its quality. Evaluation of the implementation and effectiveness of the Police Act over the past 100 years can only be described as negative. In 1902, a report by the Police Commission stated that the public had little confidence in the police. Police were described as examples of a corrupt and oppressive police force (Hakeem 2008). More recent critiques of the Indian police have expressed frustration that things have gotten progressively worse and that the police have remained as corrupt, prone to political influence, and grossly incompetent (Bayley 1969; Dhillon 2005).

There appears to be many reasons for the lack of progress in policing. First, the organizational structure, culture, and even many of the rules and regulations, which were developed for the benefit of the British, have remained unchanged since the implementation of the Police Act almost 150 years ago. Much of what was stated in the rules (e.g., regulations for hiring, training) is now outdated and does not reflect a modern democratic police force. Second, it appears that despite the establishment of a democratic government, the effects of the long struggle and the many conflicts with the British remain in the minds of many Indians, which seriously hampers police-citizen relations. Third, it appears that the Indian leaders themselves have decided to continue and adapt the British model of colonial-style policing for their own political advantage. For example, some politicians have been known to use the police to help them harass adversaries or suppress dissent. Even police officials have misused their power to advance their own wealth and professional status. Low salaries, especially for constables, create conditions where police often extort citizens for special treatment and free goods. As a result, a majority of Indian citizens still view the police as exemplars of corruption, brutality, and indifference to law and order (Verma 1999).

In addition to the problems with the police, high poverty and the feeling the government is only interested in the ruling class, has led to considerable citizen discontent in India. Daily street protests, demonstrations, and conflicts between various ethnic and religious groups are common occurrences throughout India. As a result, the police have a large role to play relative to civil order control.

To handle this monumental problem, the IPS has developed an extensive array of armed police units at both state and federal levels. Every state has its own paramilitary unit that is called upon for civil order maintenance; it cannot be used, however, for normal police work. The state armed police are drilled like military regiments, are equipped with automatic weapons, and live in barracks ready to be called up at short notice (Verma 2009). The federal government also can summon their own police under the supervision of the Central Police Organization (CPO). The CPO is divided into two units. The first is a variety of unarmed agencies that serve the research, records, and intelligence functions of the Indian police. The second, called the Central Paramilitary Force (CPMF), is a variety of armed forces, each with their own mission, e.g., border control, railway protection, protection of public sector utilities, and combating terrorism. Among the largest CPMFs is the Central Reserve Police (CRP). Established by the British in 1939, the CRP was originally formed to assist the state police and the army in handling internal disturbances. They continue as a force for maintaining law and order but recently have been called upon to assist in anti-terrorist and additional security, e.g., elections or VIP visits (Hakeem 2008, 177).

Despite the large variety and increasing number of armed federal and state police agencies, the Indian police have been unable to quell the considerable unrest occurring throughout the country. In fact, the chaos has grown considerably in recent years, fueled by caste-based and extremist militias that have terrorized citizens as well as the police. To further complicate matters, terrorist threats from outside the country, most notably Pakistan and Bangladesh, continue to cause tension. Unfortunately, it appears that the growth of the federal and state armed militias has come at the expense of deviance control, and narrowed the confidence of the people in the police, thus increasing the probability of future conflicts between the police and the citizens they serve.

Policing in a Civil Law Country: France

Historical Background

Policing in France has a long history, dating back to at least the year 580 CE when night watch systems were common. In 1306 King Phillip le Bel formed the first criminal investigation unit and around that time the first mounted military police called the *maréchaussée* were formed. Between 1697 and 1699, Louis XIV asserted his authority as king over policing and the *maréchaussée* became the formal law enforcement arm of the country. In 1791, they formally became the *Gendarmerie* and in 1789 Napoleon gave them their military flavor (i.e., military structure, discipline, uniforms, etc.). In 1903 they were established as a local military force (Dupont 2008). The second leg of a highly centralized national police structure, created in 1966 and previously called the *Sûreté Nationale,* is the *police nationale.* The *Gendarmerie* and *Police Nationale* will each be described in more detail below.

The current police organization of France has its roots in the Napoleonic system of internal spying and policing that consolidated the power of the nineteenth-century dictator. Despite reform efforts, its reputation as a repressive force has continued; to some it appears that the police have little concern for the rights of the average citizen. In contrast to England, where the stated philosophy is policing by consent, the French police see themselves more as acting on behalf of the state (i.e., the country). Moreover, the conception of police agency power in France historically involves the regulation of society and the maintenance of order as well as the traditional police functions of the prevention and detection of crime.

During the first few years of the twenty-first century it appears that the conservative political faction has moved to address the growing crime issue as well as increasing civil unrest in France. In 2003 the French Parliament passed police reform legislation that called for increasing police powers as well as designating new laws for prostitution, hostile gatherings, and begging. The legislation also contains measures to strengthen the role of the local governments in the coordination and supervision of the police and to reduce the rights of suspects who are detained after arrest. For some in France, this legislation was viewed to be contrary to the ideals of a free Republic and a direct effort to criminalize the poor, the young, immigrants, and those with variant lifestyles (Hodgson 2005, 57).

Structure, Organization, and Training

France's twenty-two administrative regions are divided into ninety-six provinces that act as conduits to the central government. Each province is administered by a *prefect*, selected by the government to enforce the laws of the nation. Legislation during the early 1990s attempted to decentralize authority, giving a broader range of powers to local elected officials. Although local governments can now hire their own officers, the prefect still retains general power over law and order (Terrill 2003). The organization of the French police is an unusual one, with both military and civilian bureaucracies. In France, policing is centralized—all police power rests in one agency, with the police involved in such additional tasks as public health regulation, housing regulations, and population registration.

As mentioned, there are really two French police organizations, the *Police Nationale* (PN), and the *Gendarmerie Nationale* (GN). The PN operates within the Ministry of the Interior, whereas the GN operates within the Ministry of Defense. The leadership of both is centralized in Paris. Both have conventional deviance control responsibilities, although in different places, with the PN responsible for Paris and other urban areas and the GN responsible for small towns and rural areas with fewer than 10,000 inhabitants.

The GN oversees ten geographical regions with two main administrative divisions: the departmental and the mobile *gendarmerie*. The *Departmental Gendarmerie*, with a total strength of over 105,000, performs all basic police tasks for nearly half of the French people. Members of the *Gendarmerie Mobile* are assigned to civil disorder and other large-scale problems that involve the possibility of violence. Curiously, working for the GN, the police arm of the military, carries greater prestige than working for the PN under the Interior Ministry. GN training is slightly different: they live in barracks and their training has greater emphasis on the military aspects of police work. For this reason, the GN feels that, as a law enforcement agency, it is more disciplined than and superior to the PN (Terrill 2003, 218). In addition, a number of specialized units within the GN provide assistance in areas such as security of public officials, maritime and overseas support, airport security and transport, and training.

The PN is the largest police force with over 150,000 personnel divided into nine departments. The Division of Information controls the flow of information that has political, economic, and social significance. The Division of the City Police (also called Public Security) is responsible for urban law enforcement. The Central Branch of the Judicial Police coordinates searches for dangerous juvenile delinquents and investigates serious offenses. The Division of Territorial Surveillance is responsible for state security. The Republican Security Companies (CRS) are the equivalent of the *Gendarmerie Mobile* in that they respond to civil disorder. The *Inspectorate* investigates complaints against the police. The Division of Immigration oversees illegal movement of people and materials. The Personnel and Training Division and the Equipment Division are self-explanatory.

Recruitment and training for the PN and GN are handled separately by each organization. The PN requires police recruits to take written and physical agility tests. If selected, the recruit attends an eight-month training period at one of the eight regional National Police Schools, followed by a four-month in-the-field training period. The recruit is then assigned to a town, city, or Republican Security Company. Longer periods of training and additional schooling are required for those interested in becoming police inspectors or administrators (Terrill 2003, 222).

The French police organization is closer to the way policing worked in the days before large urban police departments were developed in the late nineteenth century. In earlier times, policing the countryside and controlling citizen unrest were the responsibility of a militia allied to the military. Policing urban areas, the task of local watchmen or watch societies, did not have the comprehensive nature of modern police work. The smaller cities of those times generally found such an arrangement adequate for their needs.

Recent legislation has allowed local governments to hire their own police officials and officers. These police forces, called *Police Municipale*, carry out duties (specified by the mayors and town councils) related to crime prevention, public order, security, and public safety. The 18,000 officers in the *Police Municipale* remain under the supervision and jurisdiction of the Minister of the Interior.

When it comes to civil order control, the GN and the PN each have specialized forces that perform this task. In the PN, the Republican Security Companies assume responsibility. In the GN the *Gendarmerie Mobile* are assigned to civil disorder and other large-scale problems that involve the possibility of violence. Both of these specialized civil order control branches operate independently of conventional police work of patrol and criminal investigations.

Civil order control is an essential component of French policing, probably more so than in any of our model countries. The French have a long history of taking to the streets to express their unhappiness about social and political issues. In 1789 the French masses stormed the Bastille and it sparked the French Revolution. In 2000, there were more than 1,700 demonstrations in Paris alone. In addition to simple demonstrations, politically motivated acts of violence are a major concern for citizens, with many of the problems stemming from labor unions protesting government cutbacks of services and benefits. Several violent riots have taken place recently, and attacks on police officers and other public officials are not uncommon. The most damaging of these occurred in 2005 when three weeks of nightly rampages in the suburbs of Paris and several other cities left extensive damage including 10,000 burned cars and 300 damaged buildings. Police arrested more than 6,000 people during the riots that left 220 police injured (Stinson 2006).

The impact from riots and demonstrations in the City of Paris alone is considerable. The primary problem is the chaos created for traffic and those trying to work around the city during these demonstrations. Another issue is the tremendous costs associated with civil order control. In Paris there are over 5,000 police officers assigned to handle civil order control (Walt 2001). Because of the historical importance of being able to express dissent, there is little chance that demonstrations and civil order disputes will become fewer in number in the near future.

Current Issues of Concern for French Police

In addition to the major issues of concern related to civil order control, the French police also have to deal with the issues of drugs, terrorism, and immigration. With the collapse of its North African colonial empire, France has experienced a large immigration of Arabs from its former colonies of Algeria, Tunisia, and Morocco. Racial tension and cultural conflict have resulted, with attendant problems for law enforcement and judicial operations. With the largest Jewish population in Western Europe, France has also experienced an increase in the number of verbal and physical attacks on Jews. And with its central location and fine transportation system, France is also a crossroads for terrorist activity, from both internal and external sources.

Drugs are also a major social problem because France is both a transshipment point for and consumer of South American cocaine and southwest Asian heroin. Crime statistics in France report that since the 1990s there has been an increase in the overall crime rate. At that time then President Jacques Chirac called for a policy of zero tolerance on crime, similar to that adopted by some U.S. cities (BBC News 2001).

Policing in a Civil Law Country: Germany

Historical Background

The first organized police force in Germany dates back to the early nineteenth century when some of the German kingdoms adopted a force similar to the one developed by Napoleon in France (Feltes 2004). During the reign of Otto von Bismarck in the 1870s the Germans developed a more centralized government and the culture of a strong and civil service system that developed survives to this day. The police were an important part of that elite system. German police strength grew from 200,000 to 1.5 million between 1933 and 1945, the years when Germany was under the rule of Hitler and the National Socialist (Nazi) Party. This force, which included the Gestapo, much of the *Schutzstaffel* (better known as the "SS"), and other Nazi agencies, acted as a private army for Hitler, ruthlessly stamping out dissent, running death camps in the occupied territories, and otherwise acting in a way that made the organization synonymous with evil in the modern world. Little wonder that one of the first items of business for the occupying authorities after the defeat of Germany in World War II was a thorough overhaul of the police apparatus (Dammer, Fairchild, and Albanese 2006).

Immediately after the war the German police were placed under the supervision of the military regional governments of the Allies. With the new German constitution of 1949 and the formation of eleven *Länder* (states) in western Germany, each state gained the power to establish their own police forces. In East Germany the German Democratic Republic (GDR), under the authority of the Soviet government, established one central police force. The police of the GDR were dissolved after reunification in 1990 and many of the former People's Police (*Volkspolizei*) of the GDR were subsumed into the police forces of the new states. The exceptions were when any police member had close ties to the secret police of the GDR, which were called the *Ministerium für Staatssicherheit* (Ministry for State Security or, more commonly, the "Stasi"). Today the police of Germany are part of a decentralized executive force. Since reunification, each of the sixteen German states has its own police law and its own police force. The police laws of the sixteen states deal with the prevention of crime, the preservation of public security and order, and warding off impending danger.

Organization, Structure, and Training

Today's German police were organized during the postwar period in response to the new realities of a democratic Germany. The basic police structures, however, were familiar to Germans because they were essentially the same as those that existed during the Weimar Republic, the democratic government that took power following the fall of the German Empire in 1918 (Fairchild 1988).

The German constitution (Article 20: 3) allows each *Land* (state) to have its own police law and force. Each of the sixteen *Länder* controls their force from that state's Interior Ministry. The police in the *Länder* are not decentralized to municipalities or other units of local government. Thus, the German system occupies a middle level of decentralization between the highly centralized French system and the highly decentralized and fragmented U.S. system.

Within each *Land* are several kinds of police. The *Schutzpolizei* ("Schupo") are the equivalent of municipal police; they are the first to arrive at the scene of most crimes and handle all general aspects of law enforcement and simple investigations. The *Kriminalpolizei* ("Kripo") are plainclothes police who handle serious crime investigations and situations that require developing a case against a suspect. The *Bereitschaftspolizei* ("Bepo") are actually officers-in-training living in barracks, but they serve as civil order police when the situation arises.

The German federal government also has some police agencies at its disposal. The Federal Police (*Bundespolizei*, or "BPol"), previously known as the Federal Border Police (*Bundesgrenzschutz*, or "BGS"), are organized along military lines but are under the supervision of the Federal Ministry of the Interior, not the Ministry of Defense. Their major functions include border control, sea patrol, and airport and railroad security. However, the BPol may also assist *Länder* police in controlling some inner cities and dealing with major civil disturbances that are beyond the scope of the *Länder* police, provide some intelligence gathering activities, and lend support to UN peacekeeping operations. Since 2008 the BPol have become the law enforcement agency that deals with illegal migrants and asylum seekers. Included within the BPol is a special task force, called Special Group 9 (BGS-9) that handles terrorist incidents. Since the end of 2004, the BPol is part of the Joint Center for Defense against Terrorism (*Gemeinsames Terrorismusabwehrzentrum* [GTAZ])—together with members of the *Länder* police and representatives of the BKA, Federal Office for Migration, Customs, and the Military Counter-Intelligence Service (MAD).

Germany also has an agency similar to the FBI called the Federal Criminal Investigation Office (*Bundeskriminalamt* [BKA]). The BKA collects and compiles crime statistics, acts as a clearinghouse for criminal records, and provides support to the *Länder* relative to criminal investigations, forensics, and research. The current BKA handles a large number of international organized crime cases.

In addition to federal and state law enforcement agencies, private security forces have become common in Germany. There are some 3,000 security agencies that employ more than 150,000 people. Their main tasks are securing (private) buildings and property, transporting money, and providing security services at mass events such as soccer games or concerts. Most private security guards are not armed, but neither are they trained very well. The German law demands only a few weeks of training. More and more, the public police are cooperating with private police, e.g., in train stations or during mass events. The results of the World Football Championship in 2006, in which 20,000 private security personnel were involved, showed that the cooperation can be successful. More and more cities outsource security tasks to private companies, but mainly in connection with the protection of buildings.

Entry into the German policing profession is one of the most demanding and comprehensive training experiences in the world. Common for all *Länder* and Federal Police is that all training and education is organized in special schools under the control of the (federal or state) Ministries of Interior. Only few officers, for very special tasks (e.g., chemical analysis, DNA-tests), are educated with a degree from a university outside the current system.

For an individual who aspires to a career of policing, there are different paths they may take depending on the *Land* where he or she lives. Generally speaking, there are two paths of entry into the *Länder* police. Both require twelve or thirteen years of school and a diploma from a German secondary school that qualifies them for entrance into a college or university. In some *Länder* there is a three-level career entry system: The first two years are spent at a police academy (*Polizeischule*) undergoing basic training. A small part of this training focuses on riot control; the rest involves conventional school subjects, law and law enforcement, psychology, sociology, criminology, and criminalistics. After one year at the police academy young officers may be used for civil order control work either in their own *Länder* or, if the need arises, in other *Länder*. After the two years of basic training and civil order control work, the officers begin street patrol work. With few exceptions, recruits must go through the street patrol experience for at least a few years. After that time, some of them may undergo two more years of education at a police college (*Polizei-Fachhochschule*) to become either criminal investigators or middle-management supervisors. After completing the street patrol the officers receive a university diploma in public administration-policing.

Candidates for the highest management positions (the top 3 percent of recruits) go through another two years of training, with one year at the German Police University (DHPol) in Münster where they meet and work with top management candidates from other *Länder*. Since 2008, they can receive a master's degree in public administration/management. Plans are in progress to offer a Ph.D. for police administrators. Since 2007 the German Police University has offered a degree in police science, and since 2003 a second university (in Ruhr-Bochum) has offered a degree in criminology and police science (Feltes 2009).

The division between civil order control structures is different from their civil law partners the French, although both have separate units that handle this kind of work. In Germany, all officers live in barracks and handle civil order control incidents before going on to do street patrol work. In France, civil order work is performed by special units in both the National Police and the *Gendarmerie*. Presumably, the French system produces officers who are more experienced in handling demonstrations and riots because they are older and more specialized. In practice, however, the German structures seem to work well, with few instances of police losing control in the highly charged and provocative atmosphere that exists at many demonstrations.

Current Issues of Concern for German Police

The reunification of Germany in 1990 posed some organizational problems for police because at that time East Germany was broken up into its former states, and police organizations had to be decentralized to the state level. The process was facilitated by the fact that the new organizations were similar to those of West Germany. Personnel issues were more problematic, because many East German police had collaborated closely with the Stasi, and therefore were not allowed to become part of the new police. Some police, especially among the leadership ranks, were purged. As we mentioned earlier, most of the rank-and-file East German police were incorporated into the new organizations (Dammer, Fairchild, and Albanese 2006).

Unfortunately, the problem of Stasi infiltration into the new police ranks has not been resolved. In 2009, after media reported that 17,000 of the 230,000 police officers in Germany had been members of the Stasi, a discussion started on whether all police officers (and politicos) should be cleared for their background again. Aside from some spectacular cases, most of the 17,000 former Stasi-members are believed to have worked for the Stasi in a minor capacity, e.g., a driver or a clerk.

More recently the major problem for the German police has been related to the large numbers of immigrants entering the country since 1990. Since the fall of the Berlin Wall the number of foreigners that registered in Germany went from 4.2 million in 1987 to 7.4 million in 1997 (Ewald and Feltes 2003). In 2008 the number declined to 7.2 million; however, these numbers do not reflect the emigrants from Russia, Poland, Romania, and other former Eastern Bloc countries that claimed German ancestry and are thus counted as German citizens, nor do they include the significant number of Turks with migrant parents. After an initial rise in crime immediately after the unification, overall crime has stabilized in Germany and has actually declined since 2004.

Another problem that arose during the 1990s was hate crimes. The influx of foreigners inspired hostile reactions from some Germans, primarily young, working-class youths, who felt that those from other countries were a threat to their lifestyle and future. After 1990 the number of violent offenses recorded by police as having xenophobic or right-wing connections rose. In 2008 the police registered nearly 14,000 cases with right-wing or extremist characteristics including 735 crimes of violence. German human rights advocates have estimated that 136 people have been killed by right-wing violence between 1990 and 2005 (Feltes 2009).

Policing in a Socialist/Mixed Law Country: China

Historical Background

The history of the police in China is a long one, with records going back to *Shun* monarchy in 2255 BCE when the geographic area we know now as China was not a united kingdom but a loose configuration of tribes in which local officials were designated to handle disputes and maintain order. For the most of the 2,000 years and during long periods of dynastic rule, policing in China remained a grassroots affair that was handled by local officials or, in special situations, by the military of the emperor who were called in to handle civil disorder (Wong 2009). During the Zhou dynasty in the years 1100–771 BCE the first Ministry of Justice and professional policing institution was formed to help the local officials address security and social order (Bayley 1985). The Qin dynasty (221–207 BCE) was important because during this time policing became more formalized and bureaucratic with a central administration and uniform laws (Wong 2009). But even with the beginnings of a bureaucratic and governmentally supported formal police force, China was always a country where social control is first addressed in the family, in the community, and then by state officials. This societal trait has continued through the overthrow of the dynastic period in China in 1911 by the *Kuomintang* (Nationalist Party) and through the tumultuous times that followed.

After gaining power in 1949 the Communist Party handed over policing to three groups: (1) public security forces, which provided basic police services, (2) militia groups, which monitored the border regions, and (3) the People's Liberation Army (PLA), which was the military wing of the Communist Party (Terrill 2003, 568). In the 1950s, as the Communist Party became more entrenched, and formal mechanisms for law enforcement were developed based on the principles outlined in the first constitution of the People's Republic of China in 1954. Basically, the Chinese government formulated a Soviet-style criminal justice system with overall control in the hands of the Communist Party. From the mid-1950s until 1966, there was little crime or civil disorder in China. But the Cultural Revolution of 1966 changed all that.

Along with Mao's attempt to reform the Communist Party came attacks on police officials and police stations and seizures of courts by the followers of Mao and the Red Guard. Local police were placed under the control of local Communist Party officials. Eventually, Mao had to call on the PLA to restore some semblance of order. This period of lawlessness and disorder continued until the late 1970s when Deng Xiaoping reestablished the rule of law and restored the police as the main enforcers of law. This return of law and order to the police was reinforced by the Police Law of 1995, which replaced the previous law of 1957. The new law outlined the organizational structure, authority, and duties of police in China and defined the modern roles of police including maintaining social order, safeguarding state security, protect personal safety, protecting personal freedom and property, and guarding against and punishing law violators (Yisheng 1999).

Some feel that the focus of the police in China has changed in the last decade. Although the local aspect of policing remains important and the neighborhood stations remain strong, police have now begun to concentrate more on crime fighting and order maintenance, and less on dealing with political dissent and the provision of social services. Also, the police have become more centralized, professional, and accountable; they have also made an effort to recruit without politics as criteria; and they have made an effort to follow the new rule of law emphasis that was put forth in the 1995 Law on People's Police of the People's Republic of China (Wong 2002).

Structure, Organization, and Training

The Chinese police are centrally monitored by the Ministry of Public Security. The Ministry formulates policies and regulations, coordinates police work and operations among the twenty-two provinces, and provides technological and specialized assistance to local police (Du 1997). The Chinese police are divided into five main components: Public security police, state security police, prison police, judicial procuratorates police, and judicial people's courts police. Although this organization may seem straightforward, what confuses our understanding of the Chinese police is the myriad of levels under which they operate. Although the five police agencies are directly answerable to the Ministry of Public Security, they are also under the authority of the individual provinces, 450 prefects, 1,904 county security bureaus, and thousands of local police stations (Guo, Xiang, Zongxian, Zhangun, Xiaohui, and Shauang-shuang 1999). Thus, in theory, the police fall under the leadership of the Ministry of Public Security; in practice, the day-to-day administration is governed by a corresponding agency. In many cases, local levels of government can determine their own policing priorities and appoint and promote their own officers (Xiancui 1998).

The Public Security police (*gongan;* literally "public peace") provide not only basic uniformed patrol but also twelve other specialized functions, including supervising probationers and parolees, criminal investigations, fire control, border patrol, and monitoring of all modes of transportation (Cao and Hou 2001; Wang 1996, 155). They make up almost 90 percent of all the police in China. State security police, established in 1983, are responsible for preventing and investigating espionage, sabotage, and conspiracies. Prison police supervise convicted offenders in prisons. The judicial procuratorates police escort suspects in cases investigated by the procuratorates (similar to prosecutors). Finally, the judicial police in the people's courts maintain security and order in the various courts and also may carry out death sentences.

Since the 1950s, the Chinese national police force has moved to decentralize police to thousands of neighborhood stations to help them control crime and build the socialist welfare state (Cao and Hou 2001; Jiao 1995, 72). There over 38,000 neighborhood stations, called *Paichu Suo,* which were possibly the forerunner of the Japanese *koban* system (Wong 2002).

Most Chinese police graduate from one of the 300+ police universities, colleges, or police academies located in the individual provinces, all of which are coordinated by the Ministry of Public Security (Wong 2009). Recruits with special skills may be hired without this training but all must be at least twenty-five years of age and have a strong physique. Training lasts for an average of six months, but it will vary depending on officers' future positions and specialization. Potential officers are trained directly by the Ministry of Public Security at one of the three major police universities whereas nonofficers are trained by their respective governmental offices: province, county, prefect, or municipality (Wong 2009; Guo et al. 1999).

When there is a civil order dispute in China, the Ministry of Public Security generally calls upon the main public security police in that jurisdiction. However, when the matter requires strength in numbers, the Ministry may turn to the Chinese People's Armed Police, which serve as part of the army with dual responsibilities to the Central Military Commission and the Ministry of Public Security.

Issues of Concern for Chinese Police

Since the end of the Cultural Revolution, the government has implemented significant reforms in many social and economic areas. With a free market economy and an increase in individual wealth have come the social ills of crime and corruption. As a result, the Communist Party, fearing a total breakdown of control, has sometimes felt it necessary to call on the police to crack down on crime through the implementation of various "get tough" policies. Citizens have responded with calls for increased civil rights and democratic participation. These calls have not been received well by the Communist Party, and there have been frequent and sometimes violent confrontations between police and citizens. The most famous occurred in 1989 in Tiananmen Square, Beijing, when over 800 people died in a hail of gunfire from the Red Army in response to a mass demonstration in favor of democracy and freedom. Despite the international furor that followed, Chinese officials defend their actions to this day, stating that they were necessary to maintain public order.

National surveys in the late 1990s suggested that the public still viewed the police in a positive way and had confidence in their abilities (Ma 1997). However, according to other sources, since the Cultural Revolution public attitudes toward the police have shifted. The Chinese people now seem to view police with more distrust and to see them as bullies or tyrants. The number of complaints against police has increased considerably, and physical confrontations with citizens have become more frequent (Cao 1995). One more recent example of this distrust is the story of a 28-year-old man who was convicted of killing six police officers in 2008. Yang Jia entered a Shanghai police station then stabbed and killed the officers after he claimed he was beaten over stealing a bicycle in October 2007. What happened that surprised many was that during his two trials many supporters gathered outside the courthouse, wore t-shirts with his image, and called him a hero because he stood up to the police and government injustice (Barboza 2008).

Recently, at least in public announcements, the Chinese government has begun to recognize the rule of law over the rule of those in political power.

But this change is happening too slowly for many Chinese, especially young citizens, who are calling for more individual freedoms. These combination of challenges—economic growth, growing crime, and the call for more citizen rights, will undoubtedly be of great concern for the Chinese government and especially the police in the coming decades.

Policing in an Islamic Law Country: Saudi Arabia

Historical Background

The Saudi Arabia Police, a highly centralized force, is responsible for the maintenance of peace and order throughout the country. Prior to the late 1920s, policing in Saudi Arabia was primarily a tribal affair. A *sheik,* appointed to supervise a certain region, would have the authority to handle matters related to public safety. He would hire and financially support the local police as well as provide himself with additional security. This power was granted to the *sheiks* by the different kings that ruled the region between invasions and occupations of the Ottoman Empire. The sheiks even had the power to punish offenders of the civil law. But in 1927 under the first king of the modern Saudi Arabia, Abdul-Aziz, the country was consolidated and the first recognized police force was established. The current police force, established by royal decree in 1950 by King Abdul-Aziz, is called the Department of Public Safety. The Minister of the Interior, who is appointed by the king, is responsible for the administration of all police matters in the country. Police in the Department of Public Safety handle most of the daily law enforcement functions in the country. This force can seek help from the military forces in times of need. The structure of the Saudi police will be discussed in greater detail below.

Organization, Structure, and Training

Saudi Arabia is divided into fourteen provinces (or "emirates") that make up the country's administrative divisions. Each of the emirates is run by a governor, and the police are directly administered by a general manager who controls the activities of the police within that area. The managers are responsible to the provincial governors, who are directly answerable to the overall director of public safety. The director is actually the head of the Saudi police and is a high-ranked official in the Ministry of the Interior. The director appoints most of the managers and officers of the local police forces.

The police department is divided into three kinds of police: the regular police, the *mubahith,* and the *mutawa.* The regular police, on the provincial and municipal (local) levels, consist of officers that handle the deviance control functions of average police officers. The *mubahith* (secret police) are the special investigative police of the General Directorate of Investigation (GDI). The *mubahith* conduct criminal investigations and handle matters pertaining to domestic security and counterintelligence.

The Department of Public Safety police also has a morals force or religious police force known as *mutawa* (or *mutaween*), which ensures that Saudi citizens live up to the rules of behavior derived from the *Qur'an*. This agency, also called the Saudi Arabia's Commission for Promotion of Virtue and Prevention of Vice, has a membership of around 20,000 men who are usually bearded men who wear traditional Arabic white robes (*kamees*). They are not armed and not trained as law enforcement personnel. Their roles are many and outlined in the Commission's regulations. Among them are to maintain strict separation of the sexes in Saudi public life, pressure women to wear the traditional long black robes and face coverings, and stop women from driving cars in certain locations. The *mutawa* also ensures that businesses are closed during prayer hours, cover up advertising that depicts attractive women and regulate alcohol use. They have also been known to disperse gatherings of women in public places designated for men and prevent men from entering public places designated for families. Although the regulations do include a variety of behaviors describing what is "right and wrong" the *mutawa* are sometimes left to their own interpretation of the regulations. As a result there are numerous reports of the mistreatment and harassment of many Saudi citizens, especially women and foreign workers.

Saudi police make a strong distinction between commissioned officers and rank-and-file police. The commissioned officers receive three years of training at King Fahd Security College and are promoted through the ranks from second lieutenant to general. The director of public safety, who heads the Saudi police, usually is a relative of the king (as are many heads of executive agencies in Saudi Arabia). Rank-and-file police personnel must be literate and spend three months in training. They are not eligible to become commissioned officers (Alobied 1989).

Saudi Arabia has a separate "special forces" division to handle civil order control functions. One use of these special forces, called the Pilgrims and Festivals Police Force, is used to control the large throngs that gather during the annual pilgrimage to the cities of Mecca and Medina. When civil order situations go beyond the control of the special police, the National Guard and Saudi Army are called in (Ross 1996).

As the guardian of the holy cities, Saudi Arabia must maintain order, sanitary conditions, and food distribution channels among the approximately two million Muslims from other countries, as well as Saudi Arabia, who go on the pilgrimage each year. In past years, the pilgrimage has been marred by high crowd concentrations and riots resulting in many deaths and serious foreign relation problems among Saudi Arabia, Iran, and Pakistan (Dammer, Fairchild, and Albanese 2006).

Current Issues of Concern for Saudi Police

A major challenge for Saudi Arabian police is how they balance the need for maintaining civil order within an Islamic system of justice while staying within the bounds of international human rights standards. Many international organizations (e.g., Amnesty International and Human Rights Watch) have publicly excoriated the Saudis for numerous examples where it was believed that the police crossed the line to abusive methods of policing. On one level this can be viewed as merely a public relations problem that has little or no impact on the daily practices of the police. However, the issue can become increasingly problematic if Saudi citizens begin to call for more rights and protections, or if the international community exerts pressure on the police—through political and economic sanctions—to bring human rights policies and practices more in line with other countries.

Another significant concern for the Saudi police is the constant threat of terrorism. This is an internal problem for the Saudis: they are highly susceptible to terrorist activity because of the numerous oil fields and the concomitant infrastructure changes they have made from oil producing wealth. In addition, current and former citizens of Saudi Arabia, including Osama bin Laden, have created complications for the Saudi government because such individuals and groups associated with terrorism have caused countries to question the safety of their interests in the region. Saudi Arabia has taken a number of steps to improve its internal security and support the fight against terrorism. In addition, Western countries and groups have begun to call for a liberalization of politics and social policies, e.g., better treatment of women and more human rights for those who commit crime. However, religious extremists have moved strongly, even to the point of violence, to prevent these possible changes. As a result the Saudi government, and especially the police, has the difficult task of keeping internal peace while maintaining positive relations and upgrading their international reputation.

Web Sources

1. Official site of the International Criminal Police Organization: http://www.interpol.int/
2. The Metropolitan Police Force of London England: http://www.met.police.uk
3. Video clip about German immigration police (Bundespolizei, BPol): http://www.bundespolizei.de/cln_116/nn_719704/EN/Home/Film/film__DSL__wmv,templateId=raw,property=publicationFile.wmv/film_DSL_wmv.wmv
4. The UN Code of Conduct for Law Enforcement Officials: http://www.legislationline.org/documents/action/popup/id/7787
5. Video clip providing visual images about the Police in China: http://video.google.com/videosearch?q=Chinese+Police&hl=en&um=1&ie=UTF-8&ei=NGKASqOVDuKntgeU-pToAQ&sa=X&oi=video_result_group&ct=title&resnum=10#

Discussion Questions

1. Select one unique historical development that you feel was instrumental in the formation of the police in each of our selected countries.
2. Which of the six selected nations do you believe has the most effective police force? Why?
3. How does the United States deal with problems related to civil order control? How do these methods compare and contrast with our selected countries?
4. The *mutawa* in Saudi Arabia are a type of police not found anywhere else in the world. What makes them unique and why do they not exist in most other countries?
5. Based on the information provide in this chapter, as well as your knowledge about policing around the world, what do you believe are the biggest challenges police face in the twenty-first century?

References

Alobied, Abdullah. "Police Functions and Organizations in Saudi Arabia." *Police Studies* 10 (1989): 80–84.

Barboza, David. "Police Officers' Killer, Hero to Some Chinese, is Executed." *New York Times,* November 27, A18, 2008.

Bayley, David. *The Police and Political Development in India.* Princeton, NJ: Princeton University Press, 1969.

_____. *Patterns of Policing: A Comparative International Analysis.* New Brunswick, NJ: Rutgers University Press, 1985.

BBC News. "Big Jump in Crime in France." *BBC News,* February 2, 2001. Accessed March 10, 2001. http://news.bbc.co.uk/1/hi/world/europe/1150193. stm.

Cao, Guanghui. "Bringing Police in Hunan Provide to Account: Before and After." *Outlook Weekly Beijing* 49, 1995.

Cao, Liqun, and Charles Hou. "A Comparison of Confidence in the Police in China and in the United States." *Journal of Criminal Justice* 29 (2001): 87–99.

Commonwealth Human Right Initiative. "Police Organisation in India." Accessed March 28, 2009. http://www.humanrightsinitiative.org/publications/police/police_organisations.pdf, 2003.

Dammer, Harry R., Erika Fairchild, and Jay S. Albanese. *Comparative Criminal Justice Systems* (3rd ed.). Belmont, CA: Wadsworth/Thomson Learning, 2006.

Dhillon, Kirpal. *Police and Politics in India: Colonial Concepts, Democratic Compulsions: Indian Police 1947–2002.* New Delhi, India: Manohar Press, 2005.

Diaz, S. M. "Police in India." In *Police Practices: An International Review,* edited by Dilip K. Das, 181–229. Metuchen, NJ: Scarecrow Press, 1994.

Du, Jinfeng. "Police-Public Relations: A Chinese View." *The Australian and New Zealand Journal of Criminology* 30, no. 1 (1997): 87–94.

Dupont, Benoit. "The French Police System: Caught Between a Rock and a Hard Place—The Tension of Serving Both the State and the Public." In *Comparative Policing: The Struggle for Democratization,* edited by M. R. Haberfeld and Ibrahim Cerrah, 247–276. London: Sage, 2008.

Ewald, Uwe, and Thomas Feltes. "Multicultural Context, Crime and Policing in Germany: Challenges after Unification." *Police and Society* 7 (2003): 167–198.

Fairchild, Erica. *German Police.* Springfield, IL: Thomas Publishing, 1988.

Feltes, Thomas. "Police Forces of Germany." In *Encyclopedia of Law Enforcement,* edited by Larry Sullivan, 1073–1078. Thousand Oaks, CA: Sage, 2004.

_____. Personal Interview with Thomas Feltes, Chair of Criminology and Police Science at the Ruhr University-Bochum and former Rector of the Fachhochschule for Polizei, Villingen-Schwenningen. July 10, 2009.

Gregory, Frank, E. C. "The British Police System: With Special Reference to Public Order Problems." In *Police and Public Order in Europe,* edited by John Roach and Jürgen Thomaneck, 33–72. London: Croom-Helm, 1985.

Guo, Jianan, Guo Xiang, Wu Zongxian, Xu Zhangun, Peng Xiaohui, and Li Shauangshuang. "China." In *The World Factbook of Criminal Justice System*. Washington, DC: Department of Justice. Accessed July 1, 2009. http://www.ojp.usdoj.gov/bjs/pub/ascii/wfbcjchi.txt, 1999.

Hakeem, Farrukh. "Emergence of Modern Indian Policing: From Mansabdari to Constabulary." In *Comparative Policing: The Struggle for Democratization*, edited by M. R. Haberfeld and Ibrahim Cerrah, 169–182. London: Sage, 2008.

Hodgson, Jacqueline. *French Criminal Justice: A Comparative Account of the Investigation and Prosecution of Crime in France*. Portland, OR: Hart, 2005.

Home Office. *Policing: Building Safer Communities Together*. London: Home Office, Performance Delivery Unit, 2003.

Jiao, Allan Y. "Community Policing and Community Mutuality: A Comparative Analysis of American and Chinese Police Reforms." *Police Studies: The International Review of Police Development* 18, no. 3/4 (1995): 69–91.

Jones, Trevor, and Tim Newburn. "The Transformation of Policing? Understanding Current Trends in Policing Systems." *British Journal of Criminology* 42 (2002): 129–146.

Joyce, Peter. *Criminal Justice: An Introduction to Crime and the Criminal Justice System*. Portland, OR: Willan, 2006.

Ma, Yue. "The Police Law of 1995: Organization, Functions, Powers, and Accountability of the Chinese Police." *Policing: An International Journal of Police Strategy and Management* 20 (1997): 113–135.

Mayhew, Pat, David Elliot, and Lizanne Dowds. *The 1988 British Crime Survey*. London: Home Office Research Study. Accessed July 2, 2009. http://www.met.police.uk/recruitment, 1989.

Muir, H. "Yard Expands Civilian Policing Scheme Despite Problems." (Manchester, UK) *The Guardian* October 7, p.4, 2003.

Ross, Jeffrey Ian. "Policing in the Gulf States: The Effect of the Gulf Conflict." In *Policing Change, Changing Police: International Perspectives*, edited by Otwin Marenin, 79–106. New York: Garland, 1996.

Stinson, Jeffrey. "Fear of replay of '05 riots has French on edge." *USA Today*. October 27, 2006. Accessed July 2, 2009. http://www.usatoday.com/news/world/2006-10-26-france-riot-anniversary_x.htm.

Southgate, P. "Alternate Forms of Patrol: Innovations in the UK." Paper presented at the annual meeting of the American Society of Criminology, Boston, Massachusetts, November 1995.

Terrill, Richard. *World Criminal Justice Systems: A Survey* (5th ed.). Cincinnati, OH: Anderson, 2003.

United Nations Asia and Far East Institute. "Effective Administration of the Police System." In *Annual Report for 2001 and Resource Material Series No. 60*, 182–183. Fuchu, Tokyo, Japan: Author, 2003.

Verma, Arvind. "Cultural Roots of Police Corruption in India." *Policing: An International Journal of Police Strategies and Management* 22, no. 3 (1999): 264–279.

_____. "Democratic Policing in India: Issues and Concerns." In *Policing Developing Democracies*, edited by Mercedes S. Hinton and Tim Newburn, 119–140. New York: Routledge, 2009.

Walt, Vivienne. "Every Day is May Day for the Police Of Paris." *USAToday*, June 19, 2001. Accessed July 2, 2009. http://www.usatoday.com/news/world/ 2001-05-01-paris-usat.htm.

Wang, Zheng. "The Police System in the People's Republic of China." In *Comparative and International Justice Systems*, edited by Obi N. I. Ebbe, 155–168. Newton, MA: Butterworth-Heinemann, 1996.

Watt, Ian. *Police Higher Education and Training in the United Kingdom*. Chicago: Office of International Criminal Justice, 1988.

Wong, Kam C. "Policing in the People's Republic of China: The Road to Reform in the 1990s." *British Journal of Criminology* 42 (2002): 281–316.

_____. *Chinese Policing: History and Reform*. New York: Peter Lang, 2009.

Yisheng, Dai. "Policing Reform in China." *Crime & Justice International* 15, no. 34 (1999). Accessed August 31, 2009. http://www.cjimagazine.com/ archives/cji98a8.html?id=335.

Chapter 6

Policing Subordinate Sovereignties: Policing in Democratic Societies

L. Edward Wells

Introduction

The institution of the police presents a perennial, never-fully-resolved puzzle for societies with liberal democratic political systems, especially nations in the English Common Law tradition that value individual freedom and are wary of "police states." An inherent conflict arises between the society's need to preserve social-political order and the democratic culture's desire to preserve individual freedoms. As the agency formally charged with using the coercive power of the state to maintain internal civil order, the police are at the core of this conflict. The basic issue is: How to organize the police to exercise collective control over citizens' activities so that social order is maintained but so that the rights and freedoms of individuals are preserved? Moreover, can this be done in a way that is consistent with the basic principles and values of a democratic society?

We note that *policing* is a general governance function required of every society or community to maintain the collective well-being of the community and to regulate the behaviors of its members. The basic policing tasks are found in all societies—e.g., maintaining social order, enforcing moral codes, and protecting public safety—but there are a multitude of ways that societies may set up formal police systems to carry out these tasks, and some traditional kinship-based societies may not have any formal police systems. Conventional police scholars point to a fundamental dichotomy of how police systems might be implemented in different societies, differentiating between autocratic and democratic policing. *Autocratic* police are those imposed upon the community or society from above by a ruler or ruling elite (which stands apart from and above the community). An autocratic police system derives its authority to enforce the law and use force from the political legitimacy or the military power of the ruler. This kind of ruler-imposed policing may be described as "policing from the top down." Familiar historical examples of this kind of police are the *gendarmes* of postrevolutionary France or the MVD police of prerevolutionary tsarist Russia. *Democratic* police systems represent the second basic format, in which the authority of the police and their license to use coercive force derive from public support of the community being policed. This type of police is developed "from the bottom up" as an extension of the community's own efforts to regulate and protect itself. Familiar historical models for democratic police are the early Frankpledge system of Anglo-Saxon England and the later urban Constable-Watch systems of post-Elizabethan England.

Which type of policing system is better? Modern liberal political ideology favors democratic over autocratic forms of governance, but does that imply that democratic policing is inherently better than autocratic policing? Critical analysis suggests that neither form is inherently superior in all respects; what works best may depend on the particular context where it is used. Autocratic policing is not invariably despotic, nor is democratic policing invariably more just or popular or corruption-free. Each form of policing has its strengths and weaknesses, and the relevant question is when to use one versus the other, with conventional wisdom presuming that the form of the police system should match the form of the political system (e.g., Reith 1975; Cole 1999; Marenin 2000). Thus, conventional policing theory presumes that democratic governance systems require democratic police systems to function well as democracies. The argument is that autocratic police systems would fundamentally contradict and politically undermine the legal basis for democratic governance. Although this seems intuitive, it proves oversimplified when we consider the wide diversity of policing arrangements found in societies around the world where "mismatches" between government and police systems are common. Many modern democracies are recent and gradual conversions from governments that previously were monarchies, theocracies, or dictatorships. At any point in history, the government will be a mixture of old and new structures, containing many traditional elements left over from prior systems as familiar and customary practices—including their justice and police systems (Kratcoski 2000). Conversely, many autocratic governments, in order to placate public opinion and stay in power, have modified their police system to make them (or make them seem) more democratic and egalitarian. In many autocratic political systems at the present time, policing is actually provided by a number of independent community-based militias (e.g., the Taliban) operating separately from the state police (which serves primarily as a security force for the ruling elite).

Policing in Neocolonial Societies

A mismatch between the police and the government structures seems especially problematic in modern societies that have democratic governance and police systems, but who nonetheless rely on autocratic police systems for order maintenance and law enforcement among some minority populations within those societies. This inconsistency occurs notably in modern democratic nations that are "neocolonial states"—i.e., former colonial states formed as a result of military or political conquest of indigenous peoples who were sovereign nations prior to their conquest and colonization. During colonization, the sovereignty and lands of indigenous peoples were taken without their consent and they were annexed into a new nation where they are a distinct and disadvantaged minority. Although such nations may be modern liberal democracies today (e.g., United States, Canada, or Australia), the aboriginal subgroup remains an internally colonized people, because they were not consulted in the formation of the nation and they have not freely consented to be governed or policed. Attention to policing in situations like the one described above is important, because more than half the world's population live in postcolonial states (Cole 1999). Here the police systems are products of their colonial histories and do not really fit the idealized models of policing drawn from Western countries. How does this colonial experience affect the types of policing systems found in postcolonial and neocolonial societies?

Colonial systems are describable as either *pacified* or *resettled* colonies—reflecting how the colonizer nation appropriated the colonized land (Cole 1999). In "pacified colonies," extensively found in Africa, Asia, and the South Pacific, sovereignty over the colonized countries was asserted by European colonizers merely for economic gain—e.g., trade, marketing advantages, and/or the extraction of natural resources. The pacified colonies were largely exploited and administered from afar as distant economic resources. They were populated mostly by indigenous people who eventually regained political sovereignty over their lands when colonization ended. In "resettled colonies" the colonizer nation used the colonized country for geographic expansion of its population, its political and cultural sovereignty, and its economic fortunes. This pattern is notably found in the Americas, especially North America, as well as Australia and New Zealand. In resettling the colonized land, the colonizer nation has taken over the territory of the colonized people by transferring large numbers of its population to the new land as settlers so that they outnumber the indigenous peoples (often helped by European diseases that decimated the indigenous population). By exerting social, as well as political and economic, dominion over the colonized territory, the colonizer rewrites the identity of the land in its own cultural terms. When the colonial period ends and the re-settled colony is granted its independence as a separate nation, the original in-digenous occupants do not regain their sovereignty over their land. They have become an internally colonized minority within the newly sovereign state. Their relegation to a colonial status is permanent: they remain racially, eco-nomically, socially, and political subordinate within their own homelands. This pattern is found throughout the world, including many modern, wealthy, politically stable, liberal democracies.

How the colonization was initially implemented can have important legal consequences for the colonized populations. Where the colonizing was ac-complished substantially through treaties and formal political agreements be-tween the colonizer and indigenous nations (e.g., the United States and Canada), rather than by simple invasion and military conquest (e.g., Latin America or Aus-tralia), then the colonized peoples retain some legal claims over their own sov-ereignty as a people or a nation. Although national and international courts have been inconsistent, they generally acknowledge that the original treaties es-tablish the political sovereignty of the colonized peoples that persists to some degree in the present day (Nettheim 1991; Popic 2005; Washburn 1995; Wilkins and Lomawaima 2001). Without formal treaties establishing some prior legal recognition of their sovereignty, however, indigenous peoples are regarded merely as demographic minority groups (to which sovereignty claims do not apply).

The sovereignty granted to indigenous tribal groups constitutes a limited form of political sovereignty called *subordinate sovereignty*. This grants some legal protection and autonomy to indigenous peoples' traditional identities, communities, territories, and ways of life, but they remain subordinate to the legal system of the nation in which they are located. They have some legal right to political autonomy and self-governance (including self-policing), although the terms of their self-government cannot violate or contradict the terms of the larger national law. The recognition of subordinate sovereignty applies to the native tribal peoples of the United States and Canada for whom special Native American or First Nation citizenship status is recognized in national law, but it does not apply to the indigenous tribal peoples of Mexico or most Latin American countries. It applies to the indigenous Maori people of New Zealand, but not to the aboriginal tribes of Australia with whom the British did not negotiate treaties (Perry 1996; Popic 2005). The precise legal meaning of "subordinate sovereignty" is a complex and evolving issue in international law that likely will remain unsettled for decades to come. However, it sits at the center of attempts to formulate equitable and effective police systems for neo-colonial indigenous groups, exemplified by recent efforts in the United Nations to formulate international law regarding the legal rights of indigenous peoples (United Nations 2007).

Autocratic Policing of Indigenous Peoples

The fundamental problem for the policing of subordinate sovereign tribal populations in neocolonial democracies is how to achieve democratic police systems when the colonized people did not consent to become members of the state and the justice structures are culturally foreign to them. Modern nation-states are formulated on an assumption of common political interests and ideological consensus among the governed groups, but native communities present an obstacle in this process. Because enduring populations of indigenous people generally seek to preserve their traditional territories, governmental practices, and cultures—and because native world-views may be radically at odds with "modern" world-views—they often present strong resistance to the national processes of inclusion, compromise, accommodation, and unification upon which democratic states are formed. As a result, native communities in former resettled colonies find themselves marginalized and autocratically governed by the larger states in which they are located, even in the most liberal democratic nations.

From a governance and policing standpoint, the presence of a distinct and incongruous indigenous minority presents the modern postcolonial state with two options: removal or assimilation. The first option, *removal,* represents the most drastic and controversial solution, although it has proven frequently popular as a fallback option when assimilation programs were unsuccessful or too slow. In its most extreme form, removal of an indigenous minority may involve its physical elimination by genocide or ethnic cleansing—as occurred to native peoples in Tasmania and Newfoundland (Perry 1996). In less severe form, removal may involve physically transporting a native minority population to some distant location where they no longer represent a policing problem because they are outside jurisdictional boundaries or are too distant to be noticeable. A prime example of this occurred in the United States during the 1830s, when numerous Indian tribes were removed from Eastern states and relocated to "Indian country"—an area located outside the borders of the non-native settled states. Beyond physical relocation, removal may also rely on symbolic elimination of the indigenous minority by a legal procedure of redefining its political status, i.e., from protected and special to ordinary. That is, the legal definition of a specific indigenous group is legislatively rewritten (or withdrawn) so that it no longer exists as a semi-sovereign governmental entity with special legal claims. This form of removal occurred in the United States during the so-called "Termination Era" of the mid-1950s when the U.S. Congress withdrew federal recognition from dozens of Native American tribes, essentially defining them out of existence as federally identifiable populations.

Removal of indigenous populations from their native lands without their consent represents an unsatisfactory solution for nations who purport to be democratic societies. Achieving democratic policing of tribal populations in postcolonial states hinges mainly on the second option, *assimilation,* which means incorporating indigenous peoples into the political systems as participating and contributing citizens. The difficulty is that many (if not most) indigenous peoples have sought to retain their traditional native cultural practices and structures, and they have actively resisted assimilation (Perry 1996). Thus, several different strategies might be used to bring about assimilation and incorporation of reluctant indigenous populations and to achieve at least the appearance of democratic governance.

The traditional, most elementary, and most commonly used strategy is *assimilation by coercion,* which relies on physical force, violence, and fear to secure behavioral accommodation. Based on the "power of the stick," it is appealing because of its directness and forcefulness. But coercion invariably proves an ineffective way to police a community, because it yields compulsory rather than voluntary compliance. It produces conformity in behavior but not genuine assimilation and cultural acceptance. Moreover, history shows that reliance on violence and military force engenders hostility and resentment; in general, it is not viewed by those being policed as legitimate, and it often results in violence, brutality, and rebellion. All of these are inconsistent with the idea of democratic policing.

An alternative strategy, more compatible with the idea of democratic governance, is *assimilation by conversion,* which relies on education and indoctrination to change peoples' minds and resocialize their behaviors. This strategy is embodied in the universal reliance on religious missionaries to bring civilization into indigenous colonial societies throughout the world. Especially during the seventeenth, eighteenth, and nineteenth centuries, "civilizing the natives" meant converting them to Christianity, as well as converting them to Western ideas of morality and politics. Education also has figured prominently and universally in assimilation politics. The common practice in Australia, North America, and Africa was to remove indigenous children from their natural families and send them to boarding schools where their Native languages, behaviors, and outlooks could be extinguished and replaced by more civilized habits, and beliefs. In this way, the second generation of indigenous peoples would be assimilated to think, speak, pray, work, and act like their European colonizers; traditional native cultures and habits would naturally become extinct after the first generation.

Assimilations by conversion are criticized when they are imposed and involuntary, contradicting the basic tenets of democratic participation and amounting to cultural imperialism. A slightly different and/or more modern strategy is *assimilation by cooptation* in which the appearance of voluntary participation is maintained. Relying on the carrot rather than the stick, cooptation involves the creation of economic or political conditions that reward the adoption of approved behaviors and values while disadvantaging the retention of native cultural traditions. Policies are set up to make receiving the necessities of a comfortable (or at least tolerable) life contingent upon following nonnative practices and adopting a nonnative cultural framework. Social and governmental programs are set to provide money, food, and legal privileges to those native populations who adopt officially approved practices, whereas those who retain traditional native practices experience the resulting poverty, hunger, illness, and political disenfranchisement. Tribal communities that choose to reorganize themselves following federally mandated guidelines for governmental and policing structures receive monetary grants and aid to sustain their communities; otherwise, they struggle in poverty and anomie. In these terms, indigenous populations will "voluntarily" choose to assimilate to the mainstream culture to receive its benefits rather than persist in the disadvantages of traditional ways.

Neocolonial Policing of American Indians in the United States

The conditions and histories of colonized indigenous peoples around the world vary greatly, and they have been called by different labels (e.g., aboriginals, native peoples, First Nation peoples, indigenous peoples). Nonetheless, they share similar experiences and political processes, whether in the New World, the Old World, the northern hemisphere, or the southern hemisphere (Perry 1996; Wilkins and Lomawaima 2001; Champagne 2005). To highlight the difficulties of indigenous peoples in modern neocolonial democracies, this analysis focuses on arguably the best example (or best documented example) of the difficulties of policing subordinate sovereign populations. This occurs among Native American tribes in the United States, who in popular reference and in formal federal law are called "American Indians." Note, however, that the insights and conclusions are by no means limited to this particular population; the historical details may be specific to the United States but the underlying processes are universal, as Perry's (1996) global review shows.

Surprisingly, the first pattern to notice is that indigenous tribal peoples seldom have police (in the meaning that the term has today). Most scholars on law and justice among Native American tribes argue that policing " ... in the way that it has been practiced in Indian Country during the twentieth century, is a foreign concept to most Native American communities" (Luna 1998, 75).

Policing did not occur among Native American peoples as a distinct and identifiable activity but was accomplished as an integral function of the social order of daily social interactions and relationships among tribal members. It did not require a separate, formally designated and specialized police force or justice system to maintain social order, and no Native American group had a tribal position identifiable as a "policeman" or organization identifiable as "the police." In its aboriginal form, policing in American Indian tribes was accomplished through informal social control mechanisms reliant upon embarrassment, shaming, and social appeals to a collective "harmony ethic" to control most deviant behavior (French 2005; Peak 1989). Interpersonal transgressions, such as insults, thefts, assaults, and even homicides, were viewed as civil disputes or harms between the involved individuals and their families—i.e., more as torts—to be settled between the conflicting kinship groups by compensation or conciliation. They were seldom regarded as crimes, in the sense of legal wrongs against the entire tribe to be formally adjudicated and punished by tribal institutions.

On those occasion when stronger, more forceful enforcement actions were needed to deal with more serious violations and threats to the communal safety of the tribe, these were accomplished without formal ceremony by the elders of the tribe or by warrior subsocieties, e.g., the *akicita* of American Great Plains tribes (Barker 1998; Humphrey 1942; Wissler 1916). The latter were sometimes empowered to apprehend and punish offenders, but these policing powers were limited in scope, rarely used, and only temporarily assigned to groups who had other primary functions. These did not constitute an identifiable police force. Thus, the Anglo-European concept of policing as a specialized function of a formally designated police agency was unknown or unneeded, because policing occurred as an organic element of communal tribal life and social structure.

Scholarly research on policing suggests that *the police* as a separate, formal mechanism of social control and rule-enforcement is historically linked to the emergence of *the state* as a formal, specialized political structure and the development of *the law* as a formal codified body of rules and procedures (e.g., Robinson, Scaglion, and Olivero 1994). In kinship-based, tribal, stateless societies like most Native American tribes, operating with unwritten codes and traditions, such elaborations are unnecessary and absent. Thus, the history of policing in American Indian communities reflects a progressive and lopsided conflict between traditional kinship-based democratic values of Indian tribal societies and the modern autocratic state-based values of colonizer nations. It represents an evolving autocratic process in which policing systems were externally imposed on Native American communities, rather than the democratic process by which police systems emerged out of community practices.

To illustrate this process the following sections provide a summary historical overview of the policing of American Indian/Native American tribes over the past three centuries. For reference, Figure 1 provides a summary chart of the major periods or eras in U.S.-Indian relations and policies over this period.

Figure 1 Major Eras in U.S. Policy toward Indian Tribal Policing

I. *Vassal State Era* (up through early 1800s)

Indian tribes were regarded as *semi-sovereign nations* to be dealt with militarily— either through use of military force or through treaties negotiated by military officers. Harmful actions occurring between Indians and non-Indians were "international" issues to be corrected through military or diplomatic interventions. Harmful actions occurring between Indians were regarded as internal matters resolved within the Indian nations.

II. *Removal Era* (1820s through 1840s)

Indian tribes were redefined as *domestic dependents* who could be moved out of the way for economic and political expansion of Indian lands. The military remained the primary police agency to insure using military force that tribes were relocated to the designated Indian Territory west of the Mississippi River and stayed within that territory.

III. *Reservation Era* (1850s through early 1880s)

Reservations were developed under the Department of Interior, and policing was shifted from exclusively military to increasingly civilian agencies. Late in this period, many tribes developed their own tribal police to handle crimes between Indians and to maintain order on the reservation. By 1880 most reservation had their own tribal police forces, organized and administered by the local Indian Affairs agent but staffed by Indians.

IV. *Allotment and Assimilation Era* (late 1880s through early 1920s)

Reservation lands were converted into individual property parcels and allotted to individual tribal members to become their personal property. A majority of tribal lands were sold or forfeited away to non-Indians; tribal memberships were dramatically reduced through allotment of private property; tribal governments were dramatically weakened. Tribal police forces fell into disuse or misuse, and most were discontinued.

V. *Reorganization Era* (1930s and 1940s)

The arrival of the New Deal brought a shift in federal attitudes about Indian tribes and the *Indian Reorganization Act of 1934.* This reversed the policies of allotment and assimilation, and it provided federal support for reorganizing tribal governments and reestablishing tribal justice systems, including police, under BIA guidelines and direction. These reforms were cut short by World War II and were cut off in the ideological changes that followed the war.

VI. *Termination Era* (1950s and 1960s)

Federal recognition was withdrawn for many tribes through congressional acts; *Public Law 83-280* in 1953 transferred legal jurisdiction over Indian tribes in six "mandatory" states from federal to state governments; another nine "optional" states accomplished the transfer of jurisdiction over Indian tribes by formal requests from state legislatures. For tribes in the affected states, these changes put Indian tribes under local justice authority and police jurisdiction; they ended all federal support and funding for tribal police forces.

VII. *Self-Determination Era* (1970s through 1990s)

The civil rights movement of the 1960s prompted another renewal of support for recognizing Indian tribes and tribal self-governance. Passage of the *Indian Self-Determination and Education Assistance Act* in 1975 (*Public Law 93-638*) provided federal funding for tribal governments and allowed PL-280 states to retrocede jurisdiction over Indian reservations and lands back to the Federal government. Other legislation restricted application of PL-280 to optional states and required tribal consent for changes in jurisdiction. Increased formal recognition of tribal groups also increased to over 500 tribes.

The Vassal State Era (late 1770s–1820s)

With the arrival of Europeans in North American in the seventeenth and eighteenth centuries, the occurrence of social control and rule enforcement in Native American populations as organic parts of tribal life did not change much. Indigenous tribes were regarded by the colonizing British and French governments as sovereign nations whose domestic social control practices were internal tribal matters to be decided by the tribes themselves. The initial relations between European and Indigenous nations were based on treaties between them, involving mutual recognition of sovereignty by which each recognizes the national autonomy of the other and agrees to "live and let live" according to their separate laws and customs (Washburn 1995; Williams 1990).

After independence was gained from England, the view of Indian tribes as sovereign nations continued but with an additional overlay of federal domination. Increasing numbers of nonnative settlements and military forces shifted the balance of political power more strongly toward the newly established and expanding nation. In this context, Indian nations were not seen as equals but "semi-sovereign vassal states"—separate and nominally autonomous nations but subordinate to the U.S. government. "Indian affairs" were viewed as military matters under the jurisdiction of the War Department of the U.S. government, where the Office of Indian Affairs was initially located. Such matters entailed the regulation of interactions between Indians and non-Indians as a military responsibility of the national government. In contrast, the internal governance of Native tribal communities and policing of interactions among tribal members remained an internal matter to be handled by tribal communities themselves following their own traditional practices (Barlow 1994; Deloria and Lytle 1983; French 2003).

Most native tribes continued to follow traditional customs after the European arrival; however, some Indian tribes adapted to the increasing colonial influence by adopting many social customs and practices of Anglo-European society. Most notable were the "Five Civilized Tribes" of the Cherokee, Chocktaw, Chickasaw, Creek, and Seminole—so called because they more readily adopted many of the social practices and structures of Euro-American society; these included such non-Indian customs as written languages, Christianity, and the practice of slavery. The adaptation also included some use of rudimentary tribal police forces, which appeared first among these tribes in the late 1790s and early 1800s in an effort to control horse theft. The first permanent Indian police force in the United States seems to have occurred with the creation of the Lighthorse Guard by the Cherokee tribe in 1808 (French 2005; Hagan 1966); its name denoted a type of mounted cavalry, suggestive of an English paramilitary unit. Other than these, Indian tribal policing remained traditional and an internal matter for each tribe to determine according to its cultural traditions.

The Removal Era (1830s–1840s)

With dramatic growth and expansion of the United States during the first decades of the nineteenth century, tribal lands increasingly attracted non-Indian interest for their natural resources as well as the land itself. This resulted in increased conflict, acts of aggression, and warfare between Native tribes and nonnative settlers. In this context, continued recognition of Indian tribes as semi-sovereign nations became increasingly unpopular and subject to political reinterpretation. A series of legislative enactments and court decisions extended federal jurisdiction over events in Indian lands until Indian tribes were redefined as "domestic dependents" (as a child to a parent) rather than as autonomous-but-subordinate sovereigns. The legal terms of prior treaties with Native tribes were reexamined and revised, so that tribal populations became increasingly subject to federal regulation and control, despite the egalitarian terms of prior treaties. This culminated in widely popular support (especially in the Southern states) for a national policy of "Indian removal" to relocate Indian tribes outside the land area coveted for nonnative expansion efforts.

Responding to the growing demands for native-occupied land, the U.S. Congress passed the *Indian Removal Act* of 1830 mandating the relocation of Indian tribes to the area west of the Mississippi River, designated as "Indian country" and covering the modern-day states of Oklahoma, Kansas, and Nebraska. The *Removal Act* authorized the federal government to negotiate treaties with all Eastern Indian tribes in which they would exchange their traditional tribal lands in the East for new lands in the West, and then to enforce their migration to their new territory. The relocation treaties were accomplished with many, but not all, tribes and often with considerable pressure and subterfuge by federal agents. The treaty with the Cherokee tribe was not actually negotiated with the elected tribal leadership but with a smaller faction of tribal members agreeable to relocation. Other tribes, such as the Seminoles and the Creeks, aggressively resisted signing treaties, but ultimately were militarily subdued and compelled to migrate. These migrations, accomplished under the military authority of the U.S. Army, were devastating in their effects on tribal populations and social structures. For example, during the "Trail of Tears" relocation of the Cherokee from Georgia to Oklahoma in 1838–39, an estimated one-fourth of the original population died from exposure, disease, and starvation. During this period, the U.S. Army served as the de facto police agency for social control of Indian tribes and continued in this role even after relocation to their new territories in the West.

The Enculturation Era (1850s–early 1880s)

The relocation of Eastern Indian Tribes to new territories in the West in the 1830s and 1840s changed the nature of the "Indian problem" for the U.S. government and the policing problem for tribal communities. The process of relocation into new locations severely disorganized traditional tribal structures and social orders, and left tribal communities weakened and dependent. In the new ecological settings Indian tribes were unable to sustain traditional economies and became increasingly "wards of the state," dependent on the U.S. government for sustenance and support. In 1849, Congress transferred the Indian Affairs Office from the Department of War to the newly created Department of the Interior, reflecting the transformation of "the Indian problem" from a military problem of handling conflicts with external nations into an internal problem of managing domestic populations. In these terms, solving "the Indian problem" meant civilly controlling the populations of people exiled in Indian country, while encouraging these populations to become more "American" and less "Indian."

Initially during this period, policing of Native populations was handled as a matter of martial law with policing provided by the U.S. Army. This practice was less than ideal, because military force may be effective in compelling people to travel from one place to another, but it is ineffective in making them assimilate. However, military policing was maintained even after the transfer of Indian Affairs to the Department of Interior because there were few administrative alternatives. There were no federal civil mechanisms for administering peacetime autocratic police authority over internal populations of U.S. residents or for governing colonized territories. Traditional tribal mechanisms of social control had been severely weakened or neutralized by the Western dislocation, and the Office of Indian Affairs included no separate agency for policing Indian reservations.

The reliance on the army to provide policing became especially problematic when tribal lands and communities were formally organized into reservations in the late 1860s, which were intended to bring about assimilation and protection of native populations. To deal with the absence of civil policing mechanisms, tribal police officers began to appear on many reservations in the early 1870s to provide some measure of tribal law enforcement, independent of the U.S. military. The first use of tribal police officers occurred among the Iowa, Sac, and Fox tribes in Nebraska in 1869, followed by the Navaho tribe in Arizona in 1872 and the San Carlos Apache reservation in Arizona in 1874 (Peak 1989). The effectiveness of these tribal police agencies gradually convinced even skeptics of their utility (over the continued reliance on military force). In fact, the San Carlos Apache police force accomplished what the U.S. Army could not—namely, the surrender of the renegade leader Geronimo without bloodshed (Wachtel 1982). During the 1870s, tribal police were established by Indian agents on many of the major reservations (Barlow 1994) and by 1881 almost three quarters of all Indian reservations in the U.S. had tribal police forces (Peak 1989).

The adoption of Euro-American-style justice and law enforcement practices by Indian tribes was a central part of the nineteenth-century philosophy of "civilizing the Indian tribes" to adopt more modern Western cultural values, customs, and social structures while abandoning their native heathen traditions. The ultimate goal was the *assimilation* of Native Americans into U.S. society as modernized, civilized citizens, although complete equality was not really expected given the racial ideologies of the era that viewed Indians as generally inferior.

Although the development of tribal police forces in the 1870s and 1880s suggests a serious federal policy of encouraging increased tribal self-governance and self-policing, this is somewhat illusory. The tribal police forces, although staffed by Native American officers, were set up by Indian Affairs agents who administered and controlled their activities. The Native tribal police officers were poorly supported and were responsible for providing their own weapons and horses. Moreover, the administrative process by which tribal police officers were appointed and supervised by nonnative Indian Affairs agents effectively undermined traditional tribal governance and leadership structures. It made the selection of important tribal positions (such as police officers or judges) outside of traditional tribal democratic processes and dependent on pleasing federal administrators.

Moreover, tribally administered police and courts were permitted only as long as they yielded outcomes agreeable to outside nontribal interests, especially to the sensibilities of the large nonnative community outside the reservation. When tribal actions or decisions diverged from Anglo-European ideas of justice, support for autonomous tribal police and courts quickly faded. Following the particularly controversial Crow Dog case in the mid-1880s in which the tribal courts assigned a sentence consistent with tribal laws but at odds with outside non-Indian law, the federal government reasserted outside control over reservation justice processes. Congress enacted the *Major Crimes Act* in 1885, which assigned the federal government exclusive legal jurisdiction over almost all major crimes occurring within Indian lands and reservations (including those between tribal members). It left only minor crimes or violations of tribal codes involving only tribal members under Indian police jurisdiction. This greatly diminished the authority and importance of the tribal police and it gave the Office of Indian Affairs much greater autocratic police control over what went on within Native American reservations and communities. It also blocked Native tribal communities from using traditional justice procedures and punishments for criminal acts committed by Indians on Indian land (Peak 1989), a limitation that continues to the present day.

The Allotment Era (late 1880s–1920s)

The changes in the mid-1880s (e.g., the *Major Crimes Act, 1885*) signaled an ideological shift in the general strategy for civilizing American Indian populations—namely, a move away from the policy of assimilation by gradual conversion to a more immediate strategy of tribal dissolution by eliminating the salience and importance of tribal memberships and by dismantling reservations as federally protected tribal homelands. The intent was to diminish tribes as the organizing principle of Indian life and to force Native Americans to be individual U.S. citizens rather than Native tribal members. The means by which Native Americans were to be detribalized and individualized as independent, productive American citizens was through the ownership of *private property*. The prevailing ideology of the era was that ownership of private property had "mystical magical qualities about it that lead people directly to a 'civilized state.' The expressed feeling was that teaching the Indian the value of private property and individualism was an essential step toward integration" (Barlow 1994, 149).

This was formally accomplished in 1887 by federal passage of the *Dawes Severalty Act* (also called the *General Allotment Act*). This act authorized the division of tribal reservations into separate 160-acre parcels, which were allotted to individual tribal members who would eventually acquire them as personal private property (if they lived, farmed, and paid taxes on the parcels for ten years). The policy of allotment directly detribalized Native American peoples in several fundamental ways. The first was the physical reduction of reservation lands that had been owned in common by tribal members and had been protected from encroachment or alienation by federal law. Dividing up the tribal land into smaller privately owned parcels removed this protection, and resulted in the loss of most of tribal lands and transfer to nonnative ownership. Many individual parcels were sold to nonnative buyers or were lost to tax foreclosures. "Surplus" tribal land (i.e., not allotted to individual tribal members) was sold off, invariably to nontribal, nonnative owners. The second effect of the loss of tribal lands was cultural or spiritual, because the tribes' sense of community, tribal culture, and social structure were dependent on communal ownership of the lands on which tribal members lived together. As the land was divided and individually allotted, the basis for tribal unity and traditional leadership was greatly reduced. Individual ownership of property reinforced individuality and self-interest, which were foreign to most Native American cultures. Allocation of rewards and resources was also a traditional way in which tribes implemented their leadership structures. The federally mandated allotment completely invalidated this process and weakened achievement of stable tribal leadership. A third result was dramatic reduction in tribal membership by the removal of Native individuals from the tribes as they received their personal shares of tribal land. As tribal members accepted ownership of their allotted individual land parcels, they simultaneously lost their official status as communal members of federally protected Indian tribes. They officially became mere property-holding citizens, rather than Native American tribal members. By this process, Indian tribes were gradually reduced in population size, as well as in social organization, political influence, and property ownership.

The policy of detribalization through allotment continued from the late 1880s through the first three decades of the twentieth century. The impact of allotment on the social, political, and economic conditions of American Indian populations was devastating. Many smaller tribes were simply erased, while even larger, better organized tribes struggled to maintain tribal social organization and identity. Reserved tribal land holdings were dramatically reduced from 138 million acres in the late 1880s to about 48 million acres in the 1920s through a combination of politically misguided and malfeasant processes. Tribal memberships lapsed and blurred, and most members moved away from tribal lands where they fared badly as an economically and politically marginal racial minority. Although the *Allotment Act* (1887) was avowedly enacted to force Native Americans to become "typical American citizens," they were not formally granted full national citizenship until 1924 and did not gain full citizenship (e.g., right to vote) in some states until the 1940s (Wilkinson 2005; Deloria and Lytle 1983).

The Reorganization Era (1930s–1940s)

By the 1920s, the wisdom of allotment was being questioned by a number of governmental commissions that acknowledged the failure (and in some cases malignity) of the allotment and assimilation policies (Waldman 2000). The growth of New Deal politics in the 1930s under President Franklin Roosevelt and the appointment of John Collier—an active opponent of allotment—as commissioner of Indian Affairs resulted in a marked reversal of the prior policies. In 1934 Congress passed the *Indian Reorganization Act* (also called the *Wheeler-Howard Act*), aimed at reversing the destructive policies of the preceding four decades and restoring tribal self-governance. This act formally ended the policy of allotment and restored the federal recognition of tribal identity and limited sovereignty. It also provided for reacquisition of tribal lands lost through allotment and reestablishment of tribal self-governments, including the restoration of tribal justice and police systems. Although the *Indian Reorganization Act* was a radical reversal of the strategy of allotment, it reflected some inevitable political compromises that moderated its accomplishments and it continued to receive strong political opposition and criticism. Although aimed at increasing tribal autonomy, the *Indian Reorganization Act* actually extended federal jurisdiction over many activities within Indian Country, although with more benign motives. Although it authorized and funded Native American reservations to reorganize their tribal governments, they did so only by adopting federally approved practices and Anglo-American legal values, rather than traditional tribal ways. Almost all tribal policy creation and governance practices were subject to approval or veto by officials in the federal Office of Indian Affairs. The reorganized Indian courts and police were limited in their jurisdiction to less serious crime and legal matters as a continuing legacy of the *Major Crimes Act*. Serious crimes and legal decisions remained under the jurisdiction of the federal government, as they still are today.

The Termination Era (late 1940s–early 1960s)

Overall, the *Indian Reorganization Act* was an important rejection of the tribally destructive policies of the late nineteenth and early twentieth centuries and initiated the development of tribal self-policing. However, the well-intentioned reforms it introduced were short-lived. They fell into neglect during the World War II (with a dramatic reduction in the number of tribal police officers funded) and were radically overturned during the Eisenhower administration (1953–60). In the political and economic recovery after World War II, a policy of "termination" was initiated by which tribes as federally protected, legally sovereign communal entities would be eliminated and replaced by economically viable corporate enterprises made up of economically autonomous citizens. With this policy, members of Indian tribes would be assimilated into the general population as free and equal participants in the national economy, Indian communities would be liberated from the onus of federal supervision and intrusion, and the federal government would be liberated from the onus of managing Indian reservations. Termination of tribal sovereignty arguably would lead to more freedom, less federal government, more economic prosperity, and greater local integration of Indian peoples into the states where their reservations were located.

The political doctrine of "termination" was formally implemented in several major pieces of federal legislation in the early 1950s. *House Concurrent Resolution 108* was passed in 1953, and it explicitly resolved that assimilation of Native Americans into U.S. society would occur by terminating federal recognition, responsibility, and treaty obligations for many native tribes. It gave official expression to federal intention to terminate the subordinate sovereign status of native peoples. *Public Law 83-280* (PL-280) was passed later the same year, and mandated the transfer of federal jurisdiction over Indian tribes in six states to their state governments and removed the special federal trusteeship status of the Native tribes in those states. Beyond the six mandatory transfer states, the law also provided an option to the remaining states to implement a similar transfer of jurisdiction over Native peoples and lands within their borders if they enacted appropriate enabling legislation. Ten additional states did so. Passage of PL-280 was followed by a flurry of additional federal legislation aimed at withdrawing federal recognition of specific American Indian tribes and of making their lands available as private property.

Under PL-280 transfers, tribal members living on Native-owned lands were policed by state and local nonnative police agencies, and they were subject to state and local legal systems, like all other residents of the states where the reservations or lands were located. They retained no special protection or recognition as semi-sovereign groups with whom legal treaties had been signed. In total, the federal trusteeship relationship with hundreds of Native tribes and tribal bands was terminated (Waldman 2000, 221) and many lost ownership of almost all of their tribal reservation lands. As Jimenez and Song (1998) note:

> By enacting Public Law 280, Congress disregarded the historical trust relationship that existed between the Federal Government and the Indian tribes. Indian country law enforcement was exclusively a federal-tribal responsibility, but with Public Law 280, Congress ignored history and tradition and treated Indians *like any other citizens,* removing their historic insulation from state authority (1664).

The PL-280 legislation had several major shortcomings as major legislation for reversing two centuries of American Indian policy. One was that Indian tribes had no voice in whether or not this policy was implemented. It was merely forced on them without consultation or consent by the U.S. Congress in the mandatory states and by the state legislatures in the optional states. This resulted in a profound sense of injustice and illegitimacy among many tribes. The second problem was that PL-280 provided no funds to the states for assuming the additional responsibilities of policing lands within Indian reservations, so it represented an unfunded and generally unfulfilled mandate. Where previously they had weak and inconsistent federal police services, most affected reservations and tribes now found themselves with no police services at all. A third problem was the prejudiced and often hostile relationships that existed between Natives and nonnatives in many areas where PL-280 was applied, making tribal members even more subject to abuse and discrimination, and even more wary of and hostile to law enforcement. A fourth problem was the arbitrary selectivity it enacted into the law—i.e., applying mandatorily to some states but optionally to others, as well as applying to only some tribes in affected states. This meant that the confusing patchwork of legal jurisdiction over criminal offenses involving Native American persons or lands became even more complex, varying drastically from one state to the next and even from tribe to tribe within a single state.

The Self-Determination Era (late 1960s–present)

Although the impact of PL-280 was demonstrably harmful, the policies of the termination strategy were also short lived, lasting less than a decade. Several developments in the 1960s encouraged abandoning termination as government policy and led to the renewed promotion of "Indian self-determination."

One factor was the resurgence of New Deal politics in the Great Society programs under Presidents Kennedy and Johnson. These featured a renewed activist role for the federal government in protecting the interests and fortunes of disadvantaged minorities, resulting in the passage of the *Indian Civil Rights Act* (ICRA) in 1968 to promote tribal self-governance and self-determination. Beyond affirming that the Bill of Rights and the *Civil Rights Act* of 1964 applied to residents of Indian reservations, the *Indian Civil Rights Act* amended PL-280 to significantly restrict the optional transfer of legal jurisdiction over Indian tribes from federal to state governments by requiring tribal approval for the transfer to occur. Significantly, after this latter limitation was enacted, no tribe consented to such a jurisdictional transfer. The ICRA also amended the original provisions of PL-280 by allowing states to "retrocede" jurisdiction over Indian tribes back to the federal government upon passage of appropriate legislation by state governments. Eventually thirty tribes in PL-280 states were retroceded back to federal jurisdiction. Also in 1968, Congress passed the *Omnibus Crime Control and Safe Streets Act* that, which, although primarily aimed at reducing urban crime problems in large cities and major metropolitan centers, included significant funding for the rebuilding of Indian criminal justice systems, especially the courts and policing agencies.

Because the 1960s were a period of considerable social activism regarding civil rights—Indian tribes themselves provided a major impetus for revising and liberalizing federal Indian affairs policies. Many tribes, as well as pantribal organizations like the American Indian Movement (AIM), adopted a more activist, confrontational, militant stance in demanding a greater degree of tribal self-determination as well as fair compensation for past wrongs by the U.S. government. These activities, along with a growing number of critical reports produced by various governmental commissions, led to the passage of the *Indian Self-Determination and Education Assistance Act* in 1975, also known as *Public Law 93-638* (PL-638). This law authorized a political mechanism for tribes to assume responsibility for many of the governance services administered by the federal government. *Public Law 98-638* provided for tribal self-governance to be accomplished through contracts negotiated by each tribe with federal agencies, such as the Department of the Interior and the Department of Health and Human Services, that provide federal funding for tribally administered agencies, including social services, tribal courts, and police forces. Critics noted that, although this does provide for tribal self-governance and self-policing, it does so under terms that determine the kinds of police agencies being adopted—namely, following modern Anglo-American, nonnative police procedures.

In response to criticisms of PL-638, additional amendments (i.e., the *Indian Self-Governance Act* of 1994) subsequently provided for more liberalized avenues of self-governance. According to Waldman (2000), federal programs supporting tribal development declined somewhat during the 1980s and 1990s due to cutbacks in funding for domestic programs generally; however, "the federal government continues to back nominally the principles of Indian self-determination" (Waldman 2000, 224), at least in principle. Of particular note in this regard was the dramatic expansion during the 1990s in officially granting federal recognition to Indian tribes. By 1996, approximately 500 tribes had been granted official federal recognition (Luna 1998), and by 2008 the number of federally recognized "tribal entities" had reached 564 (Bureau of Indian Affairs [BIA] 2008).

Calling this most recent phase in U.S. Indian Affairs the era of "Self-Determination" perhaps overstates the case for the changes made, which provide only partial and limited self-determination. However, it has been a notable era of "Reestablishment," in which tribal recognition, federal trusteeship, and some measure of tribal self-governance were reestablished after being nearly extinguished during the decade of termination. Governance and policing of Native American reservations has remained fundamentally autocratic and under federal control, even as tribal governance has been encouraged. It can be argued that during this period the administrative and bureaucratic reach of the Bureau of Indian Affairs (BIA) expanded and extended over a wider range of tribal operations, as well as becoming more centralized for more efficient federal supervision of tribal concerns. The *Indian Civil Rights Act* of 1968 extended federal oversight and legal restrictions over tribal courts. The *Indian Law Enforcement Reform Act* of 1990 enhanced the administration of law enforcement services within the BIA, shifting the administration of federally provided tribal police forces from local to national command and centralizing the training of tribal police officers in a national training academy under the auspices of the FBI. The federalization of tribal policing provides for more services and support to Native American communities, but it limits tribal autonomy and sovereignty by providing nationally standardized and supervised supports.

Surprisingly, after all the legislative enactments and tribal lobbying in recent decades, PL-280 remains on the books. It was never rescinded or repealed, despite considerable legislative reforms to modify its harmful effects, and it still greatly limits Native tribal efforts in affected states to govern and police themselves. The *Major Crimes Act* (1885) also remains in effect, and it continues to hinder Native American efforts at self-policing by limiting Indian tribal jurisdiction to enforcement of mainly minor or tribal crimes occurring between tribal members. The jurisdictional complexities created by the *Major Crimes Act* and greatly magnified by PL-280 have not been substantially reduced or clarified. Arguably they have been made even more complicated by recent court cases and by the selective, incomplete pattern of retrocessions of some Native tribes in states affected by PL-280 back to the federal government. The retrocessions in the 1980s and 1990s of many tribes in PL-280 states from state jurisdiction did not grant them full autonomy, but rather returned them to federal jurisdiction and trusteeship. In most cases, that led to better funding due to deeper federal pockets and to more resources. However, it also led to greater federalization and national standardization of federal support, which works against restoration of substantial tribal autonomy. Critics have noted that the overall posture of the federal government toward Indian tribes remains somewhat paternalistic, bureaucratic, and elitist, and that it is still pervasively distrusted by many tribal members who favor self-government on tribal terms.

Contemporary Forms of Tribal Policing

What kinds of police system currently apply to Native Americans in the United States? For the majority of Native Americans, policing is ordinary and nontribal, because almost two-thirds of persons identified as "American Indian/Alaskan Native" in the United States live outside of areas considered "Indian country" (i.e., formally designated as tribal areas or reservations) (Perry 2005). The majority of Native Americans, even formally enrolled tribal members, live in general population communities and are policed by the local general-jurisdiction police departments of the state in which they live. Because they live outside designated tribal areas, they are not subject to tribal or reservation police jurisdiction, except when they travel on reservation land. Thus, the issue of distinctive Native or tribal policing is only relevant to the approximately 36 percent of the Native American population who live on tribal reservations or other federally reserved areas. For those living in identified Native American reservations, policing occurs in three basic forms, depending on who has jurisdiction over the community and who is responsible for administering the police agencies. The first two represent autocratic policing by outside governments and sovereignties, although the third represents more democratic self-policing by the tribes themselves.

The first policing format is found in reservations that are under PL-280. Here the police are externally provided by local nontribal governments in whose legal jurisdiction the tribal reservations are located—state, county, and (sometimes) municipal. It is difficult to tell how many Native tribal communities in the United States this involves and how well it works for these communities, because there are no governmental statistics available on this issue and little independent research has been done on policing PL-280 reservations (Gold-berg and Singleton 1998). Because PL-280 has been applied selectively to tribes—some tribes have been retroceded back to federal jurisdiction, some have not—there is no definite list or count of tribes in this situation. Luna (1998) estimates that there were 145 tribal communities in 1996 with this type of po-lice service, but this seems low considering the more than 200 tribal villages and communities in Alaska (a mandatory PL-280 state). This form of policing is an explicitly autocratic form of tribal policing, which is dependent on rela-tionships with local nontribal populations and on local nonnative govern-mental policies. According to anecdotal information, this form of policing sometimes results in heavy-handed, racially oppressive policing of tribal pop-ulation by local police, whereas in others it results in an absence of policing of tribal communities (which are left to fend for themselves). Where reservations and their surrounding communities have more positive, cooperative relations, this type of tribal policing may be satisfactory even if autocratic and external.

The second form of external policing applies to reservations that are not under PL-280 and thus under federal jurisdiction and protection. Here, police departments are often supplied and administered by the BIA, an external fed-eral agency within the U.S. Department of the Interior. This is an "old" method of policing Native communities, going back to the Indian reservations of the late 1800s, when reservation superintendents or Indian Agents appointed and supervised local groups of officers (both tribal and nontribal) to maintain order on the reservations. As the BIA was expanded and bureaucratically cen-tralized in the twentieth century, this form of policing became more prevalent and professional. It was the most prevalent form of tribal policing through the 1990s when federal programs began to encourage and support tribes devel-oping their own tribally administered police departments. According to re-ports by Luna (1998) and Wakeling, Jorgensen, Michaelson, and Begay (2001), a substantial number of reservations are still policed mainly by external BIA po-lice departments, but, again, there are no public statistics and little published research. It seems plausible that BIA-provided policing is gradually being re-placed by more democratic forms of tribal self-policing, given the increased fed-eral funding and support for it. However, it is also possible that tribal self-administered police are supplementing, rather than replacing, the tradi-tional federally administered reservation police. Autocratic police systems his-torically have proven resistant to removal and replacement, often being retained even as more democratic forms as implemented. Research and data on the op-eration of BIA-administered police on Native American reservations has been effectively shut down for more than a decade due to a lawsuit by Native tribal members against the Department of the Interior over their past management of tribal resources and monies.

The third format for policing Native American communities involves police administered locally by the tribes or reservations themselves. This is the most democratic arrangement for providing police Native American reservations, because the police are accountable to and controlled by the tribal community itself, rather than outside governments or organizations. According to recent surveys (Hickman 2003; Luna 1998; Perry 2005), this form of policing arrangement has noticeably increased over the past several decades, made possible by a number of political and legal developments (listed earlier). Tribally administered police departments may be further distinguished by the funding source for the tribal agencies. External money for tribal administration often comes with "strings attached," which limits the ability of tribal governments to be completely independent of outside direction or influence. When the funding comes from the tribes' own revenue sources, police agencies operate more autonomously, constrained only by the legal limitations or requirements imposed by federal law (because tribal sovereignty is subordinate to the sovereignty of the national government). In recent years, the ability of some tribes to be sufficiently self-supporting to fund their own governmental programs—such as police departments—has improved with the expansion of tribal-based casino gambling as well as increased tribal investment in other economic ventures. Thus, a significant number of reservations (at least sixty, involving mainly larger and longer established tribes) are able to both fund and administer their own police (Luna 1998; Wakeling et al. 2001). This is the most democratic situation for tribal policing, because it affords the greatest autonomy and self-sufficiency to the tribal community.

The other method of funding tribally self-administered police relies on the availability of federal grants and contracts implemented to support self-governance by Native American tribal communities. The principal means by which this is done is through the *Indian Self-Determination and Education Assistance Act* of 1975—also known as *Public Law 638* (PL-638). Using federal program, tribes apply to the BIA to receive contracts that provide the funds for the tribal police departments; the agencies are administered locally by the tribal governments under conditions set out in the PL-683 contracts. According to recent studies (Luna 1998; Wakeling et al. 2001), this represents the most common arrangement for tribal self-administration, with over half of the tribal police agencies in the U.S. administered under PL-683 contracts. The trend seems to be increasing numbers of this format, because additional federal sources of funding for tribal police and justice systems have been developed, notably the Community Oriented Policing Services program. Under PL-638 arrangements, the federal funding source retains some oversight over the general structure and operation of tribal police departments to ensure that the terms of the PL-638 contract are met, but does not provide "hands-on" administration of the police departments. Thus, the extent to which PL-638 or similar contracts can actually produce democratic police systems on Native reservations depends on the flexibility with which the funding is provided. To date these programs seem to have been successful in shifting the policing of indigenous tribal communities from strongly autocratic (imposed by outside governments) to increasingly democratic (administered by the tribal communities themselves). This trend is supported currently by most political interests in the United States, whether conservative or liberal, and it can be noted in a number of similarly neocolonial countries around the world, most obviously in Canada, New Zealand, and Australia.

Conclusion

This chapter presented an overview of the history of political efforts in the United States to create police systems for maintaining order in Native American tribal communities and reservations. This has been a vexing problem for a democratically governed nation with a colonial past—namely, how to carry out policing of an internally colonized subordinate sovereign people without setting up an autocratic police state. Although the discussion focused on one particular nation, the United States, the results are certainly not unique. Perry (1996) notes that similar patterns can be found in many other modern countries (and regions) with histories of colonial settlement and displacement of indigenous minorities, including the United States, Canada, Australia, New Zealand, Central and South America, the South Pacific, southern Africa, East Africa, and even Siberia. They do not have exactly identical patterns, but they are surprisingly similar in their basic problems and developments.

Although the overall history of policing Native American communities in the United States has clearly favored autocratic systems, this has not remained constant but varied noticeably over the last 200 years. The changes in policing Native American communities has not been a gradual evolutionary transition from autocratic to democratic systems. Rather, the history displays a pattern of oscillation rather than evolution—i.e., repeated switching back-and-forth between different forms of autocratic policing with an occasional and brief attempt at more democratic policing practices. The historical flip-flop pattern in tribal policing appears to correlate strongly with historical shifts in political ideology, in popular attitudes toward Native Americans as a racial minority, and in economic fluctuations (when native property or resources became more valuable). The changes in attitudes about policing Native Americans matches the wide swings between conservative and liberal governance eras that are characteristic of popular democracies (which are famous for their responsiveness to large shifts in popular sentiments and ideological moods). Those historical eras when the federal government viewed Native American tribes as *subordinate sovereigns* within a trustee-beneficiary relationship—i.e., having legitimate rights to claims of political autonomy, self-governance, and territorial integrity—correspond to the liberal periods for Native American communities when federal police systems were less oppressive and autocratic. The historical eras when Native Americans were seen as *domestic dependents* in a ward-guardian relationship—as children to a parent who needs to exercise firm control and strong discipline to ensure proper development—correspond to more autocratic, dictatorial, aggressively strategies for controlling Native Americans and reflect a more conservative view of native sovereignty (Wilkins and Lomawaima 2001). Thus, the historical record suggests a strong link between policing and governance methods, a pattern that seems to be repeated in many other neocolonial countries.

Web Sources

1. Annotated Bibliography for an Understanding of Tribal Governance (Wilkinson & Ulrich):
    http://muse.jhu.edu/journals/wicazo_sa_review/v017/17.1wilkinson.html
2. Indigenous Peoples Issues and Resources (world-wide)
    http://indigenouspeoplesissues.com
3. Aboriginal People of Canada:
    http://www.geocities.com/SoHo/Atrium/4332/abor2.htm?200927
4. Indigenous Peoples and the Law:
    http://www.kennett.co.nz/law/indigenous/
5. Indian Country Tribal Jurisdiction in the United States:
    http://tribaljurisdiction.tripod.com/index.html
6. Law Enforcement and Tribal Courts—National Congress of American Indians:
    http://www.ncai.org/Law-Enforcement-and-Tribal-Cou.34.0.html
7. Public Law 280: Tribal Court Clearinghouse:
    http://www.tribal-institute.org/lists/pl280.htm
8. National Criminal Justice References Service—Tribal Justice Publications:
    http://www.ncjrs.gov/publications/tribal/index.html

Discussion Questions

1. What are the basic differences between *autocratic* and *democratic* policing? How are these related to the types of governments found in different societies? Do people care which kind of police they have? Which kind of policing is more effective?
2. What does the legal term *subordinate sovereignty* mean and how does this determine a society's ability to govern and police itself? What might be some examples of subordinate sovereignty in other countries?
3. What are *aboriginal* or *indigenous peoples?* What are the legal issues raised by the national governance of such groups of people in modern-day nations such as United States, Canada, or Australia? Are there indigenous peoples located in other countries beside these?
4. What is the difference between *pacified colonies* and *settled colonies?* How might this affect the way that former colonies are policed?
5. Why is democratic policing difficult to implement in many neocolonial societies (e.g., United States, Canada, or Australia) that contain enduring populations of aboriginal or indigenous tribal peoples?
6. According to the discussion of Native Americans in the United States, what would seem to be linkage between the type of governance in a society and the type of police system?

References

Barker, Michael L. *Policing in Indian Country*. Guilderland, NY: Harrow and Heston, 1998.

Barlow, David E. "Minorities Policing Minorities as a Strategy of Social Control: A Historical Analysis of Tribal Police in the United States." *Criminal Justice History: An International Annual* 15 (1994): 141–163.

Bureau of Indian Affairs (BIA). *Tribal Leaders Directory, Winter 2008*. U.S. Department of the Interior, Washington, D.C. Accessed July 20, 2009. http://www.doi.gov/bia/TLD-Final.pdf, 2008.

Champagne, Duane. "Rethinking Native Relations with Contemporary Nation-States." In *Indigenous Peoples and the Modern State*, edited by D. Champagne, K. J. Torjesen, and S. Steiner, 3–23. Walnut Creek, CA: Alta Mira Press, 2005.

Cole, Bankole A. "Post-colonial Systems." In *Policing Across the World: Issues for the Twenty-First Century*, edited by Rob I. Mawby, 88–108. London: UCL Press, 1999.

Deloria, Vine, Jr., and Clifford M. Lytle. *American Indians, American justice.* Austin: University of Texas Press, 1983.

French, Laurence A. *Native American Justice.* Chicago: Burnham, 2003.

_____. "Law Enforcement in Indian Country." *Criminal Justice Studies* 18, no. 1 (2005): 69–80.

Goldberg, Carole, and Heather Valdez Singleton. "Research Priorities: Law Enforcement in Public Law 280 States." Paper presented to Crime and Justice Research in Indian Country Strategic Planning Meeting, National Institute of Justice, U.S. Department of Justice, Portland, OR, 1998. Accessed July 20, 2009. http://www.ncjrs.org/pdffiles1/nij/grants/209926.pdf.

Hagan, William T. *Indian Police and Judges: Experiments in Acculturation and Control.* New Haven, CT: Yale University Press, 1966.

Hickman, Matthew J. *Tribal Law Enforcement, 2000.* Washington, D.C.: U.S. Department of Justice, Bureau of Justice Statistics, 2003.

Humphrey, Norman D. "Police and Tribal Welfare in Plains Indian Cultures." *Journal of Criminal Law and Criminology* 33, no. 2 (1942): 147–161.

Jimenez, Vanessa J., and Soo C. Song. "Concurrent Tribal and State Jurisdiction under Public Law 280." *American University Law Review* 47 (1998): 1627–1707.

Kratcoski, Peter C. "Policing in Democratic Societies: An Historical Overview." In *Challenges of Policing Democracies: A World Perspective,* edited by Dilip K. Das and Otwin Marenin, 23–41. Amsterdam: Gordon and Breach, 2000.

Luna, Eileen. "The Growth and Development of Tribal Police." *Journal of Contemporary Criminal Justice* 14, no. 1 (1998): 75–86.

Marenin, Otwin. "Democracy, Democratization, Democratic Policing." In *Challenges of Policing Democracies: A World Perspective,* edited by Dilip K. Das & Otwin Marenin, 311–331. Amsterdam: Gordon and Breach, 2000.

Nettheim, Garth. "Sovereignty and Aboriginal Peoples." *Aboriginal Law Bulletin* 53, no. 2 (1991): 4–11.

Peak, Ken. "Criminal Justice, Law and Policy in Indian Country: A Historical Perspective." *Journal of Criminal Justice* 17 (1989): 393–407.

Perry, Richard J. *From Time Immemorial: Indigenous Peoples and State Systems.* Austin: University of Texas Press, 1996.

Perry, Steven W. *Census of Tribal Justice Agencies in Indian Country, 2002.* Washington, D.C.: U.S. Department of Justice, Bureau of Justice Statistics, 2005.

Popic, Linda. 2005. "Sovereignty in Law: The Justiciability of Indigenous Sovereignty in Australia, the United States and Canada." *Indigenous Law Journal* 4, no. 1 (2005): 117–157.

Reith, Charles. *The Blind Eye of History: A Study of the Origins of the Present Police Era*. Montclair, NJ: Patterson Smith (first published 1952, London: Faber & Faber), 1975.

Robinson, Cyril D., Richard Scaglion, and Michael J. Olivero. *Police in Contradiction: The Evolution of the Police Function in Society*. Westport, CT: Greenwood Press, 1994.

United Nations. "United Nations Declaration on the Rights of Indigenous Peoples (General Assembly Resolution 61/295)." Accessed July 20, 2009. http://www.un.org/esa/socdev/unpfii/en/drip.html, 2007.

Wachtel, David. "Indian Law Enforcement." In *Indians and Criminal Justice*, edited by Laurence A. French, 109–120. Totowa, NJ: Allanheld, Osmun, 1982.

Wakeling, Stewart, Miriam Jorgensen, Susan Michaelson, and Manley Begay. *Policing on American Indian Reservations: A Report to The National Institute of Justice*. Washington, DC: U.S. Government Printing Office, 2001.

Waldman, Carl. *Atlas of the North American Indian*. Rev. ed. New York: Checkmark Books, 2000.

Washburn, Wilcomb E. *Red Man's Land/White Man's Law: The Past and Present Status of the American Indian*. 2nd ed. Norman: University of Oklahoma Press, 1995.

Wilkins, David E., and K. Tsianina Lomawaima. *Uneven Ground: American Indian Sovereignty and Federal Law*. Norman: University of Oklahoma Press, 2001.

Wilkinson, Charles. *Blood Struggle: The Rise of Modern Indian Nations*. New York: W.W. Norton, 2005.

Williams, Robert A. *The American Indian in Western Legal Thought*. New York: Oxford University Press, 1990.

Wissler, Clark. *Societies of the Plains Indians*. New York: American Museum of Natural History, 1916.

Legislation

Dawes Severalty Act (see General Allotment Act).

General Allotment Act (1887) 14 Stat. 388, as amended 25 U.S.C. §§ 331–359.

House Concurrent Resolution 108 (1953).

Indian Civil Rights Act (ICRA) (1968) 25 U.S.C. §§ 1301–1322.

Indian Law Enforcement Reform Act (1990) 25 U.S.C. § 2801–2809.

Indian Removal Act (1830) 14 Stat. 411–413.

Indian Reorganization Act (1934) 48 Stat. 984, codified 25 U.S.C. § 461 et seq.

Indian Self-Determination and Education Assistance Act (1975) Public Law 93-
    638.
Indian Self-Governance Act (1994) Public Law 103-413.
Major Crimes Act (1885) 18 U.S.C. A.§ 1153.
Omnibus Crime Control and Safe Streets Act (1968) 42 U.S.C. § 3789d.
Public Law 83–280 (1953) 18 U.S.C. 1162, 28 U.S.C. § 1360 & 25 U.S.C.
    §§ 1321–1326.
Public Law 93–638 (1975) 88 Stat. 2203–2802, codified 25 U.S.C. §§ 450a–450n.
Wheeler-Howard Act (see *Indian Reorganization Act*).

Chapter 7

Correctional Systems, Philosophies, and Innovations: A Comparative Perspective

Sesha Kethineni & Sarah McCullough

Introduction

A comparative perspective of correctional population in various countries tells a story about a country's philosophy of punishing offenders. For example, a Pakistani anti-terrorism court recently ordered the noses and ears of two men to be cut off after they had done the same thing to a young woman when her parents refused a marriage proposal from one of the men. In addition to sentencing each man to fifty years in prison, the court ordered the offenders to pay several thousand dollars as compensation to the victim (Associated Press 2009). In India, a female medical student and her male companion were lured by five men and a juvenile onto a bus in New Delhi. They gang raped her and assaulted her with a metal rod, which led to her death a few days later. Of the five men, one committed suicide in jail, four men received the death penalty, and the juvenile (who was seventeen at the time) was given the maximum sentence available for juveniles—three years. Both are examples of violence against women from two different countries with different correctional goals. Pakistan, for example, has elements of Islamic law embedded in their penal code that awards harsh penalties based on retributive philosophy. India, on the other hand, uses common law and harsh penalties are reserved for the most serious offenses. Although there may be some similarities in the punishment of violent offenders worldwide, overall prison population, number of penal institutions, prevention measures, rehabilitation programs, and number of executions provide a better picture of a country's correctional system. This chapter first provides the world imprisonment rates, followed by a discussion of five correctional goals, applicable international standards, sentencing options, including the death penalty, and recent innovations in correctional programs.

World Imprisonment Rates

Worldwide prison populations and imprisonments are compared using the incarceration rates (number incarcerated/total population) × 100,000. The tenth edition of the *World Prison Population List* provides detailed information on the number of prisoners held in 222 countries and the rate of incarcerations. The most recent report covers data through September 2013. According to the report, there are more than 10.2 million people confined in various penal institutions, which include pretrial detainees and convicted offenders. These figures exclude[1] detainees in detention centers in China and prison populations from Eritrea, Guinea Bissau, North Korea, and Somalia. Of the total world prison population, the United States (2.24 million), China (1.64 million), and Russia (0.68 million) account for almost half of the inmates. In addition, these three counties make up just over a quarter of the world's population of 7.1 billion (Walmsley 2013).

Of the countries in the world, the United States is by far the biggest user of prison with a rate of 716 per 100,000 of the population. England and Wales have an incarceration rate of 148 per 100,000, which represents 50 percent more than France, Germany, Ireland, and The Netherlands. Many of the developing countries, including India and Nigeria have low imprisonment rates. India, with a population of over 1.2 billion, has an imprisonment rate of 30 per 100,000 (International Center for Prison Studies [ICPS] 2012a), followed by Nigeria (32) and Japan (51) (ICPS 2012b). China, with a population of 1.35 billion, has an imprisonment rate of 121 per 100,000 (ICPS 2012c; World Population Statistics 2013). When compared to juvenile incarcerations, Mexico has the highest percentage (14%) of incarceration, followed by Canada (4.9%). A higher percentage of females are incarcerated in the United States (8.7%), followed by Russia (8.3%) and Japan (8%). See Table 1 for incarceration rates in the world. Many factors explain these high rates of incarcerations, such as the "get tough on crime" policies, increases in juvenile populations, and public and professional support for harsh punishments.

---

1. While the detention center data for China were incomplete, the prison data for four other countries—Eritrea, Guinea Bissau, North Korea, and Somalia—were unavailable.

Table 1 Comparison of Prison Population in Selected Countries

Country	Prison Population	Population per 100,000	Pretrial Detainees (%)	Minors/ Young Persons	Women Prisoners (%)
United States	2,239,751	716	19.9	0.4	8.7
Canada	40,544	118	35	4.9	5.1
France	67,050	100	25.4	1.1	3.3
Germany	63,317	77	16.7	3.0	5.8
China	1,640,000	121	N/A	N/A	5.5
Russia	681,050	475	16.7	0.9	8.3
Brazil	548,003	274	38	0.0	6.4
India	385,135	30	66.2	0.0	4.4
Mexico	246,226	210	42.1	14.0	4.9
South Africa	156,370	294	28.1	0.3	2.3
Poland	83,295	216	8.3	0.7	3.4
England/Wales	85,382	149	12.9	1.2	4.6
Japan	64,932	51	10.7	0.5	8.0
Kenya	52,000	121	36.0	0.5	5.3
Turkey	140,716	184	20.3	1.3	3.6
Nigeria	53,841	32	68.7	1.0	2.0
Australia	8273	98	20.1	1.6	6.4
Scotland	7,808	146	18.7	0.7	5.1
Northern Ireland	1,874	102	28.5	0.0	3.4
Saudi Arabia	47,000	162	58.7	0.9	5.7

Source: International Center for Prison Studies (2013). Retrieved December 2013 from http://www.prisonstudies.org/.

Four Goals of Corrections

The four goals of corrections have traditionally been: (1) retribution, (2) deterrence, (3) incapacitation, and (4) rehabilitation. These goals have received political and public support over a period of time. The restorative justice concept has recently gained popularity in Canada, France, Germany, New Zealand, and the United States.

- Retribution (deserved punishment) is a punishment inflicted on a person for violating a criminal law. To be effective, the punishment should be proportionate to the harm caused or to the extent the offender had made others suffer. It is based on the premise that the offender must "pay his debt" (Dammer and Albanese 2011). It does not, however, focus on deterring the offender from future criminality or reforming the offender. Although some claim that the notion of retribution has lost its influence with "the age of reasoning and the development of utilitarian approaches to punishment" (Clear, Cole, and Reisig 2013, 66), others argue that the desire to take revenge against those who harmed them is a human nature. If the government fails to punish those wrongdoers, the victims' family members, friends, or the community may take revenge against the perpetrator. This idea is deeply rooted in Islam. Since 1970s, there is a renewed interest in the concept of retribution mainly because of the lack of success with rehabilitation programs. Using a new term, "just desserts" (deserved punishments), scholars contend that punishment is a moral response to crime (Clear et al. 2013) and the government should punish the wrongdoers.
- Deterrence defines punishment as a threat aimed at averting criminals from committing crimes in the future. There are two type of deterrence: general and specific deterrence. General deterrence is meant to deter members of the general public who realize, from observing the punishments of others, that there are severe consequences for committing crimes and that the cost of committing crimes outweighs the benefits gained. Specific deference, on the other hand, is aimed at preventing the specific individual who has already been convicted of a crime from repeating. In order to be effective, the punishment should be sufficiently severe so that the offender avoids committing further crimes.
- Incarceration is a temporary or permanent removal of offenders from society as a way to restrict their ability to commit further crimes. In the eighteenth and nineteenth centuries, the British transported convicted offenders to Australia and other British colonies. With the development of modern penitentiaries, incarceration became the primary method of punishment. Other forms of incapacitation include dismemberment of body parts, such as chemical or surgical castration of sex offenders, which is used in at least seven states in the United States. For example, fifteen California sex offenders recently asked for surgical castration to avoid

long-term incarceration. South Korea recently used chemical castration on a sex offender who had raped young girls. The Czech Republic also uses surgical castration for convicted sex offenders (Park 2012). The idea behind castration is to prevent dangerous sex offenders from reoffending. In England and Wales, attendance center orders are given for youthful offenders under the age of 21. The goal is to restrict the leisure time of at-risk youth by engaging them in productive activities (Barton 2005). Finally, the ultimate sanction is capital punishment. It is justified as a form of deterrence, although studies have shown the contrary.

- The theme of rehabilitation has been persistent throughout the history of American corrections as well as in the correctional systems of Japan, India, and China. Efforts to strengthen the rehabilitation goal resulted in the implementation of the indeterminate sentence (no fixed term), parole, probation, and separate juvenile justice systems in many parts of the world. The support for rehabilitation diminished in the 1980s in the United States with the publication of Robert Martinson's (1974) "nothing works" essay, which criticized correctional programs as ineffective in reducing recidivism. Others argue "that broader social transformations led people at this particular historical juncture to be open to the message that rehabilitation was ineffective" (Cullen and Gendreau 2000, 111). Despite skepticism, the public, however, continues to view rehabilitation as a viable goal, especially for juveniles and nonviolent offenders (Sundt, Cullen, Applegate, and Turner 1998).

- Restoration (or restorative justice) is based on the premise that offenders accept responsibility for their actions, take reparative measures to repair the damage caused to the victim and the community, and reintegrate offenders back into the community through providing help needed to live crime free (Clear et al. 2013). This concept and its application is not new. Indigenous people in precolonial Africa, New Zealand, North America, and Australia have used a variation of this concept. Restorative justice is typically associated with victim-offender reconciliation programs (VORPs). It is a relatively new concept to many Western countries. Canada, for example, established VORPs in the early 1970s, whereas the United States experimented with VORPs much later. Correctional Services of Canada (CSC) has embraced the concept and has implemented it at various levels. For example, some of the programs develop reintegration plans prior to offender release, whereas other programs help offenders at the post-incarceration stage (Bell and Trevethan n.d.). These programs are primarily intended for property offenders, juvenile offenders, and their victims. In recent years, these programs, at least the concept, has been extended to adult offenders (Galaway and Hudson 1996).

International Standards on Corrections

ICPS (n.d.) reported problems with penal systems such as overuse of pre-trial detention when release into the community would be more appropriate; corruption due to lack of transparency and ineffective oversight; human rights abuses such as overcrowding, scarcity of resources, infectious diseases, violence and brutality; and severe lack of rehabilitative programs. To address these issues, countries enter into bilateral agreements (between two countries) or multilateral agreements (among three or more countries). In addition, there are international (i.e., United Nations) and regional conventions (i.e., European Union) prohibiting inhuman and degrading punishment or treatment of inmates. This chapter primarily focuses on the following six UN documents: International Covenant on Civil and Political Rights (1966), The Second Optional Protocol to the International Covenant on Civil and Political Rights (1989), UN Standard Minimum Rules for the Treatment of Prisoners (1977), Convention against Torture and other Cruel, Inhuman or Degrading Treatment or Punishment (1984), UN Standard Minimum Rules for Noncustodial Measures (1990), and the Optional Protocol to the Convention against Torture and other Cruel, Inhuman or Degrading Treatment or Punishment (2002).

International Covenant on Civil and Political Rights (1966) (came into force in 1976)

In addition to recognizing civil and political rights, the Covenant states that every person has the inherent right to life. This principle is in conflict with countries still using the death penalty. In such cases, the death penalty may be imposed for the most serious offenses and it shall be given only by a competent authority. It states that the sentence of death shall not be given to persons under the age of eighteen or to pregnant women. It also contains strict provisions under which imprisonment with hard labor may be given. Finally, it also includes several procedural rights such as presumption of innocence, right to appeal, and right against self-incrimination (Office of the High Commission for Human Rights 1976).

The Second Optional Protocol to the International Covenant on Civil and Political Rights, Aiming at the Abolition of Death Penalty (1989) (came into force in 1991)

This Protocol is an attempt at the international level to abolish the death penalty. Article 1 asserts that no one within the jurisdiction of a State Party to the Protocol shall be executed. Each State Party shall take every effort to abolish the death penalty within its jurisdiction. It is a clear affirmation by the United Nations and the ratifying states to abolish the death penalty (Office of the High Commission for Human Rights 1989).

UN Standard Minimum Rules for the Treatment of Prisoners (1977)

These Rules provide guidelines for the treatment of prisoners and the management of penal institutions. Specifically, the rules emphasize (1) the separation of offenders in institutions using classifications based on sex, age, criminal record, type of offenders (i.e., those awaiting trial vs. convicted) and treatment needs; (2) the use of single cell occupancy whenever possible; (3) regular supervision of inmates at night; and (4) the appropriate maintenance of institutions through providing proper sanitation, ventilation, exercise, medical service, nutritious food, and discipline. In addition, useful work and training should be made available, including vocational and educational training (Standard Minimum Rules for the Treatment of Prisoners 1977).

Convention against Torture and other Cruel, Inhuman or Degrading Treatment or Punishment (1984) (came into force in 1987)

The Convention requires the States Parties to respect and promote human rights and fundamental freedoms. In addition, they should take legislative, administrative, judicial, or other measures to prevent all forms of torture in their respective jurisdictions. It also stipulates that States should ensure that acts of torture are offenses under the criminal law (Office of the High Commission for Human Rights 1987).

UN Standard Minimum Rules for Noncustodial Measures ("The Tokyo Rules") (1990)

These Standards were intended to promote the use of noncustodial measures as well as minimum safeguards for those who were given alternative sanctions in lieu of imprisonment. In addition, it recommends greater community involvement in the treatment of offenders and greater offender accountability. The Standards seem to embrace the restorative justice principles, for example, a balance between the rights of offenders, rights of victims, and ensuring public safety (UN General Assembly 1990).

Optional Protocol to the Convention against Torture and Other Cruel, Inhuman or Degrading Treatment or Punishment (2002) (came into force in 2006)

This Protocol was adopted to further strengthen the earlier commitment to prevent torture and inhumane treatment of persons. In addition, the objective of the Protocol is to establish regular visits by national and international monitoring bodies (i.e., subcommittee on prevention) to places where people are deprived of liberty, or faced torture or cruel or inhumane treatment. It also requires that the subcommittee be given unrestricted access by the States to places of detention, detainees, or any other pertinent information (Office of the High Commission for Human Rights 2006).

Sentencing Options

Depending upon the nature of the offense and the countries' laws, types of punishments awarded for similar offenses vary. In most countries, for example, a theft is considered a nonviolent property offense and the offender receives a fine or a jail term, whereas in countries such as Nigeria and Saudi Arabia, an offender's right hand will be cut off for theft. Flogging or lashing with a whip is used in Iran, Sudan, the United Arab Emirates, and Bahamas for theft. Similar variations in punishments exist for other, more serious offenses. Worldwide punishments can be classified into noncustodial and custodial sanctions. Noncustodial sanctions include financial sanctions such as fines and day fines, confiscation of property, restitution to the victim/compensation, community service, house arrest and/or electronic monitoring, probation, or a combination of these sanctions. Custodial sanctions include detention/jail and prison sentences.

Table 2 Correctional Goals by Countries

Correctional Goals	England & Wales	China	Japan	Saudi Arabia
Retribution		Yes	Yes	Yes
Deterrence				Yes
Incapacitation	Yes			
Rehabilitation	Yes	Yes	Yes	Yes
Restoration	Yes*	Yes*	Yes	

* Primarily used in juvenile cases.

Source: Dammer, Harry R., and Albanese, Jay. *Comparative Criminal Justice.* (4th ed.). Belmont, CA:Wadsworth, Cengage Learning, 2011.

These sanctions are reviewed in the correctional context in England and Wales, China, Japan, and Saudi Arabia. Although these countries incorporate more than one correctional goal, the priority given to each of the goals tends to vary. For example, the goals of the correctional system in England and Wales are twofold: rehabilitation and incapacitation. In addition, a restorative goal is used in the juvenile justice system (see Table 2). China and Japan model their correctional system based on retribution, rehabilitation, and restoration goals. Saudi Arabia's correctional system is grounded on *sharia* law, which has elements of retribution, rehabilitation, and deterrence, whereas the United States embraces all five goals of corrections (Dammer and Albanese 2011).

Noncustodial Sanctions

The specific international standards applicable to noncustodial sanctions are the United Nations Standard Minimum Rules for Noncustodial Measures ("The Tokyo Rules") (1990); the United Nations Standard Minimum Rules for the Administration of Juvenile Justice ("The Beijing Rules") (1985); and the Declaration of Basic Principles of Justice for Victims of Crime and Abuse of Power (1985). The following section presents non-custodial sanctions in selected countries.

England

Fines and Restitution. Of all the noncustodial sanctions, the fine is the most common form of punishment imposed by the courts. A fine is money paid to the courts as a punishment for a crime or other offense. The amount of a fine can be determined on a case by case basis, depending on the nature of the crime and the financial status of the offender. In some instances, the law sets fixed amounts for specific offenses. Although fines are commonly given for violation of traffic laws or local ordinances, a huge sum of fines can be ordered for financial fraud. Fines can be a stand-alone sanction or they can be linked to other sanctions. In England and Wales, the use of fines is strengthened with the passage of the Criminal Justice Act of 1967. The Act increased the amount that magistrate courts could give from £100 to £400. To increase the effectiveness of the collection of fines, offenders were given more time to pay and they could not be sent to prison for failure to pay unless all measures had been taken to collect the fine. In some cases, the courts could collect fines directly from a person's wages as a means of enforcement. With the rise in the prison population and the incarceration costs, England reevaluated the use of fines as an option. Two primary issues were discussed: (1) how to assess the level of fines for a given offender and a given offense; and (2) how to enforce the fine. In regards to the level of the fine, they reviewed the Swedish day-fine system. Under this system, the gravity of the offense determines the number of days fined, and the financial status of the offender is used to determine the amount of fine per day. Although impressed with the Swedish system, England decided, at that time, not to adopt it because of the anticipated difficulty in establishing the financial status of the offenders (Gillespie 1980). Later, the Criminal Justice Act 1991, which came into force in 1992, briefly introduced a day-fine system. It was suspended shortly thereafter because of the opposition from the judiciary (Albrecht n.d.). The Sentencing Council of England currently provides approaches for assessing a fine as well as enforcement strategies. For example, the amount of a fine must be based on the seriousness of the offense and the financial status of the offender (i.e., the amount the offender is able to pay in twelve months). The maximum fine allowed in a magistrate court is £5,000; in the Crown Court, the amount is unlimited (Sentencing Guidelines Council 2008). In any given year, approximately 66 percent of offenders receive fines.

In addition, courts can impose restitution/compensation to the victim as a stand-alone order, or ordered as a condition of probation, or other sentences. The concept of restitution is based on tort law where a person who injured another person due to negligent is liable for damages (Benson 1996). Similar to tort cases, criminals are held responsible for causing intentional harm against the victims. Earlier in the British system of justice, the primary legal institutions (tithings and hundreds) assumed the duty to pursue thieves. The hundreds were further organized into shires and together they adjudicated disputes. In some cases, restitution was awarded and failure to pay restitution resulted in ostracizing the offender. The sanction was reinstated in legislation in 1846. Restitution is currently ordered either to benefit the victim or the public (i.e., community service order).

For example, a defendant convicted of vandalism may be ordered to pick up trash in a park as a form of restitution to the general public.

Probation. It is one of the oldest noninstitutional sanctions given to nonviolent offenders. Its purpose is to allow the offender to serve the sentence in the community while under the supervision of a probation officer. During the pretrial phase, the probation officer compiles information for the prosecutor and the court to assist them in making a bail decision. Once the finding of guilt is made, a presentence report is made by the probation officer to assist with sentencing. The report includes an analysis of the offense, the criminal behavior of the offender, and an assessment of the risk of reoffending. All of these factors are considered by the judge in making the decision. The National Probation Service (NPS) for England and Wales is responsible for the administration of noninstitutional programs. There are approximately forty-five local probation authorities monitoring offenders in the community. At any given time, probation services monitors approximately 200,000 adult offenders in the community. Of these offenders, ninety percent are men and about nine percent are ethnic minorities (National Probation Service for England and Wales 2005).

The probation orders (or community orders) are standard orders such as remaining crime free, maintaining contact with the probation officer, no contact with specific people or stay away from certain locations, or complete the recommended assessments/treatments. If the offender has no place to reside, the court may order the offender to reside at an Approved Premise (i.e., Hostels). These facilities are either run by the NPS or voluntary organizations. The offender can work outside the facility during the day and return at night. The term of a probation order ranges from one year to three years. In addition to hostels, probation centers were established to provide basic skills, which will enable offenders to obtain employment. Failure to comply with the probation conditions result in a fine or an order to perform community service (Terrill 2013).

In the 1970s, community service as a sanction was introduced with rehabilitation in mind. Offenders who are between the ages of sixteen and twenty-one and have received probation or other custodial sanctions in the past are given this sanction. Offenders are ordered to serve from 40 to 240 hours of unpaid community service. This could include working at a hospital, caring for the elderly, working at the employment bureau for ex-offenders, or involvement with youth organizations. These orders continue to be popular although concerns have been raised by probation officers. First, the officers perceive that their role in the supervision of offenders is limited once the offender is placed with an organization in the community. Second, the community service orders can be viewed as punitive, rehabilitative, or a form of compensation to the community. This muddles the purpose of the sanction (Terrill 2013).

China

In China, punishments are classified into principal punishments, supplemental punishments, and administrative sanctions. Principal punishments include public surveillance, criminal detention, a fixed term of imprisonment, life imprisonment, and the death penalty. Supplemental sanctions consist of fines, deprivation of political rights, and confiscation of property. Administrative penalties are warnings, fines, and detention for up to fifteen days. Public security agencies are authorized to give administrative sanctions. Of the principal punishments, public surveillance is a noncustodial sanction and as such is discussed under this category.

Fines. According to Section 6 of the Criminal Law of the People's Republic of China (1997), the amount of fine depends on the circumstances of the case. The fine can be paid one time or in installments (Laws of the People's Republic of China, 1997).

Deprivation of political rights. Section 7 of the Criminal Law of the People's Republic of China (1997) lists the following political rights:

(1) the right to vote;
(2) the rights of freedom of speech, of the press, of assembly, of association, of procession, and of demonstration;
(3) the right to hold a position in a state organ; and
(4) the right to hold a leading position in a state-owned company, enterprise, or institution, or people's organization.

Any person endangering national security, or who has committed murder, rape, arson, explosion, robbery, or other serious crimes shall be given a sanction of deprivation of political rights as a supplemental punishment. The term of deprivation ranges from one to five years. In all other cases, the derivation of political rights will stay as long as the offender is serving the principal punishment. For example, a person sentenced to life imprisonment is deprived of political rights for life (Chen 2013). Finally, Section 8 of the Law explains the offenses for which a person's property can be confiscated.

Public Surveillance. This sanction is imposed on those who do not require a term of imprisonment. As a condition, offenders have to report to the local public security agency. In addition, if the offender is employed, the employer will be notified of the sanctions and required to monitor the offender at work. The surveillance could typically last from three months to two years. In the case of criminal detention, the sentence could be suspended from two months to one year. If the sentence is for a fixed term, it can be suspended from one to five years. During the suspension, the offenders are monitored either by the local public security agency or the offender's work unit (Terrill 2013).

Japan

Japanese correctional philosophy is based on retribution and rehabilitation. The concept of restorative justice is also deeply rooted in the Japanese correctional philosophy. Although the Japanese justice system is concerned with the individual offender, it also focuses on how the sanctions benefit the society. Citizens trust the agents of the criminal justice system and view them as protectors of society's morals rather than as enforcers of the law. All agents of the criminal justice system have wide discretionary powers. The police often decide whether a minor infraction should be handled through a citation or an apology. Prosecutors can suspend the prosecution irrespective of the nature of the offense. The judges have the authority to modify the sanction of a formally adjudicated offender. The decision to punish offenders is based on the severity of the offense and the culpability of the offenders. At the time of sentencing, information about the offender (similar to a presentence report) is prepared by the prosecutor, not by the probation officer. The correctional goal of retribution is achieved through shaming the offender and alienating the offender from the group. The second goal—rehabilitation—is achieved through awarding shorter sentences for nonviolent offenders. This is to show the offender that the court is serious about the offender's rehabilitation (Terrill 2013).

Fine. The Japanese use fines in over 95 percent of cases. Two types of fines can be awarded based on the nature of the offense. Minor fines range from ¥20 to ¥4,000, and regular fines are typically ¥4,000 and above. Those who fail to pay fines are detained in a workhouse; the length of the detention is based on the size of the fine.

Restitution. In Japanese culture, it is common to give blood or condolence money (*mimaikin*) to a victim's family. In a recent case involving the murder of Lucie Blackman, the father of the victim accepted £450,000 as blood money from the accused killer. In this case, the accused, Obara, a 54-year-old man, admitted taking Miss Blackman on a date to his apartment but denied killing her. Her dismembered body was found seven months later in a beach cave about 200 meters from the defendant's apartment. The lawyers for the defendant expect that the judges would consider the actions of the father and the defendant at the time of judgment (Ryall 2007).

Probation. The use of probation in Japan is in some respects similar to that of England and Wales. For example, like England, Japan utilizes voluntary probation officers. The Japanese parliament (Diet) recently revised the criminal code to release drug offenders earlier than usual and place them on a longer probation term so that they can be rehabilitated with the support of the probation officer (Osaki 2013).

Saudi Arabia

Saudi Arabia, like many Islamic countries, follows the *Sharia* law. *Sharia* means "path" or "way." *Sharia* regulates almost everything from worship, ritual, purity, marriage and inheritance, criminal offense, commerce to personal life. It is considered God's revealed law and therefore binding on individuals, society, and state in all aspects (Jansen 2012). "Sharia law is not a practical system of law developed in courts ..." and therefore does not deal with the practical concerns of the judge, prosecutors or defenders (Jansen 2012, ¶8). It divides human acts into permitted (*halal*) and prohibited (*haram*) acts.

Offenses under Islamic law are classified into two main categories: determined offenses and discretionary offenses. The determined offenses and corresponding punishments have been specified either by God in the *Quran* or by the Prophet Mohammad in *Sunna* and as such cannot be changed by humans. The discretionary offenses, although not specifically mentioned in either the *Quran* or the *Sunna*, offer examples of sanctions in the aforementioned sources. The determined offenses are categorized into two types: *Hudud* and *Quesas* offenses. *Hudud* offenses and the corresponding punishments (*hadd*) are specified in the religious texts and no one is permitted to change them. *Hudud* offenses are considered the most serious offenses and include theft, highway robbery, rebellion against legitimate authority, adultery/fornication, defamation, apostasy (rejecting Islam), and drinking alcohol. The punishment for these offenses involve mutilation to death (which is discussed below). The second type of determined offenses, *Quesas*, are offenses that violated rights of individuals and are considered revenge crimes. These offenses are considered private wrongs and the prosecution is brought upon by the victim. These include murders and physical assaults and the punishment for such acts shall be punishable by retaliation (i.e., retribution) or in some cases compensation (*diyya*). In Saudi Arabia, the concept of retribution is based on the older Draconian laws, "an eye for an eye" and "a tooth for a tooth." It is known as *Quesas* or equal retaliation in *Sharia* law (Poladian 2013). For example, in 2010 a Saudi court ruled that a man who paralyzed his best friend should be crippled. He was fourteen years old when he committed the crime and has served ten years in prison. In the same year, a man who lost his foot in a fight with his brother asked the court for "an eye for an eye" punishment. In 2000, an Egyptian worker's eye was surgically removed in a Saudi hospital when he hurt another person by throwing acid at him.

The discretionary offenses are referred to as *Tazir* offenses (the least serious) and include offenses such as fraud and sodomy. Saudi Arabia allows the judge (*qadi*) to set the *Tazir* crime and associated punishments (Terrill 2013).

In Islamic and Arab traditions, the *Quran* specifies that one should seek compensation instead of retaliation. In place of retribution in the form of "an eye for an eye," "a nose for a nose," and "an ear for an ear"; victims can seek financial compensation known as *Diyya* (blood money). *Diyya* is based on tort laws where the injured party has to show that someone has caused the damage and does not have to show the intent. These are allowed for *Quesas* offenses such as murder and other forms of physical violence. In Saudi Arabia, for example, the heirs of the victim have a right to settle the case for *Diyya*, instead of the execution of the murderer. The prescribed blood money for killing a person in Saudi Arabia is as follows:

- 100,000 riyals if the victim is a Muslim man (US$1.00 = 3.7 Saudi Riyal)
- 50,000 riyals if the victim is a Muslim woman
- 50,000 riyals if the victim is a Christian man
- 25,000 riyals if the victim is a Christian woman
- 6,666 riyals if the victim is a Hindu man
- 3,333 riyals if the victim is a Hindu woman (Malone 2009)

Diyya also applies to other forms of injuries and the amount of *Diyya* depends on the injury. For example, loss of a normal hand is worth more than the loss of a hand with one finger missing. Arms and legs are basically worth the same. *Diyya* has to be approved by the judicial authority. Moreover, if the injury occurs during holy time, the value is much higher. Other forms of noncustodial sanctions include counseling, fines, public or private reprimand, confiscation of property, and suspended sentences are commonly given for *Tazir* offenses. Public reprimand is achieved by shaving the head of the accused and parading him by making him sit on the back of a donkey.

Custodial Sanctions

The international standards applicable to custodial sanctions are: The UN Convention against Torture and Other Cruel, Inhuman or Degrading Treatment or Punishment (1987); the UN International Covenant on Civil and Political Rights (1966) (came into force in 1976); the Second Optional Protocol to the International Covenant on Civil and Political Rights, aiming at the abolition of death penalty (1989) (came into effect 1991); and the Safeguards Guaranteeing Protection of the Rights of Those Facing Death Penalty. The following section describes custodial sanctions in selected countries.

England and Wales

Prisons. In the sixteenth and seventeenth centuries, prisons were used to hold pretrial detainees or those awaiting punishment. In the mid-eighteenth century, imprisonment with hard labor was used for petty offenses. Transportation of convicted offenders to British colonies such as Australia, America, or Tasmania was common until the mid-eighteenth century. Other forms of punishment such as hard labor or holding convicts in houses of correction were practiced. Prison hulks (ships) anchored in the Thames, Portsmouth, and Plymouth were used to hold offenders at night. Due to terrible conditions in the hulks, many inmates contracted diseases and died. This practice was eventually ended. By the mid-nineteenth century, imprisonment replaced capital punishment for serious offenses. New state prisons were built during this time and the trend continued into the twentieth century (Howard League for Penal Reform n.d.). Penal servitude, hard labor, and flogging were abolished with the passage of the Criminal Justice Act (1948).

In the 1970s, like many countries, England and Wales experienced a financial crisis due to high unemployment, inflation, and employee strikes. These crises exacerbated the problems of the already overcrowded prisons. For example, the inmate population after World War II was 20,474. By 1980, it had increased to 42,264. The 1990s did not see much of an increase but then took an upward trend that continues to the present day. In 2012, the number of inmates increased to 86,634, an increase of 4.8 percent from the previous year (Berman and Dar 2013). Estimates from the Ministry of Justice show that the prison population was projected to increase to as high as 90,900 in the next five years. With the improved economic conditions, the British embarked on building new prisons. In 2013, the country opened the largest jail, the Victorian Wandsworth Prison in south London, with a capacity to hold 1,605 inmates. On January 2014, the Justice Secretary has announced plans to build Britain's biggest prison, one capable of housing 2,000 inmates (Perry 2014).

The administration of prisons currently falls under the jurisdiction of the Ministry of Justice with the Lord Chancellor as the head. The home secretary, a civilian politician was previously responsible for the position. The National Offender Management Service (NOMS), the Office of Chief Inspector of Prisons, Independent Monitoring Boards, and Prison and Probation Ombudsman are all responsible to the Ministry of Justice. The NOMS identifies the gaps in

the system and develops strategies to improve it. The Office of the Chief Inspector of Prisons serves as a prison oversight committee and periodically in-
spects young offender institutions. The other oversight committee is the
Independent Monitoring Board. The members are citizens appointed by the Ministry of Justice. The Ombudsman reviews prisoner's complaints and serves as
a final source of appeal regarding internal disciplinary complaints. The Ministry of Justice is also responsible for the Prison Service, National Probation Service, and the Parole Board.

There are five types of prisons: (1) remand centers, (2) local prisons, (3)
closed and open prisons, (4) high security prisons, (5) open and closed young
offender institutions. Remand homes hold those awaiting trial or sentence.
Since 1948, England has made efforts to incorporate rehabilitation by transforming all prisons into correctional training centers (Terrill 2013). As of June
2013, one-third of the inmates were serving determinate sentences of more
than four years, and one-fifth of the inmates were serving indeterminate sentences (including life sentences). Of all the offense categories, irrespective of
gender, violence against persons accounted for the largest proportion of the
total sentenced inmates (Berman and Dar 2013). The restorative justice concept is more visible in the juvenile justice system than in the adult system.

China

Unlike the centralized administration of the correctional system in England
and Wales, three different agencies are responsible for overseeing different correctional institutions in China. The Ministry of Justice oversees prisons and
reform-through-labor camps (*Laogai*), public security agencies are in-charge
of criminal detention centers, and the Local Commission of Reeducation Reform oversees reeducation-through-labor camps.

Prisons. The Prison Law of the People's Republic of China (1994) stipulates
that the Ministry of Justice be in charge of all prisons in the country. The Ministry, through the Bureau of Prison Administration, administers the prisons. Offenders sentenced to a fixed-term of more than ten years, a life sentence, or the
death penalty with two-year suspension, and political prisoners are housed in prisons. These offenders are considered a threat outside the prison environment.

The Reform-through-Labor Camps (Laogai). These were established during
Mao Zdeong's reign in the 1950s, and were modeled after the Soviet "Gulag."
The camps were meant to punish and reform offenders and, at the same time,
provide economic gain to the state. Offenders who were not considered a risk
outside the facility, those who received a sentence of at least one year, and

those who were considered a threat to state safety (i.e., political prisoners) may be sent to these camps (Pejan 2000).

Criminal Detention Centers. These centers are administered by local public security agencies. Offenders awaiting trial or those who received less than two years of imprisonment serve their sentence in detention centers. These are similar to jails in other countries.

Reeducation-through-labor Camps. These camps are run by a commission with representatives from the public security agency, department of labor, and department of civil affairs. The intent of the original legislation, the Decision of the State Council Relating to Problems of Reeducation-through-labor, was to offer education as well as to reform. Amnesty International states that these camps, which fall outside of the formal prison system, are used to persecute human rights activists, intellectuals, or any person who oppose the government policies. In January 2013, the Chinese government announced that it would terminate these camps (Park 2013).

Death Penalty. In Maoist China, capital punishment was used as a tool by politicians to curb political unrest in the country. Later on it was used as a crime-fighting strategy. Although other countries such as the United States and India use capital punishment, China topped the list of pro-death-penalty countries. Miao (2013) discussed capital punishment during three time periods in Chinese penal history—the Maoist era (1949–late 1970s), the Deng-Jiang era (late 1970s–early 2000s), and the Hu-Wen administration (early 2000–2012). Mao Zedong used capital trials as "a vehicle for political propaganda and mass 'education' to strengthen public confidence" in the new party (Miao 2013, 235). During the Deng-Jiang administration, the country experienced an increase in rural-urban migration and social and economic reforms. The authorities feared that such changes could bring an increase in crime and as such toughened up the capital punishment policies. In the third phase, the country experienced economic inequality and political and social instability. The political leaders, concerned that the situation could spiral out of control, decided to make limited changes in the area of corrections. One such reform was the review of capital cases by the Supreme People's Court, starting from 2007. The current law (Criminal Law of the People's Republic of China 1997) lists the offenses that qualify for the death penalty and they include homicide, arson, causing explosions, causing serious injury, causing heavy losses to public or private property, sabotage, hijacking an aircraft, rape, trafficking of human beings, kidnapping, armed robbery, embezzlement, drug trafficking, and impairing government defense (Terrill 2013, 520). The offender must be at least eighteen years of age to be executed. If a person is sixteen years of age and has committed a serious offense, the sentence is suspended for two years. If the offender repents and does not commit an intentional crime during the time of suspension, the sentence is commuted to life imprisonment. The executions are carried out by shooting or lethal injection. Due to the secret nature of the executions, the Dui Hua Foundation (2011) estimates around 4,000 executions in 2011, whereas others estimate as high as 10,000.

Japan

In 1908, Japan passed the Prison Law and Penal Code, which were considered progressive because the laws stipulated that inmates be provided with supplies, hygiene and medical care, and education. After World War II, a new constitution was passed and the Prison Law was revised to include correctional treatment and reentry. Again, the Penal Code was revised to include treatment services for remand inmates. As of 2008, the rate of incarceration was 63 per 100,000, which is much lower than England and Wales or China. Of the 80,523 incarcerated inmates, pretrial detainees constitute 10.5 percent. Rehabilitation programs as well as substance abuse counseling, job assistance, sex offender counseling, and education to make the offender see from the victim's perspective are provided (Hill 2009).

Prisons. The Correctional Bureau and the Rehabilitation Bureau come under the authority of the Ministry of Justice. The Corrections Bureau oversees both adult and juvenile institutions. The Bureau has several divisions, including the treatment division, industry division, medical and classification division, and education division. Compared to other countries, Japan has developed an elaborate system of classification. The first classification is based on different populations: females, foreigners, those sentenced to imprisonment without compulsory labor, those receiving sentences of no more than eight years, adults under twenty-five years, and juveniles. The second classification is based on the offenders' criminal tendencies. The third classification identifies those with special needs. The fourth classification focuses on treatment needs (Terrill 2013).

Sanctions of incarceration include imprisonment with or without compulsory labor and penal detention. Imprisonment with or without labor can be for a fixed term or for life. A fixed term is typically fifteen years but can be extended for up to twenty years. Offenders who receive penal detention serve one to twenty-nine days in a house of detention. Life in prison is regimented with strict discipline, and prisons use a progressive system to reward offenders. For example, Grade 1 allows offenders to be free from body searches or search of their cells. In addition to offering educational and vocational opportunities for inmates while in prison, the Rehabilitation Bureau oversees the release of inmates, including parole.

Capital punishment. Around the fourth century, Japan was influenced by the Chinese judicial system and slowly adopted different types of punishments, including the death penalty. During the Nara period (710–794 BCE), the death penalty was rarely used due to the belief in Buddhist teachings. It came into force during the Kamakura period (1192–1333) and capital punishment was used as a tool to suppress crime. The cruel punishments were embraced with the introduction of Chinese penal law. Executions were carried out by hanging, slaying, decapitation, crucifixion, burning, and boiling. During the Ashikaga period (1392–1490), the death penalty became the primary choice of punishment. More cruel methods of executions, such as spearing, being torn apart by oxen, and submerging in water, were used. These types of cruel punishments continued until the early years of the Meiji period (1868–1911). In 1868, it was decided that enforcement of laws should proceed as before (Schmidt 2001).

In 1928, Japan introduced the jury system that lasted until 1943. In the 1990s, Japan started reforming its judicial system due to high-profile death-row acquittals in the 1970s and 1980s. It was found that many death-row inmates had been wrongfully convicted and suffered decades of imprisonment. The first reform focused on how to increase citizen involvement and confidence in the criminal justice system. In 2004, the Lay Assessor Act was passed, which created a mixed jury system comprised of professional judges and lay jurors. The mixed jury was to review serious cases and decide who deserves death based on the Nagayama guidelines articulated by the Japanese Supreme Court in 1984 (Métraux 2009). These are: (1) the severity of crime; (2) the motive for committing crime; (3) the cruelty and the heinousness of the murder; (4) the number of victims involved; (5) the feelings of the victims and survivors; (6) the social impact of the crime; (7) the age of the defendant; (8) the prior history of the defendant; and (9) what happened to the defendant after the crime was committed (e.g., felt remorse and apologized) (Schmidt 2001). Although there were discussions of abolishing the death penalty in recent years, Japan executed eight people in 2013 and has 129 inmates on death row (McCurry 2013). Currently, hanging is the method of execution.

Saudi Arabia

In Saudi Arabia, the criminal justice system is based on the state's interpretation of the *Sharia* law. Corporal punishments such as flogging, maiming, and beheading are common for *Hudud* offenses as well as for some *Quesas* offenses. In addition to noncustodial sanctions, *Tazir* offenses could qualify for flogging, imprisonment, or death (see Table 3).

Table 3 *Hudud* offenses in Saudi Arabia and Punishments

Hudud Offenses	Sanctions
Theft	1st offense: Amputation of the right hand at wrist 2nd offense: Amputation of the left hand at wrist 3rd offense: Amputation of foot at ankle or imprisonment
Highway Robbery	1st offense: Amputation of the right hand and left foot 2nd offense: Amputation of left hand and right foot Homicide during attempted robbery: Beheading by sword Homicide during robbery: Death by crucifixion
Adultery	Stoning to death or lashes (50–100) or both
Defamation (False Accusation of Unlawful Intercourse)	Freemen: 80 lashes Slave: 40 lashes
Drinking of Wine	Freemen: 80 lashes Slave: 40 lashes
Rebellion against Authority	Execution by Sword
Apostasy	Death by Beheading

Source: O'Connell, Kelly. Crime & Punishment in Islamic Law. Canada Free Press. September 26, 2010; Dammer, Harry, and Jay Albanese. Comparative Criminal Justice Systems, Belmont, CA: Wadsworth-Cengage Learning, 2011.

Amputation and Flogging. For theft and highway robbery, offenders are punished with amputations. If an offender commits a theft, his right hand is amputated at the wrist. For robbery, cross-amputation (e.g., right hand and left foot) is a punishment. For many offenses, flogging is used as a common punishment under *Sharia.* The more severe the crime, the harder the flogging. Males are whipped standing and females are punished sitting and it is carried out in public (O'Connell 2010).

Death Penalty. Amnesty International reports that executions in Saudi Arabia tripled from twenty-seven in 2010 to seventy-nine in 2012 (Amnesty International 2013). Saudi Arabia uses different methods of execution such as beheading by sword in a public place, death by stoning, or death by crucifixion, hanging, immolation by fire, or buried alive. Of these methods, beheading is the most common method of execution. If killing occurs during an attempted robbery, the offender is beheaded by a sword and, if murder occurs during an actual theft, the offender is executed by crucifixion. For the offense of apostasy, the offenders are given three days to reflect and are then beheaded by a sword. In addition, executions may be used in place of blood money if the victim's family requests retribution.

Death by stoning is often given to adulterous women. In most cases, a hole big enough to cover the woman up to her waist is dug and the stones are thrown until she dies. The size of the stone should not be too small, which would delay the death or too big, which would kill the woman too quickly. For sodomy (a *Tazir* offense), offenders receive death by sword, or are thrown from a high building, or buried alive. The Saudi government recently began considering the use of firing squad (O'Connell 2010).

Conclusion

Many countries around the world have moved away from cruel and inhumane treatment of offenders and made major strides through improving the conditions of correctional institutions and the treatment of inmates. Developing countries have also made efforts to incorporate guidelines, rules, and provisions enumerated in various UN documents pertaining to the humane treatment of offenders and right of inmates. In addition, many countries have eliminated traditional sanctions such as corporal punishment and banishments, instead choosing alternative sanctions such as probation, community service, restitution, and fines. Islamic countries, such as Saudi Arabia and Iran, continue to use corporal punishments and the death penalty in place of imprisonment. The legal system in these countries is based on *Sharia* law, and therefore major changes in sentencing policies are not to be expected. The increased use of *diyya* in place of executions for *Quesas* offenses could reduce the number of executions in Saudi Arabia.

Public perception of crime, changes in social and economic conditions, and political and professional views about the effectiveness of correctional treatment programs resulted in reevaluating various correctional goals. In the first seven decades of the twentieth century, rehabilitation was considered the primary goal of corrections in the United States. This view changed in the 1970s and was replaced with the "just desserts" goal. During the 1980s and 1990s, sentencing practices in the United States embraced a "crime control" model, which advocated imprisonment as a way to reduce crime in the community. Other countries have also faced similar dilemma. With the increase in prison costs, many countries, including the United States, are reassessing their correctional policies. China, for example, decided to eliminate reeducation-through-labor camps; Japan included more rehabilitation programs for offenders; the United

States closed down several prisons and youth institutions and has been allocating additional funding to extend the availability of community-based programs for moderate to low-risk offenders; and England is placing more offenders in community-service programs. Finally, the number of inmates held in correctional institutions are on the rise. To address the problem, countries such as England are building new prisons. The United States has taken that path before but with less success. It is time for countries with high inmate populations and overcrowded prisons to review their sentencing policies.

Web Sources

1. Prison condition in Japan is available at:
   http://www.hrw.org/sites/default/files/reports/JAPAN953.PDF
2. Information on death penalty is available at:
   http://www.amnesty.org/en/death-penalty/numbers
3. Information on National Correction Service in England is available at:
   http://www.syscon.net/Solutions/national-corrections-services
4. World Prison Statistics is available at:
   http://www.prisonstudies.org/news/more-102-million-prisoners-world-new-icps-report-shows

Discussion Questions

1. Discuss the significance of the UN documents pertaining to the custodial treatment of inmates.
2. Explain the four goals of corrections and how they complement (or contract) each other.
3. What are the two main types of crimes in *Sharia* law and how are they different?
4. Compare and contrast the death penalty in Japan, China, and Saudi Arabia.
5. What is *diyya* and how is it different from a fine?

References

Albrecht, Hans-Jörg. "Sanction Policies and Alternative Measures to Incarceration: European Experiences with Intermediate and Alternative Criminal

Penalties." Accessed December 15, 2013. http://www.unafei.or.jp/english/pdf/RS_No80/No80_07VE_Albrecht.pdf, n.d.

Amnesty International. *Death Sentences and Executions 2012.* London, UK. Amnesty International Publications, 2013.

Associated Press. "Pakistani Court Orders Noses of Spurned Men to be Cut Off." *The Guardian,* December 22, 2009. Accessed December 5, 2013. http://www.theguardian.com/world/2009/dec/22/noses-cut-off-pakistan-court.

Barton, Alana. "Incapacitation Theory." In *Encyclopedia of Prisons & Correctional Facilities,* edited by Mary Bosworth (464–466). Thousand Oaks, CA: Sage, 2005.

Bell, Amey, and Shelley Trevethan. *Restorative Justice in Corrections.* Correctional Services of Canada. Accessed December 10, 2013. http://www.csc-scc.gc.ca/text/pblct/forum/e151/151k_e.pdf, 2013.

Benson, Bruce L. Restitution in Theory and Practice. *Journal of Libertarian Studies* 12, no. 1 (1996): 75–97.

Berman, Gavan, and Aliyah Dar. *Prison Population Statistics: England and Wales.* The Offender Management Statistics Quarterly Bulletin and Ministry of Justice Publication, 2013.

Chen, Jianfu. *Criminal Law and Criminal Procedure Law in the People's Republic of China.* Leiden, The Netherlands: IDC Publishers, 2013.

Clear, Todd R., George F. Cole, and Michael. D. Reisig. *American Corrections.* 10th ed. Belmont, CA: Wadsworth-Cengage Learning, 2013.

Criminal Manual. Lucknow, India: Eastern Book Company, 1995.

Cullen, Francis T., and Paul Gendreau. "Assessing Correctional Rehabilitation: Policy, Practice, and Prospects." *Criminal Justice* 3 (2000): 109–175.

Dammer, Harry R., and Albanese, Jay. *Comparative Criminal Justice Systems.* (4th ed.). Belmont, CA: Wadsworth, Cengage Learning, 2011.

Dui Hua Foundation. "Dui Hua Estimates 4,000 Executions in China, Welcomes Open Dialogue." Accessed December 20, 2013. http://duihua.org/wp/?page_id=3874, 2011.

Galaway, Burt, and Joe Hudson. "Introduction." In *Restorative Justice: International Perspectives,* edited Burt Galaway and Joe Hudson, 1–16. Monsey, NY: Criminal Justice Press, 1996.

Gillespie, Robert W. *Fines as an Alternative Sanction to Incarceration: An International Perspective.* Urbana-Champaign, IL: College of Commerce and Business Administration, University of Illinois, 1980.

Hill, Gary "Japan's Correction Bureau." *Corrections Compendium* 34, no. 4 (2009): 36–38.

Howard League for Penal Reform. "History of the Prison System." Accessed December 15, 2013. http://www.howardleague.org/history-of-prison-system/, n.d.

International Center for Prison Studies. "Penal Reform and Gender." Accessed December 15, 2013. http://www.icpa.ca/tools/download/1013/DCAF_Penal_Reform_and_Gender.pdf, n.d.

International Centre for Prison Studies. "India." Accessed December 2, 2013. http://www.prisonstudies.org/country/india, 2012a.

International Centre for Prison Studies. "Japan." Accessed December 2, 2013. http://www.prisonstudies.org/country/japan, 2012b.

International Centre for Prison Studies. "China." Accessed December 2, 2013. http://www.prisonstudies.org/country/china, 2012c.

Jansen, Hans. "What is Sharia?" *Frontpage Magazine,* July 16, 2012. Accessed December 2, 2013. http://www.frontpagemag.com/2012/dr-hans-jansen/what-is-sharia/.

Laws of the People's Republic of China. "Criminal Law of the People's Republic of China, 1997." Accessed December 25, 2013. http://www.asianlii.org/cn/legis/cen/laws/clotproc361/, 1997.

Malone, Noreen. "How Does Blood Money Work? What an Arm and a Leg Cost You." Accessed December 2, 2013. http://www.martinfrost.ws/htmlfiles/mar2009/blood-money.html, 2009.

Martinson, Robert. "What Works? Questions and Answers about Prison Reform." *The Public Interest,* 35 (1974): 22–54.

McCurry, Justin. "Japan Condemned for "Secret" Executions." *The Guardian,* December 12, 2013. Accessed December 15, 2013. http://www.theguardian.com/world/2013/dec/12/japan-condemned-secret-executions.

Métraux, Daniel A. "The Nagayama Criteria for Assessing the Death Penalty in Japan: Reflection of a Case Suspect." *Southeast Review of Asian Studies* 31 (2009): 282–289.

Miao, Michelle. "Capital Punishment in China: A Populist Instrument of Social Governance." *Theoretical Criminology* 17 (2013): 233–250.

O'Connell, Kelly. "Crime and Punishment in Islamic law." *Canada Free Press,* September 26, 2010. Accessed December 5, 2013. http://www.canadafreepress.com/index.php/article/28083.

Office of the High Commission for Human Rights. "International Covenant on Civil and Political Rights." Accessed December 20, 2013. http://www.ohchr.org/en/professionalinterest/pages/ccpr.aspx, 1976.

Office of the High Commission for Human Rights. "Convention against Torture and Other Cruel, Inhuman or Degrading Treatment or Punishment."

Accessed December 2013. http://www.ohchr.org/EN/ProfessionalInterest/Pages/CAT.aspx, 1987.

Office of the High Commission for Human Rights. "Second Optional Protocol to the International Covenant on Civil and Political Rights, Aiming at the Abolition of the Death Penalty." Accessed December 5, 2013. http://www.ohchr.org/EN/ProfessionalInterest/Pages/2ndOPCCPR.aspx, 1989.

Office of the High Commission for Human Rights. "Optional Protocol to the Convention against Torture and other Cruel, Inhuman or Degrading Treatment or Punishment." Accessed December 20, 2013. http://www.ohchr.org/EN/ProfessionalInterest/Pages/OPCAT.aspx, 2006.

Osaki, Tomohiro. "Volunteer Probation Officers Face Uphill Battle." *Japan Times,* August 29, 2013. Accessed December 25, 2013. http://www.japantimes.co.jp/news/2013/08/28/national/volunteer-probation-officers-face-uphill-battle/#.UuClofbnapo.

Park, Madison. "Using Chemical Castration to Punish Child Sex Crime." *CNN Health,* September 5, 2012. Accessed December 10, 2013. http://www.cnn.com/2012/09/05/health/chemical-castration-science/.

Park, Madison. "China Eases One-Child Policy, Ends Labor Camps." *CNN,* December 28, 2013. Accessed January 5, 2013. http://www.local10.com/news/china-eases-onechild-policy-ends-labor-camps/-/1717324/23678176/-/2ac9me/-/index.html.

Pejan, Ramin. "Laogai: Reform through Labor in China." *Human Rights Brief* 7, no. 2 (2000): 22.

Perry, Keith. "Chris Grayling Plans to Build Britain's Biggest Prison." *The Telegraph,* January 5, 2014. Accessed January 5, 2014. http://www.telegraph.co.uk/news/uknews/crime/10552614/Chris-Grayling-plans-to-build-Britains-biggest-prison.html, 2014.

Poladian, Charles. "Saudi Man Sentenced to Paralysis for Decade-Old Crime." *International Business Times,* April 4, 2013. Accessed December 15, 2013. http://www.ibtimes.com/saudi-man-sentenced-paralysis-decade-old-crime-1170947.

Ryall, Julian. "Lucie's Father Helped Killer by Accepting Blood Money." *Daily Mail (London),* April 21, 2007. Accessed December 25, 2013. http://www.highbeam.com/doc/1G1-162408862.html.

Schmidt, Petra. *Capital Punishment in Japan.* Leiden, The Netherlands: Brill, 2001.

Sentencing Guidelines Council. "Magistrates' Court Sentencing Guidelines." Accessed December 20, 2013. http://sentencingcouncil.judiciary.gov.uk/docs/MCSG_Update9_October_2012.pdf, 2008.

Standard Minimum Rules for the Treatment of Prisoners. Accessed December 1, 2013. http://www.unodc.org/pdf/criminal_justice/UN_Standard_Minimum_Rules_for_the_Treatment_of_Prisoners.pdf, 1977.

Sundt, Jody L., Francis T. Cullen, Brandon K. Applegate, and Michael G. Turner. "The Tenacity of the Rehabilitative Ideal Revisited: Have Attitudes toward Offender Treatment Changed?" *Journal of Criminal Justice and Behavior* 25, no. 4 (1998): 426–442.

Terrill, Richard. World Criminal Justice Systems (8th edition). Waltham, MA: Anderson Publishing, 2013.

The National Probation Service for England and Wales. Accessed December 20, 2013. http://www.cumbriaprobation.org.uk/files/publications/document_134.pdf, 2005.

UN General Assembly. "United Nations Standard Minimum Rules for Non-Custodial Measures (The Tokyo Rules)." Accessed November 30, 2013. http://www.un.org/documents/ga/res/45/a45r110.htm, 1990.

U.S. Department of Justice. "Criminal Program: Antitrust Division 2013 Criminal Enforcement Update." Accessed December 20, 2013. http://www.justice.gov/atr/public/division-update/2013/criminal-program.html, 2013.

Walmsley, Roy. *World Prison Population List.* (10th ed.). International Centre for Prison Studies, London: United Kingdom, 2013. Accessed December 2, 2013. http://www.prisonstudies.org/sites/prisonstudies.org/files/resources/downloads/wppl_10.pdf, 2013.

World Population Statistics. Accessed December 2, 2013. http://www.worldpopulationstatistics.com/china-population-2013/, 2013.

Chapter 8

Juvenile Justice:
A Comparative Perspective

Sesha Kethineni, Sarah McCullough & Richard Charlton

Introduction

Violence committed by juveniles has been a concern in both developing and developed countries. The contributing factors for the increase in violence include high urban growth rates, densely populated neighborhoods, high concentration of slums, and street gang activity among youth in urban areas. According to United Nations Habitat report (UN HABITAT 2006/07), one out of every three city dwellers—amounting to one billion people—lives in slums. These slums are distinctive of developing countries and these areas are deprived of social support systems, housing, sanitation, etc. The regions with the highest concentration of slums are sub-Saharan Africa, Southern Asia, Eastern Asia, Latin America, and the Caribbean. In addition, the presence of street children begging, peddling on the streets or committing petty crimes are common in urban areas of the developing countries, especially in sub-Sahara Africa, Latin America, and India (UN Factsheet n.d.). The street youth who participate in criminal activities often form gangs for sharing of profits as well as for security.

Worldwide, the youth gangs are more likely to participate in acts such as theft, robbery, and rape and less likely to engage in more violent offenses such as murder. In some parts of the world, youth gangs are known to control entire cities, compete over territories, and even collaborate with other criminal organizations for profits, trafficking activities related to prostitution, weapons, drugs, etc. In the sub-Saharan Africa, countries such as Mozambique, Niger, Madagascar, Tanzania, Kenya, and Burkina-Faso are faced with high growth of urban populations. This growth is primarily concentrated in semi-urban and slum areas (Urban Management Programme 2000). In addition to the lack of adequate housing, proper sanitation, and clean drinking water, many of the street children in these areas come from single-parent households. The absence of coherent social policies to address the urban poor, which include street children, youth crime and gang activity seem to thrive in these areas.

Although India is one of the countries with a high concentration of street children, juvenile crime constitutes only 1.2% of total crimes reported to police (National Crime Records Bureau 2012), which is much lower than many countries with similar levels of poverty and the number of street children. In 2012, 27,936 juveniles were apprehended for violating the Indian Penal Code, of which 5–8% of juveniles were apprehended for serious offenses such as murder and rape, while about 65% were apprehended for property offenses such as theft and burglary (Raha 2013). India, compared to other countries, does not have a major youth gang problem.

In the Caribbean, for example, gangs are 35 times more likely to collaborate with drug dealers than non-members (UNODC and World Bank 2007). Latin American countries, such as Argentina, Brazil, Chile, El Salvadore, and Mexico experienced an increase in youth crime, including gang violence (Center for International Conflict Resolution n.d.). In Mexico City alone, there are about 1,500 street gangs. Some operate locally with few members, while others are much larger and have ties to well-known international gangs such as *Mara Salvatrucha* (MS-13) and 18th Street Gang (M-18). Honduras, a Central American country, is also faced with the biggest gang problem in the region with over 36,000 gang members; many of them have affiliations with MS-13 and MS-18. The UNICEF reported over 4,700 children and young people belong to gangs in Honduras (González 2012).

Youth crime, however, is not limited to developing countries. A developed country such as the United States has high rates of juvenile crime. In 2010, 1.6 million juveniles (under age eighteen) have been arrested. In comparison to all persons arrested, juveniles in the United States represented one-fourth (24%) of arrests for robbery, about 14% for forcible rape, and 11% for aggravated assault, and 9% for murder in 2010 [Office of Juvenile Justice and Delinquency Prevention (OJJDP) 2010]. Studies have shown that 14% to 30% of adolescents in the United States join gangs and the age range of these youth is about twelve to twenty-four (Howell 1997). The 2011 National Youth Gang Survey estimates that there are 782,500 gang members located in 3,300 jurisdictions throughout the United States. A large percentage of these gang members (75%) are concentrated in urban areas (Egley and Howell 2013). In addition to juvenile crime rates, historical, cultural, religious, and political views about the treatment of juveniles and public attitude towards deviance, explain the creation and the evolution of the juvenile justice system of a country.

This chapter first compares the Unites Nations' (UN) role in the development of rules and guidelines for the administration of juvenile justice. Second, it provides variations in the age of criminal responsibility. Third, it explains different models of juvenile justice and countries that belong to each of the models.

United Nations' Role and Juvenile Justice

The UN has taken initiatives to improve the administration of juvenile justice and the humane treatment of juveniles throughout the world. It developed several rules, guidelines, principles, standards, and conventions to assist and encourage countries to incorporate them in their juvenile justice systems. The rules, guidelines, principles, and standards are non-binding on Member States and no penalties are attached for non-compliance. The conventions, on the other hand, are binding on ratifying Member States, or else they face sanctions (Dammer and Albanese, 2011). The following are four important documents pertaining to juveniles:

- The UN Standard Minimum Rules for the Administration of Juvenile Justice, 1985 (commonly known as the Beijing Rules)
- The UN Convention on the Rights of the Child (CRC) 1989, which entered into force in 1990
- The UN Guidelines for the Prevention of Juvenile Delinquency, 1990 (also referred to as the Riyadh Guidelines)
- The UN Rules for the Protection of Juveniles Deprived of their Liberty, 1990 (commonly known as the JDL Rules)

The UN Standard Minimum Rules for the Administration of Juvenile Justice, 1985

The rules were adopted by the UN at a meeting in Beijing, China in 1985 and referred to as the Beijing Rules. The Beijing Rules were considered historical in significance because they were the first international standards that provided a framework for the administration of juvenile justice for nations to follow (Dammer and Albanese 2011). The rules defined juvenile offenders as a child or young person who was accused of committing or who had committed an offense. Although not binding on Member States, the Rules emphasized that the juvenile justice system shall focus on the well-being of juveniles, and shall take into consideration the circumstances of the offender and the offense (i.e., the principle of proportionality). The consideration of proportionality should be based on the seriousness of the offense as well as the individual circumstances of the offender, including social status, family environment, and their willingness to change. The Rules recommended diversionary programs; right to privacy; procedural safeguards, including presumption of innocence; counselling, community service or probation; and discouraged the use of institutionalization unless it was intended for rehabilitating young people (United Nations Standard Minimum Rules 1985).

The UN Convention on the Rights of the Child (CRC), 1989

Many of the Rules enumerated in the Beijing Rules were incorporated in the CRC. The CRC defines a child as anyone under the age of eighteen. The CRC not only guarantees children's rights to survival, proper development, and protection from abuse and exploitation, but also includes right to participation. The right to participation accords the children access to appropriate information and the freedom of thought and expression, conscience, and religion. States that are party to the CRC are obliged to develop and undertake all necessary actions and policies to promote the best interests of children (Bullis 1991). As of 2012, 193 countries ratified the CRC (United Nations Treaty Collection 2011). By ratifying the CRC, the countries are morally and legally obligated to uphold the principles enumerated in the CRC. Only two countries, Somalia and the United States, have not ratified the CRC. Somalia is currently unable to ratify it because it has no recognized government. The United States, although signed the CRC, has yet to ratify it (UNICEF 2011b). Opponents of the treaty contend that it conflicts with the U.S. privacy laws and family rights, particularly the rights of parents to educate and discipline their children (Blanchfield 2009).

Specifically, Articles 37 and 40 provide procedural rights and humane treatment of juveniles. Article 37 prohibits torture, cruel, inhuman treatment, or punishment; capital punishment; or life imprisonment without the possibility of release. It also states that arrest, detention or imprisonment of a child shall conform to the law, and shall be used only as a measure of last resort and for the shortest period deemed appropriate. Article 40 provides many protections to children, including the presumption of innocence until proven guilty, right to prompt and appropriate legal assistance, right not to be compelled to give testimony or to confess guilt, and right to maintain privacy throughout the judicial process (United Nations Convention 1990).

The UN Guidelines for the Prevention of Juvenile Delinquency, 1990 ("The Riyadh Guidelines")

The Riyadh Guidelines were not standalone guidelines and, according to the UN, should be incorporated within the broad framework instruments such as the Universal Declaration of Human Rights; the International Covenant on Economic, Social and Cultural Rights; the International Covenant on Civil and Political Rights; the Declaration of the Rights of the Child and the Convention on the Rights of the Child; and the United Nations Standard Minimum Rules for the Administration of Juvenile Justice which are meant to protect the rights, interests and well-being of all children and young persons (United Nations General Assembly 1990a). The primary focus of the Guidelines was prevention of delinquency through the development of progressive delinquency prevention programs. Those programs should include early childhood delinquency prevention, offering educational opportunities, safeguarding the well-being of children, and developing community-based programs. In addition, juvenile justice agencies and professionals should have awareness of labelling young persons as "deviant," "delinquent," or "pre-delinquent" and the contributing effect of such labels on young people. They also emphasize the importance of family, community, and the media as positive role models for children. Since families play an integral role in the socialization of children, governments should give utmost importance to the needs of all family members. Communities should provide opportunities for young people such as community development centers and recreational facilities for at-risk children, drug counselling centers for young drug users, and shelter facilities for homeless children. In addition to government organizations, non-governmental organizations should be given funding to provide necessary services to young persons (UN General Assembly 1990a).

The UN Rules for the Protection of Juveniles Deprived of Their Liberty, 1990

Concerned about the institutional confinement of juvenile offenders with adult offenders, as many countries do not differentiate the juvenile and the adult system and possible abuses resulting from such confinement, the UN invited Member States to adapt the Rules. The deprivation of liberty includes detention or imprisonment or placement in a public or private institution by an order of any judicial, administrative or public authority. Juveniles deprived of liberty should not be denied the civil, economic, political, social, or cultural rights to which they are entitled to under national or international law. The Rules also stipulate that detention prior to trial should be limited to extraordinary circumstances, and if detained, it should be for the shortest time possible. In addition, juveniles should have access to (1) legal counsel and to free legal aid when needed, and (2) educational and recreational opportunities while in detention. Other regulations include proper physical conditions of facilities; notification to parents and juveniles; separation of juvenile offenders from adult offenders; limitations on use of force and physical restraint;

prohibition of cruel, inhuman, or degrading treatment of juveniles while confined; and reintegration of juveniles into the community (UN General Assembly 1990b).

In addition to the above documents, the UN in 1995 adopted the World Programme of Action for Youth (WPAY). Through WPAY, the UN puts forth policy action to promote well-being and livelihood of young people between the ages of fifteen and twenty-four. Of the fifteen priority areas, prevention of delinquency and rehabilitation of youth offenders are relevant to juvenile justice. The UN has not only involved in developing policies concerning the treatment of juveniles, it actively participates in the implementation of those policies into practice. For example, the UN Interregional Crime and Justice Research Institute (UNICRI) had worked with local governments in Angola and Mozambique in institutional building and social activities. In Mozambique, the UNICRI assisted in the drafting of a Code of Conduct for the Community Courts; strengthening of juvenile agencies; and training of juvenile justice personnel, including para legal personnel and non-governmental (NGO) volunteers (UNICRI n.d.-a). In Angola, the UNICRI, with the financial support from the Italian Ministry of Foreign Affairs, launched a two-phase project. In Phase I, the UNICRI strengthening its juvenile justice system by assisting the government in establishing the juvenile court, a network of prevention/rehabilitation centers, and strengthening their database on the situation of children in their country (UNICRI n.d.-b). In Phase II, the UNICRI organized courses for juvenile justice personnel and provided skill training for magistrates, police, prosecutors, and other related personnel.

Age of Criminal Responsibility

Determining the age at which a juvenile becomes an adult in the eyes of the law varies from country to country and, in some instances, differs from state to state within a country. Even the UN does not set the minimum age of criminal responsibility. The UN Standard Minimum Rules states that the beginning age of criminal responsibility should not be set too low, keeping in mind the emotional, mental, and intellectual maturity of juveniles. The age of criminality ranges from seven to eighteen, depending on the country (see Table 1). Making matters even more complicated is the act of setting different age criteria for boys and girls and using more than one age of criminal responsibility based on the nature of the offense committed. Iran, for example, considers age nine for girls and age fifteen for boys. In Pakistan, the 1979 Hudood ordinances (intended to bring punishments of hadd offenses into criminal law) hold all citizens, regardless of age, responsible for offenses such as rape, adul-

Table 1 Age of Criminal Responsibility in Selected Countries

Age 7	Age 8	Age 9	Age 10	Age 12
Belize	Bermuda	Ethiopia	Australia	Canada
Cyprus	Cayman	Iran*	(except	Greece
Ghana	Islands	Malta	Tasmania)	Jamaica
India	Gibraltar	Philippines	England and	Morocco
Ireland	Indonesia		Wales (UK)	Netherlands
Liechtenstein	Kenya		Fiji	San Marino
Malawi	Northern		Guyana	Turkey
Myanmar	Ireland (UK)		Kiribati	Uganda
Nigeria	Scotland (UK)		Malaysia	
Pakistan	Sri Lanka		Nepal	
Papua New	Western Samoa		New Zealand	
Guinea	Zambia		Ukraine	
Singapore			Vanuatu	
South Africa				
Sudan				
Switzerland				
Tasmania				
(Australia)				
Thailand				

Age 13	Age 14	Age 15	Age 16	Age 18
Algeria	Austria	Czech Republic	Argentina	Belgium
France	Bulgaria	Denmark	Andorra	Brazil**
Poland	Germany	Estonia	Macau	Colombia**
Uzbekistan	Hungary	Egypt	Poland	Luxembourg
	Italy	Finland	Portugal	Peru**
	Japan	Iceland	Spain	
	Latvia	Norway		
	Lithuania	Slovakia		
	The P. Rep.	Sweden		
	China			
	Mauritius			
	Romania			
	Slovenia			
	Taiwan			
	Vietnam			

* In Iran, the age is 9 for girls, 15 for boys.

** In Brazil, Colombia, and Peru, the official age of criminal responsibility is 18; from age 12 children's actions are subject to juvenile legal proceedings.

Source: Unicef (n.d.) *International juvenile justice and related issues.* Accessed December 3, 2013. http://zimmer.csufresno.edu/~haralds/LECTURENOTES/crim109/lec11juvyjust.htm.

tery, substance abuse, theft, armed robbery, and slander. For all other offenses, criminal responsibility begins at age seven (Unicef n.d.). In the United States, the age of criminal responsibility is established by each state. Of the fifty states, only thirteen states set the minimum age limits, which range from six to twelve, while the majority of the states follow the common law age limit of seven (Unicef 2007).

Models of Juvenile Justice

The two primary theoretical models of juvenile justice have been the welfare and the justice models. The welfare model focuses on rehabilitating juveniles, while the justice model emphasizes procedural (due process) rights and offender accountability. More recently, the restorative model has gained popularity in some countries. This model emphasizes that offenders accept responsibility for their criminal behavior and its impact on victims and the community (Australian Law Reform Commission n.d.). Several scholars (Cox, Allen, Hanser, and Conrad 2013; Corrado, Bala, Linden, and LeBlanc 1992; Reichel 1994, 2005; and Winterdyk 2002) have developed models for classifying juvenile justice systems. Winterdyk (2002) explained six different models—participatory, welfare, corporatism, modified justice, justice, and crime control. Reichel's (2005) more recent classification scheme seems the most viable. That scheme had four models—welfare, legalistic, corporatist, and participatory. This following section discusses two countries for each model; however, it should be noted that any country is likely to have aspects of several models as laws and public opinion can change over time (see Figure 1).

Figure 1 Models of Juvenile Justice

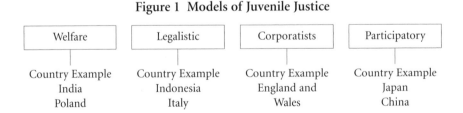

| Welfare | Legalistic | Corporatists | Participatory |

Country Example	Country Example	Country Example	Country Example
India	Indonesia	England and	Japan
Poland	Italy	Wales	China

Welfare Model

The welfare model was based on the principle of *parens patriae*, wherein the king intervened in place of parents to remove children from parental authority if they could not take care of them (Martin 2005). This doctrine originated in England in 1600s was applied in English Chancery courts. The recognition that every society must consider children's well-being gave rise to the separation of juvenile and adult criminal court proceedings as well as detention facilities, procedural safe guards, and reforms in many countries, including the countries examined in this chapter: India, Poland, Australia, New Zealand, and the United States.

India

Between 1850 and 1919, India, similar to the United States, was experiencing rapid social changes, population increases, and industrial developments. These changes created a new class of delinquent, neglected, and dependent children needing formal intervention. In India, the Penal Code (1860), the Code of Criminal Procedure (1861), and the Reformatory School Act (1876) changed juvenile penal philosophy from punishment to reformation (Kethineni 2005). The Indian Penal Code (IPC) (1860), although not a specific legislation dealing with juveniles, has a provision to address offenses committed by juveniles. Section 82 of the IPC considers children under seven years of age are incapable of committing crime, while those seven to twelve years of age get qualified immunity (Prakash 2013). The Reformatory School Act of 1876 established special schools (i.e., reformatory schools) for young criminals. In 1919, a jail committee recommended separate legislation for juveniles, which were enacted in different provinces. After India's independence from the British in 1947, the Children Act (1960) was passed. This Act was to provide care, protection, maintenance, welfare, training, and education of neglected and delinquent children; however, it was applicable only in Union Territories (i.e., areas directly under the Central Government Rule).

In 1974, India passed a National Policy for Children, which gave priority to the best interest of the child and highlighted the importance of protecting children from abuse, neglect, cruelty, and exploitation. In 1986, the country developed the first comprehensive Juvenile Justice Act (1986) and brought uniformity in the application of the juvenile law. In addition, the Act provided for the care, protection, treatment, development, and rehabilitation of neglected and delinquent juveniles throughout the country. It created separate procedures for addressing juveniles accused of committing crimes and those in need of care and protection (i.e., abused and neglected). Two separate authorities—juvenile courts to deal with delinquents and welfare boards to handle neglected/dependent minors—were created (Kethineni and Klosky 2000). Due to a controversial age determination issue in the legislation (upper age limit for boys was below sixteen and for girls below eighteen to be considered a juvenile), as well as limited procedural rights available for juveniles, the Juvenile Justice (Care & Protection) Act (2000) was passed (Kethineni 2005).

The 2000 Act incorporated many of the provisions enlisted in the Convention on the Rights of the Child, the UN Standard Minimum Rules for the Administration of Juvenile Justice, and the UN Rules for the Protection of Juveniles Deprived of their Liberty instruments. This Act continues to emphasize a welfare approach with the inclusion of noncriminal justice terminologies (e.g., "juvenile" refers to a child who has committed an offense; "child" means a young person under eighteen years of age in need of care and protection), fixing the age of juvenile justice jurisdiction up to eighteen years, regardless of gender, adoption of a child-friendly approach in adjudication and disposition, and a strong emphasis on rehabilitation through various institutions established under this enactment. Juvenile Justice Boards (previously juvenile courts) now handle juveniles in conflict with the law and Child Welfare Committees (previously child welfare boards) process children in need of care and protection. In addition, special homes meant to house adjudicated juveniles, were established by state government or a voluntary organization. Similarly, juvenile homes were created for housing children in need of care and protection.

The 2000 Act also included additional procedural rights for juveniles, including bail irrespective of the nature of the crime unless such a release exposes the juvenile to moral, physical, or psychological danger or result in association with known criminals; fair trials; and prohibition against death penalty or life imprisonment. Similar to adults, juveniles may be represented by attorneys of their choice as soon as they are taken into custody. If juveniles or their parents are unable to afford such representation, then the courts ensure provision of free legal aid. Each board is composed of a magistrate and two social workers, one of which must be a woman. Magistrates representing the board must have special knowledge or training in child psychology or child welfare and the social workers must be involved in health education or welfare activities for at least seven years prior to their appointment. The board members have wide discretionary authority in sentencing ranging from an admonition to a fine, probation, or placing juveniles in special homes (for up to three years). Overall, the system maintains the welfare approach, with recent emphasis on procedural (due process) rights irrespective of whether the individual is a juvenile or a child [Juvenile Justice (Care and Protection of Children) Act 2000].

Poland

After regaining independence in 1918, Poland unified both the penal and civil laws. First, a legislative commission was set to draft the Penal Code. The commission stressed that children and youth who had violated the law should not be treated as "little adults," and as such, should not receive the same penalties as adults. The Penal Code was passed in 1932 containing a separate chapter on juveniles. The Code defined a juvenile as a person who had committed an offense under the age of seventeen. Juveniles under thirteen years of age who had committed an offense could not be held accountable. For such children, authorities could only impose educational measures, ranging from a reprimand to the supervision of parents to placement in educational institutions (Stando-Kawecka 2004). Juveniles between thirteen and seventeen years of age who were competent enough to understand the nature of their offenses were sentenced to houses of correction. It was possible, however, to impose education measures if the court deems fit. Placing juveniles in such institutions became a matter of controversy as some of these juveniles could be sent to a house of correction until they reach the age of twenty-one. Some lawyers criticized such practices as educational-preventive measures, whereas others argued that such practices constitute punishments (or quasi-punishments) with elements of both retribution and rehabilitation (Stando-Kawecka 2006). In addition to the Penal Code, the Code of Criminal Procedure (1928) also introduced separate proceedings for juveniles. However, there were only a few juvenile courts operating in Poland until the 1960s.

At the time when many Western nations were moving away from a welfare model to a more legalistic approach emphasizing personal accountability in the early 1980s, Poland took an even more paternalistic welfare approach with the Juvenile Act of 1982 (Wojcik 1995). Some claim the Act broke most of the links that previously connected the criminal law and the provisions pertaining to juveniles. First, it provided reasons for intervention: (1) the juvenile committed a criminal act; and (2) the juvenile shows symptoms of demoralization (i.e., prostitution, truancy, vagrancy, participating in criminal gangs, etc.). Second, the Act categorized juveniles into three groups: first, a child under eighteen years of age who shows symptoms of demoralization; second, a child between the ages of thirteen and sixteen who committed a crime; and third, juveniles under twenty-one who were involved in demoralizing acts or criminal deeds. Juveniles who fall into the first group are handled in the family court using civil law proceedings. Juvenile cases in the second group are heard by the family court applying either the civil law proceedings or criminal proceedings. For the last group of juveniles (under 21), both educational and corrective measures of the Juvenile Act are applied (Krukowski 1987).

An important aspect of Poland's welfare approach to juvenile crime is the active role played by family judges who conduct and control all stages of family court proceedings (Stando-Kawecka 2004). The educational measures that the family courts can use are: warning, and accountability of the juvenile to specific conduct. The latter includes restoring the damage, apologizing to the victim, refraining from alcohol and drugs, etc. The courts may also send the case to mediation. In serious cases, the court may use correctional measures such as placement at the correctional institution up to the age of twenty-one (Utrat-Milecky 2005). The welfare approach is achieved by bringing about positive changes in juveniles' personalities and behaviors and ensuring the appropriate discharge of parents' (or guardians') and the public's duties and obligations. The public is represented in this system by two laypersons whom, along with a judge, must agree to any sanctions imposed.

Legalistic Model

The legalistic model to juvenile justice focuses on offenses rather than offenders, and the enforcement of the law over the welfare of youth. Reichel (2005) contends that the legalistic model is not less humanitarian than the welfare model; rather, it recognizes when and how the law should be applied.

Indonesia

Indonesia is an extreme example of the legalistic model. The legal basis in dealing with juveniles is the Juvenile Court Act (1997). Similar to India, Indonesia also has ratified the CRC. The Juvenile Court Act and other national legislations define a "juvenile" as a person under the age of eighteen who has not been married, and the age of criminal responsibility is set at age eight. The Act is also applicable for persons up to the age of 21. The law identifies two categories of children: "status offenders" (considered an offense only for children who engage in truancy or running away from home), and "juvenile delinquents" (those who have committed crimes). The goals of the juvenile justice system are to keep citizens safe and rehabilitate delinquents, however, the policymakers and citizens are unclear on which of the two goals should receive priority (Mardite n.d.). Another issue is the lack of implementation of the Juvenile Justice Law. Although the law was approved in 1997 to create a special court system and a criminal code for handling juvenile cases, the special courts are still not established. Recent reports claim that the current law offers limited hope for children (Andriyanto 2010).

The period of detention for juveniles is shorter than what was stipulated in the Criminal Code. In addition, the legal sanctions are classified into criminal sanctions and measures. Criminal sanctions include imprisonment, detention, fine and supervision. The maximum penalties for juvenile delinquents who are convicted of serious crimes is two-thirds the punishment given to adults for the same crimes. In capital cases, juveniles can receive a maximum of ten years in prison. Measures include returning the juveniles to their parents, referring them to the State for education, or delivering them to the Social Department for education or training, For minor offenses, juveniles may be given suspended sentences, probation, or conditional discharge.

Italy

Italy represents a more typical legalistic model. The juvenile justice system relies primarily on the legalistic model with focus on the rehabilitation of juveniles. In recent years, the Italian public has been skeptical about the rehabilitative efficacy and the benefits to convicted offenders who receive lenient sentences.

Italy did not establish juvenile courts with jurisdiction over youths until 1934. Under 1956 and 1962 legislation, juveniles considered "wayward" were sent to rehabilitative institutions administered by the juvenile courts. The 1956 model combined penal intervention, punishment, and welfare. These institutions, according to many, did not differ in organization or atmosphere from penal detention centers, despite legislative intent to the contrary (Gatti and Verde 1997). A 1977 presidential decree brought sweeping changes in the administration of the juvenile justice system. It gave local authorities more control over implementing community interventions. The magistrates insisted on greater control over juveniles, including the use of closed institutions and other coercive methods in the treatment of juveniles, while the local authorities stressed rehabilitation (Gatti and Verde, 1997). The 1988 presidential decree (Decreto del Presidente della Repubblica, D.P.R) resulted in the passing of the New Code of Criminal Procedure for Minors. The new code was a marked shift from an inquisitorial to an accusatorial model, which opened cross-examination, independent investigation by the defense, and guaranteed legal assistance.

Article 97 of the Italian Penal Code (1934) states juveniles under fourteen years of age at the time of commission of a crime cannot be punished. The Penal Code (Article 98) also stipulates those juveniles between the ages of fourteen and eighteen and have committed offenses may be given a custodial sentence, but are usually given lenient sentences (Commissione per le Adozioni

Internazionali 2005; Crime and Society 2005; Marongiu and Biddau 2005). Although sentences are served in the juvenile institutions until the age of twenty-one, the court could maintain supervision of the youth until they turn twenty-five years of age. In addition, juvenile offenders cannot be sentenced to life imprisonment as per the rule of the Italian Constitutional Court.

Italian juvenile courts have broad jurisdiction (Gatti and Verde 1997). The courts are divided into three sectors: penal, civil, and administrative or rehabilitative. Each court is composed of four individuals—two professional magistrates and two citizens, typically one man and one woman. The two citizens are considered as consultants with expertise in biology, education, humanities and social sciences (Commissione per le Adozioni Internazionali 2005). A special public prosecutor is present at hearings, but the accused is questioned directly by the magistrate in a private setting. Moreover, to avoid further trauma, the minor may not be cross-examined. The accused can request an "abbreviated" trial, in which the findings of the preliminary hearing are accepted and the accused then is entitled to a one-third reduction in sentence (Kethineni 2005).

"Accelerated" trials apply to minors who have confessed or been arrested in the commission of their crimes (Gatti and Verde 1997; Reichel 2005). Such minors are eligible for preventive detention in the family homes, public group homes, or, in the worst case, a one-month prison term. In civil matters, the courts deal with prejudice against or abandonment of children and may assume parental authority. Children engaged in prostitution or other deviant behaviors are dealt with administratively, and rehabilitative measures are favored over criminal punishments. The last option is to request an "immediate" trial with no preliminary hearing. The case then goes directly to trial (Gatti and Verde 1997).

During the criminal proceedings against minors, the prosecutor and magistrate are required to review the juvenile's personal, family, social, and economic resources. This information is used to decide if charges should be filed, the extent of the juvenile's responsibility, and, if appropriate, to determine the penalty. The court can impose sentences applicable to adults as well as the punishments particularly designed for juveniles (Gatti and Verde 1997). The specific penalties for juveniles include: judicial pardon, suspension of the trial with imposition of probation, and custodial sanctions. The custodial sentences are generally reduced by one-third of what an adult would receive and are served in special prisons for juveniles (Gatti and Verde 1997).

Along with this strict adherence to legality, Italy's juvenile justice system provides opportunities for informality. For example, when an offense is petty and the behavior is out-of-character, the prosecutor may request the judge to dismiss the case so that the minor's education and rehabilitation would not be interrupted (Gatti and Verde 1997). In 1989, the country introduced a new form of probation for minors, which enabled a large percentage of youth to receive re-education measures instead of punitive sanctions (Maffei and Betsos 2011). In addition, mediation is encouraged in some cases.

Overall, there is an interesting contrast between Italy's strict interpretation of the law presuming that similar offenses should receive similar penalties and its informality in dealing with juveniles who sometimes receive individualized punishments based on levels of maturity (Lemert 1986). This combination provides Italy with a juvenile justice system with elements of "formal rigidity tempered by informal adaptability" (Reichel 2005, 344).

Corporatist Model

Typically when countries attempt to incorporate the two opposing goals (welfare v. legalistic), societal acceptance and bureaucratic mechanisms have to be in place to effectively integrate these models. When these models are almost reaching success, yet another variable, "just dessert," presents itself resulting in our third model: corporatist. Thus the corporatist model uses a combination of welfare, legalistic, and punishment in its approach to treatment of juveniles. Pratt (1989, p. 246) defines "corporatist" as "centralization of policy, increased government intervention, and the cooperation of various professional and interest groups into a collective whole with homogenous aims and objectives." England and Wales, Egypt, Israel, and Hong Kong are typical examples of the corporatist model. The section describes the England and Wales's model below.

England and Wales

In the eighteenth and early nineteenth centuries, the treatment of juveniles accused of committing crimes was no different than for adult offenders. They were subjected to punishments such as imprisonment, transportation to colonies, or death (Gelsthorpe and Fenwick 1997). The belief that extreme poverty is the root cause of crime resulted in the passing of a series of laws known as poor laws. The laws were intended to aid destitute children and to protect society from beggars and vagrants (Terrill 2007). In 1908, the Children's Act created a special sitting of the magistrate court (branch of an adult criminal court) with both criminal and civil jurisdiction pertaining to juveniles. This special sitting signified a symbolic change in attitudes towards juveniles. In spite of this change, procedures and dispositions in juvenile cases were basically the same as adults for decades to come.

After World War II, England established a child-orientated juvenile justice system. The 1961 Criminal Justice Act prohibited juvenile courts, with a few exceptions, from sentencing young offenders to prison for more than six months (Graham 2002). Eight years later, the Children and Young Persons Act (1969) was passed prohibiting juvenile offenders younger than fourteen from being referred to the juvenile court. The Children's Act of 1989 made children's welfare a significant part of the juvenile justice system (Reichel 2005). The 1989 Act abolished the use of care orders in criminal proceedings and removed the offense condition as a justification of state intervention in the life of a family (Wakefield and Hirschel 1996). The Criminal Justice Act (1991), however, moved towards a "just desserts" approach. This approach shifted the focus from the offender and his background, to the nature and the seriousness of the offense (Graham and Moore 2006). The Act brought seventeen-year-olds under the jurisdiction of new youth courts, which replaced juvenile courts. The Act distinguished between "children" and "young persons" (between ages fourteen and seventeen). Children are further divided into two groups: those under ten years of age and those between ten and thirteen (Terrill 2007). The Act also included a two-track system in dealing with young offenders: a track for dealing with violent, dangerous, and persistent offenders for whom custody was recommended; and a track for petty property offenders for whom community-based sentences were deemed appropriate.

The Criminal Justice and Public Order Act (1994) further introduced strict penalties for juveniles, including long-term detention for 10–13-year-olds and secure-detention orders for persistent offenders who are 12–14 years of age. The research showed that a small percentage of persistent offenders (3%) were committing over a quarter of the offenses, and that juveniles do not grow out of crime when they reach adulthood, and the publication of Misspent Youth report criticizing the efficacy and effectiveness of overall youth justice system prompted the enactment of the Crime and Disorder Act (CDA), 1998 (Graham and Moore 2006). The CDA provides the basis for the current juvenile justice system in England (Reichel 2005). The act's primary objective was to prevent offending and reoffending, resulting in unifying the practitioners "towards a common and shared purpose" (Graham and Moore 2006, 66). The act also abolished the age-based criteria for culpability. For example, previously, those under ten years of age were completely immune from criminal responsibility, those between ten and thirteen were not regarded as criminals unless proven otherwise, and those above thirteen were considered responsible for their actions, but subject to different procedures and punishments. The act also established a new Youth Justice Board with overseeing powers, and a network of more than 155 multi-agency youth offending teams (YOTs) to coordinate juvenile justice services. The new

thinking was to include parents in the process, incorporate the restorative justice approach, make the offender realize the consequences of his/her actions,
and help offenders develop a sense of reasonability (Graham and Moore 2006).

Juvenile trials are held in magistrates' courts sitting as youth courts. The
courts used the same adult procedures whether they are in trial on indictment
or summary proceedings. Trials are closed to the public. Parents have to attend
all of the proceedings and the youth may also bring their attorneys either to defend their case or to provide an explanation to the court. Victims and members of the youth offending team (YOT) may also be present (Terrill 2007).
YOTs play a significant role in assisting juveniles in fulfilling one of the main
objectives of the CDA—accountability. The 1999 Youth Justice and Criminal
Evidence Act introduced referrals to youth offender panels (consisting of two
volunteers from the local community and a member from the local YOT) (Goddard 2003). They provide pre-court and court services; community supervision; and assist offenders' follow through with special orders such as *reparation*,
wherein young offenders assist victims, write apologies, or clean graffiti; *action plan orders* that require offenders and their parents to address causes of offending behavior; and *referral orders* for participation in programs designed
for first-time offenders to help recognize the consequences of their behavior.

Currently, there are five types of custodial sanctions available: (1) youth
custody orders, (2) detention and training orders, (3) supervision order, (4)
care orders, and (5) attention center orders. Youth custody is designed for juveniles fifteen to twenty years of age. If the youth are under seventeen, the
length of confinement should not exceed twenty-four months. Detention training order applies to offenders between the ages of twelve and seventeen and
the order could last anywhere from twelve months to three years. A supervision order is for serious offenders and could be given for up to three years. A
care order places a juvenile with a local authority and removes parental rights.
Technically, the attendance centers are not custodial in nature. They are open
on weekends and teach juveniles constructive ways to spend their time (Terrill
2007). The range of sanctions reflects a conglomeration of "just desserts" and
restorative justice principles making the juvenile justice in England and Wales
a corporatist model.

Participatory Model

The participatory model of juvenile justice involves active participation of
citizen and community organizations to prevent deviant behavior. Its primary
goal is to integrate troubled youths into the mainstream society without any
significant or formal legal interventions (Reichel 2005). Compared to the mod-

ern industrialized countries with similar populations, Japan records the lowest crime rate. Homogeneity of the population, family cohesiveness, respect for authority, the low rates of unemployment, and the stigma of shame placed on law violators explain its low crime rate (Terrill 2007). The model is popular in traditional societies, such as Japan and China.

Japan

In Japan, legislations such as the Criminal Code of One Hundred Articles of 1742 had provisions for reduced punishments for young people up to age fifteen. After the Meiji restoration in 1868, however, Japan enacted the Penal Code of 1880, which set the minimum age of criminal responsibility at twelve (Yokoyama 1997). The postwar Code of Criminal Procedure (1948) guaranteed human and due process rights to juveniles. The juveniles are classified into three categories: First, "juvenile offenders" between the ages of fourteen and twenty (previously the upper age limit was eighteen) who have committed delinquent or criminal acts; second, "child offenders" (those juveniles aged fourteen or younger) who have committed delinquent or criminal acts; and third, "pre-delinquent" (covers juveniles aged twenty or younger) who have not yet committed any criminal or delinquent acts. Unlike many industrialized countries, the Japanese people have always relied on informal social controls to maintain order and prevent juvenile delinquency. In rural areas, people have relied on informal social controls implemented by families and neighborhoods. In urban areas, people have been involved in informal social control mechanisms such as town associations that conduct festivals, athletic meetings, or traffic safety training (Yokoyama 1997). Those informal efforts are complimented by formal social controls such as juvenile guidance centers and law enforcement agencies. Guidance center members patrol streets, counsel juveniles and their parents, and help the overall social environment. In addition, there are many volunteer probation officers who supplement the formal system of justice.

Typically, pre-offense juveniles and law breaking children are referred by the police to either the Family Courts or the Child Guidance Centers. More serious cases are reviewed by the public prosecutor. Once the case is received, a Family Court judge initiates an investigation and assigns a probation officer to compile life histories, home environment, and the personal background of the juvenile. When the investigations are complete, cases are heard either in the Family Courts or referred to the Child Guidance Centers for treatment. Although the Family Courts have primary jurisdiction over all juveniles, in exceptional cases, the judge can send a case to the public prosecutor to be prosecuted in an adult (district) court (Tonioka and Goto 1996; Kethineni 2005). Proceedings in juvenile courts are informal, where the judge's main focus is not the determination of guilt but to find ways to provide treatment (Terrill 2007). The juvenile justice system's goal of protecting, educating, and rehabilitating young offenders is reflected in the type of dispositions given. These sanctions range from probation, to referring juveniles and their parents to the Child Guidance Center, commitment to homes where juveniles receive education and live in a protective environment, to juvenile training schools operated by the Ministry of Justice. Finally, juveniles tried in a district court are sent to a juvenile prison where work, academic and educational aspects are encouraged (Terrill 2007).

People's Republic of China

As in many countries, China experienced upward and downward trend in delinquency (Terrill 2007). The first period was between 1949 and 1965 during which China experienced an increase in adult crime and the scholars have attributed the increase to the founding of the People's Republic of China. The juvenile crime rate during this period, however, was low. The second period was from 1966–1976 (the period of the Cultural Revolution), and China reported high rates of delinquency (Zu-Yuan 1988). The increase in juvenile crime was attributed to the Cultural Revolution and the country's modernization efforts. The third period started in 1984 and continues to the present day. The one-child policy, high rates of unemployment, an increase in school dropouts, and migration of young people from rural to urban areas were thought to be the reasons for the increase. The one-child policy was believed to have created young troublemakers who were spoiled by their parents, or they were left alone with no emotional support because they have no older sibling to rely on when parents are at work. The increase in juvenile crime, although very low compared to many countries, prompted the Chinese Communist Party to crack down on juvenile delinquency, known as the "severe blows" campaign (Terrill 2007; Kethineni 2005).

In China, the term "juvenile delinquents" refer to those between the ages of fourteen and twenty-five, and the term "juvenile criminals" applies to those between the ages of eighteen and twenty-five years (Terrill 2007). In addition to the above broad classification, young people (those who are fourteen and sixteen) who commit serious offenses (i.e., murder, aggravated assaults, robbery, rape, arson, drug trafficking) are criminally responsible. Additionally, youth who are between fourteen and seventeen receive lighter sentences (Wong, 2004).

Like the Japanese juvenile justice, China utilized both formal and informal mechanisms of social control. Because of heavy emphasis on informal social controls, China did not see the need for a separate juvenile court or a separate juvenile law until the mid-1980s (Kethineni 2005). The first juvenile court was initiated in the City of Shanghai in 1984, comprising of a collegial bench to hear juvenile cases (Zhang 2008). As of 2008, there were about 3,300 juvenile courts in the country. The juvenile justice system continues to develop with the passage of two significant laws: Juvenile Protection Law (1991) and Preventing Juvenile Delinquency Law (1999). The aim of the Juvenile Protection Law was to provide "comprehensive protection of minors' rights and interests" (Zhang 2008, 154). The Preventing Juvenile Delinquency Law emphasized prevention through providing moral and legal education to three groups of juveniles: (1) pre-delinquents; (2) delinquents before they become serious offenders, and (3) recidivists before they become chronic offenders (Zhang 2008). The law outlines responsibilities of parents, schools, law enforcement, social service agencies, and neighborhood committees in preventing misbehavior of children. In addition, juveniles who are in need of close supervision may be sent to juvenile detention centers (known as the reeducation-through-labor) (Wong 2004).

As many jurisdictions do not have separate juvenile courts, formal proceedings against juvenile offenders are held before a basic people's court (a lower-level trial court) where the proceedings are similar to the adult system with a few exceptions. For example, if a minor under the age of eighteen commits a crime, the minor and his/her legal representative are notified to be present at the time of interrogation and trial. In contrast, an adult defendant is not allowed to have legal representation until after the initial interrogation (Terrill 2007).

Those who were sent to a period of incarceration are either sent to a juvenile reformatory or to a reform-through-labor camp, depending on the age and the nature of the offense. Juveniles between the age of fourteen and sixteen are sent to reformatories. The goal of reformatories is to include education and work as a daily routine. Juveniles over the age of sixteen are typically sent to a reform-through-labor camp. Similar to reformatories, offenders at the reform-through-labor camp are required to perform physical labor. In addition to these formal sanctions, juveniles can be administratively sanctioned by the State Council Relating to Problems of Reeducation-Through-Labor to a reeducation-through-labor camp for up to three years (Terrill 2013). The Ministry of State Education established work and study schools. The work-study schools are quasi-judicial in nature (Kethineni 2005). Juveniles who are between the ages of twelve and eighteen and have committed minor offenses, or are habitually truants, or have had disciplinary issues at school are referred to the schools by parents, police, or other community members. In addition to providing education, the schools focus on discipline (Terrill 2007).

Historically, China has relied on an informal system of social control to address misbehavior of children. One of the informal strategies is the use of the neighborhood committee. These committees operate in neighborhoods, schools, and factories. The two main purposes of these committees are responsible for: maintaining public order and mediate disputes. If there is a dispute between a young person, a family member, or a neighbor, the neighborhood committee tries to resolve the issue. The other informal strategy is the establishment of a local committee (*bang-jiao*) for community supervision and educational assistance. It is a grassroots effort to prevent, as well as address, delinquency in the local community. A bang-jiao typically consists of the juvenile's parents, a member of the local neighborhood committee, a school administrator (even if the juvenile is no longer attending the school), a member of the work group (if the juvenile is currently working or had worked), and a local public security officer (i.e., police). The group actively participates both in preventing delinquency as well as in assisting in the rehabilitation of a released offender (Terrill 2007).

The participatory approach is more visible in China's commitment in prevention of delinquency through early intervention programs. Younger and less serious offenders are referred to various informal organizations to provide guidance and supervision (Wong 2001). A similar philosophy is applied even when young persons commit serious offenses. Instead of referring such cases to the neighborhood organizations, offenders are sent to surveillance and rehabilitation centers to reform and to obtain education (Kethineni 2005).

Conclusion

This chapter discussed the important UN documents pertaining to the juvenile justice system, the age of criminal responsibility in different countries around the world, and the four models of juvenile justice—welfare, legalistic, corporatist, and participatory. For all practical purposes, juvenile personnel should first look to the CRC and then to the Riyadh Guidelines for preventing children from coming in to conflict with the law; second, they should look to the CRC and the Beijing Rules when dealing with children alleged or accused of having come in to conflict with the law; and third, the personnel of the criminal justice system should look to the CRC and the JDL Rules for dealing with children found to be in breach of the criminal law.

The age of criminal responsibility differs from country to country as well as within the same country. Although most of the common law countries set their minimum age at seven and the maximum age at eighteen, China, Germany, Italy, Japan, and Russia set the minimum age at fourteen. Within the United States, Oklahoma State sets the minimum age at seven, while Nevada sets minimum age at eight. In addition, a vast majority of states in the United States have no specific minimum age. Even the UN did not set the minimum age in any of the rules, guidelines, or conventions pertaining to children. This lack of uniformity and clarity diminishes the protections accorded to children.

Finally, while each of the four models of juvenile justice stresses the best interest of the child as its primary focus, each take a different approach to achieve the goal. Countries such as India and Poland primarily emphasize the welfare of the child through providing care, development, education, and treatment of juvenile offenders rather than punishment. India, however, recently incorporated several aspects of due process rights without jeopardizing the welfare goal in accordance with the UN international standards, including the CRC.

As the welfare approach was criticized for its paternalism, violation of rights, and discriminatory treatment, countries such as Indonesia and Italy have favored a legalistic model. These countries have exchanged informal approaches to addressing juvenile offenders for more formal court procedures and procedural rights. Although juveniles are accorded the same procedural rights as adults, they have not completely ignored the consideration of individual needs (Kethineni 2005).

Public concern over increase in youth crime and limited success with rehabilitating persistent offenders, countries such as England and Wales moved towards a new model—the corporatist model. In addition to giving due process rights, the new model highlighted the importance of public protection. One such effort was to create specialized courts to address a specific group of offenders. England and Wales, for example, created youth courts to handle serious offenders and gave the administrative agencies the responsibility to provide treatment for less serious offenders where the public still favors treatment (Kethineni 2005).

Finally, the participatory model emphasizes a community-based approach to prevent and rehabilitate juvenile offenders. Although formal systems exist to address serious offenses, countries such as Japan and China rely heavily on informal systems of crime control. Neighborhood committees and voluntary organizations operate in rural and urban areas to provide mediation, supervision, and delinquency prevention programs. Active involvement of parents, school administrators, and other community members are essential part of the informal system.

Web Sources

1. Information on UN convention on CRC is available at:
   http://www.ohchr.org/en/professionalinterest/pages/crc.aspx
2. Information on juvenile justice in China is available at:
   http://duihua.org/wp/?page_id=131
3. Recent changes in youth justice in Japan are available at:
   http://ir.lib.hiroshima-u.ac.jp/metadb/up/kiyo/AN0021395X/HLJ_33-4_90.pdf
4. Crime in India is available at:
   http://ncrb.nic.in/
5. Information about the Youth Justice Board in England is available at:
   http://www.justice.gov.uk/about/yjb

Discussion Questions

1. What is the significance of the UN Convention on the Rights of Children?
2. What are the controversies regarding the age of criminality of the juveniles?
3. Which of the UN documents provide due process rights for juveniles? What is the importance of those rights?
4. Discuss the Indian juvenile justice system and its model. How is it different from the Italian system?
5. Compare and contrast the four models of juvenile justice and explain the fundamental principles that guide each of the models.

References

Andriyanto, Heru. "Indonesia's Juvenile Justice System Offers Little Justice for Children." *Jakarta Globe,* February 21, 2010. Accessed November 4, 2013. http://www.thejakartaglobe.com/archive/indonesias-juvenile-law-system-offers-little-justice-for-children/.

Australian Law Reform Commission. *Children Involvement in Criminal Justice Process: Juvenile Justice Models.* Accessed December 15, 2013. http://www.alrc.gov.au/publications/18-childrens-involvement-criminal-justice-processes/juvenile-justice-models, n.d.

Center for International Conflict Resolution. *Youth Violence in Latin America.* Accessed December 5, 2013. http://www.cicr-columbia.org/research/past/youth-violence/, n.d.

Commissione per le Adozioni Internazionali. *The Juvenile Courts*. Accessed January 5, 2005. http://www.commissioneadozioni.it/site/en-GB/The_Institutional_actors/The_Juvenile_Courts/http://www.akf.dk/eng98/juvenile.htm, n.d.

Corrado, Raymond R., Nicholas Bala, Rick Linden, and Marc LeBlanc. *Juvenile Justice in Canada: A Theoretical and Analytical Assessment*. Toronto: Butterworths, 1992.

Cox, Steven M., Jennifer M. Allen, Robert D. Hanser, and John J. Conrad. *Juvenile Justice: A Guide to Theory, Policy, Practice*. Thousand Oaks, CA: Sage, 2013.

Crime and Society: A Comparative Criminology Tour of the World. *Italy*. Accessed November 12, 2013. http://www-rohan.sdsu.edu/faculty/rwinslow/europe/italy.html, 2005.

Dammer, Harry R., and Jay S. Albanese. *Comparative Criminal Justice Systems*. (4th ed.). Belmont, CA: Wadsworth Cengage Learning, 2011.

Egley, Arlen, Jr., and James C. Howell. *Highlights of the 2011 National Youth Gang Survey*. Washington, DC: U.S. Department of Justice, Office of Juvenile Justice and Delinquency Prevention, 2013.

Gatti, Uberto, and Alfredo Verde. "Comparative Juvenile Justice: An Overview of Italy." In *Juvenile Justice Systems: International Perspectives*, edited by John A. Winterdyk, 177–204. Toronto: Canadian Scholar's Press, 1997.

Gelsthorpe, Loraine, and Mark Fenwick. "Comparative Juvenile Justice: England and Wales." In *Juvenile Justice Systems: International Perspectives*, edited by John A. Winterdyk, 77–112. Toronto: Canadian Scholar's Press, 1997.

Goddard, Jim. "Youth Justice Policy in the United Kingdom." *Criminal Justice Studies* 16, no. 4 (2003): 329–338.

González, Marcos. *UNICEF-Supported Study Sheds Light on Gangs in Honduras*. Accessed October 2013. http://www.unicef.org/infobycountry/honduras_65204.html, 2012.

Graham, John. "Juvenile Crime and Justice in England and Wales." In *Juvenile Justice Systems: An International Comparison of Problems and Solutions*, edited by Nicholas M. Bala, Joseph P. Hornick, Howard. N. Snyder, and Joanne J. Paetsch, 67–106. Toronto: Thompson Educational Publishing, 2002.

Graham, John, and Colleen Moore. "Beyond Welfare Versus Justice: Juvenile Justice in England and Wales." In *International Handbook of Juvenile Justice*, edited by Josine Jungar-Tas and Scott H. Decker, 65–92. New York: Springer, 2006.

Howell, James C. *Youth Gangs*. Washington, DC: U.S. Department of Justice, Office of Juvenile Justice and Delinquency Prevention, 1997.

Juvenile Justice (Care and Protection of Children) Act. Accessed December 4, 2013. http://www.law.yale.edu/rcw/rcw/jurisdictions/assc/india/india_juv_just.pdf, 2000.

Kethineni, Sesha. "Comparison of Juvenile Justice Models." In *Introduction to International Criminal Justice*, edited by Mangai Natarajan, 61–70. New York: McGraw-Hill, 2005.

Kethineni, Sesha, and Trisha Klosky. "The Impact of Juvenile Justice Reforms in India." *International Journal of Offender Therapy and Comparative Criminology* 44, no. 3 (2000): 321–325.

Krukowski, Adam. "Criminological and Legal Problems of Juvenile Delinquency in Poland." *EuroCriminology* 1 (1987): 113–129.

Lemert, Eric M. "Juvenile Justice Italian style." *Law and Society Review* 20 (1986): 509–544.

Maffei, Stefano, and Isabella M. Betsos. "Crime and Criminal Policy in Italy: Tradition and Modernity in a Troubled County." *European Journal of Criminology* 4, no.4 (2011): 461–482.

Mardite, Harlan. *The Juvenile Justice System in Indonesia.* Accessed December 3, 2013. http://www.unafei.or.jp/english/pdf/RS_No68/No68_16PA_Mardite.pdf, n.d.

Marongiu, Pietro, and Mario Biddau. *World Factbook of Criminal Justice Systems: Italy.* Accessed November 5, 2013. http://www.bjs.gov/content/pub/pdf/wfbcjsit.pdf, 2005.

Martin, Gus. *Juvenile Justice Process and Systems.* Thousand Oaks, CA: Sage, 2005.

National Crime Records Bureau. *Crime in India 2012.* Accessed December 10, 2013. http://ncrb.nic.in/, 2013.

Office of Juvenile Justice and Delinquency Prevention (OJJDP). *Statistical Briefing Book: Juvenile Arrests.* Accessed December 5, 2013. http://www.ojjdp.gov/ojstatbb/crime/qa05102.asp?qaDate=2010, 2010.

Prakash, Haveripeth. "Juvenile Justice: A Hard Look." *International Research Journal of Social Sciences* 2, no.1 (2013): 38–40.

Pratt, John. "Corporatism: The Third Model of Juvenile Justice." *British Journal of Criminology* 29 (1989): 236–254.

Raha, Swagata. "Busting Misconceptions on Juvenile Justice." *The Hindu,* August 26, 2013. Accessed December 4, 2013. http://www.thehindu.com/opinion/op-ed/busting-misconceptions-on-juvenile-justice/article5061398.ece.

Reichel, Philip L. *Comparative Criminal Justice Systems.* Englewood Cliffs, NJ: Prentice Hall, 1994.

Reichel, Philip L. *Comparative Criminal Justice Systems* (4th ed.). Upper Saddle River, NJ: Pearson, 2005.

Stando-Kawecka, Barbara. *The Juvenile Justice System in Poland: Report Prepared for the European Society of Criminology.* Accessed December 2, 2103. http://www.esc-eurocrim.org/files/juvenile_justice_system_in_poland.doc, 2004.

Stando-Kawecka, Barbara. "Continuity in the Welfare Approach: Juvenile Justice in Poland." In *International Handbook of Juvenile Justice*, edited by Josine Junger-Tas and Scott H. Decker, 351–376. New York: Springer, 2006.

Terrill, Richard. *World Criminal Justice Systems* (6th ed.). Newark, NJ: Lexis-Nexis, 2007.

Terrill, Richard. *World Criminal Justice Systems* (8th ed.). Newark, NJ: Anderson Publishing, 2013.

Tanioka, Ichiro, and Hiroko Goto. "Japan." In *International Handbook on Juvenile Justice*, edited by Donald Shoemaker, 191–206. Westport, CT: Greenwood Press, 1996.

UN Factsheet on Youth. *Fact Sheet on Juvenile Justice.* Accessed December 5, 2013. http://www.un.org/esa/socdev/unyin/documents/wyr11/FactSheetonYouthandJuvenileJustice.pdf, n.d.

UNICEF. *South Asia and the Minimum Age of Criminal Responsibility.* Accessed December 5, 2013. http://www.unicef.org/rosa/Criminal_Responsibility_08July_05(final_copy).pdf, n.d.

UNICEF. *Children's Rights and Journalism Practice: A Right-Based Perspective.* Accessed December 5, 2013. http://elearning-events.dit.ie/unicef/index.htm, 2007.

United Nations Office on Drugs and Crime (UNODC) and the Latin America and the Caribbean Region of the World Bank. *Crime, Violence, and Development: Trends, Costs, and Policy Options in the Caribbean.* Accessed December 3, 2013. http://www.unodc.org/pdf/research/Cr_and_Vio_Car_E.pdf, 2011.

UN Treaty Event. *2011 Treaty Event: Towards Universal Participation and Implementation.* Accessed December 5, 2013. https://treaties.un.org/doc/source/events/2011/Publication/publication-English.pdf, 2011.

United Nations. *UN Convention on Rights of Children.* Accessed December 3, 2013. http://www.ohchr.org/Documents/ProfessionalInterest/crc.pdf, 1990.

United Nations. UN Standard Minimum Rules for the Administration of Juvenile Justice ("The Beijing Rules"). Accessed December 2, 2013. http://www.achpr.org/files/instruments/un-standard-the-beijing-rules/standard_minimum_rules_for_the_administration_of_juvenile_justice.pdf, 1985.

United Nations General Assembly. *United Nations Guidelines for the Prevention of Juvenile Delinquency (The Riyadh Guidelines).* Accessed December 2, 2013. http://www.un.org/documents/ga/res/45/a45r112.htm, 1990a.

United Nations General Assembly. *United Nations Rules for the Protection of Juveniles Deprived of their Liberty.* Accessed November 3, 2013. http://www.un.org/documents/ga/res/45/a45r113.htm, 1990b.

United Nations Human Settlement Report (UN-HABITAT). *State of the World's Cities 2006/07.* Sterling, VA: Earthscan, 2006–2007.

United Nations Interregional Crime and Justice Research Institute (UNICRI). *Juvenile Justice in Mozambique.* Accessed November 5, 2013. http://www.unicri.it/topics/juvenile_justice/mozambique/, n.d.-a.

United Nations Interregional Crime and Justice Research Institute (UNICRI). *Juvenile Justice in Angola.* Accessed November 5, 2013. http://www.unicri.it/topics/juvenile_justice/angola/, n.d.-b.

Urban Management Programme. *Street Children and Gangs in African cities: Guidelines for Local Authorities.* Nairobi, Kenya: Urban Management Programme and the United Nations Centre for Human Settlement (Habitat). Accessed November 5, 2013. http://www.ucl.ac.uk/dpu-, 2000.

Utrat-Milecky, J. *The Polish Approach to Juvenile Delinquency: Context and Tendencies.* Accessed December 4, 2013. http://www.dvjj.de/sites/default/files/medien/imce/documente/veranstaltungen/dokumentationen/polizei2/milecki.pdf, 2005.

Wakefield, William, and J. David Hirschel. "England." In *International Handbook on Juvenile Justice*, edited by Donald Shoemaker, 90–109. Westport, CT: Greenwood Press, 1996.

Winterdyk, John A. "Introduction." In *Juvenile Justice Systems: International Perspectives,* edited by John A. Winterdyk, vii–xxx. Toronto: Canadian Scholar's Press, 2002.

Wojcik, Dobrochna. "Juvenile Delinquency and Victims of Crime." In *Crime Control in Poland,* Jerzy Jasinski and Andrzez Siemaszko, 73–76. Warsaw: Oficyna Naukowa, 1995.

Wong, Dennis S. "Changes in Juvenile Justice in China." *Youth and Society* 32, no. 4 (2001): 492–509.

Wong, Dennis S. "Juvenile Protection and Delinquency Prevention Policies in China." *Australian and New Zealand Journal of Criminology* 37 (2004): 52–66.

Yokoyama, Minoru. "Juvenile Justice: An Overview in Japan." In *Juvenile Justice Systems: International Perspectives,* edited John A. Winterdyk, 1–28. Toronto: Canadian Scholar's Press, 1997.

Zhang, Lening. "Juvenile Delinquency and Justice in Contemporary China: A Critical Review of the Literature over 15 years." *Criminal Law and Social Change* 50 (2008): 149–60.

Zu-Yuan, H. "Juvenile Delinquency and Its Prevention. *Criminal Justice International* 4, no. 5 (1988): 5–6, 8, 10.

Chapter 9

The Global Normative Order: International Individual Rights, States and Justice

Gabriel Rubin[1]

Introduction

How are international justice and international law different from domestic justice or domestic law? The main difference that theorists have inferred is that in the international order, the basic units of legal jurisprudence or justice are nation-states or peoples, not individuals. In this chapter, I will argue that this is a foolish contention and that international legal rights must be derived at the individual level. In making this argument, this chapter will be written as a riposte to the theory proposed in John Rawls's *The Law of Peoples* (1999), which presents the preeminent theorist's conception of justice on the international scale.

Theorists of international justice seek to describe what a just international legal and political system should look like. They call this project that of conceiving of and describing the just global normative order. Once Utopianism is eschewed, this task proves to be an exceedingly difficult one. "The perpetual peace," Immanuel Kant famously wrote. "A Dutch innkeeper once put this satirical inscription on a signboard, along with the picture of a graveyard. We shall not trouble to ask whether it applies to men in general, or particularly to heads of state (who never have enough of war), or only to philosophers who blissfully dream of perpetual peace" (Kant 1991, 93). Of course, those who seek international justice seek a world that is more peaceful.

Because theorists of international justice seek to construct a just global normative order, one of the main questions with which they grapple is: How

---

1. I thank Josh Cohen for his help in the conceptualization of this chapter.

should the international order be politically and legally organized? I will keep this chapter normative by arguing that international rights should be derived at the individual level and not at the level of the state or of the "people." This is a novel argument because today rights are derived at the state level both domestically and internationally. This chapter has two goals. First, to show, contrary to John Rawls's narrative in *The Law of Peoples,* that it is only logical to derive fundamental rights at the level of individuals rather than at the level of groups. Second, to determine whether democracy or liberal rights should be fundamental rights for all people in a just global normative order given that rights are derived at the individual level. Along the lines of Rawls's calls for mutual respect between just and decent peoples, even if a powerful argument exists in favor of democracy or liberalism, the conclusion will attempt to answer whether other societal forms should be tolerated. The question that will inevitably be left open is how these international legal and political rights should be enforced; the conclusion of this chapter will present some ideas on this matter. In the end, this chapter will make an argument for a world composed exclusively of liberal democracies.

A World of States

Let us begin with a discussion of states to show how the world got where it is today before turning to normative issues. In today's world, international justice is elusive. States determine the legal codes and rules for their inhabitants and usually protect their inhabitants, as much as they can, from international law and the laws of other states. In a world of states, international justice is present only in its most rudimentary forms since human beings are beholden to the laws and codes of their particular state.

Whereas women in the Western world have equal rights to men,[2] women in Saudi Arabia cannot leave the house without a male chaperone nor can they drive (see Husain 2011). In other parts of the world, such as India and the Democratic Republic of Congo, women are blamed and ostracized for being raped (Kristoff and WuDunn 2009 and Harris 2013). In North Korea, the people suffer from abject malnourishment and are punished for three generations for speaking against the government (Cooper 2012). This is all to say that rights

---

2. Of course, feminists will argue this point, but it cannot be contended that women in the West are more or less equal (at least in the eyes of the law) to men whereas women and girls in many parts of the developing world are clearly second-class citizens or treated like property. In other words, feminists are right to push for greater equality for the sexes everywhere, but there are great disparities in how women and girls are treated the world over.

and justice are incredibly uneven in a world of states. While liberal democratic values are given frequent lip service the world over, for instance in the United Nations' Declaration of Human Rights (https://www.un.org/en/documents/udhr/), many states treat their people terribly.

One only has to look at the Democratic Republic of Congo to see a perfect example. The DR-Congo is a land rich in minerals, wildlife, and beauty and yet it is one of the poorest countries in the world with one of the world's lowest life expectancies. This is because it is very hard to rule a land the size of Western Europe, which includes the second-biggest rainforest in the world, and because the government there preys on the people and uses the land to aggrandize itself to the detriment of its citizens (see Stearns 2011). Contrast this with Somalia, a land without a structured government, where the people are forced to fend for themselves (Leeson 2007).

So how did we get to this world where states are the key actors in international relations and the nation-state you live in determines what laws you follow? Human society began with tribes and clans based on familial and tribal membership. Tribes still exist in many parts of the world, including parts of Africa, South America, and pockets of the Middle East and Southeast Asia. Tribal rule is characterized by the rule of a chieftain or tribal elder who may hold advisors but no other formal officials [states, by contrast, have many formal officials: the U.S. government employs about two million people (Dinan 2010)]. Tribes also typically have no set territory. They are nomadic or semi-nomadic. They may stick to a certain region or set of regions (Wilkinson 2007, 13).

In Africa, tribal rule was characterized by an emphasis on controlling people not land. Since there was a lot of land and not many people, wars would be fought to capture one's opponents' people. The African map was one where a ruler controlled circles of land, and sometimes concentric circles, and where people were welcome to leave that land to live in the bush or the jungle (Herbst 2000).

The next unit of rule was the city-state. Aristotle, Socrates and Thucydides lived in city-states in Ancient Greece and the city-state remained as a typical form of rule for at least 1500 years. Machiavelli, writing in the late 1400s and early 1500s, describes an Italy divided into a multitude of city-states. City-states like Andorra, Vatican City and Luxembourg in Europe exist to this day. A city-state is exactly what it sounds like. It is a city that is ruled as if it were its own country. It has its own government, its own army, its own tax collectors, and so on. It has all the characteristics of a country today only it is the size of a city.

At the same time, empires formed usually around religious doctrines. An empire is a large group of territories and peoples controlled by a single monarch or a group of monarchs, empires varied in how much rule they exacted over the territories they controlled: some allowed their conquered lands to rule themselves, others did not. The Islamic empire stretched from Persia (today's Iran) to Spain. The empire expanded out of the Middle East from the seventh century to the sixteenth century and was later replaced by the Ottoman Empire, which controlled large parts of the Middle East until its destruction after World War I. The Holy Roman Empire ruled much of Europe during the Middle Ages. The Mongol Empire controlled much of Asia at one point in the thirteenth century. Colonial empires formed in more recent times like the British Empire that controlled America, India, and parts of Africa among other territories.

The modern state system began in 1648 with a series of treaties called the Peace of Westphalia. These treaties ended the Thirty Years' War, which had been fought between the Holy Roman Empire and the European monarchies such as France and it established states in France, Spain and England as well as other areas of Europe (Wilkinson 2007, 14–17).

From there, the state system expanded. America became an independent country. World War I saw the fall of the Ottoman Empire and the creation of a European map that looks very similar to today's map. Countries in the developing world, such as in the Middle East, became independent after World Wars I and II. By the end of World War II, almost all of humanity lived in a world of nation-states.

So what is a state? Max Weber says that a state is an entity which claims a monopoly over the legitimate use of violence in a given territory (Weber in Gerth and Mills 1948). Charles Tilly argued that, "Wars make states," and states make war (Tilly 1985, 170). Through wars, states expanded their territory—or really the groups that ruled those states did. Through wars, states developed the apparatus of officials to collect taxes (for the war effort originally) and to punish their citizens (for not fighting in wars and for disloyalty originally).

Today we have two kinds of states: states created by war like those in Europe where borders and territories were fought over for centuries. And states created by colonialism, like those in Africa and the Middle East, where borders were literally just drawn on a map by colonial leaders. In fact, Europeans actually had a conference to draw up who would control what African territory wherein the map of Africa we know today was created (see Herbst 2000, 59–77 on the Berlin West African Conference).

States, and the governments that control them, are the primary guarantors of justice in the world today due to the (sometimes dubious) legitimacy their governments have in the eyes of their people (but more so in the eyes of other governments) and the sovereignty states hold. As the state system has grown, people have banded together to fight for their own, many times ethnically segregated, states. South Sudan is just the newest addition to the likes of Kosovo, Serbia, Bosnia, Israel, the Palestinian Authority, the Czech Republic, Slovakia, Pakistan, and Bangladesh. Calls to split Iraq along ethnic lines were loud in the immediate aftermath of the recent American invasion there (see, for instance, Ignatieff 2007 and Lawson and Thacker 2003).

A world of segregated states raises walls—many times literally—between people and causes tension, miscommunication, and misunderstanding. The ideologically divided Korean Peninsula is just one such example. With states too there is a norm of indivisibility since existing states like China, Russia, and the United States do not want to establish a precedent of easy state formation. This makes states shapes on a map that can be conquered like individual properties ready to be invaded and drained of their resources. The recent history of the Central African Republic is just one such example (Mezyaev 2013).

For these reasons and others many have called for an end to a world of states. Amos Oz derides his fellow Jews for falling into the trap of wanting a state like everyone else—especially when it comes at the cost of a state for another people. In many ways, Oz champions peoplehood over statehood and sees the project of each "people" being glued to a territory on a map as being silly and, perhaps, fleeting (Oz 1983). George Monbiot rightly declares in the first sentence of his *Manifesto for a New World Order,* "Everything has been globalized except our consent" (Monbiot 2003, 1). Monbiot calls for a world parliament made up not of governments, like the United Nations, but of people. He writes that, "in the UN General Assembly, the 10,000 people of the Pacific island of Tuvalu possess the same representation as the one billion people of India. Their per capita vote, in other words, is weighted 100,000-fold" (Monbiot 2003, 74). Immanuel Kant did not call for the creation of a world state, but rather of a federation of peoples that sounds like it would look a lot like the United Nations. Kant assumed that people had chosen to organize themselves into nation-states and, thus, judged nation-states as "individual men living in a state of nature" (Kant 1991, 102). Such a supposition is highly problematic, of course. Many nation-states were created through the conquest of indigenous peoples, many, particularly postcolonial nation-states, have poorly drawn borders that do not even attempt to capture the territory of a single "people," and, then, there is the question of who decides on the membership of a people. The individual people themselves? The government? Ideally, it would be the former, but in today's world that is certainly not the case.

Though the concept of international justice conjures images of a world state, it will not be the focus of this chapter. Instead, the focus will be on conceiving of a just global normative order that consists of either states or peoples wherein international rights are derived at the individual level. The reasoning behind this decision is that international justice and international law today exist in a world of states and, despite the poststatist aspirations of authors such as Thomas Friedman (2005) and George Monbiot, states are still necessary and will be necessary for the foreseeable future. Martin Wolf provides the following legal and economic reasons for the necessity of the state: "for people to be successful in exploiting the opportunities afforded by international integration, they need states, at both ends of their transactions. This is why failed states, disorderly states, weak states and corrupt states are shunned states— they are the black holes of the global economic system" (Wolf 2004, 277).

While it remains to be seen whether or not states will allow for international individual rights, the goal here is to argue for their necessity. This is the same mission behind the United Nations Declaration of Human Rights. Establishing an ideal to aspire to can lead to dramatic change. This is evident in the fast-changing opinion of same-sex marriage in America (Socarides 2013) and the reinforcement of a human right to democracy seen most recently in the Arab Spring uprisings.

Rawls's *The Law of Peoples:* A First Encounter

In *The Law of Peoples,* John Rawls attempts to describe an ideal international system of justice or, as he puts it, a realistic Utopia (Rawls 1999, 11). Rawls conceives of what he calls a Society of Peoples, his terminology for the just global normative order that he prescribes. He uses "peoples," as Kant did, rather than states because, unlike Kant, Rawls believes that attributing "moral motives" to states is problematic (17). John Rawls describes the reasoning behind his Society of Peoples thus: "This account of the Law of Peoples conceives of liberal democratic peoples (and decent peoples) as the actors in the Society of Peoples, just as citizens are the actors in domestic society" (23). Rawls assumes that rights in the international system are derived differently than they are in domestic society. Specifically, rights are derived on the level of peoples internationally and on the individual level domestically. This is Rawls's attempt at conceiving of a just international order.

As Rachel Brown asserts, "To focus on peoples rather than on states enables Rawls to begin a response to certain theories of international relations, namely those that emphasize the 'non-moral' characteristics of states as presenting a barrier to relations of justice between them" (Brown 1999, 23). So, for instance, Rawls does not endow peoples with the "traditional sovereignty" of states, thus freeing them from the yoke of the realist perception of international relations. As Rawls professes,

If a state's concern with power is predominant; and if its interests include such things as converting other societies to the state's religion, enlarging its empire and winning territory, gaining dynastic or national prestige and glory, and increasing its relative economic strength— then the difference between states and peoples is enormous (Rawls 1999, 28).

Rawls's statement, given his inclusion of quests for relative economic strength and national prestige in the forum of states rather than peoples, differentiates the Society of Peoples drastically from the state system we know today. In addition, peoples as we know them today—Brown uses the example of Jews— also seek relative economic strength and national prestige to varying degrees. So Rawls is using peoples as a foil to combat the arguments of international relations realists such as John Mearshimer. Entering this argument is not the goal of this chapter, but it is important to note Rawls's motivations and the almost selfless aims he requires of peoples.

Four Problems with Deriving Fundamental Rights at the Group Level

Fundamentally deriving rights at the level of groups such as peoples is problematic for a number of reasons; here I enumerate four of them. Although Charles Beitz (1979) believes that justice needs to be promoted in states, he defines justice as the promotion of individual autonomy. As Beitz avers, "a government is legitimate if it *would be* consented to by rational persons subject to its rule"[3] (80). Moreover, he argues that a state's moral entitlement not to be interfered with is derived entirely from its ability to promote justice (76–77). Promotion of state rights, in Beitz's view, is a means to an end. That is, state rights are only necessary as a means to achieving individual rights. Beitz quotes Michael Walzer's assertion that "the rights of states rest on the consent of their members" (77). If the role of states is to promote the wellbeing of individuals, then there exists a powerful logic for deriving rights on the state level because the individual gains resources and rights as part of the state. But giving a state or a group rights does not necessarily ensure that those

---

3. This argument, depending on how one understands it, follows the "hypothetical" or implicit consent model forwarded by state of nature theorists. These theorists hold that we agree to the government either through our actions (by, say, voting or accepting government benefits) or through our admission that we *would* agree to the government's rule if given the choice (see Wolff 2006, 42–45).

rights will trickle down to all individuals—indeed they may be captured and controlled by political elites.

This takes us to the first problem with deriving rights at the group level, which is that basing the derivation of rights at the level of the group can easily lead to cooptation by elites. In Benedict Anderson's *Imagined Communities* (1991), nationalism is first created through the establishment of Creole nations, but then becomes a model called "official nationalism" that political elites use to concretize their zones of control and justify their rule. In Anderson's words, "official nationalism [is] an anticipatory strategy adopted by dominant groups which are threatened with marginalization or exclusion from an emerging nationally-imagined community" (101). Deriving rights at the group level in the age of nationalism has thus been a tool for controlling the masses. The easiest way to forge a group has frequently been to point to the existence of an "other" group and to label them an "enemy." This brings us to the second problem with deriving rights at the group level: the overpoliticization of identity.

The overpoliticization of identity means that when deriving rights at the group level, a group is more likely to use its communal identity for the purposes that Rawls warns against in his definition of peoples, such as the attainment of empire, relative economic gain, or national pride. The use of group identity as a tool for achieving economic, territorial, or political gain is tantamount to the politicization of identity. A certain level of identity politicization may be necessary in order to define a group. However, deriving fundamental rights at the group level leads to overpoliticization of group identity because under such a system groups must compete with one another for goods and resources, and thus must explicate claims of dessert regarding these substances. The following deleterious effects can be caused by overpoliticization of identity: the potential creation of an "other" group, spurious group formation, and, most importantly, particularistic nationalism and group competition over resources. These factors all have the potential to yield racism, violence, and resource inequality. Let us now examine each of these negative effects and the overpoliticization of identity that flows from such a decision.

First, the overpoliticization of identity can easily lead to the creation of an "other" group and thus to an increase in human suffering. Most generally, a politically charged group identity can lead to ethnic conflict. As the former Bosnian President Alija Izetbegovic stated, "Will we accept peace at any price in Bosnia, bend our heads once and for all, because of peace accept an inferior position for the next fifteen years, or shall we say, we want sovereignty, risking a conflict" (Burg and Shoup 1999, 77). Because, in the example, the right to self-determination is derived at the group level, groups must define themselves and reify their differences, thus creating an "other" or enemy group, in order to stake claims to this right.

Thus, deriving rights at the group level calls for groups to form platforms and characterize themselves in order to prove that they are groups. In a non-ideal world in which resources and territories are limited, the formation and characterization of groups that must prove their "groupness" in order to derive rights is problematic. Here I am thinking of the rights to secession and self-determination. Not only is it difficult to determine which groups "deserve" states, but it is also difficult to determine who belongs in what group or where new states should begin and end. In today's world, the right to self-determination in practice is predicated on a group *proving* that it indeed consists of a coherent "people." The most salient way of doing this has been the use of violence against the state from which the new group would like to secede. This violence is the product of the need to overpoliticize a group's identity in order to gain the rights to, in this instance, a state. However, the problem of defining who belongs in a group and thus who deserves certain rights remains, even in a world with no states but limited resources.

This ties into the second problem with the overpoliticization of groups: by deriving rights at the level of the group, groups are apt to pop up simply in order to request the rights that come with being a group. The process of group formation simply for the gain of goods or rights is similar to what Gayatri Spivak (1987) calls "strategic essentialism." Jean Jackson (1995) contends that some Indian groups (e.g., Colombia's Tukanoans) deliberately self-essentialize because "they increasingly need to demonstrate Indianness to obtain benefits from both government and NGOs" (12). Thus, the Tukanoans choose to simplify and folklorize the culture they preserve "to make it easier for outsiders to understand" it (15). Jackson writes that groups like the Tukanoans end up learning to use culture as a "commodity" (16). It is true that groups in need do exist and that, in many instances, it is most efficient for these groups to request aid at the group level. However, by deriving rights at the group level, spurious groups may form simply to obtain the rights that come with being a group. In and of itself this is not a bad outcome; however, these groups may strategically essentialize in order to prove their status as a "people," which in some instances may require them to define themselves against others. This can easily lead to conflict.

Moreover, Thomas Pogge (2002, 119) points to the fact that overly particularistic nationalism not only leads to chauvinism and racism, but also to unjustifiable "human misery and premature deaths." Pogge's most powerful argument supporting the latter point is that particularistic nationalist groups have incentives to only (or almost only) care about themselves in terms of resource extraction and economic gain. As Pogge writes, "Affluent people use vastly more of the world's resources, and they do so unilaterally, without giving any compensation to the global poor for their disproportionate consumption" (202). Pogge concludes this line of argument with the following rhetorical question: "what entitles a global elite to use up the world's natural resources on mutually agreeable terms while leaving the global poor empty-handed?" (202). When rights are derived at the group level, the rights of certain people are undermined simply because of their group affiliation—deserved or not. Deriving rights at the group level leads to group competition that leads at least to minor economic or political inequality and at most to violence. Strategic essentialism and an emphasis on group affiliation as the basis for achieving fundamental rights can thus lead to unequal resource distribution and, consequently, human misery.

By contrast, if rights were derived at the individual level internationally, groups would not have to compete or prove their "groupness" in order to obtain rights. This circumvents the problem of group creation simply for obtaining fundamental rights and minimizes the amount of politically charged groups that will be created, thus limiting the incidence of violent conflict. The problem described here is one prevalent today in international politics because in order for a "people" to gain certain rights they must form a state. The most prominent example is the creation of the Jewish state on the grounds that without it the Jewish people may cease to exist. Michael Ignatieff's (2001) assertion that, "nationalism solves the human rights problems of the victorious national groups while producing new victim groups, whose human rights situation is made worse" holds here (15). Still, an end to deriving rights at the group level will most probably not lead to an end to violent conflict.

There will surely still be reasons for people to form groups and for people to disagree. Indeed, Isaiah Berlin (1969) averred that, "If, as I believe, the ends of men are many, and not all of them are in principle compatible with each other, then the possibility of conflict—and of tragedy—can never wholly be eliminated from human life, either personal or social" (169). It is not the act of group formation that is troublesome here; rather it is the type of groups, in my jargon: overpoliticized ones, which form under a system in which groups are the fundamental derivers of rights. By establishing fundamental rights at the individual level, then the incidence of overpoliticized group formation will be minimized because individuals will have less incentive to form such groups because their rights as individuals are assured. The incidences of war and resource inequality will thus be limited. This leads to the third problem with basing rights at the group level: minority rights.

In the words of Onora O'Neill (2000, 173), "if identities matter, minority identities matter." This points to the arbitrary nature of deriving rights at the group level. It is unclear how minority identities are dealt with in Rawls's decent societies. Rawls (1999) writes, "all persons in a decent hierarchical society are not regarded as free and equal citizens, nor as separate individuals deserving equal representation ... they are seen as decent and rational and as capable of moral learning as recognized in their society" (71). Moreover, decent societies "must admit a sufficient measure of liberty of conscience and freedom of religion and thought, even if these freedoms are not as extensive nor as equal for all members of the decent society as they are in liberal societies" (74). In this chapter, decent and liberal societies are used as proxies for societies in which fundamental rights are derived at group and individual levels, respectively. In the decent/group-rights-based society, minorities would be allowed to be part of society but would be systematically established as second-class citizens[4]—an arrangement reminiscent of the Islamic *dhimma* system. Under the Islamic system, *dhimma* status is applied to followers of non-Islamic monotheistic faiths deemed worthy of toleration (Lewis 1984, 20). Bernard Lewis defines the *dhimma* system this way:

> In Muslim law and practice, the relationship between the Muslim state and the subject non-Muslim communities to which it extended its tolerance and protection was regulated by a pact called *dhimma*.... By the terms of the *dhimma*, these communities were accorded a certain status, provided that they unequivocally recognized the primacy of Islam and the supremacy of Muslims. This recognition was expressed in the payment of the poll tax and obedience to a series of restrictions defined in detail by the holy law (Lewis 1984, 21).

Though the *dhimma* system was meant on one level to protect non-Islamic minorities, it is clear that the *dhimma* were treated as inferiors. According to Mordechai Ha-Cohen, a prominent Libyan Jew who lived in the late nineteenth and early twentieth centuries, "The Muhammadans of the villages [did] not have religious hatred toward the Jews, but, nevertheless [were] very proud. They [would] not allow a Jew to pass in front of them, mounted on an animal, nor [would] they permit him to carry a weapon" (quoted in Goldberg 1990, 10, 12). Though these slights are minor, they establish a hierarchical order within a society that, as Brown posits, could easily prove humiliating to the minority or disenfranchised group (Brown 1999, 47). For example, Bernard Lewis

---

4. Second-class citizenship could portend varying degrees of rights. But the fact that decent societies do not necessarily provide for individual equality and rather derive rights at the group level would yield a system in which one group rules another. Indeed, decent societies are characterized by decent consultation *hierarchies.*

(1984, 25) notes that under the *dhimma* order, "Christians and Jews were to wear special emblems on their clothes. This, incidentally, is the origin of the yellow badge, which was first introduced by a caliph in Baghdad in the ninth century and spread into Western lands in later medieval times." The fact that this yellow badge was used as a way of singling out Jews for humiliation and oppression in Hitler's Germany illustrates how the establishment of a group's status as second-class citizens can quickly regress into scapegoating and mass violence.

Therefore, the very fashioning of the group as the fundamental deriver of rights could lead to pushing people outside the sphere of rights that group members acquire. Thus, deriving rights at the group level potentially limits who can justifiably stake a claim to these rights. This can lead to societal structures that justify discrimination on grounds of membership, tradition, or other similar reasons. Thus, the rights of a woman or a resident alien might be explicated to be justifiably less than those of a requisite citizen because those persons do not fulfill the notion of the group regarding who deserves rights. In such a system, Rawls's Society of Peoples for instance, the greatest slight to a person may be banishment.

Moreover, even if these hierarchical structures are agreed to, they could also lead to conflict and resource inequality. For example, say there is a drought in a decent society in which Muslims are the superior group and Jews the inferior. If Jews are not allowed to hold political office, then resources may go predominantly to Muslims in times of crisis in order to please the people that "really matter." In such a situation Jews are forced to starve or rebel. Indeed, no less a source than the caliph 'Umar I declared, in justifying a poll tax against the *dhimma* class, that "the Muslims of our day will eat [from the work of] these people as long as they live, and when we and they die, our sons will eat [from] their sons forever" (quoted in Lewis 1984, 31). Moreover, the proof may be found in the fact that Muslims' attitudes and behavior toward their "subject communities" worsened whenever the status of Muslims worsened economically or politically (169). Therefore, in practice, a system wherein one group is privileged over another can easily lead to inequality in a variety of public spheres. It can lead to violence, discrimination, and even genocide practiced against the subject group because the society is based on a philosophy that one group is superior to the other.

This hierarchical notion is akin to Aristotelian justice. Aristotle called for "equality for equals." He contended, for instance, that men were superior to women and masters superior to slaves. So, he inferred, different rules should apply to different classes of people (Aristotle in Everson 1996, 27–29). Of course, such a system has been proven to rest on faulty logic and faulty science.

The fourth and final problem with deriving fundamental rights at the group level, the indivisible nature of the individual and the comparatively arbitrary definition of the group, brings the first three problems (elite cooptation, over-politicization of identity, and minority representation) together. As seen above, national groups and peoples are not as primordial in nature as they purport to be.[5] Moreover, group identity can easily be co-opted by elites and can lead to a subversion of minority rights. Basing rights at the level of the indivisible individual has a more powerful logic than doing so at the level of the group. After all, what is the group? As O'Neill writes, "How can those who argue for principles of justice of universal scope, or for human rights, endorse structures that entail that the rights people actually have depend on where they are, or more precisely on which place recognizes them as citizen rather than alien" (O'Neill 2000, 170)? This question cuts to the issues of a) who decides who belongs to a group and b) how one earns rights if he does not view himself, or if his group does not view him, as part of the group with whom he resides. The definition of "group," "people," or "national community" is a muddled one. Where does a group begin or end? Who counts as part of the group and who does the counting? Is it not arbitrary to count groups or peoples only territorially? How about defining groups ethnically or religiously?

The individual, by contrast, is not an arbitrary unit. It can plainly be seen where an individual starts and ends, and who she is. Beitz asserts that, "the individual is in a better position than anyone else, and certainly than any government, to determine his own interests" (Beitz 1979, 84).

One may argue, as some communitarians do, that individuals are "nothing" without societies because they cannot live in a vacuum. As O'Neill mentions, "such arguments are typically strengthened by pointing out that a feeling of affiliation to nations or communities is not a mere matter of preference, but the basis of the very sense of self and identity of the persons so linked" (O'Neill 2000, 173). However, in my estimation, the meaning and identity that one can derive from a group is inversely related to the level to which that person is forced to be in said group. For example, religion can provide powerful meaning in a person's life. However, if one is forced to sit in church every Sunday simply because one "has to," the meaning that can be derived from such a situation is markedly reduced. One may counter that simply by going to church, forced or not, one will eventually learn the truth and that a person does not always enjoy or find meaning in activities the first time he partakes

---

5. Anderson asserts that "the *new* imagined communities ... conjured up by lexicography and print capitalism always regarded themselves as somehow *ancient*" (Anderson 1991, 109; italics added).

of them. However, one can only begin to find meaning in a life situation when he chooses to accept it.[6] Lest this dialogue go too far, let it be underlined that what is being proposed here is not akin to the end of societies but rather the end of fundamental human rights being derived at the group level. Nevertheless, I do not think that a strong empirical case can be made that countries in today's world that derive rights at the group level have, on the whole, more robust civil societies or that the people in those societies live more meaningful lives.

Now that the arguments against deriving rights at the group level have been established, the discussion turns to what rights individuals should have. Specifically, in a just global normative order, should individuals have a right to democracy and the liberal rights that some argue flow from democracy?[7] I will begin this discussion by defining democracy before turning to the heart of the argument. The first step in the argument will be to ascertain whether there is sufficient logic or reasoning to establish an individual's right to democracy and the liberal rights that it entails given the problems with deriving rights on the group level (discussed above). The second step will be to face Rawls's argument about the need for a mutual respect between liberal and decent peoples to see if it holds in this case.

Should There Be an Individual Right to Democracy?

To begin a discussion on whether individuals should have a fundamental right to democracy in a just global normative order, a definition of "democracy" must be established. Though there is wide disagreement on what electoral systems best provide for democracy,[8] the actual rules of democratic systems are secondary to the argument here. It is important, instead, to focus on what

---

6. This may be a narrow definition of "meaning," but I contend that the element of choice cannot be divorced from the notion of meaning completely. Can a being that lives solely on instinct, such as a goldfish, feel meaning? In my estimation, the goldfish cannot feel meaning because it has no free will. Then again, many would argue that humans also lack free will, so I will leave that argument for another day.

7. For a strong argument for establishing liberal rights in a democracy, see William Riker's *Liberalism Against Populism* (1982). Riker contends "in the populist interpretation of voting, the opinions of the majority *must* be right and *must* be respected because the will of the people is the liberty of the people. In the liberal interpretation, there is no such magical identification. The outcome of voting is just a decision and has no special moral character" (14).

8. Disagreements over democratic systems are focused on whether the electorate is best served in presidential or parliamentary systems and whether it is best to conduct voting on

rights democracy provides for individuals and whether it is moral to forward these rights to all people.

One point that most experts on democratic electoral systems do not disagree on is that democracy needs to include universal suffrage. It is true that this is a relatively new idea, even in the United States, but without universal suffrage then some individuals are left out of the electorate and thus we return to the problem of minority rights and in-group, out-group dynamics. Moreover, suffrage must include some level of free speech for elections to run effectively.

A democracy is a system whereby, in the words of Article 21(1) of the Universal Declaration of Human Rights (UDHR), "Everyone has a right to take part in the government of his country, directly or through freely chosen representatives." Article 21(1) of the UDHR points to the reasoning behind seeing democracy simply as a system of universal suffrage. But what about the rights that liberalism portends? As Rachel Brown (1999, 67) asserts, "Liberalism is centrally defined by a commitment to respect and protect individual liberty. To secure this, liberalism claims that each individual holds certain basic rights and liberties, and gives a high priority to their protection." In a system wherein individuals are the key derivers of fundamental rights, certain liberal rights need to be guaranteed so that the rights of individuals are protected. Most basically, these are the rights to life, liberty, equality, and security. Simple democracy would allow for a system whereby the majority could vote to disenfranchise a specific group. This goes against the arguments for why fundamental rights should be derived individually, thus such a democracy could not be part of the normative order that I am proposing. Perhaps, then, democracy is a necessary but not sufficient condition for establishing a just global normative order.

First, we must examine whether democracy—that is, universal suffrage—is necessary for the establishment of a normative order that is based on individual rights. Simply providing individuals with the right to choose their rulers by majority or otherwise does not guard against the oppression of minorities, elite cooptation of individual rights, or the overpoliticization of group identity.[9] These factors, plus the indivisibility of the individual as a requestor of rights, have been established to necessitate the need to base fundamental rights at the individual level. Universal suffrage provides individuals with the right to choose their rulers, but there is no guarantee implied in it that: a) their

---

a plurality (i.e., "first-past-the-post") or a proportional representation system. See Lijphart (1992) and Shepsle and Bonchek (1997).

9. Even in proportional representation systems, coalitions form that forward the rights of certain groups over others.

choice will be a substantive one, b) that their rulers will not opt to undermine their rights, and c) that the ruler they vote for will be the one that ultimately wins. Thus, it should be added that a democracy is a system whereby individuals are ordained with universal suffrage and wherein elections contain multiple parties. Moreover, free speech, and, by proxy, a free press, should be ensured so that elections are substantive and transparent. Even this broader definition of democracy, however, does not necessarily provide for minority rights. Thus, we must turn to the tenets of liberalism to safeguard the rights of the individual. A second encounter with Rawls will parse out whether, in order to be just in the global normative order I am describing, societies must be both liberal and democratic, or simply democratic.

Rawls's *The Law of Peoples:* Decent versus Liberal Peoples

Rawls defines two societal forms that he sees as just, namely, decent and liberal societies. In the second part of his ideal theory in *The Law of Peoples,* Rawls (1999) states that although "liberal constitutional democracy is, in fact, superior to other forms of society" (62), it is important that the relationship between decent and liberal peoples be characterized by mutual respect. In rebutting arguments that emphasize the fundamental importance of liberal rights, Rawls asserts that "a liberal people should have confidence in their convictions and suppose that a decent society, when offered due respect by liberal peoples, may be more likely, over time, to recognize the advantages of liberal institutions and take steps toward becoming more liberal on its own" (62). In essence Rawls is stating that even if we find decent societies to be unjust by liberal standards, their societies look enough like liberal societies to necessitate mutual respect between the two groups. Even if we reject this argument, Rawls would counter that at least decent societies should be respected because respecting them is the quickest route to getting decent societies to see the virtues of liberalism. Closer scrutiny of these assertions requires a definition of "decent societies."

Rawls characterizes "decent peoples" as those whose societal structures include *decent consultation hierarchies* that allow for a right to dissent. The decent consultation hierarchy is to be informed by a "common good idea of justice." Further, though people in decent hierarchical societies "are not regarded as free and equal citizens, nor as separate individuals deserving of equal representation, ... they are seen as decent and rational and as capable of moral learning as recognized in their society" (Rawls 1999, 71). Rawls is careful to note that though people in decent societies have a right to voice dissent, they do not have complete freedom of speech. In decent societies, dissent "is permissible provided it stays within the basic framework of the common good idea of justice" (72). He further requires that decent societies "admit a sufficient measure of liberty of conscience and freedom of religion and thought." But Rawls allows the established religion to be privileged above others in decent societies as long as other religions are tolerated (74). Thus, decent hierarchical societies look a lot like the Muslim *dhimma* system described above because they establish the superiority of a single group through the establishment of a hierarchy but intend to act benevolently toward minorities.

The *dhimma* system could be justified on the basis that it protects some minorities. It can easily lead, however, to the humiliation and disenfranchisement of unprivileged groups through, for example, inequalities in resource distribution. Brown proffers the following principle of humiliation:

> A justification of institutional practices is properly regarded as humiliating to some class of persons X when it strongly negates the political conception of the person that all decent societies may reasonably be expected to endorse in the light of their guiding principles and ideals, and justifies treating members of X as less than this conception recommends (Brown 1999, 45).

The example of Jewish life in Muslim Libya above illustrates the humiliating form that institutionalized second-class citizenship can take. Moreover, Brown rejects Rawls's statement that decent hierarchical societies should be tolerated because of their consensual nature and allowance of dissent. A disenfranchised group's virtual exclusion from political life, Brown asserts, is doubly unjust in decent consultation hierarchies because the ruling group in such societies recognizes the unjustness of the secondary group's treatment but still allows itself to view the disenfranchised group as unequal. Moreover, the exclusion of certain groups from the political process by proxy excludes them from political life. As Brown states, "recognition followed by rejection is just as humiliating as no recognition at all" (Brown 1999, 47). The fact that decent societies allow for consent and dissent is akin to paying lip service to minority or unrepresented groups while concretizing their lower social status through the establishment of a hierarchy. Decent societies, therefore, understand the logic of treating all people equally but do not actually believe in the equality of individuals. In my mind, then, decent societies are ones that have been co-opted by relatively benevolent elites.[10]

---

10. These elites are benevolent compared to those of less just societal forms described in Rawls's *The Law of Peoples:* outlaw states, societies burdened by unfavorable conditions, and benevolent absolutisms (Rawls 1999, 63).

This leads to the argument for providing all people in a democratic society with the right to vote. One can point to "virtual representation," as the British did regarding the American colonies, all one wants but a system such as a decent hierarchical society where one is considered, but is not truly, represented is endemically faulty. The structure of the household with a husband at the top who takes the wife's views into consideration but ultimately makes decisions on his own could only be reasonably believed to be justly arranged if we attribute certain qualities to each gender. The assumptions underlying such a system would have to be either structural or qualitative. Examples of qualitative arguments using the household analogy are: a) that men are better at making decisions (because they are smarter, less emotional, etc.), or b) that men are fit for certain roles and women for others. Qualitative arguments point to biological or priori differences between people to rationalize a hierarchical system. Structural arguments, on the other hand, include the notion that having a hierarchical structure in place maximizes efficiency. Structural arguments focus on the efficiency, tradition, or economical sense of the structure in place, rather than focusing on the differences between individuals. Qualitative arguments are especially pernicious, even if they are meant to be benign, because they can quickly regress into discrimination and oppression. Because all people are equally capable, given the right opportunity, they should be allowed access to societal institutions on an equal basis. The qualitative rationale for rigid hierarchical structures unduly limits the opportunities for an individual's personal advancement, be it psychologically, professionally, or otherwise. Structural arguments are more malleable because, at their most benign, they assume that certain structures are more efficient. Within all societies there exist varying degrees of hierarchy, but the efficiency or traditional nature of hierarchical arrangements does not justify the establishment of an inferior group.

Regardless of the rationale, it is clear that the establishment of a hierarchical societal structure can lead to myriad problems. The nature of such hierarchies in practice normally leads to some degree of oppression of the minority or disenfranchised group. Further, by deriving rights at the group level, individuals are not judged by who they are but by what they are. Group identities may be overpoliticized in order to show that they deserve certain rights, elites may co-opt the rights of individuals, and minorities may be disenfranchised.

Still, Rawls believes that decent societies should be tolerated because they are nonaggressive, bestow their people with the powers of consent and dissent, and because they protect human rights. Above I make clear the weaknesses in a system that allows for consent and dissent without universal suffrage. Namely, such a system may purport to give individuals rights, but ultimately it does not. Following Brown's arguments and the example of virtual representation, even though these second-class citizens have some rights in decent consultation hierarchies, ultimately they only have the right to be heard, but not to be listened to. Decent societies, therefore, provide only weak rights for individuals and it is unclear whether these rights would provide sufficient human rights protections.

Decent Societies and Human Rights

Indeed, there is a contradiction within Rawls's definition of decent peoples. On the one hand, in decent societies "the established religion may have various privileges" as long as adherents of other faiths are neither persecuted nor "denied civic and social conditions permitting [their religious] practice in peace and without fear" (Rawls 1999, 74). On the other hand, Rawls states that, "one condition of a decent hierarchical society is that its legal system and social order do not violate human rights" (75). If certain groups may be privileged in decent societies, how could these societies be said to be forwarding human rights? The first sentence of the first article of the UDHR states that "[a]ll human beings are born free and equal in dignity and in rights." This statement is unequivocal regarding both the equality and the dignity a society must ensure individuals in it for it to be deemed a protector of human rights. The placement of this statement as the first sentence of the first article of the UDHR demonstrates its central importance in the assurance of human rights. However, Rawls's system does not claim to adhere to the UDHR.

Rather, Rawls draws up human rights of his own: the rights to life, liberty, property, and "formal equality as expressed by rules of natural justice (that is, that similar cases be treated similarly)" (Rawls 1999, 65). It is important to note that Rawls states that "similar cases be treated similarly," which allows him considerable "wiggle room" regarding equality. One interpretation of this phrase is that one group may be privileged in its treatment; it just cannot be egregiously privileged. If a person from the ruling group and one from the disenfranchised group are hungry, then Rawls's argument might require decent societies to provide that both people eat but does not require them to provide both with the same food. Another interpretation of Rawls's right to formal equality is that decent societies are required to explicate the differences between peoples such that they can justify different treatments for different groups. Such a system smacks of discrimination, a societal structure that is far from tolerable. Formal equality may also mean equality in the political or public sphere, in which case "equality" may not be ubiquitous. Regardless of the interpreted meaning of "similar cases be treated similarly," the fact that Rawls allows certain groups in decent societies to be systematically "privileged" through the establishment of a hierarchy proves that such societies are unequal and thus violate human rights as framed in both the UDHR as well as any other rational definition of equality. Rawls himself "does not argue" with the contention that "full democratic and liberal rights are necessary to prevent violations of human rights" as established by "empirical fact supported by historical experience" (Rawls 1999, 75fn.16). Such empirical arguments could be based on the *dhimma* example and, therefore, show that in practice human rights are not secured by a decent consultation hierarchy.

Rawls foresees these arguments and offers a final caveat: "in view of the possible inequality of religious freedom [in decent societies], if for no other reason, it is essential that a hierarchical society allow and provide assistance for the right to emigration" (Rawls 1999, 74). Simply providing for the right to emigrate, however, does not make a society tolerable, though it certainly makes it more tolerable. If we are to accept societies that do not provide for liberal rights, then it is fair to say that these societies must at least prove that the people who live in them do so by choice. Thus, the right to emigration is essential to Rawls's argument that decent peoples must be tolerated because, as Joseph Carens demonstrates, freedom of movement is "essential for equality of opportunity" (Carens 1994, 145). However, as Carens indicates, the right to emigrate "does not imply a right to enter any particular place" (146). The potential inability of citizens of a decent society to enter more equal societies poses a problem for Rawls's realistic utopia because if persons from a decent society cannot enter societies in which they will have greater equality, then decent societies are charged with the burden of providing commensurate equality for their citizens. This is because if the right to emigration does not provide for a range of reasonably just societies for a citizen to choose from, then an individual in the decent society may stay in that society not by choice but because it is the best option available. Because in order for decent societies to be most just they should be based on the choice of their citizens to live by their rules, decent societies in a world where emigration is not a tenable option are less just.

Moreover, a large part of Rawls's reasoning behind tolerating decent societies is their existence in a world alongside liberal societies. Thus, liberal societies provide a potential demonstration effect for decent societies and are charged with the duty to tolerate decent societies—not vice versa. However, in a world bereft of liberal peoples, the justness of decent societies erodes because, first, the possibility of becoming liberal due to the example of other societies is gone. Second, decent consultation hierarchies are not just in themselves; Rawls makes clear that liberal societies are more just (Rawls 1999, 62). Therefore, in a world without liberal societies, the burden shifts from liberal societies needing to tolerate decent ones to decent societies needing to adhere to liberal rights. The burden is shifted because liberal societies are the most just societies and thus in a world where they do not exist, the duty to tolerate decent societies is nonexistent because the toleration of their existence is premised on the existence of liberal societies in a Society of Peoples.

Without a Society of Peoples, we are left with only the duties to "honor the laws of peace" and adhere to human rights (Rawls 1999, 67). In such a scenario, the argument that decent societies should be allowed to change in their own way no longer applies because there are only people who live in decent and less just societies. Because decent societies are less just than liberal societies, the inequality of opportunity in such a world would necessitate the enfranchisement of subject groups. Though it may be important to tolerate decent peoples in the Society of Peoples, given that these societies limit the rights of certain individuals, why should their citizens, second-class or otherwise, tolerate them? So we see the right to emigrate does not justify the toleration of decent societies internally by their citizens.

Rawls states in his introduction, however, that immigration in the Society of Peoples for reasons of "persecution of religious and ethnic minorities" and "the denial of human rights" would no longer be of urgent necessity (Rawls 1999, 9). As previously argued, the right to consultation and dissent in decent societies does not necessarily provide for the right for groups to take part in government. The example of the *dhimma* system was used in this case. Yet if we are to take Rawls at his word that the Society of Peoples that he envisions would be free of human rights violations and persecution of minorities, then how does this society look? For one, it is clear that though decent societies might not blatantly persecute minorities or deny human rights, their conception of the group as the fundamental requestor of rights limits the rights of individuals. Rawls spills much ink calibrating the level to which individual rights are limited in decent societies because he attempts to "conceive a reasonably just Law of Peoples that liberal and nonliberal peoples could together endorse" and yet admits that he is partial to liberalism. Thus in his example of a decent society called Kazanistan, he states that such a society is not "perfectly just," but rather perfectly "decent." He further equivocates with regard to religious minority rights in Kazanistan, a place that sounds like it is run by something akin to the *dhimma* system, declaring that Kazanistan "is an enlightened society in its treatment of religious minorities." A decent society such as this, says Rawls "is the best we can realistically ... hope for" (78).

Rather than turning down the path of asking whether a place like Kazanistan could actually exist, I think it is important to ask whether such a place should be tolerated. Does a decent society that allows for a limited degree of equality but intends to treat its members well deserve the respect of liberal constitutional democracies? The answer appears to be yes, given the limited range of alternatives. An answer in the negative would have to be combined with a course of action to take against decent societies, such as economic sanctions or military intervention. Further, Rawls does not ask that liberal peoples accept decent societies, only that they tolerate and respect them. Charles Beitz states that a "true believer would not accept as neutral a principle protecting religious liberty" for all people, because his "most deeply held beliefs [entail] that certain actions protected by the liberty principle should not be permitted to take place." He concludes that "[d]espite its nonneutrality from the point of view of, for example, a true believer, the equal-liberty principle might be defended by showing that it is required to protect the pursuit of self-determined ends by autonomous agents, which is itself a central feature of an ideal of social life that is based on the criterion of respect for persons" (Beitz 1979, 89). Though Beitz does not believe that the rationale behind an equal-liberty principle could hold in international relations, he concludes that "[t]he most that can be said is that considerations analogous to those that support the equal-liberty principle [in domestic society] protect against those states whose institutions conform to appropriate principles of justice and those whose institutions are more likely to become just in the absence of outside interference than with outside assistance" (90). Decent societies, as Rawls conceives them, fit into this second group.

Because life in decent societies appears to run smoothly and because these societies are ruled by relatively benevolent, if not completely consented to, elites, there appears to be little logical argument that can be made in defense of aggressively condemning, attacking, or attempting to uproot such societies. Rawls's argument is simply that if laws that are not completely, but sufficiently, just rule a society then that society should not be actively interfered with. At least the logic of Rawls's argument that tolerating and respecting (but not necessarily accepting) such a society would be more likely to yield liberalism in it holds here.

Toleration, Liberalism, and Democracy

One way to get at whether individuals should have a right to democracy and what the term "democracy" portends is to enumerate the benefits of democracy and then see whether these benefits are provided simply by the mechanism of universal suffrage. The first benefit of democracy is that through the mechanism of elections, democracy provides governments with the verifiable consent of the people. In Thomas Franck's view, the contemporary international community has asserted, through the Soviet and Haitian cases of the early

1990s, "that *only* democracy validates governance" (Franck 1992, 47). The consent of the governed, therefore, provides rulers with legitimacy both internally and internationally. The systematic institutionalization of a superior group based on factors other than the consent of the people differentiates decent societies from democracies. However, the "tyranny of the majority" that Alexis de Tocqueville points to, which is present in democracies, could also fashion a system whereby a minority group becomes relatively disenfranchised. There are two arguments that can be employed to distinguish democracies from decent consultation hierarchies in this case. The first is that democracies allow for shifting majorities so that, in theory at least, no one group is established as supreme for all time as they are in hierarchical societies. The second argument states that in order for democratic governments to be deemed to hold the consent of the people, they must secure the rights of individuals so that minority group rights are not eroded. In this case, however, democracy must be coupled with liberal rights.

A second purported benefit of democracy is that the mechanism of free speech creates a dialogue between the rulers and the ruled that creates transparency within societies. Transparency allows the people and their government to share information, motivations, and goals in a way that best furthers the goals of a society and ensures that the government is acting in the people's interests. Thus, Amartya Sen sees a free press as an integral component of democracy. Sen writes that "rulers have the incentive to listen to what people want if they have to face their criticism and seek their support in elections." He further points out that "no substantial famine has ever occurred in any independent country with a democratic form of government and a relatively free press" (Sen 1999, 152). Sen's example illustrates how the mechanisms of free speech and a free press translate into a better standard of living for people. It is important to note, however, that though consent and legitimacy are attained simply through universal suffrage, transparency is gained through the liberal rights to free speech and a free press. Thus, this second benefit, although attributed to democracy, is actually achieved through liberalism.

Conclusion

The crux of the argument in this chapter has been to prove that rights should be derived at the individual level. From this vantage point, it is difficult to come up with a legitimation of democracy without liberalism. Though democracy provides for government legitimacy, in order for a democracy to secure individual rights, it must provide for a certain degree of liberal rights such as, most fundamentally, the right to free speech and the rights to life, liberty, equality, and security. If a society allows for these liberal rights without providing elections, then under my rubric it would be found to be just. The legitimacy that a government gains from democracy both internally and internationally is an advantage, but I believe that this legitimacy could be achieved simply by providing liberal rights. One may counter that a monarchy that provides the polity with liberal rights is not just because the government is not consented to by the people. However, as previously stated, providing for democracy alone does not ensure any rights for individuals at all.

A hierarchy of justness should be established with liberal democracy at the top, liberal nondemocracy (if such a system could actually exist) in the middle, and nonliberal democracy on the bottom. In my judgment, of these three, only nonliberal democracy should not be tolerated because it has the potential for elite cooptation, disenfranchisement of certain social groups, and overpoliticization of identity in addition to all the other unjust things that a government could do, including infringing on a person's right to property, judging people without a fair trial, etc.

Democracy alone does not yield the human rights necessary for the creation of a just society. Deriving rights at the group level also does not provide these rights. A system run according to the dictates of liberalism provides these rights for individuals and, democracy or not, is therefore just. Some societies that are nonliberal, however, should be tolerated. In the real world, these should be judged on a case-by-case basis to determine whether members of these societies are afforded the choice to remain in them, whether they are nonaggressive, whether their rulers are benevolent, and whether tolerating them is the best way to get them to see the virtues of liberalism. The definition of Rawls's decent society has its problems, but the concept that there could exist societies that are not liberal constitutional democracies but still should be tolerated holds.

A world where international rights are derived at the individual level, not the state-level, may sound a lot like one controlled by a world government. But this need not be the case. It is true that a world government that is truly democratic would be an improvement on the current international legal system—as Monbiot argues above. Yet a world made up of democracies wherein people are endowed with a robust set of liberal rights would be a vast improvement on the current global order. Democracies do not suffer from the problems of decent hierarchical societies, failed states, or outlaw states. It is true that minority rights are of special concern in a democracy, but these could be secured through a liberal constitution. Theorists have long divided the international and the domestic realm when discussing justice and law, and wrongfully so. The individual is the basis of law domestically and she should be the basis internationally as well.

Web Sources

1. Information on Universal Declaration of Human Rights is available at: http://www.un.org/en/documents/udhr/
2. Information about what is *dhimma*, who are *dhimmis*, and what are the rights and restrictions of *dhimmis* in Moslem countries are available at: http://www.peacefaq.com/dhimma.html

Discussion Questions

1. What does your vision of a just global normative order look like? Does it include a world state, a world of democracies, or something completely different?
2. Do you think that governments that are not democratic or liberal, such as Rawls's decent hierarchical societies, should be tolerated by democratic regimes? Do you agree with Rawls that tolerating such governments, despite the problems they pose to minorities, is the best way of liberalizing them?
3. In your estimation, how just is the current global order? Do you think that the United Nations is arranged in a fair manner? Do you think that it is fair that what country one is born into determines everything from their life expectancy to their rights and opportunities? If you do not think the current system is fair, then what should be done about it?
4. Is there hope for perpetual peace internationally or, as Isaiah Berlin contends, are the interests of people too different to ever hope for a world of perpetual peace? On a related subject, do you think that an international system that does not include states would be a more just and peaceful system than the current one?
5. Should rights be derived differently internationally than domestically? Why do you think this way?

References

Anderson, Benedict. *Imagined Communities: Reflections on the Origin and Spread of Nationalism.* (Rev. ed.) New York: Verso, 1991.

Beitz, Charles. *Political Theory and International Relations.* Princeton, N.J.: Princeton University Press, 1979.

Berlin, Isaiah. "Two Concepts of Liberty." In *Four Essays on Liberty*, edited by Isaiah Berlin, 169–172. New York: Oxford University Press, 1969.

Brown, Rachel. "The Extension of Liberalism beyond Domestic Boundaries: Three Problem Cases." Ph.D. diss., Massachusetts Institute of Technology, Cambridge, Mass, 1999.

Burg, Steven L., and Paul S. Shoup. *The War in Bosnia-Herzegovina: Ethnic Conflict and International Intervention*. Armonk, N.Y.: M.E. Sharpe, 1999.

Carens, Joseph H. "The Rights of Immigrants." In *Group Rights*, edited by Judith Baker, 142–162. Toronto, Canada: University of Toronto Press, 1994.

Cooper, Anderson. "Horrors Revealed at North Korean Prison Camp," *60 Minutes, CBS News*. November 30, 2012. Accessed November 30, 2012. http://www.cbsnews.com/8301-18560_162-57556456/horrors-revealed-at-north-korean-prison-camp/.

Dinan, Stephen. "Largest-Ever Federal Payroll to Hit 2.15 Million," *The Washington Times*, February 2, 2010.

Everson, Stephen (ed.). *Aristotle: The Politics and the Constitution of Athens*. Cambridge, UK: Cambridge University Press, 1996.

Franck, Thomas. "The Emerging Right to Democratic Governance." *American Journal of International Law* 86, no. 1 (1991): 46–91.

Friedman, Thomas L. "It's a Flat World, After All." *New York Times*, April 3, 2005. Accessed November 20, 2012. http://www.nytimes.com/2005/04/03/magazine/03DOMINANCE.html.

Gerth, Hans H., and C. Wright Mills. *From Max Weber: Essays in Sociology*. London, UK: Routledge, 1948.

Goldberg, Harvey E. *Jewish Life in Muslim Libya: Rivals and Relatives*. Chicago: University of Chicago Press, 1990.

Hanna, Michael Wahid. "The Seven Pillars of the Arab Future." *Democracy Journal*, no. 28, (Spring 2013). Accessed November 20, 2012. http://www.democracyjournal.org/28/the-seven-pillars-of-the-arab-future.php?page=all.

Herbst, Jeffrey. *States and Power in Africa: Comparative Lessons in Authority and Control*. Princeton, NJ: Princeton University Press, 2000.

Husain, Ed. "Why Women's Rights in Saudi Arabia are Still So Bad." *The Atlantic*, September 28, 2011. Accessed November 20, 2012. http://www.theatlantic.com/international/archive/2011/09/why-womens-rights-in-saudi-arabia-are-still-so-bad/245780/.

Ignatieff, Michael. *Human Rights as Politics and Idolatry*. Princeton, N.J.: Princeton University Press, 2001.

Ignatius, David. "Dividing Iraq to Save It," *The Washington Post*, October 4, 2007.

Jackson, Jean E. Culture, Genuine and Spurious: The Politics of Indianness in the Vaupés, Colombia. *American Ethnologist* 22, no. 1 (1995): 3–27.

Kant, Immanuel. "Perpetual Peace: A Philosophical Sketch." In *Kant: Political Writings* (2nd ed.), edited by Hans S. Reiss, 93–125. Cambridge: Cambridge University Press, 1991.

Kristoff, Nicholas D., and Sheryl WuDunn. *Half the Sky: Turning Oppression into Opportunity for Women Worldwide.* New York: Vintage Books, 2009.

Lawson, Chapell, and Strom Thacker. "Democracy? In Iraq?," *Hoover Digest*, July 30, 2003. Accessed November 20, 2012. http://www.hoover.org/publications/hoover-digest/article/7533.

Leeson, Peter T. "Better off Stateless: Somalia Before and After Government Collapse," *Journal of Comparative Economics*, 35, no. 4 (2007), 689–710.

Lewis, Bernard. *The Jews of Islam.* Princeton, N.J.: Princeton University Press, 1984.

Lijphart, Arend (ed). *Parliamentary versus Presidential Government.* Oxford: Oxford University Press, 1992.

Mezyaev, Alexander. "Central African Republican: Another Western Backed Coup d'Etat," *Global Research*, April 4, 2013. Accessed April 5, 2013. http://www.globalresearch.ca/central-african-intrigue-another-western-backed-coup-detat/5330013.

Monbiot, George. *Manifesto for a New World Order.* New York: New Press, 2003.

O'Neill, Onora. *Bounds of Justice.* Cambridge: Cambridge University Press, 2000.

Oz, Amos. *In the Land of Israel.* New York: Harcourt Brace & Co, 1983.

Pogge, Thomas. *World Poverty and Human Rights.* Malden, Mass.: Blackwell Publishers, 2002.

Rawls, John. *The Law of Peoples.* Cambridge, Mass.: Harvard University Press, 1999.

Riker, William. *Liberalism against Populism: A Confrontation between the Theory of Democracy and the Theory of Social Choice.* Prospect Heights, Ill.: Waveland Press, 1982.

Sen, Amartya. *Development as Freedom.* New York: Anchor Books, 1999.

Shepsle, Kenneth A., and Mark S. Bonchek. *Analyzing Politics: Rationality, Behavior, and Institutions.* New York: Norton, 1997.

Socarides, Richard. "Momentum and Gay Marriage, from Paris to SCOTUS" *The New Yorker*, April 24, 2013.

Spivak, Gayatri. *In other Worlds: Essays in Cultural Politics.* New York: Routledge, 1987.

Stearns, Jason K. *Dancing in the Glory of Monsters: The Collapse of the Congo and the Great War of Africa.* New York: PublicAffairs, 2011.

Tilly, Charles. "War-Making and State-Making as Organized Crime." In *Bringing the State Back in,* edited by Peter Evans, Dietrich Rueschemeyer, and Theda Skocpol, 169–186. Cambridge: Cambridge University Press, 1985.

United Nations. "The Universal Declaration of Human Rights." Accessed November 20, 2012. http://www.un.org/en/documents/udhr/, n.d.

Wolf, Martin. *Why Globalization Works*. New Haven, Conn.: Yale University Press, 2004.

Wolff, Jonathan. *An Introduction to Political Philosophy*. New York: Oxford University Press, 2006.

Chapter 10

International Human Rights Movement

Satenik Margaryan

Introduction

We are all entitled to human rights because of the simple fact that we are all human. We share these rights equally, regardless of our race, sex, religion, national origin, economic class, or any other factor. Human rights have been defined in detail in numerous international treaties and conventions. The Universal Declaration of Human Rights (UDHR), however, was the first instance of countries coming together and recognizing the importance of upholding human rights in the international arena and establishing a universal expression of the human rights. In 2008 we celebrated the sixtieth anniversary of the adoption of the UDHR. This milestone presents us with an occasion for introspection. The Declaration, translated into 360 languages, is the foundation of international human rights law and an inspiration for constitutions of newly independent states. A document released by the United Nations (UN) (2007, iii) for this occasion declares that the Universal Declaration "has become a yardstick by which we measure respect for what we know, or should know, as right and wrong."

Nonetheless, the sixtieth anniversary of the Universal Declaration underscores the vast challenges facing the protection of human rights in every corner of the world. Reports of flagrant violations of the most basic human rights flood mass media sources, causing us to question the viability and effectiveness of the institutionalized human rights apparatus. In the last decade of the twentieth century, the bloody events in Rwanda, Kosovo, East Timor, Iraq, the West Bank, and other places challenge the idea we are able to protect the most basic human rights.

In this chapter, we will briefly review the history of human rights and international human rights movements. We also examine the provisions of international instruments of human rights by focusing on the International Bill of Rights—the Charter of the United Nations, the UDHR, the International Covenant on Economic, Social and Cultural Rights, and the International Covenant on Civil and Political Rights. Finally, the challenges of the international human rights movement will be discussed.

The History of Human Rights

The histories of the human rights and the human rights movement are distinct. We can trace the antecedents of modern thought about human rights in religious works and writings of philosophers. The human rights movement, however, did not materialize until the beginning of the twentieth century. Thus, although the modern understanding of human rights is predominantly the product of seventeenth and eighteenth centuries, there were religious and philosophical antecedents that shaped and directed the development of our understanding of human rights. Next, we will describe the major thinkers of the twentieth century who influenced how we think of human rights today.

Controversies are numerous[1] when we talk about the history of human rights. One controversy, according to Ishay (2004), concerns the origins of human rights. When did the humanity start concerning itself with rights inherent to the human race? Are human rights handed down to us by the world's religions from the time immemorial? Sellars (2002, vii) writes that "human rights are as old as civilisation itself. Or so we are often told." To answer these questions we need to deal with a semantic problem. The term "human rights" is a relatively recent formulation that became prominent in the 1940s (Cmiel 2004). If we were to restrict our historical foray to the antecedents of "human rights" or "the rights of the man," we would overlook vast areas of religious, ethical, and philosophical thoughts that do not contain the words mentioned above but do deal with the rights and freedoms of people. We should, however, also be cognizant of the pitfalls of an expansive approach to human rights, i.e., viewing them as anything positive and good. Cmiel (2004, 119) warns us this approach can result in classifying Buddha and Jesus as human rights activists.

All of the major religions have addressed questions of right and wrong, justice and fairness, the dignity of each person, and the brotherhood of human beings. These issues influenced our conception of human rights. The central tenet of most religions speaks to the inherent dignity of a human being. And the sacredness of a human being entitles him or her to dignified treatment. For example, Genesis (the first book of the Pentateuch or the Old Testament)

---

1. Ishay (2004) was able to distill these controversies into six distinct groups.

emphasizes the sacredness of the individual because human beings were created in God's image (Kaplan 1980).

Likewise, most religions speak of the duties and obligations of humans towards God, their kin, and beyond, rather than focusing on individual rights and freedoms. In the ancient texts of Hinduism, the sacred nature of all human life and the importance of human duty towards people beyond oneself or one's family are underscored (Lauren 1998). Nasr (1980, 97) argues that, according to Shari'a (the body of Islamic religious law), human rights are "a consequence of human obligations and not their antecedents." Thus, only by fulfilling our obligations to God, nature, and other people, can human beings gain rights and freedoms (Nasr 1980). The maxim of the Golden Rule, found in most world religions, recognizes that one has a right to be treated justly and has a responsibility to ensure justice for others (Nowak 2003). Most scholars of human rights, however, do not support the notion that modern human rights are equivalent to the ancient religious understanding of the common good (Ishay 2004). Sellars (2002) argues that historians have found no evidence that ancient societies believed that all people possessed inherent rights. Nevertheless, we cannot overlook the contribution of religion to our conception of human rights.

The main philosophical antecedent to human rights ideas is found in the doctrine of natural law, which grants individuals natural, inherent, and inalienable rights. As Rosenbaum (1980, 8) points out, "the history of the evolution of human rights is associated with what may be called the natural law tradition." According to philosophers, the roots of natural law are found in classical Greek philosophy. Mahoney (2007, 3) states that "the earliest stage of Western ethical reflection contains two deeply significant features that contributed to the eventual emergence of human rights: the centering of human morality on the idea of justice; and the recourse to human nature as a source of moral knowledge." The concepts of justice and human virtue are found in the works of Aristotle and Plato. Aristotle and Plato, in their philosophical tractates, introduced a number of conceptions of equality that became key elements of modern human rights theory: equal respect for all citizens, equality before the law, equality in political power, equality in suffrage, and equality of civil rights (Rosenbaum 1980).

The idea of natural law was further developed by Roman Stoic philosophers such as Seneca and Cicero. According to them, natural law required societies to implement rational governance that was egalitarian and universal. Cicero wrote in De Re Publica that natural law "binds all human society" and applies to "the whole human race" without distinction and that "eternal and unchangeable law will be valid for all nations and all times" (quoted in Lauren 1998, 12).

In the Middle Ages, the doctrine of natural law became entrenched in Christian theology by redefining the natural law as divine in which humanity was subject to the authority of God as well as mankind. Moreover, the Christian theology of this era posited the universal brotherhood of the humankind, thus viewing an individual as something apart from his or her membership in a state (Lauren 1998). Rosenbaum (1980, 11) argues that this separation is "the conceptual precursor to the emergence of both individualism as a political theory and the notion of 'freedom' rights, each exerting its influence on the formation of the human rights concept." The Magna Carta ("Great Charter") of 1215, one of the most significant legal documents of the Middle Ages, sought to limit the powers of royal government and guaranteed the respect of rights by the king (Lauren 1998).

During the era of the Enlightenment, a European philosophical movement of the late seventeenth and eighteenth centuries, the doctrine of natural law reached its apogee. The doctrine was endorsed by social contract theorists, who argued that individuals enter into an implicit social union and form a society that protects the individual's natural rights. Hobbes's, Locke's, and Rousseau's theories of social contract viewed individuals as possessing natural rights— e.g., the right to life, liberty, property, security, and happiness—and the state was required to protect these rights (Nowak 2003). Of the three philosophers, scholars consider Locke to be the most influential on modern rights theories (Tierney 2005). Locke articulated that natural rights to life, liberty, and property are enforceable only in a civil society that recognizes an obligation to protect those rights. Locke's theory of the social contract had an enormous impact on the philosophers of the eighteenth century, most notably Thomas Jefferson. Rosenbaum (1980) points out that Jefferson modified and expanded Locke's natural rights to life, liberty, and property and included them in the American Declaration of Independence (1776) as unalienable rights to "life, liberty, and the pursuit of happiness" (quoted in Rosenbaum 1980, 12).

The theories of Enlightenment philosophers fueled the American and French revolutions. The American struggle for independence allowed for the implementation of European ideas of natural rights in the Declaration of Independence, the Constitution, and the Virginia Declaration of Rights (1776). The French Revolution, which followed the American Revolution, radically advanced the cause of universal rights in the Declaration of the Rights of Man and Citizens (1789) and became one of the basic charters of human rights (Ishay 2004). The Declaration affirms the equality of men (Article 1), and guarantees the rights of liberty, private property, security, and resistance to oppression (Article 2); the right to participate (directly or indirectly) in legislation (Article 6); freedom from unlawful arrest and prosecution (Article 7);

the presumption of innocence (Article 9); and freedom of religion (Article 10) and speech (Article 11). The Declaration went beyond its American predecessors by asserting that rights are based on principles that are fundamental to man and therefore universally applicable (Lauren 1998).

The civil and political rights found in eighteenth-century declarations were manifested in a number of national constitutions. As Nowak (2003, 14) points out, "the development of human rights is closely linked with the era of constitutionalism." In these constitutions, countries such as the United States provided a legal basis not only for the organization of the highest governing bodies and the structure of the state, but also for the protection of fundamental human rights. The U.S. Constitution (1787), along with the ten amendments of the Bill of Rights (1791) and the French Constitution of 1789, are considered to be the first comprehensive constitutions. Before the World War II, a number of nations solidified human rights in their respective constitutions. These constitutions placed the protection of universal human rights within the jurisdiction of states. As Cmiel (2004, 126) points out, "as far as the international community was concerned, nations could still do what they wanted inside their borders."

The ideas developed in the seventeenth and eighteenth centuries had an enormous impact on our conception of human rights. In fact, Morsink (1999, 281) states that "even a casual reader of the Universal Declaration will see that there is a similarity of language between this 1948 United Nations document and the classical declarations of the eighteenth century." The preamble and Article 1 use Enlightenment-inspired language, and speak of "inherent dignity" and of "equal and inalienable rights."

The History of International Human Rights Movement

The international human rights movement is relatively recent. There have been two waves that influenced the idea of human rights in politics and government (Burgers 1992). Burgers (1992) argues that the first wave began in the seventeenth century and finished at the end of the eighteenth century. As discussed above, the language of human rights emerged during the French and American revolutions. However, the rhetoric at the end of the eighteenth century did not have significant impact on how countries were governed (Mazower 2004). Thus, for two centuries, the human rights movement was essentially moribund until the beginning of the twentieth century. The second wave began in the twentieth century and is, perhaps, continuing still (Burgers 1992). The twentieth century brought changes to our understanding of human rights in modern society and the role of the international community in monitoring those rights. A number of historical antecedents led to the internationalization of the issue, which culminated in the UDHR and subsequent international instruments.

Early international human rights activism consisted of various campaigns to promote the protection of basic rights across national borders. The anti-slavery movement of the early nineteenth century was one such example. The reduction and eventual abolition of the slavery in the nineteenth century was achieved not only through national anti-slavery movements and legislation banning slave trade and emancipating the slaves, but also through international law (e.g., Declaration on the Slave Trade of 1815), several bilateral treaties, and the Quintuple Treaty of London of 1841, and the Suppression of the African Slave trade (Nowak 2003). The prohibition of slavery and the slave trade by the Slavery Convention of 1926 adopted under the auspices of the League of Nations is "one of the first universal treaties for the protection of human rights under international law" (Nowak 2003, 20).

Humanitarian international law concerned with care of the wounded and other protections afforded to people in armed conflicts is another example of an early historical antecedent of the human rights movement. Beginning in the 1860s, minimum treatment standards exist for prisoners of war, wounded and sick persons, former combatants, and civilians affected in armed conflict. Such instruments include the 1863 Instructions for the Government of Armies of the United States in the Field (i.e., the Lieber Code), the Geneva Conventions for the Amelioration of the Condition of the Wounded in Armies in the Field (1864, 1929, 1949), the Geneva Convention Relative to the Treatment of Prisoners of War (1929, 1949), the Geneva Convention relative to the Protection of Civilian Persons in Time of War of 1949, and the Additional Protocols of 1977 (International Committee of the Red Cross 2005). Compared to the international human rights law, the international humanitarian law is narrower in its scope of protections afforded to people affected by international armed conflicts. First, the humanitarian law is activated only during international armed conflicts, and thus they are inactive in peaceful times. Second, the humanitarian law is based on the principle of reciprocity, meaning that parties of an armed conflict agree to treat each other prisoners of war favorably, for example. Basically, if we follow the rules, our enemy will also abide by them. The international human rights law, on the other hand, expects every signatory to a convention or a treaty abide by its provisions. Nonetheless, the international humanitarian law set up an important precedent of international involvement in the issues concerning rights of individuals.

The period between World War I and World War II included a few scattered international campaigns to protect basic human rights (Cmiel 2004). Most associate the international human rights movement with the consequences of the World War II. However, the impact of World War I on the movement cannot be underestimated. As Sellars (2002, ix) argues, the human rights movement was propelled to act "by the shock of being plunged into another catastrophic conflict less than a quarter of century after the First World War."

Normand and Zaidi (2008) point out that the human rights discourse from the turn of the century until World War II was focused on the collective rights, including the rights of minorities, workers, and women. After World War I, the issue of minority rights was at the forefront of the early human rights campaign.[2] The League of Nations, an intergovernmental organization founded after World War I, took it upon itself to supervise protection for minorities guaranteed by bilateral peace or other treaties between the countries (Burgers 1992). The significance of the minority clause binding states as proposed by the League of Nations was that it put "the unprecedented limitations on national sovereignty under international law" (Burgers 1992, 450). The precedent of international pressure and international jurisdiction over human rights was set.

A number of individuals sought to move human rights to the international level between the two world wars. These sought to publicize the importance of human rights and lobbied for binding mechanisms at the international level, e.g., international human rights treaties. André Mandelstam, a Russian émigré living in Paris, an international lawyer, former diplomat under the Tsarist government, and an active proponent of human rights, is considered one of the most prominent pioneers of the international human rights movement (Burgers 1992; Normand and Zaidi 2008). His involvement with human rights issues was reportedly triggered by the Armenian genocide Mandelstam witnessed as a Tsarist diplomat posted in Turkey (Normand and Zaidi 2008). Among his accomplishments was the creation of a commission to study the protection of minorities and general human rights under the International Law Institute in 1921 (Burgers 1992). The purpose of the International Law Institute and similar organizations was to increase the profile of human rights issues and establish binding human rights system at the international level. In 1929, upon Mandestam's initiative, the Institute adopted a Declaration of the International Rights of Man that delineated the state's obligations in preserv-

---

2. In this time period, being a member of a minority group meant that he or she differed in language, religion, or race from the majority of the population (Burgers 1992; Normand and Zaidi 2008).

ing individual rights in its territory (Burgers 1992). This landmark declaration, which proclaimed the importance of individual rights to life, liberty, religious freedom, and property, was one of the first international declarations of this kind. A number of articles written by Mandelstam publicized the Declaration and the philosophy of human rights (Burgers 1992).

Mandelstam's colleague from the International Law Institute and fellow Russian émigré, Boris Mirkine-Guetzévitch, made an important contribution to giving human rights international status by researching human rights provisions in national constitutions of all countries and publishing the results in 1929 (Burgers 1992). Another organization important for the promotion of international human rights, the Diplomatic Academy, was established by Antoine Frangulis, another pioneer of the international human rights movement. He was a Greek émigré and a former Greek delegate to the League of Nations (Burgers 1992). According to Burgers (1992), the Academy set up a commission to study the question of the protection of human rights. Due to the efforts of Mandelstam, Mirkine-Guetzévitch, and Antoine Frangulis, as well as organizations like the International Law Institute and the Diplomatic Academy, the issue of international human rights was well publicized in the 1920s and 1930s, which created the fertile grounds upon which the Universal Declaration was created a decade later.

By the beginning of World War II, one of the most influential global campaigns to bring international human rights to the forefront of the international community was undertaken by Herbert G. Wells, the famous British author (Normand and Zaidi 2008). In 1939, in spite of the Nazi march through Europe, Wells drafted a bill of human rights that he circulated among the most notable intellectuals in the world,[3] soliciting their comments. He also published the initial draft of the declaration in the *Times* of London in 1939, which presented a comprehensive list of social, economic, civil, and political rights. This declaration in its subsequent iterations and publications in various international outlets kept the world's intellectuals' attention on human rights despite World War II.

The unrelenting work of pioneers like Mandelstam, Mirkine-Guetzévitch, Frangulis, Wells, and many others, resulted in the eventual acceptance of international human rights. However, as Norman and Zaidi (2008) point out, activism in the 1920s and 1930s was on the political periphery, and it was the atrocities of World War II occupied the minds of the public, not the human

---

3. H.G. Wells had the bill translated in more than thirty languages so that intellectuals across the world could understand the declaration in their own language (Normand and Zaidi 2008).

rights. The eventual victory of the international human rights movement was predicated on the victory of the Allied forces. Norman and Zaidi (2008) argue that "only when human rights were taken up during the war as part of an ideological offensive by the Allied coalition, in particular the United States under Roosevelt's leadership, did the issue begin to be taken seriously as a basis for planning the postwar order" (78).

The new wave of international human rights activism comes from nongovernmental organizations (NGOs). These groups spearhead contemporary efforts to combat violations of human rights throughout the world. The Universal Declaration was a direct product of the work done by these organizations. A number of drafts of international bills of rights were submitted by different NGOs to the UN Commission of Human Rights during the drafting stage of the Universal Declaration. Articles from these international bills of rights appeared in the final draft of the Universal Declaration because, as Morsink (1999) points out, John P. Humphrey, the first drafter of the Declaration, freely borrowed articles and whole phrases from these bills.

In the last decades of the twentieth century, human rights NGOs rather than the UN emerged as main players in the international human rights activism (Cmiel 2004). Amnesty International (created in 1961) and Human Rights Watch (created in 1978), among the most prominent human rights organizations, monitor states' obligations under international human rights instruments and publicize violations and human rights abuses. The agenda of an exponentially increasing number of Western and non-Western human rights NGOs currently include health rights, women's rights, economic justice, environmental justice, and indigenous people's rights. For instance, Amnesty International's Web site lists more than twenty topics of interest and runs four global campaigns to control arms, counter terror with justice, stop violence against women, and abolish the death penalty (Amnesty International 2009).

It is difficult to assess what has been accomplished by recent human rights activism. Human rights abuses persist despite international instruments and mechanisms created to prevent them. Although the vast majority of countries have signed treaties protecting human rights of children, women, and men, governmental and nongovernmental violations of human rights are epidemic (Hafner-Burton and Tsutsui 2005). Cmiel (2004, 134), in his overview of the recent history of human rights, poses a question: "What if claims made in the name of universal rights are not the best way to protect people?" Hafner-Burton and Tsutsui (2005) find evidence that could deny this pessimism. They argue that though countries ratify treaties as "window dressing," the governments' pro forma agreement to human rights standards energizes human rights advocates within countries to improve actual human rights practices. They call this phenomenon "the paradox of empty promises" (Hafner-Burton and Tsutsui 2005, 1378). To understand the role of NGOs in contemporary international human rights activism, a spiral model of human rights change has been proposed (Risse, Ropp, and Sikkink 1999). Risse, Ropp, and Skikkink (1999) propose to look at interactions between domestic NGOs, international non-governmental organizations (INGOs), international institutions, and national governments to see how international norms affect domestic policies. Thus, the emerging global legitimacy of human rights, coupled with the creation of strong civil societies, replete with NGOs, can foster improvement in states' human rights practices.

The International Bill of Rights

The foundation of international human rights law consists of the Charter of the United Nations (1945), the International Covenant on Economic, Social and Cultural Rights (1966), the International Covenant on Civil and Political Rights, the International Convention on the Rights of the Child, and the Torture Convention (Skogly 2006). Rather than presenting a single international bill of human rights at once, the United Nations moved slowly by first adopting the Charter of the United Nations, then the Universal Declaration of Human Rights (UDHR), and only then the two UN Covenants. In the following sections, we will review the provisions of the UDHR, the International Covenant on Economic, Social and Cultural Rights, and the International Covenant on Civil and Political Rights.

The Universal Declaration of Human Rights

The document known as the UDHR was adopted in 1948 by the UN General Assembly in Paris. It was a culmination not only of a two-year drafting and preparation process carried out by the UN Commission on Human Rights, but also increasing national and international pressure since the World War II to introduce an international bill of human rights (Morsink 1999). The Declaration is a landmark document in the history of human rights because, for the first time, the nations agreed to a single expression of fundamental human rights that should be universally protected.

The Charter of the United Nations, the predecessor of the Declaration, was signed in June 1945, in San Francisco, at the conclusion of the UN Conference on International Organization, and came into force in October 1945 (UN 2009). The Charter included seven references to the need for international recognition and protection of human rights (Morsink 1999). For instance, in the second paragraph of the preamble, the Charter states that its purpose is "to reaffirm faith in fundamental human rights, in the dignity and worth of the human person, in the equal rights of men and women and of nations large and small." The Charter, nonetheless, did not include any means of implementation of human rights, nor defined the term "human rights," nor created a specific body to deal exclusively with human rights (Nowak 2003). The Charter, instead, created the Economic and Social Council (Chapter X, Articles 61–72). The Charter mandates, among other tasks, that the Economic and Social Council promote "respect for, and observance of, human rights and fundamental freedoms for all" (Article 62[2]). In 1946, the Council, in turn, delegated human rights to the Commission on Human Rights[4] and tasked it with creation of an international bill of human rights.

Upon the creation of the Commission on Human Rights in 1946, the two-year drafting process of the Universal Declaration began. The work of the Commission on Human Rights on the Universal Declaration started in 1947. The Commission was chaired by Eleanor Roosevelt, the widow of President Franklin D. Roosevelt. The multinational Commission was made up of eighteen persons representing Australia, Belgium, the Belorussian SSR, Chile, China, Egypt, France, India, Iran, Lebanon, Panama, Philippine Republic, the UK, the United States, the USSR, Uruguay, and Yugoslavia (Morsink 1999).

In the two-year drafting process, there were several drafts of the declaration were prepared. The preliminary draft of the Declaration was prepared by the Canadian John P. Humphrey, the director of the Secretariat's Division on Human Rights. In writing the first draft of the Declaration, Humphrey conducted extensive cross-country research and relied on a collection of proposals and drafts of bills of rights submitted by countries and various NGOs to the United Nations (Morsink 1999; Glendon 2004). According to Morsink (1999), he borrowed freely from these documents, looking for the best articles. Humphrey also included articles of national constitutions that matched to the rights in the draft. This draft became the basis for all other drafts of the Declaration. The subsequent draft was prepared by René Cassin, the delegate from France. The drafts were presented and debated during sessions of the Human Rights Commission, which were attended by a great number of NGOs. Member states that were not represented on the Human Rights Commission also had an opportunity to participate during the meetings of the Third Committee of the General Assembly in 1948 (Morsink 1999). Thus, the creation of the

---

4. In 2006, the UN Commission on Human Rights was replaced by the Human Rights Council (Commission on Human Rights 2006).

Declaration was truly a multinational effort. The final draft of the Universal Declaration was presented to the Third General Assembly in Paris on December 10, 1948. The Universal Declaration was adopted the same day, with forty-eight countries voting for it, no country voting against it, and eight countries abstaining.[5]

The Universal Declaration consists of a preamble, which lays out the foundation and principles of the document, and the articles, which present a comprehensive catalogue of the rights. The structure of the Universal Declaration possesses an organic unity (Morsink 1999). René Cassin, the second prominent drafter of the Universal Declaration, explaining the structure of the Declaration, compared it to the portico of a temple. The distinct parts of the Declaration are interrelated and the relative order or placement of articles was not crucial. Rather, rights need to be interpreted in the context of the whole Declaration.

According to Cassin's analogy, as described by Glendon (2004), the preamble's seven clauses represent the steps leading to the entrance of temple, and provides the reasons for adopting the Declaration. The first paragraph of the preamble underscores the belief that "in recognition of the inherent dignity and of the equal and inalienable rights of all members of the human family is the foundation of freedom, justice and peace in the world." The words "inherent" and "inalienable" point to the Enlightenment ideas.

The drafters' moral outrage about the Holocaust provided them with the motivation to proclaim, in the preamble, that the atrocities of the World War II had a devastating impact on the "conscience of the mankind." They then establish the four freedoms—freedom of speech, freedom of belief, freedom from want, and freedom from fear—that are "proclaimed as the highest aspiration" of the people. The expression of these four essential freedoms was a tribute to the President Franklin Roosevelt who called for the protection of these freedoms in his 1941 State of the Union address (Morsink 1999).

In addition, the preamble states that human rights "should be protected by the rule of law" so people do not resort to a rebellion when living in tyranny and oppression. The fourth paragraph underscores the importance of friendly relations between nations. The fifth paragraph ties the Declaration to the UN Charter in which member states have already expressed their "faith in fundamental human rights, in the dignity and worth of the human person and in the equal rights of men and women and have determined to promote social progress and better standards of life in larger freedom." The sixth paragraph af-

---

5. The eight abstaining countries were the Soviet bloc, consisting of the USSR, the Ukrainian SSR, the Belarusian SSR, Czechoslovakia, Yugoslavia, Poland; South Africa; and Saudi Arabia (Morsink 1999).

firms that all UN member states have pledged to achieve, with the cooperation with the United Nations, "the promotion of universal respect for and observance of human rights and fundamental freedoms." The seventh paragraph underscores the importance of a "common understanding" of the rights set forth in Declaration. The preamble ends with a statement that the Universal Declaration should be viewed "as a common standard of achievement for all peoples and all nations." Morsink (1999) argues that the drafters did not think of the Declaration as a legally binding document, but offered it as an educational tool to "promote respect for these rights and freedoms."

The first two articles of the Declaration, which proclaim the basic principles of dignity, liberty, equality, and brotherhood, represent the foundation blocks, according to Cassin's temple analogy (Glendon 2004). Article 1 of the Declaration ascertains that "all human beings are born free and equal in dignity and rights. They are endowed with reason and conscience and should act towards one another in a spirit of brotherhood." This article, although it appears first, was the last one to be added to the Declaration (Morsink 1999).

In the Cassin's temple, four columns of rights are built on the foundation of dignity, liberty, equality, and brotherhood: individual rights; the rights of individuals in relation to each other and to various groups; spiritual, public, and political rights; and economic, social, and cultural rights (Glendon 2004). Specifically, among the rights found in the Declaration are the right to be free from discrimination (Article 2); the right to life, liberty, and personal security (Article 3); the right to be free from slavery and servitude (Article 4); and the guarantee of freedom from torture or cruel, inhuman, or degrading treatment or punishment (Article 5). Morsink (1999) argues that these rights were not only the reflections of Enlightenment ideas, but also the drafters' reaction to the treatment of people in concentration camps during the World War II.

Articles 6 through 12 guarantee legal human rights. Morsink (1999) argues that the drafters were convinced that the only way to stop systematic human rights violations was to guarantee the rights for individuals before the law (Article 6); persons will be equal before the law and be protected from any discrimination (Article 7); the right to a legal remedy if individual's rights are violated (Article 8); to be free from arbitrary arrests, detention, or exile (Article 9); to "a fair and public hearing by an independent and impartial tribunal" (Article 10); to be presumed innocent until proven guilty (Article 11 [1]); to be convicted only of those acts that had been previously codified as crimes in national and international law (Article 11 [1]); and to be protected by the law against interference with individual's privacy, family, and correspondence (Article 12).

Furthermore, the Universal Declaration protects the freedom of movement and residence, the right to an asylum from persecution in another country, and the right to a nationality. The rights contained in Articles 13, 14, and 15 were the direct reflection of the persecution of Jews, the Roma, and others who were unable to leave the Nazi Germany (Morsink 1999).

The Universal Declaration also protects the family by proclaiming that "the family is the natural and fundamental group unit of society and is entitled to protection by society and the State" (Article 16 [3]). It promotes the freedom of people of the age of consent to marry and form a family regardless of race, nationality, or religion (Article 16 [1]) and [2]). The Declaration also protects the right to own property alone or in association with other people and to be free from the arbitrary deprivation of property (Article 17).

The Universal Declaration encompasses a comprehensive protection of second-generation rights, including political and civil rights. Article 18 grants absolute freedom of religion for members of both majority and minority religious groups (Morsink 1999). According to the Declaration, people have the right of free speech (Article 19) and the freedom of peaceful assembly and association (Article 20). Article 21(1) guarantees freedom of participation in the government directly or indirectly through elected officials. Moreover, this article protects the right of equal access to public service (Article 21 [2]) and the will of the people as expressed in periodic and universal suffrage elections that "shall be the basis of the authority of government" (Article 21 [3]). Morsink (1999) argues that Article 21, in conjunction with Article 2's prohibition of discrimination, calls for a multiparty system.

The Universal Declaration protects economic, social and cultural rights. Article 22 introduces these rights by declaring:

> Everyone, as a member of society, has the right to social security and is entitled to realization, through national effort and international cooperation and in accordance with the organization and resources of each State, of the economic, social and cultural rights indispensable for his dignity and the free development of his personality.

Articles 23 through 27 provide a comprehensive review of rights in economic, social, and cultural spheres. The rights in the economic sphere include the freedom of choosing employment (Article 23[1]), equal pay (Article 23[2]), forming and joining a union (Article 23[4]), leisure and paid holidays (Article 24), the right to be healthy, the right to security in cases of unemployment, sickness, disability, and other circumstances, and protections of mothers and children (Article 25 [3]).

Educational rights are covered in Article 26. First, the article guarantees the right to education, including free and compulsory elementary education. Second, the article maintains that education should be aimed towards the "full development of the human personality" and the development of respect for human rights and fundamental freedoms. Article 26 also argues for human rights education, which should promote "understanding, tolerance and friendship among all nations, racial or religious groups, and shall further the activities of the United Nations for the maintenance of peace." Parents are given priority in deciding the kind of education their children should receive. Morsink (1999) argues that Article 26 (3) is of special importance for parents who are members of minority groups because the Article gives them the freedom to bring up their children in accordance with the teachings of their linguistic, religious, or ethnic groups. Article 27 deals with dual cultural rights. First, everyone is entitled to the right to freely participate in culture, enjoy the arts, and share the benefits of scientific advances. Second, the article offers protections of intellectual property of scientists, artists, and authors.

The last three articles of the Declaration set out the general conditions necessary for the realization of the rights described in the Declaration. These articles, the crown of the portico for Cassin, place the rights of the Declaration in the "context of limits, duties, and the social and political order in which they are to be realized" (Glendon 2004, 68). Article 28 provides that everyone has the right to social and international order "in which the rights and freedoms set forth in this Declaration can be fully realized." Article 29 deals with "the communitarian dimension of rights possession" (Morsink 1999, 336) and describes the individual's duties to the community. The article also provides that limitations on exercising the rights and freedoms contained in the Declaration can be enacted by law for purpose of protecting the rights and freedoms of others and for maintaining morality, public order, and the general welfare. Article 29(3) prohibits the exercise of the rights and freedoms "contrary to the purposes and principles of the United Nations." Finally, Article 30 prohibits any action on the part of a state, group, or person aimed at "destruction of any of the rights and freedoms set forth herein." Morsink (1999) points out that the Universal Declaration introduced the individual human being into international law in Article 30, which was unprecedented because international law previously concerned only countries.

It is important to note that the Universal Declaration is not a legally binding treaty.[6] Instead, it is a declaration of fundamental human rights without a mechanism of binding obligations. According to the definitions provided by the UN Treaty Collection (2009a), the Universal Declaration originally was

------

6. Treaties are the primary sources of international law and contain rights and obligations for countries (Skogly 2006).

not intending to have binding force, and its provisions gained this power later on (UN Treaty Collection 2009a, 2009b, 2009c). Nevertheless, the legal status of the Universal Declaration does not diminish its far-reaching importance: it has influenced and has been referred to by other international human rights treaties and national constitutions and legislation (Skogly 2006). Specifically, the International Covenants on Economic, Social, and Cultural Rights serves the purpose of binding member states not only to the provisions of the Covenant but to the provisions of the Universal Declaration.

International Covenant on Economic, Social, and Cultural Rights

The International Covenant on Economic, Social, and Cultural Rights is a multilateral treaty that was adopted by the General Assembly on December 16, 1966, and came into force on January 3, 1976, after a sufficient number of countries had ratified it. Currently, there are 160 state parties to the Covenant (UN Treaty Collection 2009b).

The Covenant was drafted by the UN Commission on Human Rights within the Economic and Social Council after work on the Universal Declaration had been completed. Initially, the Commission intended to draft a single legally binding instrument that would include all the rights of the Universal Declaration. However, disagreements between Western and socialist states ensued. The Socialist states argued that human rights were indivisible and were independent. Western states demanded for the rights to be divided into social, economic, and cultural rights and into civil and political rights and put into two distinct covenants (Nowak 2003). In 1952 the decision was made to draft two Covenants on Human Rights against the resistance of the Social states, one with a focus on social, economic, and cultural rights, and the other on political and civil rights (Skogly 2006).

The purpose of the International Covenant on Economic, Social, and Cultural Rights was to develop a legally binding treaty that would solidify the rights referred to in the Declaration and would expand human rights to include "second generation" rights in economic, social, cultural, political, and civil spheres. The Covenant on Economic, Social, and Cultural Rights, in fact, is considered the most important international treaty on economic, social, and cultural rights (Nowak 2003).

The Covenant, in particular, guarantees economic rights. Article 6 recognizes the right to work. The right to "just and favourable conditions of work" contained in Article 7 of the Convention includes a right to fair wages, safe working conditions, equal opportunity for promotion, and a right to rest, paid vacation, and public holidays. The Covenant provides for a right to form and join a union (Article 8b) and a right to strike (Article 8d).

The Covenant includes a number of social rights. The Covenant recognizes a right to social security (Article 9). Article 10 reaffirms the importance of the family and provides for family protection and assistance, including a right to a paid maternal leave. A right to an adequate standard of living is provided by Article 11, including a right to "adequate food, clothing and housing, and to the continuous improvement of living conditions." A right to physical and mental health is guaranteed by Article 12, which also compels states to undertake a number of steps to improve the health of the population. For instance, the Article mandates that states improve environmental conditions and reduce industrial pollution.

Among cultural rights, the Covenant recognizes the right to education (Article 13), making primary education compulsory (Article 14) and secondary and higher education accessible to all (Article 14). Article 15 not only recognizes the right to participate in cultural life but also requires the protection of the intellectual property of artists and scientists as well as freedom of scientific research and creative activity. Furthermore, the Covenant includes the right of all people to self-determination, meaning that people have a right to "freely determine their political status and freely pursue their economic, social and cultural development" (Article 1). The Covenant prohibits discrimination based on race, sex, language, religion, political or other opinion, national or social origin, property, birth, or other status (Article 2). Finally, Article 3 emphasizes gender equality in the economic, social, and cultural rights contained in the Covenant.

The Covenant provides a number of obligations for the ratifying states. Article 2(1) sets out their general obligations:

> Each State Party to the present Covenant undertakes to take steps, individually and through international assistance and co-operation, especially economic and technical, to the maximum of its available resources, with a view to achieving progressively the full realization of the rights recognized in the present Covenant by all appropriate means, including particularly the adoption of legislative measures.

It is important to note that the Covenant mandates international cooperation and assistance in protecting human rights and emphasizes the role of international organizations. In fact, the Covenant calls upon industrialized nations to help developing nations guarantee social, economic, and cultural rights (Nowak 2003; Skogly 2006).

One of the most potent criticisms of the Covenant is its weak international monitoring mechanisms (Nowak 2003). Article 16 mandates that the states report on the measures undertaken to protect rights outlined in the Covenant. The article establishes that the state reports need to be submitted to the UN Secretary General, who will transmit them to the Economic and Social Council, "one of the principal political organs of the United Nations" (Nowak 2003, 82). Since 1985, a special committee, the UN Committee on Economic, Social and Cultural Rights (CESCR), made up of eighteen independent experts, has been responsible for monitoring the implementation of the International Covenant on Economic, Social, and Cultural Rights by the states parties (CESCR 2009). The CESCR carries out the provision of Part IV of the Covenant, issues general comments on various rights included in the Covenant, examines the state reports, and issues recommendations to the STATE party (CESCR 2009). Nowak (2003) argues that the weakness of this arrangement is that the CESR's preoccupation with state reports diverts the Committee's attention from the protection of rights underlined by the Covenant. In response to this criticism, in 2008 the CESR was empowered through an Optional Protocol to the International Covenant on Economic, Social, and Cultural Rights[7] to receive and review individual complaints (CESCR 2009). This will necessarily increase its monitoring powers by ensuring that violations of social, economic, and cultural rights are brought to the attention of the Committee.

International Covenant on Civil and Political Rights

As discussed above, due to disagreements between Western and socialist nations about implementation of rights, it was decided to split the legally binding treaty on human rights in the Universal Declaration into two covenants. The UN Commission on Human Rights worked on both Covenants simultaneously and presented drafts of proposals to the General Assembly in 1954. The International Covenant on Civil and Political Rights was adopted for signatures and ratifications by the UN General Assembly in 1966. Ten years after the adoption of the Covenant, it came into force in 1976. Currently, there are 164 state parties to the Covenant (UN Treaty Collection 2009c).

The Covenant on Civil and Political Rights contains essential civil and political rights. These rights contain the right of self-determination of peoples (Article 1) and protection from gender, religious, racial, or other forms of dis-

---

7. The Optional Protocol was adopted by the General Assembly on December 10, 2008 and will be open for signatures in 2009 (CESCR 2009).

crimination (Articles 2 and 3).[8] The Covenant protects individual's physical integrity by guaranteeing the right to life (Article 6[1]) by protecting against execution (Article 6), torture or cruel, inhuman, or degrading treatment, or punishment, or medical or scientific experimentation without consent (Article 7), arbitrary arrest or detention (Article 9), or slavery (Article 8). Article 6 places limitations on the use of the death penalty. The Second Optional Protocol to the Covenant of 1989 prohibits the death penalty. The Covenant also guarantees procedural fairness in legal proceedings (Articles 9 and 10), e.g., rights concerning arrest, trial, and treatment in detention, rights to a lawyer, and impartial process in trials.

Political and civil rights guaranteed by the Covenant include protection of individual freedom of thought, conscience, and religion (Article 18), expression (Article 19[2]), association (Article 22[1]), and the right to hold assemblies (Article 21). The Covenant prohibits propaganda for war and incitement to national, racist and religious discrimination, hostility, or violence (Article 20). Article 25 guarantees individuals the right to political participation in the conduct of public affairs, voting, and being able to be elected at periodic elections. Article 27 protects the rights of ethnic, religious, or linguistic minorities to enjoy and practice their own culture, religion, or language in a community with other members of the group.

Human Rights Committee established by Article 28 of the Covenant is in charge of monitoring state parties' human rights treaty obligations. Human Rights Committee is made up of eighteen independent experts with recognized competence in the field of human rights. In accordance to Articles 28 and 39 of the Covenant, members of the Committee are elected to a term of four years by state parties.[9] The Human Rights Committee performs four monitoring functions. First, under article 40 of the Covenant, the Committee examines reports submitted by state parties. The countries prepare an initial report within one year of accession or ratification of the Covenant and file subsequent "periodic reports" on the implementation of obligations and responsibilities. Second, the Human Rights Committee releases general observations interpreting

---

8. Article 26 of the Covenant provides for equality before the law and equal protection of the law without discrimination based on any grounds, including "race, colour, sex, language, religion, political or other opinion, national or social origin, property, birth or other status."

9. The members of the Human Rights Committee, although elected by state parties, do not represent their respective countries in the Committee. Article 38 of the Covenant requires a public declaration of impartiality in an open committee before the member takes over his or her duties.

the provisions of the Covenant (Human Rights Committee n.d.). Under the First Optional Protocol to the Covenant (1966), the Human Rights Committee also has a mandate to receive and examine individual complaints about violations of rights guaranteed by the Covenant (Human Rights Committee 2009). According to 2004 data, 1,295 individual complaints had been registered by the Committee, and they found violations of the Covenant in 349 cases (Human Rights Committee n.d.). Finally, the Human Rights Committee is empowered by Article 41 to handle complaints from countries that are party to the Covenant about failures of obligations assumed under the Covenant. As Nowak (2003) points out, there have not been any cases of interstate complaints. It is important to point out that, notwithstanding the mandate, the Human Rights Committee is a quasi-judicial body whose decisions are not legally binding and are not politically enforceable (Nowak 2003).

Other International Human Rights Instruments and Bodies

In addition to the two Covenants, there are other important international human rights treaties that form foundation of the international human rights law. Five UN human rights treaties are focused on individual substantive topics or issues: the International Convention on the Elimination of All Forms of Racial Discrimination (1965); the Convention on the Elimination of All Forms of Discrimination against Women (1979); the Convention against Torture and Other Cruel, Inhuman or Degrading Treatment or Punishment (1984); the Convention on the Rights of the Child (1989); and the 1990 International Convention on the Protection of the Rights of All Migrant Workers and Members of Their Families (Human Rights Committee n.d.). These treaties and conventions resemble the covenants in structure: they contain a normative part specifying the rights and freedoms guaranteed by the convention, and they create independent committees like the Human Rights Committee to monitor the implementation of obligations by the state parties.

In addition to the UN instruments, a number of other international human rights treaties and bodies operate in various regions of the world. The Organization of American States (OAS), which is made up of thirty-five sovereign states[10] of the Americas, provides human rights system for people in the

---

10. The members of the OAS are Antigua and Barbuda, Argentina, the Bahamas, Barbados, Belize, Bolivia, Brazil, Canada, Chile, Colombia, Costa Rica, Cuba (although a member, Cuba's government has been excluded since 1962), Dominica, Dominican Republic, Ecuador, El Salvador, Grenada, Guatemala, Guyana, Haiti, Honduras, Jamaica.

Americas who have suffered violations of their rights by the state (OAS 2009). The two pillars of the OAS human rights system are the Inter-American Commission on Human Rights (located in Washington, D.C.), and the Inter-American Court of Human Rights (located in San José, Costa Rica) (OAS 2009a). According to the OAS (2009b), these institutions apply regional law on human rights, i.e., the nonbinding American Declaration of the Rights and Duties of Man (1948)[11] and the American Convention on Human Rights (1969), which established the Inter-American Commission on Human Rights and the Inter-American Court of Human Rights.

In Europe, the Council of Europe promotes human rights in the forty-seven member states.[12] Established in 1949, the Council of Europe is an intergovernmental organization and is called upon to promote parliamentary democracy, rule of law, and human rights based on cooperation of the member states. The entrance of new members into the Council of Europe is conditional on ratification of several legally binding treaties and conventions, e.g., the European Convention for the Protection of Human Rights and Fundamental Freedoms, the European Convention for the Prevention of Torture, Protocol 6 (abolishing the death penalty), and the Framework Convention for the Protection of National Minorities. The European Court of Human Rights, established by the Convention for the Protection of Human Rights and Fundamental Freedoms in 1959, is a powerful international body that reviews individual and interstate complaints about human rights violations from member states. Unlike the UN Human Rights Committee, the European Court of Human Rights is a judicial body and its decisions are legally binding (Nowak 2003).

Other regional international organizations called upon to protect human rights include the African Union (rights guaranteed in the 1981 African Charter on Human and Peoples' Rights), the Organization of the Islamic Conference rights contained in the nonbinding Cairo Declaration on Human Rights of 1990 and the League of Arab States (Nowak 2003).

Mexico, Nicaragua, Panama, Paraguay, Peru, Saint Kitts and Nevis, Saint Lucia, Saint Vincent and the Grenadines, Suriname, Trinidad and Tobago, the United States, Uruguay, and Venezuela (OAS 2009).

11. It was issued before the Universal Declaration of Human Rights (Nowak 2003).

12. Members of the Council of Europe are Albania, Andorra, Armenia, Austria, Azerbaijan, Belgium, Bosnia and Herzegovina, Bulgaria, Croatia, Cyprus, Czech Republic, Denmark, Estonia, Finland, France, Georgia, Germany, Greece, Hungary, Iceland, Ireland, Italy, Latvia, Liechtenstein, Lithuania, Luxembourg, Malta, Moldova, Monaco, Montenegro, Netherlands, Norway, Poland, Portugal, Romania, Russian Federation, San Marino, Serbia, Slovak Republic, Slovenia, Spain, Sweden, Switzerland, "the former Yugoslav Republic of Macedonia," Turkey, Ukraine, and the United Kingdom.

The aforementioned international human rights instruments are primarily targeted at countries' responsibilities to uphold human rights at the national level. As Nowak (2003) states, however, the gross violators of human rights—e.g., dictators, heads of juntas, and police chiefs—have reigned in impunity even if they were complicit in genocide, torture, or forced disappearances. Even with all the international human rights protections in place, atrocious violations of the most essential human rights have taken place in countries all over the world, and most perpetrators have been able to escape responsibility. Thus, it has become clear that there is a need to focus on individual responsibility for cases of serious human rights violations. Since the 1990s, the United Nations has set up a few *ad hoc* international tribunals to investigate and adjudicate serious and systematic violations of humanitarian law and human rights. These international tribunals include the International Criminal Tribunal for the former Yugoslavia (1993), the International Criminal Tribunal for Rwanda (1994), the Special Court for Sierra Leone (2002), and the Extraordinary Chambers in the Courts of Cambodia or Khmer Rouge Tribunal (2005). The major shortcomings of these tribunals were their temporary nature and their focus on a specific time frame and a specific conflict.

A permanent and independent International Criminal Court (ICC), governed by the Rome Statute of 1998, came into force in 2002. The ICC is responsible for criminal prosecutions of international crimes—e.g., genocide, crimes against humanity, and war crimes—defined in the Rome Statute (ICC 2009a). Currently, the prosecutor of the ICC has opened and is conducting investigations into four situations where grave crimes were allegedly committed: by the Lord's Resistance Army in Uganda; in the Democratic Republic of Congo; in Darfur, Sudan; and in Central African Republic (ICC 2009b).

Conclusion

Human rights have ancient roots, were formulated in the seventeenth to eighteenth centuries, and were codified in the middle of the twentieth century. Human rights have become a global phenomenon and a vast number of countries have ratified international treaties concerning human rights. The Universal Declaration, the covenants, and all the treaties and conventions that followed them have entrenched themselves into our understanding of the modern world. A great number of international bodies and NGO promote and monitor how countries meet their human rights obligations. Newly independent states, such as countries of the former Soviet Union, have adopted the language of human rights in their constitutions. The ICC is poised to conduct trials of some of the worst violators of human rights in the recent past.

Nonetheless, the challenges of human rights persist. The protection of ordinary people's basic human rights remains a priority among national NGOs and international organizations. The ratification of human rights treaties does not automatically translate into governmental respect for human rights and sometimes even provides cover for violating citizens' rights (Hafner-Burton and Tsutsui 2005). However, pessimism about the global success of human rights is premature. Scholars have pointed out that it turns out that the key to success in human right activism lies with strong civil societies within countries that, with the support of the global force, work relentlessly to improve human rights practices.

Web Sources

1. United Nations: Human Rights:
   http://www.un.org/en/rights/
2. Office of the UN High Commissioner for Human Rights (OHCHR):
   http://www.ohchr.org/EN/Pages/WelcomePage.aspx
3. University of Minnesota, Human Rights Library:
   http://www1.umn.edu/humanrts/
4. Human Rights Watch:
   http://www.hrw.org/
5. Amnesty International:
   http://www.amnesty.org/
6. A Web-based project created by Professor Peter Danchin of Columbia University, the Center for the Study of Human Rights about the Universal Declaration of Human Rights:
   http://www.columbia.edu/ccnmtl/projects/mmt/theUniversal Declaration/index.html

Discussion Questions

1. The International Bill of Rights includes the Universal Declaration, the Covenant on Social, Economic, and Cultural Rights and the Covenant on Civil and Political Rights. These international instruments cover the protection of human rights in most spheres of life. What are some of the enforcement mechanisms that ensure that human rights are respected by nations?
2. What are some examples of early international activism efforts that contributed to the rise of the international human rights movement?
3. What documents constitute the International Bill of Rights? What is the difference between the Universal Declaration of Human Rights and the two Covenants?
4. What is the significance of the International Criminal Court in promoting human rights? Why was the creation of the ICC heralded as one of the most important achievements?
5. What are the current challenges facing the international human rights movement?

References

Amnesty International. "Campaigns 2009." Accessed July 18. 2009. http://amnesty.org/en/campaigns, 2009.

Burgers, Jan Herman. "The Road to San Francisco: The Revival of the Human Rights Idea in the Twentieth Century." *Human Rights Quaterly* 14, no. 4 (1992): 447–477.

Cmiel, Kenneth. "Recent History of Human Rights." *American Historical Review* 109, no. 1 (2004): 117–135.

Commission on Human Rights. "Commission on Human Rights: 62nd Session, Geneva." Accessed June 14, 2009. http://www2.ohchr.org/english/bodies/chr/index.htm, 2006.

Committee on Economic, Social and Cultural Rights (CESCR). "Monitoring the Economic, Social and Cultural Rights." Office of the UN High Commissioner for Human Rights. Accessed June 14, 2009. http://www2.ohchr.org/english/bodies/cescr/, 2009.

Declaration of the Rights of Man and of Citizens. Approved by the National Assembly of France, August 26, 1789. Accessed July 18, 2009. http://www.constitution.org/fr/fr_drm.htm.

Glendon, Mary Ann. "The Rule of Law in the Universal Declaration of Human Rights." *Northwestern University Journal of International Human Rights,* 2 (2004): 67–81.

Hafner-Burton, Emilie M., and Kiyoteru Tsutsui. "Human Rights in Globalizing World: The Paradox of Empty Promises."*American Journal of Sociology,* 110, no. 5 (2005): 1373–1411.

Human Rights Committee. "Monitoring Civil and Political Rights.": Office of the UN High Commissioner for Human Rights (OHCHR). Accessed June 14, 2009. http://www2.ohchr.org/english/bodies/hrc/, 2005.

_____. "Civil and Political Rights: The Human Rights Committee. Fact Sheet No. 15 (Rev. 1)." Office of the UN High Commissioner for Human Rights (OHCHR). Accessed June 14, 2009. http://www.ohchr.org/Documents/Publications/FactSheet15rev.1en.pdf, n.d.

International Committee of the Red Cross. "International Humanitarian Law—Treaties & Documents: Victims of Armed Conflicts." Accessed June 20, 2009. http://www.icrc.org/ihl.nsf/TOPICS?OpenView#VictimsofArmedConflicts, 2005.

International Criminal Court. "ICC at a Glance: Jurisdiction and Admissability." Accessed June 14, 2009. http://www.icc-cpi.int/Menus/ICC/About+the+Court/ICC+at+a+glance/Jurisdiction+and+Admissibility.htm, 2009a.

_____. "ICC: Situations and Cases." Accessed June 14, 2009. http://www.icc-cpi.int/Menus/ICC/Situations+and+Cases/, 2009b.

Ishay, Micheline. *The History of Human Rights: From Ancient Times to the Globalization Era.* Berkeley and Los Angeles: University of California Press, 2004.

Kaplan, Abraham. "Human Relations and Human Rights in Judaism." In *The Philosophy of Human Rights: International Perspectives,* edited by Alan S. Rosenbaum, 53–85. Westport, CT: Greenwood Press, 1980.

Lauren, Paul Gordon. *The Evolution of International Human Rights: Visions Seen.* Pennsylvania studies in human rights. Philadelphia: University of Pennsylvania Press, 1998.

Mahoney, John. *The Challenge of Human Rights: Origin, Development, and Significance.* Malden, MA: Blackwell, 2007.

Mazower, Mark. "The Strange Triumph of Human Rights, 1933–1950." *Historical Journal,* 47, no. 2 (2004): 379–398.

Morsink, Johannes. *The Universal Declaration of Human Rights: Origins, Drafting, and Intent.* Pennsylvania Studies in Human Rights. Philadelphia: University of Pennsylvania Press, 1999.

Nasr, Seyyed Hossein. "The Concept and Reality of Freedom in Islam and Islamic Civilization." In *The Philosophy of Human Rights: International Per-*

spectives, edited by Alan S. Rosenbaum, 103–112. Westport, CT: Greenwood Press, 1980.

Normand, Roger, and Sarah Zaidi. *Human Rights at the UN: The Political History of Universal Justice*. UN intellectual history project. Bloomington: Indiana University Press, 2008.

Nowak, Manfred. *Introduction to the International Human Rights Regime*. Leiden, The Netherlands: Martinus Nijhoff, 2003.

Organization of American States. "OAS in Brief: Protecting Human Rights." Accessed June 14, 2009. http://www.oas.org/key_issues/eng/KeyIssue_Detail. asp?kis_sec=2, 2009a.

_____. *OAS member states and permanent missions*. Accessed June 14, 2009. http://www.oas.org/documents/eng/memberstates.asp, 2009b.

Risse-Kappen, Thomas., Stephen C. Ropp, and Kathryn Sikkink, eds. *The Power of Human Rights: International Norms and Domestic Change*. Cambridge Studies in International Relations, vol. 66. New York: Cambridge University Press, 1999.

Rosenbaum, Alan S. "Introduction: The Editor's Perspectives on the Philosophy of Human Rights." In *The Philosophy of Human Rights: International Perspectives*, edited by Alan S. Rosenbaum, 3–41. Westport, CT: Greenwood Press, 1980.

Sellars, Kirsten. *The Rise and Rise of Human Rights*. Stroud, UK: Sutton Publishing, 2002.

Skogly, Sigrun I. *Beyond National Borders: States' Human Rights Obligations in International Cooperation*. Anwerpen, Belgium: Intersentia, 2006.

Tierney, Brian. "Historical Roots of Modern Rights: Before Locke and After."*Ave Maria Law Review*, 3(2005): 34–57.

United Nations. *The Core International Human Rights Treaties*. New York: Author, 2006.

_____. "60th Anniversary Special Edition Booklet of The Universal Declaration of Human Rights." Accessed June 8, 2009. http://www.un.org/events/humanrights/udhr60/pdf/60th_booklet_final.pdf, 2007.

_____. "Charter of the United Nations." Accessed June 8, 2009. http://www.un.org/en/documents/charter/index.shtml, 2009.

UN Treaty Collection. "Definition of Key Terms Used in the UN Treaty Collection." Accessed June 8, 2009. http://treaties.un.org/Pages/Overview.aspx?path=overview/definition/page1_en.xml, 2009a.

_____. "Status of Treaties: International Covenant on Economic, Social and Cultural Rights." Accessed June 8, 2009. http://treaties.un.org/Pages/

ViewDetails.aspx?src=TREATY&mtdsg_no=IV-3&chapter=4&lang=en# EndDec, 2009b.

————. "Status of Treaties: International Covenant on Civil and Political Rights." Accessed June 8, 2009. http://treaties.un.org/Pages/ViewDetails. aspx?src=TREATY&mtdsg_no=IV-3&chapter=4&lang=en#EndDec, 2009c.

Chapter 11

War Crimes: International Response to Genocide

Ralph Weisheit

Introduction

There is nothing new about mass killings. It has been suggested that modern man may have exterminated the Neanderthals; the Old Testament books of Exodus and Deuteronomy specifically name ethnic groups that God ordered exterminated (Kiernan 2007). There is no period in history that was free of mass killings. Although it would be nice to think that as civilizations have advanced the practice has diminished, all evidence points to the contrary. It has been argued that more people have been killed through genocide in the past 100 years than in any 100-year period in history (Heidenrich 2001).

Although mass killings may have occurred throughout history, the word "genocide" is relatively new. Until recently actions we now call genocide may have been immoral and horrific, but they were not considered international crimes. Most words in the English language have an obscure origin. For example, we may know that the word "homicide" was created by combining the Latin word for "man" (*homo*) and the Latin word for "killing" (*cide*), but we do not associate a particular person or date with its creation. The word "genocide," however, was created in 1944 by Raphael Lemkin. Lemkin was a Polish legal scholar who studied the Nazis' efforts to wipe out Jews and Gypsies in Europe during World War II, having lost 49 members of his large family to the Holocaust (Charny 1999). The term "genocide" is the result of combining the Greek word *genos* (race, tribe) and the Latin *cide* (killing) (Lemkin 1946).

Although most people seem to know what is meant by the term genocide, it has been surprisingly difficult to define in precise terms and academics have argued about what should be included in the definition. In his original statement on the issue, Lemkin (1944, 79) defined genocide as "a coordinated plan of different actions aiming at the destruction of essential foundations of the life of the national groups, with the aim of annihilating the groups themselves." His definition referred to actions carried out by people working under the authority of the state and included such nonlethal actions against the group as efforts to destroy a group's "culture, language, national feelings, religion, and the economic existence ... and the destruction of the personal security, liberty, health, [and] dignity" (79).

Genocide as an International Crime

Although the word genocide may have been created in 1944, it was just a word—it had no legal authority behind it. Lemkin worked hard with the United Nations to create a law recognizing genocide as an international crime. His efforts culminated in the *Convention on the Prevention and Punishment of the Crime of Genocide,* adopted by the United Nations on December 9, 1948, and set to take effect on January 12, 1951. By January 2009 the *Convention* had been ratified by 140 nations (Office of the United Nations High Commissioner for Human Rights 2009). The United Nations' legal definition is contained in Article 2 of the *Convention* (Office of the United Nations High Commissioner for Human Rights n.d.):

> In the present Convention, genocide means any of the following acts committed with intent to destroy, in whole or in part, a national, ethnic, racial or religious group, as such:
> (a) Killing members of the group;
> (b) Causing serious bodily or mental harm to members of the group;
> (c) Deliberately inflicting on the group conditions of life calculated to bring about its physical destruction in whole or in part;
> (d) Imposing measures intended to prevent births within the group;
> (e) Forcibly transferring children of the group to another group.

The crime includes genocide, attempts to commit genocide, conspiracy to commit genocide, public incitement to commit genocide, and complicity in genocide, thus including a wide range of behaviors that directly or indirectly play a role in mass killings. The scope of the law was limited, however, in that it could not be applied retroactively, thus exempting atrocities committed during World War II. A further limit of the law was that "[I]f the perpetrator did not target a national, ethnic, or religious group *as such,* then killings would constitute mass homicide, not genocide" (Power 2002, 57).

Genocide: Limits of the Legal Definition

The United Nations thus created a law that, for the first time, recognized genocide as an international crime. The law, however, has many critics, who argue the law has few teeth. Chalk and Jonassohn (1990, 11), for example, argue that although the law "has undoubted symbolic value, it has never had any practical effect." In fact, although legally taking effect in 1951, the United Nations has been slow to charge member nations with genocide or to act against those engaged in genocide. The U.S. Congress did not ratify the Convention until 1988 and the first conviction under the law did not occur until August 2001, when a Bosnian Serb general was convicted for killing as many as 8,000 Bosnian Muslims in 1995 (Court Rules Genocide was Committed in Srebrenica 2001). Discussing the criticisms of the UN definition is a useful exercise because it can clarify why the United Nations has sometimes been slow to act in situations where genocide has been alleged and because the discussion can highlight some of the difficulties in defining genocide in the law.

One problem with the United Nations' definition is that it omits the mass killing of political and social groups, thus excluding a substantial number of contemporary genocides (Totten, Parsons, and Charny 1997; Chalk and Jonassohn 1990; Kuper 1981). Thus, as Heidenrich (2001, 2) observes, the definition excludes the case of Cambodia:

> In Cambodia in 1975–79, the Khmer Rouge followers of Communist leader Pol Pot murdered people for "political" reasons as inane as for simply wearing eyeglasses. The Khmer Rouge, being Communists, wanted to eliminate all bourgeois intellectuals—and they assumed that any Cambodian who wore eyeglasses must be one. In their effort to socially re-engineer Cambodian society using terror and killing, later dramatized in the motion picture *The Killing Fields*, the Khmer Rouge murdered an estimated 1.7 million Cambodians out of an original population of only 7 million. In per capita terms, the Cambodian nation suffered the worst mass murder ever inflicted upon a population by its own government. Yet according to the international legal definition of genocide, the great majority of those victims were not victims of "genocide" because they were killed according to a purely political, not a racial, criteria.

By any measure of common sense Cambodia represents an example of genocide, but technically it does not fit the legal definition. Lemkin fought to include such politically motivated killings in the legal definition, but gaining the cooperation of multiple nations with their individual interests necessitated compromise. This does not mean that such killings are beyond the reach of international law. Those who engage in politically motivated mass killings may still be tried for committing "crimes against humanity," an offense codified in the Nuremburg charter following World War II, and more recently in the charter for the International Criminal Court (ICC) (Gutman and Rieff 1999). In 2009, more than thirty years after the killings in Cambodia, some (5–10) of the surviving perpetrators have been put on trial for committing crimes against humanity, though many reports have mislabeled the proceedings as genocide trials (e.g., Peck 2009).

A second problem with the United Nations' definition is that it is unclear how many people must die for genocide to have taken place. It is obvious if the numbers are in the millions or even in the tens of thousands. What if 5,000 people are killed? What about 500? What about 5? Is it a proportion of the group's members, such as more than one quarter or more than one half? Likewise, what if there is an attempt to wipe out a group but the attempt fails, killing no one, or killing only 50 of the group's 2 million members? Although only a small proportion of the group was killed, the intent may have been to wipe out everyone. The law provides no guidance on this.

A third problem is that the UN definition requires there be intent. In other words, it is essential to know what was in the minds of the killers. In some cases, such as the killing of Jews, Gypsies, and homosexuals by the Germans, there was abundant documentation to show intent. A more common circumstance has been for the killers to deny that destroying the group was the intent. Instead, they will argue the killings were the result of police actions to restore order, or that the victims were the casualties of war, not of genocide. Unless there is evidence to the contrary, one may avoid being charged with genocide under international law by simply denying intent and carefully avoiding documentation of intent.

Most scholars make a distinction between acts of war and acts of genocide. War involves killings that result from battles between two or more groups, each of which is in a position to fight. In contrast, genocide involves victims who are unable to defend themselves or to otherwise engage in battle. However, neither the United Nations' definition nor most other definitions of genocide facilitate making a straightforward distinction between war and genocide. For example, on August 6, 1945, during World War II, the United States dropped atomic bombs on Japanese civilians in Hiroshima and Nagasaki, killing at least 140,000 men, women, and children. Another 130,000 civilians were killed in the firebombing of Tokyo. The bombings took place in time of war and were against a civilian population unable to defend itself. While some scholars argue that the bombings should be called acts of genocide (e.g., Kuper 1981), others disagree (Fein 1994), and still others confess they have difficulty resolving the issue (Charny 1994).

Another criticism of the *Genocide Convention* is the vague and brief description of the procedures used to try those accused of genocide. Article V calls for countries that ratify the *Convention* to enact their own laws within the guidelines of their individual constitutions and to base penalties on those constitutional guidelines. Article VI calls for genocide trials to be carried out in the country where the genocide occurred (which would be unlikely in cases in which the killers emerge victorious) or in an unspecified "international penal tribunal." These international tribunals, and now the ICC, appear to be the primary mechanism by which genocide trials will be held, but they have been slow to develop: the first trials did not occur until more than fifty years after the *Convention* was passed.

Some argue that the systematic study of genocide must not be limited by the legal definition of the term (e.g., Hagan and Rymond-Richmond 2009; Hagan and Rymond-Richmond 2008; Hagan, Rymond-Richmond, and Parker 2005). Although there are numerous cases in which this makes sense, it is also possible to expand the working definition beyond the bounds of common sense. The term "genocide" has become part of our everyday vocabulary and its popularity may be partly attributable to the powerful images it conveys. Describing killings as genocide makes them seem more sinister, calculated, and far-reaching. Perhaps this is why it has been applied in a number of areas that some scholars of genocide would deem inappropriate, including family planning, race mixing, drug distribution, cocaine addiction, abortion, bisexuality, medical research, dieting, and language regulation in the schools (Chalk and Jonassohn 1990; Fein 1994; Porter 1982). At present there is no universally accepted definition of genocide that can be easily applied across a range of specific situations.

Although the definition of genocide offered in the United Nations' *Genocide Convention* has been frequently criticized, many of those same critics use the UN definition in their own work. For example, although Leo Kuper (1981; 1985) wrote a great deal on the limitations of the UN definition, he resigned himself to working with that definition in his research. This is because the UN definition is one of the few internationally recognized definitions of genocide and because it has been codified in international law. As a result, the *Genocide Convention* is likely to serve as the basis for international actions against genocide.

Genocide and War Crimes

As noted above, the *Genocide Convention* makes no distinction between acts of genocide and acts of war. This problem merits further discussion. Most scholars make a distinction between acts of genocide and acts of war. Although the two acts are different, periods of war may facilitate a society's genocidal tendencies. There are several reasons for this: First, in times of war normal restrictions on government behavior are lifted and the state is granted the authority to take actions that might not otherwise be allowed. Moreover, in times of war citizens are more likely to support this expanded authority.

Second, the perceived threat to society posed by a group (e.g., the Jews in World War II Germany) may seem much greater in times of war, when people are naturally sensitive to threats to their national security.

Third, the leaders of a country at war may find that the presence of a hated group is a useful tool for mobilizing the masses, as Hitler did with Jews during World War II.

Fourth, the "fog of war" may make what is happening on the ground unclear to the outside world, only to be more fully understood after the killing has ended. The horrors of genocide may be less immediately apparent to other countries, whose focus is on the war and who might well be initially fooled by claims that the killing is an act of war rather than of genocide. The result is a reluctance of other countries to intervene. Separating genocide and war may be particularly difficult within the context of civil war in which a faction seeks to break away and form an independent state, and where those seeking independence are of a different religious or ethnic group. In such cases the government may claim they are merely using force to maintain a unified nation, as was claimed in the genocides in Bosnia and the Sudan (discussed below).

Finally, there are times when major powers are themselves engaged in war elsewhere. In such cases those powers may be distracted or may have limited additional resources to contribute to a military intervention. The Allied powers in World War II, for example, focused many of their military resources on battlefronts and that may explain, in part, their inability or unwillingness to intervene in the Holocaust as it was happening. It is possible that one reason the United States has been reluctant to send military forces into the Sudan is because its military resources are already spread thin in Afghanistan and Iraq.

Even when the behavior of the governing authority is heinous and morally reprehensible it is not always obvious whether the actions constitute genocide or war crimes. War crimes are generally actions in which individual killers are criminally responsible, whereas genocide implies responsibility at higher levels. Fein suggests conditions that distinguish between war crimes and genocide. In Fein's view, a case can be made for genocide when:

1. There is a sustained attack, or continuity of attack, by the perpetrator to physically destroy group members.
2. The perpetrator is a collective or organized actor or commander of organized actors.
3. The victims are selected because they are members of a group.

4. The victims are defenseless or are killed regardless of whether they surrendered or resisted.
5. The destruction of group members is undertaken with intent to kill and the murder is sanctioned by the perpetrators (Fein 1993, 37–38).

Fein also identified two conditions that facilitate genocide: 1) the presence of ideologies and beliefs that legitimize or justify genocide and 2) the absence of rules that prohibit such killings or the absence of any mechanism to enforce such rules.

The guidelines suggested by Fein are helpful, but do not fully resolve the problem. This is particularly true in modern warfare, which is different from warfare of the past. Civilians are increasingly caught in military conflicts and are increasingly the targets of military actions. As Singer noted:

> Whereas wars were once fought almost exclusively between soldiers, in recent decades the worldwide percentage of victims from wars has become predominantly civilian. In World War I, the percentage of casualties that were civilian was under 10 percent of the total; in World War II, the percentage had risen to nearly 50 percent. The evolution continued through the next fifty years, to the point that now the overwhelming majority of those killed in conflicts are civilians instead of soldiers. For example, of all the persons killed in African conflicts in the late twentieth century, the overwhelming preponderance (92 percent) were civilians (Singer 2006, 4–5).

In this context it is easier than ever for a genocidal killing to be presented to the world as an unfortunate consequence of war.

The discussion now shifts to three modern examples of genocide. These examples highlight the limitations of the *Genocide Convention*. In each case there have been extended debates in the international community about whether the actions constituted genocide. These cases also illustrate the conditions that both lead to and facilitate genocide. They also illustrate the reluctance of powerful nations to intervene, even in the face of clear evidence that genocide has occurred.

Bosnia-Herzegovina (1992–95)

The genocide in Bosnia-Herzegovina resulted in the deaths of at least 200,000 people and the creation of 2 million refugees. At that time the population of Bosnia was "about 44 percent Muslim, 31 percent Serbian, and 17 percent Croatian" (Cox 2002, 144). Most victims were Muslims killed by Serbs acting under the authority of the Yugoslavian government, though Croats were also targeted by Serbs. Croats, in turn, also targeted Muslims and some Serbs. The killings were described in the press as "ethnic cleansing," introducing a new term into the lexicon of genocide. The genocide took place within the context of a regional war in which regions of Yugoslavia sought independence. For the most part, powerful Western nations stood by and let it happen.

Understanding what happened and why requires some historical background on the region. Bosnia-Herzegovina is situated in a region of southeastern Europe with longstanding tensions among religious and ethnic groups, including ethnic Albanians (also known as *Bosniaks,* most of whom are Muslims), Serbs (predominantly Orthodox Christian), and Croats (predominantly Catholic). Following World War I, the Western Allies brought these groups together under a single nation called "Yugoslavia." During World War II, German forces conquered Yugoslavia and partitioned the country. "German units and the Croatian puppet Ustashe regime killed approximately 65,000 of Yugoslavia's Jews and half a million Serbs" (Kiernan 2007, 588). The intent was to exterminate these groups as well as the Gypsies. The defeat of Germany was followed by the reunification of Yugoslavia under the leadership of Communist strongman Josip Tito.

Ruling with an iron fist, Tito was able to suppress religious and ethnic violence, creating enough stability that the 1984 Winter Olympic games were held in Sarajevo, Yugoslavia. Tito's death in 1980 left a power vacuum, though it took nearly a decade for the country to begin to come apart. Throughout the 1980s Slobodan Milošević, a Serb, used appeals to nationalism and religious hatred to build a power base, becoming president of Yugoslavia in 1989. As president he controlled Yugoslavia's military, which was made up primarily of Serbs. In the 1990s regions within Yugoslavia began to break away, declaring their independence. Milošević responded with military force. Although presented as a civil war intended to preserve a united Yugoslavia, Milošević's soldiers disproportionately targeted old enemies of the Serbs. In 1991 the army attacked the breakaway republic of Croatia, starting "… the first mass executions of the conflict, killing hundreds of Croat men and burying them in mass graves" (History Place n.d.). Only years later would the extent and ferociousness of the killing come to be understood (Shattuck 2003).

After a negotiated cease-fire with Croatia in late 1991, Milošević and the Yugoslavian army turned their attention to Bosnia, whose independence was recognized by the international community in April 1992. For Milošević losing Bosnia meant losing a key base of his support. Muslims in Bosnia were particularly targeted, with Islam depicted "as a 'malignant disease' threatening to 'infect' Europe" (Kiernan 2007, 589). State-controlled radio spread false stories of Bosnian towns being attacked by Muslim extremists, rallying Serbs against Muslims and creating the illusion that it was Serbs who were victims (Power 2002). John Shattuck, who served as U.S. Assistant Secretary of State for Democracy, Human Rights, and Labor during this period described the reports he received on one of his fact-finding missions to the region:

> I have heard credible eyewitness accounts of mass executions of men and boys by Bosnian Serb soldiers with many of the victims buried in mass graves dug on the spot by bulldozers. I have also heard first-hand accounts of horrible brutalities committed against people who were trying to flee, including slitting of throats, cutting off of ears, noses, jaws and limbs of persons still alive, and tying people to landmines. I have heard many credible accounts of the shelling of large columns of civilians attempting to flee, and four separate accounts of the possible use of chemical weapons that severely disoriented fleeing people, causing several to commit suicide. Information was presented to me by both victims and witnesses of rape and sexual abuse of Muslim women by soldiers. I also heard several accounts of Bosnian Serb soldiers luring Muslim residents to follow them by wearing U.N. helmets and then attacking them (Shattuck 2003, 117).

Not all Croats and Muslims were subject to immediate extermination. Many were sent to concentration camps run by the Serb military. Some 10,000 people perished in these camps. Some of these were "rape camps" where women were abused, whereas in other camps prisoners were tortured and starved. Although Western journalists heard about the camps from refugees, the stories were so horrific that at first they did not believe them (Power 2002).

Croats also began seeking out and killing Muslims in Bosnia. Under the guidance of their president, Franjo Tudjman, Croatian forces inflicted upon Bosnian Muslims some of the same horrors to which they themselves had been subjected, while also taking the opportunity to exact revenge on Serbs living in Bosnia (Shattuck 2003).

Although the war and the genocide that accompanied it began in 1992, for the most part the rest of the world stood by until late 1995. An arms embargo imposed by the United Nations in 1991 was intended to limit the fighting but in practice left Muslims with a limited ability to fight the well-armed Serbian and Croatian military machines (Power 2002). Early in the fighting the United Nations dispatched a peacekeeping force to monitor the cease-fire in Croatia, protect innocent civilians, and safeguard humanitarian aid shipments. However, the UN force numbered only 12,500 and its authority was so restricted that it could not even protect food and medical shipments to civilians in the war torn region. The extent of the killing and its focus on "ethnic cleansing" should have led Western nations to label the actions genocide early in the war. Instead, there was debate about whether the term "genocide" was appropriate

(Burg 1997), and the debate only served to further delay an effective response. The term "genocide" was only publicly applied after the killing had largely ended. Western leaders were concerned that labeling the mass killings genocide might obligate them to intervene, possibly risking their own military casualties (Shattuck 2003).

The reluctance of Western nations to intervene emboldened Serbian leaders, in effect giving them permission to do what they wanted without fear of reprisal. The United Nations had created safe areas where Croat and Muslim civilians could find shelter from the violence, but Serb forces took these areas one by one. Western inaction and the willingness of Serb forces to take advantage of it was illustrated again in May 1995. North Atlantic Treaty Organization (NATO) forces conducted limited air strikes against Serb artillery units that were targeting civilians in Sarajevo. In response, Bosnia Serbs seized 350 UN soldiers as hostages, sharing images of them chained to trees or waiving white flags of surrender. The soldiers were released after assurances by the United Nations and NATO that air attacks against Serb forces would end (Shattuck 2003).

Serb forces did not simply wish to prevent the creation of new states, but sought to destroy all traces of Croats and Muslims in the region. As part of the campaign of ethnic cleansing, Bosnian Serb soldiers set about destroying cultural and religious sites and killing Muslim and Croat intellectuals, musicians, and professionals in an effort to erase any remnants of their culture (Power 2002). Civilians were deliberately targeted with a particular focus on killing young and able-bodied men. Serb women who had married Croats or Muslims were also targeted for rape, mutilation, and killing by Serb militias. Serb military units forced Croats and Muslims to leave their communities and become refugees in neighboring states, after which their homes were either burned or taken by Serbs as their own.

> The armed [Serb] marauders sought to sever permanently the bond between citizens and the land. Thus, they forced fathers to castrate their sons or molest their daughters; they humiliated and raped (often impregnating) young women. Theirs was a deliberate policy of degradation; destruction so this avowed enemy race would have no homes to which to return.... (Power 2002, 251).

One of the sad realities of the genocide in Bosnia is that world leaders knew about it even as it unfolded but refused to take actions to stop it, behavior that would be repeated in Rwanda and the Sudan. The human rights group Helsinki Watch (later to become Human Rights Watch) sent teams of investigators to the scene shortly after the war broke out. Only four months into the war they produced a lengthy and detailed report describing conditions on the ground as an indication of genocide (Power 2002). Press coverage began soon after the fighting started and provided the world with grisly details of the events on the ground. In the United States, the killings were not only known but were anticipated, yet for the first three years of the genocide the United States refused to put troops on the ground and Western nations contributed only token peace-keeping forces through the United Nations. As one observer noted, "[N]o other atrocity campaign in the twentieth century was better monitored and understood by the U.S. government" (Power 2002, 264).

Finally, at the end of August 1995, some three and a half years after the genocide began, the international community was ready to intervene. The United States and its European allies began sustained air strikes against Bosnian Serb military sites. At the same time there was growing international support for war crimes tribunals to hold the leaders of Bosnia and Croatia accountable for the mass killings. Until this point, Western nations had relied on public criticism and embargos, with little to show for their efforts. Now diplomatic efforts were being reinforced by military strikes and by the threat of prison for those orchestrating the genocide. Facing the consequences of their actions, Serb and Croat leaders became willing to negotiate an end to the fighting. In November 1995, Milošević, Tudjman, and Izetbegovic (president of Bosnia and a Muslim) came to Andrews Air Force Base in Dayton, Ohio, to determine how the three ethnic-religious enclaves would peacefully share Bosnia. The killing—at least killing that could be classified as genocide—had ended.

The Aftermath of Genocide in Bosnia

The wheels of justice grind slowly. As early as 1993 the United Nations created the International Tribunal for the Prosecution of Persons Responsible for Serious Violations of International Humanitarian Law Committed in the Territory of the Former Yugoslavia since 1991. The tribunal is more commonly known as the International Criminal Tribunal for the former Yugoslavia (ICTY). The tribunal has no powers to arrest and the maximum penalty it can administer is life in prison. At the beginning of 2009 the tribunal had indicted 161 people, had concluded 120 cases, and two indicted leaders remained at large (ICTY 2009).

The two leaders most responsible for the genocide managed to escape punishment. Tudjman remained free and president of Croatia until his death in 1999. He never faced charges before the ICTY, although he likely would have been charged had he lived. Milošević remained a free man and continued to serve as president of Yugoslavia until 2000, when he lost his bid for reelection. In 1998, just two years after the Dayton Accord, he launched a series of attacks on Kosovo, a province whose large Muslim population was seeking independence.

This time the international community responded with military force. In March 1999 NATO forces began bombing Serbia, with the threat that bombings would continue until Milošević accepted the autonomy of Kosovo. "It was the first time in history that the United States or its European allies had intervened to head off a potential genocide" (Power 2002, 448).

In 2001, just one year after his political defeat, Milošević was arrested and sent to The Hague to stand trial for genocide and for crimes against humanity. Throughout his trial he remained defiant, insisting on serving as his own attorney and arguing that the killings were committed by paramilitary groups beyond his control. In 2006, five years after his arrest, Milošević died from a heart attack in his prison cell in The Hague, Netherlands, forever escaping justice for his actions.

Rwanda (1994)

The genocide in Rwanda is unique among genocides in the modern era. It was the first genocide with images of the killing captured on video. It has become the subject of an acclaimed feature-length film, *Hotel Rwanda,* and has been the subject of documentary film makers who followed the aftermath of the genocide. Rwanda, located in west-central Africa, is slightly smaller than the state of Maryland, only about 125 miles across at its widest point and only about 100 miles long at its longest point (Central Intelligence Agency [CIA] 2001). At the time of the genocide it was among the most densely populated countries in Africa. Rwanda is among the poorest nations in the world and in 1994 it was facing a drought in which "it was estimated that as many as 800,000 people would need food aid to survive" (Des Forges 1999, 1).

There are two major ethnic groups in Rwanda. The Hutus make up about 85 percent of the population; most of the remaining people are Tutsi. These groups had lived in the region for over 2,000 years and over time developed a shared language and culture. The Tutsi, although far fewer in number, had historically held positions of power in Rwanda, whereas the Hutu were generally commoners. Rwanda came to be ruled by Belgium after World War I and in the 1920s Belgian authorities ordered that only the Tutsi, who already held most positions of leadership, should be officials in the Rwandan government. This required differentiating between Hutu and Tutsi and beginning in the 1930s Rwandans were required to register with the government and declare their ethnicity (Des Forges 1999). By the 1950s tensions between the Hutu and the Tutsi had grown and the Belgium government sought to bring peace by placing some Hutu in positions of power. In 1961 Rwandans voted to establish a republic in which citizens elected their own representatives. Because of their overwhelming numbers, these elections placed many Hutu in positions of power. At this time the Hutu began to attack the Tutsi who had previously held power and drove as many as 10,000 from the country. The Hutu depicted the refugees as enemies of Rwanda and eliminated any powerful opponents within Rwanda. The Catholic Church, which had supported the Tutsi and had many Tutsi among its priests, shifted allegiance and threw its support behind the new Hutu leadership. Other Christian churches remained officially neutral but openly worked with Hutu officials (Des Forges 1999).

Tutsi refugees would periodically launch attacks against Hutu-led Rwanda. They also orchestrated the slaughter of the Hutu in neighboring Burundi in 1972, killing as many as 200,000. By the late 1980s the number of Tutsi exiles had grown to nearly 600,000 people (Des Forges 1999).

By the late 1980s Rwanda was at war with the Rwandan Patriotic Front (RPF), an organization led by refugees from Rwanda, many of whom were Tutsi. The RPF invaded Rwanda on October 1, 1990 and between that date and the victory of the RPF over the Hutu government in July 1994, "the killings wiped out one-tenth of Rwanda's population of seven million" (Lemarchand 1997, 408). Although Rwanda was in a state of war beginning in 1990, the killings on each side were limited until spring 1994.

On April 6, 1994, the Hutu president of Rwanda was killed when his plane was shot down. The genocide of the Tutsi in Rwanda began in earnest with that event and lasted for thirteen weeks, during which time as many as 800,000 people were killed. Although the primary target of the genocide was the Tutsi, Hutu who were sympathetic to the Tutsi or who refused to take part in the killing were also targeted. Throughout the genocide the Hutu couched their actions as necessary for self-defense in their civil war against the RPF. Although the killing of Rwanda's president appeared to be the trigger for the genocide, it has been argued that planning for the genocide began months earlier. It has also been argued that the president's plane may have been shot down by Hutu extremists hoping to use the event to mobilize citizens against the RPF and stir them to genocide (Lemarchand 1999).

Rwandan military personnel often began the killing, later to be joined by Hutu citizens. At first they moved from house to house, but later they arranged to bring victims together in groups—in churches, schools, and other public sites—where they could be massacred on a larger scale (Des Forges 1999). The Hutu government also made extensive use of the media, including radio, television, newspapers, and magazines, to stir up anti-Tutsi sentiments (Taylor 1999). Before the genocide at least 29 percent of Rwandan homes owned a radio. Immediately before and during the genocide government officials handed out free radios to Hutus and used radio broadcasts to incite the public by reporting fabricated stories about massacres committed by the RPF. Radio broad-

casts were also used to persuade Hutu citizens that killing Tutsi and Tutsi sympathizers was their patriotic duty (Des Forges 1999).

At the time of the genocide poverty was extreme and a drought left many
in Rwanda starving. The government responded by delivering food, drink,
and clothing to those willing to kill. Killers operating in the countryside were
often promised land, a scarce and valuable commodity. Hutu willing to take
property and destroy the homes of Tutsi were sometimes threatened with punishment or even death if they did not also kill the inhabitants. The original
slaughter, described to the outside world in the language of war, focused on young
males. Later the killing would be extended to women, children, and the elderly (Des Forges 1999).

The killing of Tutsi women was often accompanied by sexual and physical
abuse. "Tutsi women were often raped, tortured, and mutilated before they
were murdered" (Des Forges 1999, 10), although some managed to escape
with their lives by giving the killers sexual favors. Violence was particularly
fierce against Tutsi women who had married Hutu men (Taylor 1999). Such
marriages were defined as race mixing, and it was believed that children produced from such a marriage would be part Tutsi and thus would be racially
impure (Taylor 1999; Des Forges 1999).

In preparation for their war with the RPF, the Hutu government had supplied both guns and machetes to civilian Hutu males, and had provided training for many of them. Although guns were more efficient killing tools, the
machetes were often utilized because of the terror they caused. Many victims
were simply hacked to death, or beaten to death with hammers or clubs. Victims sometimes had both Achilles tendons cut in their legs before they were killed,
so they were unable to run away.

It is now clear that other world powers were not only aware of the genocide as it was happening, but knew about it in advance. In addition to a large
number of early indicators that preparations were being made for genocide,
the head of the UN Assistance Mission in Rwanda (UNAMIR) specifically
warned the United Nations of a plan to annihilate all Tutsi (Des Forges 1999).
This information was available to the United States, France, and Belgium, all
of whom had peacekeeping troops in the country. The response was not to
strengthen peacekeeping forces and protect Tutsi citizens, but to withdraw all
forces, including diplomatic representatives (Lemarchand 1999). The withdrawal included UN soldiers guarding refugee camps within Rwanda. As a result, the camps were raided and their inhabitants killed soon after the UN
troops left. The United Nations and other countries did not fail to act because
they were unaware of the genocide. They failed to act because Rwanda was not
of critical economic or political importance to them. As Lemarchand (1999, 511)

observed, "That a carnage of this magnitude could have been going on day after day, week after week, without interference from the international community speaks volumes for the lack of resolve to deal with massive human rights violations."

The genocide in Rwanda is striking because it was so thoroughly planned and executed, because the methods were extremely cruel and brutal, because it is among the first modern genocides in which a number of the killings were captured on videotape—making it easier for the outside world to directly see the horror of the killing; and because other nations failed to intervene when human decency dictated otherwise. Unlike the genocide in Bosnia, other countries could not credibly claim that the "fog of war" obscured what was really happening. In fact, there were no credible excuses.

The Aftermath of Genocide in Rwanda

The genocide ended in Rwanda in July 1994, but the killing continued on a smaller scale. This time, however, scattered fragments of the Tutsi-led RPF were now doing the killing and the Hutu were now fleeing the country for safety. In an ironic reversal of roles, some of the Hutu directly involved in the genocide of the Tutsi were refugees and became leaders organizing military forays into Rwanda in an effort to destabilize the government. The RPF, for its part, launched attacks against these refugee camps, driving hundreds of thousands of Hutu back into Rwanda and killing thousands in the process. Meanwhile, some of the Hutu who returned to Rwanda organized guerrilla groups to attack the government (Taylor 1999). Although nothing as organized as, or on the scale of, the 1994 genocide has occurred, each side has engaged in smaller massacres, with little interference from other nations.

The international community has been slow to act. The United Nations created the International Criminal Tribunal for Rwanda (ICTR) in November 1994, five months after the mass killings ended. By the end of 1998 only two people had been convicted, both sentenced to life in prison (ICTR 2009). By the end of June 2009, there had been a total of seventy-nine arrests, thirty-seven convictions, and six acquittals (ICTR 2009). Among those charged by the ICTR included political leaders, military leaders, high-level government bureaucrats, business leaders, journalists, a physician, a military chaplain, a Protestant minister, a Catholic priest, and an Anglican bishop (ICTR 2009). In a separate proceeding, in June 2001 a Belgian court convicted four people of war crimes for their actions in Rwanda. One was a factory owner, one a college professor, and two were Catholic nuns. The nuns "were charged with helping Hutu extremists kill more than 5,000 people at their convent" (Two Nuns Guilty in Genocide 2001).

Although the ICTR was well-funded and was able to hand down lengthy prison sentences, the Tribunal was capable of handling only a minuscule number of offenders. By some estimates 135,000 suspects were jailed in Rwanda for their part in the killings, a number that not only overwhelmed the ICTR, but the Rwandan court system as well. By January 2002 only 5,000 of those in jail had been tried in Rwanda and it was estimated that at that pace it would take 200 years to try the rest (Harman 2002). In response, Rwanda turned to traditional tribal courts, known as *gacaca,* in which victims confront offenders in public and are judged by tribal elders. The focus of these courts is to uncover truth, rather than to administer punishment. Thus, they operate much like truth and reconciliation commissions (Minow 1998).

Sudan (2003–Present)

In February 2003 a conflict began in the western region of Sudan known as Darfur. Some have labeled this conflict a civil war, whereas others have called it genocide. As time has passed evidence of genocide has increased and the number of people and groups defining the conflict as genocide has grown. Nevertheless, the international community has been reluctant to commit the resources necessary to stop the fighting. As is so often the case, hard numbers are difficult to come by, but most estimate that as many as 200,000 people have been killed and another 2–4 million people have become refugees in surrounding countries, including Ethiopia and Chad.

Sudan is a country about one-fourth the size of the United States and with a population of approximately 41 million people. The Darfur region is one of the least developed regions of the Sudan, which itself is among the twenty-five poorest countries in the world (Totten 2009). The two largest ethnic groups are Black (52%) and Arab (39%). Seventy percent of the population is Sunni Muslim. Muslim Arabs dominate national politics and have engaged in a series of civil wars with non-Muslim and non-Arabs in southern Sudan since the country's independence in 1956 (CIA 2009). This civil war was not only about Arab hostility toward Black Africans, but was also fueled by oil reserves in the region. The Chinese government had invested heavily in the oil industry in this region (Hagan, Rymond-Richmond, and Parker 2005), and it is perhaps no coincidence that the Chinese government has been among those reluctant to have the United Nations intervene with military force. Though the civil war in southern Sudan was supposed to have ended in 2005, a June 2006 report by Human Rights Watch indicated the killing of innocent civilians by Sudanese military units has continued (Human Rights Watch 2009a).

In a separate action, in 2003 citizens of Darfur came under attack by Sudanese military units and by the *Janjaweed*, nomadic Arab tribes that are technically beyond the control of the government but who are believed to be armed and guided by the government. The term *Janjaweed* roughly translates as "evil horsemen" and the group included bandits, common criminals released from jail, unemployed young men, and former military personnel (Prunier 2008). Although the Sudanese government claimed to be targeting rebel groups in Darfur, there is considerable evidence that the killings are motivated by a desire to "cleanse" the region of Black Africans.

As was true during the killings in Bosnia and Rwanda, the outside world has debated whether the killings in Darfur constitute genocide. Things have changed since those earlier genocides, however. In Bosnia and Rwanda major world powers were hesitant to label the killings genocide out of concern that it would require them to respond and perhaps place their own soldiers at risk. In the Sudan, several world powers, including the United States, France, and Israel, have publicly declared the killings in Darfur to be genocide, but have felt little compulsion to intervene. Apparently, inaction by powerful nations is no longer cause for shame. For its part, the United Nations has been reluctant to label the killings genocide, citing a lack of evidence of intent on the part of the Sudanese government, despite mounting evidence to the contrary and a report to the United Nations by the chief prosecutor of the ICC that "the entire Darfur region is a crime scene" (MacFarquhar 2008). He also noted that the Sudanese government had been bombing schools, markets, and water installations, and that if the number of villages being burned was going down it was only because there were fewer left. Sudanese and *Janjaweed* forces in Darfur have poisoned wells, raped, gang raped, and murdered women, killed young men, most of whom were Black Africans, and have burned villages to the ground while generally leaving adjacent Arab villages alone.

The Sudanese government learned much from the Rwandan genocide. Much of the world's reaction to the killing in Rwanda was prompted by the video footage of killings and by the reports of journalists on the scene. To blunt criticism and promote their own view of events on the ground, the Sudanese government banned journalists from Darfur. In July 2008 the president of Sudan was charged in the ICC with war crimes, genocide, and crimes against humanity. This was the first time that a sitting head of state was charged with crimes before the ICC. On March 4, 2009, the ICC issued an arrest warrant for the president of Sudan without the genocide charges, though there was no mechanism for carrying out the warrant. The next day the Sudanese government announced the expulsion of aid agencies from Darfur (Human Rights

Watch, 2009b), further endangering the health and lives of innocent civilians and further complicating efforts to unveil government actions there.

One of the distinguishing features of the genocide in Darfur is the extent to which science and technology have been brought to bear to document the situation on the ground. In 2007 the world could turn to Google Earth to view satellite images of burned-out villages—evidence of what was literally a "scorched earth policy" (Labott 2007). In addition, it is only the second genocide to be documented through the use of modern survey research methods. (The first was a survey of refugees from Kosovo [Hagan and Rymond-Richmond 2009].)

To better understand what was happening in Darfur, the U.S. State Department funded a 2004 survey of 1,136 refugees from the region. The Atrocities Documentation Survey (ADS) was based on multistage cluster sampling in twenty refugee camps or clusters in eastern Chad in which respondents were asked a series of questions about what they had seen and experienced in Darfur (Howard 2006). A brief summary of the survey's findings provided the impetus for U.S. Secretary of State Colin Powell's 2004 testimony before the United Nations in which he explicitly called the killings in Darfur genocide. This was the first time a victimization survey influenced U.S. foreign policy. John Hagan and his colleagues undertook a more elaborate analysis of the data and their findings provide broad support for labeling actions in Darfur genocide (Hagan, Rymond-Richmond, and Parker 2005; Hagan and Palloni 2006; Hagan and Rymond-Richmond 2008; Hagan and Rymond-Richmond 2009). In particular, they utilize statistical analysis and qualitative interview data to cite nine crucial elements supporting a claim of genocide in Darfur:

"The first element is the background of tension between Arab and Black groups in Darfur. The Sudanese state, especially in recent years, has implemented Arab-Islamic supremacist and demonizing policies that pit Arabs and Blacks against one another in an 'us' against 'them' kind of conflict" (Hagan and Rymond-Richmond 2009, 5). The second element was the arming of *Janjaweed* militias by the Sudanese government. The third element was the bombing of Black villages by the Sudanese government using Russian aircraft and helicopters. The fourth element was the ground attacks in which Sudanese soldiers raided villages, killing boys and young men while raping—and sometimes killing—women and young girls. These were often joint ventures between Sudanese military forces and *Janjaweed*. The fifth element was the specific targeting of Black tribes. During these attacks racial epithets made it clear that people were being targeted because of the color of their skin and not because of their participation in rebel actions. The sixth element was the widespread use of sexual violence against Black women, including gang rape and the mutilation of sex organs. The seventh element was "the confiscation of property—

including animals, grains, seed, farm equipment, household items, and money. These possessions are required to sustain and reproduce a way of life for individuals and groups; indeed, they are necessary for physical survival" (Hagan and Rymond-Richmond 2009, 11). The eighth element was displacing Black Africans from the land, preventing their return, and prohibiting them from making a livelihood. The ninth element was evidence that when Black Africans were driven from the region Arab groups quickly moved in and resettled the area, often with the help of the Sudanese government. Some dispute this last point, arguing that it is unlikely that nomadic herdsmen would suddenly become interested in agriculture (Prunier 2008).

The sheer brutality of the attacks is illustrated in the following quotes from interviewed refugees:

> First vehicles attacked the village. After one hour, planes came and bombed; after this military came on camels and horses and began shooting at random. They cut open the stomachs of pregnant women and split the throats of male fetuses. Bombs from airplanes killed a lot of animals and people. The military took women away. The village was burned and destroyed.... Three boys were caught and slaughtered. Their throats were cut, a foot was cut open from big toe to the ankle, hands were cut off, brains removed, sexual organs cut off. Boys were 5, 6, and 7.... The 7-year-old's stomach was slit open and his clothes were torn off. A man who tried to return to the village was caught and killed. His skin was removed (Hagan and Rymond-Richmond 2009, 7–8).

Although the global community has done little to directly intervene in Darfur, concern is growing as the killing extends beyond the borders of Sudan into the refugee camps in surrounding countries, and as food and medical crises escalate in the camps. Hollywood celebrities, including Mia Farrow, George Clooney, Brad Pitt, and Don Cheadle (who also starred in the film *Hotel Rwanda*) have traveled to the refugee camps in Chad in an effort to draw the world's attention to the plight of the refugees and the killing in Darfur, but with little effect to date.

The discussion of genocide in Bosnia and Rwanda concluded with an overview of events following the genocide, but for the ongoing genocide in Sudan there is, as of this writing, no immediate end in sight. In 2009 the ICC issued an arrest warrant for the president of Sudan on five charges of crimes against humanity and two charges of war crimes, and in 2010 he was charged with three counts of genocide in Darfur. This was the first time the International Criminal Court issued genocide charges. However, there is little indication that any nation or group will step forward to enforce that warrant. In July of 2011 a peace agreement was signed between Sudan and a Darfur rebel group and there was hope that the bloodshed would end. That did not happen, however, and the violence against innocent civilians continues (Human Rights Watch 2013).

Conclusion

"Never again" is a phrase that followed the Nazi Holocaust and that is frequently repeated today in remembrance of that tragic event. Unfortunately, the phrase has a hollow ring to it, as one genocide has followed another in modern times. In case after case powerful nations have been slow to respond, if they have responded at all. It is important to bring those who orchestrate genocide to justice, even if such justice takes years to enforce. John Shattuck has articulated three reasons why it is important to hold such leaders accountable:

> *First,* the spiral of retribution must be stopped. If responsibility is covered up or ignored, it will never be possible to have peace, reconciliation or democracy. Those who have seen their parents, brothers or sisters targeted for ethnic killing are never going to reconcile with killers who are not identified and brought to justice. *Second,* the oppressive atmosphere of collective guilt must be lifted. The air must be cleared so that those who are innocent can breathe freely and not be seen to be responsible. Collective guilt not only destroys individuals, it makes whole peoples the target for retribution. Those who were the planners and instigators of genocide must be held responsible for their actions; those who were misled by them should not be punished by collective guilt. *Third,* international human rights law must be enforced. If these crimes against humanity can be committed with impunity, there can be no rule of law and no deterrent against any conceivable form of international terrorism (Shattuck 2003, 143).

The wheels of justice grind slowly, but in the case of genocide they too often move at a snail's pace. Jeremy Fowler notes the contradiction between the urgency that a finding of genocide implies and the inaction that typically accompanies the global awareness of genocide. He faults the UN's *Genocide Convention* itself:

> After calling for international cooperation "to liberate mankind from such an odious scourge," the Convention proceeds to define the crime of genocide in terms that, from the perspective of "preventing" or "suppressing" genocide, are problematic. It then offers only the vaguest

sense of what should be done when genocide is imminent or actually underway (Fowler 2006, 127).

John Hagan has lamented the inattention to genocide by the field of criminology (Hagan and Rymond-Richmond 2009). Although it is hard to dispute his claim, the subject has not been ignored by scholars. There are genocide studies programs at dozens of universities in the United States, including Yale, University of Minnesota, University of South Florida, and University of North Dakota. There are also numerous programs outside of the United States, including programs in Australia, Denmark, England, Germany, Poland, and Sweden. In 2009 Rwanda became the first African nation to provide a master's degree in genocide studies (Musoni 2009). There are at least two journals dealing with genocide: *Genocide Studies and Prevention* and *Holocaust and Genocide Studies,* and there is a continuing stream of books on the topic. Such efforts promise a more educated public about the warning signs of genocide and about what can be done to prevent genocides and stop genocides in progress. However, it is not clear that a greater understanding of the issue has done much to prompt powerful nations to act. Countervailing forces may make genocides more frequent. For example, P. W. Singer has argued that the rise of private armies, equipped with advanced technologies for killing, and drawing on a global market in arms, has made it possible for even minor dictators to undertake short-term wars (Singer 2003). It requires no stretch of the imagination to foresee these same developments facilitating genocide and increasing its likelihood.

Aside from private militaries, technological advances alone can facilitate genocide. Improved communications make it easier for governments to coordinate killing and to maintain records of where targeted groups live. Technological advances also make weapons of war lighter and more affordable. Advanced tools of war can now be made by those with little technical skill, for relatively little money, and with off-the-shelf materials (Singer 2009).

Another factor is the growing global competition for valuable resources, including water, land, oil, and precious minerals; competition that sparks wars between nations (e.g., Klare 2001) can also spark drives to eradicate groups of people. For example, the number of wars over access to water has increased in each of the past three decades, and this trend is likely to continue (Gleick 2000).

Following the Holocaust of World War II much progress has been made in understanding the conditions that lead to and facilitate genocide. At no time in history has there been more awareness of the issue. Advances in communication technology have meant that the world is increasingly aware of genocide as it occurs. Despite these advances, however, powerful nations appear no more willing than in the past to step in and end the killing. Creating the term "genocide" was not enough. Making genocide an international crime was not enough. Increasing awareness of genocide was not enough. What is needed now is a mechanism to compel other nations to act.

Web Sources

1. A full text of the *Genocide Convention,* including the definition of genocide and procedural issues, is available at: United Nations Office of the High Commission for Human Rights.
    http://www.unhchr.ch/html/menu3/b/p_genoci.htm
2. The documentation on past and ongoing genocides is available at: Human Rights Watch.
    http://www.hrw.org
3. A wealth of information about genocide, including databases, satellite images, and publications are available at the Genocide Studies Program at Yale University.
    http://www.yale.edu/gsp

Discussion Questions

1. What are some of the arguments for and against having genocide as an international crime?
2. What are some of the weaknesses of the *Genocide Convention*? How might these be corrected?
3. What is a proper punishment for those convicted of genocide?
4. What can be done to get major world powers to act more quickly when there is evidence that genocide is occurring?
5. What factors make it likely that genocides will continue to take place, and may even increase in number?

References

Burg, Steven. "Genocide in Bosnia-Herzegovina?" In *Century of Genocide: Eyewitness Accounts and Critical Views,* edited by Samuel S. Totten, William S. Parsons, and Israel W. Charny, 424–433. New York: Garland Publishing, 1997.
Central Intelligence Agency (CIA). "The World Factbook: Rwanda." Accessed September 26, 2001. http://www.cia.gov, 2001.

_____. "*The World Factbook: Sudan.*" Accessed September 26, 2001. http://www.cia.gov//, 2009.

Chalk, Frank, and Kurt Jonassohn, eds. *The History and Sociology of Genocide: Analysis and Case Studies.* New Haven, CT: Yale University Press, 1990.

Charny, Israel W. "Toward a Generic Definition of Genocide." In *Genocide: Conceptual and Historical Dimensions,* edited by George J. Andreopoulos, 64–94. Philadelphia: University of Pennsylvania Press, 1994.

_____. "The Dawning of a New Age of Opposition to Genocide." In *Encyclopedia of Genocide,* Vol. I, edited by Israel W. Charny, xi–xxiv. Santa Barbara, CA: ABC-CLIO, 1999.

Court Rules Genocide was Committed at Srebrenica. *Los Angeles Times,* August 2, 2001. Accessed August 2, 2001. http://www.latimes.com.

Cox, John K. *The History of Serbia.* Westport, CT: Greenwood, 2002.

Des Forges, Alison. *Leave None to Tell the Story: Genocide in Rwanda.* New York: Human Rights Watch, 1999.

Fein, Helen. "Discriminating Genocide from War Crimes: Vietnam and Afghanistan Reexamined." *Denver Journal of International Law and Policy* 22, no. 1 (1993): 29–62.

_____. "Genocide, Terror, Life Integrity, and War Crimes." In *Genocide: Conceptual and Historical Dimensions,* edited by George J. Andreopoulos, 95–107. Philadelphia: University of Pennsylvania Press, 1994.

Fowler, Jerry. "A New Chapter of Irony: The Legal Definition of Genocide and the Implications of Powell's Determination." In *Genocide in Darfur: Investigating the Atrocities in the Sudan,* edited by Samuel Totten and Eric Markusen, 127–139. New York: Routledge, Taylor & Francis Group, 2006.

Gleick, Peter H. 2000. "The World's Water: Water Conflict Chronology." Accessed February 8, 2003. http://www.worldwater.org/conflict.htm, 2000.

Gutman, Roy, and David Rieff. (eds.). *Crimes of War.* New York: Norton, 1999.

Hagan, John, and Alberto Palloni. "Death in Darfur." *Science* 313 (2006): 1578–1579.

Hagan, John, and Wenona Rymond-Richmond. "The Collective Dynamics of Racial Dehumanization and Genocidal Victimization in Darfur." *American Sociological Review* 73 (2008): 875–902.

_____. *Darfur and the Crime of Genocide.* Cambridge: Cambridge University Press, 2009.

Hagan, John, Wenona Rymond-Richmond, and Patricia Parker. "The Criminology of Genocide: The Death and Rape of Darfur." *Criminology* 43, no. 3 (2005): 525–562.

Harman, Danna. "Rwanda Turns to Its Past for Justice." *Christian Science Monitor,* January 30, 2002. Accessed January 30, 2002. http://www.csmonitor.com.

Heidenrich, John G. *How to Prevent Genocide: A Guide for Policymakers, Scholars, and the Concerned Citizen*. Westport, CT: Praeger, 2001.

History Place. "Genocide in the 20th Century: Bosnia-Herzegovina, 1992–1995." Accessed June 15, 2009. http://www.historyplace.com. n.d.

Howard, Jonathan P. "Survey Methodology and the Darfur Genocide." In *Genocide in Darfur: Investigating the Atrocities in the Sudan*, edited by Samuel Totten and Eric Markusen, 59–74. New York: Routledge, Taylor & Francis Group, 2006.

Human Rights Watch. "*No One to Intervene: Gaps in Civilian Protection in Southern Sudan*." Accessed June 21, 2009. http://www.hrw.org, 2009a.

_____. "Darfur and the ICC: Myths versus Reality." Accessed June 22, 2009. http://www.hrw.org, 2009b.

_____. "World Report 2013: Sudan." Accessed April 17, 2013. http://www.hrw.org, 2013.

International Criminal Tribunal for the Former Yugoslavia (ICTY). Accessed June 21, 2009. http://www.icty.org, 2009.

International Criminal Tribunal for Rwanda (ICTR). 2009. Accessed June 22, 2009. http://www.ictr.org, 2009.

Kiernan, Ben. *Blood and Soil: A World History of Genocide and Extermination from Sparta to Darfur*. New Haven, CT: Yale University Press, 2007.

Klare, Michael T. 2001. *Resource Wars: The New Landscape of Global Conflict*. New York: Henry Holt, 2001.

Kuper, Leo. *Genocide: Its Political Use in the Twentieth Century*. New Haven, CT: Yale University Press, 1981.

_____. *The Prevention of Genocide*. New Haven, CT: Yale University Press, 1985.

Labott, Elise. "Google Earth Maps Out Darfur Atrocities." *CNN*, April 15, 2007. Accessed June 23, 2009. http://www.cnn.com.

Lemarchand, Rene. "The Rwanda Genocide." In *Century of Genocide: Eyewitness Accounts and Critical Views*, edited by Samuel Totten, William S. Parsons and Israel W. Charny, 408–423. New York: Garland Publishing, 1997.

_____. Rwanda and Burundi, Genocide. In *Encyclopedia of Genocide*, vol. II, edited by Israel W. Charny, 508–513. Santa Barbara, CA: ABC-CLIO, 1999.

Lemkin, Raphael. *Axis Rule in Occupied Europe*. Washington, D.C.: Carnegie Endowment for International Peace, 1944.

_____. 1946. "Genocide." *American Scholar* 15, no. 2 (1946): 227–230.

MacFarquhar, Neil. "Security Council Members Push to Condemn Sudan." *New York Times*, June 6, 2008. Accessed June 22, 2009. http://www.nytimes.com.

Minow, Martha. *Between Vengeance and Forgiveness: Facing History after Genocide and Mass Violence*. Boston: Beacon Press, 1998.

Musoni, Edwin. "Rwanda: Country to Offer Master's Degree in Genocide Studies." *NewTimes*, June 15, 2009. Accessed June 23, 2009. http://www.allafrica.com/stories/200906150144.html.

Office of the United Nations High Commissioner for Human Rights. "Convention on the Prevention and Punishment of the Crime of Genocide." Accessed June 10, 2009. http://www.unhchr.ch/html/menu3/p/p_genoci.htm. n.d.

_____. 2009. "Seminar on the Prevention of Genocide." Accessed June 11, 2009. http://www2.ohchr.org/english/events/RuleofLaw/index.htm, 2009.

Peck, Grant. "Khmer Rouge Horrors Detailed at Opening Trial." *ABC News*, March 30, 2009. Accessed June 12, 2009. http://abcnews.go.com.

Porter, Jack. "Introduction." In *Genocide and Human Rights: A Global Anthology*, edited by Jack Porter, 9–10. Washington, D.C.: University Press of America, 1982.

Power, Samantha. *A Problem From Hell: America Find the Age of Genocide*. New York: Basic Books, 2002.

Prunier, Gerard. *Darfur: A 21st Century Genocide*. (3rd ed.). Ithaca, NY: Cornell University Press, 2008.

Shattuck, John. *Freedom on Fire: Human Rights Wars and America's Response*. Cambridge, MA: Harvard University Press, 2003.

Singer, P.W. *Corporate Warriors*. Ithaca, NY: Cornell University Press, 2003.

_____. *Children at War*. Berkeley and Los Angeles: University of California Press, 2006.

_____. *Wired for War: The Robotics Revolution and Conflict in the 21st Century*. New York: Penguin Press, 2009.

Taylor, Christopher. *Sacrifice as Terror: The Rwandan Genocide of 1994*. Oxford: Berg, 1999.

Totten, Samuel, William S. Parsons, and Israel W. Charny. eds. *Century of Genocide: Eyewitness Accounts and Critical Views*. New York: Garland Publishing, 1997.

Totten, Samuel. "The Darfur Genocide." In *Century of Genocide: Critical Essays and Eyewitness Accounts*, 3rd ed., edited by Samuel Totten and William S. Parsons, 555–607. New York: Routledge, Taylor & Francis Group, 2009.

Two Nuns Guilty in Genocide. *Los Angeles Times*, June 8, 2001. Accessed June 8, 2009. http://www.latimes.com.

Chapter 12

Specific Crimes against Humanity: Groups and Minority Rights

Sesha Kethineni & Gail Humiston

Introduction: The Status of Dalits

The first part of this chapter describes the historical and current plight of Dalits in India, including the social and economic challenges they face. It provides specific examples of violations against the Dalits. Second, it reviews economic, social, and cultural rights in general and how they are applicable to Dalits. Third, it looks at India's efforts to fulfill its commitment to human rights. Fourth, it examines India's implementation and enforcement of Dalits' rights. Finally, it discusses the various recommendations made by human rights organizations and scholars. The second part addresses the rights of the Roma in Europe.

The Dalits (also known as "Untouchables," *Harijan*, or "Scheduled Castes") have historically been poor, deprived of basic human rights, and treated as social inferiors in India. They still face economic, social, cultural, and political discrimination in the name of caste. "Centuries of this 'hidden apartheid' that has perpetuated discrimination and denial of their human rights, has resulted not only in Dalits representing a disproportionate amount of the poor in India, but also in the creation of numerous other obstacles that hinder Dalit's ability to change their situation" (Artis, Doobay, and Lyons 2003, 9).

Gandhi first recognized the Dalits' struggles and brought them to the attention of the Indian national government in the 1930s. Concern for the Dalits led to a more radical movement headed by Dr. B. R. Ambedkar. Gandhi viewed "the Dalits problem" as a social one, whereas Dr. Ambedkar saw it as a political and economic problem created by upper castes. When Dr. Ambedkar became the first law minister, he created progressive legal reforms and incorporated these reforms into the Indian Constitution (Prashad 2001).

To understand the Dalits' position in Indian society, one needs to understand the caste system (*varna vyavastha*). The caste system, which has dominated Indian society for over 3,000 years, was developed by the *Brahmins* (Hindu priests) to maintain their superiority over the less educated and less skilled. Over time, the caste system was formalized into four distinct classes (*varnas*). At the top of the hierarchy are the Brahmins, who are considered arbiters in matters of learning, teaching, and religion. Next in line are the *Kshatriyas*, who are warriors and administrators. The third category is *Vaisyas*, who belong to the artisan and commercial class. Finally, the *Sudras* (Backward Caste) are farmers and peasants. These four castes are socially and religiously important because they are said to have divine origination—they came from different parts of the Hindu god *Brahma*, the creator. The Brahmins came from the mouth of Brahma, the Kshatriyas from his arms, the Vaisyas from his thighs, and Sudras from his feet (Izzo, 2005; National Campaign on Dalits Human Rights [NCDHR] n.d.-a).

Beneath the four classes, there is a fifth group, which is not included as part of the caste system. Individuals from this group are literally untouchable for the rest of the castes. The *Dalits* (broken people) compose this untouchable society. The term "broken" has meant oppression for many radical Dalits who have used the term in their struggle for liberation. Gandhian liberals referred to them as *Harijans* (children of god) and the Government of India officially calls them "Scheduled Castes." "Scheduled" means they are on a government schedule that entitles them to certain protections and affirmative actions (Prashad 2001).

For centuries, Dalits were not treated as part of the mainstream Indian society, and they were traditionally assigned menial and degrading jobs (NCDHR n.d.-a, 3). Some traditional roles, such as removing dead animals or playing drums at religious ceremonies, are expected to be carried out without compensation. Despite protections in the Indian Constitution (see Articles 39, 41, and 16 [sections 2 and 4]), attempts by Dalits to be treated fairly in the workplace are often countered by violence and social or economic boycotts by the other castes (Human Rights Watch 2003a).

Although the concept of untouchability was made illegal after India gained independence in 1947, the persecution and alienation of the Dalits has not stopped. In fact, it is reported to be at an all-time high. Entire villages in many Indian states are segregated by caste with the intent to keep Dalits away from the higher castes. For example, it is common in many rural areas to have a designated area called "Dalit Street," which is the only place Dalits are allowed to live (Artis, Doobay, and Lyons 2003). Dalits typically live in locations more distant from village roads, an indication of segregation and a reminder of their untouchability.

Dalits are not allowed to fetch water from the same wells used by higher castes, visit the same temples, drink from the same cup at local tea shops, or use land that is legally theirs. Dalit children who attend school must sit in the back of the classrooms. Moreover, the villages where Dalits live have limited or no access to public transportation, health care, or educational, political, or legal institutions (Human Rights Watch 1999).

Existing Conditions of Dalits

Dalits make up approximately 170 million of India's billion people (Minority Rights Group International 2006). Many are agricultural laborers. They have a limited share of India's agricultural holdings and an even more limited share of its irrigated land holdings. "Most of them are merely agrestic [rural] slaves or serfs ... or crop-sharing tenants-at-will" who were not placed on official records until recently (Neelima 2002, 123).

Education

It is often argued that the quality of education in public schools is inadequate compared to private schools. The poor quality of education, especially in rural areas, can be attributed to inadequate infrastructure, the lack of accountability of teachers to the local community (teachers' salaries are controlled by the state), and inadequate work conditions for teachers (teachers are often compelled to teach more than one grade at a time). Of all Indian children, Dalit children suffer the most. For example, school attendance in 1998–99 was 65.7 percent for Scheduled-Caste children ages 7–17, compared to 81.3 percent for high-caste children (Jenkins and Barr 2006). Furthermore, the completion rate of five years of schooling for Scheduled-Caste children between 2002 and 2004 was 34 percent, compared to 44 percent for children from higher castes (Jenkins and Barr 2006).

Employment Opportunities

Although outlawed, approximately two-thirds of bonded laborers (debt servitude or forced labor) are from the Dalit community. Of the 40 million bonded laborers in India, 15 million are children (Human Rights Watch 1999). Bonded labor is the traditional expectation of free labor or inadequate compensation for work. Because they are unable to afford basic necessities, such as health care, Dalits often become indebted to employers after accepting loans that they are unable to repay due to insufficient wages (Human Rights Watch

2007; Larson 2004). The forced bonded labor was abolished by Article 23 of the Constitution and the Bonded Labour (System) Abolition Act of 1976, but the practice continues. According to the Act, all bonded laborers were to be released and rehabilitated, and their debts were to be cancelled (NCDHR 2006).

Women and children are primarily engaged in "civic sanitation work" (e.g., manual scavenging, even though this has been outlawed), followed by leather fraying in tanning and footwear manufacturing. Of the 1.3 million Dalits employed as manual scavengers, most of these are women Dalits whose duty is to clear human excrement from dry pit latrines. In many villages, Dalits are lowered into manholes without protection to clear blocked sewers, which has resulted in the death of over 100 Dalits each year from the inhalation of toxic gases or drowning in fecal matter and urine (Human Rights Watch 2007). Those who engage in scavenging are seen as the lowest of the Dalits, being discriminated against within their own caste (Human Rights Watch 1999). Moreover, entrepreneurial opportunities are extremely limited for Dalits as they lack both capital and the collateral to secure loans. Even if they are successful in opening small businesses, non-Dalits will not patronize those shops (Artis, Doobay, and Lyons 2003).

Migration

Dalits often migrate in search of work. Although poor non-Dalits migrate in search of employment, Dalits migrate much more. The main cause of this migration is lack of land ownership, exacerbated by droughts. The majority of Dalits in rural areas have no financial recourses, such as loans, to survive economic hardships (Fernando, Macwan, and Ramanathan 2004).

Specific Instances of Abuse

Neelima (2002) has listed four primary causes of atrocities against Dalits: Land disputes, lack of civic facilities, untouchability-related crimes, and self-assertion. Of these, land is the most important.

Land Dispute

These disputes relate to land redistribution, allotment of housing sites by the government, cultivable land, irrigation rights, and land alienation (e.g., land grabbing). For example, Dalits lose their land in acquisition or to irrigation projects under the guise of development. Use of common pasture and farming in community lands in the villages has also led to disputes between higher-caste landlords and Dalits. Most often, the powerful upper castes encroach upon Dalits' lands and resistance is met with violence. About 75 percent of Dalits are considered completely landless (Human Rights Watch 2007). Some examples: In 2003, 7,000 Dalits were forced from their homes in Calcutta so that plans for beautification and development could be undertaken. Bulldozers, fire brigades, ambulances, and a 500-man Rapid Action Force entered the community and demolished hundreds of houses, temples, statues, and a school. Seven hundred families were with nowhere to live (International Secretariat of the World Organization against Torture 2003). In 2007, violence erupted in Nandigram when efforts were made to impose an unjust land acquisition law on Dalits. Although accounts varied, police records confirmed the deaths of fourteen people and the gang rape of three women as a result of the action (India Together 2007).

Lack of Civic Facilities

Atrocities pertaining to civic facilities are frequently related to lack of essential facilities or limited access to facilities in Dalit localities. For example, in the central state of Madhya Pradesh an entire village was set on fire by a mob of 300 people, resulting in the death of three Dalits. The incident was provoked by the installation of a new hand-pump for a water-starved Dalit village. In the southern states of Tamil Nadu and Andhra Pradesh, the dead bodies of two aged women were held on the pathway because of disputes regarding access to the segregated Dalit burial ground (Neelima 2002). Less than 10 percent of households belonging to a Scheduled Caste have access to sanitation, and 20 percent lack a safe source of drinking water (Human Rights Watch 2007).

The Dalit Rights Movement

In response to India's failure to provide economic and social rights, young Dalits in the late 1960s took inspiration from the Black Panther movement in the United States and the resurgent militant left-wing uprising in India. By 1972, the Dalit Panthers emerged as a militant political organization whose demands included land distribution, increased wages, free education, and an end to economic corruption. Unable to secure wide support at that time, the Dalit Panthers could not make a mark on the national political scene.

A more recent Dalit political party that emerged at the national front is the Bahujan Samaj Party (BSP). The BSP, unlike previous Dalit-rights organizations, is well-organized and committed to protecting the rights of Dalits. However, their efforts have shown minimal success. Dalits are still victims of human rights violations.

Concerned about Dalits' plight in India and Blacks' struggle in other countries, activists want to make a connection between caste and race. Afrocentrics and Dalitocentrics claim that Dalits are *Negritos* who suffered oppression in the hands of "Aryans," much like Blacks in the United States. Others contend that, unlike Blacks in the United States and South Africa, Dalits generally are not distinguishable from other Indians. Dalits face apartheid-like conditions determined by occupation and descent, not by appearance (Prashad 2001). Furthermore, "the agenda of social justice is not identical, since the social context of the fights are separate; where the human rights agenda of civic justice may be more important in one context, the fight for land rights may be central in the other" (Prashad 2001, 13). What they have in common is they all have faced some form of oppression at the hands of a powerful upper class.

Between 1980 and 1996, Dalits gained the support of small nongovernmental organizations (NGOs), such as the Chennai (Madras)-based Dalit Liberation Education Trust and the Volunteer in Service to India's Oppressed and Neglected, but they were unable to garner assistance from larger NGOs, the United Nations, or other international organizations until 1996. Dalit advocates finally gained international attention in 1996 when the UN Committee on the Elimination of Racial Discrimination (CERD) criticized India for its lack of protection of Dalit human rights. The International Convention on the Elimination of All Forms of Racial Discrimination of 1965 (ICERD) (which was ratified by India in 1968) defines "racial discrimination" as:

> ... any distinction, exclusion, restriction or preference based on race, colour, descent, or national or ethnic origin which has the purpose or effect of nullifying or impairing the recognition, enjoyment or exercise, on an equal footing, of human rights and fundamental freedoms in the political, economic, social, cultural or any other field of public life (Bob 2007, 177).

The CERD's scrutiny of India's treatment of Dalit atrocities attracted the attention of Human Rights Watch, and Dalit activist organizations became more organized. Human Rights Watch began preparing its major report, *Broken People,* in 1997, and it received widespread attention from the media following publication in 1999. The National Campaign on Dalit Human Rights (NCDHR) was created in 1998 to link dozens of Dalits' rights groups from fourteen states in India.[1] In 2000, the International Dalit Solidarity Network

---

1. NCDHR currently has chapters in Bihar, Delhi, Gujarat, Haryana, Himachal Pradesh, Karnataka, Kerala, Madhya Pradesh, Maharashtra, Orissa, Pondicherry, Punjab, Rajasthan, and Uttar Pradesh.

(IDSN) was formed to share information on the international level. The UN Human Rights Commission's Subcommission for the Promotion and Protection of Human Rights enacted a resolution forbidding discrimination on the basis of work and descent. In 2001, the Goonesekere Report (2000) stimulated international debate by closely examining worldwide discrimination based on "work and descent" and how the custom infringes on international human rights laws. Dalit activism has benefited from international deliberations as the argument of discrimination has shifted away from the religion of Hinduism and its caste system and toward discrimination on the basis of "work and descent" (Bob 2007).

Economic, Social, and Cultural Rights

Dalits claim that their economic, social, and cultural (ESC) rights, as well as their civil and political rights, have been violated by the government and its entities for centuries. They argue that the government should recognize and enforce ESC rights. Furthermore, they contend that violations should be punished.

ESC, civil, and political rights are internationally recognized human rights. For example, ESC rights are recognized in the Universal Declaration of Human Rights (1948) and the International Covenant of Economic, Social and Cultural Rights (ICESCR 1966). Articles 1–21 recognize what are commonly considered civil and political rights, e.g., rights to life, liberty, and property. These rights were drawn from liberal constitutions, primarily those of the United States and European nations. Later, the International Covenant on Civil and Political Rights (ICCPR) added provisions relating to the right of people to self-determination and to the sovereignty over their natural wealth and resources.

Empirical Conceptualization of ESC Rights

International attention to descent-based discrimination extended the empirical discussion of the conceptualization and measurement of the human rights indicators of economic, social, and cultural rights. For empirical purposes, the primary elements of ESC rights impose a duty on the government to respect, protect, and fulfill citizens' rights to food, housing, health, education, and work, if the government has the resources available to fulfill basic needs. The right to food includes sustainable access to safe food and information regarding nutrition (Green 2001). Self-administration of land and natural resources also falls within the realm of adequate food (Hansen 2000). The right to housing includes access to adequate housing, along with rights to security and privacy. The health indicator encompasses access to health care; individual control over health-care choices, including reproductive freedom and freedom from torture; and issues of underlying determinants, such as clean water, sanitation, healthy workplace environments, and information regarding health. Citizens should have the right to education, which includes free and compulsory primary education, the right to make individual choices, and the right to establish schools and teach. Finally, the right to work includes freedom from forced labor, labor union rights, adequate working conditions and leisure, and the right to fair wages and equal compensation (Green 2001).

Individual versus Collective Rights

The international community has grappled with the issue of collective (i.e., group) rights. The international human rights movement and the international law of human rights address only individual rights. For example, the Universal Declaration (Article 20) states that everyone is entitled to freedom of peaceful assembly and associations, but does not define "association." Likewise, Article 18 of the Declaration recognizes the freedom of everyone to practice their own religion, either as an individual or in a community with others. The Article, however, does not describe rights of religious communities.

The Optional Protocol to the ICCPR, the Convention on the Elimination of All Forms of Racial Discrimination, and the European and the American Conventions on Human Rights provide certain remedies for individuals. For example, individuals can report to an international treaty body (e.g., the Human Rights Committee established by the ICCPR, or the Committee Against Torture established by the Torture Convention) (Henkin, Neuman, Orentlicher, and Leebron 1999). More recently, the literature on human rights has addressed collective rights after the outbreak of ethnic hostilities and genocide in the former nation of Yugoslavia (Henkin et al. 1999). Moreover, continued ethnic fighting in the former Soviet Union and Sri Lanka, religious conflict in India between Hindus and Muslims, and tribal animosities in Africa have also brought about discussion of minority issues in international forums.

India's Efforts to Fulfill Its Commitment to Human Rights

To overcome the historical discrimination of Dalits, India has taken several steps to prohibit the practice of untouchability. These steps include constitutional guarantees, legislative enactments, and policy measures.

Constitutional Provisions

The Indian Constitution, in its Bill of Rights, guarantees all citizens basic civil and political rights and fundamental freedoms. In addition, the Constitution has special provisions prohibiting discrimination based on caste. These provisions are found under the Right to Equality (Articles 15, 16, and 17), the Right Against Exploitation (Article 23), Cultural and Educational Rights (Article 29:2), and prohibition against disenfranchisement in elections based on one's religion, race, caste, or sex (Article 325).

Articles 330 and 333 permit Union and state legislatures to reserve seats for members of the Scheduled Castes and Scheduled Tribes (indigenous people) based on their population in each constituency. Article 338 mandates the creation of a National Commission for Scheduled Castes and Scheduled Tribes to monitor the safeguards provided to them. Finally, Article 341 makes possible the governmental identification of different subcategories of Scheduled Castes in relation to each state. The list of Scheduled Castes or subgroups within the Scheduled Castes, published by the president through public notification, is deemed final.

Legislative Enactments

To fulfill the constitutional provisions pertaining to Scheduled Castes, India has passed various laws to protect their rights. These include the Protection of Civil Rights (Anti-Untouchability) Act (1955); the Bonded Labour (Abolition) Act (1976); the Scheduled Castes and Scheduled Tribes (Prevention of Atrocities) Act (1989) and Rules (1995); the Employment of Manual Scavenger and Construction of Dry Latrines (Prohibition) Act (1993); and various land-reform laws to redistribute community land to the landless. Finally, to monitor enforcement of some of these laws, the Central (i.e., federal) Government established the National Commission for Scheduled Castes and Scheduled Tribes and the National Human Rights Commission in the early 1990s (NCDHR n.d.-b.).

Implementation and Enforcement of Laws and Policies

Land Reforms

Lack of access to agricultural land for cultivation is a major barrier to progress among Dalits. They become economically vulnerable; their dependency is exploited by upper- and middle-caste landlords; their lack of political power leads to abuses by the police and politicians. From 1948 to the 1970s, 34.9 million acres were given to farmers, of which only 0.5 percent was given to Dalits and Scheduled Tribes (NCDHR 2006). The NCDHR report on Caste, Race, and the World Conference Against Racism (WCAR) shows that out of an estimated 30 million hectares of harvestable surplus land, only 7.5 million acres have been declared surplus, and only a small portion has been given to Dalits. Large tracts of land are being sold at well below market value to multinational corporations and the World Bank, which has resulted in the displacement of many Dalits and Adivasis who had been living on the land (NCDHR 2006). Shah, Meander, Thorat, Deshpande, and Baviskar (cited in NCDHR 2006) found that Dalits in 21 percent of the villages surveyed were denied access to common property resources (CPRs), e.g., lands and fishing ponds.

In 2004–2005 only one-fifth (20 percent) of all Scheduled-Caste households were able to cultivate land as independent agricultural workers, whereas upper-caste households represented twice that number (see Table 1). The limited access to land and capital due to the ongoing discrimination against Dalits resulted in greater levels of poverty among this group. For example, the level of poverty was reported to be 60 percent among agricultural laborers, a vast majority of whom are Dalits (Thorat 2002).

Employment Reservations Policy

The government implemented the "reservations" policy to create job opportunities for Dalits and other disadvantaged groups. However, the reservation system has only minimally benefited the Dalits. This is partly because the system applies only to the government sector. Moreover, the system is reported to be flawed because many jobs are left unfilled and because of a lack of commitment on the part of a government dominated by upper-caste politicians (Artis, Doobay, and Lyons 2003). For example, most of the reservations are in low-skill, low-paying jobs. It is often difficult for Dalits to make the transition from their traditional jobs to mainstream jobs. To allow for proportional representation, the Constitution reserves 22.5 percent of seats in government jobs, state legislatures, the lower house of the Parliament, and government educa-

Table 1 Occupational Pattern: Scheduled Caste, Scheduled Tribes, Backward Castes, and Other (by percentage)

Social Groups in Rural India				
Occupational Category	SC	ST	OBC	OTHER
Self-employed in Agriculture	20.2	39.3	38.7	43.3
Self-employed in Nonagricultural Work	14.1	06.4	17.6	18.1
Self-employed (Subtotal)	34.2	45.7	56.2	61.4
Agricultural Wage Labor	40.5	34.0	22.4	15.6
Nonagricultural Wage Labor	15.4	11.3	10.4	07.7
Rural Wage Labor (Subtotal)	56.0	45.3	32.7	23.3
Others	09.8	08.9	11.0	15.3
Occupational Category Social Groups in Urban India				
Self-employed	29.3	26.3	40.3	38.6
Regular Wages/Salaried	41.1	41.8	36.7	44.8
Casual Labor	21.8	17.3	14.5	06.2
Others Wage	07.7	14.5	08.4	10.3
All	100	100	100	100

SC = Scheduled Caste; ST = Scheduled Tribes; OBC = Other Backward Caste; Others = Non SC/ST/OBC (excluding Scheduled Caste, Scheduled Tribe, and Other Backward Castes)

Source: National Sample Survey Organization Ministry of Statistics and Programme Implementation (2006). *National Sample Survey Report No. 516: Employment/unemployment situation among social groups in India, 2004–2005, Delhi.*

tional institutions for Scheduled Castes and Scheduled Tribes. Of the total reservations for Scheduled Castes in the central government, 54 percent remain vacant. The situation is worse in other public sector jobs, with 88 percent remaining unfilled (NCDHR n.d.-c).

Local Government Reservations

India's Constitution created formal governmental institutions (*Panchayatis Raj*) in an effort to foster democratic representation and control at the grassroots level. The reservation policy applies to these governing bodies, but they have been unable or unwilling to implement measures that facilitate their constitutional duties of promoting equality (Menon 2007). Dalits were forbidden from entering polling booths in 12.3 percent of the 565 rural villages surveyed. Census officers refuse to register Dalits in public records to deprive them of government representation and benefits (Asian Legal Resource Center n.d.). Higher-caste members control elections by permitting their chosen candidates to file nomination papers, while threatening, coercing, or bribing unapproved candidates into removing or not filing their nomination papers (Pur 2007). Upper-caste citizens react violently during elections to prevent Dalits from running for office. In 1996, Murugesan and his supporters from a Dalit community were dragged from a bus and killed because Murugesan ran in the *Panchayat* elections against a member of the dominant caste in Tamil Nadu. Four Panchayat districts in Tamil Nadu were unable to hold elections due to violence between 1996 and 2005 (NCDHR 2006). The control over candidates often results in unanimous, uncontested elections of informal leaders into the formal leadership positions, effectively eliminating meaningful Dalit representation at the local level (Pur 2007).

Dalits who manage to become elected officials within their local governments are covertly and overtly forced into early resignations to allow non-Dalits to assume leadership. Dalit representatives may not be allowed to sit in their assigned seats at government meetings or eat or drink with non-Dalit representatives (NCDHR 2006). Upper-caste members stop the day-to-day activities within their jurisdictions to exert control. Dalit *Panchayat* presidents resign prematurely from their elected positions because they are unable to exercise any influence over higher-caste personnel and representatives (Menon 2007). If Dalits cannot be harassed into voluntary resignations, they may be accused of embezzlement (NCDHR 2006). An example of harassment of a Dalit elected official is Ms. Munia Devi of the Koirajpur village, who was elected in 2005 as village head in the *Panchayati Raj,* a position that required her to become custodian of the village records. She was chased away by the former village head, Mr. Lal Chand, and she did not receive the records. The next year, Ms. Devi was physically and verbally abused by Lal Chand and his men. When she attempted to register a complaint, the police officers also chased her away (Asian Legal Source n.d.).

Prosecution of Offenders

India's criminal justice system has been negligent in its conviction of persons who violate the rights of Scheduled Castes and Scheduled Tribes. In 2005, there were 31,840 alleged criminal incidents reportedly committed against Scheduled Castes and Scheduled Tribes, as defined by the IPC and Special

Laws. Although the charge-sheet rates for crimes against Scheduled Castes and Scheduled Tribes were similar to the national means, the average conviction rates for offenses against Scheduled Castes and Scheduled Tribes were 29.8 and 24.5 percent, respectively, compared to national rates of 42.4 percent for IPC crimes and 84.5 percent for Special Law Crimes. Police personnel act with impunity, as evidenced by the fact that 61,560 complaints were alleged against police personnel in 2005. Only 225 police personnel were tried that year, and only 97 police personnel were actually convicted (National Crime Records Bureau n.d.). Unfortunately, the protection of Dalits' human rights fails in practice due to the impunity of higher-caste groups and police corruption.

Food Programs

Approximately 55 percent of Scheduled-Caste and Scheduled-Tribe children are undernourished, compared to 44 percent of children in other communities (OneWorld South Asia 2006). India implemented the National Programme of Nutritional Support, also known the "midday meal scheme" (MMS), in 1995 after the Supreme Court directed the national government to create such a program, and participation grew from 33.4 million to 105 million children between 1995 and 2004. However, the number of Scheduled-Caste children participants fell from 22,638,260 to 22,004,919 between 2003 and 2005. The states of Rajasthan and Tamil Nadu have been notably deficient in providing the MMS to Dalit children, because Dalit children are hesitant to enter hostile areas inhabited by higher castes. Unfortunately, higher-caste members usually block Dalits from being hired as cooks and participating in the distribution of the MMS. If a Dalit is hired as a cook, non-Dalit parents send sack lunches with the children to school. Higher-caste members may also attempt to have the Dalit cook fired or campaign to close the school (NCDHR 2006).

India's Targeted Public Distribution System (TPDS or PDS) is the largest system of food distribution in the world, and Fair Price Shops (PDS shops) are responsible for allocating food to the villagers. Dalits have less access to distribution centers because 17 percent of the shops are located in Dalit colonies and 70 percent are in dominant-caste areas, with the remaining 13 percent being located elsewhere. Shop owners discriminate against Dalits in terms of quantity and price (NCDHR 2006). Food subsidies meant for the poor are often sold on the black market, and ration shop licensees bribe police officers so that complaints are not registered. For example, hundreds of complaints have been filed against a distributor in Belwa, but the police did not register the complaints and the distributor has not been prosecuted (Asian Legal Resource Centre n.d.).

Health Programs

The central government adopted the National Health Policy in 1983, and finally put those policies into action in 2002. The national government aids states by providing funds to combat major diseases, but most of the burden of health care is delegated to the states (Republic of India 2006). Dalits are less likely to benefit from the meager health-care benefits provided by the government. According to India's National Family Health Survey of 2005–2006, Dalit infants had a mortality rate of 83 deaths per 1,000 children, compared to the non-Dalit rate of 61 per 1,000. The Dalit child mortality rate was 39 per 1,000, compared to the average of 22 per 1,000. OneWorld South Asia (2006) reported under-5 mortality rates for Scheduled-Caste and Scheduled-Tribe children were 127 and 119 per 1,000, respectively, compared to 92 per 1,000 for other children. In 1998 and 1999, more than half of Dalit children were malnourished, and 75 percent of Dalit children and 56 percent of Dalit women were anemic. Maternal health care is free in India, but Dalit women receive less prenatal care than upper-caste women (NCDHR 2006), and Dalit mothers were less likely to receive postnatal care within two days of their last birth (Ministry of Health & Family Welfare n.d.). Unfortunately, some states, such as Uttar Pradesh, Bihar, and Rajasthan, are not making efforts to improve prenatal care (NCDHR 2006). Finally, Dalit men and women are more likely to be underweight (Ministry of Health and Family Welfare n.d.).

Education Program

As a result of the 86th Amendment (2002), India initiated the *Sarva Shiksha Abhiyan* (SSA) (also known as Education for All [EFA]), to achieve the mission of universal elementary education (UEE). The basic goal of SSA is to create quality community-owned elementary education schools for children 6–14 years of age with universal retention by 2010, with a special focus on girls, Scheduled Castes, Scheduled Tribes, and other disadvantaged groups (Republic of India 2006). According to the Ministry of Human Resource Development, India's touted SSA program is not effective for Dalit children due to discrimination. Moreover, teachers maintain discriminatory attitude and practices (NCDHR 2006). In one such incident in 2001, the officiating headmaster of a government secondary school in Rajasmand, located in the northwestern Indian state of Rajasthan, committed suicide as a result of the harassment and beatings he received at the hands of school staff and teachers (National Human Rights Commission [NHRC] n.d.) Elementary education is not accessible to Dalits, as illustrated by an incident in 2005 in which Ms. Jhaman (a 45-year-old woman from Tenare village in Uttar Pradesh) was chased away by the *Panchayat* secretary and village head. Ms. Jhaman had requested that her children be given registration and birth certificates and they be allowed to sit among the upper-caste children in school (Asian Legal Resource Centre n.d.).

Work

India passed the National Rural Employment Guarantee Act in 2005; however, it has not yet been implemented. It is the first national safeguard regarding the right to work (Republic of India 2006). Meanwhile, Dalits are still forced into degrading occupations, such as the manual scavenging, bonded labor, and child labor discussed previously. Child labor is also forced labor, and the National Sample Survey Organization Report of 1999–2000 estimated that there are over 10 million child laborers in India; however, unofficial sources estimate that the total number of working children is closer to 100 million. Child labor laws, wages, and safety standards are not monitored because employers bribe law enforcement officials (NCDHR 2006).

Dalits who are not forced into degrading occupations are discriminated against by means of lower wages, longer periods of unemployment, and fewer opportunities for work. Dalits have more difficulty getting hired by others because business owners normally prefer to hire those from their own caste. Some Dalits are excluded from crop processing, residential construction, and restaurant work. Dalit agricultural laborers earn less money on average, work less often, and are paid later than non-Dalit workers. In nonagricultural positions, Scheduled Castes, Scheduled Tribes, and other backward castes (e.g., Sudras) work fewer days and earn a lower daily wage than higher-caste laborers (NCDHR 2006).

Recommendations

The CERD criticized India in 1996 for its lack of protection of Dalit human rights. India did not respond for ten years, but eventually submitted a compilation of the fifteenth through the nineteenth reports to the CERD (which had been due on January 4, 1998, 2000, 2002, 2004, and 2006). The Committee made several recommendations to India at its seventieth session in 2007 regarding the amount of information provided by India, the repeal of suppressive laws, and the effective enforcement of current legislative acts. Despite India's contention that " 'caste' cannot be equated with 'race' or covered under 'descent' under Article 1 of the Convention" (Republic of India 2006, 6), the Committee maintained its position that caste-based discrimination falls within its jurisdiction. Also, India needs to address the lack of information regarding castes by providing "disaggregated data on the percentages of the Union, State and district budgets allocated for that purpose and on the effects of such measures on the enjoyment by members of Scheduled Castes and other tribes of the rights guaranteed by the Convention" (CERD 2007, 2). The Committee recommended that India repeal the Habitual Offenders Act and the Armed Forces (Special Powers) Act, which allow government agencies to search and arrest people and seize their property without procedural restraint. The CERD also noted that there are numerous human right laws already in place that need to be effectively enforced.

The CERD (2007) recommended that India fully implement existing laws designed to protect the civil, political, economic, social, and cultural rights of Indian citizens of all caste groups. The CERD made the following recommendations regarding the enforcement of civil and political rights:

1. Implement the Protection of Civil Rights Act, which gives the government the authority to punish those who practice "Untouchability" and take action against segregation in schools, residential areas, places of worship, medical facilities, water sources, and other public places (CERD 2007, 3).
2. Under the Scheduled Castes and Scheduled Tribes Act, officials should provide effective protection to Scheduled Castes and Scheduled Tribes, and mandatory training should be provided to police, prosecutors, and judges. Victims who report violent incidents should be protected from retaliation. Complaints should be registered. Offenders must be prosecuted and sentenced, and victims should be compensated. Information regarding the justice process should be collected and reported (CERD 2007, 4).
3. Reservation policies must be effectively enforced by providing safe voting conditions and allowing Scheduled Castes and Scheduled Tribes employment in all public service positions, including the judiciary (CERD 2007, 5).

The CERD (2007) made the following recommendations regarding the enforcement of ESC rights:

1. The ILO Convention No. 107 on Indigenous and Tribal Populations (1957) stipulates that tribal communities' ownership of land must be respected, and government land projects must gain the prior informed consent of the communities. Land owners must be equitably compensated for their land, and the government is to aid in the protection of tribal lands from encroachment by other parties. The Committee

gave the example of a 2002 order by the Indian Supreme Court to close the road through the *Jarawa* reserve, which had not yet been enforced (CERD 2007, 5).

2. The Scheduled Castes and Scheduled Tribes Act (1989) should be used as a means of punishing those who commit violence in land disputes (CERD 2007, 6).
3. The Recognition of Forest Rights Act of 2006 should be implemented to provide "adequate safeguard against the acquisition of tribal lands" (CERD 2007, 6).
4. Given that Scheduled Castes and Scheduled Tribes are disproportionately affected by malnutrition and diseases, they must be guaranteed equal access to "ration shops, adequate health-care facilities, reproductive health services, and safe drinking water" (CERD 2007, 7).
5. India should take effective actions toward reducing student dropout rates through the use of scholarships and grants (CERD 2007, 7).
6. Dalit children should be given nondiscriminatory access to the Mid-Day Meal Scheme and schools with competent teachers and adequate facilities (CERD 2007, 7).

Finally, the CERD (2007) made the following recommendations regarding descent-based work:

7. Forced occupations, such as manual scavenging, child labor, and debt bondage, must be addressed by the effective implementation of the "Minimum Wages Act (1948), the Equal Remuneration Act (1976), the Bonded Labour (System) Abolition Act (1976), the Child Labour (Prohibition and Regulation) Act (1986) and the Employment of Manual Scavengers and Construction of Dry Latrines (Prohibition) Act (1993)" (CERD 2007, 6).
8. The reservation policy should be extended to private employment positions.
9. Job cards should be issued under the National Rural Employment Guarantee Scheme (2005), and the effects should be measured and reported.
10. Public education and awareness campaigns should be used to promote social acceptance of the equalization of Scheduled-Caste and Scheduled-Tribe human rights.

At the international level, India has failed to meet its obligations enumerated in the Universal Declaration of Human Rights (UDHR); the International Covenant on Economic, Social and Cultural Rights (ICESCR); International

Covenant on Civil and Political Rights (ICCPR); International Convention on Elimination of All Forms of Racial Discrimination (ICERD); and the Convention on the Rights of Child (CRC), to which India is a party. India has also failed to protect Dalit workers in accordance with its obligations in the International Labor Organization Convention, which India ratified in 1958 (Hanchinamani 2004).

It is surprising to see that India, which took the initiative to secure UN consideration of the problem of apartheid in South Africa, has attained minimal success in the case of Dalits. India pressured the United Nations to take action against the South African apartheid regime, but has refused to admit that discrimination against Dalits is similar to racial discrimination (Measures taken by India for the elimination of apartheid n.d.).

Many believe there is a lack of political will to implement the laws. The rising middle class may well not want any additional competition, and the wealthy, land-owning upper-class, which is dependent on cheap labor provided by Dalits, effectively lobbied politicians not to give priority to human rights issues. As a result, the country has failed to promote human dignity or improve education among Dalits, and has failed to provide ESC rights. Frustrated with the situation, some Dalit rights activists want to hold an international forum to discuss caste-based discrimination. The Indian government, on the other hand, insists that caste is an internal matter and must be dealt with internally. According to Prashad (2001, 4), "caste … is not 'internal,' but a form of social discrimination.…" India's systematic and violent discrimination against Dalits would be an embarrassment if the matter were presented before the international community.

The question is: Can Dalits apply the provisions of the apartheid convention of 1973 to fight for their rights? The Convention has already been applied, at least theoretically, to contexts outside South Africa. The following discussion provides some insights into how its provisions can be used in the Dalits' situation.

Boyle (2003, 161) argued in favor of applying the Apartheid Convention to end Israel's suppression of Palestinians. He contends that "the absolute prohibition on apartheid is a requirement both of customary international law and of *jus cogens*—a preemptory norm of international law.…"

The following articles to the Convention are applicable in the Indian context: Article 1 (1) considers apartheid a "crime against humanity and that inhuman acts resulting from such policies and practices of racial segregation and discrimination" are crimes against the principles of international law (Boyle 2003, 161). Article 1(2) declares "criminal those organizations, institutions, and individuals committing the crime of apartheid" (161).

According to the Article II of the Convention, the term "apartheid" includes "policies and practices of racial segregation and discrimination as practiced in southern Africa," (Boyle 2003, 162) and shall apply to any inhuman acts committed for the purpose of exercising domination by one racial group over another, as well as systematic oppression. The Article lists some of the acts: "(a) denial to a member or members of a racial group or groups of the right to life and liberty of person" (162) by (i) murder; (ii) serious bodily injury or mental harm, subjecting them to torture, or subjecting them to cruel, inhuman, or degrading treatment or punishment; (iii) arbitrary arrest and imprisonment; (b) inadequate living conditions; (c) preventing a racial group or groups from participating in any political, social, economic and cultural elements of the country; and denying those groups basic human rights and freedoms, such as right to work, right to form trade unions, right to education, right to travel, right to nationality, right to freedom of movement and residence, right to freedom of expression, and right to freedom of assembly and association (163); (d) any legislative or other measures meant to segregate the population by creating a separate reserves and ghettos for any racial groups, prohibition of mixed marriages; and the exploitation of landed property belonging to a racial group or groups; (e) submitting a racial group or groups to bonded labor; and (f) persecution of organizations or people, by denying their fundamental rights and freedoms, because they oppose apartheid (163).

Dalits in India can claim that they have, and are facing, all of the atrocities prohibited in Article II of the Convention. There is documented evidence of discrimination and violence against Dalits compiled by human rights activists and the Human Rights Commission in India. Many newspaper reports published over the decades have numerous articles on inhuman treatment of Dalits by upper-caste Hindus, as well as by agencies of the criminal justice system.

Article III of the Convention places criminal responsibility, regardless of motives, on "individuals, members of organizations, and institutions and representatives of the State: when (a) they commit, participate, incite, or conspire in the commission of the acts, or (b) directly abet, encourage, or cooperate in the commission of crimes mentioned in Article II" (Boyle 2003, 164). Article III is clearly applicable to the Indian situation. As per the article, any individual, members of organizations or institutions, government or otherwise, who commit, participate, incite or conspire, directly abet, encourage, or cooperate in the commission of the crime of apartheid are international criminals. There are documented cases where individuals, including politicians, and governmental organizations have been directly involved in crimes committed against Dalits. Those individuals and members of the organizations with involvement in atrocities should be held as international criminals (165).

Article IV of the Convention states that the parties to the Convention must undertake: (a) legislative or other measure to suppress and prevent any encouragement of apartheid and punish those guilty of that crime; (b) "legislative, judicial, or administrative measures to prosecute, bring to trial, and punish" (Boyle 2003, 165) those who committed acts listed in Article II irrespective of whether those individuals live in the State or are stateless persons. Article IV creates universal jurisdiction by governments to prosecute. In the Indian context, the government has adopted legislative measures to suppress, prevent, and prosecute those who commit the crime of apartheid. However, enforcement has clearly been lax.

Article V states that persons charged with the acts listed in Article II may be tried by a competent tribunal, which may acquire jurisdiction over the accused person. Accordingly, any Indian official (or other individuals) who have committed the crime of apartheid can be prosecuted by any one of the member states who has signed the Apartheid Convention.

The international penal tribunal that has jurisdiction over apartheid crimes is the International Criminal Court (ICC). The ICC considers "the crime of apartheid" a "crime against humanity" (Boyle 2003, 166). However, some argue that the treatment of Dalits in India is not similar to the oppression of Palestinians, where the oppression is institutionalized, systematic, and racial in nature. Dalits certainly can argue, however, that caste-based oppression is, to some extent, institutionalized in India (Boyle 2003).

Article VI requires the state parties to the Convention to accept and carry any decisions taken by the UN Security Council in its efforts to prevent, suppress, and punish the crime of apartheid. Article VII requires state parties to submit periodic reports concerning legislative, judicial, and administrative efforts undertaken by the parties. Given that India became a party to the Convention in 1977, it should abide by all its provisions. Any deviations from those provisions should be strictly dealt with by member states.

Racial Discrimination of Roma/Gypsies of Europe

Racial discrimination of an ethnic group descended from nomadic Indians called "Roma" or "Gypsies" has become an issue in the international arena. The estimated 10 million Roma who live throughout Europe make up the largest, most visible, and possibly second oldest minority group after Jews (Brearley 2001). The end of communism in the former Soviet Union and the demise of the Council for Mutual Economic Assistance (COMECON) in the early 1990s resulted in massive unemployment and oppression of the Roma. Former Communist countries that have recently joined the European Union (EU) are required to ensure democracy, rule of law, human rights, and protection of minorities. However, the Roma continue to experience social exclusion and racial discrimination in terms of employment, housing, education, and other social services in both old and new EU member states (European Commission 2004).

The oppression of Romani people is best understood within its historical context. Sometime between the 3rd and 7th centuries C.E, nomadic Indians from north-west India migrated west, settling throughout Europe. The dark-skinned newcomers were unique in appearance, language, and culture, and local majority populations often valued the Roma for their skills in weaving, basket-making, and smelting, as well as their musical and equestrian talents (Fraser 1992). Some Roma in Hungary were able to work as blacksmiths, horse traders, carpenters, and barbers during the Ottoman occupation until the late seventeenth century (Human Rights Watch/Helsinki 1996). In the sixteenth century, however, Church and state authorities began anti-Roma campaigns due to the popularity of the Romanies' renowned skills in healing and fortune telling (Brearley 2001).

Anti-Roma propaganda eventually led to anti-Roma laws. Romanies were outlawed, and several countries, such as England, executed both male and female Roma. Organized Roma hunts became common in many countries, such as the Netherlands, and male Roma were sentenced to serve as chained oarsmen in royal galleys. In England, Spain, Germany, and Hungary, young children were forcibly taken from their parents and given to non-Roma families so the children would be raised in accordance with majority norms. Switzerland continued the practice of displacing Roma children until 1973. Spain, France, and Portugal enslaved the Roma and shipped them to America and Africa. Princes and monasteries in Eastern Europe treated the Roma like chattel and kept them as slaves until the 1860s (Brearley 2001). The Enlightenment tempered the harsher methods of dealing with the "Gypsy problem" during the eighteenth century (European Commission 2004). "Efforts to exterminate or expel Gypsies were gradually replaced by forcible assimilation and eradication of the Romany language and identity" (Brearley 2001, 589).

The persecution of the Roma ebbed in the nineteenth century as scholars became interested in Romani language, culture, and music, but Social Darwinism labeled Roma "noble savages." The Roma were stigmatized as racially inferior, and in 1876 Cesare Lombroso included the Roma in his description of criminal atavists in *L'uomo delinquente* (Criminal Man) (Fraser 1992, 249). Police agencies became more organized during this period and created Roma registries to track the whereabouts of Roma, because they were believed to be inherently deviant (European Commission 2004).

In the early twentieth century, there was resurgence in the use of extermination as a means of dealing with the "Gypsy nuisance" in Western Europe (Brearley 2001) when Hitler came to power in Germany (1933–45). The Roma were not only victims of racial subjugation in Nazi-occupied countries, but also in cooperative countries that covertly favored the elimination of the Roma. According to Kenrick, between 200,000 and 500,000 Roma were put to death in extermination camps by Nazis, Croats, Slovaks, Hungarians, and Romanians (cited in Brearley 2001).

Following World War II, many European nations resumed their efforts to assimilate the Roma. Western European nations attempted to incorporate the Roma into mainstream society by means of sterilization, placement of Romani children in state care, and forcible settlement of nomadic Roma. State socialism in Central and Eastern European nations called for the proletarianization of all citizens, which resulted in intense assimilation programs. For example, Poland and Czechoslovakia mandated the settlement of nomadic Roma, whereas some governments sterilized Romani women and segregated school children (European Commission 2004). Assimilation efforts also included banning political organizations, self-employment, and use of the Romani language (Brearley 2001). However, the Roma have been averse to majority conformity and assimilation and prefer to maintain their cultural beliefs (Barany 1994).

The end of communism in Eastern European countries in 1989 also brought an end to strong central governments that did not allow open discrimination, along with the end of socialistic economies that guaranteed employment, education, health care, and housing for citizens (Brearley 2001). In communist states, political ideals dictated that all citizens, including the Roma, become useful workers within society, which in turn decreased economic exclusion by providing guaranteed, compulsory employment, free medical care, and subsidized housing (Barany 1994). Some Eastern European governments (e.g., Albania, Bulgaria, Czech Republic, Germany, Hungary, Poland, Romania, Russia, Slovakia, Ukraine, and Yugoslavia) blamed the Romani people for the collapse of public order, which resulted in organized persecution, racist movements, and violence against Romani people. Widespread incidents of racial discrimination and violence in the former Eastern Bloc resulted in the Roma seeking refuge in Western European countries (e.g., Belgium, Finland, France, Germany, Ireland, Italy, the Netherlands, Norway, Spain, Switzerland, and the United Kingdom) (European Commission 2004).

Western European countries were not receptive to the Roma seeking refuge from the East. Media reports of "Gypsy invasions" legitimized discrimination against the Roma (Erjavec 2001) and triggered public panic and legislative action preventing the Roma from gaining asylum. For example, in October 1999, the Belgian government expelled Roma asylum-seekers from Slovakia based on a narrow interpretation of its obligations under international treaties, such as the International Convention on the Elimination of All Forms of Racial Discrimination (ICERD) (Cahn and Vermeersch 2000).

In July 2001, British immigration officials were stationed at Prague's Ruzyne Airport to screen passengers, and 120 people, mostly Roma, were not allowed to board flights to England. Between January and September of that same year, none of the 1,200 claims for asylum by Czech Roma citizens were accepted (Human Rights Watch 2006a). In 1992, Germany signed a treaty with Romania to repatriate 40,000 Romanian asylum-seekers, most of whom were Roma (Witte 1993).

Specific Instances of Violence

Under communism, the strong centralized government and police state suppressed overt majority intolerances of minority groups like the Roma. "Hatred of Roma, latent but suppressed under communism, can now be expressed openly. This hatred combines racism, contempt for Roma poverty, resentment for perceived past favoritism toward Roma under communism, and newly found nationalism" (Brearley 2001, 592). Racist violence reflects the ethnocentric beliefs of the majority, who exact "justice" on minority groups, such as the Roma, who are characterized as thieves, rapists, and exploiters of social welfare programs (Björgo and Witte 1993). For example, government subsidies for children are often the main source of income for the Roma due to their inability to find employment (Barany 1994). Much like violence against Dalits, community violence against the Roma is often overlooked by the police, and the police violate Roma civil rights with impunity.

Endemic aggressions and vigilantism may be in response to perceived social injustices and are committed by mobs and individuals with the tacit agreement of police. For instance, 170 Roma of Hadareni, Romania, fled for safety when they were violently attacked in 1993. Moreover, no arrests had been made even after several months although investigators claimed to have sufficient evidence against several suspects (Human Rights Watch 2006b). The Roma may be collectively penalized for the transgression of a single individual (Reemtsma 1993). In 1994, a mob of at least 800 villagers in Racsa, Romania, raided nine Roma homes and set them on fire in retaliation for two Roma teenagers who were arrested after robbing and murdering a Romanian shepherd. Thirty-eight people were arrested on only minor charges of theft, destruction, and illegal entry of a residence (Human Rights Watch 2006b). In 1997, five Roma were beaten by a mob of at least 100 people in front of the mayor's office in Sredno Selo, Bulgaria, in response to the theft of cattle. That same year, a Roma woman died after she and her 12-year-old son were attacked by four teenage boys in Slivan, Bulgaria (Human Rights Watch n.d.). In 1999, ethnic Albanians forced Serbs and Roma to leave their homes in Kosovo through the use of harassment, intimidation, beatings, abductions, arson, destruction of property, and murder (Human Rights Watch 2003b). The Albanians' ethnic cleansing campaign displaced an estimated 120,000 Roma (European Commission 2004).

Acts of violence against the Roma are often committed by a racist sect known as "skinheads." On May 1, 1995, in Kalocsa, Hungary, a small group of skinheads assaulted a Rom at a community celebration, which resulted in several Roma giving chase and being ambushed by a large group of fighting skinheads shouting racial hate speech. The police finally arrived more than two hours after the fight began, and despite eyewitness testimony, no one has been charged under Hungarian hate crime laws (Human Rights Watch/Helsinki 1996). In 2001, a Romani man was stabbed by a skinhead in Svitavy, Czech Republic. The racist gang member was a repeat offender who had received a suspended sentence for the same offense in 1997. In the town of Novy Bor, Czech Republic, a group of twenty Romani men were attacked by forty-five skinheads with baseball bats, and eight Roma were injured (Human Rights Watch 2006a).

A series of racially motivated violent acts in the town of Gyöngyös, Hungary, culminated in Molotov cocktails being used on Roma families. During the first incident on February 11, 1993, three young Roma women were battered by a group of twenty-five young men carrying brass knuckles, pipes, and baseball bats who had set out that evening to beat up some Gypsies. Eighteen defendants were charged with a minor offense of hooliganism, which completely disregarded the motivation of the attack. In July 1994, several Roma were injured when they were attacked in their home by a group of twenty to thirty young men with closely shaven heads dressed in military attire, carrying baseball bats, pipes, cables, and broken bottles. Although the media described the assailants as skinheads, the police claimed that the incident was the result of a personal conflict and denied the existence of skinheads within the community. Finally, in November of that same year, a group of fifteen youths terrorized two Roma families by attacking their homes and bombing them with Molotov cocktails. Investigators later found numerous weapons and Nazi paraphernalia in the homes of the suspects who admitted to being skinheads. The subsequent trials were closed to the press by the National Police Headquarters (Human Rights Watch/Helsinki 1996).

In addition to the aforementioned examples of police apathy, passivity, and negligence, police officials also act with brutality. In 1993, sixty policemen assaulted a Roma community in Örkény, Hungary, when local residents protested the search of a Romani home, which resulted in several injuries, including a woman who had a miscarriage. In 1994, six Roma were beaten while being interrogated during the investigation of a petty theft in Nagyfüged, Hungary (Human Rights Watch/Helsinki, 1996).

Social, Economic, and Cultural Discriminations and Recommendations

Notwithstanding the endemic violence of the majority, the end of communism has in some ways diminished the political and cultural marginalization of the Roma, but increased their social and economic exclusion (Barany 1994). The Roma now have the legal right to declare their ethnicity, create political organizations, and participate in democratic political processes; however, there is little ethnic solidarity and Roma political groups are often uncoordinated. Romani politicians vie for leadership positions are unable to work well with state officials. Government authorities are therefore able to divide and manipulate Romani leaders (Barany 2005). The Roma have become the biggest "losers" in the transition from communism to democracy (Vermeersch 2005).

The European Union (EU) has grown considerably after the fall of communism. Prior to 2004, the EU consisted of fifteen member states (Austria, Belgium, Denmark, Finland, France, Germany, Greece, Ireland, Italy, Luxembourg, Netherlands, Portugal, Sweden, and the United Kingdom). Since then, twelve Central and Eastern European countries have joined the EU (Bulgaria, Cyprus, Czech Republic, Estonia, Hungary, Latvia, Lithuania, Malta, Poland, Romania, Slovakia, and Slovenia). Croatia, the former Yugoslav Republic of Macedonia, and Turkey have also applied for membership (Europa n.d.). Soon after the admittance of most of the new member states, the European Commission (2004) published its findings regarding the situation of the Roma in Europe. In its report, the European Commission addressed the issues of economic, social, and cultural rights of the Roma, which included an evaluation of education, employment, housing, and health care.

The European Commission (2004) found that few of the member states measure the educational achievement of Roma children. They are often classified as mentally disabled and placed in remedial classes apart from mainstream students. For example, the Czech government has estimated that 75 percent of Romani primary school children were assigned to remedial schools.

Overrepresentation of Romani children in "special" schools has also been found in Slovakia, Hungary, and Bulgaria. Western European nations, such as Spain, France, and the United Kingdom, are also guilty of segregating Romani school children from the majority population. Special programs for the Roma have been funded by the European Social Fund and the Community Action Programme, but the initiatives are limited. The European Council has called for improvement in education by meeting the following five benchmarks by 2010: (1) a dropout rate of less than 10 percent; (2) a 15 percent increase in math and science graduates; (3) a minimum graduation rate of 85 percent among 22-year-olds from upper-secondary education; (4) a decrease in the illiteracy rate of 20 percent among 15-year-olds; and (5) participation of at least 12.5 percent of adults (ages 25–64) in a Lifelong Learning program.

Employment is the primary means of poverty eradication and social inclusion. According to the European Commission (2004), every member state was required to enact laws that prohibit labor discrimination based on race and ethnicity and adopt National Action Plans that reflect the EU's employment policies. As of 2003, however, the Roma were not specifically included in the National Action Plans for employment in Austria, Belgium, Finland, Germany, France, Sweden, Spain, Ireland, or the United Kingdom. The Roma remain disproportionately unemployed. In Slovakia, more than 85 percent of the Roma were unemployed in 2003, compared to an unemployment rate of less than 15 percent for the entire nation. Unemployment rates for the Roma in the Czech Republic ranged from 50 to 80 percent, whereas the unemployment rate for the general population was under 11 percent. The EU's Employment Strategy calls for an employment rate of 70 percent by 2010. The EQUAL Community Initiative is a primary EU program that has funded forty-five employment projects for the Roma; however, Denmark, Luxembourg, the Netherlands, Belgium, and Finland had not implemented any EQUAL projects by 2004.

The EU's Race Directive unequivocally bans racially motivated discriminatory practices in housing, but the issue of housing is not addressed thoroughly by the EU because it requires large financial resources. Many Roma live in slum ghettos or homes with few, if any, utilities, e.g., sewage, water, or electricity. High rates of unemployment for the Roma translate into high eviction rates due to their inability to pay rent. Many live in remote settlements that effectively segregate them from public service institutions, e.g., schools, post offices, and medical facilities. Municipalities perform massive expulsions of the Roma due to the sale of social housing developments, and because there is often a lack of public land, nomadic Roma must camp unlawfully. Lack of a permanent residence, along with a lack of personal documents (e.g., birth certificates, passports), contribute to the social exclusion of the Roma by creating a condition of "statelessness" in which they are denied citizenship and access to basic public services. Some housing programs have been successful, such as those undertaken by UN Habitat, EU Phare programme, and various NGOs. The European Regional Development Fund can provide funding for infrastructural projects, but it is unable to bear the entire financial burden of providing adequate resources for building homes throughout Europe. Therefore, it is imperative that political leaders at the national level provide municipalities with explicit guidelines regarding their obligations for providing housing for marginalized groups, like the Roma. The Romani people must be included in the planning and implementation of housing projects, which is imperative for successful social inclusion (European Commission 2004).

Racial discrimination is explicitly prohibited by the EU Race Directive in the field of healthcare, and the EU Directorate General of Public Health is responsible for developing common health indicators for measuring public health, including disease incidence and access to the health-care system. Although there is a lack of statistical data concerning Roma health, their minority and socioeconomic status indicate that they may be at greater risk for sexually transmitted diseases, HIV/AIDS infections, and drug use. The data show that the Roma have a higher prevalence of hepatitis A, hepatitis B, tuberculosis, and asthma. In 1997, 40 percent of Roma children living in several remote Spanish towns had not received any type of vaccination. Poland and Slovakia have experimented with mobile health units as a means of addressing the healthcare issue, but EU member states must implement systematic policies that would allow the Roma to receive preventative, primary, and emergency health-care services on a consistent basis. There is considerable argument that the EU should develop healthcare indicators, as well as social indicators, which specifically measure data concerning the health of the Roma population (European Commission 2004).

The European Commission (2004) concluded that the formal legislation and policies of EU members have failed to include the Roma in programs and initiatives created for the benefit of marginalized groups. Rather than assuming that the Roma are included in blanket anti-discrimination policies and social programs, the EU and member states must explicitly include the Roma in social inclusion legislation, policies, and programs. The Roma must be educated and included in policy making, implementation, and the assessment of EU and member state government processes and initiatives. There is a dire need for the EU and member states to raise awareness of the problems of anti-Romani racism and social exclusion practices. The deficiencies in the collection of ethnic and racial statistical data regarding employment, education, housing, and health-care must be addressed, as well as the evaluation of EU and national projects targeting the Roma. The EU must continue sanctions against member states that fail to pass and enforce anti-discrimination and equal employment directives.

Both the Dalits of India and the Roma of Europe have become the international "litmus test" groups for racial discrimination. They have been deprived of their political, civil, economic, social, and cultural rights by majority groups and police agencies through the use of violence and exclusion from governmental processes, civic facilities, employment, education, land, food, housing, and health care. The movements for human rights for both groups have been hindered by a lack of solidarity among political groups, yet they have advanced their causes by garnering international attention. The Dalits have managed to transform their argument from a religious issue to a descent-based work issue in the UN forum, and the migration of the Roma from Eastern and Central Europe to Western Europe has created a climate of cooperation among the member states of the European Union. The methods of marginalization and oppression of the Dalits and the Roma are strikingly similar, yet their goals for overcoming social exclusion seem to be different. Dalits share the same religion and ethnicity of the majority, and are striving for social inclusion and assimilation. The Roma, however, have resisted majority conformity and assimilation. Therefore, the Roma must be socially included while also being allowed to maintain their unique cultural beliefs.

Web Sources: Dalits

1. Center for Human Rights and Global Justice: New York City School of Law
   http://www.ohchr.org/english/index.htm
2. Constitution of India
   http://indiacode.nic.in/coiweb/welcome.html
3. Human Rights Watch: Asia
   http://www.hrw.org/doc?t=asia&c=india
4. Human Rights Watch homepage
   http://www.hrw.org/
5. India's Directory of Government Websites
   http://goidirectory.nic.in/
6. India Law & Government Law Research
   http://www.lawresearch.com/v10/GLOBAL/ZIN.HTM
7. India's National Human Rights Commission, New Delhi, India
   http://nhrc.nic.in/nhrc.asp

8. International Dalit Solidarity Network
   http://www.idsn.org/
9. National Campaign on Dalit Human Rights
   http://www.ncdhr.org.in/
10. United Nations' homepage
    http://www.ohchr.org/english/index.htm
11. United Nations Millennium Project
    http://unmillenniumproject.org/index.htm

Discussion Questions

1. Discuss the economic, social, and cultural discriminations perpetrated against Dalits.
2. Discuss the different methods used by Dalits and advocates of Dalits' rights to obtain justice within their own communities and nation. What was the reaction?
3. Discuss the Dalits' movement at the international level. How have the United Nations and other nongovernmental organizations (NGOs) argued for Dalits' human rights? How has India responded?
4. What types of programs has India used to address the economic, social, and cultural rights of Dalits, and have they been effective?
5. Discuss how the situation of Dalits' human rights could be applied to the Apartheid Convention.
6. Discuss the economic, social, and cultural discriminations perpetrated against the Roma of Europe.
7. What is European Union's role in providing assistance to the Roma?
8. What was the criticism leveled against the European Union by the European Commission regarding the Roma?

References

Artis, Ellyn, Chad Doobay, and Karen Lyons. *Economic, Social and Cultural Rights for Dalits in India: Case Study on Primary Education in Gujarat.* Workshop on Human Rights: From Grassroots Courage to International Influence, the Woodrow Wilson School of Public and International Affairs, Princeton, NJ, 2003.
Asian Legal Resource Centre. "A Supplementary Document Concerning Caste Based Discrimination in India Submitted by the Asian Legal Resource Cen-

tre: For Consideration by the United National Committee on the Elimination of Racial Discrimination, 70th Session in Geneva." Accessed September 5, 2007. http://www.ohchr.org/english/bodies/cerd/docs/ngos/ALRC-report. pdf, n.d.

Barany, Zoltan. "Living on the Edge: The East European Roma in Postcommunist Politics and Societies." *Slavic Review* 53, no. 2 (1994): 321–344.

Barany, Zoltan. "Ethnic Mobilization in the Postcommunist Context: Albanian in Macedonia and the East European Roma." In *Ethnic Politics after Communism*, edited by Zoltan Barany and Robert Moser, 78–107. Ithaca, NY: Cornell University Press, 2005.

Björgo, Tore, and Robe Witte. "Introduction." In *Racist Violence in Europe*, edited by Tore Björgo and Rob Witte, 1–17. New York: St. Martin's Press, 1993.

Bob, Clifford. 2007. "Dalit Rights are Human Rights: Caste Discrimination, International Activism, and the Construction of a New Human Rights Issue." *Human Rights Quarterly* 29 (2007): 167–193.

Boyle, Francis. *Palestine, Palestinians and International Law*. Atlanta, GA: Clarity Press, 2003.

Brearley, Margaret. "The Persecution of Gypsies in Europe." *American Behavioral Scientist* 45, no. 4 (2001): 588–599.

Cahn, Claude., and Peter Vermeersch. "The Group Expulsion of Slovak Roma by the Belgian Government: A Case Study of the Treatment of Romani Refugees in Western Countries." *Cambridge Review of International Affairs* 13, no. 2 (2000): 71–82.

Committee on the Elimination of Racial Discrimination [CERD]. "Consideration of Reports Submitted by States Parties under Article 9 of the Convention: Concluding Observations of the Committee on the Elimination of Racial Discrimination, May 5." Accessed September 6, 2007. http://www.ohchr.org/english/bodies/cerd/docs/CERD.C.IND.CO.19.doc, 2007.

Constitution of India. "Schedules." Accessed March 15, 2005. http://indiacode.nic.in/coiweb/coifiles/p04.htm, n.d.

Erjavec, Karmen. "Media Representation of the Discrimination against the Roma in Eastern Europe: The Case of Slovenia." *Discourse and Society* 12 (2001): 699–727.

Europa. "European Countries." Accessed January 20, 2008. http://europa.eu/abc/european_countries/index_en.htm, n.d.

European Commission. 2004. "The Situation of Roma in an Enlarged European Union." Accessed January 18, 2008. http://www.errc.org/db/00/E0/m000000E0.pdf, 2004.

Fernando, Franco, Jyotsna Macwan, and Suguna Ramanathan. *Journeys to Freedom: Dalit Narratives*. Mumbai, India: Popular Prakashan, 2004.

Fraser, Angus. *The Gypsies.* Oxford: Blackwell Publishing, 1992.

Goonesekere, Rajendra K.W. *Prevention of Discrimination and Protection of Indigenous People and Minorities: Working Paper.* New York: United Nations, Economic and Social Council, Sub-Commission on the Promotion and Protection of Human Rights, 2000.

Green, Maria. "What We Talk About When We Talk About Indicators: Current Approaches to Human Rights Measurement." *Human Rights Quarterly* 23 (2001): 1062–1097.

Hanchinamani, Bina B. "Human Rights Abuses of Dalits in India." *Human Rights Brief* 8, no. 2 (2004): 1–5.

Hansen, Stephen A. 2000. "Thesaurus of Economic, Social and Cultural Rights: Terminology and Potential Violations." Accessed September 12, 2007. http://shr.aaas.org/thesaurus/help.htm, 2000.

Henkin, Louis, Gerald L. Neuman, Diane F. Orentlicher, and David W. Leebron. *Human Rights.* New York: Foundation Press, 1999.

Human Rights Watch. "Bulgaria: Human Rights Developments." Accessed January 20, 2008. http://www.hrw.org/worldreport/Helsinki-06.htm, n.d.

———. "Broken people: Caste Violence against India's 'Untouchables.'" Accessed March 10, 2005. http://www.hrw.org/reports/1999/india/India994.htm, 1999.

———. "Small Change: Bonded Child Labor in India's Silk Industry." Accessed September 25, 2007. http://www.hrw.org/reports/2003/india/india0103.pdf, 2003a.

———. "Harassment and Violence against Serbs and Roma in Kosovo." Accessed January 20, 2008. http://hrw.org/english/docs/1999/08/03/serbia1022.htm, 2003b.

———. "Czech Republic: Human Rights Developments." Accessed January 20, 2008. http://www.hrw.org/wr2k2/europe8.html, 2006a.

———. "Romania: Human Rights Developments." Accessed January 20, 2008. http:www.hrw.org/reports/1995/WR95/HELSINKI-12.htm, 2006b.

———. "Hidden Apartheid: Caste Discrimination against India's 'Untouchable.'" Accessed September 12, 2007. http://www.hrw.org/reports/2007/india0207/india0207web.pdf, 2007.

Human Rights Watch/Helsinki. *Rights Denied: The Roma of Hungary.* New York: Author, 1996.

India Together. "Nandigram, an Atrocity on Dalits." Accessed September 11, 2007. http://www.indiatogether.org/2007/may/soc-nandigram.htm, 2007.

International Covenant on Economic, Social and Cultural Rights. University of Minnesota, Human Rights Library. Accessed August 4, 2009. http://www1.umn.edu/humanrts/instree/b2esc.htm, 1966.

International Secretariat of the World Organization against Torture (OMCT) and the Coordination Office of Housing and Land Rights Network of Habitat International Coalition (OMCT/HIC-HLRN). "Joint Urgent Action Appeal: Forced Eviction of 7,000 Dalits in India, July 24, 2003." Accessed September 25, 2007. http://www.hlrn.org/cases_files/IND-FE%20%20240703.doc, 2003.

Izzo, John F. "'Dalit' Means Broken." *America* 192 (2005): 11–15.

Jenkins, Rob, and Eimar Barr. (2006). "Social Exclusion of Scheduled Caste Children from Primary Education in India." Accessed November 24, 2008. http://www.unicef.org/policyanalysis/files/Social_Exclusion_of_Scheduled_Caste_Children_from_Primary_Education_in_India.pdf, 2006.

Larson, Desi. "India." In *Child Labor: A Global View*, edited by Cathryne L. Schmitz, Elizabeth K. Traver, and Desi Larson, 101–112. Westport, CT: Greenwood Press, 2004.

"Measures Taken by India for the Elimination of Apartheid." Accessed September 11. 2005, http://www.anc.org.za/ancdocs/history/solidarity/indian, n.d.

Menon, Sudha Venu. "Grass Root Democracy and Empowerment of People: Evaluation of Panchayati Raj in India." *Munich Personal RePEc Archive*, paper no. 3839, June 17. Accessed September 11, 2007. http://mpra.ub.uni-muenchen.de/3839/01/MPRA_paper_3839.pdf, 2007.

Ministry of Health & Family Welfare. "2005–2006 National Family Health Survey (NFHS-3): National Fact Sheet India." Accessed July 10, 2009. http://www.nfhsindia.org/pdf/IN_WICT.pdf, n.d.

Minority Rights Group International. "Less Protection for Those Who Change Religion Will Deepen Discrimination for India's Most Marginalized Group, Says MRG." Accessed September 11, 2007. http://www.minorityrights.org/?lid=671, 2006.

National Campaign on Dalit Human Rights [NCDHR]. "Communities Across the World Discriminated against on the Basis of Caste, or Work and Descent." Accessed February 14, 2005. http://www.dalits.org/globalcastesystems.htm, n.d.-a.

_____. "Dr. Ambedkar's Interventions on Caste Discrimination before the British Round Table Conference, 1930–1932." Accessed March 15, 2005. http://www.dalits.org/AmbedkarViews.html, n.d.-b.

_____. "Broken Promises and Dalits Betrayed: Black Paper on the Status of Dalit Human rights." Accessed February14, 2005. http://www.dalits.org/Blackpaper.html, n.d.-c.

_____. "Alternate Report to the Joint 15th to 19th Periodic Report of the State Party (Republic Of India): To the Committee on the Elimination of Racial Discrimination." Accessed September 6, 2007. http://www.ohchr.org/english/bodies/cerd/docs/ngos/shadow-report.pdf, 2006.

National Crime Records Bureau. "Crime in India." Accessed September 15, 2007. http://ncrb.nic.in/crimeinindia.htm, n.d.

National Human Rights Commission. "Death of Officiating Headmaster of Government School, Rajasmand: Rajasthan." Accessed September 11, 2007. http://nhrc.nic.in/DalitCases.htm#No15, n.d.

National Sample Survey Organization, Ministry of Statistics and Programme Implementation Government of India. "Employment and Unemployment among Social Groups in India, 2004–05." Accessed November 22, 2008. http://mospi.gov.in/national_data_bank/pdf/516_final.pdf, 2006.

Neelima, B. N. "Atrocities on Dalits: Need for Human Rights Education." In *Human Rights and Criminal Justice Administration*, edited by R. Thilagaraj, 121–134. New Delhi, India: A. P. H. Publishing, 2002.

OneWorld South Asia. *Social Inequality in MDGS: Disparities in Levels and Progress Among Social Groups in India.* Paper presented at the meeting of the International Multidisciplinary Conference on Equality and Social Inclusion in the 21st Century: Developing Alternatives, Belfast, Northern Ireland, February 2006.

Prashad, Vijay. "Cataract of Silence: Race on the Edge of Indian Thought." Paper Prepared for the United Nations Research Institute for Social Development (UNRISD) Conference on Racisms and Public Policy. Durban, South Africa, 2001.

Pur, Ananth K. "Rivalry or Synergy? Formal and Informal Local Governance in Rural India." *Development and Change* 38 (2007): 401–421.

Reemtsma, Katrin. "Between Freedom and Persecution: Roma in Romania." In *Racist Violence in Europe*, edited by Tore Björgo and Rob Witte, 194–206. New York: St. Martin's Press, 1993.

Republic of India. "Reports Submitted by States Parties under Article 9 of the Convention." Accessed September 6, 2007. http://www.ohchr.org/english/bodies/cerd/cerds70.htm, 2006.

Thorat, Sukhadev. "Hindu Social Order and the Human Rights of Dalits." Accessed March 10, 2005. http:www.indiatogether.org/combatlaw/issue4/hinduord. 2002.

Vermeersch, Peter. "Marginality, Advocacy, and the Ambiguities of Multiculturalism: Notes on Romani Activism in Central Europe." *Global Studies in Culture and Power* 12 (2005): 451–478.

Witte, Rob. "Racist Violence: An Issue on the Political Agenda?" In *Racist Violence in Europe*, edited by Tore Björgo and Rob Witte, 139–153. New York: St. Martin's Press, 1993.

Chapter 13

International Terrorism

Jeffrey Ian Ross & Michael Stohl

Introduction

Since 9/11, both the phenomenon and study of international terrorism—also known as transnational terrorism—has become more prominent in government, media, scholarly, and educational circles. This chapter provides a brief overview of international terrorism, including domestic and international responses to the phenomenon. This approach includes a discussion of laws, treaties, intelligence, and military-led activities. The chapter also delineates some of the possibilities for the future of international terrorism.[1]

We should recognize that although terrorism is not a new kind of political violence or crime, during the last six decades terrorism has become a major problem in domestic and international politics. Although some political actors (e.g., individuals, groups, countries, and geographic regions) are more affected than others, almost every country in the world has experienced terrorism. Moreover, terrorism is not a static phenomenon as new players utilize terrorism and compete for scarce resources (e.g., the attention spans of the public, news media, and government). Predictably, terrorism and reactions to it has ebbed and flowed. This is largely the result of previously established and well known terrorist organizations that have disbanded and new terrorist groups that have taken their place. These new actors acquired and used improved communications and more destructive technology in their operations. Before analyzing the subject of terrorism, we must ask the logical and necessary question: What is terrorism?

---

1. The reader is advised that the number of acts of international terrorism pales in comparison to incidents of state and domestic terrorism (see Ross 2000a; 2000b; Stohl 2006).

Defining Terrorism

Numerous people and organizations have attempted to define terrorism. Indeed, the proper definition of terrorism has led to considerable debate, in part because there are several drawbacks to developing a definition that would lead to widespread agreement (Ross 2006, 2–5). Thus, no internationally accepted definition of terrorism exists. In the early 1980s, Alex Schmid conducted an exhaustive analysis of fifty experts' definitions of terrorism. Concluding that there was no "true or correct definition" (Schmid 1983, 110), Schmid developed a five-part consensus definition:

> Terrorism is a method of combat in which random or symbolic victims serve as ... *target[s] of violence....* Through [the] previous use of violence or the credible threat of violence other members of that group ... are put in a *state of chronic fear (terror)....* The victimization of the target ... is considered extranormal by most observers ... [which in turn] creates an ... audience beyond the target of terror.... The purpose of [terrorism] ... is either to immobilize the target of terror in order to produce disorientation and/or compliance, or to mobilize secondary *targets of demands* (e.g., a government) or *targets of attention* (e.g., public opinion) (Schmid 1983, 111; emphases in original).

Schmid's definitional quest highlighted many of the difficulties in achieving a consensus definition and earned much respect among scholars and policy makers (Ross 2003). However, for the purposes of this analysis we prefer Stohl's (1983) more parsimonious definition: The purposeful act or the threat of the act of violence to create fear and/or compliant behavior in a victim and/or audience of the act or threat. This definition, when applied within the political context, eliminates the characterization of the perpetrator or actor and focuses on the act itself and includes not only acts of violence, but threats (implying credible threats) of violence as well, so that all acts of instrumental violence that intend to influence an audience (through fear of further violence if they do not comply with whatever demands are being made) would be included.

It is also crucial in all discussions of terrorism to understand that we must distinguish the victims of the violent act from the targets (the audience of the violence) and in so doing distinguish terrorism from "simple" acts of violence (e.g., armed robbery). In this sense terrorism (state or oppositional, domestic or international) may be seen as a process (see Walter 1969) in which (1) threatened or perpetrated violence is directed at some victim; (2) the violent actor intends that violence induce terror in some witness who is generally distinct from the victim (the victim is instrumental); and (3) the violent actor

Table 1 Typology of Political Terrorism

		Direct involvement of nationals/citizens more than one state	
		Yes	No
Government Controlled or Directed	Yes	Interstate/State-sponsored terrorism	State terrorism
	No	International/Transnational terrorism	Domestic terrorism

intends or expects that the terrorized witness will effectuate a desired outcome, either directly (in which case the witness is the target) or indirectly (in which case the witness and the target are distinct; the witness is also instrumental). What distinguishes terrorism from other acts of violence are its instrumentality and its targets. It distinguishes direct and indirect victims and it is crucial to understand that whether we are examining insurgent or state terrorism, how the audience reacts is as important as the act itself and the instrumental victims who are its direct casualties.

Types of Terrorism

Much like definitions of terrorism, typologies of terrorism have proliferated over the past four decades. One of the most popular, flexible, and useful typology is the one developed by Mickolus (1981). He distinguishes four types of political terrorism—interstate, domestic, state, and international/transnational—based on degrees of government control, direction or influence, and whether nationals/citizens of more than one state are involved, as either perpetrators or victims (Mickolus 1981) (see Table 1).

International and transnational terrorism are actions carried out by autonomous non-state actors and affect nationals of at least two states (when, in 1972, for example, the Palestinian terrorist group Black September traveled to Munich, kidnapped then killed Israeli athletes).[2]

---

2. According to Johnson (1982), "Analysts invented the terms 'international terrorism' to refer to terrorist actions carried out by individuals or groups controlled by a sovereign state (e.g., Cuba or Libya) and 'transnational terrorism' to refer to terrorist actions carried out by basically autonomous actors (e.g., the Baader-Meinhoff gang)" (162). Over the years, this distinction has been ignored.

Tracing the Historical Trajectory and Contemporary Trends

Introduction

Both state and oppositional political terrorism have occurred since the dawn of human history. But the nature of this type of political violence and crime has changed over time, evolving from localized and domestic activities to regional and international events (Laqueur 1977; Weinberg and Davis 1989, Chapter 2). Consequently, terrorism has become an experience shared by many individuals, organizations, and states.

Although domestic terrorism dates back to tribal modes of political organization, and most acts of terrorism remain local (not to mention the highest rates of casualties), international terrorism is the product of the modern state and has been made much more possible by the advances in technology and transportation that have accompanied the processes of globalization. More specifically, international terrorism has been synonymous with world politics since the 1960s. Since 1968, there has been a sustained increase in the number of terrorist incidents, terrorists, and terrorist groups. Terrorism in this period has been more violent (as measured by number of individuals injured and killed). Many new groups are better organized and more sophisticated than those operating in previous historical eras. Terrorism since the 1960s is also better documented and studied. Moreover, there is more public, political, and national security awareness of terrorism.

Rapoport (2003) has argued that there have been four waves of terrorism in the past 125 years. In general, there are important differences between the terrorism of the contemporary period and previous terrorist waves. The transformation in communication and transportation capabilities have created much greater opportunities for terrorists to operate in a much wider set of locations while guaranteeing them a real-time global audience for their most spectacular events and terrorists have adapted their tactics to take advantage of both the latest technical changes to influence audiences and to operate globally as target opportunities arise.

In general, we can divide the history of terrorism during the past six decades even further, into four overlapping time periods. During the 1960s and extending into the 1970s, a number of revolutionary/nationalist-separatist and left-wing terrorist groups operated. From the mid-1970s and into the 1980s a handful of right-wing terrorist organizations came to public attention. Some, but not all, of the groups engaged in international terrorism. Although many of these organizations, particularly those connected to unresolved ethno-nationalist conflicts, still exist, since the 1980s most of the new groups that emerged have been dominated by religious fundamentalism concentrating in the Middle East and Asia. Authorities also highlighted the rise of "narco-terrorism" in South America, in which it was charged that terrorist groups and drug lords made common cause in criminal operations, which enabled the financing of terrorist operations. A similar pattern emerged in the post-Soviet era in the Caucasus and other locations along the "Old Silk Road, the traditional route of smugglers and traders for more than a millennium" (Picarelli and Shelly 2002).

The 1980s: State-Sponsored, Religious Fundamentalist, and Single-Issue Terrorism

By the mid-1980s, largely based on circumstantial evidence put forth by Claire Sterling (1981),[3] many Western politicians, and most vociferously the Reagan administration, claimed that a disproportionate amount of terrorism was sponsored, if not directed, by the Soviet Union with ties to Cuba, Iran, Iraq, Libya, and North Korea. This created quite a political clamor. One of its residual effects was to force the U.S. State Department to create a list, updated each year, of both terrorist groups and countries that support terrorism.

In 1979, the Shah (King) of Iran was overthrown by a loose coalition of students, Islamic fundamentalists, and small business owners. The Ayatollah Khomeini became the leader of Iran and established the first modern Islamic theocracy (i.e., government rule based on religion). At the same time, the U.S. embassy in Tehran was occupied by so-called student activists and the remaining embassy staff held hostage. This lead to a full year of intense media coverage of "America Held Hostage, Day XXX," a true made-for-television spectacular, which helped end the reelection hopes of Jimmy Carter and that morphed into the long-running ABC late-evening news program "Nightline" at the conclusion of the crisis.

By the mid-1980s, a number of Islamic fundamentalist and Middle Eastern terrorist groups formed. Three of the most prominent are Hezbollah, Islamic Jihad, and Hamas. Both Hezbollah (*Shia*) and Hamas (*Sunni*) draw their main strength from and focus upon the particular territory in which they are based (southern Lebanon and the Gaza Strip, respectively). In addition to their fiery rhetoric and social service activities within their base areas, they have carried out numerous suicide bombings, many of which have taken place in Is-

---

3. See the critique of Sterling in Stohl (1984). In particular, Sterling was "fed" much of her information as part of a CIA disinformation campaign—the information was part of "an old, small-scale CIA covert propaganda operation" (see Woodward 1987, 125–27).

rael. Some of them have been supported by the post-1979 Iranian regime, and others, particularly in the name of their social service activities, by a number of Arab regimes.

During the 1980s, analysts also noted the presence and increase in the number of individuals and groups in Western countries that resorted to terrorism in furtherance of narrow political goals or "single-issue terrorism" (Smith 1998). Three issues attracted radicals who resorted to terrorism: animal rights (e.g., Animal Liberation Front), pro-life/anti-abortion, and protection of the environment (e.g., Earth First). Individuals and groups wedded to these causes have engaged in violence ranging from property damage to assault, bombings, and murder. In these cases there is a fine line between direct action (typically confined to property damage) and political terrorism.

The 1990s: Narco-Terrorism

In the early 1990s, "narco-terrorism" was the focus of some terrorism experts. The term referred to the "use of drug trafficking to advance the objectives of certain governments and terrorist organizations"—identified as the "'Marxist-Leninist regimes' of the Soviet Union, Cuba, Bulgaria, and Nicaragua, among others" (Hoffman 1998, 27). Regimes in less-developed countries, communist states, and powerful illegal drug cultivators and traffickers formed alliances with terrorist groups for mutual benefit. Regions that have generated interest by politicians, practitioners, and scholars in the narco-terrorism phenomenon are South America, Middle East, Africa, and Asia, each of which contains countries that are major cultivators, distributors, and processors of drugs. However, the majority of interest focused on Latin America and on Colombia in particular, where the cocaine cartel needed protection and rebel forces wanted resources (primarily money, in this case). This relationship, sometimes labeled "convergence theory," combined the essential elements of not only terrorism, but also organized crime and state sponsorship, especially when the state (or those in positions of power) was corrupt. In many respects, ideological concerns were placed on hold and access to money prevailed (Hoffman 1998; Picarelli and Shelly 2002; Schmid 1996).

The 2000s: Dark Networks

Finally, a relatively new term, "dark networks," is being used to describe alliances (temporary and/or long standing) that may exist among terrorist groups, criminal organizations, and regional warlord factions (Raab and Milward 2003). In some cases it is believed that these "alliances" employ the Internet to help coordinate their activities (Arquilla and Ronfeldt 2001). Because these networks are "dark" the nature of their actual linkages is the subject of considerable debate and it is not clear if their interactions are simply opportunity-driven "normal" criminal exchanges of money for services (e.g., weapons, transport, and safe haven) or if they represent an emerging organizational form (see Stohl and Stohl 2007).

Contemporary Trends in Terrorism

In order to get a better sense of the amount of international terrorism it is wise to consult empirical evidence and review recent trends. The following section reviews data sources and trends.

Data Sources[4]

Prior to the mid-1970s, the majority of information on terrorism was presented in case studies of particular individuals, groups, and movements that used terrorism and in analyses of countries that experienced terrorism. In the mid-1970s, however, some scholars, private research companies, and governmental departments attempted to systematically collect data on the actions and characteristics of terrorism. The majority of these efforts were rudimentary quantitative studies, which, unlike descriptive studies, allow us to speak with greater precision about terrorist phenomena. The most basic statistics for the study of terrorism are "events data," i.e., important information gathered on each incident over a specified period of time.

This approach to the study of terrorism has allowed researchers and policy makers to understand the frequency of terrorism and, occasionally, to test hypotheses. The two most widely used data sources on terrorism are the RAND/St. Andrews dataset and ITERATE. ITERATE has always focused on international terrorism events, whereas the RAND dataset concentrated on international events until 1997 and on both domestic and international events from 1998 on.

The reader is asked to keep in mind that these databases are composed of only a small percentage of the sum total of terrorist events. Transnational or international terrorism is relatively infrequent as compared to domestic terrorism; there are very few accessible domestic terrorism databases and no comprehensive cross-national domestic terrorism database. Compiling these databases is extraordinarily resource intensive.

In April 2005, the U.S. State Department formally announced that it would no longer disseminate their "Patterns of Global Terrorism" statistics.[5] Instead,

---

4. This section builds on Ross (2004; 2006).

5. In June 2004, it came to public attention that the data presented in the 2003 annual report had serious problems and had underreported the amount of terrorism that occurred.

this function would be handed over to the National Counter-Terrorism Center, which is part of the Central Intelligence Agency. The data were managed by the National Memorial Institute for the Prevention of Terrorism (MIPT), located in Oklahoma City. This dataset was composed of data from the RAND Terrorism Chronology 1968–1997; RAND-MIPT Terrorism Incident database (1998–present); Terrorism Indictment database (University of Arkansas), and DFI International's research on terrorist organizations.

Since spring 2008, when the federal government decided to discontinue MIPT's Terrorism Knowledge Base (TKB) terrorism database, the general public no longer has access to easily digestible data on oppositional political terrorism. One must go either to the NCTC database, copy each act of terrorism in the database, and then perform basic descriptive statistics, or download the University of Maryland's START database and do the same. This is asking quite a bit of the average person, student, and expert.

The statistics presented below are based on a variety of sources, including information from the State Department's "Patterns of Global Terrorism" reports, and the now inactive MIPT's TKB data base.

Annual Statistics of International Events

Between 1968 and June 30, 2005, there were approximately 9,718 international political terrorist events, ranging from a low of 103 incidents in 1969 and 2000 to a high of 440 in 1985 with an average of about 259 incidents each year (MIPT, 2005). The prevailing impression given by the media, public officials, and some experts concerned with international terrorism, however, is that terrorism is on the increase. For the most part, increases are relative to the time period under investigation; increases are not linear, as media accounts might imply. In 2004, the most recent complete year for which statistics are available, the total number of international terrorist incidents was 330—56 events more than in 2003. However, not all events are of the same magnitude and intensity. For example, the magnitude of the attacks on the World Trade Center and the Pentagon on September 11, 2001, might lead to the conclusion that there has been a steep increase in the number of terrorist events overall, which is not actually the case; the peak years were actually 1985 and 1991.

The U.S. Department of State took responsibility, but argued, however, that in the interests of getting the report to the printer in time, data collection efforts were suspended before the year's end. On June 22, 2004 the revised database was released, and it is from this report the figures discussed in this chapter are drawn.

Geographic Spread

Although terrorism is experienced throughout the world, some regions currently suffer a disproportionate amount of the world's international terrorism. Regions experiencing the largest number of terrorist activities change almost every year. Between 1968 and 2005 (June 30), for example, the Middle East received the brunt of terrorist attacks (6,743), and East and Central Asia incurred the fewest incidents (198) (MIPT, 2005). About 20 countries account for between 75 and 90 percent of all reported incidents. The top three countries that experience the largest amount of terrorism (approximately 75 percent) are, in descending order of frequency: Israel (including the Gaza Strip and the West Bank), Pakistan, and Colombia. We should also note that is often the case that authorities (a well as scholars) are ambivalent on whether to categorize incidents as domestic or international. For example, during the first five years of the U.S. war in Iraq the question of whether the bulk of terrorist incidents were domestic or international was clouded by the Bush administration's need, on the one hand, to demonstrate that Al-Qaeda (in the guise of the renamed group Al-Qaeda in Iraq), was international, while arguing that the administration was reducing the number of international attacks overall.

Targets

Since the 1960s, the range of terrorist targets has expanded. Although spectacular events make us think that most of the terrorist attacks are aimed at people and increasing numbers of casualties, the profile has not changed much; more than half of the events continue to be unclaimed bombings. A considerable amount of public and media attention has been directed toward the possibility of terrorist attacks on nuclear facilities and the potential resulting fallout. Indeed, although there have been breaches of security at these places, most of the incidents were carried out by anti-nuclear protestors trying to halt or delay the construction of new nuclear facilities rather than destroy existing ones and should be considered protests, not terrorism.

Americans, the British, the French, Israelis, and Turks account for approximately half of all the nationalities victimized by international terrorists.[6] The individuals attacked include diplomats, military personnel, tourists, businesspeople, students, journalists, children, nuns, priests, and the Pope. The

---

6. Why is this the case? Israel, because of its seemingly unending conflict with the Palestinians, and the Americans, French, and British largely because of their transnational corporations.

MIPT / TKB statistics indicate that since 1968 the majority of targets have been private citizens and property (3821) rather than government officials, buildings, or property.

Between 1968 and June 30, 2005, out of the 22,457 incidents, there were a total of 75,245 injuries and 29,642 fatalities (MIPT 2005). The 2004 State Department figures indicate that approximately 16 percent (2,998 individuals) of the victims were U.S. citizens. By the end of 2001, largely because of the events of September 11, the number of deaths rose to approximately 3,000. Nevertheless, few terrorist incidents involve fatalities. Suicide bombings, though newsworthy, are typically rare. Thus, Brian Jenkins's 1979 observation, "terrorists want a lot of people watching rather than a lot of people dead" (Jenkins 1979, 169) remains the continuing distinguishing feature for terrorist groups who, by definition, seek to influence an audience much wider than the immediate victims.

Tactics

It is interesting that although new technologies have altered the ease of communication, and transportation capabilities have made it easier to enlarge the geographic scope of terrorist attacks, and weapons and explosives have become more powerful, terrorists continue to operate with a fairly limited repertoire of attacks. Seven basic tactics have accounted for 97 percent of all terrorist incidents: bombings (13,217), assassinations (2,182), armed assaults (3,657), kidnappings (1,652), arson (868), hijackings (232), and barricade and hostage incidents (201) (MIPT 2005). In short, terrorists blow things up, kill people, or seize hostages. Every incident is essentially a variation on these activities. Bombings appear to be the most deadly.

Although the use of chemical, biological, radiological, and nuclear weapons is a topic of constant concern, bombings of all types continue to be the most popular terrorist method of attack. Approximately 50 percent of all international events are bombings (and this has been consistent for the past 40 years). This is followed, in terms of numbers, by armed attacks, arsons, and kidnappings. In addition, the number of arson incidents, bombings, attacks on and assassinations of diplomats has increased in the past few years.

Although the majority of bombs are simple incendiary devices, terrorists have made and often use more sophisticated explosive weapons. Rudimentary bombs in particular are easy to construct. Bombings also typically involve the least amount of group coordination and thus are one of the easiest terrorist tactics to employ. In addition, they are relatively cheap; the group can get a considerable amount of "bang for its buck" through using bombs, particularly if their main intent is to demonstrate the capacity to attack rather than to create large numbers of casualties.

Terrorist Groups

Some terrorist organizations show considerable endurance, operating for a lengthy period of time, replacing their losses, preparing for new attacks, and turning into semi-permanent subcultures. Other groups have fleeting existences. For example, Crenshaw (1991) examined the longevity of seventy-six terrorist organizations. She found that many groups exhibited remarkable stability and tenacity, but almost half of the organizations no longer existed or no longer committed acts of terrorism. However, at least 10 groups—including al-Fatah, the Popular Front for the Liberation of Palestine-General Command, and Euszkadi Ta Askatasuna (Basque Fatherland and Freedom, ETA)—were in operation for twenty years (Crenshaw 1991). The MIPT database (2005) lists 792 terrorist organizations, with probably no more than 200 are active in any given year. Although many of the new emerging groups since Crenshaw's research may be characterized, as per classification of Rapoport (2003), as part of the fourth wave of religious fundamentalist groups, the most enduring organizations continue to be those that are tied to ethno-nationalist causes such as ETA, Fatah, and the recently apparently defeated Tamil Tigers.

Over the past 37 years most terrorist incidents are attributed to "other group" or "unknown group." This means that the organizational affiliation could not be positively identified. In situations where the organization was positively identified, Hamas (446), ETA (387), and the National Liberation Army (in Columbia) (282) have committed the greatest number of international incidents. The groups that are responsible for the highest number of fatalities are Al-Qaeda (3,521), Hezbollah (821), Tanzim Qa'idat al-Jihad fi Bilad al-Rafidayn (a Palestinian group) (615), and Hamas (577).

Combating Terrorism

Introduction

A variety of strategies are used in combination to prevent, deter, respond to, and combat terrorism. States react to terrorists and their groups through antiterrorist and counterterrorist measures. The former responses are proactive (or defensive) actions designed to prevent or deter terrorist incidents from happening and include, among other things, special legislation (Alon 1987). The latter are reactive (or retaliatory) measures a government takes after terrorism has occurred, and usually includes the use of force, as in air strikes or selective assassination.[7] Most observers and practitioners blur the distinction and use these terms interchangeably (Townshend 2002, 114–15).

We must also recognize that in any security environment, tradeoffs must be made between the risk of attack, including its possible effects, and the cost of preventing the incident (Sloan 1993). Most security decisions are made in a political and economic context where reason often is subjugated to expediency (Schneier 2003). If, for example, you examine the history of emergency legislation passed in Canada, the United Kingdom, and the United States, one of the threads that connects these events is that they were passed immediately in the wake of major terrorist incidents without the benefit of calm and rational discussion.

Contextual Issues

The reactions to terrorism in general, and to counterterrorism in particular, come from a host of political actors (e.g., policy makers, practitioners, law enforcement and national security personnel, and citizens) with competing resources, agendas, and interests. Interpreting and balancing what these constituencies want and need is no easy task. One central question is whether government agencies should or must adhere to the rule of law, or—given the unusual nature of terrorism—whether they may circumvent state-based constitutions and internationally mandated human-rights documents and practices by responding with extraordinary force. The dilemma is not easily resolved in a manner that makes all parties happy but we would agree with the conclusions of the Club of Madrid's (the organization of the former presidents and prime ministers of the world's democracies) Summit on Terrorism that the rule of law should be adhered to even under the most difficult circumstances if democracies are to be successful in combating terrorism in the long run (see Club de Madrid 2005).

Another question asks whether we should approach terrorism as a policy problem to be addressed primarily by government organizations that deal with issues of justice and law enforcement, or as a security issue to be answered by bureaucracies that oversee national security and armed conflict. The answer will determine, to a large extent, which state agency should take the lead role. In the United States, the natural choices have been between the Federal Bureau of Investigation (FBI) and the Central Intelligence Agency (CIA). Prior to September 11, 2001, the FBI was responsible for monitoring major crimes, particularly those that affected more than one U.S. state, including domestic

---

7. This seems to be a regular feature of the current Palestinian-Israeli conflict.

terrorism. The law enforcement approach of the FBI seeks to gather evidence to enable the capture of suspected perpetrators to bring them to justice. The CIA, on the other hand, was considered responsible for gathering intelligence that would aid foreign policy, including monitoring external threats like terrorists from abroad and assisting in the "combating" of terrorism. Traditionally, if terrorism occurred in the United States, it was an FBI matter; if it was external to the country, it was a CIA concern. After September 11 and the declaration of the "war on terror," the traditional debate intensified as the war was propagated primarily by the secretary of defense and the armed forces with the intelligence and justice agencies in subsidiary roles.

With the creation of the Department of Homeland Security (DHS), much of the debate moved inside the newly created organization, but the Obama administration has now reversed the Bush administration approach and emphasized a law enforcement rather than war fighting approach and eliminated the "war on terror" lexicon from its vocabulary (Goldsmith 2009). In addition, because local law enforcement is often a "first responder" (the first point of contact in a crisis), it's appropriate role in terrorism and the question of jurisdictional primacy also creates tensions between national and local authorities in the context of a crisis.

The primary opportunity to control terrorism is in the country of origin, at the hands of their own governments. This is done through local, state, and federal police forces, or a public security agency, e.g., the Canadian Security Intelligence Service in Canada or the DHS in the United States. Things become more complex at the global level. One of the international bodies that have taken up the responsibility in the fight against terrorism is Interpol, the international police agency. As some analysts have pointed out, however,

> Interpol's effectiveness is limited by several factors. First although it maintains a data bank on criminal activity around the world, it is under-funded and understaffed. Second, it is generally not supposed to get involved in political problems—and most international terrorist activities are highly political. The European Union has developed a European police force (Europol) with similar aims. However, it will be years before Europol has the political, technical, and financial support needed to tackle not only organized crime, but terrorism as well (Duncan, Jancar-Webster, and Switky 2002, 283).

The United Nations has also attempted to impose itself in the combating of terrorism but often the underlying political issues that gave rise to the conflicts associated with the terrorism prevent the United Nations from engaging in effective actions or support for other regional associations and nations.

Problems in Combating Terrorism

Some of the difficulties that stand in the way of countering the terrorist threat include a lack of a definition commonly accepted by government agencies, and a lack of cooperation—not only among state agencies with an interest in monitoring and responding to terrorism, but also among countries that may have helpful intelligence. Most of these entities are reluctant to share information, especially national security agencies, unless they believe that it is in their own short-term political interests.

Countries and their national security agencies must also carefully balance citizens' individual freedoms in their pursuit of terrorists. Deviations from established rules of law and repressive actions by state agencies lead to the alienation of the citizenry and to questions of the legitimacy of the existing regime. In reprisals for terrorist actions, there is always the possibility of the unwarranted killing and injury of innocents often labeled as collateral damage by the perpetrators to "soften" the public relations impact (Ross 2000a; 2000b). This outcome is an all-too-familiar consequence of the United States' involvement in Afghanistan and Iraq, and was also evident during the summer of 2005 with respect to the United Kingdom's shoot-to-kill policy after the London bombings.

Finally, measuring the effectiveness of combating terrorism is a thorny issue. According to Townshend (2002), "[i]f we look for precise evaluation of the effectiveness of antiterrorist policies we find it is surprisingly thin on the ground. Very few indeed of the many writers on terrorism have produced a statistical analysis of key countermeasures" (133). Policy makers and practitioners would be well advised to keep these factors in mind when they comment on or propose and implement measures designed to combat terrorism. As Enders and Sandler (1993) make clear the choice of one counterterrorism strategy may have the unintended effect of making other targets and strategies more attractive to terrorists because their first choice of target or tactic has been made more difficult.

Typical Measures

As with the general study of terrorism, scholars have developed categories to combat terrorism. Pillar (2001) identifies five instrument sets: diplomacy, criminal law, financial controls, military force, and intelligence. These responses include reactive as well as proactive strategies, e.g., the hardening of physical targets, including port security (for people and products); the creation of better financial regulatory and forensic policies; weapons control and acquisition policies; creation and use of "third forces" (i.e., special military units or SWAT teams to handle terrorist situations); changing police policies and practices regarding the use of force; development and use of antiterrorist technology; approval and implementation of new international treaties; passage and enforcement of new laws against terrorism, both nationally and internationally; the increased use of intelligence and surveillance of suspected terrorists and their supporters; military responses; and decisions as to whether to pursue these strategies in a unilateral or multilateral context. Associated with these policies are decisions that address the relationship of "normal" criminal law and the prosecution of terrorist crimes as well as the sentencing and incarceration policies that accompany a successful prosecution.

These methods to combat terrorism should be interpreted as a menu from which counterterrorist practitioners can choose. The power to experiment with as many strategies as possible—while at the same time keeping track of the costs and benefits—will inevitably minimize the future occurrence of terrorism. What remains, however, are regular systematic analyses and testing of counterterrorist strategies (e.g., Hewitt 1984) as terrorism evolves and counterterrorist methods improve.

The post-9/11 bombings mean that we must continue to harden our societies against terrorist attacks, and expand our efforts domestically and internationally to take down and destroy terrorist networks. We need to protect vulnerable targets, improve cooperation with our allies, and minimize or address grievances held by groups that have difficulties with the United States, the United Kingdom, and their allies. This includes increasing transatlantic cooperation in a number of key areas, e.g., penetrating terrorist organizations, arresting or eliminating terrorist operatives, destroying the links between transnational crime and terrorism, and halting recruitment into terrorist organizations or providing realistic alternatives to young men susceptible to these groups' appeals (Ross 2005a; 2005b).

The Bush administration created the "war on terrorism" to characterize its counterterrorism approach. Components of the approach included the creation of the DHS and the wars in Afghanistan and Iraq. Despite the administration's argument that "war on terror" kept the United States safe from further attacks, much has been written on why the war metaphor is a counterproductive rhetorical and tactical strategy (e.g., Alam 2005; Heymann 2003; Lakoff 2001; Smith 2002). Scholars, pundits, and even military leaders have argued that the war metaphor undermined the ability of the United States to manage the problem of terrorism in the long term and, in particular, made it difficult to bring suspects to justice. In addition, many have argued that the Bush administration's approach harmed the standing of the United States internationally and its ability to work multilaterally on the problem of terrorism. President Obama changed the rhetoric to "overseas contingency operations" in the initial days of his administration and has argued for a law enforcement rather than military approach to the problem of counterterrorism (Alam 2005; Heymann 2003; Lakoff 2001; Smith 2002).

Successes and/or Failures in Fighting Terrorism at Home and Abroad

The Bush administration, and in particular former Vice President Cheney, have argued that they were very successful in fighting terrorism because there were no further attacks on U.S. soil. This claim, however, is very difficult to judge. In 2003 former Secretary of Defense Donald Rumsfeld wrote, "Today, we lack metrics to know if we are winning or losing the global war on terror. Are we capturing, killing or deterring and dissuading more terrorists every day than the madrassas and the radical clerics are recruiting, training and deploying against us?" (Rumsfeld 2003, ¶ 7). As Stohl (2010) has argued, this simple body-count approach to measuring the war on terror is the most prevalent in governmental and media discussions. However, when considering the effectiveness of counterterrorism, appropriate measures must also include the perceptions of the various audiences affected and their attitudes to both terrorism and counterterrorism in their names. Thus, when one looks beyond the number of attacks on U.S. soil to the numbers of terrorist attacks worldwide, the declining standing of the United States in public opinion polling since the War on Terror began, with the particularly negative spikes surrounding the release of the Abu Ghraib photos and the incarceration of prisoners at Guantanamo, the verdict becomes far more difficult to render (Stohl 2010).

The Future of Terrorism

Two basic and competing perspectives characterize the future of terrorism: optimistic and pessimistic. In terrorism studies, in an optimistic scenario, the frequency, intensity, and lethality of terrorism will subside until terrorism becomes a far less frequent occurrence. In the pessimistic alternative, terrorism will increase, and terrorists will eventually resort to utilizing more dangerous and destructive weapons. In all likelihood the reality will be somewhere in the middle between these positions (Ross 2006: Chapter 9).

Future Causes of Terrorism

Around the world, small civil wars, population growth, natural disasters, conflicting values, and limited or unequal access to food, unemployment and underemployment, and depletion and destruction of natural resources are prime motivators for mass migrations, refugee problems, and unaddressed grievances. These conditions will encourage what Holden-Rhodes and Lupsha (1993, 5) have characterized as "grey area phenomena": "threats to the stability of sovereign states by non-state actors and non-governmental processes and organizations." Over time, these factors, and the organizations that choose to exploit them for political gain, will place a greater burden on governments, and individuals and groups whose needs are not addressed by countries are more likely to resort to terrorism to make themselves heard.

All these factors, in combination, may fuel the future course of terrorism. But which individuals or groups might in the future continue or resort to terrorism?

Future Perpetrators

The challenge posed by alienated Islamic fundamentalists will not subside in the near future. In countries with majority or significant minority Islamic populations, with republican governments (e.g., Algeria and the Philippines) or monarchies (e.g., Jordan and Saudi Arabia), governments are being challenged by indigenous religious fundamentalists who resort to violence to back up their demands. In addition to the local sources of conflict in these societies, the Palestinian/Israeli conflict will continue to provide opportunities to link the local with the international and stoke a sense of resentment within the aggrieved Muslim community.

There is also fear that fringe members of the anti-globalist movement may, for a variety of reasons, strike out with terrorism. The violent (but nonterrorist) outbursts in Seattle (1999), Québéc City (2001), Gothenburg (2001), and Genoa (2001) during meetings of the World Bank and the International Monetary Fund have led some analysts to believe that some of the anti-globalist cadre will turn to terror tactics in the future. In addition, since the 1990s, particularly in the former Soviet republics, the number of nationalist and ethnic groups seeking independence from their home countries has increased. Tensions among certain nationalities (especially among Indians, Sikhs, and Pakistanis) are bubbling below the surface. The Pakistani Army, in their efforts to root out suspected Taliban and Al-Qaeda members from the isolated tribes along the border with Afghanistan, is creating anti-Pakistani sentiments. Some doomsayers have also prophesized the possibility of the emergence of the "third position," "a coalition between the extreme left and extreme right, between nationalism and socialism" (Laqueur 2003, 220). Within this scenario these two ideological camps may find enough common ground to temporarily suspend their antagonism towards each other and form a short-term alliance to achieve a mutual goal.

Finally, others worry that individuals and small groups with narrow issues from the ecology (Nilson and Burke 2002), animal-rights (Smith 1998), and anti-abortion movements may also resort to terrorism if opportunities arise. A new development in terrorist identity is that these violent actions are increasingly being committed by criminally, psychologically, and socially hardened but inexperienced youth with their own agendas. In sum, the number of possible perpetrators with grievances is considerable.

Future Targets

A considerable amount of recent public dialogue has been devoted to the possibility of cyberterrorism (e.g., Weimann 2004). There is much confusion in the discussion as the term is used to include everything from terrorists using the Internet "ranging from psychological warfare and propaganda to highly instrumental uses such as fundraising, recruitment, data mining, and coordination of actions" (Weimann 2004, 1), as well as including attacking critical computer networks, destroying power transmission capabilities, air controller networks, nuclear facilities, and other critical infrastructure as well as disabling a country's ability to counter terrorist groups. Although the terrorists do take advantage of the cyber infrastructure for communication, propaganda, and organizing, there have yet to be any actual cyberterrorism events and most analysts believe that critical infrastructure has been the subject of sensible security measures (Green 2002; Stohl 2007).

Solutions

Although we cannot predict the number of future terrorist attacks or their location, there are policy options that could be chosen to minimize the possibility of terrorism and/or lessen the amount of property damage, injuries, and deaths when this kind of political violence strikes.

What Won't Help?

Although bilateral treaties and cooperation among countries do occur in the fight against terrorism, the problem of sharing intelligence not only inside a country, between its own agencies, but also beyond its borders, between countries, looms large. It is doubtful that this problem will be consistently solved in the near future. Government agencies, because of turf wars, scarce resources, competition, or simply suspicion of the intelligence collection procedures and products, are not willing to trust outsiders.

It is also often the case that diplomatic and economic sanctions are often not sufficient in and of themselves to deter countries from helping terrorist groups (or oppositional actors that engage in violence) when states deem those oppositional actors to be acting in their interest. Whether it is a "pariah" state such as North Korea, or a state engaged in a long-running conflict with a geographically adjoining state such as Pakistan and India, or a superpower such as the United States or the former Soviet Union, states will support terrorists (whom they often define as freedom fighters) if it is perceived to be in their national interest (Stohl 1984).

Technological fixes, although often making it more difficult to attack a particular target, might assist in deterring or detecting possible terrorists in some cases but often will simply point the potential terrorist to a new less protected target (Enders and Sandler 1993). Law enforcement utilizes multiple screening systems, including driver's licenses, passports, fingerprints, and so on but all the systems are tied to the quality of the training of the screeners and the willingness of the public (and policy makers) to tolerate the inevitable delays and inconvenience that any screening system imposes. As fear of an immediate attack, tolerance for inconvenience declines markedly amongst both.

Another idea, proposed in the immediate wake of 9/11, was for national ID cards to be issued. This suggestion was hotly debated, its civil liberties infringements highlighted, and ultimately rejected as redundant. Finally, target hardening will not deter the most dedicated individuals from attacking. But until more sophisticated antiterrorist measures are taken, it is the least risky first step in an antiterrorism strategy.

What May Help?

What is going to win the day in the fight against terrorism? Clearly, a multipronged approach is most appropriate.

One way of minimizing future attacks is, if discernable and relatively painless, to address the legitimate grievances of the terrorists (Reeve 1999, 264). In April 2003, the United States finally announced that it would remove the nearly 5,000 troops that have been stationed in Saudi Arabia since the 1991 Gulf War. Although it is not completely clear that this has led to a cessation of anti-American terrorist attacks, it is probably a step in the right direction.

Another important improvement would be the timely collection and analysis of intelligence, so that attacks can be prevented and perpetrators caught (Clarke 2004). But technologically gathered intelligence can only do so much. Thus, in terms of intelligence, countries will need to rely more on good informants and the cooperation of the communities within which terrorists seek safe haven. National security agencies' inability to cultivate appropriate sources and their lack of expertise in appropriate foreign languages make it difficult for them to obtain detailed and credible information on terrorist groups, especially when compounded by the secretive nature of antiterrorist organizations (Baer 2003) and the often closed and ethnic and clan-based societies within which many long-standing groups are based and organized.

In any case, the intelligence needs to be gathered in a manner that protects civil liberties, although not in a manner that gives terrorists an unfair advantage. States are also well advised to build a functional national database to track suspected terrorists and to allow criminal justice agencies to develop the appropriate infrastructure for it to be useful. At a lower level, the personal motivations of law enforcement officers are often neglected; clearly, those officers who are truly attentive and care about their jobs are more likely to catch the "bad guys." Research needs to be initiated to determine what particular qualities or skills these individuals have and then try to improve the skills of current employees or seek out new hires with these qualities.

Tolerating Terrorism

Finally, although terrorism has created a considerable amount of controversy and has cost governments and corporations substantial resources, perhaps there a tolerable level of terrorism with which a society can live (Gal-Or 1991). For example, during the 1960s and 1970s, citizens in advanced industrialized countries were constantly reminded through the media, educators, and personal experience that street crime was increasing. This created a furor of public indignation and governmental responses that manifested in a "war on crime." Although the rate of crime has increased and decreased in a cyclical fashion since those times, and the methods by which we gather crime data and how we interpret it have been debated, the crisis of *response* seems to have abated, or been replaced by "the war on terrorism." No one has seriously posed the question of whether or not there are tolerable levels of violence that we can live with (Gal-Or 1991). Terrorist attacks are disruptive to the normal functioning of the government's, businesses', and individuals' daily lives. However, policy makers and practitioners, as much as possible, need to avoid simplistic responses that can create a more dangerous environment or lead to needless expenditure of resources.

Researchers, policy makers, and practitioners need to be cautious about going down blind alleys or targeting as terrorists those individuals and groups who engage in legitimate advocacy, protest, and dissent. Needless to say, we must recognize that, in some constituencies, there is absolutely nothing the United States or any other country can do. In this case, neither accommodation nor eradication of terrorist enclaves will entirely eliminate this most salient form of political violence and crime. About the best we can do, at the very least, in this scenario is use our power to be informed, to seek out reliable information, and to question that which seems confusing or based on faulty reasoning while adopting sensible policies that make it harder for attacks to succeed and build cooperation with other nations to share information that might make attacks less likely.

Web Sources

1. Federal Bureau of Investigation on counterterrorism is available at: http://www.fbi.gov/terrorinfo/counterrorism/waronterrorhome.htm
2. Central Intelligence Agency and the war on terrorism is available at: https://www.cia.gov/news-information/cia-the-war-on-terrorism/index.html
3. Federal Emergency Management Agency, general information on terrorism is available at: http://www.fema.gov/hazard/terrorism/info.shtm
4. UN action to counter terrorism is available at: http://www.un.org/terrorism/
5. Memorial Institute for the Prevention of Terrorism is available at: http://www.mipt.org/

Discussion Questions

1. Why is developing a definition of terrorism difficult?
2. When did international terrorism become an issue for governments?
3. Why is international terrorism a concern for governments?
4. How can governments combat international terrorism?
5. What are three future targets in international terrorism?

References

Alam, Shahid M. "The Meaning of the Grand Metaphor for War. Terrorism: America Defines its Targets." *Counterpunch*, July 25, 2005. Accessed August 4, 2009. http://www.counterpunch.org/2005/07/25/terrorism-america-defines-its-targets/.

Alon, Hanan. "Can Terrorism be Deterred? Some Thoughts and Doubts." In *Contemporary Trends in World Terrorism*, edited by Anat Kurtz, 125–131. New York: Praeger, 1987.

Arquilla, John, and David Ronfeldt, eds. *Networks and Netwars: The Future of Terror, Crime and Militancy.* Santa Monica, CA: RAND, 2001.

Baer, Robert. *See No Evil: The True Story of a Ground Soldier in the CIA's Fight against Terrorism.* New York: Three Rivers Press, 2003.

Clarke, Richard. *Against All Enemies.* New York: Free Press, 2004.

The Club de Madrid Series on Democracy and Terrorism. June 8, 2005. Accessed August 4, 2009. http://english.safe-democracy.org/causes/the-club-de-madrid-series-on-democracy-and-terrorism-.html.

Crenshaw, Martha. "How Terrorism Declines." *Terrorism and Political Violence* 3, no. 1 (1991): 69–87.

Duncan, Raymond W., Barbara Jancar-Webster, and Bob Switky. *World Politics in the 21st Century.* New York: Longman, 2002.

Enders, Walter, and Todd Sandler. "The Effectiveness of Anti-Terrorism Policies: Vector-Autoregression-Intervention Analysis." *American Political Science Review* 87, no. 4 (1993): 829–844.

Gal-Or, Noemi. *Tolerating Terrorism in the West: An International Survey.* New York: Routledge, 1991.

Goldsmith, Jack. "The Cheney fallacy: Why Barack Obama is Waging a More Effective War on Terror than George W. Bush." *New Republic,* May 18, 2009. Accessed July 29, 2009. http://www.tnr.com/politics/story.html?id=1e733cac-c273–48e5–9140–80443ed1f5e2.

Green, Joshua. "The Myth of Cyberterrorism." *Washington Monthly,* November 2002. Accessed August 4, 2009. http://washingtonmonthly.com/features/2001/0211.green.html.

Hewitt, Christopher. *The Effectiveness of Anti-Terrorist Policies.* Lanham, MD: University Press of America, 1984.

Heymann, Philip. *Terrorism, Freedom, and Security: Winning Without War.* Cambridge, MA: MIT Press, 2003

Hoffman, Bruce. *Inside Terrorism.* New York: Columbia University Press, 1998.

Holden-Rhodes, Jim, and Peter Lupsha. "Grey Area Phenomena: New Threats and Policy Dilemmas." *Criminal Justice International* 9, no.1 (1993): 11–17.

Jenkins, Brian M. "The Potential for Nuclear Terrorism." In *Studies in Nuclear Terrorism,* edited by Martin H. Greenberg and August R. Norton, 170–171. Boston: G. K. Hall, 1979.

Johnson, Chalmers. *Revolutionary Change.* Stanford, CA: Stanford University Press, 1982.

Lakoff, George. "Metaphors of Terror." *In These Times,* October 29, 2001. Accessed June 6, 2006. http://www.press.uchicago.edu/News/911lakoff.html.

Laqueur, Walter. *Terrorism.* Boston: Little, Brown, 1977.

_____. *No End to War: Terrorism in the Twenty-First Century.* New York: Continuum, 2003.

Memorial Institute for the Prevention of Terrorism (MIPT). "Terrorism Knowledge Base." Accessed June 30, 2005. http://www/tkb.org/, 2005.

Mickolus, Edward. *Combating International Terrorism: A Quantitative Analysis.* PhD diss., Yale University, 1981.

Nilson, Chad, and Tod Burke. "Environmental Extremists and the Eco-Terrorism Movement." *ACJS Today* 24, no. 5 (2002): 3–5.

Picarelli, John T., and Louise Shelly. "Methods Not Motives: Implications of the Convergence of International Organized Crime and Terrorism." *Police Practice and Review: An International Journal* 3, no. 4 (2002): 305–318.

Pillar, Paul R. *Terrorism and U.S. Foreign Policy.* Washington, D.C.: Brookings Institution Press, 2001.

Raab, Jörg, and H. Brinton Milward. "Dark Networks as Problems." *Journal of Public Administration Research and Theory* 13, no. 4 (2003): 413–439.

Rapoport, David. C. "The Four Waves of Rebel Terror and September 11." In *the New Global Terrorism: Characteristics, Causes, Controls,* edited by Charles W. Kegley, Jr., 36–59. Upper Saddle River, NJ: Prentice Hall, 2003.

Reeve, Simon. *The New Jackals.* Boston: Northeastern University Press, 1999.

Ross, Jeffrey Ian. *Controlling State Crime* (2nd ed.). New Brunswick, NJ: Transaction, 2000.

Ross, Jeffrey Ian, (ed.). *Varieties of State Crime and Its Control.* Monsey, NY: Criminal Justice Press, 2000b.

_____. "Defining terrorism: An international consensus, a critical issue after 9/11." In *Encyclopedia of World Terrorism,* edited by F. G. Shanty and R. Picquet, 12–16. Armonk, NY: M. E. Sharpe, 2003.

_____. Taking stock of research methods and analysis on oppositional political terrorism, *American Sociologist* 35, no. 2 (2004): 26–37.

_____. "Post 9/11: Are We Any Safer Now?" In *Terrorism: Research, Readings, and Realities,* edited by L. L. Snowden and B. C. Whitsel, 380–389. Upper Saddle, NJ: Prentice Hall, 2005a.

_____. "Reacting to 9/11: Rational Policy and Practice versus Threat-of-the-Week Syndrome." In *After 9/11: Terrorism and Crime in a Globalized World,* edited by G. Walker and D. Charters, 306–321. Joint Publication of the University of New Brunswick's Centre for Conflict Studies and Dalhousie University's Center for Foreign Policy Studies, 2005b.

_____. *Political Terrorism: An Interdisciplinary Approach.* New York: Peter Lang, 2006.

Rumsfeld, Donald. "Rumsfeld's War-on-Terror Memo." *USA Today,* October 16, 2003. Accessed February 1, 2006. http://www.usatoday.com/news/washington/executive/rumsfeld-memo.html.

Schmid, Alex P. *Political Terrorism: A Research Guide to Concepts, Theories, Data Bases and Literature.* New Brunswick, NJ: Transaction, 1983.

_____. "The Links between Transnational Organized Crime and Terrorist Crimes." *Transnational Organized Crime* 2, no. 4 (1996): 40–82.

Schneier, Bruce. *Beyond Fear: Thinking Sensibly about Security in an Uncertain World.* New York: Copernicus Books, 2003.

Sloan, Stephen. "U.S. Anti-Terrorism Policies: Lessons to be Learned to Meet an Enduring and Changing Threat." *Terrorism and Political Violence* 5, no. 1 (1993): 106–131.

Smith, Brewster M. "The Metaphor (and Fact) of War." *Peace and Conflict: Journal of Peace Psychology* 8 (2002): 249–258.

Smith, Davidson (Tim) G. "Single Issue Terrorism." *Commentary,* 74(Winter 1998). Publication of the Canadian Security Intelligence Service. Accessed August 2, 2009. http://www.pa-aware.org/who-are-terrorists/pdfs/C-17.pdf.

Sterling, Claire. *The Terror Network: The Secret War of International Terrorism.* New York: Holt, Rinehart, and Winston, 1981.

Stohl, Michael. *The Politics of Terrorism* (2nd ed.). New York: Marcel Dekker, 1983.

_____. National interests and state terrorism *Political Science* 36, no. 2 (1984): 37–52.

_____. *The State as Terrorist: Insights* and Implications. *Democracy and Security* 2, no. 1 (2006): 1–25.

_____. "Cyber terrorism: A Clear and Present Danger, the Sum of All Fears, Breaking Point or Patriot Games." *Crime, Law and Social Change* 46, no. 4–5 (2007): 223–238.

_____. "Winners and Losers in the War on Terror: The Problem of Metrics." In *Coping with Contemporary Terrorism: Origins, Escalation, Counter Strategies and Responses,* edited by Rafael Reuveny and William R Thompson, 349–368. Albany: State University of New York Press, 2010.

Stohl, Michael, and Cynthia Stohl. "Networks of Terror: Theoretical Assumptions and Pragmatic Consequences." *Communication Theory* 17, no. 2 (2007): 93–124.

Townshend, Charles. *Terrorism: A Very Short Introduction.* New York: Oxford University Press, 2002.

Walter, Eugene V. *Terror and Resistance: A Study of Political Violence with Case Studies of Some Primitive African Communities.* New York: Oxford University Press, 1969.

Weimann, Gabriel. *How Modern Terrorism Uses the Internet.* Washington, D.C.: U.S. Institute of Peace, 2004.

Weinberg, Leonard, and Paul B. Davis. *Introduction to Political Terrorism.* New York: McGraw-Hill, 1989.

Woodward, Bob. *Veil: The Secret Wars of the CIA, 1981–1987.* New York: Simon & Schuster, 1987.

Chapter 14

Transnational Corruption in the 21st Century: Context and Countermeasures

Michaelene Cox

Introduction

One of the leading issues of the millennium is undoubtedly the internationalization of crime. Here we are speaking of illicit activities that are performed across national borders or, if committed in one country, will affect others. These include offenses such as smuggling of weapons, drugs and other goods, human trafficking and sex slavery, piracy, terrorist activities, and cybercrime. Transnational crimes also include those that violate international norms or values, such as crimes against humanity, genocide and war crimes (Mueller 1999; Hill 2005; Dandurand 2007). This lawlessness is compounded by the role that corruption generally plays in enabling these exploits. Indeed, a significant challenge to criminal justice systems everywhere is curbing corruption itself. The magnitude of global corruption seems daunting, with mixed outlooks about the ability of domestic and international efforts to stymy its scope and impact. This chapter provides an overview of corruption as criminal behavior. A summary of its typologies, causes, and consequences prepares the reader for appreciating the contemporary nature of, and countermeasures to, the phenomena of transnational corruption. We might begin by considering general views about the definition and extent of corruption. Examples of corruption include bribery, kickbacks, embezzlement, and fraud. Is it becoming worse? A look at recent news reports, public opinion polls, and country reports suggest that the fight against corruption appears bleak. We have little evidence of positive trends in curbing transnational corruption, despite optimism among some observers about domestic and international efforts.

Contextualizing Corruption

Virtually every academic treatise on the topic of corruption today begins with a caveat—there simply is not a universally accepted definition, primarily because the concept is subject to different interpretations across time and culture. Certainly, it is an age-old problem in both Western and non-Western societies. Some of the most ancient writings document the problem of corruption, with perhaps the earliest found on a hieroglyphic inscription dated from the reign of Egyptian Pharaoh Haremheb (circa 1306–1292 BCE). The decree specifies punishments for those involved with fraudulent practices, and the abuse or theft of people or goods meant for the royal palace (Redford 2001). Again from antiquity, we hear from an Indian statesman and philosopher, Kautilya (370–283 BCE), who detailed forty ways to embezzle the government and even then hinted at transnational corruption by addressing a connection between trade and corruption. Commenting on the problem in a treatise to the king, he writes:

> (The king) shall protect trade routes from harassment by courtiers, state officials, thieves and frontier guards ... (and) frontier officers shall make good what is lost ... Just as it is impossible not to taste the honey or the poison that finds itself at the tip of the tongue, so it is impossible for a government servant not to eat up, at least, a bit of the king's revenue (Kangle 1969, 91).

While Kautilya argues for greater administrative strictness and control, he is pessimistic about curbing illicit behavior. He adds, "[J]ust as fish moving under water cannot possibly be found out either as drinking or not drinking water, so government servants employed in the government work cannot be found out (while) taking money (for themselves)" (Kangle 1969, 91). But for some early Western political philosophers like Aristotle (384–322 BCE), corruption is a pathological activity and more than embezzlement of public funds; it is a "general disease of the body politic" (Barker 1946, 373). We find that Machiavelli, a sixteenth-century Florentine, brings together these concepts of corruption by addressing two sorts. He deliberates on the attitudes and behaviors of a corrupt state, as well as that of depraved individuals (Shumer 1979). Thus, we might examine a type of political system as corrupt in itself, such as a republic with its citizens, leaders and institutions altogether participating in an iniquitous structure, or look at individuals participating alone or in organized criminal groups. This latter focus on nefarious individual or subgroup behavior is found in most contemporary analyses of corruption.

Definitions

Over time, corruption becomes a recurrent theme in discourses about good governance with nearly all discussants first energetically tackling the dilemma of defining corruption. Most definitions reflect such malfeasance as a social or political dysfunction (Vargas-Hernandez 2011), although contemporary definitions of corruption illustrate a wide divergence in the interpretation and scope of the phenomenon. Observers often remark that search for a precise definition of corruption compares to the exhausting and futile pursuit of the Holy Grail (Cox 2008). We can look to Webster's College Dictionary and find a long list of perturbing descriptives for the noun: corruption is moral perversion; depravity; dishonesty; debasement; putrefaction; and rottenness (Random House 2010). Consequently, whether local or global, archaic or contemporary, corruption is a phenomenon that generally refers to a transgression of law and/or morality (Pardo 2004; Nuijten and Anders 2007). The legal approach to viewing an act as corrupt considers whether or not civil or criminal law on a particular matter is broken. If there is no law prohibiting the behavior, performance of the act may be unethical but not corrupt (Gardiner 1993). For example, until passage of the Foreign Corrupt Practices Act in 1977, it was not unlawful for U.S. companies or citizens to bribe foreign officials. Such acts of bribery may have been viewed as unscrupulous and wrong from a moral perspective, but nevertheless were not corrupt from the legal perspective and so not subject to prosecution. Here then is a simple classification that distinguishes acts as corrupt based on legal or moral traditions. For purposes of this chapter, we will examine transnational corruption from legal frameworks.

Lack of consensus in defining corruption means there is no universally agreed-upon typography of the phenomenon. Classification schemes vary because there are multiple dimensions of corruption. A popular approach to sorting the concept is in terms of the sector in which the activity occurs; that is, as public or private. Our quest here is not to settle for an all-embracing definition of corruption but to understand some of the assorted ways that individuals, groups, states, and institutions may subvert the rule of law and so obstruct international justice and stability.

Public Corruption. Public corruption, also popularly called political corruption, focuses on the undermining of public trust by a government official. This includes civil servants and anyone holding a legislative, executive, administrative or judicial office, whether they are paid or not, or elected, appointed, or hired. Corruption is the misuse of power tied to official duties. A three-prong approach frequently taken to classifying political corruption centers on the public interest, the market, and public office (Heidenheimer 1989). Here, one variation of the definition of public corruption finds that the corrupt public official is one "induced to take actions which favor whoever provides the rewards and thereby does damage to the public and its interest" (Friedrich 1966, 74). Deciding what is public interest, especially in a tightly integrated global community and in modern pluralistic societies composed of special interest groups, can be ambiguous and open to interpretation. A second definition of public corruption is to define it based on exchange principles, so that a corrupt public official is one who relies on his position to bring him maximum personal gains. The description reveals a rational motivation for corrupt behavior. Definitions of corruption using this approach are usually broad, because they may incorporate a variety of nuances. For example, corrupt exchanges might include, among other things, undue influence. One social scientist thus defines political corruption as "an extra-legal institution used by individuals or groups to gain influence over the actions of the bureaucracy ... to a greater extent than would otherwise be the case" (Leff 1989, 389). Perhaps more frequently embraced, however, is a third approach which defines political corruption as the deviation of public office norms, often expressed as

> ... behavior which deviates from the normal duties of a public role because of private-regarding (family, close private clique), pecuniary or status gains; or violates rules against the exercise of certain types of private-regarding influence. This includes such behavior as bribery (use of reward to pervert the judgement of a person in a position of trust); nepotism (bestowal of patronage by reason of ascriptive relationship rather than merit); and misappropriation (illegal appropriation of public resources for private-regarding uses) (Nye 1967, 419).

There appears less ambiguity in defining political corruption in terms of public office duties. This widely-employed definition also incorporates elements of the former two approaches; it refers to the maximizing of gain, as well as to the subversion of public concerns by private interests (Cox 2008). However, even this concept of political corruption is troublesome. Critics say that cultural bias creeps into the definition, because public office norms in all countries are not alike, and not all subjected to Western-style legislative processes that define and enforce those norms. In some developing states, the notion that public duty and private interest are distinct is a foreign concept. Public office is often an acceptable means for self-enrichment, and public accountability is sometimes less important than loyalty and obligations to extended family or ethnic groups (Mbaku 1996; Hao 1999). For instance, the customs of gift giving and patronage vary in propriety from country to county; it may be culture that distinguishes a bribe from a gift. It appears that a separation of the public and private spheres lies at the heart of Western concepts of corruption (Theobald 1990).

Using public opinion as a basis for determining what is political corruption may avoid such bias in definitions. In this way, an act is corrupt if the local culture or society determines it to be so. Nevertheless, problems arise from this scheme, too. Perhaps elite and mass opinions differ, or perhaps what constitutes illegal behavior changes as readily as government administrations. It is not clear what constitutes public opinion any more than it is clear what constitutes public interest. Different groups may have unique perspectives on what is and what is not specifically a corrupt act, but there is no dispute that corruption itself denotes illegitimate or wrongful behavior. Reports on the incidences and perceptions of political corruption generally reflect those judgments about public behavior. Further, taking a comparative approach to the study of political corruption poses minor difficulty because legal standards of appropriate public behavior in nearly all countries today derive substantially from Western traditions (Bayley 1966; Nye 1967; Klitgaard 1987). It is important to note, however, that these legal standards may or may not reflect cultural values. As still more developing countries adopt anticorruption programs based on Western norms, the corruption literature addresses the cultural relativity argument less often.

Despite the challenges faced by researchers and practitioners in formally defining political corruption, and the shortcomings found in any single interpretation of the concept, most studies generally converge upon one serviceable definition. Drawn essentially from the public-office-norms approach introduced by Nye, it refers to illegal administrative behavior. Misuse of government power may take the form of bribery, embezzlement, fraud, kickbacks, or extortion, for example. Some definitions of political corruption exclude certain public activities, such as police brutality or intimidation. Others include misconduct by law enforcement officers as corrupt if the act is designed for career advancement, such as falsifying evidence to secure convictions, or for personal financial gain, such as soliciting bribes for not reporting unlawful activities. In the face of dissimilar classifications and descriptions, many scholars and governmental and nongovernmental organizations fall back on The World Bank's straightforward definition of political corruption as "the abuse of public office for private gain" (World Bank n.d.-a). When linked to the state, the illegal use of political authority is regarded as especially insidious in its ability to perpetuate widespread effects in domestic and international spheres. Public corruption may certainly foster transnational criminal activities when broadly defined as thus.

Private Corruption. Private sector corruption is also seen as an aberration of laws with potentially equal deleterious effects. There is often overlap between the public and private sector when government officials and company employees are both embroiled in an illegal act, but here we look specifically at corruption as it is committed by businesses or non-governmental organizations. One commentator cleverly notes that essentially there is little difference. "In the private sector, the consequences of fraud and corruption are borne, in general, by two parties: investors in a company and clients of a company. In the public sector, the consequences of fraud and corruption are borne similarly, except that for investors, read taxpayers, and for clients, read citizens" (Vegter 2012, ¶8). However, most scholars attempt to establish a clear distinction between the two, particularly when discussing corruption in developed countries. Challenges in effective law enforcement persist in those countries where lines between laws and social practices are not clearly established (McNab and Bailey n.d.). This ambiguity between private and public spheres is frequently linked to high levels of corruption (Johnston 2004; Wedel 2002).

Corporate corruption refers to illegal acts committed by individuals on behalf of a business or nongovernmental entity. Those entities, however, are also subject to various domestic and international laws because apart from their representatives, they have separate legal personalities themselves and are liable for criminal actions. Accordingly, both natural persons and corporations are held accountable for the same kind of transgressions. It is important to remember, however, that laws vary between state jurisdictions. Some corporate activities may be viewed as ruthless or injurious, and even in violation of civil or administrative law, but not be regarded as criminal in all jurisdictions. Insider trading is not illegal in all jurisdictions, for example. Coining the term "white-collar crime" in the mid-twentieth century, Sutherland addresses class-based offenses which we generally associate with corporate crime (Sutherland 1949). These may include intentional or unintentional regulatory violations, only some of which would be regarded as corruption today. Just as there are countless approaches to defining and classifying corruption, so there are with white-collar crime. This exemplifies the complex and slippery nature of corruption. The U.S. Federal Bureau of Investigation, for instance, defines white-collar crime as "those illegal acts which are characterized by deceit, concealment, or violation of trust and which are not dependent upon the application or threat of physical force or violence. Individuals and organizations commit these acts to obtain money, property, or services; to avoid the payment or loss of money or services; or to secure personal or business advantage" (USDOJ 1989, 3). Some of these illegal acts include embezzlement, bribery, forgery, cyber-crime, violation of intellectual property rights, money laundering, racketeering, and fraud. Like public sector corruption, private sector corruption can weave a tight thread of illicit activities across state borders.

Causes and Consequences

There is a voluminous, and yet still flourishing, body of research devoted to investigating the causes and consequences of various dimensions of corruption. Attempts to better understand the complexities of domestic and international corruption, along with mounting anticorruption efforts, have spawned an "industry" in which increasing interest and resources are devoted to those causes (Sampson 2010). Still, the literature includes mixed empirical evidence and does not definitively resolve many academic and policymaking debates about the associations between corruption and quality of governance, levels of economic development, other kinds of criminal activities, armed conflict, and so forth. Demands for further study continue to swirl about our heads. After all, there is no consensus on how to define corruption; the practice is by nature secretive and difficult to measure; and further, the possible influence of one factor must be evaluated in light of other stimuli. These challenges continue to spur the industry. We have seen that corruption is not a new phenomenon, yet it has attracted considerable attention of late. There are several reasons to explain the renewed interest. In part, a heightened awareness of corrupt activities sparks this interest; new information technologies and data-gathering methods, more rigorous monitoring and reporting, and less public tolerance for government and corporate malfeasance increases exposure of corruption. Once the shroud cast by the Cold War lifted, there was less reluctance to talk about the matter. What had been essentially regarded as taboo and ignored, especially when it pertained to politically strategic states, is now a topic of concern in all camps. The post-Communist years brought with them systemic changes in many countries that weakened or nullified political, legal, and social institutions. These transitions expand opportunities for widespread corruption in a myriad of ways. Conspicuous examples of corrosive effects following the shift from command economies to free market economies are in Eastern Europe and Russia where corruption is now pervasive and seemingly irrepressible. By all accounts, however, no country or region is exempt from corruption scandals. Corruption emerged as an international issue most visibly in the early 1990s, when numerous governmental and nongovernmental organizations, most prominently The World Bank, International Monetary Fund, and Organization for Economic Cooperation and Development (OECD), placed the matter on their agendas for discussion, and for fostering anticorruption reform. Likewise, some effects of global integration arguably may be responsible for this apparent surge in corruption. Contact is often more frequent between countries with little corruption and those with a high level, and an integrated world economy lends itself to the perception that common market forces are a contagion for further corruption (Cox 2008). It is probable that bureaucratic or institutional self-interest, the professionalization of grassroots movements, and concurrent international interest in related issues such as human rights and environmental protection also intensifies the focus on corruption (Sampson 2010). In this era of "corruption eruption," the subject found its way more frequently into theoretical and empirical literature as well. At the cusp of the millennium, more than 200 journal articles were published on corruption in 1999 alone, which was four-fold of that reported ten years previously (Cox 2008). Most notably, perhaps, the increasing pace of globalization and the perceived extent and costs of transnational corruption continues to prompt further quantitative and qualitative studies about its causes and consequences.

Corruption can emerge in virtually any political, social or economic environment in which there are incentives for illicit activities. We might look to social, economic, political, and psychological concepts to examine the causes of criminality. Here, we consider the relatively large body of literature that uses the principal-agent model and rational choice theory as a framework for explaining corruption (Rose-Ackerman 1978; Kiser and Tong 1992; Braguinsky 1996; Jain 1998; Shleifer and Vishny 1998; and Szanto 1999). Jensen and Meckling (1976) describe the principal-agent relation as a "contract under which one or more persons (the principal) engage another person (the agent) to perform some service on their behalf which involves delegating some decision-making authority to the agent" (308). Governments or corporations grant individuals decision-making authority, for example, but there is no guarantee that these agents will always act in the interest of the public, the clientele or the company. There are, after all, incentives for agents to maximize their own welfare at cost to the principal. Speaking of political leaders in particular and their cohorts who prosper at the expense of their impoverished nations, Bueno de Mesquita (2002) observes that, "Plainly, effective public policy does not serve the personal political interests of such leaders nearly as well as venality and corruption" (4). The failure of the principal-agent relationship is generally explained by the inability of the principal to enforce its contract with the agent. The primary objective of the principal, therefore, is to control the agent's behavior so that it conforms to the principal's goals. For example, the state may limit the discretion or authority of the agent, although to avoid giving monopolistic power to some low level agents in the field such as policemen or housing inspectors may be impossible (Rose-Ackerman 1978). The state may also establish specific rules forbidding agents use of their positions to advance personal interests, rules such as those outlawing bribery and embezzlement. A system of monitoring and sanctioning generally accompanies these efforts. However, checks and balances put into place by the principal can be circumvented by agents who themselves have control over the system (Rose-Ackerman 1978; Jain 2001). Taking this rational-choice approach to explain the determinants of corruption, Jain identifies three necessary conditions for corruption to occur. First, there must be agents who have discretionary power over the regulation or delivery of a good or service. Second, the agent must be able and willing to misuse that power. Third, the agent must have an incentive to do so. In essence, then, rational choice theory tells us that the corrupt act simply reflects a balancing of the expected benefit against the expected cost. Expected benefits might include monetary or other gains, while costs include the probability of being caught, the severity of legal and social penalties, and even the moral cost of doing wrong (Klitgaard 1987). Thus, in corruption control efforts the principal seeks to raise the cost and subsequently minimize the gains of illegal agent behavior at the lowest cost possible. Fertile ground that affects the costs and benefit analyses of agents might include such factors as low salaries of public officials, high unemployment, social norms or political pressures such as giving gifts in exchange for favors, weak criminal justice systems, access to rich resources such as minerals or oil, incompetence or mismanagement of governments or corporations, excessive regulations and complicated licensing systems, lack of adequate border controls, and a thriving shadow economy. It is impossible to eliminate all incentives for individuals or groups to engage in corrupt activities, of course. Later in this chapter we will review some anticorruption strategies based on the principal-agent and rational choice models.

The impact that corruption has on the economy alone is much studied, but nevertheless debated. Most observers note that both public and private sector corruption creates unfair competition and undermines free market principles. It hinders economic development and trade, and is especially pernicious for developing countries. Government and corporate corruption is found to be more widespread in transitioning economies, with protection of property rights and attraction for potential investors impaired. In fact, one of the most destructive effects is on investment (Mauro 1995). The World Bank reports that lower income per capita is correlated with higher levels of corruption, and that state spending is diverted to military spending and other capital budgets where it is easier to extract bribes (Klitgaard 1987; Mauro 1996). It is found that some areas in the public and private sectors, especially in developing economies, appear to be more susceptible to corruption. These include real estate, metals and mining, aerospace and defense, and power and utilities (Ernst & Young 2013). Others argue that in the long term, private corruption will be punished by the market because illicit behavior will have a negative effect on corporate profits and shareholder values, company reputation, and investor confidence. This self-correcting mechanism is usually not found in the public sector. Therefore, some argue that we ought to be less concerned about private sector corruption than about political corruption because the latter undermines the very rule of law and institutions that provide foundations for free market principles and just application of rules and regulations (McNab and Bailey n.d.). The interplay between public and private corruption is incontrovertible. Perhaps a more cynical view of this relationship suggests that corruption is sometimes a useful method for circumventing bad government policies, especially those policies that favor the few instead of the public at large. In this vein, Leff (1964) argues that corruption is a hedge against ineffective, inefficient, or unfair government policy. Through corruption, entrepreneurs can pursue other routes that may be more cost effective and efficient. Huntington (1968) also states that corruption provides certain benefits to society. Corruption can stimulate economic development by enabling entrepreneurs to evade rigid and oppressive administrative regulations, and thus be a "welcome lubricant easing the path to modernization" (69). By replacing political action with economic transactions, corruption can even serve as a substitute for violent revolution; in this way new groups more peacefully enter the political system, Huntington adds. With few exceptions, however, scholars and practitioners view corruption in an unfavorable light. The common perception is that public and private corruption is detrimental to economic growth and societal well-being. It is seen as a serious threat to democratic governance because it weakens public integrity and confidence in both the public and private sector. Nonetheless, research on the causes and consequences of corruption is fragmented and generally does not take an interdisciplinary approach. Holistic insights to the genesis and endurance of corruption within different countries or on the global stage are not readily discernible by anecdotal, case study, or statistical analyses. Perhaps this is in large part due to considerable disagreement about how to measure it.

Measuring the Extent of Corruption

Obtaining reliable measures of domestic and global corruption evades us. By its very nature corruption is secretive, and thus all incidences are not observable or reported. One observer notes that, "If corruption could be measured, it could probably be eliminated" (Tanzi 1998, 560). Another quips that,

"Like pornography, corruption is difficult to quantify, but you know it when you see it" (Wei 1999, 4). The lack of comprehensive hard data would seemingly make the task of analyzing corruption a futile enterprise. However, despite there being no direct ways to reliably measure public or private malfeasance there are a number of indirect methods to obtain information to guide our understanding. But before examining various ways that may be helpful in estimating the extent of corruption, we might revisit the notion that classification of corruption is diverse, too. In addition to categorizing such acts as a transgression of law and/or morality, or as public or private corruption, we can further distinguish between the types of corruption as petty or grand in terms of their scale (Rose-Ackerman 1978, 2006).

Petty corruption entails low level or bureaucratic violations that often occur on a relatively frequent basis. This might take the form of small favors or bribery on a limited scale, and occurs within established legal or regulatory frameworks such as agencies or lower levels of government. If it involves the exchange of money, petty corruption refers to fairly modest sums. Everyday petty corruption is especially pervasive in developing countries. It is often committed when individuals regard the violation as insignificant and even part of a social norm, such as offering bribes to police or local licensing authorities. Petty corruption might be seen as the grease to facilitate convenient and efficient transactions, but still poses a serious threat to the rule of law and transparency in governance. On the other hand, grand corruption appears to evoke greater concern since it can subvert political, legal, and economic systems in more immediate and major fashion. Grand corruption is most often viewed as taking place at the top levels of government. Some observers classify these acts as grand regardless of the sums of money involved because they are committed by high-ranking officials who are positioned to influence public policies and rules. The reach of malfeasance has been as high as the presidency and prime minister in several countries over the past few decades. Others, however, take into account the magnitude of the illicit exchange, and even append the label of grand corruption to major illegal corporate activities. For instance accounting fraud, embezzlement and securities violations committed by a host of large domestic firms and multinational corporations have cost investors and the public billions of dollars. Lastly, another way to gain an appreciation for the extent of corruption in a particular country or across borders is to determine if the corruption is systemic. The scope and impact of systemic corruption is far more pronounced than the illegal acts of individuals since it points to pervasive failings in a government or society by which corrupt individuals or groups routinely dominate the system. Endemic corruption of this nature is tightly integrated in all aspects of major institutions and state processes. Here, "corruption becomes the rule rather than the exception" (Znoj 2009, 53–54). Participants in petty and grand corruption exploit specific opportunities, whereas systematic corruption is entrenched so that there are few if any alternatives for most people to deal with corruption.

Is corruption becoming worse? Accounts do suggest overall that domestic and global corruption is escalating, but what are the sources of this claim? Some studies measure corruption as the number of individuals or corporations convicted of corruption charges. One cross-national data set of reported crimes such as embezzlement, bribery, and fraud is assembled by the UN Crime Prevention and Criminal Justice Division in Vienna. However, conviction rates are not sufficient indicators since they may only reflect a country's enforcement policies or quality of judicial system. Neither arrests nor convictions mirror undiscovered incidences of corruption. Alternately, some researchers suggest that there may be useful information about corrupt activity from news sources. But again, the media cannot report what is undetected. There is wide variation, too, among countries in the news content selected for public consumption. Perhaps the most widely used, and indirect approach, to measuring corruption is survey data. Questionnaire-based data is subjective; it tabulates respondents' perceptions of or experiences with corruption. Drawn from these samples, a variety of indices ranking countries by degree of perceived corruption serve as indicators of the phenomena. Although there are differences in methodologies and in coverage among countries, there are high correlations among various corruption indices (Treisman 2000). Arguably, measurements based on perceptions may in fact merely reflect widely shared biases. Nevertheless, perceptions are important. The following sections introduce us to some of the ways that public perceptions are shaped, and how they are used to estimate the extent of corruption.

In the News. It is rare not to find headlines each day shrieking of investigations or convictions connected to public and private corruption. After a decade of global attention focused on fighting public and private malfeasance, the millennium began with a series of scandals tied to corruption. We recall a Christian Democrat Party leader in Germany hanging himself in January 2000 after leaving a suicide note stating that he participated in an embezzlement of the party's finances. Within the next two months, China executed a former vice-governor for taking more than $600,000 in bribes; the interior minister of Thailand resigned after charges were levied against him for fabricating a million-dollar loan to conceal his assets; and the astonishing precious jewels of an Indian politician and former movie star were catalogued as accessories to alleged public corruption crimes. The media continues to chase what appears to be an intensifying crime spree around the world. Just a few headlines and news abstracts from the first month in 2014, for example, illustrate the various types and extent of corruption that still persist. "Turkish corruption probe deepens" in which 350 police officers were dismissed in the capital Ankara in the biggest shake-up since a recent corruption inquiry targeted government allies. "Eighty retired New York cops, firefighters charged in disability fraud," whereby the police and firefighters were charged in a disability scam in which dozens of people allegedly claimed falsely to have been traumatized by the September 11 attacks. "China's top drug distributor Sinopharm says ex-VP detained," reports that the former vice president of the country's largest pharmaceutical distributor was detained as part of a probe into alleged corruption. "Malawi prepares for $100m 'cashgate' corruption trial," a mass trial being conducted of 100 civil servants, politicians and business people involved in allegedly looting more than $100m from government coffers. "Pope removes cardinals in shake-up of Vatican bank," in which Pope Francis removed four of five cardinals from an oversight body connected with the scandal-plagued Vatican bank. "Four former Yara executives to be tried in bribery case," reports that the executives of the fertilizer maker, including its former chief executive and top legal counsel, were indicted by Norwegian police for allegedly paying about $8 million in bribes in Libya and India.

With no relief from the flood of such news stories, it would seem reasonable to suspect that corruption today is everywhere and commonplace. We would imagine that the public is disenchanted with the lack of probity among its politicians and the business community, and policymakers everywhere doubtlessly strategizing how to constrain what seems to be runaway corruption. Several different opinion polls test our perception that corruption is not decreasing and instead seems to be accelerating. Transparency International (TI), a non-profit watchdog nongovernmental organization based in Berlin, was established in the 1990s by World Bank lawyer and economist Peter Eigen. With more than 90 chapters worldwide, TI is renowned for its global anticorruption efforts. Among other things, it publishes survey results to suggest trends in political and public malfeasance. One TI publication states that, "The corrupt are running out of places to hide ... empowered by technology—essential to the prompt and accurate flow of information—the media and the public are increasingly calling businesses and politicians to account" (TI 2014a, ¶ 1). Below are summaries from three popular TI indices based on perceptions about corruption.

The Corruption Perceptions Index. One of the most widely used measures of corruption in research comes from the annual Corruption Perceptions Index (CPI). The index was first published in 1995 and covered 99 countries; the most recent 2013 index includes 176 countries. Unlike other TI instruments that rely on public opinion surveys or outside experts and businessmen to ascertain political corruption levels, the CPI index draws upon more than a dozen different surveys and expert assessments from a number of institutions such as the African Development Bank, the Economist Intelligence Unit, Freedom House, and The World Bank. At least three sources must assess a country before it is ranked, and so the CPI is often described as a "poll of polls." The surveys capture the perceptions of domestic and foreign business people, risk analysts, journalists and other experts about the incidence or perception of corruption occurring in a country. Countries are ranked on a scale from 100 (very clean) to 0 (highly corrupt). Counterintuitively, then, a lower score in one country reflects perceptions that corruption is more of a problem there than in one with a higher score. The 2013 CPI shows Denmark and New Zealand, each with a score of 91, are ranked number 1 as the least corrupt states. The index over time consistently reflects higher scores primarily among the Scandinavian countries. The United States receives a score of 73 and is still ranked relatively near the top at 19. Ranked at the bottom of the index are Zimbabwe and Myanmar, each with a score of 21, and so seen as the most corrupt of countries included in that year's ranking. TI also groups countries by region and reports the percentage of countries in each region with scores that fall below 50—a red flag that corruption is prevalent among those areas. In the European Union and Western Europe 23 percent fall below 50, providing the impression that less than a quarter of European states are assessed as particularly corrupt, and so this region is seen as the cleanest in the world. In contrast, 66 percent or two-thirds of countries in the Americas fall below 50. Asia Pacific fares about the same with 64 percent. Most worrisome are the other regions in the world. In the Middle East and North Africa 84 percent of countries there fall below 50; in Sub-Saharan Africa it is 90 percent; and at the very bottom is Eastern Europe and Central Asia with 95 percent of those countries scoring below 50. This paints a different picture than the long list of single country scores from which we might speculate that African states are generally perceived as most corrupt. In truth, the Eastern European and Central Asian region is viewed worse. TI provides us with a global perspective as well. Altogether, two-thirds of all countries ranked fall below 50, indicating a significant worldwide problem with corruption (TI 2013b).

Global Corruption Barometer. This most recently devised TI annual index has caused a bit of a stir since its first release in 2008. Survey responses from the 2013 report come from more than 114,000 people in more than 100 countries, not from institutional experts as the CPI index above. This is the world's largest public opinion poll about corruption, with respondents providing their views and their own experiences with corruption. Here are some of the key findings taken directly from the latest Global Corruption Barometer (TI 2013a), some of which seem quite surprising. One in four people surveyed said they paid a bribe over the past twelve months when accessing key public institutions and services. Of those who reported paying a bribe, 40 percent said they did so "to speed things up," and more than a quarter said "it was the only way to obtain a service." Political parties are considered the most corrupt institution, followed by the police and the judiciary. Globally, religious institutions are seen as least corrupt. In Israel, Japan, Sudan and South Sudan, however, religious bodies were seen to be highly corrupt. Nearly two-thirds of respondents said they believe personal contacts and relationships help get things done in the public sector in their country. In ten countries, including Israel, Italy, Malawi, Russia and Vanuatu, this figure was more than 80 percent. Wealthier respondents reported paying bribes more often than their poorer counterparts, and globally, slightly more men than women reported paying a bribe. However, in some countries such as Nepal and Pakistan, many more men reported paying bribes than women. As we might expect, there are often differences of opinions and experiences between people in various countries.

Of great concern, TI found that a significant percentage of people surveyed said that basic services provided by their government were withheld if they could not afford to pay a bribe. Thus, fundamental rights appear to be at risk with the prevalence of corruption and the expectation to participate in illegal activities such as bribery. Despite nine out of ten people willing to report incidences of corruption so that action might be taken against the perpetrators, this latest corruption survey indicates that most people believe their governments are losing the fight against corruption.

Bribe Payers Index. Unlike the aforementioned survey which reports aggregate responses from citizens around the world, the Bribe Payers Index (BPI) ranks 28 of the leading exporting countries on the probability that multinational corporations in those countries will offer bribes when operating abroad. The countries represented on the index produce almost 80 percent of the total world outflow of goods, services and investments. The ranking is based on an average of survey responses to two questions from business executives in those countries. One question asks for the country of origin for foreign-owned companies doing the most business in their own country. The second question asks, "In your experience, to what extent do firms from the countries you have selected make undocumented extra payments or bribes?" Answers are given on a scale of 1 (bribes are common or mandatory) to 10 (bribes are unknown); thus if highly ranked, a country is less likely to use bribery. The first BPI was distributed in 1999, with the most recent ranking published in 2011. Key findings taken directly from the latter indicate no overall improvement since 2008 in the incidence of corporate corruption. Bribery is prevalent across various business sectors, but is seen as more common in public works contracts and construction. Business people claim that business integrity matters but there is clear evidence of significant bribery between private companies. Interestingly, the perceived likelihood of companies to bribe abroad is closely related to views on the level of business integrity and perceptions of corruption in the public sector at home. Thus, home country governance matters. The index shows that there are perceptions of corruption in all 28 countries. At the top of the BPI with the cleanest record, although still with room for improvement, are The Netherlands and Switzerland, with Belgium, Germany and Japan closely behind. The United States, France, and Spain are ranked near the middle, while over time India, Mexico, China and Russia remain at the bottom of the index. That China and Russia are viewed as the most likely to pay bribes is disconcerting to Transparency International analysts. They say that the importance in international trade and investment is rapidly growing in the two countries, and conclude that there will be significant impacts on the ability of companies to compete fairly in those markets (TI 2012). Perhaps it is the Bribe Payers Index that offers us a clearer picture of the extent of corruption believed to be occurring between states. This then prepares us for a discussion of corruption that transpires across state jurisdictions.

Transnational Corruption

Up until fairly recently, corruption literature generally focused on the role of the state in perpetuating or in fighting public and private corruption. True enough, the work on organized crime points to a longstanding international concern with much of that early research focused on criminal behavior such as drug trafficking, arms dealing, and the like across borders, rather than corruption *per se*. Yet it has only been within the past decade or so that the internationalization of corruption became a buzzword. The "globalization of corruption" or "transnational corruption" has since found a secure place on the agenda of researchers and policymakers alongside some of the most important ongoing studies about globalization (Glynn et al. 1997; Eigen 2002). There is considerable discussion about why the matter has become an international sensation. Certainly there are multi-faceted perspectives, but most observers simply point to increased opportunities since the end of the twentieth century for cross-border corruption to simultaneously flourish alongside significant increases in political and economic interdependence. More specifically, some scholars help us to understand why fraud and other such abuses appear to run rampant now that the state no longer has exclusive control over economic activities. First, they say, global economic integration provides fertile ground for additional corruption opportunities, which subsequently leads to widespread negative spillover effects. Second, it becomes exceedingly difficult to deter opportunities and costs of corruption facilitated by international electronically networked financial systems. Lastly, we witness a significant increase in the numbers of sectors that work collaboratively across borders. These economic alliances suggest that the "global economy resembles a complex worldwide network of interfirm agreements" and so pose challenges to anticorruption efforts (Glenn et al. 1997, 12). Others see structural defects and a resistance to extraterritorial legal constraints as a problem. The World Bank and other international organizations, for instance, argue that a lack of effective domestic institutions and rules has enabled the growth of corruption across jurisdictions.

Just as detecting the causes and extent of domestic corruption remains a thorny issue, so is monitoring trends in the internationalization of corruption. Once again we are faced with inconsistent methodologies and unreliable empirical evidence to assess interstate behavior. Regardless of the reasons for its apparent growth, however, the impact of transnational corruption is already felt (World Bank 2014b). The World Bank declared that corruption is the largest obstacle to development in emerging economies. In part this is due to pervasive bribery from multinational corporations in influencing local laws and governance in those weak states. When state capacity to maintain the rule of law is undermined, the door is opened for transnational criminal groups to respond to global demands for cheap or illicit goods and services. Wedded with the prevalence of transnational crime is greater corruption. The Millennium Project, an independent nonprofit international think tank, estimates the current value of organized crime income in just half of the countries in the world to be over $3 trillion. This includes the drug trade, human trafficking, prostitution, environmental crimes, counterfeiting and intellectual property piracy, money laundering, and the like. More than half of that amount, $1.6 trillion, is the estimated value attached to corruption and bribery alone (Millennium Project n.d.). The World Bank provides additional estimates. Focusing only on the extent of bribery to governments from firms and individuals, a conservative figure given for annual worldwide bribery is about $1 trillion. This figure does not include other forms of corruption, such as embezzlement of public or private funds, theft of public assets, or tainted procurement (World Bank n.d.). The U.S. Department of State acknowledges that in the space of seven years, from 1994 to 2001, there were allegations of bribery in more than 400 international contract bids valued at $200 billion by firms in more than 50 countries to more than 100 buyer countries (USDS 2001). The staggering economic cost of corruption clearly impacts political and social development projects. In 2012, UN Secretary-General Ban Ki-moon appealed to the international community to take such costs to heart as it works to achieve the Millennium Development Goals (MDGs). In light of the ambitious project to halve extreme poverty rates, halt the spread of HIV/AIDS, and providing universal primary education by 2015, he declared that "addressing the problem of corruption becomes all the more urgent." The Secretary-General added that a sustainable future required the exposure and rejection of corruption (UN 2012, ¶2). The message was made in observation of International Anti-Corruption Day which is designated on 9 December.

Countermeasures to Transnational Corruption

The designation of International Anti-Corruption Day by the United Nations in 2003 was to raise global awareness about the deleterious effects of both domestic and transnational corruption, and the need to combat and prevent it. The observatory day accompanied passage of the UN Convention Against Corruption on 31 October of the same year. An active anticorruption movement around the world was well underway by this time. Paradoxically, while political and economic integration appears to be the culprit in facilitating the spread of public and private corruption across borders, globalization also emerges as a potential champion to address the problem—one which is now regarded as a collective-action problem. With hopes for greater cooperation in the fight against corruption, a surge of attention has focused on galvanizing actors at every level. This section of the chapter reviews some of those efforts to date. It is important to note, however, that while research suggests a general pattern in the relationship between political and economic integration and corruption, successful reforms necessarily require customized approaches (United Nations 2012).

Global Civil Society. At the heart of fighting corruption is learning more about it. Literature on the phenomenon has fairly exploded over the past few decades, with more attention paid these days on the internationalization of corruption. The need for better understanding the links between various illicit activities around the globe has prompted creation of several academic institutions devoted to that cause. The first such program in the United States is the Terrorism, Transnational Crime and Corruption Center at George Mason University. A number of similar educational and research programs are found in Europe, such as a joint research center in Italy called Transcrime. International organizations including The World Bank, United Nations, and Transparency International produce volumes of corruption studies themselves, and as indicated herein, there are a host of scholars busy researching various aspects of public and private sector corruption. Still, there is much more to do. A report submitted to the U.S. Department of Justice in 2005 points to a "myriad of barriers" to investigating transnational crime, including corruption. The authors claim to be unaware of any systematic data collection techniques to adequately study the capabilities of domestic law enforcement agencies in identifying and addressing illegal activities of this nature (USDOJ 2005). We notice, too, that better informed about the nature and prevalence of corruption at home and abroad, grassroots movements and the general public have become more vocal in their demands for cleaner government and fairer dealings in the private sector. We can recall massive demonstrations in Ankara at the beginning of 2014 which drew more than 20,000 protesters. Corruption probes into the Turkish government sparked international furor as well. Public reaction that is so strongly opposed to bribery, embezzlement and other corrupt activities may signal a cultural change that in the end may be more effective in curbing corruption than legal changes (Byrne 2007). Transnational civil associations, such as the International Chamber of Commerce, is recognized for being one of the first such organizations to prioritize the fight against transnational corruption like bribery and extortion in business transactions. Observers point to the vital role that a strong civil society, its academic institutions, media, and other nongovernmental associations play in tackling corruption. At the same time, civil society—or any other one sector—cannot be a sufficient tool in promoting good governance. There is consensus that collaborative approaches to battling corruption stands to be the best approach.

Anticorruption Law and Enforcement. Other partners in the effort certainly include domestic and international legal frameworks and systems for monitoring compliance. While public fervor against corruption may be especially emotive and not morally neutral, ideally the legal approach to regulating public and private transactions in order to minimize corruption is. This, of course, is assuming that legislative and judicial bodies themselves are public-minded and not corrupt themselves. Even still, we must be cautious about the limitations to legislate behavior. One scholar notes that "a corrupt act can be camouflaged by lawful justification … undue emphasis on narrow legalism has obscured more subtle yet costly manifestations of misgovernance … where 'legal corruption' may be more prevalent than illegal forms" (Kaufmann 2006, ¶ 2). Policies, laws, regulations, and programs are only words, and not necessarily accompanied with political will and commitment to anticorruption efforts.

Domestic. Some critics note that states have failed to coordinate their policies and enforcement policies and practices with the international community.

And indeed, they have failed to adequately attend to the matter at home. Some states address corruption in their criminal or penal codes, without having adopted legislation specifically targeting corruption. Others in succession over the past several decades have amended current laws, passed new ones or are in the process of doing so. An early attempt to reform its legal framework was Pakistan's The Prevention of Corruption Act in 1958. The Foreign Corrupt Practices Act in the U.S. trailed two decades later in 1977, and then India's Prevention of Corruption Act in 1988. These moves anticipated the flurry of anticorruption legislation that subsequently followed during the 1990s. The turn of the twenty-first century notably witnessed Nigeria's Corrupt Practices and Other Related Offenses in 2000, and Russia's passing federal legislation in 2008 called On Corruption Counteraction. Most recently, China amended its criminal law so that it was directed at international bribery of foreign public officials in 2011, and Afghanistan passed the Law of Campaign Against Bribery and Official Corruption in 2012. For a sense of the nature of some of these anticorruption laws, we can look at The Foreign Corrupt Practices Act which governs U.S. business dealings with foreign countries. The Act prohibits bribery of foreign officials by companies listed on the U.S. securities exchange and requires companies to maintain accurate books and records. Whistleblowers that report violations of the Act can recover a large reward. Similarly, China's amendment to the Criminal Law makes it an offense for Chinese companies and citizens to bribe foreign government officials. Previously the law had no extraterritorial application and only applied to bribing Chinese government officials. Legislation such as this at the national level may be influenced by intolerable levels of corruption in the country, and/or by global/regional anticorruption campaigns.

Regional. The 1990s also saw a number of collaborative projects among states to check corruption, particularly those illegal activities that crossed borders and began impacting their immediate region. The earliest of these was The Inter-American Convention against Corruption of the Organization of American States (1997), with quick succession of others including The Civil Law Convention on Corruption of the Council of Europe (1999), The Criminal Law Convention on Corruption of the Council of Europe (1999), and the Anti-Corruption Initiative for Asia-Pacific (1999). With passage of The African Union Convention on Preventing and Combating Corruption (2002), all regions had devised cooperative frameworks among neighboring states. Related collaborative projects have also sprung up. For instance, The Group of States Against Corruption (GRECO) in 1999 agreed upon certain principles in the fight against corruption; compliance of members in meeting these anticorruption standards are monitored through mutual evaluation procedures. Assessments are presented by the Council of Europe to indicate the progress of national legislative bodies in the region to combat corruption.

International. Perhaps most visible on the landscape of transnational corruption reform are multilateral agreements between states. From the number of and scope of these agreements over the past few years, we might expect that international frameworks are beginning to make a difference. But keen observers note that progress is stymied by the failure of national laws to adequately integrate those international standards (Hill 2005). Here we take a look at major international agreements, some binding on state signatories and some not, that demonstrate growing attention paid to transnational corruption. Initiating the global anticorruption movement is the UN Declaration Against Corruption and Bribery in International Commercial Transaction (1996). Passed by the General Assembly, the declaration does not have the force of law but is a political commitment made by UN members. It reaffirms the right of states to adopt anticorruption legislation, and to investigate and take appropriate legal action, in accordance with their national laws and regulations. The Declaration calls upon all Governments to cooperate to prevent corrupt practices, including bribery. The OECD Convention on Combating Bribery (1999) is a binding instrument that prohibits bribery of foreign public officials in international business transactions. But along with the OECD Working Group on Bribery to assess performance of the Convention, Transparency International publishes an annual progress report on foreign bribery enforcement in the 40 parties to the Convention. Both reports maintain that there is little or no actual enforcement against foreign bribery, although there is variation among the member states. Further, the Convention does not apply to bribery among private sector actors, raising questions about the limitations of the instrument. The UN Convention against Transnational Organized Crime (2003) and its three Protocols is the main international instrument in combatting international organized crime. To date the multilateral treaty, also called the Palermo Convention, has been ratified by 179 states and is binding on those members. Members agree to integrate the criminalization of certain transnational acts, including corruption activities, into their domestic legislation. They also agree to work cooperatively in law enforcement. Finally, the UN Convention Against Corruption (2005) has been ratified by 154 countries to date. It requires member states to take preventative measures and to criminalize a wide range of corrupt acts, including bribery of foreign officials. Terms of the Convention must be integrated with the policies, laws, and practice of member states. It is notable that three leading economies, Germany, Japan, and Saudi Arabia, have not ratified the Convention yet. Still, it is the first global multilateral binding instrument devoted to fighting corruption. It was with this Convention that the UN declared 9 December as Anti-Corruption Day.

In short, alarm about the proliferation of corruption across borders is expressed by a number of governmental and nongovernmental bodies along with civil society in general. Consequently the fight against transnational corruption is seen as one of great urgency, although to date there are mixed views about the progress being made. One scholar finds an interesting development underway in transnational anticorruption efforts—they are increasingly becoming privatized (Hall 2013). Important regulatory measures are being created by the likes of banks, development agencies, corporations, technical experts, and other nonstate groups, with the result that global anticorruption standards and guidelines are assuming a significant role in determining the anticorruption laws adopted by states. But this can be a good thing, she argues, since anticorruption regulation is becoming "harmonized" and influencing governance in positive ways.

Conclusion

This chapter attempts to provide an introduction to political, economic and social challenges posed by public and private corruption, particularly in view of the growing impact of transnational corruption in the new millennium. It is necessarily limited in its ability to cover many nuances of the phenomenon, and so does not address the wide range of significant issues and debates within academic literature or in practice. Perhaps, however, this treatment will spark interest in readers to learn more. In conjunction with lively discussion about how to best define and measure corruption, budding and energetic anticorruption programs from various camps will place us in a better position to gauge progress down the road in curbing malfeasance and in strengthening democratic governance and the rule of law.

In the meanwhile, there are at least three fundamental principles we ought to keep in mind. First, we must acknowledge that the specific nature and determinants of corruption varies among countries and regions, and so anticorruption strategies must build upon case-specific understandings. In regard to efforts by Asian-Pacific governments to form a regional alliance to combat corruption, for instance, one OECD official said that because the character of corruption does vary from place to place, "Countries have to generate the domestic will and move at their own pace to address it effectively" (Geiger 2001, 1). To a degree, the statement reflects the belief by some observers that states, not the international community, ultimately remain the primary actor in even transnational matters. The second principle to note is that reformers acknowledge the critical importance of domestic—and international—political will to effectively counter avarice. Adoption of and compliance with anticorruption policies and programs requires sustained commitment from both public and private sectors. Some observers ambitiously propose that structuring a successful anticorruption program even requires a change in public perceptions and values. The World Bank argues, for example, that the view of corruption in some countries must be changed from simply being a means to prospering to being perceived as "aberrant and immoral" (Stapenhurst and Kpundeh 1999). Third, reformers generally agree that the opportunities for government and corporate workers to engage in corrupt behavior must be curtailed. Transparency in the public and private sector is frequently cited as a key means to discourage the abuse of power, with accountability including the ease in determining the legitimacy of decision-making processes. One researcher writes that in many countries where corruption is visible, "rules are often confusing, the documents specifying them are not publicly available, and at times, the rules are changed without properly publicized announcements. Laws or regulations are written in a way that only trained lawyers can understand" (Tanzi 1998, 569). In similar light, anticorruption strategies also frequently focus on reducing incentives for illegal behavior. Some observers suggest that corrupt bargaining relationships depend partly on institutional political arrangements such as legislative and electoral processes (Shleifer and Vishney 1993). Competition in the marketplace as well as the political system may serve to restrain some forms of corruption; for instance, term limits might foster corruption by putting public officials in "an end game in which they are sure that they will not be returned to office" (Rose-Ackerman 1978, 58).

Specific strategies for controlling corruption are plentiful but generally incorporate those principles discussed earlier that reform must be tailored to individual countries and circumstances, acquire commitment from both the public and private sector, and limit the opportunities and incentives of wrongdoers. Reform initiatives are also often based on a particular viewpoint about the nature and causes of corruption. Cultural perspectives suggest attitudinal changes be made. Institutional perspectives suggest that effective institutional controls, such as term limits, be placed on actors. But how effective might we anticipate these reforms to be? After all, reforms must give individuals and groups adequate incentives to forego illicit activity that is in their self-interest for that of the public.

Some scholars and practitioners cast a wary eye at the anticorruption laws and programs adopted by countries. National legal frameworks and criminal justice systems do not appear able to effectively combat domestic crime, much less transnational crime. Based on public opinion polls and indices constructed by organizations such as Transparency International, even ambitious anticorruption strategies currently proposed by the global community appear futile, at least in the short term. Corruption control "may be just a temporary fad," retorts Rose-Ackerman (1999, 178). Incentives for public officials and those in the private sector to engage in illegal activities will persist as long as they have discretionary authority, and so reform will only be effective by compensating or marginalizing those individuals or groups, she adds. Therefore, economic perspectives about the nature and causes of corruption suggest reform strategies that focus on cost and benefit analyses. Subsequently, the rational choice and principal-agent model explains the basic dynamics of illicit exchanges and so may suggest realistic approaches to curbing corruption. The benefits of collective action may help to counter corruption. Incentives for collective action might be extended to business associations, nongovernmental organizations and government agencies. Indeed, growing dissent among the business community about unfair competition in a corrupt marketplace suggests a willingness to apply collective pressure on countries tolerating bribery and other forms of corruption. Singly, reform initiatives such as institutional checks and balances, decentralization, greater competition, and an informed electorate and international community are no guarantees for success. Speedy integration of domestic and international prevention and enforcement measures may be the best hope for curbing corruption. As governments in developing countries attempt to boost economic development, they might keep in mind that development is closely intertwined with corruption, and as research demonstrates, greatly harmed by it. At the same time, the suggestion here is not that the link between economic and political integration and corruption is automatic. Perceived corruption and the analyses resting on them can only suggest one picture of transnational corruption, its determinants, and its consequences.

Web Sources

1. International Association of Anti-Corruption Authorities is available at: http://www.iaaca.org/AntiCorruptionLaws/ByCountriesandRegions/
2. International Chamber of Commerce is available at: http://www.iccwbo.org/about-icc/
3. Terrorism, Transnational Crime and Corruption Center is available at: traccc.gmu.edu/
4. Transparency International is available at: http://www.transparency.org/

5. United Nations is available at:
   http://www.un.org/en/
6. World Economic Forum
   http://www.weforum.org/

Discussion Questions

1. In your view, what are likely reasons that transnational corruption is receiving so much attention today from the international community?
2. Drawing upon the various typologies of corruption discussed in this chapter, how would you categorize the high-profile corruption cases that were briefly mentioned here?
3. Which of the three indices published by Transparency International seem to capture the extent of corruption best? Why? What alternative methods might researchers and practitioners use to monitor transnational corruption?
4. In what way(s) does transnational corruption enable the commission of other transnational crimes?
5. Do you feel that legal countermeasures established by states and international organizations are effective mechanisms to curb public and private sector corruption? Why or why not?

References

Barker, Ernest, ed. *The Politics of Aristotle*. Oxford, UK: Clarendon Press, 1946.

Bayley, David H. "The Effects of Corruption in a Developing Nation." *Western Political Quarterly* 19 (December 1966): 719–732.

Braguinsky, Serguey. "Corruption and Schumpeterian Growth in Different Economic Environments." *Contemporary Economic Policy* 14 (July 1996): 14–26.

Bueno de Mesquita, Bruce. "Domestic Politics and International Relations." *International Studies Quarterly* 46 (March 2002): 1–9.

Byrne, Elaine. *The Moral and Legal Development of Corruption: Nineteenth and Twentieth Century Corruption in Ireland*. PhD diss., University of Limerick, 2007.

Cox, Michaelene. "A Primer in Political Pathologies: Corruption and Its Correlates," In *State of Corruption, State of Chaos: The Terror of Political Malfeasance*, edited by Michaelene Cox, 3–12. New York: Lexington Books, 2008.

_____. *Assessing the Impact of Trade, Foreign Direct Investment, and Foreign Aid on Political Corruption*. PhD diss., University of Alabama, 2002.

Dandurand, Yvon. "Strategies and Practical Measures to Strengthen the Capacity of Prosecution Services in Dealing with Transnational Organized Crime, Terrorism and Corruption." *Crime Law and Social Change* 47 (2007): 225–246.

Eigen, Peter. "Corruption in a Globalized World." *SAIS Review* 22, no. 1 (2002): 45–59.

Ernst & Young. "Bribery and Corruption: Ground Reality in India. A Survey by EY's Fraud Investigation & Dispute Services Practice." Accessed January 10, 2014. http://www.ey.com/Publication/vwLUAssets/Bribery_and_corruption:_ground_reality_in_India/$FILE/EY-FIDS-Bribery-and-corruption-ground-reality-in-India.pdf, 2013.

Friedrich, Carl. "Political Pathology." *Political Quarterly* 37 (January–March 1966): 70–85.

Gardiner, John A. "Defining Corruption." *Corruption and Reform* 7, no. 2 (1993): 111–124.

Geiger, Rainer. "Asian and Pacific Governments Adopt Regional Plan to Fight Corruption." OECD press release, November 30, 2001. Accessed January 10, 2014. http://unpan1.un.org/intradoc/groups/public/documents/apcity/unpan014285.htm#2001.

Glynn, Patrick, Stephen J. Korbrin, and Moises Naim. "The Globalization of Corruption." In *Corruption and the Global Economy*, edited by Kimberly Elliott, 7–27. Washington, DC: Institute for International Economics, 1997.

Hall, Kath. "Strategic Privatisation of Transnational Anti-Corruption Regulation." *Australian Journal of Corporate Law* 28, no. 1 (2013): 13–14.

Hao, Yufan. "From Rule of Man to Rule of Law: An Unintended Consequence of Corruption in China in the 1990s." *Journal of Contemporary China* 8 (November 1999): 405–424.

Heidenheimer, Arnold J., Michael Johnston, and Victor T. LeVine, eds. *Political Corruption: A Handbook.* New Brunswick NJ: Transaction Publishers, 1989.

Hill, Cindy. "Measuring Transnational Crime." In *Handbook of Transnational Crime & Justice*, edited by Philip Reichel, 46–65. Thousand Oaks: Sage, 2005.

Huntington, Samuel P. *Political Order in Changing Societies.* New Haven: Yale University Press, 1968.

Jain, Arvind K., ed. *Economics of Corruption.* Norwell, MA: Kluwer Academic Publishers, 1998.

_____. "Corruption: A Review." *Journal of Economic Surveys* 15, no. 1 (2001): 71–121.

Jensen, Michael C., and William H. Meckling. "Theory of the Firm: Managerial Behavior, Agency Costs, and Ownership Structure." *Journal of Financial Economics* 3 (1976): 305–360.

Johnston, Michael. "Corruption." In *The Oxford Companion to Politics of the World*, 2 ed., edited by Joel Krieger, 177–178. Oxford: Oxford University Press, 2004.

Kangle, R. P., ed. and trans. *The Kautilya Arthashastra*. Bombay, India: University of Bombay, 1969.

Kaufmann, Daniel. "Corruption, Governance and Security." In *World Economic Forum. Global Competitiveness Report*, 2006. Accessed January 16, 2014. http://mpra.ub.uni-muenchen.de/8207/, 2006.

Kiser, Edgar, and Xiaoxi Tong. "Determinants of the Amount and Type of Corruption in State Fiscal Bureaucracies: An Analysis of Late Imperial China." *Comparative Political Studies* 25 (October 1992): 300–332.

Klitgaard, Robert. "Combating Corruption." *UN Chronicle* (Spring 1998): 90–93.

_____. *Controlling Corruption*. Berkeley and Los Angeles, CA: University of California Press, 1987.

Leff, Nathaniel H. "Economic Development through Bureaucratic Corruption." In *Political Corruption: A Handbook*, edited by Arnold J. Heidenheimer, Michael Johnston, and Victor T. LeVine, 389–403. New Brunswick, Canada: Transaction Publishers, 1989.

Mauro, Paolo. *The Effects of Corruption on Growth, Investment, and Government Expenditure*. IMF Working Paper 96/98. International Monetary Fund, Washington, D.C., 1996.

Mbaku, John Mukum. "Bureaucratic Corruption in Africa: The Futility of Cleanups." *CATO Journal* 16 (Spring/Summer1996): 99–119.

McNab, Robert, and Kathleen Bailey. "Defining Corruption." Accessed January 25, 2014. http://www.nps.edu/About/ USPTC/pdf/Faculty_Publications/Manuscript%202%20%20Defining%20Corruption%20-%20McNab-Bailey%20(17%20Sep).pdf, n.d.

Millennium Project. "Global Challenges Facing Humanity." Accessed January 5, 2014. http://www.millennium-project.org/millennium/Global_Challenges/chall-12.html, n.d.

Mueller, Gerhard O. W. "Transnational Crime: An Experience in Uncertainties." In *Organized Crime: Uncertainties and Dilemmas*, edited by S. Einstein and M. Amir, 3–19. Chicago: Office of International Criminal Justice Press, 1999.

Nuijten, Monique, and Gerhard Anders, eds. *Corruption and the Secret of Law: A Legal Anthropological Perspective*. Burlington, VT: Ashgate Publishers Ltd., 2007.

Nye, J. S. "Corruption and Political Development: A Cost-Benefit Analysis." *The American Political Science Review* 61 (June 1967): 417–427.

Pardo, Italo, ed. *Between Morality and the Law: Corruption, Anthropology and Comparative Society*. Burlington, VT: Ashgate Publishers Ltd., 2004.

Random House Webster's College Dictionary. New York: Random House, Inc., 2010.

Redford, Donald B., ed. *The Oxford Encyclopedia of Ancient Egypt.* Vol. II. Oxford, UK: Oxford University Press, 2001.

Rose-Ackerman, Susan. *Corruption: A Study in Political Economy.* New York: Academic Press, 1978.

_____. "Introduction and Overview." In *International Handbook on the Economics of Corruption*, edited by Susan Rose-Ackerman, xiv–xxxviii. Cheltenham, UK: Edward Elgar, 2006.

Sampson, Steven. "The Anti-Corruption Industry: From Movement to Institution." *Global Crime*, 2 (2010): 261–278.

Shleifer, Andrei, and Robert W. Vishny. "Corruption." *Quarterly Journal of Economics* 108 (August 1993): 599–619.

_____. *The Grabbing Hand. Government Pathologies and Their Cures.* Cambridge, MA: Harvard University Press, 1998.

Shumer, S. M. "Machiavelli: Republican Politics and Its Corruption." *Political Theory* 7, no. 1 (1979): 5–34.

Stapenhurst, Rick and Sahr J. Kpundeh. *Curbing Corruption: Toward a Model for Building National Integrity.* Washington, D.C.: The World Bank, 1999.

Sutherland, Edwin H. *White Collar Crime.* New York: Holt, Rinehart & Winston, 1949.

Tanzi, Vito. "Corruption Around the World: Causes, Consequences, Scope and Cures." *International Monetary Fund Papers* 45 (December 1998): 559–589.

Transparency International [TI]. "Global Corruption Barometer 2013." Accessed January 23, 2014. http://www.transparency.org/research/gcr/gcr access_to_information, 2013-a.

_____. "Corruption Perceptions Index 2013." Accessed January 23, 2014. http://www.transparency.org/cpi2013/results, 2013-b.

_____. Transparency International [TI]. "Bribe Payers Index Report 2011." Accessed January 23, 2014. http://bpi.transparency.org/bpi2011/results/, 2012.

Treisman, Daniel. "The Causes of Corruption: A Cross-National Study." *Journal of Public Economics* 76 (June 2000): 399–457.

United Nations [UN]. "Secretary-General, in Message for International Anti-Corruption Day, Says Prevention Critical to Securing Rule of Law." Accessed January 26, 2014. http://www.un.org/News/Press/docs/2012/sgsm 14703.doc.htm, 2012.

U.S. Department of Justice [USDOJ]. *State and Local Law Enforcement Response to Transnational Crime.* Task Order T-046, Final Report prepared by Caliber Associates. Accessed January 8, 2014. https://www.ncjrs.gov/pdf-files1/nij/grants/209521.pdf, 2005.

U.S. Department of Justice [USDOJ], Federal Bureau of Investigation. *White Collar Crime: A Report to the Public.* Washington, D.C.: Government Printing Office, 1989.

U.S. Department of State [USDS]. *Fighting Global Corruption: Business Risk Management* Washington, D.C.: Government Printing Office, 2001.

Vargas-Hernandez, Jose G. "The Multiple Faces of Corruption: Typology, Forms and Levels." *Contemporary Legal & Economic Issues* (2011): 269–290.

Vegter, Ivo. "Do We Tolerate Private Sector Corruption?" *Daily Maverick* November 26, 2012. Accessed January 20, 2014. http://www.dailymaverick. co.za/opinionista/2013-11-26-do-we-tolerate-private-sector-corruption/ #.UuLHCz_napo.

Wedel, Janine R. "Blurring the Boundaries of the State-Private Divide: Implications for Corruption." Paper presented at the European Association of Social Anthropologists Conference in Copenhagen, August 14–17, 2002. Accessed January 19, 2014. http://www.anthrobase.com/Txt/W/ Wedel_ J_01.htm.

Wei, Shang-Jin. "Corruption in Economic Development: Beneficial Grease, Minor Annoyance, or Major Obstacle?" Working paper of The World Bank (February 1999). Accessed January 20, 2014. http://elibrary. worldbank.org/ doi/book/10.1596/1813-9450-2048, 1999.

World Bank. "Helping Countries Combat Corruption: The Role of the World Bank: Corruption and Economic Development." Accessed January 24, 2014. http://www1.worldbank.org/publicsector/anticorrupt/corruptn/cor02.htm, n.d.-a.

_____. "Six Questions on the Cost of Corruption with World Bank Institute Global Governance." Accessed January 5, 2014. http://web.worldbank.org/ WBSITE/EXTERNAL/NEWS/0,,contentMDK:20190295~menuPK:34457~ pagePK:34370~piPK:34424~theSitePK:4607,00.html, n.d.-b.

Znoj, Heinzpeter, "Deep Corruption in Indonesia: Discourses, Practices, Histories." In *Corruption and the Secret of Law: A Legal Anthropological Perspective,* edited by Monique Nuijten and Gerhard Anders, 53–54. Burlington, VT: Ashgate Publishers Ltd., 2009.

Chapter 15

International Drug Trafficking

Melanie-Angela Neuilly

Introduction

One hundred years have elapsed since the use of drugs first became a concern of the international community. The first step toward a coordinated action against drugs was taken in 1909 at the International Opium Commission in Shanghai (International Narcotics Control Board [INCB] 2009) at the initiative of the United States (Buxton 2006; Fields, Holt, and Ferrell 2005). Since then, international bodies of drug control have developed to carry out the international treaties signed throughout the twentieth century. They have coordinated and guided the various national strategies and administrations aimed at regulating the issues raised by the cultivation, manufacture, transportation, distribution, and consumption of illicit substances that constitute the complex nexus of what is broadly referred to as "drug trafficking" (Johnson, Hamid, and Sanabria 1992; Natarajan 2005). Since 1909, the number of substances identified as dangerous and controlled has multiplied from a few dozen to over 200 (INCB 2009); levels of consumptions have become more and more precisely measured [UN Office on Drugs and Crime (UNODC)] 2008e); and the issue of international drug trafficking has continually evolved, not only in scope but also in nature (Buxton 2006; Fichtelberg 2008; Natarajan 2005). This chapter identifies patterns and trends in international drug trafficking, provides a contextual explanation of the strategies and actors at play, and outlines the multilayered levels of existing legal and institutional responses.

International Drug Trafficking and Consumption Patterns and Trends

In order to establish the need for policies, as well as to decide on the nature of those policies, one first needs to examine whether or not there is a problem, its extent, and its nature. This is when the use of statistics comes in handy. Of course, any student of criminology knows that policy often precedes or ignores detailed studies of criminological issues, and drugs are no exception (Walker 2006). It is also true that in order for a social phenomenon to emerge and be studied it must first be defined, and this definition often happens at the legal level within the field of criminology (Best 2001; Bogdan and Ksander 1980). In that respect, how drugs are perceived in a given society will influence how they are defined and measured, and therefore like other topics of interest in international criminology, local variations make compilations and comparisons perilous. Bearing this in mind, a number of resources are available and they allow for a number of characteristics to emerge regarding the issue of drugs at the global level.

Patterns and Trends

Drug Consumption

According to the 2010–2011 U.S. National Survey on Drug Use and Health (NSDUH) (formerly known as the National Household Survey on Drug Abuse) and conducted by the Substance Abuse and Mental Health Services Administration (SAMHSA), 22.6 million (almost 9 percent) of Americans age 12 or older had used an illicit drug within a month of the survey (SAMHSA 2012). Meanwhile, data from 2010 or later reported by European member states, Norway, and candidate states Croatia and Turkey to the European Monitoring Center for Drugs and Drug Addiction (EMCDDA), show that over 12 million people reported the use of cannabis within one month prior to data collection, or 3.6% of people aged 15 through 64, around 1.5 million (or 0.5%) for cocaine, and 2 million within the past year for ecstasy and amphetamines (EMCDDA 2012).

On a global level, the UNODC 2012 World Drug Report notes a continually stable trend in illicit drug consumption. Since the 1990s, use prevalence has varied between 4.7 and 5 percent of the world adult population (15–64 years of age), and in 2010, the period covered by the 2012 report, the annual prevalence of drug use was reported at 5 percent or about 230 million people, whereas the monthly prevalence of drug use was 2.6 percent.

Cannabis remains the most commonly used drug in the world, with prevalence rates stable overall between 2.6 and 5 percent (UNODC 2012). Variations are seen between developed and developing countries. The EMCDDA outlines what appears to be a loss of popularity, most acutely perceived amongst youth, and tentatively explained as correlated with the decrease in tobacco consumption due to repeated public health campaigns (in Europe, cannabis is smoked in combination with tobacco) (EMCDDA 2012). In developing countries, however, cannabis consumption is increasing (UNODC 2012). Prevalence is nonetheless highest in developed countries, particularly in North America, Europe, and Oceania. Amphetamines are the second most common with prevalence of use between 0.3 and 1.2 percent. Opioid consumption, driven up by high estimates in Asia, is between 0.6 and 0.8 percent of the population (more than half being heroin and opiate users), and cocaine use prevalence is between 0.3 and 0.4 percent. While the latter has remained constant, heroin has been fluctuating, with increases in Asia and decreases in Europe (UNODC 2012).

Two developing new trends are the non-medical use of opioid-based prescription drugs, and the manufacture of synthetic psychoactive substances. Non-medical use of prescription drugs is emerging in various ways, with monthly prevalence use of 2.7 percent in people aged 12 and older in the United States in 2010 (SAMHSA 2012). In Australia the rates have increased from 3.7 percent in 2007 to 4.2 percent in 2010 in persons 14 and older (Australia Institute of Health and Welfare 2011). Other data have further shown that such prevalence rates are higher for females than males, and this across a broad range of countries, from Afghanistan, Morocco, Algeria, South and Central American countries, to European countries (UNODC 2012). As per the development of synthetic psychoactive substance, the goal is to imitate the effects of other existing controlled substances, while remaining within the domain of uncontrolled substances. These include, most notably, the methcathinone analogue 4-methyl-methcathinone (also known as mephedrone) and methylenedioxypyrovalerone (MDPV) used as Amphetamine-Type Stimulant (ATS) replacements, and Spice, the herbal smoking blend aimed at emulating the effects of cannabis (UNODC 2012).

Markets

All cultivation and transportation pattern changes can be better understood within a historical context. As a matter of fact, the major shifts have usually occurred in reaction to historical events, making the drug problem an intensely political one. Changes in cultivation and transportation patterns have led to changes in consumption patterns. Some of those major trends are outlined below, but overall, the global drug market has remained stagnant in recent years, aside from the return to high levels of opium production in Afghanistan after a disease decimated poppies in the region in 2010 (UNODC 2012).

Opium Cultivation. Opium cultivation has its historical origins in the Middle East. It was then introduced in Egypt, before Arab merchants brought it to India, which became the main producer until the late nineteenth century, when China legalized its consumption and trade and started cultivating it. During the same period Siam (Thailand) and Burma also started opium cultivation in the Golden Triangle. The Golden Triangle (i.e., modern day Laos, Burma, and Thailand) became the main opium producer following the 1949 revolution in China (Buxton 2006; Ryan 2001; UNODC 2008a). Countries in the Golden Crescent (i.e., Afghanistan, Iran, and Pakistan) have traditionally been involved in opium cultivation, particularly Turkey and Persia (Iran) (Ryan 2001), but they really started to emerge after the Iranian revolution of 1979, which caused poppy cultivation to relocate to the neighboring countries of Pakistan and Afghanistan. When the so-called "French connection," in which Turkish opium was transformed into heroin in the south of France, using chemical precursors locally available (thanks to the perfume industry prominent in that area), and then shipped to New York, was broken down in the mid-1970s, the Golden Triangle, Golden Crescent, and Mexico swiftly stepped up to fill the gap created in the American heroin market (Ryan 2001). The Golden Triangle heroin was then distributed by Chinese organized crime through Hong Kong (Williams 1993). The fall of the Golden Triangle as main producer of heroin can partly be linked with the return of Hong Kong to China in 1997. The continued ascent of the Golden Crescent, and in particular Afghanistan, as the world's purveyor of opium occurred during the United States' attacks on the Taliban in Pakistan and the invasion of Iraq following 9/11, and recent events involving the Taliban in Pakistan cannot be ignored when considering this fact [Filkins 2009; General Accounting Office (GAO) 2006; Tavernise, Oppel, and Schmitt 2009].

As of today, the consequences of the Afghani opium crisis of 2010 remain unclear. While the opium market is generally considered to be back to 2009 levels, prices are continuing to go up, and users have had to switch to other substances such as desomorphine (krokodil) or acetylated opium (kompot) (UNODC 2012). Afghanistan and Burma continue to be the primary cultivation location for poppies, but trafficking routes are switching away from the traditional Balkan route (from Afghanistan through Central Europe) and toward the African coastal markets and countries of South-East Asia (UNODC 2012).

Coca Cultivation. Unlike opium, which has been cultivated in many areas, provided conditions are favorable, coca is native to the Andean region of South America, and its cultivation never really developed elsewhere (there was some production in Indonesia and Japan during the first part of the twentieth century) (Buxton 2006; UNODC 2008a). It is, however, not native to Colombia, where it was introduced only in the 1980s, but which is now the largest producer (Buxton 2006). According to UNODC, almost all of the world's cocaine is produced in South America (specifically Peru, Bolivia, and Colombia), and most of that is consumed in North America (UNODC 2008d).

Traditionally, coca leaves were grown for chewing as a mild stimulant, medicinal remedies, and rituals, and archeologists have found evidence of coca cultivation and consumption dating back to precolonial Inca civilization (Arias 2005; Fichtelberg 2008). Cocaine was first extracted from the coca leaf in 1859, and was used in the soft drink Coca-Cola until it was banned in the 1920s; however, it is not until the 1970s that its use began to soar in the United States. Distribution changed from individual "mules" (i.e., carriers) transporting small quantities on their person or by swallowing wrapped packages or in simple suitcases, to a global and complex system run by Colombian cartels (described later in this chapter).

Much like opium, the cocaine trade needs to be understood within its larger political context. As a matter of fact, whereas coca cultivation is a traditional element of Peruvian and Bolivian culture, it is the political instability, and even civil wars in the case of Peru and Colombia, which have allowed the illegal cocaine trade to flourish (Arias 2005; Fichtelberg 2008). The rise and fall of the drug cartels has to be understood within that context, but, in addition, in both Peru and Colombia, revolutionary and reactionary terrorist groups such as the *Sendero Luminoso* (Shining Path) in Peru, and the United Self-Defense Forces and the Revolutionary Armed Forces of Colombia (FARC) in Colombia are involved in the drug trade and use its revenues to finance their fight. The cocaine drug market has recently shifted away from Colombia, back to Peru and Bolivia, and the cocaine consumption, while remaining mostly in North America, Europe, and Oceania, has seen declines in the United States, leading to increases in prices, while Europe has seen increases in consumption with a stable pricing (UNODC 2012).

There are three main transit routes for cocaine, the first two go to North America, one through Mexico (the largest one), and the other through the Caribbean; the third route goes to Western Europe, and uses transshipment points in West Africa. Recent shifts in the market seem contradictory, with the increased consumption in Europe being coupled with decreased seizures on the traditional routes, which would indicate the development of new trafficking modes, possibly including an increased use of containers (UNODC 2012).

Cannabis Cultivation. Although international and governmental organizations abound with information concerning a wide range of aspects concerning heroin and cocaine cultivation, production, distribution, and consumption, they lack comparable information about cannabis. This is posited to be due to the ambivalent attitude toward cannabis in recent history. Because of the ambivalence towards cannabis as a drug, only a few countries have aggressively pursued its eradication: Mexico, the United States, Canada, the European Union, Egypt, Morocco, and Lebanon (UNODC 2008a).

Unlike opium and coca, cannabis can be cultivated everywhere. It is a versatile and prolific plant cultivated in temperate and tropical climates all over the world. Its origin is unknown, but it has been posited that it first grew in temperate regions of Central Asia from where it was spread through trade and invasions (Booth 2005). Cultivated as far back as prehistorical times, cannabis not only yields the drug it is famous for, but also a durable fiber, which can be woven: hemp. Its oil-rich seeds can also be used in a variety of preparations, including drinks, or even baby food (as it is used in Sub-Saharan Africa) (Booth 2005). Thus, different varieties of the plant are grown for different purposes (see Booth 2005, for a complete history).

Cannabis' versatility and adaptation are what makes the analysis of cannabis cultivation prevalence problematic. Recent progress in hydroponics technologies and home-growing kits have amplified the issue and the main challenge now facing the world community regarding cannabis is its omnipresence. In 2006, the UNODC gathered information from 127 countries that identified themselves as producers of cannabis. Data indicate that most of the trafficking in cannabis happens at the local or intraregional level. North America and Africa are the two largest areas in which cannabis seizures occur. Although cannabis herb from Mexico makes up the bulk of the U.S. cannabis market, cannabis resin from Morocco—and increasingly from Afghanistan—is directed towards the European market.

Recent developments in the United States, with the legalization of marijuana for recreational use in Colorado and Washington State during the 2012 elections solidify a continuing pattern of liberalization toward cannabis use. These two extreme examples are to be understood within a larger context of decriminalization, development of medical marijuana legislation, as well as depenalization (Reeve & Pump 2013). It is still unclear what impact these changes will have on marijuana markets, if any, and on policy at the global level.

Amphetamine-Type Stimulants Production. ATS are a more recent drug phenomenon than plant-based drugs. Indeed, it was not until 1887 and 1888 that amphetamine and methamphetamine were first synthesized, methylenedioxyamphetamine (MDA) and 3,4-methylenedioxymethamphetamine (MDMA or Ecstasy) were synthesized in 1910 and 1913 respectively; lysergic acid diethylamide (better known as LSD) was first synthesized in 1938. These drugs did not become popular until the end of the twentieth century, but they now represent the second most prevalent type of drug (in terms of annual use) after cannabis (UNODC 2012).

Unlike opium or coca, ATS present the advantage of not being geographically limited in terms of production (UNODC 2008b). Laboratories can be set up anywhere that precursor chemicals are available. In addition, ATS manufacture does not require the level of sophistication needed for heroin or cocaine production. ATS can be made by machines, and the production line can operate much faster and with fewer controls than that of heroin or cocaine (Chin 2009). This has led to dynamics of production and distribution different from other types of drugs, but somewhat similar to cannabis. It appears, however, that in recent years the ATS market has seen a shift from intraregional trafficking to broader and more complex distribution schemes involving large criminal organizations and unusual global associations (e.g., Asian-sourced precursors, West-African and Asian traffickers, and West European and North American chemists) operating large-scale production facilities (UNODC 2008b). In addition, the Internet has emerged as a medium in ATS distribution, which adds yet another layer of difficulty in assessing patterns of manufacture, distribution, and exercising control (Buxton 2006).

In terms of market trends, 2010 marked a surge in methamphetamine seizures, surpassing amphetamines for the first time and doubling since 2008, due to local increases in Central America as well as East and South-East Asia. The European market, however, an all-time low of amphetamine seizures since 2002, but a resurgence of ecstasy, which has also been increasing in the United States, Oceania, and South-East Asia. Finally, much like with cocaine, West Africa is emerging as a new transshipment point for ATS drugs (UNODC 2012).

Drug Trafficking as Business

Organized Crime and Drug Trafficking

In the post-World War II era, and based on patterns established during the Prohibition, the Mafia was said to be responsible for 95 percent of heroin importation in the United States (reports are contradictory, however; some reports allege that the main bosses had prohibited such a low source of revenue) (Ryan 2001). Since then, however, many different types of criminal organizations have become involved in the drug trade. They vary in a variety of ways, including their organizational structure, the type of drug trade they are involved with, and the nationality or ethnicity of their members. The following is a brief presentation of three examples.

Colombian drug cartels. By the 1980s, the cocaine trade was largely dominated by the Medellin and Cali cartels from Colombia (UNODC 2008a; Arias 2005). Even though they in no way constituted cartels in the traditional sense of the term (e.g., they did not regulate prices), the term stuck and today's Mexican drug organizations are also known as cartels. Drug trafficking emerged in Columbia, like in many other countries, out of political instability, internal conflicts, and political violence in geographic areas that were physically difficult to control. The Medellin cartel, out of the town of Medellin, Colombia, was led by Pablo Escobar, Carlos Lehder, and the three Ochoa brothers (Jorge, Juan David, and Fabio). As an organization, they were known for their use of violence as well as their "Robin Hood" tendencies of providing social services in their areas of origin. The Cali cartel, out of the town of Cali, Colombia, was led by José Santacruz Londoño, Helmer Herrero Buitrago, and the Rodriguez-Orejuela brothers (Gilberto and Miguel). In contrast with the Medellin cartel, the Cali cartel put its emphasis on cultivating good relations with the people in power, and frowned upon the use of violence. Structurally speaking, cartels allow for a lowering of risks for the individual smuggler bringing together a network of criminals who can share the risks (Arias 2005). The cartels followed a top-down organizational structure, with decisions made at the top and carried out by subordinates, and their drug trafficking activities encompassed all aspects of the industry (Fichtelberg 2008). They reinvested their profits from the drug trade into a range of other activities, mostly legal.

The cartels were supposed to share the U.S. market, Medellin having Miami, Cali having New York. The situation, however, could not last and drug turf wars erupted. Soon the level of drug-related violence related to the introduction of the cheaper "crack" cocaine prompted a strong U.S. response. Under pressure from the United States to extradite the leaders of the cartels if they were not to lose their Narcotics Certification, the Colombian government cracked down on the Medellin and Cali cartels. The Medellin cartel responded with violence, killing or taking hostage government officials and judges, and allegedly blowing up a commercial airplane, killing 133 passengers. Pablo Escobar was shot and killed during a coordinated police operation between Colombian and U.S. forces. Most of the heads of the Cali cartel were brought to justice after the United States gathered intelligence alleging that Ernesto Samper's 1994 presidential campaign received funding from them, and Samper pledged to bring the cartel down. Because of their structure, once the heads of the cartels were dead or imprisoned, their operations crumbled. By the end of the 1990s, the Colombian drug cartels had ceased to exist (Arias 2005; Fichtelberg 2008).

The Case of Mexico. Because of its geographic location, as well as its political make up, Mexico is where most of the drugs consumed in the United States come from. Some of them, cannabis, methamphetamine, and heroin, are produced there; others, such as cocaine, are brought through the country on their way to the United States. The fall of the Colombian cartels in the 1990s, and the closing of the Florida smuggling route, allowed the Mexican drug cartels to grow in strength and dominate the U.S. market despite numerous enforcement efforts from both Mexico and the United States. Since the election of Felipe Calderón (see below), the level of drug-related violence has seen an upsurge, as he has declared an all-out war on the cartels (Cook 2007).

There are seven identified Mexican drug cartels: the Sinaola cartel; the Gulf cartel; la Familia Michoachana (also known as Milenio or Valencia cartel); the Juarez cartel; the Tijuana cartel; the Colima cartel; and the Oaxaca cartel (Cook 2007). Two alliances have emerged between cartels in recent years: the Tijuana and Gulf cartels are cooperating on some issues, and the Sinaloa, Juarez, and Valencia cartels have joined in what they call "the Federation" for national operations. Their activities involve all aspects of drug cultivation, production, transportation, and distribution, as well as the transportation of cocaine from South America. Their advantage lies in their knowledge and control of transit routes from Mexico to the United States, as well as their strong network of established contacts and cells in the United States (Cook 2007; Archibold 2009). They are organized into hierarchical, yet independent, cells that allow for flexibility and adaptation, as well as protecting the larger organization from law enforcement (Fichtelberg 2008). They have maintained and developed their operations using corruption and violence like the Medellin and Cali cartels.

Some of the characteristics that make the Mexican cartels of particular concern to the United States, as well as examples of mutant criminal organizations, are: (1) their use of loose gun regulations in U.S. border states in order to reinvest drug money into armaments (Archibold 2009), (2) their involvement in the production of methamphetamine and cultivation of cannabis in the United States, and (3) their involvement with Latino street gangs in the United States [e.g., Latin Kings and the Mara Salvatrucha (MS-13)] (Cook 2007).

Following an increase in drug-related violence due to turf wars between cartels, in December 2006 President Calderón began an assault on the Mexican drug cartels. This endeavor has been accompanied by a purge of the Mexican federal police; the involvement of the Mexican military force, which is usually considered the least corrupt of all government bodies; and an effort to extradite drug criminal from Mexico to the United States (Archibold 2009; Cook 2007). The cartels, however, have not taken kindly to the government's goal to bring them down and cartel-related violence reached an all-time high in early 2009 (Archibold 2009).

The United Wa State Army and the Golden Triangle. In his study of drug trafficking in the Golden Triangle, Chin (2009) provides insight in the characteristics of the opiate market from the ground up. He underscores the poverty of the opium farmers in the Wa region, who grow poppies: (1) because they have done so for generations, (2) because it allows them to overcome the deficiencies of the rice culture in that area, (3) because the Wa government requests they pay an opium tax, and (4) because it is a cash crop.

This last element should, however, not be misunderstood. Opium farmers in the Wa region are poor. They are at the bottom of the opium trade business ladder—the poorest, and those whose lives are most difficult. Opium cultivation and harvesting is a painstaking process that takes years to master (Smith and Kethineni 2007).

Chin (2009) also describes the various levels and types of opium trade within the area, contrasting low-level opium traders, who often have to walk for hours if not days to individual farmers' houses in the highlands in order to purchase opium paste, with the big heroin bosses or drug kingpins, mostly associated or directly involved with the Wa government, who live in new brick houses and drive big cars. He paints a picture of a society in which opium deals happen in individual farmers' houses or in open air markets, and in which the riches accumulated by the higher-ranking actors do not trickle down to the base. Chin (2009) also writes of a population who consume their own production and suffers from it, which is an interesting cultural contrast compared to what Smith and Kethineni (2007) describe as strict abstinence from consumption and drug use shaming among the licit opium farmers in India.

Overall, Chin (2009) underscores the fact that, although there is no question that the United Wa State Army functions as a narco-government, they do not control the opium trade in the Golden Triangle, as has been posited by the U.S. drug intelligence community, nor do the other ethnic minorities in Burma. He also argues that Chinese criminal organizations, such as the triads, are not involved in the drug trade, as opposed to what many governmental and international organizations have stated. According to him, their rigid structure does not render them amenable to the specificities of international drug trafficking. Chinese triads are indeed highly hierarchical structures in which decisions have to be made in a top-down fashion. The reach of overall structure goes beyond drug trafficking, with individuals belonging to the triads not as specialized agents, but rather as part of the hierarchy. The Asian heroin trade, in contrast and as described by Chin, is made up of a fluid mosaic of actors, each playing a role in the industry and each considering it just that: an industry. One of his subjects put it as follows:

> In the West, you view heroin production as a crime and an evil thing to do, but there [in the Kokang and the Wa areas] it is perfectly legal and normal. People in the area see the production of heroin as simply another type of business, and for local authorities it is just another way to generate income. No matter where you are from— China, other parts of Burma, Thailand, or Taiwan—as long as you are willing to pay a certain amount of money to the local authori-

ties, they are willing to allow you to get involved in the heroin production. You would get in trouble only if you do not pay .... (Chin
2009, 224)

The Structure of the Drug Trafficking Industry

Based on the previously cited cases, some broad generalizations can be made
regarding the structure of the drug trafficking industry. As far as the heroin
and cocaine drug trades are concerned, the industry's structure can be seen as
having three main levels:

- low-level suppliers, e.g., individual farmers growing coca or poppy because (a) it provides them with the best return on their investment
  (Williams 1993), (b) it is the only thing they know how to do, (c) because they have done so for generations, and (d) because their government forces them to (Chin 2009);
- high-level traffickers involved in the transformation of the raw product
  into its consumption form as well as wholesale distribution, usually organized in criminal groups (Chin 2009; EMDDCA 2008; UNODC 2008b;
  Williams 1993);
- low-level distributors and retailers, e.g., individual mules, gang members, drug dealers, and pushers who turn to crime as a means of subsis-
  tence when other avenues have failed them (Archibold 2009).

Of course, these three levels provide more of a modeling framework than
a "true-to-life" picture of the system. In reality, each level is broken down into
sublevels, and the model is less a hierarchy than a gradation of power. Overall, studies of specific drug-producing areas (Chin 2009), trade routes for specific drugs (Zaitch 2002), and trafficking in specific areas (Astorga 2001;
Griffith 1997) have shown that the structure of drug trafficking organizations
does not correspond to that of organized crime, and is generally looser, less
organized, more fragmented, but also more flexible and adaptive. Those studies have also shown that where there was a structure, it was usually that of a
family business.

Money Laundering

As a criminal enterprise, our understanding of international drug trafficking cannot be complete without an understanding of the mechanisms through
which the financial profits of the illicit trade are transformed into funds available for licit transactions. In other words, making money illegally will only get

your so far, you will need to find a way to reintroduce your illegally earned money in the legal market. This is what money laundering is.

Money laundering has been defined, at the international level, in the 1988 United Nations Convention against Illicit Traffic in Narcotic Drugs and Psychotropic Substances or Vienna Convention, the 2000 United Nations Convention against Transnational Organized Crime or Palermo Convention, and by the Financial Action Task Force on Money Laundering (FATF). These definitions all identify money laundering as the series of transactions aiming at legitimizing proceeds from illegal activities (Schott 2006).

Established in 1989 in Paris by the Group of Seven (G7), the FATF is the international organization in charge of supervising and regulating the health of the international financial system by establishing standards aimed at combating money laundering, corruption, and the financing of terrorism (FATF 2010). It comprises 34 member jurisdictions (countries and two regional organizations), eight associate members (regional bodies concerned with money laundering), and 26 observers (international organizations with central or tangential interest in money laundering).

Generally speaking, money laundering follows a three-stage process involving placement, layering, and integration. First, illegitimate cash is introduced in the financial system, often via a bank account. The second stage of the money laundering process aims at obscuring the illegitimate origin of the funds, by transferring them to another financial institution or transforming them into another financial product. Finally, the funds are invested in the legitimate economy, in the form of purchases.

While it is impossible to gather precise information on the amount of money laundered, the International Monetary Fund estimates it could represent between two and five percent of the global GDP (Schott 2006; Tanzi 1996). Some of the ways in which illegitimate funds are laundered include, but are not limited to, the use of:

- front companies: actual companies in which illegitimate and legitimate funds blend;
- shell companies: these have no other role than to obscure the origin of illegitimate funds;
- the securities sector: either at the placement stage of the money laundering process by trading illegitimate cash for securities through the use of complicit brokers, or at the layering stage, by purchasing securities with illegal funds already placed in the legal financial system;
- the insurance sector: this is very similar to the ways in which money can be laundered through the securities sector;

- the gold and diamond markets: either at the placement stage by simply purchasing gold or diamonds with illegitimate cash, or by using a gold or diamond trading company as a front company, or if the diamonds or gold are themselves the illegal proceeds of the criminal organization's activities;
- credit cards: by using illegitimate funds to pay credit card debt, or cash advance debt (FATF 2003).

Modeling the Drug Trafficking Industry

International drug trafficking markets and organizations have been analyzed using a number of different frameworks, but business and economic models have often been seen as fruitful analytical tools.

Williams (1993) compares the heroin and cocaine trafficking organizations in the 1990s with licit business organizations. Primarily using Columbian cocaine cartels and Chinese triads as his examples, he underscores the fact that they are hierarchically structured organizations that function more like franchises, rather than rigid top-down models. They also forge alliances with other criminal organizations, even though those alliances are rarely as straightforward as a merger or a contract. Williams notes that the different levels of an organization have different identities—e.g., a wholesale market is characterized by cooperation between organizations and across ethnic divides, whereas the retail level is characterized by fierce competition between and within groups—that, he contends, is not dissimilar to legitimate business models. Cooperation at the highest level and competition at the lower levels are instrumental in ensuring the profitability of the enterprise.

Markets are shaped by demand and supply. In the domain of drug control, international policies have traditionally been dominated by supply-oriented reduction strategies (Bewley-Taylor 2001; Buxton 2006; Fazey 2003), with only a few examples of demand-oriented strategies (Chatwin 2008; Gerber and Jensen 2001). It has been argued that such an orientation could be seen as the main world actors (and UNODC donors), who also happen to be the main consumers of drugs, bullying the producing regions of the world, who also happen to not do as well on the world stage (Bewley-Taylor 2001; Buxton 2006; Fazey 2003; Gerber and Jensen 2001). Demand, however, remains an integral component of the drug market, and it is with this in mind that Costa Sorti and De Grauwe (2009a) attempt to explain some perplexing recent trends in the heroin and cocaine markets through economic modeling. Indeed, in spite of consistently increasing budgets for supply reduction strategy in the two main heroin and cocaine consumption markets, and contrary to what the Bush administration maintained in the late 2000s (Walsh

2009), retail prices have consistently fallen in the past twenty years in Europe and the United States, whereas producer prices either remained stable or increased (Fries, Anthony, Cseko, Gaither, and Shulman 2008; UNODC 2008c).

Modeling the retail market, the authors show that even though an increase in drug seizures will lead to an increase in retail prices that in turn will lead to lower consumption levels, globalization increases the availability of drug dealers, which forces a price decrease, potentially resulting in a consumption increase (depending on the sensitivity to price of drug users, which the authors hypothesize to be dependent on demand-focused policies). When modeling the production market, the authors take into consideration evidence that eradication efforts in Andean countries have coincided with increases in productivity due to the impact of globalization, leading to unchanged supply levels (Costa Sorti and De Grauwe 2009b). The retail and production market models are then linked following an import-export market model. Globalization within that context is seen as explaining decreases in retail prices, increases in producer prices and production levels, increases in supply reduction efforts, and stable levels of consumption by creating more competitive market structures, lowering risk premiums because of the increased availability of low-level dealers, and increasing the efficiency at all levels of the drug business.

Responses to the Drug Problem

A Brief History of International Drug Control[1]

As mentioned in the introduction it is what came to be known as the "Chinese opium epidemic" (UNODC 2008a) that prompted an international impetus for drug control one hundred years ago. The "epidemic" was the result of the use of opium as a source of income by colonizing powers, mostly the British East India Company, during a time England was at war with its North American colonies. Opium had been brought to China from India, where it was mainly cultivated by Arab merchants, possibly around the turn of the first millennium (UNODC 2008a). Its popularity increased with two elements: first, the lower prices achieved through expanded cultivation under a monopolistic regime promoted by the Mogul emperor in India in the mid-1500s; and second, the introduction of smoked tobacco in Southeast Asia by colonials, more

---

1. A timeline of the main international drug conventions, treaties, and conferences, as well as U.S. drug policies is provided at the end of this section.

specifically, the introduction of a tobacco/opium mixture by Dutch merchants in Taiwan (the Formosa) (UNODC 2008a). Once demand was established in China, there was no shortage of suppliers, despite repeated efforts by the Chinese emperors to ban the opium trade and consumption. The British went as far as fighting the Chinese over the matter of legalizing opium trade, and, having lost, the Chinese began to cultivate opium. This led to a boom in opium production and to an increased demand in the Western markets, where grassroot temperance organizations started lobbying to stop the opium trade (Albrecht 2001; Buxton 2006; UNODC 2008a).

The Shanghai Commission of 1909 laid groundwork for what was to be a long series of treaties and conventions, first independent from any supervisory organization, then under the authority of the League of Nations, and finally under the United Nations. First, the goal was to regulate and control what was then the licit trade of narcotics. It was not until 1936 that it was made illegal, and not until 1961 that a comprehensive text was adopted, unifying the half-century worth of disparate international drug regulation (Albrecht 2001; Fields, Holt, and Ferrell 2005; UNODC 2008a). The 1961 Single Convention was 13 years in the making because of the tensions of the Cold War, but as of 2008, it has been signed by 183 states, 95 percent of all UN member states (UNODC 2008a). The Single Convention covers:

- definitions of the substances under control;
- the framework for the operations of the international drug control bodies;
- reporting obligations of states members;
- obligations regarding the production, manufacture, trade, and consumption of controlled substances; and
- actions to be taken against illicit traffic and penal provisions (UNODC 2008b, 138).

With the rise in ATS consumption following World War II, new measures were needed to place non-plant-based psychotropic drugs under international control. The 1971 Convention on Psychotropic Substances provided an answer to the emerging problem, which was different from the traditional narcotics problem because the producer countries were some of the most powerful in the world (UNODC 2008a). The Convention nevertheless found support equal to that of 1961, and created four different schedules for psychotropic substances, each establishing a different set of controls.

In the 1980s it appeared the drug problem had reached epidemic dimensions, not only in the United States but throughout the world. Between the emergence of local ATS laboratories in the United States, Europe, and Southeast Asia, and the dominance of the Medellin and Cali cartels from Colombia in the cocaine trade, the drug problem was becoming more of a security and governance problem than a criminal justice and health issue. In response to this crisis, the UN General Assembly required that a Convention take place, and in 1988, the UN Conference for the Adoption of a Convention against Illicit Traffic in Narcotics Drugs and Psychotropic Substances took place in Vienna, resulting in the 1988 Convention against Illicit Traffic in Narcotics Drugs and Psychotropic Substances. This text bolstered the international stance on drug control by putting the emphasis on legal issues, making drug trafficking as well as personal drug consumption-related behaviors criminal offenses, by focusing on money laundering, and by promoting extradition (UNODC 2008a).

Partly as a result of the strengthened international approach, but also because of the hardline attacks by the United States on the Colombian cocaine trade, by the mid-1990s the Medellin and Cali cartels had been dismantled. This, however, did not end drug trafficking and the big organizations were replaced by smaller, more flexible structures. The fall of the Iron Curtain contributed to increased consumption and trafficking levels in the former communist bloc but also in Western Europe. ATS continued to grow in popularity, and countries alongside drug transit routes started to see their consumption increase as well (UNODC 2008a). As a result, the UN General Assembly convened in a Special Session in 1998 and unanimously adopted a "Political Declaration" and "Guiding Principles on Demand Reduction." These documents reiterated the concept of "shared responsibility" first mentioned in the 1984 Declaration on the Control of Drug Trafficking and Drug Abuse, as well as the need for a "balanced approach" that was cited in the 1987 Multidisciplinary Comprehensive Outline. For the first time, drug control and fundamental freedoms were integrated, and drug trafficking was linked with terrorism. A number of targets and progress points were established, with the requirement for states to submit biennial progress reports to the Commission on Narcotic Drugs, and 2008 was made a due date for measurable progress (UNODC 2008a). By early 2000s, progress appeared to have been made in reducing cultivation areas in Peru, Bolivia, Colombia, Morocco, Thailand, Burma, and Laos (i.e., Lao PDR). Demand, however, continued to rise.

The 2008 deadline came and went, and the Shanghai Commission centennial is upon us, and yet the situation of drugs in the world continues to present many challenges. The areas under poppy cultivation in Afghanistan are at an all-time high, and the opium trade, linked with terror networks in the Golden Crescent, has not only rendered the political situation both in Afghanistan and in Pakistan more than fragile, but the market has bled locally, leading to increased consumption in the region. The connection between the U.S. market and the suppliers of cocaine, heroin, and cannabis in Mexico has led to corruption and strengthened cartels, which in turn brought on a warlike situation between the cartels and the government of President Calderon, who is resolved to bring an end to what is seen as a plague for Mexico. The new transshipment routes from South America to Europe via West Africa have opened new consumer markets to cocaine in areas ill-prepared to care for addicts. The multiplication of home-grown, high-potency marijuana at the local level makes market trends difficult to assess and control, and the continued popularity of ATS, as well as their manufacturing patterns, remain highly problematic in many areas.

Timeline

Note: The multilateral system regulating illicit drugs requires that member states ratify one of the three Conventions (1961, 1971, 1988) to align their national law with international law (UNODC, 2008a).

United States 1875: San Francisco is the first city to ban opium smoking by Chinese nationals, eleven states follow within a decade.
International 1909: International Opium Commission in Shanghai
International 1912: International Opium Convention at The Hague
    Discussed cocaine and heroin, in addition to opium and morphine.
United States 1914: Harrison Narcotics Act
    Ban on opium; and
    Established the Narcotics Division under the Treasury Department.
United States 1918: Prohibition
International 1920: League of Nations's first assembly
    Creation of an Advisory Committee on Traffic in Opium and Other Dangerous Drugs (Opium Advisory Committee), taking over the functions laid out by the Hague Convention of 1912.
United States 1922: Narcotic Drug Import and Export Act (Jones-Miller Act)
    Limited narcotics to legitimate medical use; and
    Established the Federal Narcotics Control Board under the Treasury Department.
United States 1924: Heroin Act
    Made it illegal to manufacture heroin.
International 1925: Agreement Concerning the Manufacture of, Internal Trade in, and Use of Prepared Opium signed by Britain, India, France, Japan, The Netherlands, Portugal, and Thailand.
    International Opium Convention in Geneva
      Ratified by fifty-six countries;
      Adopted the still-existing system of certified and authorized imports/exports of narcotics by competent authorities;
      Established the Permanent Central Board, precursor to the International Narcotics Control Board; and
      Inclusion of cannabis.

United States 1930: Creation of the Federal Bureau of Narcotics
          Consolidated the Federal Narcotics Control Board and the Narcotic Division established by the Harrison Narcotics Act of 1914; and Harry J. Anslinger was appointed commissioner.

International 1931: Convention for Limiting the Manufacture and Regulating the Distribution of Narcotic Drugs in Geneva
          Eventually ratified by sixty-seven countries, including the United States;
          Limited the production of narcotics to estimated medical needs, overviewed by the Drug Supervisory Body; and
          First introduction of a drug "schedule."

International 1936: Convention for the Suppression of the Illicit Trafficking in Dangerous Drugs
          First international treaty to make certain drug offenses international offenses; and
          Signed by only thirteen countries, not the United States.

United States 1937: Marijuana Tax Act
          Applied similar control to marijuana as other narcotics.

United States 1938: Food, Drug and Cosmetic Act
          Food and Drug Administration is given control over drug safety; and
          Drugs are redefined and some drugs are established as being obtainable via the use of a prescription.

United States 1942: Opium Poppy Control Act
          Prohibited growing poppy without a license.

International 1946: Transfer of the League of Nations' drug control responsibilities to the UN Commission on Narcotic Drugs

International 1948: Synthetic Narcotics Protocol
          Placed more substances under international control.

United States 1951: Durham-Humphrey Amendment
          Guidelines for prescription drugs.
          Boggs Amendment to the Harrison Narcotic Act
          Mandatory sentences for narcotics violations.

International 1953: Protocol for Limiting and Regulating the Cultivation of the Poppy Plant, the Production of, International and Wholesale Trade in and Use of Opium
          Limited to Bulgaria, Greece, India, Iran, Turkey, the USSR, and Yugoslavia to legally cultivate and export opium; and
          Signed and ratified by sixty-one countries.

United States 1956: Narcotics Control Act
          More severe penalties for narcotics violations.

International 1961: Single Convention
          Unification of all previous international drug control treaties;
          Creation of the International Narcotics Control Board (INCB) replacing the Permanent Central Board and the Drug Supervisory Body; and
          Signed by 186 states.

United States 1965: Drug Abuse Control Amendments (DACA)

Control over synthetic drugs (e.g., amphetamines, barbiturates, LSD); and

Established the Bureau of Narcotics and Dangerous Drugs.

United States 1966: Narcotic Addict Rehabilitation Act (NARA)

Allowed treatment as an alternative to jail.

United States 1968: DACA Amendments

Sentence could be suspended and records expunged if no reoffense for one year.

United States 1970: Comprehensive Drug Abuse and Control Act

Establishment of drugs "schedules."

International 1971: Convention on Psychotropic Substances

Inclusion of non-plant-based psychotropic drugs such as ATS, hallucinogens, sedative hypnotic and anxiolytics, analgesics, and antidepressant under international drug control;

Establishment of schedules; and

Signed by 183 countries.

United States 1972: Drug Abuse Office and Treatment Act

Established federally funded programs for prevention and treatment.

International 1972: Protocol to amend the Single Convention

Strengthen supply and demand reduction;

Signed by all 1961 signatories except Afghanistan, Chad, and Laos (Lao PDR); and

Creation of the U.N. Fund for Drug Abuse Control aiming at providing support in crop substitution efforts and alternative development programs.

United States 1973: Report from the Commission on Marihuana and Drug Abuse

Small amounts of marijuana should be decriminalized

Methadone Control Act;

Regulated methadone licensing;

Creation of the Alcohol, Drug Abuse, and Mental Health Administration; and

Creation of the Drug Enforcement Administration to replace the Bureau of Narcotics and Dangerous Drugs.

United States 1974: Drug Abuse Treatment and Control Amendment

United States 1978: Drug Abuse Treatment and Control Amendment

Both extend 1972 Act;

Alcohol and Drug Abuse Education Amendments; and

Set up education programs with the Department of Education.

United States 1980: Drug Abuse Prevention, Treatment, and Rehabilitation Amendments

Extended prevention education and treatment programs.

International 1981: International Drug Abuse Control Strategy

Adoption of a five-year international strategy.

United States 1984: Drug Offenders Act

Special treatment programs for offenders.

International 1984: Declaration on the Control of Drug Trafficking and Drug Abuse by the General Assembly "illegal production of, illicit demand for, abuse of and illicit trafficking in drugs impede economic and social progress, constitute a grave threat to the security and development of many countries and people and should be combated by all moral, legal and institutional means, at the national, regional, and international levels" (UNODC 2008b, 203).

International 1987: Declaration and Comprehensive Multidisciplinary Outline for Future Activities (CMO)

Established thirty-five targets falling either under prevention and reduction of illicit demand, control of supply, suppression of illicit trafficking, or treatment and rehabilitation.

United States 1988: Anti-Drug Abuse Act

Established the Office of National Drug Control Policy.

International 1988: Convention against Illicit Traffic in Narcotic Drugs and Psychotropic Substances

Made drug trafficking not only a "punishable offense" (1961 Single Convention), but a criminal offense along with personal consumption-related behaviors;

Focused on money laundering;

Included international control of precursor chemicals;

Promoted extradition; and

Signed by 182 countries.

International 1989: Creation of the Financial Action Task Force (FATF)

Under the umbrella of the Organization for Economic Co-Operation and Development (OECD); and

Targeted money-laundering activities.

United States 1992: Substance Abuse and Mental Health Services Administration replaces the ADAMHA

International 1998: UN General Assembly Special Session on Drugs (UNGASS)

Linked drug trafficking to terrorism for the first time;

Established 2008 as the target date for measurable progress;

Mandated states to report biennially on progress to the Commission on Narcotic Drugs; and

Included a special Action Plan against Illicit Manufacture, Trafficking and Abuse of ATS and their Precursors.

International 2000: UN Convention against Transnational Organized Crime

Further established definitions of money laundering;

Broadened money laundering predicate offenses beyond drug trafficking, inclusive of other types of organized criminal activities; and

Signed by 147 countries.

International 2000: UN Millennium Declaration

Regarding peace, security, and disarmament, the member states resolve: "To redouble [their] efforts to implement [their] commitment to counter the world drug problem."

United States 2012: Colorado and Washington State become the first two states to legalize marijuana for recreational use

Sources for the timeline include UNODC 2008a, Buxton 2006; Fields, Holt, and Ferrell 2005; Gerber and Jensen 2001; Goode 2007.

Institutions of Monitoring, Control, and Enforcement

In order to coordinate and administer the multitude of policies passed throughout the twentieth century regarding drug control, a number of institutions have been created and are involved at various levels of the world stage. The main organizations are listed here.

International Level

Commission on Narcotic Drugs (CND). Founded in 1946 by the Economic and Social Council, its headquarters are in Vienna, Austria. The CND is the main policy making body within the UN system on drug-related issues. It is made up of 53 members elected according to the following schema: 11 for African states; 11 for Asian states; 10 Latin American and Caribbean states; 6 for Eastern European states; 14 for Western European and other states; and additional seat that rotates among the Asian, Latin American and Caribbean states every four years. Members are selected from among the parties to the 1961 Single Convention with regard to the representation of countries involved in production as well as consumption as well as geographic representation.

Financial Action Task Force on Money-Laundering (FATF). Established at the G-7 Summit in Paris in 1989, FATF is located in Paris, France. It is a policy-making intergovernmental body in charge of promoting policies at all levels that aim to combat money laundering and terrorist financing. Its membership has evolved since its creation and currently involves 32 countries and two regional organizations.

International Narcotics Control Board (INCB). Founded in 1968 according to requirements of the 1961 Single Convention, it is located in Vienna, Austria. The INCB is an independent quasi-judicial body whose 13 members serve in their own capacity and are not government officials from member states. They are elected by the Economic and Social Council. Three of them must have medical or pharmacological experience and are chosen from a list selected by the World Health Organization. The other 10 are elected from a list of individuals selected by participating governments. Its goal is to monitor the implementation of the UN drug control conventions.

Interpol. Founded in 1923, with headquarters in Lyon, France, Interpol is the largest international police cooperation organization. Its goal is to provide support and coordination for national-level police forces on matters of international relevance. Interpol's four main functions are: (1) to secure global police communication services; (2) provide operational data services and databases for police; (3) provide operational police support services; and (4) provide police training and development. Regarding drugs, Interpol's role is to provide support and assistance to national police forces in their fight against drug production, trafficking, and abuse, as well as to identify trends in drug trafficking and criminal organizations involved in it.

UN Office on Drugs and Crime. Created in 1997 with the merger of the UN Drug Control Program and the Center for International Crime Prevention, it is located in Vienna, Austria. Its mission is to assist member states in their fight against illicit drugs, crime, and terrorism. Ninety percent of its funding comes from voluntary contributions, mostly from governments.

World Customs Organization (WCO). Established in 1952 as the Customs Co-Operation Council, and born out of a Western European post-World War II initiative, the WCO was renamed in 1994 and encompasses 174 customs administrations throughout the world. Its headquarters is in Brussels, Belgium. Similar to Interpol, its goal is to facilitate communication and cooperation between the world's customs agencies.

World Health Organization (WHO). Created in 1948 with headquarters in Geneva, Switzerland, WHO is the directing and coordinating authority for health within the UN system. With regard to drugs, its role is to provide technical expertise pertaining to the effects of substances and substance abuse.

Regional Level

Association of Southeast Asian States, ASEAN Senior Officials on Drug Matters (ASOD). Established in 1967 by the five founding countries of Indonesia, Malaysia, Philippines, Singapore, and Thailand, ASEAN now counts among its members Brunei Darussalam, Vietnam, Laos (Lao PDR), Burma, and Cambodia. The ASEAN Senior Officials on Drug Matter topic group within the organization focuses on coordinating and facilitating cooperation between member countries on the issues of drug trafficking and substance abuse.

Organization of American States (OAS), Inter-American Drug Abuse Control Commission (CICAD). Established in 1948 by 21 Western hemisphere countries, the OAS, which has its headquarters in Washington, D.C., consists of 35 countries. Its drug policy body, CICAD, was funded in 1986, and promotes cooperation and coordination amongst member states. Its goals are to (1) prevent and treat substance abuse; (2) reduce the supply and availability of illicit drugs; (3) strengthen national drug control institutions and machinery; (4) improve firearms and money-laundering control laws and practice; (5) develop alternate sources of income for growers of coca, poppy, and marijuana; (6) assist member governments to improve their data gathering and analysis on all aspects of the drug issue; and (7) help member states and the Western hemisphere as a whole measure their progress in addressing the drug problem.

European Union, European Monitoring Centre for Drugs and Drug Addiction (EMCDDA). Founded in 1993 to overcome the European Union's (EU) lack of a data and policy clearinghouse, the EMCDDA has its headquarters in Lisbon, Portugal. It provides the EU and its members information on the drug problem in the Union, as well as expertise in the area of best practices and evidence based policy.

Europol. Established in 1995, Europol acts as a coordinator in law enforcement among European member states. Located in The Hague, The Netherlands, Europol's mission focuses on illicit drug trafficking; illicit immigration networks; terrorism; forgery of money (i.e., counterfeiting of the Euro) and other means of payment; trafficking in human beings including child pornography; illicit vehicle trafficking; and money laundering. This mission is carried out via the delegation of a national unit to each member country. The national units serve as liaisons.

National Level: The United States

Drug policy, enforcement, and treatment in the United States is formalized through a variety of executive branch cabinets. Overseeing all is the White House's Office of National Drug Control Policy (ONDCP), a component of the Executive Office of the President, established by the 1988 Anti-Drug Abuse Act. The head of the ONDCP is known as the "drug czar."

Within the Justice Department, the Drug Enforcement Administration (DEA) is the main federal law enforcement agency on matters of drug crimes, with the peculiar aspect of having a large presence overseas. The National Drug Intelligence Center coordinates and consolidates intelligence on drug trafficking organization from law enforcement agencies.

Because of the international aspect of the drug problem, the State Department also has an agency dealing with issues pertaining to drugs at the international level: the Bureau of International Narcotics and Law Enforcement Affairs (BINLEA). Its role is to provide information to the President, the Secretary of State, and other U.S. agencies regarding international drug trafficking. BINLEA is also in charge of the Narcotics Certification Process, according to which U.S. aid is granted or withdrawn from countries based on their drug-control performances.

Two additional agencies in the U.S. drug-control apparatus are involved in the international aspect of the drug problem: the Department of Defense's U.S. Coast Guard, and the Department of Homeland Security's U.S. Customs and

Border Protection. Both agencies have enforcement and intelligence gathering roles in the fight against international drug trafficking.

Finally, because drugs not only pertain to law enforcement, but also to health, prevention, and treatment, the Department of Health and Human Services's Food and Drug Administration (FDA), and Substance Abuse and Mental Health Services Administrations (SAMHSA) are also key players in drug-related policy and treatment matters. The FDA is the agency in charge of establishing drug schedules according to their chemical properties and physiological effects, and SAMHSA's mission is to monitor the prevalence of drug abuse, as well as to promote, coordinate, and facilitate access to prevention and treatment programs.

Range of Responses to the Drug Problem: Looking to the Future

One of the main challenges facing the international community in its quest to resolve the drug problem is the need for a uniform and comprehensive approach. Considering the truly global aspect of the drug issue, unilateral actions are threats to the overall efforts (UNODC 2008a). Along with elements presented in this chapter and including Mexican attempts to crack down on the drug trade in that country, leading to questions regarding the legalization of marijuana, or the election of Evo Morales, the coca farmers union leader, as president of Bolivia in 2006 and his withdrawal from cooperation with the DEA, a couple of aspects pertaining to current drug policies should be underscored. In manner of a conclusion, this section presents the case of Europe, and the future of U.S. drug policy.

The Confusing Case of European Extremes

In Europe, although the overarching common goal has recently taken a turn towards harm reduction by emphasizing the need for a "comprehensive, balanced, and evidence based" set of drug policies (EMCDDA 2008), there remains a wide range of variation (Chatwin 2008; EMCDDA 2007, 2008). Specifically, a wide range of attitudes is represented within the EU, from tolerance to temperance, and they greatly affect the necessity to cooperate and coordinate policies under the requirements of the Maastricht Treaty of 1992. Some of those extremes are the Dutch, with their policy of tolerance toward "soft drugs"; the Swiss, with their emphasis on harm reduction through the establishment of heroin maintenance programs; or the Swedes, with their zero-tolerance approach to drugs (Chatwin 2008; Killias 2001).

The Dutch approach is based on pragmatism and normalization. They do not view the drug problem as one that can be solved, and therefore have opted for tolerance with the goal of better controlling behaviors perceived as harmless (i.e., the use of cannabis and mild hallucinogens) and isolating those that are problematic (e.g., severe drug addiction on "hard" drugs) in order to provide treatment and heighten security. The intriguing aspect of the Dutch approach to drug policy is that it is based on a contradiction: although the coffee shops where individuals may buy individual doses of drugs for their consumption are legal, the importation or cultivation of drugs in large amounts is illegal. Nevertheless, the contradiction appears to be a working one and allows for the Dutch's lack of tolerance toward drug trafficking (Chatwin 2008).

As far as the Swiss are concerned, they were following a U.S.-type drug policy of criminal justice enforcement until the 1990s. The threats caused by the HIV-AIDS epidemic, however, and the role of shared hypodermic needles in its transmission, caused them to question their strategies and reposition their approach. The implementation of needle-exchange programs had indeed led to a peculiar phenomenon: geographic patterns of use and associated property crime became concentrated around the needle-exchange programs outlets. Crackdowns on "needle parks" only led to displacement, and thus heroin maintenance programs emerged out of a pragmatic concern for public order, safety, and harm reduction. Those programs are carried out on a small-scale, patients are carefully screened, and the injection of the prescription heroin or substitution drug occurs on the premises, under supervision. In addition, an array of social services are available in the clinics. Such an approach has allowed for drug-use-related crime to go down overall, improved public order and safety conditions, a continued stabilization of rates of hypodermic needle HIV-AIDS transmission, and the treatment or stabilization of heroin addicts (Killias 2001).

Finally, on the other end of the European spectrum of drug policies, the Swedes find themselves at odd with the above examples. Since the 1970s, the Swedes have entirely rejected their previously liberal drug policy with the aim of abolishing the use of all drugs. In Sweden, there is no differentiation between supply-reduction and demand-reduction measures, nor is there any difference between "hard" and "soft" drugs. Drug crimes all carry sentences of imprisonment, and individuals can be prosecuted for crimes based on blood or urine samples that the police have the right to collect if they suspect use. This attitude is seen as emerging from the need for the Swedes to assert their national identity, which drugs threaten. Drugs are therefore seen as a problem coming from outside, positioning drugs as a political object, much like it has been used throughout U.S. history (Chatwin 2008).

U.S. Policy

Although drug policy in the United States has been dominated since the beginning by a well-documented and vocally criticized prohibition approach (Buxton 2006; Gerber and Jensen 2001), changes have been underway particularly regarding cannabis regulation, and accelerating since the 2008 election of Barack Obama. In March 2009, while visiting drug-violence ridden Mexico, Secretary of State Clinton stated: "Clearly, what we have been doing has not worked .... Our insatiable demand for illegal drugs fuels the drug trade, our inability to prevent weapons from being illegally smuggled across the border to arm these criminals causes the deaths of police, of soldiers and civilians" (Sheridan 2009, A01). Such a strong condemnation of previous policies is not the only thing hinting at change regarding drugs in the Obama administration. Up until 2012 the question of legalization remained contentious and raised seriously only in California (Cathcart 2009), but the 2012 election cycle proved that the winds were turning and change was happening, with the bills passed in Colorado and Washington State legalizing marijuana for recreational use. While Oregon voters rejected such a bill in the 2012 election, the legislature is moving on with a similar bill. Maine also has such a bill pending. Medical marijuana is now legal in 18 states and the District of Columbia, and being considered in Illinois. And finally, Alabama and Vermont have pending laws aiming at decriminalizing small amounts of Cannabis (Reeve & Pump 2013). It is of course too early to tell what effect such changes will have on the drug situation in the United States.

Web Sources

1. Information about the Association of Southeast Asian Nations (ASEAN) Senior Officials on Drug Matters is available at:
   http://www.aseansec.org/5682.htm
2. Bureau of International Narcotics and Law Enforcement Affairs is available at:
   http://www.state.gov/p/inl/
3. Commission on Narcotic Drugs is available at:
   http://www.unodc.org/unodc/en/commissions/CND/index.html
4. Drug Enforcement Administration (DEA) information is available at:
   http://www.usdoj.gov/dea/index.htm
5. European Monitoring Centre for Drugs and Drug Addiction (EMCDDA) is available at:

http://www.emcdda.europa.eu/html.cfm/index190EN.html
6. Information on Europol is available at:
   http://www.europol.europa.eu/index.asp?page=home&language
7. Information about the Inter-American Drug Abuse Control Commission is available at:
   http://www.cicad.oas.org/en/default.asp
8. Information about International Narcotics Control Board is available at:
   http://www.incb.org/
9. Information about Interpol is available at:
   http://www.interpol.int/
10. Information about National Drug Intelligence Center is available at:
    http://www.usdoj.gov/ndic/
11. Information about the Office of National Drug Control Policy is available at:
    http://www.whitehousedrugpolicy.gov/
12. Information about the Substance Abuse and Mental Health Services Administration (SAMHSA) is available at:
    http://www.samhsa.gov/
13. Information about the Financial Action Task Force is available at:
    http://www.fatfgafi.org/pages/0,2987,en_32250379_32235720_1_1_1_1_1,00.html
14. Information about the U.S. Coast Guard is available at:
    http://www.uscg.mil/
15. Information about the U.S. Customs and Border Protection is available at:
    http://www.cbp.gov/
16. Information about the UN Office on Drugs and Crime (UNODC) is available at:
    http://www.unodc.org/
17. Information about the World Customs Organizations is available at:
    http://www.wcoomd.org/home.htm

Discussion Questions

1. Considering the emphasis put on heroin and cocaine trade at the international level of drug control, as well as in the United States, do you think the legalization of marijuana is a possibility in the United States?
2. Discuss what powers, if any, the international organs of drug controls have on the international drug trade.
3. Discuss an ideal case scenario in solving the various aspects of the drug problem.

4. Discuss which of the international conventions has had the most impact in addressing the drug problem.
5. Design the best research in order to address one of the various aspects of the drug problem discussed in this chapter.

References

Albrecht, Hans-Jorg. "The International System of Drug Control: Developments and Trends." In *Drug War American Style: The Internationalization of Failed Policy and its Alternatives,* edited by Jurg Gerber and Eric L. Jensen, 49–60. New York: Garland Publishers, 2001.

Archibold, Randal C. "In Heartland Death, Traces of Heroin's Spread." *New York Times,* May 31, 2009, A1.

Arias, Enrique Desmond. "Drug Cartels: Neither Holy, nor Roman, nor an Empire." In *Introduction to International Criminal Justice,* edited by Mangai Natarajan, 409–418, 2005. New York: McGraw Hill.

Astorga, Luis. 2001. "Drug Trafficking in Mexico." Accessed June 15, 2009. http://www.india-seminar.com/2001/504/504%20luis%20astorga.htm.

Australian Institute of Health and Welfare. *2010 National Drug Strategy Household Survey Report, Drug Statistics Series,* No. 25. Canberra, Australia: Australian Institute of Health and Welfare, 2011.

Best, Joel. *Damned Lies and Statistics: Untangling Numbers from the Media, Politicians, and Activists.* Berkeley and Los Angeles: University of California Press, 2001.

Bewley-Taylor, D. *The United States and International Drug Control, 1909–1997.* London: Continuum, 2001.

Bogdan, Robert, and Margret Ksander. "Policy Data as a Social Process: A Qualitative Approach to Quantitative Data." *Human Organization* 39, no. 4 (1980): 302–309.

Booth, Martin. *Cannabis: A History.* New York: Macmillan, 2005.

Buxton, Julia. *The Political Economy of Narcotics, Production, Consumption, and Global Markets.* Blackpoint, Nova Scotia, Canada: Fernwood Publishing, 2006.

Cathcart, Rebecca. "Schwarzenegger Urges a Study on Legalizing Marijuana Use." *New York Times,* May 6, 2006, A21.

Chatwin, Caroline. "Drug Policy Development within the European Union: The Destabilizing Effects of Dutch and Swedish Drug Policies." In *Global Criminology and Criminal Justice: Current Issues and Perspectives,* edited by Nick Larsen and Russell Smandych, 433–450. Peterborough, Ontario, Canada: Broadview Press, 2008.

Chin, Ko-Lin. *The Golden Triangle: Inside Southeast Asia's Drug Trade.* Ithaca, NY: Cornell University Press, 2009.

Cook, Colleen W. *CRS Report for Congress: Mexico's Drug Cartels.* Washington, D.C.: Congressional Research Service, 2007.

Costa Sorti, Claudia, and Paul De Grauwe. "Globalization and the Price Decline of Illicit Drugs." *International Journal of Drug Policy* 20, no. 1 (2009a): 48–61.

_____. "The Cocaine and Heroin Markets in the Era of Globalization and Drug Reduction Policies." *International Journal of Drug Policy* 20, no. 6 (November 2009b): 488–496. doi:10.1016/j.drugpo.2009.02.004.

European Monitoring Center for Drugs and Drug Addiction (EMCDDA). *Annual Report 2007: The State of the Drugs Problem in Europe.* Luxembourg: Office for Official Publications of the European Communities, 2007.

_____. *Annual Report 2008: The State of the Drugs Problem in Europe.* Luxembourg: Office for Official Publications of the European Communities, 2008.

Fazey, Cindy S. J. "The Commission on Narcotic Drugs and the United Nations International Drug Control Programme: Politics, Policies and Prospect for Change." *International Journal of Drug Policy* 14, no. 2 (2003): 155–169.

Fichtelberg, Aaron. *Crime without Border: An Introduction to International Criminal Justice.* Upper Saddle River, NJ: Prentice Hall, 2008.

Fields, Charles B., Matthew Holt, and Gregory Ferrell. "Historical Trends and Recent Developments in International Drug Policy and Control." In *Comparative and International Criminal Justice: Traditional and Nontraditional Systems of Law and Control,* edited by C. B. Fields and R. H. J. Moore, 132–149. Long Grove, IL: Waveland Press, 2005.

Filkins, Dexter. "U.S. Set Fight in the Poppies to Stop Talibans." *New York Times,* April 28, 2009, A1.

Financial Action Task Force. "Report on Money Laundering Typologies, 2002–2003." Accessed May 23, 2013.http://www.fatf-gafi.org/media/fatf/documents/reports/2002_2003_ML_Typologies_ENG.pdf, 2003.

Financial Action Task Force. "An Introduction to the FATF and Its Work." Accessed May 22, 2013. http://www.fatf-gafi.org/media/fatf/documents/brochuresannualreports/Introduction%20to%20the%20FATF.pdf, 2010.

Fries, Arthur, Robert W. Anthony, Andrew Cseko, Jr., Carl C. Gaither, and Eric Shulman. *The Price and Purity of Illicit Drugs: 1981–2007: A Report Prepared for the Office of National Drug Control Policy.* Alexandria, VA: Institute for Defense Analyses, 2008.

General Accountability Office [GAO]. *Afghanistan Drug Control: Despite Improved Efforts, Deteriorating Security Threatens Success of U.S. Goals.* GAO-7-78. Washington, D.C.: Government Accountability Office, 2006.

Gerber, Jurg, and Eric L. Jensen, eds. *Drug War American Style: The Internationalization of Failed Policy and Its Alternatives.* New York: Garland Publishing, 2001.

Goode, Erich. *Drugs in American Society.* 7th ed. New York: McGraw Hill, 2007.

Griffith, Ivelaw Lloyd. *Drugs and Security in the Caribbean: Sovereignty Under Siege.* State College: Pennsylvania State University Press, 1997.

International Narcotics Control Board (INCB). *Report of the International Narcotics Control Board for 2008.* New York: United Nations, 2009.

Johnson, Bruce D., Ansley Hamid, and Harry Sanabria. "Emerging Models of Crack Distribution." In *Drugs, Crime, and Social Policy,* edited by Thomas Meiczkowski, 56–78. Boston: Allyn & Bacon, 1992.

Killias, Martin. "Switzerland's Drug Policy as an Alternative to the American War on Drug." In *Drug War American Style: The Internationalization of Failed Policy and Its Alternatives,* edited by Jurg Gerber and Eric. L. Jensen, 241–260. New York: Garland Publishing, 2001.

Natarajan, Mangai. "Drug Trafficking." In *Introduction to International Criminal Justice,* edited by Mangai Natarajan, 325–333. New York: McGraw-Hill, 2005.

Reeve, E., Bump, P. "A Map That Shows the Dramatic Spread of Legal Weed in the U.S." *The Atlantic Wire,* April 8, 2013. Accessed May 15, 2013. http://www.theatlanticwire.com/politics/2013/04/map-shows-dramatic-spread-legal-weed-us/63997/%20http://cdn.theatlanticwire.com/img/upload/2013/04/08/WeedLaws.ggi, 2013.

Ryan, Kevin F. "Toward and Explanation of the Persistence of Failed Policy, Binding Drug Policy to Foreign Policy, 1930–1962." In *Drug War American Style: The Internationalization of Failed Policy and Its Alternatives,* edited by Jurg Gerber and Eric L. Jensen, 19–48. New York: Garland Publishers, 2001.

Schott, Allen Paul. *An Introduction to Anti-Money Laundering and Combatting the Financing of Terrorism,* 2nd edition. Herndon, VA: World Bank Publications, 2006.

Sheridan, Mary Beth. "Clinton: U.S. Drug Policies Fail, Fueled Mexico's Drug War." *Washington Post,* March 26, 2009, A01.

Smith, Beverly A., and Sesha Kethineni. "Cultivation and Use of Opium in Rural India: Bottom-Up Insights Into Anti-Drug Efforts." *Asian Journal of Criminology* 2, no.1 (2007): 19–33.

Substance Abuse and Mental Health Services Administration (SAMHSA). *Results from the 2007 National Survey on Drug Use and Health: National Find-*

ings. Washington, D.C.: Department of Health and Human Services, Substance Abuse and Mental Health Services Administration, 2008.

Tanzi, Vito. "Money Laundering and the International Finance System." *IMF Working Paper No. 96/55*, 1996.

Tavernise, Sabrina, Richard A. Oppel Jr., and Eric Schmitt. "United Militants Threaten Pakistan's Populous Heart." *New York Times*, April 13, 2009, A1.

United Nations Office on Drugs and Crime (UNODC). *A Century of International Drug Control*. New York: United Nations, 2008a.

_____. *Amphetamines and Ecstasy. 2008 Global ATS Assessment*. New York: United Nations, 2008b.

_____. *Coca Cultivation in the Andean Region, a Survey of Bolivia, Colombia, and Peru*. New York: United Nations, 2008c.

_____. *The Threat of Narco-Trafficking in the Americas*. New York: United Nations, 2008d.

_____. *World Drug Report 2008*. New York: United Nations, 2008e.

Walker, Samuel. *Sense and Nonsense About Crime and Drugs, and Communities: A Policy Guide*. 6th ed. Belmont, CA: Thomson Higher Education, 2006.

Walsh, John. *Lowering Expectations, Supply Control and the Resilient Cocaine Market*. Washington, D.C.: Washington Office on Latin America, 2009.

Williams, Phil. "The International Drug Trade: An Industry Analysis." *Low Intensity Conflict Law Enforcement* 2, no. 3 (1993): 397–420.

Yardley, William. "Some Find Hope for a Shift in Drug Policy." *New York Times*, February 15, 2009, A13.

Zaitch, Damian. *Trafficking Cocaine: Colombian Drug Entrepreneurs in the Netherlands*. The Hague, Netherlands: Kluwer, 2002.

Chapter 16

International Crimes: *Jus Cogens* and *Obligatio Erga Omnes*

Jessie L. Krienert, Jeffrey A. Walsh & Kevin Matthews

Introduction

Universal jurisdiction is a principle of international law. The principle holds that a state may prosecute the most heinous and universally abhorrent crimes without regard to the nationality of the perpetrators or victims, or the geographic/jurisdictional location of the offense. The legitimacy of this principle is grounded in the fact that some crimes are viewed as an offense against all. While domestic crimes typically represent an offense against a specific state or its people, some of the most serious crimes are viewed as transcending national borders. The prosecutions of certain intolerable and abhorrent international offenses are made possible and/or expedited by applying the principle of universal jurisdiction, which prevents offenders from evading justice by seeking asylum in nations with ambiguous or more favorable laws. In other words, universal jurisdiction is intended to eliminate safe havens for the most serious criminals by charging all of the world's courts with the apprehension and prosecution of perpetrators of crimes such as genocide, war crimes, torture, and slavery (Macedo 2004).

Two interrelated concepts forged the way for universal jurisdiction, *jus cogens* and *obligatio erga omnes*. In its simplest form, *jus cogens* provides the criteria necessary to determine which crimes fall under universal jurisdiction, and *obligatio erga omnes* compels nations to take action against said crimes. Offenses fall under the doctrine of universal jurisdiction when conduct is characterized as "extraordinarily heinous" (Kontorovich 2004, 183).

Jus Cogens

Jus cogens, of Latin origin meaning "compelling law," describes a set of universal peremptory norms that apply to all nations. Codified in Article 53 of the Vienna Convention on the Law of Treaties in 1969, *jus cogens* supersedes all other treaties and laws and remains nonderogable, making enforcement the responsibility of all nation states (Nieto-Navia 2003). *Jus cogens* is of such importance to international justice that any treaty in violation is considered invalid. In fact, changes to rules of *jus cogens* are not possible unless a new and equal peremptory norm takes its place (Hossain 2005).

Obligatio Erga Omnes

Once elevated to *jus cogens,* the principle of *obligatio erga omnes,* meaning "obligations toward all," compels nations to take legal action in pursuit of justice for all. "In view of the importance of the rights involved, all states can be held to have a legal interest in their protection; they are obligations *erga omnes*" (ICJ Reports 1970, 32). It is the obligation of the entire international community, resulting from the acceptance of peremptory norms that lead nations to act, and to consider such actions as nonderogable duties, not optional rights (Tams 2005). Legal obligations include the duty to prosecute or extradite, the nonapplicability of statutes of limitations for such crimes, the nonapplicability of any immunities up to and including heads of state, the nonapplicability of the defense of "obedience to superior orders, the universal application of these obligations whether in time of peace or war, their non-derogation under 'states of emergency,'" and universal jurisdiction over perpetrators of such crimes (Bassiouni 1996, 63).

The next section addresses the earliest application of universal jurisdiction to the offense of maritime piracy, followed by discussions of more contemporary applications to additional offenses deemed intolerable and meeting the established heinousness principle: maritime piracy, crimes against humanity, slavery, and human trafficking—actions so deplorable that they are represented by superior fundamental principles of international law that cannot be ignored by any nation (Hossain 2005). As preemptory norms with violations so great they must be acknowledged by every society, all four offenses represent separate but unique categories of universally abhorred crimes. Each crime addressed here has had a fundamental role in creating, defining, and refining accepted universal standards for cognizable offenses meeting the established criteria of universal jurisdiction.

Maritime Piracy

There has been a tremendous amount of mainstream media attention recently covering ship hijackings and hostage negotiations on the high seas at the hands of modern-day pirates, especially in the waters off the coast of Somalia. Piracy, however, is not a new crime and we are not experiencing an aberrant resurgence of an antiquated crime. To the contrary, piracy has been a continual problem on the world's oceans and waterways for centuries. The situation has only grown more serious in recent years. Romanticized tales of old depicting swash-buckling Robin Hoods of the high seas have given way to shocking news stories from remote parts of the world where rogue bands of heavily armed (and occasionally well-trained) boys and men from deeply impoverished and desperate countries risk all to pursue tremendous financial gain through acts of maritime piracy. The victims are frequently hapless sailors crewing ships participating in international trade and commerce aboard cargo ships, or occasionally tourists who inadvertently find themselves in pirate inhabited waters.

The latest scourge of international piracy has two primary geographic fronts. Currently, the area most inundated by piracy incidents is in the Indian Ocean, off the coast of Somalia, specifically in the Gulf of Aden. The second most heavily pirated area is in Southeast Asia, near the countries of Indonesia, Thailand, and Malaysia (Huang 2007). Definitions of piracy vary slightly though fundamental principles include illegal acts of violence, detention, or depredation for private gain committed by the occupants of one ship against another (UN Convention on the Law of the Sea 1982). Occasionally, the definition has been extended to include acts occurring in ports or territorial waterways — an extension recognized by the International Maritime Board (IMB).

Two recent events stand out as largely responsible for thrusting piracy into the mainstream media. The first event was the hijacking of the Saudi Arabia-owned supertanker *Sirius Star,* taken 450 miles off the coast of Kenya in 2008. The almost 1,100-foot long oil tanker, flying a Liberian flag and carrying a 25-member multinational crew, was transporting $100 million worth of crude oil to the United States when the ship was overtaken by Somali pirates. The hijacking, one of many that occur each year, received particular attention for involving the largest vessel ever captured by pirates. The ship was also the furthest out to sea that any Somali pirates had targeted (McCann 2008). Estimates suggest that the pirates would have likely needed to travel for three or four days to reach the ship. After navigating the ship to a location near the Somali coast, brief negotiations ensued; ransom demands started at $25 million. Eventually, the pirates agreed to and received payment of approximately $3 million, paid by the ship's owners. On January 9, 2009, the ship was liberated with crew and cargo safe and intact. After fleeing from the *Sirius Star* with the ransom, the combination of high speed, due to fear of retaliatory attack by one of the nearby warships, and bad weather caused one of their small boats to capsize. Five of the pirates drowned and a portion of the money was lost as a result.

The second event was the disputed hijacking of the *Maersk Alabama* by four Somali pirates on April 8, 2009. It has been debated whether this event constitutes an actual hijacking because the crew maintains that they retained control of the ship during the incident. The captain had volunteered to go with the pirates as a hostage in order to get them off the ship and keep the crew safe. The *Maersk Alabama* was the first ship flying the U.S. flag to be "taken" by pirates in approximately 200 years, drawing immediate rebuke from the U.S. military. The captain of the *Maersk*, Richard Phillips, was taken hostage on a small covered lifeboat and held for five days while a series of negotiations took place in an effort to have the captain freed without harm. The lifeboat eventually ran out of fuel and was towed by the U.S. Navy destroyer, the *USS Bainbridge*. U.S. Navy Seal snipers simultaneously shot and killed three of the pirates while the fourth pirate was aboard the *Bainbridge* being treated for injuries sustained earlier in the ordeal. Captain Phillips was rescued unharmed and the operation was heralded a success, with popular media reporting the story as it unfolded in real time (McFadden and Shane 2009).

History

Although these two events and countless others have brought recent attention to piracy, historical accounts of such incidents date back to the earliest days of recorded sea commerce, oceanic exploration, and maritime travel. Pirates originally preyed on both seafaring ships and the ports that serviced them, frequently stealing and robbing what they could and taking captives along the way to be sold into slavery. From its earliest days, piracy has been widely regarded as among the most heinous of crimes, due in large part to the economic toll it takes on commerce and the human toll it takes in terms of violence (Chambliss 2004). An examination of early maritime piracy invokes classic images of Norse raiders (or "Vikings") travelling the high seas and taking what they wanted from whomever they wanted (Chambliss 2004). Another infamous and uniquely influential historical group was the Barbary Pirates. Operating out of the Mediterranean Sea and the Atlantic Ocean, these pirates covered much of the Barbary Coast along northern Africa from the late 1500s to the early 1800s. They became so fierce and powerful during their 250-year reign that the United States was one of many countries that paid them a sizable annual fee for safe passage of trading ships (Jarvis 2006).

The term "pirate" is somewhat of a misnomer in this instance, though, because the Barbary Pirates were technically privateers—an important distinction. Pirates attacked ships without legal authority, but privateers were authorized by a *letter of marque* to attack "enemy" merchant ships in the name of the issuing country. In other words, privateering was simply nationally sponsored piracy, unfettered by the prevailing law of universal jurisdiction (Kontorovich 2004). The end of the Barbary Pirate era came in the early 1800s when the pirates/privateers began to seize American ships and their cargo and enslave their crews, despite the safe-passage payments. The result was the establishment of the U.S. Navy for the purposes of maritime security. The first and second Barbary Wars, both decisive American victories, ushered in the end of the Barbary Pirates (Jarvis 2006).

The act of piracy is not particularly surprising when one considers the opportunity structure of the crime and the immense wealth that can be acquired. The majority of the Earth's surface is covered by water which is used by some 47,500 ships each year, servicing thousands of ports worldwide and accounting for approximately 80 percent of all global trade (Luft and Korin 2004). Today, the world's waterways are significantly underpoliced, due in part to their sheer vastness and to the diffusion of resources away from open-water security toward land-based port security in the wake of the 9/11 terrorist attacks. Taking these facts into consideration, the picture of the sea as an anarchic domain welcoming of opportunistic piratical activity becomes clear (Luft and Korin 2004).

Legal Issues: Universal Jurisdiction and *Jus Cogens*

Similar to the piracy debates taking place today regarding deterrence, apprehension, and detention, piracy once held an ambiguous status with respect to prosecutorial jurisdiction. In a commonly accepted principle of international law, a defendant cannot be tried in a court of law unless their citizenship or the crime they perpetrated links them to that country's legal jurisdiction. The first exception to this principle is found in piracy. The writings of Cicero (105–43 BCE) provide the foundation for the application of universal jurisdiction to the offense of piracy. An ancient Roman philosopher and politician, Cicero was the first to identify pirates as *hostis humani generis* (enemies of all humanity) and from that point, they were considered international criminals with the applied jurisprudence of universal jurisdiction. The act of piracy was considered to be so extraordinarily heinous and of such gravity that the pirates charged could effectively be tried in any court of law in the world once apprehended, regardless of the apprehending country or the residency of the charged pirates. The interest in abolishing piracy was so great that any and all countries were given the authority to apprehend, send to trial, and punish any pirates they encountered. The law of nations, at one time, even permitted any nation that had captured a pirate to summarily execute them at sea (Kontorovich 2004).

Today, international law continues to recognize universal jurisdiction. The legitimacy of such laws has been acknowledged by jurists and scholars of every major maritime nation with few challenges to that authority over the past several hundred years (Kontorovich 2004). How these laws are applied in practice remains somewhat ambiguous as the issue becomes further complicated by multinational involvement. The international community reaffirmed the principles of universal jurisdiction and *jus cogens* in modern times. As noted by Jarvis (2006), the 1958 Geneva Convention on the High Seas states that countries must cooperate to the fullest extent possible in the repression of piracy. It further articulates that every state has the authority to seize a pirate ship. The U.S. Code (Title 18, section 1651) provides that anyone found guilty of piracy shall serve a sentence of life in prison.

Most significant is the fact that piracy was the first offense to be considered universally cognizable, or of universal jurisdiction. Offenses that sought to expand the application of universal jurisdiction (i.e., slavery, war crimes, genocide, and crimes against humanity) have used the piracy precedent to supersede more traditional jurisdictional requirements (Kontorovich 2004). Until more recent efforts to extend the piracy precedent to other crimes were initiated, piracy as a crime of universal jurisdiction received little scrutiny. However, with courts around the world relying on the fundamental principles of universal jurisdiction and the piracy precedent to justify the extension of universal jurisdiction and *jus cogens* to other offenses deemed extraordinarily heinous, including human rights violations, the merits of the piracy precedent have been scrutinized more closely (see Kontorovich 2004). A thorough review of the critique suggests that piracy and pirates were universally cognizable not because of the seriousness of their actions, but because pirates failed to comply with licensing procedures (letters of marque) as privateers. Little distinguished the behavior of pirates from that of privateers, except that privateers were nationally sponsored (Kontorovich 2004). Pirates, in essence, were simply too rogue and their methods absent of a clear code of conduct.

Piracy Today

Modern-day piracy is clearly a threat to global commerce and security. While piracy incidents are quite frequent, rates recently reached a five-year low. According to the International Maritime Bureau (IMB), in 2012 there were 297 ships attacked by pirates, a sharp decline compared to the 439 ships attacked just a year prior in 2011. Globally 28 ships were hijacked in 2012 while 174 ships were boarded and 585 hostages taken. Consensus, however, is that pirate attacks, both failed and successful, are grossly underreported. Pirate attacks typically require an elaborate and sometimes complicated reporting procedure which, if cause for delay, can result in thousands of dollars in incurred costs related to port fees, wages, and fuel for shipping companies. Moreover, shipping companies underreport pirate attacks and associated losses in order to avoid having to pay import taxes on stolen merchandise and increased insurance premiums for crewmember safety and passage through areas deemed "dangerous" by insurance underwriters (Chalk 2008).

Pirates are becoming increasingly more brazen in their approach and method. Attacks primarily occur in territorial waters and ports due to the ease of access to ships that can be boarded while in port or anchored in the harbor awaiting a port. Evidence suggests that pirates are beginning to use more sophisticated technologies and intelligence to target larger vessels further out to sea in international waters which would otherwise have been previously unattainable (Johnson and Pladdet 2003). For example, mother ships are a relatively recent implementation that allows pirates to use larger ships to tow or carry smaller speed boats out to sea. When contact is made with the targeted ship, speedboats are used for a quick approach. This method was used to overtake the *Sirius Star* (mentioned above).

As Hanson (2009) notes, there are several mechanisms available for combating piracy, but experts agree that the measures are largely defensive and do not address the root of the problem—state instability. The options that currently exist include onboard deterrents such as fire hoses, loudspeakers, and deck patrols. Establishing naval deployments has been suggested, though to be most effective this would need to be a strong multinational security force able to police vast waters. Regional anti-piracy patrols are another consideration where the region under threat of piracy works to patrol their own interests (Hanson 2009).

Crimes against Humanity

Although atrocities that constitute "crimes against humanity" are nothing new, it was not until recently that the term was codified in an attempt to criminalize these acts on a worldwide scale. First appearing as a legal concept in the charter for the International Military Tribunal at Nuremberg in 1945, crimes against humanity were originally defined as "inhumane acts done against any civilian population, or persecutions on political, racial, or religious grounds, when such acts are done or such persecutions are carried on in execution of or in connection with any crime against peace or any war crime" (Werle 2005, 427). It was intended that only such crimes committed during a time of conflict would be punishable.

The Nuremberg Charter faced harsh criticism for its lack of any real power of enforcement within the global community. The Charter, however, provided significant precedent in international law. The legacy of the Nuremberg Trials was not fully realized until some 50 years later with the adoption of the Rome Statute in 1998. This multilateral treaty created the International Criminal Court (ICC) as a permanent body with the power to prosecute individuals who commit international offenses. The Rome Statute's definition of crimes against humanity is similar to that of its predecessor. It addresses intentional acts that cause great suffering and physical or mental injury "when committed as part of a widespread or systematic attack directed against any civilian population" (*Rome Statute of the International Criminal Court* 1998). The notable differences in this modern codification include the provision of genocide as both a separate offense, and the most serious. The statute also allows individuals to be held responsible, in addition to states, and no longer focuses solely on offenses committed during times of conflict.

It has been widely acknowledged that a need exists for clearly defined statutes to facilitate the successful prosecution of international crimes. However, seven countries voted against the adoption of the Rome Statute, including Israel and the United States. Both countries even went so far as to "unsign" the treaty, ensuring that they would no longer have obligations in connection with its provisions (McGoldrick 2004). The parties that declined to support the Statute voiced concern over whether the treaty might pose a threat to national sovereignty and differences in opinion surrounding which offenses should be treated as matters of international jurisdiction.

Despite these objections, there is a consensus that some crimes represent a threat to the entire global community and are seen as egregious offenses in all cultures and societies. Such offenses involve violations of *jus cogens* norms— universally accepted standards of conduct (May 2005, 24). This category includes three of the most serious crimes against humanity: apartheid, enforced disappearances, and gendercide. These crimes are not only universally offensive, but also share three common elements characteristic of offenses harmful enough to be considered crimes against humanity. First, the offenses are perpetrated against a civilian population. Second, the offenses are carried out as a result of a state action or policy. Third, the offenses can be characterized as widespread or systematic in scope.

Apartheid

Apartheid is defined as any number of inhumane acts that are "committed in the context of an institutionalized regime of systematic oppression and domination by one racial group over any other racial group or groups ..." (*Rome Statute of the International Criminal Court* 1998). Acts can include imprisonment, torture, rape, murder, and enslavement when part of a systematic effort to oppress a group of people of a different ethnicity. The term "apartheid" is derived from an Afrikaans word meaning "apartness" (Saunders 2003). It is also the name given to the racist regime that came to power with the election of D. F. Malan as the prime minister of South Africa in 1948. Malan was a natural-born South African citizen of European descent who endeavored to implement an official policy of racial segregation.

Apartheid developed gradually through a series of legal actions. The Population Registration Act required categorization of all citizens by race, with association judged solely on skin color. The Group Areas Act No. 41 furthered racial segregation by designating geographic boundaries by racial category. Finally, the Pass Laws Act of 1952 required that all non-White South Africans over the age of 16 carry a passbook providing proof of their right to travel, work, and live in racially specified locations (Rotberg 1980). The purpose of such laws was to redistribute the land for the economic benefit of the White and powerful. Many Blacks were forcibly relocated to less desirable areas and others became foreigners in their own homelands due to apartheid's "invented geography" (Natarajan 2005, 280).

Through the passage of additional legislation, Malan and his successors worked to design a system of oppression that sought to control every aspect of life to the advantage of the White minority. The Prohibition of Mixed Marriages Act of 1949 officially criminalized interracial relationships. A year later, the Immorality Act reached even further into personal life as police raided the homes of suspected mixed couples to arrest them for having sexual relations. Additional laws were passed that allowed the government to control the education of Blacks and prepare them for "certain forms of labor"—jobs that were considered suitable only for lower-class workers (Natarajan 2005, 280).

Apartheid was officially defined as a crime against humanity through the 1973 International Convention on the Suppression and Punishment of the Crime of Apartheid (Bassiouni 1999). Not without criticism, several countries, mainly major trade partners with South Africa, declined to support the declaration and others noted its lack of enforcement as well as the slowness to act on the part of the UN. The apartheid regime remained in place throughout the 1980s. The United States and other nations, becoming less tolerant, began to campaign for disinvestment and imposed economic sanctions. Subject to increasing attacks by militant and guerilla groups, the South African government responded by declaring a state of emergency, resulting in the detention and torture of tens of thousands of suspected contributors.

The turning point came in 1989 when President P. W. Botha suffered a stroke and was replaced by F. W. De Klerk. Throughout his five-year term, De Klerk oversaw negotiations to dismantle the apartheid system and secured the release of Nelson Mandela after twenty-seven years in prison (De Klerk 1998). Mandela was elected president in 1994, officially ending the institution of apartheid in Africa. The government no longer operates under a system of legalized racial discrimination; however, the legacy of apartheid can be felt in the racialized poverty and differential access to health care and education that remains (Treiman 2005).

Although South Africa offers the clearest example of apartheid, a modern example of an apartheid state may exist, as many have suggested, in the nation of Israel. Several official policies have been highlighted for their similarities to those used in South Africa (Davis 2003). Israel's national identification cards are comparable to Pass Laws in that they list whether the holder is Jewish and thereby determine where they are allowed to live, the availability of government welfare and services, and even the type of treatment they will receive from police and other officials (McGreal 2006). While both the South Africa of yesterday and the Israel of today present unique examples of institutionalized segregation on the basis of race/ethnicity, they also emphasize the need to establish an effective means of prosecuting states for apartheid. At present, a case must be referred by a UN council to the International Criminal Court (ICC), and the Israeli government has yet to answer for its actions. As a crime against humanity, apartheid and the inhuman acts that result from its policies violate international law and are subject to universal jurisdiction.

Enforced Disappearances

It was only recently, with the development of the ICC, that enforced disappearances were categorized as crimes against humanity (Bassiouni 1999, 363). Used extensively as a method of terror and suppression throughout the Nazi regime in World War II, the most basic component of this offense is the forced removal of an individual from society, which typically occurs when the victim is abducted or arrested and detained by state officials. Often coupled with torture or even death, enforced disappearances are defined through the government or state's attempt to conceal the whereabouts of the victim, effectively depriving them of their rights and protection of the law (UN General Assembly 2006). The victimization does not end with the disappeared; the deliberate denial to family and friends of the victim's whereabouts extends fear to the greater community. As a global phenomenon, enforced disappearances can be identified in over ninety countries; it is commonly used as a means to oppress a government's own people or to dispose of political opponents (Anderson 2006).

Since 1980, the systematic use of enforced disappearances has become more pervasive and widespread (Anderson 2006). Under the Iraqi regime of Saddam Hussein tens-of-thousands of individuals disappeared never to be accounted for in what has been described as the Kurdish Genocide. The events of 9/11 led to a dramatic increase in disappearances world-wide. The U.S. government has come under fire for the use of enforced disappearances through the secret arrest and detention of suspected terrorists (Ross 2007). Similarly, in Pakistan's Balochistan province, intelligence agencies and security forces routinely arrest and detain civilians and activists on even the slightest suspicion that they may be connected to subversive or terrorist activities. Political and human rights organizations have estimated that more than 4,000 persons remain unaccounted for (Asian Legal Resource Centre 2007). Acting without regard for international law or their own judiciary, many governments have used the U.S.-led war on terror as a justification for systematic suppression of opposition groups.

An Argentinean Example

In March 1976, Jorge Videla led a military *coup d'état* to overthrow the president of Argentina and establish a brutal dictatorship that would last for seven years (Guest 1990). Videla took over as president and launched a campaign of oppression and violence against the country's citizens. Although the regime euphemistically referred to its efforts as the "National Reorganization Process," in reality, tens of thousands of Argentineans were systematically persecuted as they were subject to random police raids and arrests, torture, enforced disappearances, and murder.

Soon after the *coup*, the regime moved to declare the government under siege in order to extend its own power. Anti-subversive operations were undertaken in order to address any perceived threats to the new state. The initial targets of this process were suspected terrorists, political opponents and dissidents, and guerilla fighters. In an attack on the legal system, Argentina's federal judges were dismissed and replaced by justices who had sworn their loyalty to the regime. To further remove any possible legal obstacles, more than 100 lawyers disappeared. Some were murdered outright; others were detained indefinitely (Guest 1990). Nearly 9,000 recorded cases of enforced disappearances were documented in Argentina, with actual numbers likely much higher (Anderson

2006). Members of labor unions, activists, students, and anyone suspected of speaking out against the government were subject to enforced disappearances.

Videla relinquished his power to a fellow military officer in 1981 and democracy was peacefully restored in Argentina two years later. Upon his inauguration, the new president vowed to prosecute members of the dictatorship. An independent commission on the disappearances revealed thousands of victims, although the total number will never be known. A subsequent report detailed the results of the investigations. Author Ernesto Sabato illustrated the fate of many:

> From the moment of their abduction, the victims lost all rights. Deprived of all communication with the outside world, held in unknown places, subjected to barbaric tortures, kept ignorant of their immediate or ultimate fate, they risked being either thrown into a river or the sea, weighted down with blocks of cement, or burned to ashes. They were not mere objects, however, and still possessed all the human attributes: they could feel pain, could remember a mother, child or spouse, could feel infinite shame at being raped in public (quoted in Kritz 1995, 5).

Videla was convicted in 1985 of a wide range of crimes including murder, kidnapping, and torture, and was sentenced to life in prison. After serving only five years, he received a presidential pardon and was granted immunity from future prosecution in connection with the offenses committed during his time in office. Videla's immunity was revoked seventeen years later, and his life sentence was reinstated. Though it was largely a symbolic gesture, "the Argentine Supreme Court ha[d] confirmed the role of human rights principles and of public international law in general in dealing with the most heinous crimes against humanity" (Bakker 2005, 1106).

Legal Ramifications

The UN General Assembly gathered in December 1978, at the height of Videla's reign, and issued a resolution expressing great concern over the growing number of reports about enforced disappearances (Lawson 1996). A similar resolution was issued in 1992, followed by the formation of a working group in 2001, created to draft a binding treaty. The group worked for five years to produce the International Convention for the Protection of All Persons from Enforced Disappearance, which has yet to take force, meeting with only limited party ratification. The Convention expands global condemnation, requiring members to take steps to prevent enforced disappearances and to bring offenders to justice.

More than 90 nations have signed the Convention; however, the United States has declined (United Nations 2013). A statement released by the State

Department specified that the Convention's definition of enforced disappearances was unacceptable as it lacked an intentionality requirement (USDOS 2009). The lack of a legally binding international treaty has made it difficult to hold offenders criminally responsible. Although the United Nations has worked diligently to create a human rights instrument that will protect individuals from enforced disappearances, the Global War on Terror has proven to be a formidable obstacle. Further attempts to gain consensus among the international community on this issue will need to account for the high priority some states place on dealing with terror suspects in a classified manner. The United Nations and its member parties are charged with the task of striking a balance between shocking acts of terrorism and the untold numbers of victims of enforced disappearances. Many of these victims have had to endure continuous violations of their most basic human rights, including life and freedom, which speaks to the severity of this crime against humanity.

Gendercide

Coined by Mary Ann Warren in 1985, gendercide is defined as "the deliberate extermination of persons of a particular sex (or gender)" (Kimmel 2004, 345). There has been limited research exploring the role of gender in mass killings. Much of the literature on gendercide has focused on its relation to genocide as if it were merely a facet or subcategory thereof. Carpenter (2002, 78) notes that gendercide is a broader categorization and that it "may indeed be a tactic of genocide, but it is not in itself genocide." The commission of murder on a sexually discriminatory basis is as reprehensible as targeting victims based on ethnic, religious, or political grounds. Motivations of gendercide are varied and may include cultural or strategic justifications. A recurring example throughout history has been the intentional slaughter of "battle-age" men and boys in an attempt to reduce an enemy's supply of soldiers and render a group defenseless (Jones 2000).

Saddam Hussein's Iraqi government may be one of the most notorious gendercidal regimes in recent history. Between 1986 and 1988, during the Anfal, also known as the Kurdish Genocide, against Kurdish rebels and the civilian population in Northern Iraq, Hussein's forces conducted anti-insurgent operations, mass deportations, bombings, and the destruction of thousands of villages. Civilian Kurds were taken to detention centers where males were separated from females. Many of the males are believed to have been killed in mass executions by firing squads or during experimentation with chemical weapons (Bruinessen 1997). Although there were many women and children among the victims, "it is apparent that a principal purpose of Anfal was to exterminate all adult males of military service age captured in rural Iraqi Kurdistan" (Black 1993, 170). Conservative estimates hold that 100,000 or more Kurds were exterminated throughout the campaign (Black 1993).

Not all gendercides occur in a military context or during a conflict. Some scholars have argued that the practice of sex-selective infanticide and feticide, which is widespread in Asian countries, can be categorized as gendercide. A male child provides potential income, support, and a continuation of the family name, whereas a female child might represent a burden. In China, many believe that the government's implementation of a one-child policy has served to reinforce a long history of preference for male children. Rummel (1997) aptly illustrates the cumulative effect that such state policies can have:

> Instances of infanticide ... are usually singular events; they do not happen en masse. But the accumulation of such officially sanctioned or demanded murders comprises, in effect, serial massacre. Since such practices were so pervasive in some cultures, I suspect that the death toll from infanticide must exceed that from mass sacrifice and perhaps even outright mass murder (66).

After many years of population engineering, "including virtual extermination of 'surplus' baby girls," China is experiencing a severe gender imbalance (Stockland 1997). In 1999, a study from the Chinese Academy of Social Sciences reported that the ratio of men to women had become so skewed that there would soon be as many as 111 million men unable to find a wife (Manthorpe 1999).

Forced abortion and involuntary sterilization accompany the government's official policy. Details about enforcement of the world's most aggressive population control program were exposed during a U.S. House of Representatives hearing in 1998 (Nie 2005, 15). Hidden behind the veil of communism are China's Planned-Birth Offices (PBOs), which keep records on the sexual histories of women in their jurisdiction (Nie 2005, 16). Women who become pregnant in violation of a planned-birth policy are brought to a PBO where they are often coerced into undergoing an abortion or held in a detention cell if they refuse. In some instances, when pregnant women have attempted to flee from PBO officials, family members have been arrested and detained instead. One woman testified that after going into hiding to protect her unborn child, PBO agents arrested her relatives, demolished their homes, and forced her to endure a sterilization procedure once she returned after giving birth. In addition, she was informed that to gain the release of her relatives and keep her child she would have to pay several exorbitant fines.

The crime of gendercide presents grave implications for the status of females in today's society. The Indian economist Amartya Sen is well known for his description of the 100 million "missing women" who would be alive today but for various types of discrimination, including infanticide and the sex-selective abortions that are common in Asian nations (Grabowski 2006). Estimates by Jha, Kumar, Vasa, Dhingra, Thiruchelvam and Moineddin (2006), suggest that as many as 10 million female fetuses have been aborted over a 20-year period of time. Other researchers have arrived at far more conservative estimates of the impact of gender selection and other discriminatory practices, suggesting that many of these supposed missing girls are simply hidden from the official census (Cai 2003). What is clear, however, is that gendercide in any form represents a serious offense against humanity.

As crimes against humanity, apartheid, enforced disappearances, and gendercide violate *jus cogens* norms. Extermination on the basis of gender, oppression on the basis of race, and the unjustified deprivation of liberty are all examples of heinous crimes that involve universal jurisdiction and should not be tolerated in any section of society. The international community has an inherent moral obligation to establish methods that allow for the effective prevention and prosecution of these behaviors. Far from being a straightforward task, it is also necessary to consider the rights of individual states as sovereign entities. Great care should be taken in defining behaviors that are universally abhorrent while respecting cultural differences. The recent establishment of the ICC can be viewed as a significant step toward achieving this objective of international law. The ICC's global sanctions are designed to complement national laws in the hope that they will "contribute to the reduction of social harm and to the preservation, restoration and maintenance of peace" (Bassiouni 1999, 808).

Human Trafficking

The term "trafficking," in all of its implied meaning, merges a wide range of illicit and often clandestine activities, all of which draw worldwide concern and admonishment for their violations of fundamental human rights. Although the majority of the conversation on national and international levels revolves around the sexual exploitation of women and children, trafficking is not unidimensional and encompasses a complex web of often interrelated activities (Gould 2007). The trade in human beings, whether for sex, servitude, labor, or goods, affects millions of women, children, and men each year. Both activities that traverse international borders and those within a country's borders can qualify as trafficking under international agreement. Recognized as a global phenomenon, all countries function as points of origin, transit, and destination (Scarpa 2004).

Although there is international agreement that trafficking meets *jus cogens* criteria, definitional issues plague the development of clear legal standards (Ould 2004). The most commonly accepted definition of trafficking comes from the 2000 Protocol to Prevent, Suppress, and Punish Trafficking in Persons. Accepted by more than 110 countries, the Protocol describes trafficking as:

> the recruitment, transportation, transfer, harboring or receipt of persons by means of threat or use of force or other forms of coercion, of abduction, of fraud, of deception, of the abuse of power, or of a position of vulnerability or of the giving or receiving of payments or benefits to achieve the consent of a person having control over another person, for the purpose of exploitation (National Human Rights Commission 2008, 4).

The Protocol expands the definition of trafficking from merely sexual exploitation to encompass other behaviors, including forced labor, slavery, servitude, and the removal of organs.

Undermining definitional agreement is a lack of baseline data. There are no comprehensive reliable data concerning the prevalence, scope, and even demographic characteristics of victims and offenders. Few governments employ systematic data collection using a universal definition (Gozdziak and Collett 2005; Laczko 2005). Similarly, the statistics that do exist are not routinely distinguished by age of victim and often focus solely on prostitution-related trafficking (Ali 2005). Given that both victims and offenders of trafficking are considered "hidden populations," it is difficult to secure reliable information about the scope and scale of the industry. Further hindering accuracy, victims often face public and private stigmatization and are likely to refuse to cooperate with officials out of a sense of self-preservation (Tyldum and Brunovskis 2005). Most published documents addressing trafficking rely on secondary, often unverified data (Laczko 2005; Ali 2005).

Becoming a Victim

Trafficking, albeit complicated, is sustained via the application of a simple and familiar economic principle: the law of supply and demand. A lack of social, economic, and educational opportunities, often coupled with political turmoil, creates a cultural surplus of potential trafficking victims. Increased demand generates economic growth, increased tourism, and increases in disposable labor (Akee et al. 2007). Second in scope only to the drug and weapons trade, human trafficking is one of the fastest growing forms of criminal activity (National Human Rights Commission 2008). Coercion into bonded occupations through factory labor, domestic work, and forced marriage affects large segments of the global population each year. Recent estimates of human trafficking suggest that there are more than 2.5 million victims, with the vast majority (1.7 million) involved in the global sex trade (Belser 2005). With profits topping billions of dollars annually, the trafficking industry is thriving. The International Labour Organisation (ILO) estimates profits from sex trafficking alone are a staggering $217.8 billion per year—an average of $23,000 per victim (USDOS 2008).

Most trafficking does not occur through large organized crime networks. Instead, individual entrepreneurs and small organized groups have become the fastest growing segment in the world of trafficking. Targeting young women and children, many traffickers coerce their victims with promises of marriage or educational opportunities, offering a chance for a better life (USDOS 2005). Some victims are tricked through offers of false employment, others are forcibly abducted, and still others are sold into slavery by their own family members including, mothers, fathers, and even husbands.

Although coercion is a defining feature of trafficking, victims often voluntarily seek international opportunities for lucrative employment and gender equality. Women in many countries around the world are prohibited from even moderate levels of employment, significantly limiting their income potential, whereas others are regarded as second-class citizens, subordinate to males. It may be difficult to discern differences between willful entrance, coercion, and exploitation. A migrant that is "voluntarily" smuggled can easily be forced into an exploitative situation. Similarly, a consensual foray into sex work may end up as sexual slavery. Globalization is an active contributor to the trafficking market. Open borders and reduced trade barriers lead to increased migration, which in turn presents increased opportunities for trafficking (Tansuhaj and McCullough 2008). Modern recruitment methods include both modeling and marriage agencies that promise financial security and then later ensure subservience through threats, violence, and monetary debt (Ould 2004; Martinez 2007):

> Lila, a 19-year-old Romanian girl who had already endured physical and sexual abuse from her alcoholic father, was introduced by an "acquaintance" to a man who offered her a job as a housekeeper/salesperson in the U.K. When she arrived in the U.K., the man sold her to a pimp and Lila was forced into prostitution. She was threatened that she would be sent home in pieces if she did not follow every order. After an attempted escape, her papers were confiscated and the beatings became more frequent and brutal. Months later, after being re-trafficked several times, Lila was freed in a police raid. She was

eventually repatriated back to Romania where, after two months, she fled from a shelter where she had been staying. Her whereabouts are unknown (USDOS 2008, 5).

Once women have crossed international borders, what begins as a choice often turns to forced compliance, leaving victims with few options and even fewer rights. Continued subservience is often maintained out of a fear of imprisonment or deportation if found by authorities (Parrot and Cummings 2008). In addition, many recruiters hail from local communities, maintaining compliance through threats and/or actual violence toward the victim and his or her family. Additional methods of control include isolation, drug or alcohol dependence, and confiscation of documentation (Martinez 2007). Once initial control has been exerted, cultural and language differences are exploited along with a lack of knowledge of available options making it nearly impossible for trafficking victims to escape.

Key Players in the Trade

There are four basic groups that form the core of the trafficking industry (Kelly 2002; Bales 2004). *Organizers* plan and structure the trafficking network. Even in small-scale operations, the organizer provides the needed financial backing to hold the system together. Without financial start-up, traffickers would not exist. *Middlemen* recruit, transport, and sell the victims. Preying on individuals from countries that are riddled with poverty, overpopulation, and social unrest, they are responsible for securing and transporting victims across borders and into the industry. *Business Operators* play a key role in the trafficking industry. Brothel and nightclub owners, agricultural enterprises, and even private households "employ" trafficked victims and keep them working in the industry through threats and other coercive tactics. Finally, *Aides* include corrupt government and law enforcement officials who participate either actively or passively in the industry. Whether it's by ignoring ongoing trafficking or active participation through ownership, they ensure industry survival.

A relatively new player in the field, women are emerging as the new face of trafficking perpetrators (UN Office on Drugs and Crime 2013). Often used as low-level organizers and recruiters, they are able to manipulate local connections for both acquisition and control. Termed "happy trafficking," female victims become successful recruiters through claims of positive personal experiences with "legitimate" employment. Happy traffickers share personal "success stories" with potential victims, detailing financial gain in foreign lands as a way to reassure new recruits the offered opportunity is legitimate. An alternative reason for increased female involvement parallels women's foray into the drug trade. Criminal organizations increasingly employ women as they are less likely to fit the developed profile of a trafficker. Moreover, even if they are caught there is widespread belief that the penalties will be less severe (USDOS 2008).

Trafficking requires minimal start-up costs and does not involve a substantial risk of arrest and prosecution for those involved. It also provides a product that can be resold and reused, offering virtually unlimited profit potential (U.S. Department of State Trafficking in Persons Report 2008, 2). Technological advances offer opportunities for expansion in an already pervasive trafficking industry. The ease of use and availability of cell phones and text messaging technologies provide for exponentially increasing opportunities for communication. The virtual world extends the scope of trafficking and creates additional obstacles for detection and enforcement. Internet technology can be used to make deals and facilitate exchanges. Chat rooms and social networking sites connect global buyers and sellers and allow for real time communication through instant messaging as a way to advertise and purchase human commodities. In addition, tracking technology, including Radio Frequency IDentification (RFID) chips and global positioning systems, offer traffickers new and innovative means of securing compliance and control (USDOS 2008; Stone 2005).

Sex Trafficking

The most common form of trafficking (an estimated 86 percent) involves the sexual exploitation of women and children, with an estimated 10–30 percent under the age of 18 (UN Office on Drugs and Crime 2012). Russia and other former Soviet Bloc countries are currently the top recruiting grounds for women entering the sex trade. However, it is a problem that affects both large and small countries (Schauer and Wheaton 2006). Victims are tricked, cheated, or coerced into traveling to another country and once there, are often forced to work in the sex trade industry. Forced prostitution and child-sex tourism are only two of the many forms of sex trafficking. The United States is the world's second largest destination/market country (after Germany) for women and children trafficked for purposes of exploitation in the sex industry (Mizus et al. 2003). Profit gained from sex trafficking tops $30 billion per year, making it one of the most lucrative industries of illegal trade (Belser 2005).

Those who are at the greatest risk for victimization include marginalized women with limited educational or employment opportunities (USDOS 2012). Many women enter the sex industry voluntarily as a way to meet familial financial obligations. Often, sex work offers greater economic opportunity than many other occupations. Working in an illegal occupation, however, only serves to further marginalize women, turning the possibility of trafficking into a job-related risk (Gould 2007). Lacking economic and social support, illegal migration adds increased vulnerability for exploitation. Whether the choice to leave their homeland is motivated by poverty, war, or limited opportunities due to gender, more women and children than ever before are making the decision to leave (Huda 2006). Cultural traditions that devalue the worth of women also serve to proliferate sexual trafficking. In India, for example, where a bride may not be able to enter into marriage without providing a payment or dowry, girls are often considered an economic liability. Dowry payments, documented at up to six times the annual household income in South Asia, can place bridal families in financial ruin (Rao 1993). In extreme cases, dowry customs have been linked to infanticide or "dowry-death," where young women are murdered or commit suicide as part of an extortion scheme to gain increased dowry (Anderson 2007). Traffickers often use the incentive of a "dowry-less" marriage as a way to gain parental consent (Ali 2005).

Sex Tourism

International travel for the purpose of obtaining sex is known as "sexual tourism." In the most common scenario, men from wealthy nations travel to less prosperous regions where lower costs, a younger age of consent, and the increased availability of child prostitutes encourage destination prostitution. Technological advances and ease of international travel have increased sexual tourism over the last twenty to thirty years. Advertisements for these kinds of services can be found using any Internet search engine in a matter of seconds:

> One of the biggest attractions in Thailand is the friendly, beautiful and exotic Thai women. Almost any Thai woman can be yours for as little as $13 US dollars. Why settle for just one when you can have 2 or 3 totally nude Thai women all to yourself in the privacy of your hotel room. Time is not an issue and you'll never be rushed as sexy Thai women are available for as little as $25 US dollars for the entire day. Enjoy them over and over again or have a different one as often as you want. You'll be pampered and treated like a king with a kingdom of thousands of beautiful eager Thai women to choose from. Join our staff of experts as well as many others who share the same interests in the pursuit of women and erotic pleasure. This is the No. 1 Thailand tour for the novice or the veteran sex traveler (Dexterhorn 2004).

It is estimated that over two million children are involved in the transnational sex trade (USDOS 2008). Each of these children may be victimized by 100 to 1,500 sex-tourist perpetrators per year (USDOS 2008). As a retired school teacher comments:

> On this trip, I've had sex with a 14-year-old girl in Mexico and a 15-year-old in Colombia. I'm helping them financially. If they don't have sex with me, they may not have enough food. If someone has a problem with me doing this, let UNICEF feed them (USDOJ 2006).

For many developing nations, sexual tourism represents a large economic opportunity similar to more conventional recreation in developed nations. In 1998, the International Labour Organisation (ILO) reported that between 2–14 percent of the gross domestic product of Indonesia, Malaysia, the Philippines, and Thailand was derived from sexual tourism. As a multi-billion-dollar industry, countries may be less willing to regulate or police international prostitution (ILO 1998).

Sex trafficking, especially sexual tourism, has serious implications for public health. These concerns extend not only to trafficked victims, but to the general public as well. Global inequalities in education and medical services are linked to the spread of HIV and other infectious diseases through international prostitution. In Thailand during the late 1980s, the profitable sexual tourism industry was used as a reason not to promote HIV education. Officials did not want to publicize the growing AIDS statistics for fear of a decrease in international sexual travel. Between 1988 and 1989, studies estimated that 44 percent of all sex workers were infected with HIV (Weniger et al. 1991). Recent numbers are no less daunting. Silverman et al. (2007) reported 38 percent of repatriated Nepalese victims were HIV positive, with higher disease prevalence (60 percent) for those trafficked prior to age 15. Ironically, it is the growing fear of HIV that makes younger children more attractive to sexual offenders. Younger children are viewed as less likely to carry HIV due to their perceived sexual innocence (Bales and Trodd 2007; Fein 2007).

Slavery

Although often regarded only as a historical atrocity, it is estimated that nearly 27 million people are enslaved today throughout the world (Bales and Trodd 2007). A thriving slave trade merges seamlessly with trafficking, with more people taken across international borders now than ever before (Kapstein 2006). Often synonymously interchanged with debt bondage, indentured labor, or domestic servitude, slavery involves the control of one person over another through violence or threat of violence (Bales 2005, 9). Currently, women make up 80 percent of the global slave market, with an estimated 50 percent under the age of 18 (Kapstein 2006).

Inextricably linked to trafficking, "debt bondage" involves using human beings as collateral for debt (Woolman and Bishop 2007). Forced to work through psychological and often physical coercion, victims of forced labor remain victimized through fraud and deception. Continued threats of death or legal action maintain bonded subservience (Belser 2005). Five industries account for the majority of forced labor. The most common includes prostitution and sexual trade, which makes up 46 percent of those in bondage worldwide. Domestic service involves 27 percent, followed by agriculture (10 percent), factory work (5 percent), and the restaurant and hotel industry (4 percent) (Bales and Trodd 2007).

Much of the focus remains on women, even though men and children also make up a significant portion of those enslaved. The use of young males as camel jockeys in the Middle East is one example. In Persian Gulf countries, camel racing is a top spectator sport, which parallels the popularity of football in the United States or soccer in Europe. Beginning in the 1970s, the practice of utilizing young migrant children as jockeys became popular practice. Children as young as 5 years old are trafficked into the United Arab Emirates (UAE) from Pakistan, Bangladesh, Mauritania, and Sudan, and are sold into the camel jockey industry (Ould 2004). Once secured, jockeys are underfed to maintain a light weight in the interest of optimum performance. Other forms of maltreatment and serious injury, including broken bones, heat exhaustion, and stunted growth are common (Caine and Caine 2005).

The advancement of modern slavery has been attributed to increased numbers of "disposable" people in the world, due to rising population growth and expanding poverty (Fein 2007). In addition, globalization has led to social and economic changes, resulting in lower prices for slaves than ever before (Bales 2005, 9). Although the United Nations estimates that the average sale price of a slave is around $12,500, earning a slave trader as much as $10,000 per victim, other figures are much lower (Kapstein 2006, 106).

> One destination for the young men purchasable for $35 on the Ivory Coast are the cocoa fields of Sierra Leone. The young men are brutalized and beaten to make them stay. They're badly fed and unpaid. In India, boys as young as 5 and 6 are kidnapped, taken hundreds of miles from their homes and locked in huts to weave carpets 14 hours a day, seven days a week. Some of those handmade carpets are sold in U.S. department stores (Jones 2001).

A hallmark of human trafficking, recruiters create an exploitive relationship, often through an initial debt, which is fraudulently labeled as a term of employment (USDOS 2008). Debts may take the form of transportation costs, uniforms, or even job skills training (Jackson 2007). These debts are often considered familial, passed down through generations of workers (Bales 2005) until the debt is paid in full. Slaves can be purchased outright or, similar to other trafficking endeavors, slavers often recruit new victims with promises of gainful employment, using threats and actual violence to force continued servitude. Slavery often adds a unique component to the bond of ownership. In many cases, the original slave and all of his or her current and future possessions—including future generations of children—are property of the slave owner. As one Indian slave describes:

> I've always lived here, so did my father and grandfather. We've always been here and we've always worked for the same master. When my father died I had to take over his debt; that was almost thirty years ago. When he died he owed the master 1,200 rupees, a lot of money (Bales 2004, 212)!

Laborers comply with forced servitude out of fear. Common threats include turning over the victims to police or immigration authorities, often confiscating their papers as a way to maintain control (Belser 2005). Current legal initiatives can exacerbate forced labor. Anti-abscondment laws typically involve arrest, incarceration, and deportation if a laborer is missing from employment (USDOS 2008). Modern slavery is propagated through contractual arrangements, often signed by the victim, making legal recourse more difficult (Jackson 2002).

Involuntary Servitude

Domestic work is the largest source of paid employment for women around the world (Anderson 2004). Millions of women migrate each year to seek domestic careers in wealthy nations. Migration fees paid to smugglers can easily lead to situations of involuntary servitude or debt bondage. Recruiters or employers may keep passports or visas as debt collateral. Frequently forced to work long hours with little pay, domestics may find themselves unable to change jobs, in essence becoming illegally confined to servitude (Ould 2004).

Domestic servants are primarily adolescents or young girls recruited through force, the lure of financial security, and even parental consent.

> My father forced me into this work by threatening that if I refused to go to work as a domestic servant he would disown me ... then I was

going to school and also learning how to sew. My father said he had no money to continue paying for my school fees, so I dropped out of school. He said he had arranged for me to go to the city to do house girl work in order to earn money. I refused but he forced me … my mother was also in support of my father (Okafor 2009, 177).

Domestics working to pay off debts often will not even receive payment for their work. Instead, all payment is given directly to the middleman or recruiter.

Mail-order bride companies are an extension of traditional servitude, which often operate under the guise of international marriage brokers (IMBs) and hide involuntary servitude behind the veil of marriage. Promoting women as marketable commodities, IMBs promise safe international passage in return for marriage. The system facilitates trafficking by essentially selling women and girls into marriage, prostitution, and/or domestic servitude, with little to no recourse (Jackson 2002). In South Korea, there were 43,121 international marriages between 2004 and 2007, with over 70 percent involving women from Southeast Asia, a central trafficking hot spot (Parrot and Cummings 2008). Often nothing more than a front for prostitution, marriage agencies are also active trafficking operations.

The International Organ Trade and Transplant Tourism

An emerging form of international trafficking involves the illegal recruitment and sale of living organs for transplant. Medical advances have created a market where the demand far exceeds the supply, leading to the development of an unregulated organ trade that mirrors other forms of human trafficking. Organ sales flow from impoverished countries (China, Pakistan, Egypt, Colombia, and the Philippines) to affluent nations, including Australia, Canada, Israel, Japan, and the United States, replicating human trafficking in a manner that the Netherlands Health Council adviser has termed "medical apartheid" (Heneghan 2007; Geis and Brown 2008; Shimazono 2007).

> In general, the circulation of kidneys follows the established routes of capital from South to North, from poorer to more affluent bodies, from black and brown bodies to white ones, and from females to males, or from poor males to more affluent males (Scheper-Hughes 2006, 20).

Organ recruitment parallels sex trafficking, preying upon similar populations. Agents/recruiters scour poor villages, luring desperate and often undereducated men and women to sell their organs as a means of achieving debt-free status and provide monetary incentives needed to survive. Possible dangers and life-long health risks are routinely left out of the recruitment pitch. Known as "kidney belts," some neighborhoods and cities become hotbeds for the trade (Scheper-Hughes 2006).

Diverging from the profile of a typical trafficking victim, adult males are the most common source of organs due to increased physical health and a greater likelihood of incarceration (Tansuhaj and McCullough 2008). China's routine practice of harvesting organs from executed criminals highlights the ethical concerns surrounding the organ trade. Reports indicate that China executes approximately 4,500 prisoners each year, with organs harvested from over 2,000 offenders (Geis and Brown 2008). In recent years, the number of executions has risen, leaving many to wonder if this increase is motivated by the desire for more organs (Tansuhaj and McCullough 2008).

Although the organ in highest demand is the kidney, other commonly trafficked parts include corneas, skin tissue, and bone. Also referred to as "transplant tourism," buyers traveling from prosperous countries and sellers traveling from poverty stricken regions meet in a third location to secure the often illicit transplant (Geis and Brown 2008). Listed as an offense in the 2000 Protocol to Prevent, Suppress & Punish Trafficking in Persons, organ trafficking has been condemned by most countries. Unfortunately, a lack of established definition, the virtual nonexistence of comprehensive data, and strong market demand make enforcement difficult (Shimazono 2007).

Legal Response and Universal Jurisdiction

Originating with maritime piracy, universal jurisdiction has been expanded to encompass many human rights violations (Kontorovich 2004). Trafficking and slavery violate universal assumptions of human decency, thus violating the heinousness principle and meeting the requirements of a universally cognizable offense. The International Criminal Tribunal for the Former Yugoslavia provided official justification for the application of universal jurisdiction to the crime of human trafficking by citing offenses that "shock the conscience of mankind" (*Prosecutor* v. *Tadic* 1995). The horrors associated with trafficking would not diminish with governmental approval; it is the inherent depravity that compels the international community to react.

Increased attention to trafficking has resulted in numerous international agreements. In the United States, the Trafficking Victims Protection Act of 2000 (TVPA) is one of the most comprehensive tools to date, offering strategies for punishment, protection, and prevention (USDOS 2008). Minimum standards of victim protection include both identification of victims and potential victims, combined with temporary care. The TVPA also requires the US State Department to issue an annual Trafficking in Persons Report that highlights the prevalence and scope of known trafficking offenses (Kapstein 2006).

Increased awareness has also led to increased funding for counter-trafficking programs. Between 2008 and 2012, the number of countries with anti-trafficking legislation doubled (UN Office on Drugs and Crime 2012). Global trafficking law enforcement agencies had a combined 7,206 prosecutions and 4,239 convictions in 2011 (USDOS 2012). Although new legislation has brought about new levels of international cooperation, law enforcement efforts are often undermined by the belief that victims are responsible for their own victimization (Farrell et al. 2008). For example, police officials may find it difficult to view prostitutes as victims, and similarly, a heavy focus on drugs and violence often deprioritizes trafficking as an area of concern. A further problem is the lack of widespread agreement on solutions to the trafficking crisis. Commonly implemented interventions, including increased controls on immigration and criminalization of existing prostitution laws could actually increase illegal trafficking (Martinez 2007). Forcing local prostitution underground provides increased opportunities for traffickers offering safe harbor and profit overseas. Similarly, countries that place a heavy focus on detention or deportation of illegal immigrants hinder reporting from trafficked victims fearing legal consequences.

Conclusion

The common elements linking all of these crimes together are the applicability of universal jurisdiction (*jus cogens*) and *obligatio erga omnes*. The act of maritime piracy, the category of offenses constituting crimes against humanity, and the various types of slavery and human trafficking taking place throughout the world are all universally despised and admonished, meeting a sufficient threshold of heinousness that warrants global interest and action. These crimes are considered to be morally reprehensible and harmful to such an extent that they must be recognized as offenses against all societies. All are seen as violations of *jus cogens* criteria, which specifically hold that these offenses should not be tolerated by any member of the global community. Further, *obligatio erga omnes* informs all nations of their moral imperative to ensure that legal action is taken against any perpetrators of these classes of crimes. Finally, universal jurisdiction allows any state to prosecute offenders for their involvement, regardless of the prosecuting state's jurisdictional connection to the actual commission of the crime or perpetrators of the crime. The severity of the offense, together with an interest in apprehension and prosecution of offenders, transcends both geographic and legal jurisdiction. By recognizing and accepting these three most essential principles of international law, nations collectively send a strong and unwavering message to their own citizens and to the global community as a whole that crimes of this magnitude of seriousness will not be tolerated.

Web Sources

Piracy

1. Additional resources about maritime piracy:
   http://www.apcss.org/core/Library/Bibliography/piracy.htm
2. The IMB Piracy Reporting Centre:
   http://www.icc-ccs.org/index.php?option=com_content&view=article&
   id=30&Itemid=12

Crimes against Humanity

3. Several videos detailing a trip through post-apartheid South Africa:
   http://www.pbs.org/kcet/globaltribe/countries/saf_journal.html#art
4. A detailed examination of a priest convicted of kidnapping, torture, and
   murder in Argentina after the Supreme Court revoked Amnesty:
   http://www.cbsnews.com/stories/2007/10/10/world/main3351642.shtml
5. Jorge Videla post-extradition:
   http://news.bbc.co.uk/2/hi/americas/110016.stm

Human Trafficking

6. An interactive map highlighting the hotspots of the organ trade:
   http://sunsite.berkeley.edu/biotech/organswatch/pages/hot_spots.html
7. The 2008 Trafficking in Persons Report:
   http://www.state.gov/g/tip/rls/tiprpt/2008/

Discussion Questions

1. With vast oceans and endless opportunities, piracy has become a lucrative profession for many in some of the world's poorest regions. Pirates act as modern-day Robin Hoods, sharing their ill-gotten gains to win support and protection from the local residents. How can countries with a

vested interest in preventing piracy combat its occurrence when the pirates have so little to lose and the residents have so much to gain?

2. For many nations, human trafficking plays an essential role to cultural stability. Families voluntarily sell their daughters into the trade in return for material goods. With familial—and often cultural—support, does this crime truly fit the definition of *jus cogens*?

3. Do you think the decriminalization of prostitution would result in a decrease in the sexual trafficking of women and children?

4. Are crimes against humanity so reprehensible that they should be prosecuted on an international level, or should they be treated as domestic crimes within each individual nation?

5. What parallels can be drawn between South Africa's system of apartheid and the social climate in the United States prior to the Civil Rights Movement?

6. How might the war on terror lead to an increase in the use of enforced disappearances in foreign countries?

References

Akee, Randall K. Q., Arnab K. Basu, Arjun S. Bedi, and Nancy H Chau. *Determinants of Trafficking in Women and Children: Cross-National Evidence, Theory and Policy Implications*. Accessed May1, 2009. http://www.iza.org/conference_files/worldb2008/basu_a3581.pdf, 2007.

Ali, A. K.M. Masud. "Treading along a Treacherous Trail: Research on Trafficking in Persons in South Asia." *International Migration* 43, no. 1/2 (2005): 141–164.

Allahbadia, Gautam N. "The 50 Million Missing Women." *Journal of Assisted Reproduction and Genetics* 19, no. 9 (2002): 411–416.

Anderson, Bridget. "Migrant Domestic Workers and Slavery." In *The Political Economy of New Slavery*, edited by Christien Van Den Anker, 107–117. New York: Palgrave, 2004.

Anderson, Kirsten. "How Effective Is the International Convention for the Protection of All Persons from Enforced Disappearance Likely to Be in Holding Individuals Criminally Responsible for Acts of Enforced Disappearance?" *Melbourne Journal of International Law* 7 (2006): 245–280.

Anderson, Siwan. "The Economics of Dowry and Brideprice." *Journal of Economic Perspectives* 21, no. 4 (2007): 151–174.

Asian Legal Resource Centre. "PAKISTAN: Council Urged to Act as Thousands Remain Forcibly Disappeared." Accessed March 11, 2009. http://www.alrc.net/doc/mainfile.php/alrc_st2007/438/, 2007.

Bakker, Christine A. E. "A Full Stop to Amnesty in Argentina." *Journal of International Criminal Justice* 3, no. 5 (2005): 1106–1120.

Bales, Kevin. *Disposable People: New Slavery in the Global Economy.* (Rev. ed.) Berkeley and Los Angeles, CA: University of California Press, 2004.

_____. *Understanding Global Slavery.* Berkeley and Los Angeles, CA: University of California Press, 2005.

Bales, Kevin, and Zoe Trodd. "All of it is Now." In *Many Middle Passages: Forced Migration and the Making of the Modern World,* edited by Emma Christopher, Cassandra Pybus, and Marcus Rediker, 222–236. Berkeley and Los Angeles, CA: University of California Press, 2007.

Bassiouni, Cherif M. "International Crimes: Jus Cogens and Obligatio Erga Omnes." *Law and Contemporary Problems* 59, no. 4 (1996): 63–74.

_____. *Crimes against Humanity in International Criminal Law.* Boston: Martinus Nijhoff Publishers, 1999.

Belser, Patrick. "Forced Labour and Human Trafficking: Estimating the Profits." International Labour Organisation, March 1, 2005. Accessed April 12, 2009. http://digitalcommons.ilr.cornell.edu/cgi/viewcontent.cgi?article=1016&context=forcedlabor, 2005.

Black, George. *Genocide in Iraq: The Anfal Campaign against the Kurds.* Human Rights Watch, 1993. Accessed February 12, 2009. http://www.hrw.org/legacy/reports/1993/iraqanfal/, 1993.

Bruinessen, Martin van. "Genocide in Kurdistan? The Suppression of the Dersim Rebellion in Turkey (1937–38) and the Chemical War against the Iraqi Kurds (1988)." In *Genocide: Conceptual and Historical Dimensions,* edited by George J. Andreopoulos, 141–166. Philadelphia, PA: University of Pennsylvania Press, 1997.

Cai, Yong. "China's Missing Girls: Numerical Estimates and Effects on Population Growth." *The China Review* 3, no. 2 (2003): 13–29.

Caine, Dennis, and Caroline Caine. "Child Camel Jockeys: A Present-Day Tragedy Involving Children and Sport." *Clinical Journal of Sport Medicine* 15, no. 5 (2005): 287–289.

Carpenter, Charli, R. "Beyond 'Gendercide': Incorporating into Comparative Genocide Studies." *International Journal of Human Rights* 6, no. 4 (2002): 77–101.

Chalk, Peter. "The Maritime Dimension of International Security: Terrorism, Piracy, and Challenges for the United States United States Air Force." Accessed April 1, 2009. http://www.rand.org/pubs/monographs/MG697/, 2008.

Chambliss, William. "On the Symbiosis between Criminal Law and Criminal Behavior." *Criminology* 42, no. 2 (2004): 241–251.

Davis, Uri. *Apartheid Israel: Possibilities for the Struggle Within*. London: Zed Books, 2003.

De Klerk, Frederik Willem. *The Last Trek: A New Beginning*. London: Macmillan, 1998.

Dexterhorn. "Thailand Tour." DH Productions. Accessed January 15, 2007. http://www.dexterhorn.com/trips/tourthai.htm, 2004.

Farrell, Amy, Jack McDevitt, Stephanie Fahy, Scott Decker, Nancy Rodriguez, Vince Webb, and Niko Passas. 2008. *Understanding and Improving Law Enforcement Responses to Human Trafficking*. National Institute of Justice. Accessed March 12, 2009. http://www.ncjrs.gov/pdffiles1/nij/grants/225202.pdf, 2008.

Fein, Helen. *Human Rights and Wrongs*. Boulder, CO: Paradigm Publishers, 2007.

Geis, Gilbert, and Gregory Brown. "The Transnational Traffic in Human Body Parts." *Journal of Contemporary Criminal Justice* 24, no. 3 (2009): 212–224.

Gould, Chandre. "Countering the 'Scourge': The Time for Evidence and Reason on Human Trafficking." *SA Crime Quarterly* 22 (2007): 7–12.

Gozdziak, Elzbieta M., and Elizabeth Collett. "Research on Human Trafficking in North America: A Review of Literature." *Internal Migration* 43, no. 1/2 (2005): 99–128.

Grabowski, Richard. *Economic Development: A Regional, Institutional and Historical Approach*. Armonk, NY: M.E. Sharpe, 2006

Guest, Iain. *Behind the Disappearances: Argentina's Dirty War against Human Rights and the United Nations*. Philadelphia: University of Pennsylvania Press, 1990.

Hanson, Stephanie. *Combating Maritime Piracy*. Council on Foreign Relations. Accessed April 22, 2009. http://www.cfr.org/publication/18376, 2009.

Heneghan, Tom. "Calls for Kidney Market as Transplant Demand Soars." *Reuters* April 3, 2007. Accessed May 9, 2009. http://www.reuters.com/article/health-SP-A/idUSL0365614720070405.

Hossain, Kamrul. "The Concept of Jus Cogens in International Law." *Daily Star*, January 16, 2005. Accessed April 3, 2009. http://www.thedailystar.net/law/2005/01/03/alter.htm.

Huang, Hua-Lun. "Piracy in Southeast Asia: Status, Issues, and Responses." *Asian Criminology* 2 (2007): 79–80.

Huda, Sigma. "Sex Trafficking in South Asia." *International Journal of Gynecology and Obstetrics* 94 (2006): 374–381.

ICJ Reports. Accessed February 5, 2009. http://www.icj-cij.org/docket/index.php?p1=3&p2=4&code=nam&case=53&k=a7, 1970.

International Labour Organisation. "Sex as a Sector: Economic Incentives and Hardships Fuel Growth." *World of Work*, no. 26 (September/October

1998). Accessed May 9, 2009. http://www.ilo.org/public/english/bureau/inf/magazine/26/sex.htm.

Jackson, Suzanne H. "To Honor and Obey: Trafficking in 'Mail-Order Brides.'" *George Washington Law Review* 70, no. 3 (2002): 475–569.

_____. "Marriages of Convenience: International Marriage Brokers, 'Mail-Order Brides,' and Domestic Servitude." *University of Toledo Law Review* 38 (2007): 895–922.

Jarvis, Robert M. "Maritime Piracy in the Modern World: Far from Hollywood, Real Pirates are Plaguing the High Seas." *Insights on Law & Society* 6, no. 3 (2006): 1–4.

Jha, Prabhat, Rajesh Kumar, Priya Vasa, Neeraj Dhingra, Deva Thiruchelvam, and Rahim Moineddin. "Low Male-to-Female Sex Ratio of Children Born in India: National Survey of 1.1 Million Households." *Lancet*, 367, no. 9506 (2006): 211–218.

Johnson, Derek, and Erica Pladdet. "An Overview of Current Concerns in Piracy Studies and New Directions for Research." Position Paper for the Piracy Panels and Roundtable at the Conference. *People and the Sea II: Conflicts, Threats and Opportunities.* International Institute for Asian Studies and the Center for Maritime Research, Amsterdam, The Netherlands, p. 4. September 4–6, 2003.

Jones, Adam. "Gendercide and Genocide." *Journal of Genocide Research* 2, no. 2 (2000): 185–211.

_____. "Global Slave Trade Prospers." *National Catholic Reporter,* May 25, 2001. Accessed May 1, 2009. http://www.natcath.com/NCR_Online/archives/052501/052501a.htm.

Kapstein, Ethan B. "The New Global Slave Trade." *Foreign Affairs* 85, no. 6 (2006): 103–15.

Kelly, Elizabeth. "Journeys of Jeopardy: A Review of Research on Trafficking in Women and Children in Europe International Organization for Migration." Accessed February 12, 2009. http://www.iom.int/jahia/webdav/site/myjahiasite/shared/shared/mainsite/published_docs/serial_publications/mrs11b.pdf, 2002.

Kimmel, Michael S. *Men and Masculinities: A Social, Cultural, and Historical Encyclopedia.* Santa Barbara, CA: ABC-CLIO, 2004.

Kontorovich, Eugene. "The Piracy Analogy: Modern Universal Jurisdiction's Hollow Foundation." *Harvard International Law Journal* 45, no. 1 (2004): 183–237.

Kritz, Neil J., ed. *Transitional Justice: How Emerging Democracies Reckon with Former Regimes.* Washington, D.C.: U.S. Institute of Peace Press, 1995.

Laczko, Frank. "Data and Research on Human Trafficking." *Internal Migration* 43, no. 1/2 (2005): 5–16.

Lawson, Edward H. *Encyclopedia of Human Rights.* New York: Taylor & Francis, 1996.

Luft, Gal, and Anne Korin. "Terrorism Goes to Sea." *Foreign Affairs Ruling the Waves: The Law and the Sea* (November/December 2004): 1–3.

Macedo, Stephen. *Universal Jurisdiction: National Courts and Prosecution of Serious Crimes Under International Law.* Philadelphia: University of Pennsylvania Press, 2004.

Manthorpe, Jonathan. "China Battles Slave Trading in Women: Female Infanticide Fuels a Brisk Trade in Wives." *Vancouver Sun,* January 11, A-1, 1999.

Martinez, Julia. "La Traite Des Jaunes: Trafficking in Women and Children across the China Sea." In *Many Middle Passages: Forced Migration and the Making of the Modern World,* edited by Emma Christopher, Cassandra Pybus, and Marcus Rediker, 204–221. Berkeley and Los Angeles: University of California Press, 2007.

May, Larry. *Crimes against Humanity.* Cambridge: Cambridge University Press, 2005.

McCann, Sarah More. 2008. "Somali Pirates Attack Tanker Loaded With Oil." Accessed March 3, 2009. http://www.csmonitor.com/2008/1117/p99s04-duts.html, 2008.

McFadden, Robert D., and Scott Shane. "In Rescue of Captain, Navy Kills 3 Pirates." *New York Times,* April 13, 2009. Accessed May 4, 2009. http://www.nytimes.com/2009/04/13/world/africa/13pirates.html.

McGoldrick, Dominic. *The Permanent International Criminal Court.* Oxford: Hart Publishing, 2004.

McGreal, Chris. "Worlds Apart." *The Guardian,* February 6, 2006. Accessed March 3, 2009. http://www.guardian.co.uk/world/2006/feb/06/southafrica.israel.

Mizus, Marisa, Maryam Moody, Cindy Privado, and Carol Anne Douglas. "Germany, U.S. Receive Most Sex-Trafficked Women." *Off Our Backs* 33, no. 7/8 (2003): 4.

Natarajan, Mangai, ed. *Introduction to International Criminal Justice.* New York: McGraw-Hill, 2005.

National Human Rights Commission. *Integrated Plan of Action to Prevent and Combat Human Trafficking with Special Focus on Children and Women.* National Commission for Women. Accessed January 12, 2009. http://ncw.nic.in/FINAL_REPORT_REVISED.pdf, 2008.

Nie, Jing-Bao. *Behind the Silence: Chinese Voices on Abortion.* New York: Rowman and Littlefield, 2005.

Nieto-Navia, Rafael. "International Peremptory Norms (Jus Cogens) and International Humanitarian Law." In *Man's Inhumanity to Man: Essays on International Law in Honour of Antonio Cassese,* edited by Lal Chand Vohrah,

Fausto Pocar, Yvonne Featherstone, Olivier Fourmy, Christine Graham, John Hocking, and Nicholas Robson, 595–640. The Hague: Kluwer Law International, 2003.

Nullis-Kapp, Clare. "Organ Trafficking and Transplantation Pose New Challenges." *Bulletin of the World Health Organization* 82, no. 9 (2004): 639–718.

Okafor, Emeka Emmanuel. "The Use of Adolescents as Domestic Servants in Ibadan, Nigeria." *Journal of Adolescent Research* 24, no. 2 (2009): 169–193.

Ould, David. "Trafficking and International Law." In *The Political Economy of New Slavery*, edited by Christien Van Den Anker, 55–74. New York: Palgrave, 2004.

Parrot, Andrea, and Nina Cummings. *Sexual Enslavement of Girls and Women Worldwide.* Westport, CT: Praeger, 2008.

Prosecutor v. Tadic. Decision on the Prosecutor's Motion Requesting Protective Measures for Victims and Witnesses, Case No.1 IT-94-1-T, T.Ch.II, August 10, 1995.

Rao, Vijayendra. "The Rising Price of Husbands: A Hedonic Analysis of Dowry Increases in Rural India." *Journal of Political Economy* 101, no. 4 (1993): 666–677.

Rome Statute of the International Criminal Court. Accessed May 7, 2009. http://untreaty.un.org/cod/icc/STATUTE/99_corr/cstatute.htm, 1998.

Ross, James. "Black Letter Abuse: The U.S. Legal Response to Torture since 9/11." *International Review of the Red Cross* 89 (2007): 561–590.

Rotberg, Robert I. *Suffer the Future, Policy Choices in Southern Africa.* Cambridge, MA: Harvard University Press, 1980.

Rummel, Rudolph Joseph. *Death by Government.* New Brunswick, NJ: Transaction Press, 1997.

Saunders, Rebecca. *The Concept of the Foreign: An Interdisciplinary Dialogue.* New York: Lexington Books, 2003.

Scarpa, Silvia. "Universalism and Regionalism: The Synergy to Fight against Trafficking in Human Beings." *Human Rights Law Review Special Issue* (Spring 2004): 4–19.

Schauer, Edward J., and Elizabeth Wheaton. "Sex Trafficking into the United States: A Literature Review." *Criminal Justice Review* 31, no. 2 (2006): 146–169.

Scheper-Hughes, Nancy. "Organs Trafficking: The Real, the Unreal and the Uncanny." *Annals of Transplantation* 11, no. 3 (2006): 16–30.

Shimazono, Yosuke. "The State of the International Organ Trade: A Provisional Picture Based on Integration of Available Information." *Bulletin of the World Health Organization* 85, no. 12 (2007): 955–962.

Silverman, Jay G., Michele Decker, Jhumka Gupta, Ayonija Maheshwari, Brian Willis, and Anita Raj. "HIV Prevalence and Predictors of Infection in Sex-

Trafficked Nepalese Girls and Women." *Journal of the American Medical Association* 298, no. 5 (2007): 536–542.

Stockland, Peter. "China's Baby Slaughter Overlooked." *Calgary Sun,* June 11, A-1, 1997.

Stone, Marjorie. "Twenty-First Century Global Sex Trafficking: Migration, Capitalism, Class, and Challenges for Feminism Now." *English Studies in Canada* 31, 2/3 (2005): 31–38.

Tams, Christian J. *Enforcing Obligations Erga Omnes in International Law.* New York: Cambridge University Press, 2005.

Tansuhaj, Patriya, and Jim McCullough. "International Human Trade: A Marketing Analysis." *Journal of Global Business Advancement* 1, no. 2/3 (2008): 225–236.

Treiman, Donald. "The Legacy of Apartheid: Racial Inequalities in the New South Africa. California Center for Population Research." Accessed February 12, 2009. http://www.ccpr.ucla.edu/ccprwpseries/ccpr_032_05.pdf, 2005.

Tyldum, Guri, and Annette Brunovskis. "Describing the Unobserved: Methodological Challenges in Empirical Studies on Human Trafficking." *International Migration* 43, no. 1/2 (2005): 17–34.

United Nations. "Treaty Collection." Accessed April 24, 2013. http://treaties.un.org/Pages/ViewDetails.aspx?src=TREATY&mtdsg_no=IV-16&chapter=4&lang=en, 2013.

The United Nations Convention on the Law of the Sea (A Historical Perspective). "United Nations Division for Ocean Affairs and the Law of the Sea." Accessed May 7, 2009. http://www.un.org/Depts/los/convention_agreements/convention_historical_perspective.htm, 1982.

UN General Assembly. "International Convention for the Protection of All Persons from Enforced Disappearance." December 20, 2006. Accessed August 17, 2009. http://www.unhcr.org/refworld/docid/47fdfaeb0.html, 2006.

UN Office on Drugs and Crime. "Global Report on Trafficking in Persons." Accessed April 24, 2013. http://www.unodc.org/documents/Global_Report_on_TIP.pdf, 2012.

U.S. Department of Justice. "Child Sex Tourism." Accessed January 12, 2007. http://www.usdoj.gov/criminal/ceos/sextour.html, 2006.

U.S. Department of State (USDOS). "Trafficking in Persons Report." Accessed April 12, 2009. http://www.state.gov/documents/organization/47255.pdf, 2005.

_____. "Trafficking in Persons Report." Accessed May 5, 2009. http://www.state.gov/documents/organization/105501.pdf, 2008.

_____. "Trafficking in Persons Report." Accessed April 24, 2013. http://www.state.gov/documents/organization/192587.pdf, 2012.

_____. "U.S. Address of the Human Rights Council on the Draft Convention for the Protection of All Persons from Enforced Disappearance." Accessed June 6, 2009. http://www.state.gov/documents/organization/124139.pdf, 2009.

Weniger, Bruce G., Khanchit Limpakarnjanarat, Kumnuan Ungchusak, Sombat Thanprasertsuk, Kachit Choopanya, Suphak Vanichseni, Thongchai Uneklabh, Prasert Thongcharoen, and Chantopong Wasi. "The Epidemiology of HIV Infection and AIDS in Thailand." *AIDS* 5, suppl. 2 (1991): 71–85.

Wenping, He. "Piracy Crackdown." *Beijing Review* 52, no. 1 (2009): 1–2.

Werle, Gerhard. *Principles of International Criminal Law.* The Hague, The Netherlands: T.M.C. Asser Press, 2005.

Woolman, Stu, and Michael Bishop. "Down on the Farm and Barefoot in the Kitchen: Farm Labour and Domestic Labour as Forms of Servitude." *Development Southern Africa* 24, no. 4 (2007): 595–606.

Chapter 17

Other International Crimes: Cyber Crime, Crimes against Cultural Heritage, Environmental Crimes, and Money Laundering

*Murugesan Srinivasan, Solomon Raja Pandian &
Arockiasamy Enoch*

Introduction

Crime appears to be a constant source of social concern, because it affects everyone in society and penetrates almost all areas of societal life. And the problem of crime assumes multiple dimensions as new forms of crimes emerge. For example, the advent of computers and the Internet—besides their use for good purposes—have created a space for the commission of crime. Likewise, during the last three decades various forms of environmental crimes—including illegal trade in wildlife; smuggling of ozone-depleting substances; illicit trade in hazardous waste; and illegal logging—have been on the rise around the globe. Next, there have been massive thefts of cultural heritages including theft of art and antiquities. Of course, a host of other transnational crimes, such as terrorism, have become rampant. However, the scope of this chapter is limited to discussion of cybercrime, crimes against cultural heritage, and environmental crimes. The chapter also discusses the issue of laundering the money generated by international crimes.

Although most crimes have always had international dimensions, in recent years, such crimes have appeared to grow, particularly as related to organized criminal activities. Some of the factors that have contributed to the increase in international crimes are: the changing sociopolitical environments in Eastern

Europe, the Middle East, and the Pacific Rim; the instability of the governments in Africa and Eastern Europe; the process of globalization, resulting in a significant increase in integrated markets; and the transnational movement of people, capital, and goods and services. This web of sociocultural, economic, political, and technological changes has yielded different kinds of effects on countries around the world (Williamson 1996; Woods 2000), including international crime. Criminal enterprises, like legitimate businesses, have expanded their geographic sphere of influence beyond national borders by adjusting to this globalized economy (Joyce 1999; Naylor 2002; Passas 2002). In many ways distance has become a nonissue (Robinson 2000), and as a result, many crimes exert influence on more than one country.

There has also been a diversification of international criminal activities. Traditional criminal activities such as drug and human trafficking, corruption, and extortion remain the same, but criminals have broadened their spheres of illicit activities (Mueller 2001; Williams 1999). Albanese (2005) stated that fraud is a characteristic of twenty-first century much like larceny characterized the twentieth century. In the year 2005, the head of the United Nations Office on Drugs and Crime (UNODC) reported that the total asset of organized crime groups was US$322 billion (Flynn and Cinelli 2009). This chapter focuses specifically on cybercrime, crimes against cultural heritage, environmental crimes, and money laundering.

Cybercrime

There has been a great deal of debate about what constitutes a computer or computer-related crime. A universal definition of computer crime has not been achieved; rather, functional definitions have been the norm. The common types of computer-related crime are: fraud by computer manipulation, computer forgery, damage to computer data or programs, unauthorized access to computer systems and service, and unauthorized reproduction of legally protected computer programs (United Nations [UN] 1999a). However, Lilley (2002) points out that most workable definition that encompasses the different forms of computer crime, as well as distinguishing between them, has three categories: (1) the computer as a target (e.g., hacking, viruses, and theft of telecommunications services); (2) the computer as a tool of the crime (e.g., fraud, money laundering, counterfeiting using new technology, and cyber stalking); and (3) the computer as an incidental accessory of the crime (e.g., a criminal's accounting records held on a computer or an anonymous letter that was composed on a computer).

An international legal definition of cybercrime used by most of the countries in Europe, North America, South Africa, and Japan was agreed to in the Convention on Cyber Crime, which came into force on July 1, 2004.[1]

- Examples of cybercrime in which the computer or network is a tool of the criminal activity include *spamming and copyright crimes, particularly those facilitated through peer-to-peer networks.*
- Examples of cybercrime in which the computer or network is a target of criminal activity include unauthorized access (e.g., *defeating access controls), malicious code, and denial-of-service attacks.*
- Examples of cybercrime in which the computer or network is a place of criminal activity include *theft of service* (in particular, *telecom fraud*) and certain *financial frauds.*
- Finally, examples of traditional crimes facilitated through the use of computers or networks include *Nigerian 419*[2] or other *social engineering frauds* (e.g., *hacking, "phishing," identity theft, child pornography, online gambling, securities fraud*). Cyberstalking is an example of a traditional crime—harassment—that has taken a new form when facilitated through computer networks.
- In addition, certain other information crimes, including trade secret theft and industrial or economic espionage are sometimes considered cybercrimes when computers or networks are involved (Council of Europe 2001).

Conceptually, the terms "cybercrime," "computer crime," and "digital crime" are not identical although they are generally used as synonyms. The term "digital crime" is a general expression that encompasses all types of crimes employing digital technology instead of conventional analog technology. Computer crime refers to any crime, the means or purpose of which is to influence the functions of a computer. It is an illegal action in which the computer is a tool.

---

1. Convention on Cyber Crime: The Convention is the product of four years of work by Council of Europe experts, but also by the United States, Canada, Japan, and other countries which are not members of organization (Council of Europe, 2001).

2. Nigerian 419 Frauds: A US$5 billion (as of 1996, much more now) worldwide scam which has run since the early 1980s under successive Governments of Nigeria. It is also referred to as "Advance Free Fraud", "419 Fraud" (Four- One- Nine) after a formerly relevant section of the criminal code of Nigeria, and "The Nigerian Connection" (mostly in Europe). However, it is usually called plain old "419" even by the Nigerians. In brief, 419 is a subclassification of Advance Free Fraud Crime in which the perpetrators are West Africans, primarily Nigerians, operating globally from Nigeria and elsewhere (http://home.rica.net/aplphae/419coal/).

Cybercrime also pertains to computer crimes committed in a networked environment, e.g., the Internet. Thus, cybercrime is a subset of computer crime, which itself is a subset of digital crime (Sahai 2004).

Bakshi (2001) enumerates some peculiarities of cybercrime:

- The intangibility of the subject matter of the offense;
- the technical character of the equipment used in, or affected by, the criminal conduct, and the conduct itself;
- the secrecy of the criminal transaction, with consequential difficulties of detection;
- absence of a definite locus; and
- multiple effects of the offense.

As far as the origin of computer crime is concerned, it is difficult to determine when the first crime involving a computer actually occurred, given that the computer has been around in some form since the abacus, which is known to have existed in 3500 BCE in Japan, China, and India. In 1801, profit motives encouraged Joseph Jacquard, a textile manufacturer in France, to design the forerunner of the computer card. This device allowed the repetition of a series of steps in the weaving of special fabrics. So concerned were Jacquard's employees with this threat to their traditional employment and livelihood that acts of sabotage were committed to discourage Jacquard from using the new technology: a computer crime had been committed (UN 1999a, 7). Though the first stored program computer was built in the 1940s, statistics on computer crimes as such have been kept since 1958. This data were recorded by the Stanford Research Institute (SRI). Rather than simply recording crimes committed using computers, the Institute kept data on what they referred as computer "abuses." These were divided into following categories:

1. Vandalism against computer hardware;
2. The theft of property of information;
3. Computer-based fraud or the theft of monies; and
4. Unsanctioned use of computer or theft and sale of computer time.

The data were not considered significant until 1968, the year when ten or more of these abuses were recorded (Mishra 2001).

One of the earliest persons to write about computer crime was an SRI scientist named Parker (1976). His somewhat unsystematic collection of news clippings culminated in *Crime by Computer*. Because *Crime by Computer* was published before the introduction of the personal computer, virtually all of the examples of computer abuse were acts against mainframe systems (Hollinger

2001). The first generation of hackers consisted of the talented students, programmers, and computer scientists from the Massachusetts Institute of Technology (MIT) and, later, the Stanford Artificial Intelligence Center (SAIC) during the 1950s and 1960s. They were academics or professionals interested in the code or sets of instructions being processed. They were often pioneers in their field. To them, the motivation for their type of hacking was the intellectual challenge (Levy 1985). But the subsequent generations of hackers, who were technological radicals in the 1970s, young people who embraced the personal computer (PC) in the 1980s, and the current generation that emerged in the late 1990s and early 2000s have all embraced criminal activity in some form or the other (Rogers 2001, 11–12).

Nature and Magnitude of Cyber Crime

Cybercrimes are on the rise around the world, and the number of Internet crime victims is increasing every year. For example, in 2007, the U.S. Internet Crime Complaint Center (IC3) processed 206,884 complaints regarding possible online criminal activity. Of these, 90,008 were referred to federal, state, and the local law enforcement for further consideration. Another study revealed that in the United States in 2005, approximately one in seven youth (13 percent) received an unwanted sexual solicitations online; 4 percent of youth received aggressive sexual solicitations online; 9 percent of youth had been exposed to distressing sexual material while online; and one in eleven youths (9 percent) reported being harassed online (Wolak, Mitchel, and Finkelhor 2006). A survey of 530 public and private sector organizations in the United States revealed that 56 percent were aware of some form of cyber attacks against their computer systems. The total financial losses incurred from these incidents were estimated at over US$200 million.

In Japan, in 2007, there were 5,473 cybercrime cases solved, up 1,048 (23.7 percent) from the previous year. These cases represented a three-fold increase since 2003. Violations of the Unauthorized Computer Access Law stood at 1,442, about 2.1 times larger than the previous year. Crimes involving computers or electromagnetic records stood at 113, down 12.4 percent from the previous year. Crimes using cyber networks stood at 3,918, up 9.0 percent from the previous year. Fraud using cyber networks slightly decreased to 1,512, down 5.3 percent from the previous year. Fraud using an Internet auction decreased, down 7.4 percent from the previous year. Distribution of obscene materials and child pornography cases stood at 395, down 10.8 percent from the previous year. Violations of the Copyright Law stood at 165, up 19.6 percent from the previous year. In 2007, police across the nation received a total of 73,193 complaints via cybercrime hotlines and other avenues, up 19.1 percent from the previous year. Complaints about fraud or unethical marketing practices, which fell in 2006, increased again in 2007. Access to "Cyber Trouble Consulting System on the Internet" at the National Police Agency (NPA) hit 420,487 counts (an average of 1,152 cases a day; up 6.9 percent from previous year) (Police Policy Research Center 2007, 15–17).

In India, 217 cases were registered under the Information Technology (IT) Act 2000 of India in 2007 compared to 142 cases in 2006, an increase of 52.8 percent. Of the 217 cases registered under IT Act 2000, 45.6 percent were related to obscene publication/transmission in electronic form (often known as "cyber pornography"). There were 76 cases of hacking computer system in 2007 (National Crime Records Bureau 2008, Ch. 18, 1–2).

According to United Kingdom (UK) government figures, hacking and viruses cost UK businesses up to £6 billion per annum. Worldwide, hacking is estimated to have cost businesses the equivalent of US$1.6 trillion in 2000 alone (Yar 2006). In the UK, it is estimated that there were 255,800 cases of online financial fraud in 2007 (up 24 percent from 2006). Online fraud on cards has risen to an estimated loss of £224 million (US$448 million; up 45 percent from 2006). Around 830,000 businesses in the UK suffered an online/computer related security incident in 2007–2008. It is estimated that there were 132,800 cases of computer misuse (excluding viruses) in 2007. Virus infection has dropped to being the fourth most common type of security incident, accounting for 21 percent of all incidents. In 2006, it accounted for 50 percent of the worst security breaches for UK businesses. It is also estimated that there were approximately 2,240,000 instances of online harassment in 2007; in the same period, 236,533 instances of harassment were officially recorded. Over 90 percent of online harassment remains unreported (Fafinski and Minassian 2008).

Most system penetrations go unreported, even though there has been adequate publicity in recent years about system risks and attacks. Corporations and government agencies are often hesitant to report and prosecute computer break-ins because of the risk of adverse publicity, loss of public confidence, and possible charges of managerial incompetence (Sharma 2003). Computer crime and security surveys reveal that financial losses due to information security incidents—e.g., denial of service, financial frauds, unauthorized access, malicious codes, and theft of proprietary information—in 2004 were between US$169 and $204 billion (Indian Computer Emergency Response Team 2006).

Global Initiatives to Deal with Cyber Crime

The first comprehensive proposal for computer crime legislation was a federal bill introduced in the U.S. Congress by Senator Abraham Ribicoff (D-CT) in 1977. The bill was not adopted, but the pioneer proposal created awareness around the world. In recent years, the question of the response of the criminal law to instances of computer misuse has come under active consideration in the UK. Initial investigations were conducted by the Scottish Law Commission, which published a consultative memorandum in 1986 and a report in 1987. The Law Commission's working paper appeared in 1988 and its final report was subsequently carried out on a similar exercise in 1989. Legislative action followed quickly when a computer misuse bill based on the Law Commission's recommendations was introduced as a private member's bill. It received the royal assent in June 1990 and came into force on August 1, 1990. The UK lagged behind many of the other major countries in introducing computer-specific legislation. Austria, France, Denmark, Finland, Italy, Luxembourg, the Netherlands, Norway, Portugal, Spain, Sweden, and West Germany enacted computer crime statutes in the 1980s.

Legislations regarding computer crimes were passed in many states in the United States, e.g., Texas Penal Code—Computer Crime Statute, 1985; Maine Criminal Code—Computer Crimes, 1989; Florida Electronic Signature Act of 1996; and Illinois Electronic Commerce Security Act, 1998. In Malaysia, the Malaysia Computer Crime Act came into force in 1997 and in 1998; and the Electronic Transactions Act was enacted in Singapore (Reed 2000). In Japan, the Unauthorized Computer Access Law (Law No. 128 of 1999) was enacted in 1999. The purpose of the law is: a) to prohibit acts of unauthorized computer access; b) to stipulate penal provisions for such acts as well as assistance measures to be taken by the Metropolitan or Prefectural Public Safety Commissions for preventing a recurrence of such acts; c) to prevent computer-related crimes that are committed through telecommunication lines; and d) to maintain the telecommunications-related order that is realized by access control functions and thereby contribute to the sound development of an advanced information and telecommunications society (Unauthorized Computer Access Law 1999).

The UN Commission on International Trade Law (UNCITRAL) adopted the Model Law on Electronic Commerce in 1996. The UN General Assembly, in resolution No. 51/162, dated January 30, 1997, recommended that all states should give favorable consideration to the Model Law when they enact or revise their own laws (UN 1997). Following the recommendations of UNCITRAL, the Government of India enacted the Information Technology Act (2000) (known as "21 of 2000") on October 17, 2000 (Information Technology Act 2005, 1, 3). A Convention on Cybercrime in Budapest in 2001 sponsored by the Council of Europe, with signatories ranging from the countries within and outside the Council of Europe became active on July 1, 2004. As of September 10, 2009, forty-six nations have signed the Council of Europe treaty on Cybercrime (Council of Europe 2001).

Characteristics of Computer Criminals

As millions of people around the world gain access to high technology, computer crimes can be committed by almost anyone with the will and the wits to break the law, or even just the ambition to learn everything possible about computer systems and software (De Angelis and Sarat, 1999). History has shown that computer crime is committed by a broad range of persons: students, amateurs, terrorists, and members of organized crime groups. The typical skill level of the computer criminal is a topic of controversy. Some claim that the skill level is not an indicator of a computer criminal, whereas others claim that potential computer criminals are bright, eager, and highly motivated subjects willing to accept technological challenges, characteristics that are highly desirable in an employee in the data-processing field. It is true that computer criminal behavior cuts across a wide spectrum of society, with the age of offenders ranging from 10 to 60 years with skill levels ranging from novice to professional. Computer criminals, therefore, are often average persons rather than supercriminals possessing unique abilities and talents. Any person of any age with a modicum of skill, motivated by technical challenge, by the potential for gain, notoriety or revenge, or by the promotion of ideological beliefs, is a potential computer criminal (UN 1999a, 9). Moreover, based on a study of computer criminals, Parker (1998) came out with various kinds of cyber criminals, which includes pranksters, hackers, malicious hackers, personal problem solvers, career criminals, extreme advocates, malcontents, addicts, and irrational and incompetent people.

Computer crime is a fairly new phenomenon with the potential for causing huge losses and damages, and its perpetrators have skills, motives, and backgrounds different from that of traditional criminals. The impact of computer crime affects almost all nations, which has caused them to enact special laws to deal with such crimes. In spite of the measures taken by law enforcement agencies, computer crimes are on the rise.

Crimes against Cultural Heritage

People have looted art and antiquities for thousands of years. However, during the past few decades the illegal market in art and antiquities has become transnational (Conklin 1994, cited in Lane, Bromley, Hicks, and Mahoney 2008). The damage caused by pilfering archaeological sites is like the harm caused when evidence is removed or destroyed prior to documenting a crime scene. The trafficking of antiquities results in the loss of valuable information that cannot be recovered. For these reasons, trafficking of antiquities is not simply considered as an offense against an object but a serious crime against peoples' heritage and culture (St. Hilaire 2007).

The Scope of the Problem

Though we do not have reliable estimates of size of illegal markets, there is no doubt that the market is massive and growing. Estimates of the illicit antiquities trade range from several hundred million to several billion dollars annually. The theft of cultural heritages around the world in the form of art and antiquities is referred to as "time crime." There are various estimates by different organizations and institutions regarding the value involved in the theft of art and antiquities. For example, Scotland Yard in London estimated the value of worldwide art theft at US$3 billion in the early 1990s. The Federal Bureau of Investigation (FBI) showed that the size of the illegal art market (including both art and antiquities) at about US$5 billion in the 1990s (Gage 2005). In late 2000s, the estimate of art theft around the world was US$6 billion.

Looting archaeological sites is a serious threat to the preservation of cultural heritage. Though the scope and frequency of looting at archaeological sites is difficult to assess, there are rough estimates and figures. Out of nearly 400 burial tombs inspected in western Turkey, 90 percent exhibited indications of looting, e.g., holes, pits, missing objects, or other damage to the site that are not part of systematic archaeological excavations (Roosevelt and Luke 2006). Gutchen (1983) found that of the 106 Belizean archaeological sites, nearly 60 percent had been looted. Between 1989 and 1990, in Beijing, Chinese officials estimated that nearly 40,000 tombs had been stripped of their antiquities (Anderson 2002; Murphy 1995; Platthy 1993). Italy's Carabinieri Cultural Heritage Protection Branch has recovered more than 326,000 objects looted from archaeological sites since 1969 (Pastore 2001).

A study on "art crime" was conducted in Australia. One of the issues was to estimate the size of the problem. Instances of theft included the disappearance of Picasso's "Weeping Woman" from the National Gallery in Melbourne, which was later returned. There were other instances where paintings were stolen from major galleries, museums, and universities. There was also the problem of counterfeit art, including fake paintings of Vermeer (Chappell, Polk, Adler, Aarons 2000).

Unlike other crimes, there is a distinctive "dark figure" problem in the study of art crime in almost all countries. For traditional crimes, e.g., assault, robbery, and burglary, there are various sources of data including official statistics, and the results of crime victimization surveys. But in the case of art crime, in most countries there are no official statistics. Although there are certain countries or places where data on art theft are available, such data have certain limitations. For example, in Australia, these offenses are not common enough to have generated data in statistical reports. Likewise, some empirical data on art theft are available in the United States (Burnham 1978; Ho 1998) and the UK (Barelli 1986).

Challenges in Dealing with Crimes against Cultural Heritage

One of the main challenges is the lack of database on the theft of art and antiquities. Major international organizations that have been active in the field have developed tools to collect data on the theft of art and antiquities. For instance, in 1995 the General Secretariat of the International Criminal Police Organization (INTERPOL) produced a new database for works of art combining descriptions and pictures. The database contains over 34,000 items as of August 2009 (Abramsohn 2009). In collaboration with INTERPOL and Paul Getty Trust, UNESCO developed the "Object ID," an easy-to-use standard for recording data about cultural and natural objects. The Object ID helps institutions, individuals, and the community to understand how to document cultural and natural objects in a uniform manner. Such documentation could assist in the recovery of objects in the event of theft or illicit export or loss. Moreover, the Object ID is a minimum standard of identification that ensures the prompt transmission of information to and from law enforcement agencies and customs officials. Terms such as cultural "property," "heritage," "goods," and "objects" are used interchangeably, but there is no universal definition for any of these terms. An exact definition for these terms and legal regime should be sought in national legislations and international conventions.

Many countries do not yet have laws and regulations to protect their cultural heritage from excessive commercial trade and theft (Calvani 2008). Although there are certain regulatory mechanisms in some countries, they are not effective. According to Alder and Polk (2005), Mackenzie (2007), and Wood

(2005), corruption and an unwillingness to enforce the existing laws are the main reasons for the limited effectiveness of regulatory systems. It should be noted that in countries in which there are high levels of theft from cultural sites, there has been direct involvement by public officials. Use of the Internet in marketing art and antiquities is another challenge. This is a popular way to create a global market. For example, sellers can use eBay and other Internet websites to distribute art and antiquities because they are not monitored or policed (Lane, Bromley, Hicks, and Mahoney 2008).

Environmental Crimes

Any illegal act that directly harms the environment can be called an *environmental crime*. Environmental crimes include illegal trade in wildlife; smuggling of ozone depleting substances; illicit trade in hazardous waste; illegal, unregulated, and unreported fishing; and illegal logging and the associated trade in stolen timber. Although environmental crimes are perceived as victimless, such crimes generate tens of billions of dollars in profits for criminal enterprises every year. Moreover, it also affects society at large. For instance, illegal logging contributes to deforestation, which deprives forest communities of livelihoods. Deforestation also causes ecological problems such as flooding. Deforestation is also a contributor to climate change. It is estimated that approximately up to a fifth of greenhouse gas emissions stems from deforestation. Other environmental crimes, such as smuggling ozone depleting substances (e.g., such as refrigerant chemicals chlorofluorocarbons (CFCs)), significantly contribute to a thinning ozone layer, which leads to human health problems, e.g., skin cancer and cataracts (Debbie et al. 2008, 1).

Its Gravity

Though estimating the cost of environmental crime is difficult, a few international organizations have collected some date. According to an estimate by INTERPOL, global wildlife crime is worth billions of dollars a year. Regarding the cost of illegal logging, the World Bank estimates the annual global market value of losses from illegal cutting of forests at over $10 billion, and annual losses in government revenues of about US$5 billion. Another form of environmental crime, the dumping of contraband waste, generates substantial profits for international criminals. For instance, a thirty-pound cylinder of colorless, odorless chlorofluorocarbons (CFC)-12 bought in China for US$40 can be sold on the U.S. black market for up to US$600 (Schmidt 2004).

Table 1 Types of Environmental Crimes and Their Value

Type of Environmental Crimes	Value (in US$ Billions)
Animals and Wildlife Trafficking	20.00
Illegal Fishing	16.50
Illegal Logging	15.00
Trash Smuggling	11.00
Gas and Oil Smuggling	6.20
Diamond Smuggling	.28
TOTAL	68.98

Source: Havocscope 2009.

The costs of various environmental crime activities are presented in Table 1. Environmental crimes are worth US$68.98 billion worldwide. The WWF (formerly known as the World Wildlife Fund) estimated total animal and wildlife trafficking to be worth US$15 billion a year (n.d.). The total value of illegal fishing losses worldwide was between US$10 and US$23 billion annually (MRAG and the University of British Columbia Fisheries Centre 2008). Brack (2006) reported that illegal logging activities may account for loss of at least US$15 billion a year. According to the U.S. International Crime Threat Assessment, trash smugglers who dump illegal trash and other hazardous materials have assets (property owned by smugglers) worth US US$11 billion. Illegal gas and oil smuggling accounts for US$6.2 billion; diamond smuggling for US$280 million (Havocscope 2009).

Developed countries generate about 400 million tons of toxic waste annually of which 60% comes from the United States. Eighty percent of the United States' internationally exported toxic waste is sent to Canada and Britain (Cass 1994, cited in Simon 2000). Such toxic wastes, in huge quantity, are often dumped in Third World nations. Recipient nations are provided handsome financial rewards by multinational corporations. In general, recipient nations are poor countries with low gross national products (GNP). One such country, Guinea-Bissau, has a GNP of US$150 million. It may take in US$150–600 million over a five-year period if it accepts toxic waste from three European nations (Simon 2000).

In general, developed nations have been successful in dumping toxic waste in Third World countries. This is mainly because the Third World government officials are bribed to establish toxic waste dumps in their countries. The Third

World nations' acceptance of waste from advanced nations has generated a host of scandals. For example, in 1991 three South Carolina metal smelting firms contracted with a waste disposal firm to send waste to Bangladesh. The waste contained life-threatening levels of cadmium and lead. Once the waste reached Bangladesh, it was used to make fertilizer used by Bangladeshi farmers (Simon 2000).

In terms of illegal logging, it is estimated that it costs developing countries up to US$15 billion a year in lost revenue and taxes (Debbie et al. 2008). Though illegal logging is one of the most pressing environmental crimes, efforts to tackle the problem have been hindered by the lack of a coherent global regulatory framework, i.e., timber considered illegal in the country of origin can be sold on to the international market without difficulty. Illegal logging is a low risk and high profit activity. It is threatening precious forests from the Amazon, through West and Central Africa, to East Asia. For instance, Indonesia's rainforests have been the victim of one of the biggest continuing environmental crimes since the late 1990s. It is estimated that 80 percent of timber coming out of Indonesia is illegal and it costs the Indonesian government US$1 billion a year (Xinhua 2007). According to the UN Food and Agriculture Organization, Nigeria has the highest rate of deforestation in the world, losing almost 55.7 percent of its forest land between 2000 and 2005. Among Southeast Asian countries, Vietnam and Cambodia have the highest deforestation rates (cited in Butler 2005).

Another form of environmental crime that calls out for attention is trafficking in wildlife. According to the U.S. Department of Justice, illegal wildlife trading generates at least US$10 billion a year worldwide. It is a financial bonanza for criminals. For instance, a single rhinoceros horn can earn several hundred dollars (Schmidt 2004).

Global Response

Both national governments and international agencies have made efforts to tackle the problem of environmental crimes. But the efforts are not proportionate to the gravity of the problem. According to Mark Measer, a criminal intelligence officer with INTERPOL, the task of investigating and prosecuting environmental crimes in developing countries is extremely challenging. He further states that though there are environmental laws on the books in these countries, local police forces are often uneducated about environmental concerns. This may be due to the fact that they are influenced by corrupt officials. Moreover, prosecution of environmental crimes is difficult due to lack of informed judges. The UN Environment Programme has expressed concern about the lack of training in environmental laws among the judiciary in different countries and has launched training programs in environmental laws. In this context, it should be noted that even with a well-trained police force, a well-informed judiciary, and the political will to implement environmental laws, environmental crimes cannot be totally prevented. Criminals will continue to indulge in illegal trading as long as they perceive a demand.

The above forms of international crimes generate huge sums of money. Such illicit cash has to be converted to a less suspicious form so that the true source or ownership is concealed and a legitimate source is created. This process is nothing but money laundering. The criminal activities that traditionally generate money laundering include drug trafficking, trafficking of women and children, smuggling, counterfeiting, tax evasion, misappropriation of public funds, corruption, and bank frauds. Other sources of money laundering include computer piracy, information thefts (cybercrimes), trafficking of works of art and antiquities (i.e., crimes against cultural heritage), and trading in species, toxic waste, and nuclear products (i.e., environmental crimes) (Agarwal and Agarwal 2004).

Money Laundering

The UN Convention against Corruption (2003), held in Mexico on October 31, 2003, sought to identify the links between corruption, organized crime, money laundering, and economic crime. In particular, drug trafficking is a main activity of the organized criminals. However, due to its illicit, clandestine nature it is generally a cash economy and therefore avoids conventional banking systems. Members of criminal organizations "clean" their funds by laundering the money through other equally illicit networks. There is a link between environmental crime and money laundering for two reasons: a) the Financial Action Task Force (FATF) has included environmental crime in the "Designated Categories of Offences" as a predicate offense to money laundering; b) the Asia Pacific group on Money-Laundering (2006) held a special seminar to look at money-laundering issues in the illegal logging industry (Debbie et al. 2008, 3).

One of the first formal definitions of money laundering to gain international recognition is that found in the UN Convention Against Illicit Traffic in Narcotic Drugs and Psychotropic Substances (commonly referred to as the 1988 Vienna Convention). The key elements of this definition include the *conversion* of illicit cash to a less suspicious form, so that the true source or ownership is *concealed* and a *legitimate source* is created. This definition was used by many countries when they drafted anti-money laundering laws (McDonell 1998).

Money laundering generally involves a series of multiple transactions used to disguise the source of financial assets, so that these assets may be used without compromising the criminals. There is a three stage process: 1) *placement*, in which dirty money is placed into the financial system through deposits, wire transfers, or other means; 2) *layering*, in which the proceeds are separated, and their criminal origin is removed by moving them through a series of financial transactions; 3) and *integration*, in which a legitimate explanation for the source of funds is created, allowing them to be retained, invested, or used to acquire goods or assets (Lal 2003).

Money laundering has become a critical issue for any criminal enterprise. Successful money laundering enables criminals to:

- remove or distance themselves from the criminal activity generating the profits, thus making it more difficult to prosecute key organizers;
- distance the profits from the criminal activity, thus preventing them being confiscated if the criminal is caught;
- enjoy the benefits of the profits without bringing attention to themselves; and
- reinvest the profits in future criminal activities or in legitimate business(es) (McDonell 1998).

According to an International Monitory Fund working paper, money laundering affects financial behavior and macroeconomic performance in a variety of ways:

- policy mistakes due to measurement errors in national account statistics;
- volatility in exchange and interest rates due to unanticipated cross-border transfers of funds;
- the threat of monetary instability due to unsound asset structures;
- effects on tax collection and public expenditure allocation due to misreporting of income;
- misallocation of resources due to distortions in asset and commodity prices; and
- contamination effects on legal transactions due to the perceived possibility of being associated with criminal enterprises (UN 1998).

Initiatives of the International Community

To combat the problem of money laundering, series of initiatives have been taken by the international community. Some of the initiatives are outlined below:

- The UN Convention against Illicit Traffic in Narcotic Drugs and Psychotropic Substances (i.e., the 1988 Vienna Convention) called for the prevention of laundering of proceeds of drug crimes and other connected activities, and the confiscation of proceeds derived from such crimes. Many countries ratified the Convention (UN 2003).
- The Paris-based Financial Action Task Force (FATF), consisting of thirty-four nations (as of 2007), was set up at the 1989 Paris Summit of the Group of Seven Countries (better known as the G7) to prevent international money laundering. In 1990, FATF developed forty recommendations that provided a complete set of countermeasures against money laundering, covering the criminal justice system and law enforcement, the financial system and its regulation and international cooperation. Then, the recommendations were revised for the first time in 1996 taking into account changes in money laundering trends and anticipating potential future threats. In 2003, the FATF completed a thorough review and update of the forty recommendations. With reference to the scope of criminal offense of money laundering, Recommendation 1 states that, "Countries should criminalize money laundering on the basis of UN Convention against Illicit Traffic in Narcotic Drugs and Psychotropic Substances, 1988 (the Vienna Convention) and UN Convention against Transnational Organized Crime, 2000 (the Palermo Convention)." It further states that countries should apply the crime of money laundering to all serious offenses, with a view to including the widest range of predicate offenses. Predicate offenses may be described by reference to all offenses, or to a threshold linked either to a category of serious offenses or to the penalty of imprisonment applicable to the predicate offense (threshold approach), or to a list of predicate offenses, or a combination of these approaches (FATF-GAFI 2003).
- The Political Declaration and Global Programme of Action was adopted by UN General Assembly in Resolution No. S-17/2 of February 23, 1990. This declaration called upon the member states to develop mechanisms to prevent financial institutions from being used for the laundering of drug-related money and for the enactment of legislation to prevent such laundering.
- A 2007 regulation aimed at combating money laundering and terrorism financing requires travelers possessing cash in the value of €10,000 or

more to declare their assets when entering or leaving a European Union (EU) country. The obligation to declare currency was first mooted by FATF. Although only fifteen constituent states of the EU are members of FATF, the European Commission, as an organizational member, is expected to implement the anti-money-laundering and counterterrorism financing measures across the entire EU. This role gains importance in view of the high incidence of fraud, corruption, and crime in many Eastern European states (Move against Terrorism Funding 2007).

- The 1990 Strasbourg Convention on Laundering, Search, Seizure and Confiscation of the Proceeds from Crime, while considering the fight against serious crime, which has become increasingly international problem, called for the use of modern and effective methods to fight serious crimes (Council of Europe 1990).
- Because the financing of terrorism is a matter of grave concern to the international community as a whole and the number and seriousness of acts of international terrorism depend on financing, the International Convention for the Suppression of the Financing of Terrorism was adopted by the UN General Assembly in January 2000 (UN 1999b).

Conclusion

According to Anderson (1989, 26, as cited in UNDPI 1995), the "global conglomerates dealing in illicit activities survive and flourish because unilateral enforcement efforts by a single country generally disable only small segments of such operations." International crimes are also facilitated by certain other factors, such as an increase in passenger volume on international commercial flights; a larger transnational flow of goods and services; increasing migration and economic hardships that migrants often face in new homelands, thereby creating fertile ground for crime networks; obstacles to international law enforcement, including language and cultural differences, variations in criminal laws, and criminal justice practices; and the reluctance of nations to share scarce resources, and their desire to protect their national sovereignty. Besides these factors, the universally exchangeable characters of some major currencies (e.g., dollar, euro, and yen) have smoothed the transition from illicit profits in one country to apparently legitimate investments in another country. Such a transition is also facilitated by electronic money transfers—trillions of dollars are exchanged through electronic transfers every day.

According to Barnet and Cavanagh (1994), half of the industrialized world's money is kept in or passes through tax havens. Under these circumstances, cooperation among the law enforcement agencies becomes crucial if we are to obtain a clear picture of criminal operations that span countries and continents. For instance, a criminal group based in one country may be smuggling valuables out of a different country and sell in one of several overseas markets. The proceeds obtained through criminal activities are likely to be invested in "front" businesses in different countries, which in turn become staging grounds for new operations. It should also to be noted that the scope of the national criminal laws is limited because what it is illegal in one country may be permissible in another.

In conclusion, it is worth quoting the former secretary general of the UN, Boutros Boutros-Ghali, who emphasized the need for a concerted global response to deal with international crimes. He stated that powerful international criminal groups work outside national or international law. These international criminal groups include traffickers in drugs, money laundering, and illegal trade in arms — including trade in nuclear materials and smuggling of precious metals and other commodities. He further stated that such criminal groups exploit both the new liberal international economic order and the different approaches and practices of states. They also induce state officials to commit unlawful acts or bribe them, making use of their vast stores of illegally obtained money. The secretary general underlined the fact that some criminal "empires" are richer than many poorer states. To deal with the many forms of organized crime, which are predominantly transnational in character, we need to have international cooperation. But law enforcement remains predominantly local and national.

Web Sources

1. Information on US cybercrime is available at:
    http://www.justice.gov/criminal/cybercrime/
2. Information on European Convention on Cybercrime is available at:
    http://conventions.coe.int/Treaty/en/Treaties/Html/185.htm
3. The UN Convention on Transnational Organized Crime is available at:
    http://www.unodc.org/unodc/treaties/CTOC/
4. The UN Environment Programme is available at:
    http://www.unep.org/
5. Information on the FBI's Art Theft program is available at:
    http://www.fbi.gov/about-us/investigate/vc_majorthefts/arttheft

Discussion Questions

1. Should the UN publish an annual compilation of statistics on international crimes, including cybercrimes, environmental crimes, and crimes against cultural heritage?
2. Should there be universal definitions for various forms of international crimes, including cybercrime, environmental crimes, and crimes against cultural heritages? Should there be a proper typology of crime under each category of international crimes?
3. Should there be a comprehensive statute on all forms of international crimes that can be enforced across national boundaries?
4. Should we broaden the scope of the INTERPOL in coordinating the member states of the UN to include enforcing laws relating to international crimes?
5. Should the International Criminal Court (ICC) assume the role of prosecuting cases of international crime?

References

Abramsohn, Jennifer. "Interpol goes Online with Database of Stolen Art." *DEUTSCHE WELLE*, August 21, 2009. http://www.dw.de/interpol-goes-online-with-database-of-stolen-art/a-4589351.

Agarwal, J. D., and Aman Agarwal. "Globalization and International Capital Flows." *Finance India, XIX*, no.1 (2004). Accessed August 4, 2008. http://www.iif.edu/director/articles/20040120art001.htm.

Albanese, Jay S. "Fraud: The Characteristics Crime of the Twenty-First Century." *Trends in Organized Crime* 8, no. 4 (2005): 6–14.

Alder, Christine, and Kenneth Polk. "The Illicit Traffic in Plundered Antiquities." In *Handbook of Transnational Crime and Justice,* edited by Philip L. Reichel, 98–113. Thousand Oaks, CA: Sage, 2005.

Anderson, Kathleen. "The International Theft and Illicit Export of Cultural Property." *New England Journal of International & Comparative Law* 8, no 2 (2002): 1–26.

Bakshi, Parvinrai Mulwantrai. "Cyber Crime." *Company Law Journal* 3 (2001): 146–48.

Banks, Debbie, Charlotte Davies, Justin Gosling, Julian Newman, Mary Rice, Jago Wadley, and Fionnuala Walravens. *Environmental Crime: A Threat to Our Future.* London: Environmental Investigation Agency, 2008.

Barelli, John J. "On Understanding the Business of Art and Antique Theft: An Exploratory Study." Unpublished Ph.D. diss., Fordham University, New York, 1986. Accessed July 22, 2009. http://fordham.bepress.com/dissertations/AAI8615718/.

Barnet, Richard, and John Cavanagh. *Global Dreams: Imperial Corporations and the New World Order.* New York: Simon & Schuster, 1994.

Brack, Duncan. *Illegal Logging: Briefing Paper.* UK: Chatham House, 2006. Accessed July 22, 2009. http://www.chathamhouse.org.uk/publications/papers/view/—id/508/.

Burnham, Bonnie, Ann Marie Cunningham, and Beth Herz. *Art Theft: Its Scope, its Impact, and its Control.* New York: International Foundation for Art Research, 1978.

Butler, Rhett A. "Nigeria has Worst Deforestation Rate, FAO Revises Figures, November 17, 2005." Accessed July 22, 2009. http://news.mongabay.com/2005/1117-forests.html.

Calvani, Sandro. "Frequency and Figures of Organized Crime in Art and Antiquities." Paper presented at the ISPAC International Conference, Courmayeur Mont Blanc, Italy, December 12, 2008. Accessed June 10, 2009. http://www.unicri.it/wwa/staff/speeches/081212_Courmayeur.pdf.

Cass, Valerie. "The International Toxic Waste Trade: Who gets Left Holding the Toxic Trash Bag?" Paper presented at the annual meeting of the American Society of Criminology, Miami, FL, November 16–20, 1994.

Chappell, Duncan, Kenneth Polk, Christine Alder, and Lisette Aarons. *An Exploration of the Illegal Art Market of Australia: A Report Submitted to the Criminology Research Council.* Parkville, Victoria: Department of Criminology, University of Melbourne, 2000.

Conklin, John E. *Art Crime.* Westport, CT: Praeger, 1994.

Council of Europe. "Convention on Laundering, Search, Seizure and Confiscation of the Proceeds from Crime, Strasbourg, 8 XI, 1990." Accessed August 18, 2006. http://conventions.coe.int/Treaty/en/Treaties/Html/141.htm.

Council of Europe. "Convention on Cybercrime, Budapest, 23 XI, September 23, 2001." Accessed January 12, 2009. http://conventions.coe.int/Treaty/EN/Treaties/Html/185.htm.

De Angelis, Gina, and Austin Sarat. *Cyber Crimes.* Philadelphia: Chelsea House Publishers, 1999.

Fafinski, Stephan, and Neshan Minassian. "UK Cybercrime Report 2008." Accessed February 10, 2009. http://www.garlik.com/static_pdfs/cybercrime_report_2008.pdf, 2008.

Financial Action Task Force (FATF). "The 40 Recommendations." Accessed September 27, 2009. http://www.fatf-gafi.org/document/28/0,3343,en_322 50379_32236930_33658140_1_1_1_1,00.html, 2003.

Flynn, Daniel, and Antonella Cinelli. 2009. Crisis Hands Crime Groups Chance to Extend Grip: U.N., Reuters, May 28, 2009. Accessed July 22, 2009. http://www.reuters.com/article/newsOne/idUSTRE54R4H720090528.

Gage, Deborah. "Art Thefts through History." Paper presented at the third annual AXA ART Conference. Rogue's Gallery: An Investigation into Art Theft, London, England, November 1–2, 2005.

Gutchen, Mark A. "The Destruction of Archaeological Resources in Belize, Central America." *Journal of Field Archaeology* 10, no. 1 (1983): 217–227.

Havocscope. "Havocscope Black Market: Online Database of Black Market Activities." Accessed July 11, 2009. http://www.havocscope.com, 2009.

Ho, T. N. "Prevention of Art Theft at Commercial Art Galleries." *Studies on Crime and Crime Prevention* 7, no. 2 (1998): 213–219.

Hollinger, Richard C. "Computer Crime." In *Encyclopedia of Crime and Juvenile Delinquency,* vol. II, edited by David Luckenbill and Denis Peck, 76–81. New York: Taylor and Francis, 2001.

IC3 (Internet Complaint Centre). "Internet Crime Report." National White Collar Crime Center and the Federal Bureau of Investigation. Accessed July 13, 2009. www.ic3.gov/media/annualreport/2007_IC3Report.pdf, 2007.

Indian Computer Emergency Response Team (CERT-In). "Computer Security Incidents." Accessed August 18, 2006. http://www.cert-in.org.in/documents/certinbros.pdf, 2006.

Information Technology Act, 2000. Delhi: Universal Law Publishing, 2005.

Joyce, Elizabeth. "Transnational Criminal Enterprise: The European Perspective." In *Transnational Crime in the Americas: An Inter-American Dialogue Book,* edited by Tom J. Farer, 99–116. New York: Routledge, 1999.

Lal, Bhure. *Money Laundering: An Insight into the Dark World of Financial Frauds.* Delhi: India, Siddharth Publications, 2003.

Lane, David C., David G. Bromley, Robert D. Hicks, and John S. Mahoney. "Time Crime: The Transnational Organization of Art and Antiquities Theft." *Journal of Contemporary Criminal Justice* 24, no. 3 (2008): 243–262.

Levy, Steven. *Hackers.* New York: Dell, 1985.

Lilley, Peter. *Hacked, Attacked & Abused: Digital Crime Exposed.* London, UK: Kogan Page, 2002.

Mackenzie, Simon. Dealing in Cultural Objects: A New Criminal Law for the UK, Amicus Curiae." *Journal of the Society for Advanced Legal Studies* 71 (2007): 8–18.

McDonell, Rick. "Money Laundering Methodologies and International and Regional Counter-Measures." Paper presented at the conference on Gambling, Technology and Society, Sydney, Australia, May 7–8, 1998.

Mishra, Abhinav. "Criminal Investigation of Computer Crimes: A Human Rights Perspective." Unpublished LLM Diss., National School of Law University, Bangalore, India, 2001.

Move against Terrorism Funding. *The Hindu*, June 22, 2007. Accessed June 25, 2009. http://www.thehindu.com/todays-paper/tp-opinion/move-against-terrorism-funding/article1859567.ece.

MRAG and Fisheries Ecosystems Restoration Research, Fisheries Centre, University of British Columbia. "The Global Extent of Illegal Fishing." April 2008. Accessed July 21, 2009. http://www.mrag.co.uk/Documents/ExtentGlobalIllegalFishing.pdf, 2008.

Mueller, Gerhard. O. W. "Transnational Crime: Definitions and Concepts." *Transnational Organized Crime* 4 (2001): 13–21.

Murphy, David. J. "Stealing China's past: The People's Republic Reports a Hemorrhage of Artifacts." *Archaeology* 48, no. 6 (1995): 71–77.

National Crime Records Bureau. *Crime in India, 2007.* Government of India. Accessed January 10, 2009. http://ncrb.nic.in/cii2007/cii-2007/Chapters.htm, 2008.

Naylor, Thomas R. *Wages of Crime: Black Markets, Illegal Finance, and the Underworld Economy.* Ithaca, NY: Cornell University Press, 2002.

Parker, Donn B. *Crime by Computer.* New York: Charles Scribner's Sons, 1976.

Parker, Donn B. *Fighting Computer Crime: A New Framework for Protecting Information.* New York: Wiley Computer Publishing, 1998.

Passas, Nikos. "Cross-border Crime and the Interface between Legal and Illegal Actors." In *Upperworld and Underworld in Cross-border Crime*, edited by P. C. van Duyne, Klaus von Lampe, and Nikos Passas, 11–42. Nijmegen, The Netherlands: Wolf Legal, 2002.

Pastore, Giovanni. "The Looting of Archaeological Sites in Italy." In *Trade in Illicit Antiquities: The Destruction of the World's Archeological Heritage*, edited by Neil Brodie, Jennifer Doole, and Colin Renfrew, 155–160. Cambridge, UK: McDonald Institute for Archaeological Research, 2001.

Platthy, Jeno. "UNESCO and Trafficking in Illicit Treasures." *Journal of Prehistoric Religion* 7 (1993): 42–48.

Police Policy Research Center. *Crimes in Japan in 2007*, National Police Academy. Accessed January 12, 2009. http://www.npa.go.jp/english/seisaku5/20081008.pdf, 2007.

Reed, Chris. *Internet Law: Text and Materials.* London: Butterworths, 2000.

Robinson, Jeffrey. *The Merger: The Conglomeration of International Organized Crime.* Woodstock, NY: Overlook Press, 2000.

Rogers, Marc. K. "A Social Learning Theory and Moral Disengagement Analysis of Criminal Computer Behavior: An Exploratory Study." Unpublished Ph.D. Diss., University of Manitoba, Canada, 2001.

Roosevelt, Christopher H., and Christina Luke. "Looting Lydia: The Destruction of an Archaeological Landscape in Western Turkey." In *Archaeology, Cultural Heritage, and the Antiquities Trade,* edited by Neil J Brodie, Morag M. Kersel, Christina Luke, and Kathryn W. Tubb, 173–187. Gainesville, FL: University Press of Florida, 2006.

Sahai, Shashank. "Cyber Crime: Modus Operandi, Counter Measures and Law Enforcement." *Indian Police Journal* 51, no. 2, (2004): 90–102.

Schmidt, Charles W. "Crimes Earth Expense." *Environmental Health Perspectives* 112, no. 2 (2004): 97–103.

Sharma, S. R. *Encyclopedia of Cyber Laws and Crime.* New Delhi, India: Anmol Publications, 2003.

Simon, David R. "Corporate Environmental Crimes and Social Inequality: New Directions for Environmental Justice Research." *American Behavioral Scientist* 43, no. 4 (2000): 633–643.

St. Hilaire, Ricardo A. "International Antiquities Trafficking: Theft by Another Name." Paper presented at the International Conference on Strategies for Saving Indoor Metallic Collections with a Satellite Meeting on Legal Issues in the Conservation of Cultural Heritage, Cairo, February 25 to March 1, 2007.

Unauthorized Computer Access Law (Law No. 128 of 1999). http://www.npa.go.jp/cyber/english/legislation/ucalaw.html, 1999.

United Nations (UN). "Model Law on Electronic Commerce Adopted by the United Nations Commission on International Trade Law (Resolution No. A/51/628 of 30 January 1997)." Accessed April 23, 2013. http://www.un.org/documents/ga/res/51/ares51-162.htm.

_____. 1998. *Money Laundering.* UN General Assembly Special Session on the World Drug Problem. Accessed June 10, 2009. http://www.un.org/ga/20special/featur/launder.htm, 1998.

_____. 1999a. "International Review of Criminal Policy: United Nations Manual on the Prevention and Control of Computer-related Crime." Accessed June 10, 2009. http://www.uncjin.org/Documents/irpc4344.pdf, 1999a.

_____. 1999b. "International Convention for the Suppression of the Financing of Terrorism." Accessed June 10, 2009. http://www.un.org/law/cod/finterr.htm, 1999b.

_____. "United Nations Convention against Illicit Traffic in Narcotic Drugs and Psychotropic Substances, 1988." Accessed June 10, 2009. http://www.unodc.org/pdf/convention_1988_en.pdf, 2003.

United Nations Department of Public Information (UNDPI). "Stop Crime: The United Nations vs. Transnational Crime." Accessed July 10, 2009. http://www.un.org/ecosocdev/geninfo/crime/dpi1644e.htm, 1995.

Williams, Phil. "Emerging Issues: Transnational Crime and Control." In *Global Report on Crime and Justice*, edited by Graeme R. Newman, 221–241. New York: Oxford University Press, 1999.

Williamson. Jeffrey G. "Globalization, Convergence, and History." *Journal of Economic History* 56, no. 2 (1996): 103–32.

Wolak, Janis, Kimberly Mitchell, and David Finkelhor. 2006. *Online Victimization of Youth: Five Years Later*. Alexandria, VA: Center for Missing and Exploited Children. Accessed July 10, 2009. http://www.missingkids.com/en_US/publications/NC167.pdf, 2006.

Wood, James. N. "Cross-border Issues Affecting Stolen Art." Paper presented at the third annual AXA Art Conference. Rogue's Gallery: An Investigation into Art Theft, London, England, November 1–2, 2005.

Woods. Ngaire. "The Political Economy of Globalization." In *the Political Economy of Globalization*, edited by Ngaire Wood, 1–20. New York, NY: St. Martin's Press, 2000.

WWF. "Wildlife Trade." Accessed July 21, 2009. http://www.worldwildlife.org/what/howwedoit/policy/wildlifeissues.html. n.d.

Xinhua. "Illegal Logging Destroying Last Strongholds of Orangutans in Southeast Asia: UN Report." Accessed June 10, 2009. http://english.peopledaily.com.cn/200702/07/eng20070207_348038.html, 2007.

Yar, Majid. *Cyber Crime and Society*. London: Sage, 2006.

Overall Conclusion

There are 196 independent countries in the world today. With a vast array of criminal justice systems and legal traditions, each country has a unique set of needs. To help satisfy these needs, the United Nations was established to provide a centralized intergovernmental organization. Within the United Nations's organizational structure, there are specialized agencies that help settle disputes between "member states." For example, the International Court of Justice (ICJ), a primary judicial arm of the United Nations, adjudicates disputes among "member states." The International Criminal Court (ICC), also created by the United Nations, is considered a forum for seeking accountability for crimes against humanity, war crimes, genocide, and crimes of aggression. The Court, headquartered in The Hague, Netherlands, prosecutes individuals who commit any of the above mentioned crimes. However, the Court's powers are severely limited for two basic reasons as pointed out by Vandiver and Jamieson: (1) lack of resources and authority to enforce the decision of the Court, and (2) no compelling reasons to abide by the decision, especially when it is against the personal or the best interest of their country.

To address human rights issues, the United Nations developed various rules, guidelines, standards, and conventions. Although conventions related to criminal justice, juvenile justice, and human rights are binding on member states who are signatories to the specific convention (i.e., ratified states), many member countries adopted the guidelines and standards in their domestic laws. Despite these progressive changes, there is a lack of political will to implement the established laws in some countries. For example, India has failed to promote human dignity or improve educational opportunities of *Dalit*. Similarly, the Roma/Gypsies of Europe face racial discrimination despite the European Union's explicit prohibition of race discrimination in the areas of housing and healthcare. Although scholars continue to debate whether human rights are derived at the individual level or group level (as presented by Rubin in Chapter 9), we all agree that these rights should be protected.

In addition to addressing human rights issues, the United Nations has also developed guidelines and rules to end the inhumane treatment of juvenile and adult offenders housed in custodial institutions, Examples include, the UN Standard Minimum Rules for the Administration of Juvenile Justice, 1985 (commonly known as the Beijing Rules) and the UN Rules for the Protection of Juveniles Deprived of their Liberty, 1990 (commonly known as the JDL Rules). The Beijing Rules advocates for diversionary program, probation, and community services for juveniles offenders in place of institutional commitments. The latter emphasizes the limited use of detention for juveniles prior to trial. The UN Standard Minimum Rules for the Treatment of Prisoners (1977) provides rules governing proper supervision of inmates, adequate accommodations, and proper maintenance of institutions. The Convention against Torture and other Cruel, Inhuman or Degrading Treatment or Punishment (1984) outlines steps that states should take to prevent torture and inhumane treatment of offenders in places of detention. Not all member states have followed these rules.

Finally, individual countries have taken measures to address transnational crimes such as terrorism, drug trafficking, human trafficking, and cybercrime on the domestic front, however, the enforcement at the international level is significantly lacking. We need a global system of international law, justice, and enforcement to effectively address many of the issues discussed in this book.

Index

People

Abd-Al-Rahman, Muhammad Ali, 48
Al-Bashir, Omar, 31–32, 50–51
Al-Nashiri, Abdul Rahim, 61
Ambedkar, B. R., 301
Anderson, Benedict, 226
Arnold, Samuel, 57
Atzerodt, George, 57
Beitz, Charles, 225, 231, 240
Bensouda, Fatou, 41
Berlin, Isaiah, 228, 243
Bin al Shibh, Ramzi, 61
Bin Laden, Osama, 71, 127
Buitrago, Helmer Herrero, 398
Bush, George W., 39, 51, 62, 63, 65,
    66, 70, 73, 89, 221, 343, 347, 349,
    350, 403
Camarena-Salazar, Enrique, 59
Carens, Joseph, 238
Carter, Jimmy, 339
Chand, Lal, 312
Chirac, Jacques, 116
Clinton, William (Bill) J., 39, 61, 63,
    416
Collier, John, 148
Collins, Shirley, 58
de Tocqueville, Alexis, 241
Devi, Munia, 312

Escobar, Pablo, 398
Franck, Thomas, 240
Frangulis, Antoine, 254
Gombo, Jean-Pierre Bemba, 48
Gonzales, Alberto, 62
Herold, David, 57
Hitler, Adolf, 117, 230, 280, 322
Ignatieff, Michael, 223, 228
Innes, James, 56
Izetbegovic, Alija, 226, 285
Jackson, Jean, 227
Jia, Yang, 124
Johnson, Andrew, 68, 151
Julian, Henry G., 57, 58
Kant, Immanuel, 219, 223–224
Kaul, Hans-Peter, 43
Kennedy, John F., 151
Ker, Frederick, 57–59
Khomeini, Ayatollah, 339
King Phillip le Bel, 113
Kourula, Erkki, 43
Kuenyehia, Akua, 43
Lehder, Carlos, 398
Lemkin, Raphael, 275–277
Lincoln, Abraham, 56, 68
Lombroso, Cesare, 321
Londoño, José Santacruz, 398
Lubanga, Thomas, 31, 48

Machiavelli, 221, 362
Madison, James, 50, 72
Mao, Zedong, 122, 179, 180
Markey, Edward J., 65
Marshal, John, 72
McCain, John, 65
Mearshimer, John, 225
Milošević, Slobodan, 282
Mmasenono, Sanji, 41, 43
Monbiot, George, 223, 224, 242
Mudd, Samuel, 57
Napier, Charles, 109
Napoleon, 5, 113, 117
Noble, Ronald, 92
O'Laughlen, Michael, 57
Obama, Barack, 67, 71, 347, 349, 416
Ochoa Brothers, 398
Peel, Sir Robert, 12, 105
Pogge, Thomas, 227–228
Pol Pot, 277
Powell, Colin, 292
Powell, Lewis, 57
Qassem, Talaat Fouad, 61
Rawls, John, 219, 220, 224–226, 229,
    230, 232, 234–240, 242, 243
Reagan, Ronald, 63, 73, 339
Ribicoff, Abraham, 465
Rice, Condoleezza, 65
Roberts, John Jr., 73
Rodriguez-Orejuela Brothers, 398
Roosevelt, Franklin, 148, 255, 257,
    258
Rumsfeld, Donald, 70, 71, 350
Samper, Ernesto, 398
Sen, Amartya, 241, 436
Shattuck, John, 282–284, 294
Song, Sang-Hyun, 41, 43
Spangler, Edman, 57
Spivak, Gayatri, 227
Surratt, John, 56, 57, 68

Surratt, Mary, 56, 57, 68
Tarfusser, Cuno, 41, 43
Tilly, Charles, 222
Tito, Josip, 282
Tomlinson, Ian, 107
Toscanino, Francisco, 58, 59
Trendafilova, Ekaterina, 43
Tsar Nicholas II, 33
Tudjman, Franjo, 283, 285
Van den Wyngaert, Christine, 43
Von Bismarck, Otto, 117
Weber, Max, 81, 222
Wells, Herbert G., 254
Wolf, Martin, 224
Wylie, Andrew B., 68
Xiaoping, Deng, 122
Zubaydah, Abu, 61

Cases

Belgium v. Senegal (ongoing), 37
Duncan v. Kahanamoku (1946), 69
Ecuador v. Colombia (ongoing), 38
Ex Parte Milligan (1866), 57, 68, 69
Ex Parte Quirin (1942), 69
Ex Parte Vallandigham (1863), 68
Frisbie v. Collins (1952), 58
Georgia v. The Russian Federation
    (2008), 38
Hamdan v. Rumsfeld (2006), 70, 71
K. M. Nanavati v. State of Maharash-
    tra (1960), 16
Ker v. Illinois (1886), 57
Lakshmi v. State (1959), 15
Marbury v. Madison (1803), 72
United States Ex Rel. Toth v. Quarles
    (1955), 70
United States v. Alvarez Machain
    (1992), 59, 60
United States v. Toscanino (1974), 58
Valentine v. U.S. (1936), 60

Countries and Unions

Afghanistan, 39, 47, 63, 64, 70, 71, 280, 348, 349, 351, 380, 393, 394, 396, 406, 409

Australia, 4, 135, 136, 138, 156, 158, 165, 166, 167, 178, 197, 198, 199, 257, 295, 393, 446, 467, 468

Austria, 80, 82, 197, 267, 325, 326, 411, 412, 465

Belgium, 37, 43, 83, 197, 257, 267, 286, 288, 322, 326, 376, 412

Bolivia, 57, 266, 394, 395, 406, 414

Bosnia, 223, 226, 266, 277, 280, 281–285, 289, 291, 293,

Bosnia-Herzegovina, 281–282

Britain, 32–34, 65, 108–109, 129–131, 178, 407, 470

Burma, 394, 400, 406, 412

Cambodia, 268, 277–278, 412, 471

Canada, 4, 41, 62, 64, 135, 136, 156, 157, 158, 164, 165, 166, 167, 197, 266, 346, 347, 395, 446, 461, 470

Chad, 37, 290, 292, 293, 409

China, 4, 7–8, 22–24, 25, 26, 34, 39, 104, 121–125, 128, 164, 165, 167,171, 174–175, 179–181, 184, 185, 193, 198, 208, 209–213, 223, 257, 272, 373, 376, 380, 393, 394, 400, 403–405, 436, 446, 447, 462, 469

Colombia, 38, 47, 197, 227, 265, 340, 343, 394, 395, 397–398, 405–406, 443, 446

Croatia, 61, 267, 281–283, 285, 325, 392

Cuba, 61, 63, 70, 266, 337, 339, 340

Czech Republic, 43, 167, 197, 223, 267, 322–326

Czechoslovakia, 258, 322

Ecuador, 38, 266

England, 4, 5, 11–14, 17, 25, 104, 105–108, 113, 128, 134, 142, 164, 166, 167, 171–173, 175, 178–179, 181, 185, 197, 198, 199, 205–207, 212, 213, 222, 295, 321, 323, 404

European Union (EU), 64, 66, 93–98, 168, 321, 325–329, 347, 374, 395, 413, 475, 483

France, 4, 5, 17–18, 25, 82, 83,90, 104, 105, 113–116, 117, 120, 134, 164, 165, 166, 197, 222, 257, 267, 288, 291, 321, 322, 325, 326, 376, 394, 407, 411, 462, 465

Georgia, 38, 47, 267

Germany, 4, 5, 6, 8, 9, 17, 19–20, 25, 43, 64, 65, 66, 69, 104, 105, 117–121, 164, 165, 166, 197, 212, 230, 260, 267, 280, 282, 295, 321, 322, 323, 325, 326, 372, 375, 381, 441

Hungary, 85, 197, 267, 321, 322, 324, 325, 326

India, 4, 11, 14–17, 25, 104, 107, 109–113, 163–165, 167, 180, 191, 192, 197, 198, 199–200, 202, 212, 213, 220, 222, 223, 257, 301–303, 305–307, 309, 311–320, 328, 329, 353, 362, 372, 373, 376, 380, 393, 400, 404, 407, 408, 425, 436, 442, 444, 445, 462, 464, 465, 483

Iran, 20, 127, 170, 184, 196, 222, 257, 339, 340, 394, 408

Iraq, 39, 47, 223, 247, 280,339, 343, 348, 349, 394, 433, 435, 436

Israel, 205, 223, 291, 318, 337, 343, 347, 351, 375, 430, 432, 446

Japan, 43, 123, 164, 165, 167, 171, 175–176, 181–182, 184, 185, 197, 198, 208–209, 210, 212, 213, 278,

375, 376, 381, 394, 407, 446, 461, 462, 463, 465

Kazanistan, 239

Lebanon, 32, 257, 339, 395

Libya, 47, 48, 229, 235, 337, 339, 373

Mexico, 59, 87, 136, 164, 165, 192, 167, 376, 394, 395, 396, 397–399, 406–407, 416, 443, 472

Morocco, 65, 116, 197, 393, 395, 396, 406

Netherlands, 31, 34, 36, 40, 93, 164, 197, 267, 286, 321, 322, 325, 326, 375, 407, 413, 446, 465, 482

New Zealand, 4, 135, 136, 156, 166, 167, 197, 199, 374

Pakistan, 61, 65, 113, 127, 163, 196, 197, 223, 343, 351, 353, 375, 380, 394, 406, 433, 444, 446

Palestine, 47, 345

Peru, 57, 58, 197, 267, 394, 395

Poland, 121, 165, 197, 198, 199, 201–202, 212, 258, 266, 295, 322, 325, 327

Romania, 121, 197, 267, 322, 323, 325, 439–440

Rome, 39, 40, 44, 81, 268, 430, 431

Russia (aka the Russian Federation), 33, 38–39, 81, 121, 134, 164, 165, 212, 223, 253, 254, 267, 292, 322, 367, 375, 376, 380, 441

Rwanda, 32, 50, 247, 268, 284, 286–293, 295

Saudi Arabia, 4, 11, 20–22, 25, 104, 125–128, 165, 170, 171, 176–177, 182–185, 220, 258, 351, 353, 381, 425

Senegal, 37

Slovakia, 197, 223, 322, 323, 325, 326, 327

Somalia, 164, 194, 221, 425

Southern Africa, 156, 319

Soviet Union (USSR), 22, 258, 269, 308, 320, 339, 340, 353, 408

Sri Lanka, 197, 308

Sudan, 170, 197, 223, 268, 280, 284, 290–294, 375, 444

Switzerland, 32, 34, 197, 267, 321, 322, 376, 412

Thailand, 90, 197, 372, 394, 400, 406, 407, 412, 425, 442, 443

Turkey, 165, 197, 253, 267, 325, 392, 394, 408, 467

United Arab Emirates (UAE), 61, 170, 444

United Kingdom (UK), 4, 11, 12, 14, 32, 43, 197, 257, 267, 322, 325, 326, 346, 348, 349, 464, 465, 468

United States of America (United States, USA), 4, 32, 34, 39, 45, 50, 51, 55–74, 80, 82–90, 92, 95, 104, 105, 128, 135–137, 139, 141–146, 149–153, 155–158, 164–167, 171, 180, 184–185, 192, 194, 198, 199, 212, 223, 233, 251, 252, 255, 257, 259, 267, 277, 278, 280, 282, 285, 286, 288, 290–292, 295, 305, 306, 307, 346–350, 353, 354, 374, 376, 378, 391, 393–399, 404–410, 413, 416, 417, 425–426, 430, 431, 434, 441, 444, 446, 447, 450, 461, 463, 465, 468, 470

Uruguay, 59, 257, 267

Wales, 4, 11–12, 14, 25, 106, 164, 165, 167, 171–173,175, 178–179, 181, 197, 198, 205, 207, 212

Yugoslavia, 32, 257, 258, 268, 281, 282, 285, 308, 322, 408, 447

Key Ideas/Concepts

Acts of War and Acts of Genocide, 278–279

Adjudication, 3, 4, 9, 11, 14, 16–18, 20, 22, 24, 44, 200

African Union, 37, 268, 380

Akicita, 140

Al-Fatah, 345

Alien Tort Statute (1789), 59

Allotment Era, 146–148
Detribalization, 147

Al-Qaeda, 61, 62, 64, 70, 343, 345, 351

America Held Hostage, Day XXX, 339

American Civil Liberties Union (ACLU), 64, 66, 74

American Convention on Human Rights, 267, 308

American Declaration of the Rights and Duties of Man, 267

American Indians, 139–141, 144–153, 155, 157
American Indian Movement, 151
First Nation Citizenship, 136
Native American, 136, 138–142, 144–148, 150, 152–157

Americanization of international police work, 97

Amnesty International, 55, 61, 66, 127, 180, 183, 255, 269

Anarchism, 80, 81

Antebellum period, 55

Anticorruption law and enforcement, 379

Anti-drug Abuse Act (1988), 410, 413

Apartheid Convention (1973), 318–320, 329

Apartheid, 301, 318–320, 329, 430–432, 437, 446, 449, 450

Armed Forces (Special Powers) Act, 316

Asia Pacific Group on Money-Laundering, 372

Asian Heroin Trade, 400

Assimilation, 137–139, 141, 145, 146, 148, 149, 321, 322, 328
By Coercion, 138
By Conversion, 138
By Cooptation, 139
Civilizing American Indian Populations, 146
Civilizing the Indian Tribes, 145

Association of Southeast Asian States (ASEAN), 412, 416

Atrocities Documentation Survey (ADS), 292

Autocratic Police System, 134
Gendarmes, MVD police, 134
See Also: Subordinate Sovereignties, 97, 133–161

Bahujan Samaj Party (BSP), 305

Black sites, 60–62, 64, 73

Bribe Payers Index (BPI), 375, 376
See Also: Bribery, 361, 363–366, 369, 371–373, 375–377, 379–381, 384

British East India Company, 109, 404

Bureau of Diplomatic Security, 85, 97

Bureau of Indian Affairs (BIA), 152–155

Bureaucratization, 80–82, 86

Cairo Declaration on Human Rights, 268

Cartels, 395–400, 403–406
Cali, 397–399, 405, 406
Colima, 399
Columbian, 403

Gulf, 399
Juarez, 399
La Familia Michoachana, 399
Medellin, 397–399, 405–406
Oaxaca, 399
Sinaloa, 399
Tijuana, 399
Caste System, 302, 307
  Brahmins, 302
  Dalits, 301–315, 318–320, 323,
    328, 329
  Kshatriyas, 302
  Sudras, 302, 315
  Vaisyas, 302
Catholic(s), 282, 287, 289
Causes of Corruption, 383, 384
  See Also: Corruption: 84, 94, 103,
    109, 110, 112, 124, 134, 168,
    305, 313, 361–385, 399, 402,
    407, 460, 469, 472, 474
Central Intelligence Agency (CIA),
    63–65, 70, 286, 290, 339, 342,
    346, 347, 355, 356
Cherokee Tribe, 143, 144
  See Also: American Indian and Na-
    tive American, 136, 138–142,
    144–157, 159, 160
Chickasaw Tribe, 143
  See Also: American Indian and Na-
    tive American, 136, 138–142,
    144–157, 159, 160
China, 4, 7–8, 22–24, 25, 26, 34, 39,
    104, 121–125, 128, 164, 165,
    167,171, 174–175, 179–181, 184,
    185, 193, 198, 208, 209–213, 223,
    257, 272, 373, 376, 380, 393, 394,
    400, 403–405, 436, 446, 447, 462,
    469
Chinese Opium Epidemic, 404
Chinese Police, 122–125, 128

Judicial People's Courts Police, 123
Judicial Procuratorates Police, 123
Militia Groups, 122
People's Assessors, 24
People's Liberation Army (PLA),
    122
Prison Police, 123
Public Security Forces, 122
State Security Police, 123
Chocktaw, 143
  See Also: American Indian and Na-
    tive American, 136, 138–142,
    144–157, 159, 160
Civil Law, 7, 17, 18, 64, 104, 113,
    117, 120, 125, 201, 380
Civil Order Control, 103, 104, 107,
    111, 112, 115, 116, 119, 120, 126,
    128
Civil Society, 250, 378, 379, 382
Civil War (other), 280, 282, 287, 290
Civil War (U.S.), 32, 55–57, 68
Club de Madrid, 346
Cold War Era, 90
Collective Guilt, 294
Collective Rights, 253, 308
Colonization, 135–136
Colonized Indigenous Peoples, 139
Colombia's Tukanoans, 227
Commission on Narcotic Drugs
    (CND), 406, 408, 410, 411, 416
Common Law, 4–5, 7, 10, 11, 14, 15,
    17, 28, 37, 62, 68, 104, 105, 107,
    109, 133, 163, 182, 198, 212
Communist Party, 22, 122, 124, 209,
    277, 282, 321, 322, 340, 406
Computer Crime, 460–462, 464–466
  See Also: Cyber Crime, 366, 459,
    461, 463–465
Consequences of Corruption, 370

Convention against Illicit Traffic in Narcotics Drugs and Psychotropic Substances (1988), 406

Convention against Torture and Other Cruel, Inhuman or Degrading Treatment or Punishment, 37, 168–170, 177, 266, 484

Convention on Cyber Crime, 461

Convention on the Elimination of All Forms of Discrimination against Women (1979), 266

Convention on the Pacific Settlement of International Disputes, 33
  Permanent Court of Arbitration, 33

Convention on the Prevention and Punishment of the Crime of Genocide, 276
  See Also: Genocide Convention, 279, 281, 294, 296

Convention on Psychotropic Substances (1971), 405, 409

Convention on the Rights of the Child, 193–195, 200, 256, 266

Convergence Theory, 340

Cooperation, 3, 10, 24, 25, 31, 41, 46, 50, 57, 61, 63, 79–90, 92–97, 105, 106, 108, 119, 205, 259, 260, 263, 267, 277, 294, 328, 348, 349, 352, 353, 355, 367, 378, 403, 411–412, 414, 448, 474, 476
  Bilateral, 80, 96, 352
  Multilateral, 79, 80, 83, 87, 88, 97

Corporate Corruption, 366, 367, 369, 376

Corruption Perceptions Index (CPI), 373, 374
  See Also: Corruption, 84, 94, 103, 109, 110, 112, 124, 134, 168, 305, 313, 361–385, 399, 402, 407, 460, 469, 472, 474

Council of Europe, 88, 267, 380, 381, 461, 466, 475

Counterterrorist Measures, 345

Court-Martial, 68

Crimes against Cultural Heritage, 459, 460, 467–468, 472, 477
  Object ID, 468

Crimes against Humanity, 40, 45, 268, 278, 286, 291, 293, 294, 301–329, 361, 424, 428–430, 432, 434, 437, 448–450, 483
  Apartheid, 301, 318–320, 329, 430–432, 437, 446, 449, 450
    Group Areas Act No., 431
    International Convention on the Suppression and Punishment of the Crime of Apartheid, 431
    Pass Laws Act of 1952, 431
    Population Registration Act, 431
    Prohibition of Mixed Marriages Act of 1949, 431
  Enforced Disappearances, 430, 432–435, 437, 450
    International Convention for the Protection of All Persons from Enforced Disappearance, 434
    National Reorganization Process, 433
  International Military Tribunal (IMT), 429

Customs Co-operation Council, 412

Cyber Crime, 366, 459, 461, 463–465
  See Also: Computer Crime, 460–462, 464–466
  Convention on Cyber Crime, 461

Global Initiatives to Deal with Cyber Crime, 465
Scottish Law Commission, 465
International Legal Definition of Cyber Crime, 461
Magnitude of Cyber Crime, 463
Peculiarities of Cyber Crime, 462
Stanford Research Institute (SRI), 462
See Also: Unauthorized Computer Access Law, 463, 465
Cyber Trouble Consulting System on the Internet, 464
Cyberterrorism, 352
Dalits, 301–315, 318–320, 323, 328, 329
Dalit Liberation Education Trust, 306
Dalit Panthers, 305
Dalit Street, 302
Dark Networks, 340
Darogas, 109, 110
Dawes Severalty Act, 147, 160
See Also: General Allotment Act, 147, 160
Decent Consultation Hierarchy, 234, 238
Decent Peoples, 220, 224, 232, 234, 237–240
Decent versus liberal peoples, 234
Declaration of the International Rights of Man, 254
Declaration on the Control of Drug Trafficking and Drug Abuse (1984), 406, 409
Democratic Police Systems, 134, 137, 156
Constable-Watch Systems, 134
Frankpledge System, 134
Department of Homeland Security (DHS, US), 347, 349

Department of Interior (US), 141, 145
Department of Justice (US), 73, 84, 379, 471
Deviance Control, 103, 104, 107, 111, 113, 114, 126
Dhimma (Second Class Citizens, Minorities), 229, 230, 235, 238, 239, 243
Elite Cooptation, 231, 233, 242
Diplomatic Academy, 254
Domestic Dependents, 141, 143, 157
Drug Cultivation, 391, 393–396, 399–400, 404 406, 408, 415
Drug Distribution, 279, 391, 395, 397, 399, 401, 408
Drug Enforcement Administration (DEA, US), 59, 84–87, 97, 409, 413, 414, 416
Drugs, 86, 87, 91, 94, 116, 191, 202, 340, 361, 391–393, 396–398, 401–403, 405–417, 440, 441, 448, 460, 472, 474, 476
Amphetamines, 392, 393, 397, 409
Amphetamine-Type Stimulants (ATS), 393, 396, 397, 405–407, 409, 410
Cannabis, 392, 393, 395–399, 406, 407, 415, 416
Cocaine, 116, 279, 340, 392–395, 397–399, 406, 407, 417, 419, 421
Ecstasy, 392, 396, 397
East India Trade Company, 109
Economic and Social Council (UN), 257, 262, 264, 331, 411
Enculturation Era, 144
England and Wales, 4, 11, 12, 14, 25, 106, 164, 167, 171–173, 175, 178, 179, 181, 197, 198, 205, 207, 212

2003 Criminal Justice Act, 12
Court of Appeal, 12
Crown Court, 12, 172
High Court, 12
House of Lords (Supreme Court), 12
Ministry of Justice, 12, 27, 178, 179
  Lord Chancellor (Secretary of State for Justice), 12, 178
English Common Law, 133
  See Also: Common Law, 4–5, 7, 10, 11, 14, 15, 17, 28, 37, 62, 68, 104, 105, 107, 109, 133, 163, 182, 198, 212
English Police, 105–107
  Community Policing, 105, 106, 108
  London City Police, 106
  London Metropolitan Police, 105–107, 128
  Metropolitan Special Constabulary (MSC), 106
  Police Authority Boards, 106
  Problem-Oriented Policing (POP), 105
  Provincial Police, 106, 107
  Reassurance Policing, 105
  Sector Policing, 105
Enlightenment, 104, 250, 251, 258, 259, 321
Environmental Crime, 94, 469–472
EQUAL Community Initiative, 326
Ethnic Cleansing, 137, 282–284, 324
European Commission (2004), 321, 322, 324–327, 329, 475
European Convention for the Prevention of Torture, 267

European Convention for the Protection of Human Rights and Fundamental Freedoms, 267
European Court of Human Rights (ECHR), 49, 267, 268
European Monitoring Center for Drugs and Drug Addiction (EMCDDA), 392–393, 413, 414, 416, 417
European Union (EU), 64, 66, 93–98, 168, 321, 325–329, 347, 374, 395, 413–414, 417, 475
Europol, 79, 84, 88, 91, 93–98, 108, 347, 413, 417
  Computer System, 94
  Drugs Unit, 94
  Management Board, 95
Europol Convention of 1995, 94–95
Extradition, 48, 49, 56, 57, 59, 62, 91, 406, 410
Extradition Treaty (1978), 57, 59
Extraordinary Rendition, 55, 63, 65, 74
Extraterritorial Abduction, 55
Extraterritorial Rendition, 55
Federal Anti-Torture Statute (1994), 60
Federal Bureau of Investigation (FBI), 84, 85, 87, 90, 98, 118, 152, 346, 347, 355, 366, 467, 476
Federal Kidnapping Act (1937), 58
Federal Recognition, 138, 142, 148–150, 152
Federal Tort Claims Act (FTCA, 1946), 59
Financial Action Task Force (on Money-Laundering) (FATF), 402, 403, 410, 411, 417, 472, 474, 475
First Congress of International Criminal Police, 82

Five Civilized Tribes, 143
    See Also: American Indian and Native American, 136, 138–142, 144–157, 159, 160
Fog of War, 280, 289
Food and Agriculture Organization (of the United Nations), 471
Foreign Corrupt Practices Act, The, 363, 380
Fox Tribes, 145
    See Also: American Indian and Native American, 136, 138–142, 144–157, 159, 160
Framework Convention for the Protection of National Minorities, 267
France, 4, 5, 17–18, 25, 82, 83, 90, 104, 105, 113–116, 117, 120, 134, 164, 165, 166, 197, 222, 257, 267, 288, 291, 321, 322, 325, 326, 376, 394, 407, 411, 462, 465
    French Code of Criminal Procedure, 18
    French Penal Code, 17, 18
French Connection, 394
French Parliament, 114
French Police, 113–116
    Departmental Gendarmerie, 114
    Gendarmerie Mobile, 114, 115
    Gendarmerie Nationale, 114
    Maréchaussée, 113
    Police Municipale, 115
    Police Nationale, 113, 114
Fugitive Slave Act, 56
Gacaca, 290
Gendercide, 430, 435–437
    Planned-Birth Offices (PBOs), 436
General Allotment Act, 147, 160
    See Also: Dawes Severalty Act, 147, 160

Geneva Convention, 61, 62, 66, 70–71, 252, 428
    Geneva Convention on the High Seas (1958), 428
    Geneva Convention Relative to the Protection of Civilian Persons in Time of War (1949), 252
    Geneva Convention Relative to the Treatment of Prisoners of War (1929, 1949), 252
Genocide Convention, 279, 281, 294, 296
    Article V, 279
    Article VI, 279
Germany, 4, 5, 6, 8, 9, 17, 19–20, 25, 43, 64, 65, 66, 69, 104, 105, 117–121, 164, 165, 166, 197, 212, 230, 260, 267, 280, 282, 295, 321, 322, 323, 325, 326, 372, 375, 381, 441
    German Civil Code, 6, 19
    German Penal Code, 19
    German Police, 80, 117–120
Global Civil Society, 378
Global Corruption Barometer (GCB), 374, 375
Globalization, 81, 85, 97, 338, 368, 376, 378, 404, 439, 444, 460
Golden Crescent, 394, 406
Golden Triangle, 394, 399, 400
Grand Corruption, 371, 372
Grey Area Phenomena, 351
Guantanamo Bay, 61, 63, 66, 67, 70, 71, 74
Gypsies, 275, 278, 282, 320–326, 483
    See Also: Roma, 260, 301, 320–329, 483
Habeas corpus, 66, 68, 69, 71
Habitual Offenders Act, 316
Hague Peace Conference of 1899, 33

Harijan, 301

See Also: Dalits, 301–315, 318–320, 323, 328, 329

Harmony Ethic, 140

Helsinki Watch, 284, 321, 324, 325

See Also: Human Rights Watch, 37, 52, 60, 76, 127, 255, 269, 284, 290, 291, 294, 296–298, 302–306, 321, 323–325, 328, 331, 451

Hierarchical Societies, 229, 234–236, 238, 241–243

Holocaust, 258, 275, 280, 294, 295

House Concurrent Resolution, 149, 160

Human Rights, 37, 42, 48, 49, 52, 60, 62, 66, 70, 75–77, 90, 92, 103, 111, 121, 127, 168–170, 180, 187, 188, 194, 208, 221, 224, 228, 231–233, 236–239, 242–273, 276, 283, 284, 289–291, 294, 296–299, 301–309, 313–315, 317–319, 321, 323–325, 328–333, 368, 428, 433–435, 437, 438, 447, 451, 452, 454, 455, 457, 480, 483

Human Rights Committee, 49, 252, 258, 265–268, 270, 271, 306, 308

Human Rights Watch, 37, 60, 127, 255, 269, 284, 290, 291, 294, 296, 302–306, 321, 323–325, 328

Human Trafficking, 24, 108, 361, 377, 424, 437–439, 445–450, 460, 484

Protocol to Prevent, Suppress, and Punish Trafficking in Persons (2000), 438

Radio Frequency Identification (RFID), 441

Hutus, 286–289

I-24/7 Communications System, 92

Illegal Extradition, 48

Illegal Immigration, 84, 86, 96, 108

Imagined Communities (1991), 226, 231

India, 4, 11, 14–17, 25, 104, 107, 109–113, 163–165, 167, 180, 191, 192, 197, 198, 199–200, 202, 212, 213, 220, 222, 223, 257, 301–303, 305–307, 309, 311–320, 328, 329, 353, 362, 372, 373, 376, 380, 393, 400, 404, 407, 408, 425, 436, 442, 444, 445, 462, 464, 465, 483

Central Paramilitary Forces (CPF), 111

Central Police Organization (CPO), 112

Code of Criminal Procedure (1861), 14, 199

Commissionerate system, 110, 111

Indian Constitution, 302, 309

Indian Evidence Act (1872), 14

Indian Penal Code (1860), 14, 15, 192, 199

Indian Police Act (1861), 110

Indian Police Service (IPS), 110–112

Panchayats, 16

Indian Affairs, 141, 142, 144–146, 148, 151, 152

See Also: American Indian, 139–141, 144–153, 155, 157

Indian Civil Rights Act (1968), 151, 152, 160

See Also: American Indian, 139–141, 144–153, 155, 157

Indian Country, 137, 139, 144, 148, 150, 153, 157

See Also: American Indian, 139–141, 144–153, 155, 157

Indian Law Enforcement Reform Act (1990), 152, 160
  See Also: American Indian, 139–141, 144–153, 155, 157
Indian Removal, 143, 144, 160
  See Also: American Indian, 139–141, 144–153, 155, 157
    Indian Removal Act (1830), 144, 160
    Trail of Tears, 144
Indian Reorganization Act (1934), 141, 148–149, 160, 161
  See Also: American Indian, 139–141, 144–153, 155, 157
Indian Self-Determination and Education Assistance Act (1975), 142, 151, 155, 161
  See Also: American Indian, 139–141, 144–153, 155, 157
Indian Self-Governance Act (1994), 152, 162
  See Also: American Indian, 139–141, 144–153, 155, 157
Informal social control, 108, 140, 208
Information Technology Act (2000, 2005) (IT Act 2000, 2005), 464, 465
Insanity, 9, 12–13, 15, 17, 19–21, 23, 25
  M'Naghten Rules, 13, 15
  Unsoundness of mind, 15, 16
  Wild Beast Test, 12
Inter-American Drug Abuse Control Commission (CICAD), 412, 417
International Agreement for the Suppression of White Slave Traffic (1904), 82
International Association of Chiefs of Police, 82

International Bill of Rights, 248, 256, 270
  Charter of the United Nations, 248, 256
International Conference of Rome for the Social Defense against Anarchists, 81
International Covenant on Civil and Political Rights (ICCPR), 168, 169, 177, 248, 256, 264, 307–308, 318
International Covenant on Economic, Social and Cultural Rights, 194, 248, 256, 262, 264, 317
International Convention on the Rights of the Child, 256
  See Also: Universal Declaration of Human Rights (UDHR), 60, 194, 221, 233, 237–238, 243, 247, 248, 252, 256, 267, 269, 270, 307, 317
International Convention for the Suppression of the Financing of Terrorism, 475
International Convention on Elimination of All Forms of Racial Discrimination (CERD), 38, 306, 315–317
International Convention on the Protection of the Rights of All Migrant Workers and Members of Their Families, 266
International Court of Justice (ICJ), 34–40, 45, 51, 52, 424, 483
International Crime Threat Assessment, 470
International Criminal Court (ICC), 31, 32, 36, 39–52, 91, 268, 269, 270, 278, 279, 291, 293, 320, 430, 431, 432, 437, 477, 483

International Criminal Police Commission (ICPC), 82, 89
International Criminal Tribunal for Rwanda (ICTR), 268, 289, 290
International Criminal Tribunal for Yugoslavia (ICTY), 268, 285, 298, 447
International Dalit Solidarity Network (IDSN), 306, 307, 329
International Drug Trafficking, 86, 391–418
International Human Rights Movement, 247–270, 308
  Anti-Slavery Movements, 252
  Declaration on the Slave Trade of 1815, 252
  History of International Human Rights Movement, 251
  Quintuple Treaty of London of 1841, 252
International Labor Organization (ILO), 316, 318, 439, 443
International Law Institute, 253, 254, 386
International Maritime Board (IMB), 425
International Maritime Bureau (IMB), 429
International Narcotics Control Board (INCB), 391, 407, 408, 411, 417
International Organ Trade and Transplant Tourism, 446–447
International Terrorism, 84, 86, 88, 90–92, 95, 97, 294, 335–355
Internationalization of Corruption, 376–378
Internet Crime Complaint Center (IC3) (US), 463

Interpol, 79, 82–85, 87–93, 95, 97, 98, 128, 347, 411, 412, 417, 468, 469, 471, 477
Iron Curtain, 406
Irregular Rendition, 55
Islam, 7, 166, 176, 229, 282
Islamic Law, 6, 7, 20–21, 104, 109, 125, 163, 176, 183
Islamic Terrorist Groups, 339
  Hamas, 339, 345
  Hezbollah, 339, 345
  Islamic Jihad, 339
  Islamic Theocracy, 339
ITERATE, 341
Janjaweed, 291, 292
Jay Treaty of 1794, 32, 51, 52
Jus Cogens, 62, 318, 423–424, 427–428, 430, 437–438, 448, 450
Kautilya, 362
Ker-Frisbie Doctrine, 58, 59
Khmer Rouge, 268, 277
Kotwals, 109, 110
Kuomintang, 121
Laissez-Passer, 46
Law of Peoples (1999), 219–220, 224, 234, 235, 239
League of Nations, 33, 252–254, 405, 408
Legal Traditions, 4–8, 11, 23, 24, 483
  Civil Legal Tradition, 4–6, 8, 9, 17, 19, 20, 22
    Code Napoléon, 5, 19
    German Civil Code of 1896, 6, 19
    Roman Law (*Corpus Juris Civilis*), 5
  Common Legal Tradition, 4–6, 9, 11, 12, 16
    Constitutions of Clarendon (1164), 5

Stare Decisis, 5
Islamic Legal Tradition, 6, 20
    Hadiths, 6
    Qur'an, 6, 7, 20, 22, 126
    Shari'a, 6, 20–22, 249
    Sunna, 6, 7, 20–22, 176
    Mixed Legal Tradition, 4, 7, 16, 22
Liberal Peoples, 224, 232, 234, 238–240
Lopez Burgos, 49
Maastricht Treaty, 93, 414
Magna Carta, 250
Major Crimes Act (1885), 146, 148, 152, 161
Mala Captus Bene Detentus, 58
Maritime Piracy, 424–426, 447–449
    Barbary Pirates, 426, 427
    Letter of Marque, 427
    Maersk Alabama, 426
    Sirius Star, 425, 426, 429
Mauryas, 109
Medellin Cartel, 398
Mid-day Meal Scheme (MMS), 313, 317
Minority Representation, 231
    Dhimma system, 229, 235, 239
    Mordechai Ha-Cohen, 229
Model Law on Electronic Commerce (1996), 465
Money Laundering, 86–88, 91, 92, 94, 96, 366, 377, 401, 402, 406, 410, 411, 412, 413, 459, 460, 472–475
Narco-Terrorism, 340
National Campaign on Dalit Human Rights (NCDHR), 302, 304, 306, 309–315, 329
National Central Bureau (NCB), 85

National Drug Intelligence Center, 413, 417
National Memorial Institute for the Prevention of Terrorism (MIPT), 342–345, 355
National Rural Employment Guarantee Act (2005), 315
National Survey on Drug Use and Health (NSDUH), 392
Nation-States, 219, 222–223
Navaho Tribe, 145
    See Also: American Indian and Native American, 136, 138–142, 144–157, 159, 160
Negotiated Relationship Agreement, 46
Neocolonial States, 135
Non-Governmental Organizations (NGOs), 35, 47, 195, 196, 269, 366
Nonrefoulement, 62
North Atlantic Treaty Organization (NATO), 284, 286
Nuremberg Charter, 429, 430
Obligatio Erga Omnes, 423, 424, 448
OECD Convention on Combating Bribery, 381
Office of National Drug Control Policy (ONDCP), 410, 413, 417
Omnibus Crime Control and Safe Streets Act (1968), 151, 161
Onora O'Neill, 228
Opium farmers, 399, 400
Organization for Economic Co–operation and Development (OECD), 367, 381, 382, 410
Organization of American States (OAS), 266, 267, 380, 412, 417
    Inter-American Commission on Human Rights, 267

Inter-American Court of Human Rights, 267
Orthodox Christian, 282
Ottoman Empire, 125, 222
Pacified Colonies, 135, 158
Palermo Convention, 381, 402, 474
Panchayat Elections, 312
Panchayatis Raj, 311
Papal Zouaves Army, 56
Patriot Act (U.S.), 66, 67
Patterns of Global Terrorism, 341, 342
Permanent Court of International Justice (PCIJ), 33, 34
Petty Corruption, 371
Pinkerton Detective Agency, 57
Police States, 133
Police System(s), 15, 104, 133–137, 140, 148, 153, 154, 156–157, 158
    Centralized, Centralized Police Systems, 104
    Decentralized, 104, 106, 117, 118, 120
    Semi-Centralized, 104
Police Union of German States, 80
Political Corruption, 363–365, 370, 374
Political Terrorism, 55, 92, 335, 337, 338, 340, 342
Popular Front for the Liberation of Palestine, 345
Prefect, 114, 123
Private Corruption, 366, 370–372, 376, 378, 382
    See Also: Corporate Corruption, 366, 367, 369, 376
Private Security forces, 109, 119
Protocol, 62, 81, 168–170, 177, 264–267, 308, 408, 409, 438, 447

Public Corruption, 363–365, 372
    See Also: Political Corruption, 363–365, 370, 374
Public Law 83-280 (PL-280), 142, 149, 161
Public Law 93-638 (PL-638), 142, 151, 161
Qin Dynasty, 121
RAND Dataset, 341, 342
Rational Choice Theory, 368, 369
Removal Era, 141, 143
Reorganization Era, 141, 148
Resettled Colonies, 135, 137
Riot Control, 103, 107, 119
Rome Statute, 39, 40, 44, 268, 430, 431
Rwandan Genocide, 50, 287, 291
Rwandan Patriotic Front (RPF), 287
San Carlos Apache Police, 145
San Carlos Apache Reservation, 145
Saudi Arabia Police, 125–127
    Department of Public Safety, 125, 126
    Mubahith, 125, 126
    Mutawa, 125, 126, 128
    Pilgrims and Festivals Police Force, 126
Scheduled Castes, 301, 302, 309, 311–317
    See Also: Dalits, 301–315, 318–320, 323, 328, 329
Scotland Yard, 107, 467
Secret Protocol for the International War on Anarchism, 81
Self-Determination Era, 150–153
Semi-Sovereign Vassal States, 142
Sendero Luminoso, 395
Sex Tourism, 441–443

Sex Trafficking, 439, 441–442, 443, 446
Shanghai Commission (1909), 405–407
Sheik, 125
Single Convention (1961), 405, 408, 410, 411
Single-Issue Terrorism, 339, 340
Slavery, 55, 143, 252, 259, 265, 361, 423–424, 426, 428, 438, 439, 443–445, 447, 448
    Debt Bondage, 317, 443–445
    International Marriage Brokers (IMBs), 446
    Involuntary Servitude, 445–446
    Prostitution, 114, 191, 201, 204, 377, 438, 439, 441–444, 446, 448, 450
Social Darwinism, 321
Society of Peoples, 224–225, 230, 239
Special Court for Sierra Leone (2002), 268
Strasbourg Convention (1990), 475
Strategic Essentialism, 227, 228
Subordinate Sovereignty, 136, 158
    Allotment Era, 146–147
    Enculturation Era, 144
    Removal Era, 141, 143–144
    Reorganization Era, 141, 148
    Reservation Era, 141
    Self-Determination Era, 150
    Termination Era, 137, 142, 149
    Vassal State Era, 141, 142
Substance Abuse and Mental Health Services Administration (SAMHSA), 392, 393, 410, 414, 417
Sunni Muslim, 290
Systematic Corruption, 372

See Also: Corruption, 84, 94, 103, 109, 110, 112, 124, 134, 168, 305, 313, 361–385, 399, 402, 407, 460, 469, 472, 474
Taliban, 70, 91, 134, 351, 394
Termination Era, 137, 142, 149–150
Terrorism, 24, 55, 61, 67, 70, 72, 84, 86–97, 103, 112, 116, 118, 127, 294, 335–355, 378, 384, 402, 406, 410, 412, 413, 435, 454, 459, 474, 475, 484
    Narco-Terrorism, 340
    See Also: International Terrorism, 84, 86, 88, 90–92, 95, 97, 294, 335–355
    See Also: Political Terrorism, 55, 92, 335, 337, 338, 340, 342
    See Also: Transnational Terrorism, 335, 337
    Single-Issue Terrorism, 339, 340
Summit on Terrorism, 346
Terrorism, Radicalism, Extremism, and International Violence group (TREVI), 93, 108
Terrorism, Transnational Crime and Corruption Center, 378, 384
Thanedars, 109, 110
Third General Assembly (1948), 258
Tiananmen Square, 124
Torture Convention, 256, 308
Torture Outsourcing Prevention Act, 65
Trafficking Victims Protection Act of 2000 (TVPA), 447, 448
Transnational Corruption, 361–385
Transnational Terrorism, 335, 337
Transparency International, 373, 376, 378, 381, 384, 385

Treaties, 36, 60, 70, 72, 136, 141–144, 150, 222, 247, 252, 253, 255, 261, 262, 266–269, 323, 335, 349, 352, 391, 404, 405, 408, 424, 476
   Bilateral Treaties, 252, 352
Tutsi, 286–289
Unauthorized Computer Access Law, 463, 465
United Self-Defense Forces and the Revolutionary Armed Forces of Columbia (FARC), 395
United States (U.S.) Department of Justice, 73, 84, 379, 471
United Wa State Army, 399, 400
Universal Declaration of Human Rights (UDHR), 60, 194, 221, 233, 237, 238, 243, 247–248, 252, 256, 267, 269, 270, 307, 317
Universal Jurisdiction, 66, 320, 423, 424, 427–428, 432, 437, 447, 448
Universal Suffrage, 233–234, 236, 240, 241, 260
Untouchability, 302, 303, 309, 316
Untouchables, 301, 331
   See Also: Dalits, 301–315, 318–320, 323, 328, 329

Utopia, 224, 238
Utopianism, 219
Vassal State Era, 141, 142
   See Also: *Subordinate Sovereignty*, 136, 158
Vienna Convention (1988), 402, 424, 472, 474
War against Terrorism, 61, 70
War Crimes Act (1996), 60
War of 1812, 32
War on Drugs, 86, 87
War on Terror, 65, 347, 349, 350, 433, 435, 450
Wheeler-Howard Act, 148, 161
   See Also: Indian Reorganization Act, 141, 148, 149, 160, 161
White Slave Trade, 82
World Bank, 192, 310, 351, 365, 367, 369, 373, 374, 377, 378, 383, 469
World Customs Organization (WCO), 412
World Drug Report (2008), 392
World Health Organization (WHO), 411, 412
Zhou Dynasty, 121